W9-CGP-628

M·A·R·K·E·T·I·N·G

M·A·R·K·E·T·I·N·G

Second Edition

David L. Kurtz
Albers School of Business
Seattle University

Louis E. Boone
Ernest G. Cleverdon
Chair of Business
and Management
University of South Alabama

The Dryden Press
Chicago New York Philadelphia San Francisco Montreal Toronto
London Sydney Tokyo Mexico City Rio de Janeiro Madrid

Acquisitions Editor: Mary Glacken
Developmental Editor: Susan Meyers
Project Editor: Russell Hahn
Managing Editor: Jane Perkins
Design Director: Alan Wendt
Production Manager: Mary Jarvis

Text and cover designer: Alan Wendt
Copyeditor: Kathy Richmond
Indexer: Kathryn Jandeska
Compositor: The Clarinda Company
Text type: 10/12 ITC New Baskerville

Library of Congress Cataloging in Publication Data

Kurtz, David L.
Marketing.

Includes bibliographical references and index.
1. Marketing. I. Boone, Louis E. II. Title.
HF5415.K849 1984 658.8 83-11544
ISBN 0-03-064087-3

Printed in the United States of America
456-032-9876543

Address orders to:
383 Madison Avenue
New York, NY 10017

Address editorial correspondence to:
One Salt Creek Lane
Hinsdale, IL 60521

CBS College Publishing
The Dryden Press
Holt, Rinehart and Winston
Saunders College Publishing

To our friends at The Dryden Press

The Dryden Press Series in Marketing

Stephen W. Brown, Consulting Editor

Blackwell, Engel, and Talarzyk
Contemporary Cases in Consumer Behavior

Block and Roering
Essentials of Consumer Behavior, Second Edition

Boone and Kurtz
Contemporary Marketing, Fourth Edition

Churchill
Marketing Research: Methodological Foundations, Third Edition

Dunn and Barban
Advertising: Its Role in Modern Marketing, Fifth Edition

Engel and Blackwell
Consumer Behavior, Fourth Edition

Futrell
Contemporary Cases in Sales Management

Futrell
Sales Management: Behavior, Practice, and Cases

Green
Analyzing Multivariate Data

Hutt and Speh
Industrial Marketing Management

Kurtz and Boone
Marketing, Second Edition

Marquardt, Makens, and Roe
Retail Management: Satisfaction of Consumer Needs, Third Edition

Rosenbloom
Marketing Channels: A Management View, Second Edition

Schary
Logistic Decisions: Text and Cases

Sciglimpaglia
Applied Marketing Research

Talarzyk
Cases for Analysis in Marketing, Second Edition

Talarzyk
Contemporary Cases in Marketing, Third Edition

Terpstra
International Marketing, Third Edition

Young and Mondy
Personal Selling: Function, Theory, and Practice, Second Edition

Zikmund, Lundstrom, and Sciglimpaglia
Cases in Marketing Research

Zikmund
Exploring Marketing Research

PREFACE

The mid-1980s are both trying and exciting times in which to begin a study of marketing. Organizations—both profit and nonprofit—are engaged in intense competition for customers, audiences, and clients. The marketplace has grown from a single village to the entire world. Rising costs and increased scarcity of energy and other needed resources have resulted in increasingly complex decision making. Marketing will play an increasing role in the United States economy. And now, organizations ranging from the local symphony orchestra to the federal government are attempting to employ marketing concepts and practices in their operations. Politicians, hospital administrators, accountants, financial institutions, and state tourism offices are studying—and applying—marketing techniques in their attempts to identify their clients and provide them with needed services.

Marketing is designed to be the textbook for the mid-1980s. It provides the reader with the following features that we believe make it one of the most thorough and comprehensive available.

Comprehensive Coverage of Marketing Planning and Strategy

Marketing is written with a strong marketing planning/strategy orientation. Several chapters deal with the vital subjects of marketing planning, forecasting, evaluation, and control. As a number of reviewers pointed out, planning occurs at the beginning of the marketing efforts, not at the end. Consequently, coverage of marketing planning and forecasting begins in Chapter 3. Two chapters are devoted to market segmentation.

Major Emphasis on Consumer Behavior and Elements of the Marketing Mix

Although the text does emphasize the importance of marketing planning, this is not done at the expense of coverage of essential marketing concepts. The vital subjects of consumer behavior and the elements of the marketing mix are stressed throughout the book. *Marketing* devotes two entire chapters to the critical subject of consumer behavior, and a third chapter is devoted to industrial buyer behavior. In addition, at least two chapters are devoted to each of the elements of the marketing mix, and separate chapter treatment of retailing, wholesaling, and physical distribution is provided.

Separate Chapter Coverage of Important Marketing Subjects

This textbook pays special attention to emerging areas of marketing. The areas of international marketing, marketing of services, industrial marketing, marketing and society, and marketing in nonprofit settings are too important to ignore in the 1980s. *Marketing* provides complete coverage of these subjects in the following chapters:

- Chapter 9 Buyer Behavior in Industrial and Government Markets
- Chapter 12 Services
- Chapter 22 International Marketing
- Chapter 23 Marketing in Nonprofit Settings
- Chapter 24 Marketing and Society.

Longer, More Comprehensive Cases

We have made a special effort to avoid simplistic, made-up cases that provide little possibility for class use. We thank the Case Clearing House and the authors of the well-known cases included at the end of each part for their assistance in obtaining them. This collection of 16 comprehensive cases makes it possible for instructors to choose from a good selection of cases of varying lengths.

Readable Text with Marketing Concepts Emphasized by Real-World Examples

Marketing is comprehensive, systematic, and rigorous. We hope it is also both practical and written in a lively, engaging manner that avoids tedious, boring prose. Readily identifiable cases and real-world examples are included to illustrate the application—correct and incorrect—of fundamental marketing concepts discussed in the text. Opening vignettes provide the reader with a flavor of the marketing concepts to be treated in each chapter. Examples following the explanation of each concept reinforce student learning. Comprehensive cases then require application of this knowledge. The book avoids sexist language and portrays women in realistic roles.

Comprehensive Teaching/Learning Package

Marketing is available in a complete educational package, designed for both instructor and student. The package includes:

Marketing Learning Guide—a comprehensive aid for students, written by Louis M. Seagull and Patricia A. Corcoran. It includes chapter overviews as well as a wealth of study and review questions. A new feature of the *Guide* is the addition of 2–4 case application exercises per chapter. These exercises are based on real-life situations and provide students with an opportunity to apply and discuss the theory of marketing to actual decision-making situations.

Instructor's Manual—the most complete manual available with any basic marketing text. The *Manual* includes lecture suggestions, a film guide, reference materials, and suggestions for using the transparency masters and acetates.

Transparencies—a complete transparency package consisting of masters as well as 50 four-color acetates.

Test Bank—2000 items organized into quiz-type and comprehensive exam-type questions. Written by Professor Michael F. Smith of Temple University, the *Test Bank* is available on floppy disk and in printed format.

Acknowledgments

The authors gratefully acknowledge the contributions of a large number of persons—colleagues, students, professional marketers in businesses and nonprofit organizations, and the fine professionals at The Dryden Press—for their invaluable critiques, questions, and advice in making the second edition of *Marketing* a reality. For their reviews of all or part of the manuscript, we would like to express our special appreciation to Professors Patricia Danaher, *San Jose State University;* Wayne Norvell, *Kansas State University;* Michael F. Smith, *Temple University;* Louis M. Seagull, *Pace University;* Robert Johnson, *University of Wisconsin–La Crosse;* Robert Benson, *St. Cloud State University;* Eldon Little, *University of Wisconsin–Oshkosh;* Ralph Weller, *University of Wisconsin–Oshkosh;* Robert D. Amason, *Texas Tech University;* Eric N. Berkowitz, *University of Minnesota;* B.C. Butcher, *California State University–Long Beach;* Joseph Chasin, *St. John's University;* Paul R. Cone, *Loma Linda University;* Lee R. Duffus, *University of Tennessee;* Calvin Duncan, *Washington State University;* Dennis S. Guseman, *University of Northern Colorado;* Roger L. Jenkins, *University of Tennessee;* James C. Johnson, *St. Cloud State University;* G.E. Kiser, *University of Arkansas;* Wade Lancaster, *University of Alabama–Birmingham;* Peter J. LaPlaca, *University of Connecticut;* Mary K. Lisko, *Augusta College;* David M. Miller, *Thiel College;* Richard L. Oliver, *Washington University–St. Louis;* William Rice, *College of William and Mary;* Robert W. Schaffer, *Whittier College;* Jack Sheeks, *Broward Community College;* Donald Stem, *Washington State University;* James L. Taylor, *University of Alabama;* Fred Trawick, *University of Alabama–Birmingham;* Richard F. Wendel, *University of Connecticut;* and David Wiley, *Anne Arundel Community College.*

David L. Kurtz
Seattle, Washington

Louis E. Boone
Mobile, Alabama

October 1983

CONTENTS

PART 2 · PLANNING THE MARKETING EFFORT

PART 7 · PROMOTION

Theodore Levitt

Whenever an instructor in an introductory marketing course decides to assign outside readings, the almost universal first choice is a brilliant article entitled "Marketing Myopia." Since the article's first appearance in the *Harvard Business Review* in 1960, it has been widely quoted and read by millions of marketing students and practitioners.

In order to avoid marketing nearsightedness and to ensure continued organizational growth, author Theodore Levitt (1925–) argues that organizations must define their industries broadly in order to take advantage of growth opportunities. He stresses the fact that, contrary to superficial appearances, there is no such thing as a growth industry. An organization or industry will survive only by viewing itself "not as producing goods and services but as buying customers, as doing the things that will make people want to do business with it." His argument is illustrated by focusing upon the railroad industry which, Levitt argues, declined inevitably with technological advancements as a result of a too-narrow definition of its "industry." He went on the suggest broadened definitions for oil companies (from petroleum to energy) and for Hollywood (from movies to entertainment).

No one questions the impact of Levitt's contribution on business and marketing thinking. On a policy level, dozens of examples abound of organizations that have redefined and broadened their "industry" definitions. On the operating level, tremendous improvements in consumer research and service have occurred as organizations cultivate what Levitt terms ". . . a greater 'external' orientation toward uses, users, and markets—balancing thereby the previously one-sided 'internal' focus on materials and methods."

Theodore Levitt is Edward W. Carter Professor of Business Administration and Head of the Marketing Area in the Graduate School of Business Administration at Harvard University.

1

THE MARKETING ENVIRONMENT

Marketing has been defined as the creation and delivery of a standard of living. Part One of *Marketing* traces the evolution of marketing as a means of identifying and responding to the consumer's needs. Essential definitions and concepts are explained in order to define the relationship of marketing to society at large.

1

INTRODUCTION

Chapter Objectives

1. To explain the types of utility and the role played by marketing in their creation.
2. To relate the definition of marketing to the concept of the exchange process.
3. To contrast marketing activities in each of the three eras in the history of marketing.
4. To explain the concept of marketing myopia.
5. To identify three reasons for studying marketing.
6. To identify the variables involved in marketing decision making and the environments in which these decisions must be made.

The chicken farmer from Maryland's Eastern Shore must be doing something right. His name is Frank Perdue, and both he and his slogan, "It Takes a Tough Man to Make a Tender Chicken," are known to millions of people in New York, New Jersey, Pennsylvania, Connecticut, Massachusetts, and elsewhere on the East Coast. His firm, Perdue Farms, Inc., is one of the largest chicken packers in the United States, and Frank Perdue markets more chickens in the New York City area than anyone else. How does he do it?

Perdue understands that a firm's production and marketing efforts must combine to create want satisfaction for consumers. For years Americans consumed an average of 41 pounds of chicken annually, paying scant attention to who packed the poultry. But Frank Perdue changed all that by converting a basic agricultural commodity into a distinguishable, brand-name purchase. Today, Perdue facilities in Maryland, Virginia, and North Carolina turn out more than 250 million birds a year.

Perdue uses computers to calculate the most inexpensive method of turning the smallest amount of feed into the most poultry. Company geneticists work at breeding bigger-breasted fowl, and veterinarians concentrate on producing healthy birds. Then Perdue's production and marketing efforts do the rest. Perdue, who is so confident of his chickens that he backs them with a money-back guarantee, says, "It costs me $1 million to give my chickens their healthy yellow color. If I'm going to spend that much money to get a bird that looks healthy, you know I'm going to bust my butt to make it healthy, too."

Frank Perdue knows that efficient production is not enough. Consequently, he has adopted an imaginative marketing strategy to ensure consumer acceptance in New York and other major urban markets on the East Coast. He offers quality, a guarantee, an identifiable product, and a premium price, but he has become best known for his commercials in which he appears as product spokesperson. Frank's folksy style and Chesapeake Bay accent proved refreshing to many consumers. He even uses the Spanish-speaking media to reach a large segment of his market. Although some question his pronunciation, "*Le necesita un hombre fuerte para hacer un polla pierna*" still comes across in Perdue's well-known style as "It takes a tough man to make a tender chicken."

Several million dollars are spent annually on promotion, but radio and television advertising are only part of Perdue's marketing strategy. Perdue and his field marketing representatives make personal calls on distributors and retailers. They openly solicit complaints about Perdue chickens. An executive at Perdue's advertising agency puts it this way:

Frank Perdue is the antithesis of the company president. Most guys talk a lot, but who do they talk to? Frank talks to butchers in a Boston ghetto at 7:30 in the morning. He knows the territory and he fights like hell to keep it.[1]

The Conceptual Framework

All organizations perform two basic functions—they produce a good, service, or idea, and they market it. This is true of all firms—from giant manufacturers such as Levi Strauss and Kellogg's to the neighborhood convenience store. It is true of profit-seeking firms and nonprofit organizations. Production and marketing are the very essence of economic life in any society.

Through the production and marketing of these goods, services, and ideas, organizations satisfy a commitment to society, to their customers, and to their owners. They create what economists call **utility,** which

[1]The Perdue success is described in Phil Patton's "Fowl Play: The Great Chicken War," *New York Times* (November 19, 1979), p. 54.

may be defined as the want-satisfying power of a product or service. There are four basic kinds of utility—form, time, place, and ownership.

Form utility is created when the firm converts raw materials and component inputs into finished products and services. Glass, steel, fabrics, rubber, and other components are combined to form a new Peugeot or Firebird. Cotton, thread, and buttons are converted into Ocean Pacific shirts. Sheet music, musical instruments, musicians, a conductor, and the facilities of Carnegie Hall are converted into a performance by the New York Philharmonic. Although marketing inputs may be important in specifying consumer and audience preferences, the actual creation of form utility is the responsibility of the production function of the organization.

Time, place, and *ownership utility* are created by marketing. They are created when products and services are available to the consumer when the person wants to purchase them, at a convenient location, and where facilities are available whereby title to the product or service may be transferred at the time of purchase.

Chapter 1 sets the stage for the entire text by examining the meaning of marketing and its importance to organizations—both profit-seeking and nonprofit. The chapter examines the development of marketing in our society and its contributions. The marketing variables utilized in a marketing strategy are also introduced.

What Is Marketing?

All organizations must create utility if they are to survive. The design and marketing of want-satisfying products, services, and ideas is the foundation for the creation of utility. However, the role of marketing in the success of an organization has only recently been recognized. Management author Peter F. Drucker emphasized the importance of marketing in his book, *The Practice of Management:*

If we want to know what a business is we have to start with its purpose. And its purpose must lie outside the business itself. In fact, it must lie in society since a business enterprise is an organ of society. There is one valid definition of business purpose: to create a customer.[2]

How does an organization "create" a customer? As Professors Guiltinan and Paul explain:

Essentially, 'creating' a customer means identifying needs in the marketplace, finding out which needs the organization can profitably serve, and developing an offering to convert potential buyers into customers. Marketing

[2]Peter F. Drucker, *The Practice of Management* (New York: Harper & Row, 1954), p. 37.

The Marketing of Rubik's Cube

Rubik's Cube, one of the major fads of the early 1980s, not only changed the life of its Hungarian professor inventor, but it meant unprecedented sales and profit success for Ideal Toy Corporation. Ideal, which had ended the decade of the 1970s with a $6 million loss in 1979, enjoyed the best sales and profit performance of its 78-year history in 1981 after it acquired the Western world marketing rights to Rubik's Cube in 1980. Stewart Sims, Ideal's vice-president of marketing, credited the product's success to the combination of a unique product and an effective marketing strategy.

Sales of the puzzle were unspectacular when it was invented in 1976 by Ernö Rubik, a Hungarian architect. A consumer trading company in his home country experienced dismal sales before selling the marketing rights to Ideal.

The product suffered from poor packaging and the wrong name, Sims said. The first thing Ideal did was change the name from Magic Cube to the more personal Rubik's Cube.

A round, jewel-like case was created to project a sophisticated, quality image. Ideal was now ready to introduce the puzzle to the trade at the American Toy Fair in New York. Buyers at the fair were encouraged to try to solve the cube, thereby involving them personally with it. Rubik appeared at the fair to demonstrate how easily the cube could be solved.

Mass consumer promotion began with a press party. To boost attendance and project a sophisticated and fun image, Ideal arranged to have Hungarian-born actress Zsa Zsa Gabor and mathematician Sol Golunk at the party.

Students tend to be trend setters, so teaser ads were placed in college newspapers. Frequent travelers, another trend-setting group, were reached by offering the cubes to first-class passengers on American Airlines transcontinental

managers are responsible for most of the activities necessary to create the customers the organization wants. These activities include:

- *identifying customer needs*
- *designing products and services that meet those needs*
- *communicating information about those products and services to prospective buyers*
- *making the products or services available at times and places that meet customers' needs*
- *pricing the products to reflect costs, competition, and customers' ability to buy*
- *providing for the necessary service and follow-up to ensure customer satisfaction after the purchase.*[3]

[3]Joseph P. Guiltinan and Gordon W. Paul, *Marketing Management* (New York: McGraw-Hill, 1982), pp. 3–4.

flights. The consumer teaser print campaign was supported with in-store demonstrations and materials such as T-shirts, bumper stickers, and solution books. National publicity reached a staggering level. Articles appeared in a wide range of publications, including *Omni, Scientific American,* and *Reader's Digest.* "NBC Magazine" and "CHiPS" gave the cube TV exposure.

The marketing plan was redesigned when the market became glutted with imitations. The package was remodeled into a brightly colored cardboard box, reducing the cost of packaging and the price. Media and consumer interest was sustained by sponsoring a national contest that culminated in the national championship on TV's "That's Incredible."

"There's no end to promoting a product once the competition has entered the picture," Sims said. "As demands increase, new strategies have to be devised to maintain market share. Proper marketing planning can help ensure that the original product will remain long after the competitors are gone."

Source: "Macromarketed Rubik's Cube Turns Around Ideal's Profit Picture with Sales of 10 Million," *Marketing News* (February 19, 1982), p. 16. Reprinted by permission. Photo courtesy of Ideal Toy Corporation.

Marketing: A Definition

Ask five persons to define marketing and five definitions are likely to be forthcoming. Due to the continuing exposure to advertising and personal selling, most respondents are likely to link marketing and selling. The Definitions Committee of the American Marketing Association, the international professional association in the marketing discipline, has attempted to standardize marketing terminology by proposing the following definition: "Marketing is the performance of business activities that direct the flow of goods and services from producer to consumer or user."[4]

[4]Committee on Definitions, *Marketing Definitions: A Glossary of Marketing Terms* (Chicago: American Marketing Association, 1960), p. 15.

Figure 1.1 Advertisement for a Nonprofit Organization

Please feed the lions
Give to The New York Public Library and get a lion's share of knowledge.
Patience, one of America's most famous lions, is looking for Friends.
Friends who'll help keep New York's great Research Library open and *free* to everyone.
Surprisingly, the Research Library is not totally tax-subsidized, but *depends on private gifts for most of its support.*
If you give now, The National Endowment for the Humanities will match one dollar for every two you contribute.
For just $25.00 or more, you can become an official Friend of the Library. Join in special events, lectures, tours. Receive discounts and library publications too!
The New York Public Library
Box M6
Fifth Avenue & 42nd Street
New York, New York 10018

Source: © 1981 The New York Public Library.

However, the definition is too narrow in its emphasis on the flow of products and services that have already been produced. Moreover, it does not consider the thousands of nonprofit organizations currently engaged in marketing activities. A broader and more descriptive view is that of the firm or enterprise as an organized behavior system designed to generate output of value to consumers. This text's definition of marketing considers the broader concept of marketing involving the activities of both profit-seeking and nonprofit organizations. **Marketing** is the development and efficient distribution of goods, services, ideas, issues, and concepts for chosen consumer segments.

The expanded conception of marketing activities permeates all organizational activities. It assumes that marketing effort will be in accordance with ethical practices and that it will be effective from the standpoint of both society and the organization. It also emphasizes the need for efficiency in distribution, although the nature and degree of efficiency depend on the kind of environment wherein the firm operates. Finally, it assumes that the consumer segments to be satisfied through the organization's production and marketing activities have been selected and analyzed prior to production. In other words, the customer, client, or public determines the marketing program. Finally, as Figure 1.1 illustrates, it recognizes that marketing concepts and techniques are applicable to nonprofit organizations as well as to profit-oriented businesses.

The Origins of Marketing

The essence of marketing is the **exchange process.** This is the process by which two or more parties give something of value to one another to satisfy felt needs.[5] In many cases, the item is a tangible good, such as a newspaper, a hand calculator, or a pair of shoes. In other cases, intangible services, such as a car wash, transportation, or a concert performance, are exchanged for money. In still other instances, funds or time donations may be offered to political candidates, a Red Cross office, or a church or synagogue.

The marketing function is both simple and direct in subsistence-level economies. For example, assume that a primitive society consists solely of Person A and Person B. Assume also that the only elements of their standard of living are food, clothing, and shelter. The two live in adjoining caves on a mountainside. They weave their own clothes and tend their own fields independently. They are able to subsist even though their standard of living is minimal.

Person A is an excellent weaver but a poor farmer, while Person B is an excellent farmer but a poor weaver. In this situation, it would be wise for each to specialize in the line of work that he or she does best. The net result would then be a greater total production of both clothing and food. In other words, specialization and division of labor will lead to a production surplus. But neither A nor B is any better off until they *trade* the products of their individual labor, thereby creating the exchange process.

Exchange is the origin of marketing activity. In fact, marketing has been described as "the process of creating and resolving exchange relationships." When there is a need to exchange goods, the natural result is marketing effort on the part of the people involved.

Wroe Alderson, a leading marketing theorist who is profiled in Part 6, said, "It seems altogether reasonable to describe the development of

[5]Richard P. Bagozzi, "Marketing as an Organized Behavioral System of Exchange," *Journal of Marketing* (October 1974), p. 77. Further work by Bagozzi on this subject appears in "Marketing as Exchange," *Journal of Marketing* (October 1975), pp. 32–39, and "Marketing as Exchange: A Theory of Transactions in the Marketplace," *American Behavioral Scientist* (March–April 1978), pp. 535–536.

exchange as a great invention which helped to start primitive man on the road to civilization."[6]

While the cave dweller example is simplistic, it does reveal the essence of the marketing function. Complex industrial society has a more complicated exchange process, but the basic concept is the same. Production is not meaningful until a system of marketing has been established. Perhaps publisher Red Motley's adage sums it up best: "Nothing happens until somebody sells something."

Three Eras in the History of Marketing

Although marketing has always been present in businesses, its importance has varied greatly. Three historical eras can be identified: the production era, the sales era, and the marketing era.

The Production Era

One hundred years ago, most firms were production-oriented. Manufacturers stressed production of quality products and then looked for people to purchase them. The Pillsbury Company of this period is an excellent example of a production-oriented company. Here is how the company's board chairman, the late Robert J. Keith, described the Pillsbury of the early years:

> *We are professional flour millers. Blessed with a supply of the finest North American wheat, plenty of water power, and excellent milling machinery, we produce flour of the highest quality. Our basic function is to mill high-quality flour, and, of course (and almost incidentally), we must hire salesmen to sell it, just as we hire accountants to keep our books.*[7]

The prevailing attitude of this era was that a good product (defined in terms of physical quality) would sell itself. This production orientation dominated business philosophy for decades. Indeed, business success was often defined in terms of production victories.

Although marketing had emerged as a functional activity within the business organization prior to the twentieth century, management's orientation remained with production for quite some time. In fact, what might be called industry's production era did not reach its peak until the early part of this century. The apostle of this approach to business operations was Frederick W. Taylor, whose *Principles of Scientific Management* was widely read and accepted at that time. Taylor's approach

[6]Wroe Alderson, *Marketing Behavior and Executive Action* (Homewood, Ill.: Richard D. Irwin, 1957), p. 292.

[7]Robert J. Keith, "The Marketing Revolution," *Journal of Marketing* (January 1960), p. 36.

reflected his engineering background by emphasizing efficiency in the production process. Later writers, such as Frank and Lillian Gilbreth, the originators of motion analysis, expanded on Taylor's basic concepts.

Henry Ford's mass production line serves as a good example of this orientation. Ford's slogan, "They [customers] can have any color they want, as long as it's black," reflected a prevalent attitude toward marketing. Production shortages and intense consumer demand were the rule of the day. It is no wonder that production activities took precedence.

The Sales Era

As production techniques became more sophisticated and as output grew, manufacturers began to increase the emphasis on an effective sales force to find customers for their output. This era saw firms attempting to match customers to their output. A sales orientation assumes that customers will resist purchasing products and services not deemed essential, and that the task of personal selling and advertising is to convince them to buy. Marketing efforts were also aimed at wholesalers and retailers in an attempt to motivate them to stock greater quantities of the manufacturer's output.

Although marketing departments began to emerge during the sales era, they tended to remain in a subordinate position to production, finance, and engineering. Many chief marketing executives held the title of sales manager. Here is how Pillsbury was described during the sales era:

> *We are a flour-milling company, manufacturing a number of products for the consumer market. We must have a first-rate sales organization which can dispose of all the products we can make at a favorable price. We must back up this sales force with consumer advertising and market intelligence. We want our sales representatives and our dealers to have all the tools they need for moving the output of our plants to the consumer.*[8]

But selling is only one component of marketing. As Theodore Levitt (whose profile begins Part 1) has pointed out: ". . . marketing is as different from selling as chemistry is from alchemy, astronomy from astrology, chess from checkers."[9]

The Marketing Era

As personal income and consumer demand for goods and services dropped rapidly during the Great Depression of the 1930s, marketing was thrust into a more important role. Organizational survival dictated

[8]Robert J. Keith, "The Marketing Revolution," *Journal of Marketing* (January 1960), p. 38.

[9]Theodore Levitt, *Innovations in Marketing* (New York: McGraw-Hill, 1962), p. 7.

"If You Build a Better Mousetrap . . ."

More than 100 years ago, the philosopher Ralph Waldo Emerson remarked, "If a man writes a better book, preaches a better sermon or makes a better mousetrap than his neighbor, though he builds his house in the woods, the world will make a beaten path to his door." The implications of this statement are that a quality product will sell itself and that an effective production function is the key to high profits. But don't tell this to Chester M. Woolworth. He knows better.

Woolworth is president of Woodstream Corporation, the nation's largest producer of mousetraps. After thoroughly researching the type of trap that would be most "appealing" to mice, Woodstream's new trap was introduced. The new model was a modern black plastic design, completely sanitary, and priced only a few cents more than the commonplace wood variety. Also, it never missed!

The better mousetrap also failed as a new product venture. While Woodstream had created a quality product, the company had forgotten the customer and the environment in which this purchase decision is made. The post-mortem analysis of this marketing disaster went something like this: men bought the majority of the newly designed plastic mousetraps. In most instances, it was also the responsibility of the male member of the household to set the trap before the family retired for the night. But the problem occurred the next morning when he failed to check the trap before leaving for work. Even though most married women work, they are most likely to check the trap—during the morning in the case of wives who are not employed outside the home, or in the afternoon when they returned home from work.

With the conventional wood trap, they would simply sweep both trap and mouse onto a dustpan and minimize the effort and time involved with this undesirable job. However, the new trap looked too expensive to throw away—even though it cost only a few cents more. Consequently, the wife was faced with first ejecting the mouse and then cleaning the instrument. In a short time the new, improved mousetrap was replaced with the wooden version.

The moral of the mousetrap story is obvious: a quality product is not successful until it is effectively marketed. Mr. Woolworth expressed it most eloquently when he said, "Fortunately, Mr. Emerson made his living as a philosopher, not a company president."

Source: The Woodstream Corporation experience is described in Chester M. Woolworth, "So We Made A Better Mousetrap," *The President's Forum* (Fall 1962), pp. 26–27.

that managers pay closer attention to the markets for their products. This trend was halted by the outbreak of World War II, when rationing and shortages of consumer goods became commonplace. The war years, however, were an atypical pause in an emerging trend that resumed almost immediately after the hostilities ceased. The marketing concept was about to emege.

Emergence of the Marketing Concept

What was the setting for the crucial change in management philosophy? Perhaps it can best be explained by the shift from a **seller's market**—one with a shortage of goods and services—to a **buyer's market**—one with an abundance of goods and services. When World War II ended, factories stopped manufacturing tanks and jeeps and started turning out consumer goods again—an activity that had, for all practical purposes, stopped in early 1942.

The advent of a strong buyer's market occasioned the need for a consumer orientation on the part of U.S. business. Goods had to be sold, not just produced. This realization has been identified as the emergence of the marketing concept. The recognition of this concept and its dominant role in business can be dated from 1952, when General Electric's annual report heralded a new management philosophy:

(The concept) introduces the marketing man at the beginning rather than at the end of the production cycle and integrates marketing into each phase of the business. Thus, marketing, through its studies and research, will establish for the engineer, the design and manufacturing man, what the customer wants in a given product, what price he is willing to pay, and where and when it will be wanted. Marketing will have authority in product planning, production scheduling, and inventory control, as well as in sales, distribution, and servicing of the product.[10]

Marketing would no longer be regarded as a supplemental activity to be performed after the production process had been completed. The marketer would, for instance, now play the lead role in product planning. Marketing and selling would no longer be synonymous.

The **marketing concept** can be defined as a company-wide consumer orientation with the objective of achieving long-run success. The key words are *company-wide consumer orientation.* All facets of the organization must be involved with assessing, and then satisfying, customer wants and needs. The effort is not something to be left only to the marketers. Accountants working in the credit office and engineers employed in product design also play important roles.

[10]*Annual Report* (New York: General Electric, 1952), p. 21.

The words *with the objective of achieving long-run success* are used to differentiate the concept from the policies of short-run profit maximization. The marketing concept is a modern philosophy for dynamic organizational growth. Since the continuity of the firm is an assumed part of it, company-wide consumer orientation will lead to greater long-run profits than will managerial philosophies geared to reaching short-run goals.

Avoiding Marketing Myopia

The emergence of the marketing concept has not been devoid of setbacks. One troublesome situation has been what Theodore Levitt called "marketing myopia."[11] According to Levitt, **marketing myopia** is the failure of management to recognize the scope of its business. Future growth is endangered when management is product oriented rather than customer oriented. Levitt cited many service industries—dry cleaning, electric utilities, movies, and railroads—as examples.

Organizational goals must be broadly defined and oriented toward consumer needs. Trans World Airlines, for example, has redefined its business as travel rather than just air transportation. The firm now offers complete travel services, such as hotel accommodations, credit, and ground transportation, in addition to air travel. Texas Instruments, a firm known for its technological innovations, completely reorganized in 1982 in an attempt to mesh its capabilities with consumer needs. As one observer noted, "The company has always developed products from a technology point of view, as opposed to what the market wanted. What we see happening now is a corporate determination to match technology prowess with what will sell."[12]

For years, the Chicago White Sox had been known as the city's South Side baseball team. The team's new management considered the White Sox to be in the entertainment business. A pay-TV plan was adopted. The White Sox implemented an aggressive marketing strategy to expand their franchise in the Chicago market. Special promotional nights were set up for the suburbs and other areas. A vice-president of marketing was hired to direct the strategy, which included extensive radio and TV advertising, an expanded ticket sales system, new uniforms and symbols, improved security at the ball park, and the acquisition of name players. Clearly, the Chicago White Sox have gone a long way toward overcoming marketing myopia.

[11] Theodore Levitt, "Marketing Myopia," *Harvard Business Review* (July–August 1960), pp. 45–56.
[12] "An About-Face in TI's Culture," *Business Week* (July 5, 1982), p. 77.

Broadening the Marketing Concept for the 1980s

Industry has been responsive to the marketing concept as an improved method of doing business. Since consideration of the consumer is now well accepted in most organizations, the relevant question has become, What should be the nature and extent of the concept's parameters?[13]

Some marketers argue that the concept should be substantially broadened to include many areas not formerly concerned with marketing efforts. Others contend that the marketing concept has been extended too far.[14] Recent experience, for instance, has shown that many nonprofit organizations have accepted the marketing concept.[15] The U.S. armed forces use advertising to recruit volunteers; the United Fund and other charitable groups have developed considerable marketing expertise; some police departments have used marketing-inspired strategies to improve their public image; and marketing efforts are, of course, necessary in political campaigns. A comprehensive discussion of marketing in nonprofit settings appears in Chapter 23.

It would be difficult to envision business returning to an era when engineering genius prevailed at the expense of consumer needs. It would be equally difficult to envision nonprofit organizations returning to a time when they lacked the marketing skills necessary to present their messages to the public. Marketing is a dynamic function, and it will no doubt be subject to continuous change. In one form or another, however, it is playing a more important role in all organizations and in people's daily lives.

[13]The current status of the marketing concept is explored in such articles as Roger C. Bennett and Robert G. Cooper, "Beyond the Marketing Concept," *Business Horizons* (June 1979), pp. 76–83; David Carson, "[illegible]tterdammerung for Marketing?" *Journal of Marketing* (July 1978), pp. 11–19; William S. Sachs and George Benson, "Is It Time to Discard the Marketing Concept?" *Business Horizons* (August 1978), pp. 68–74; Wayne Norvell, "Changing Attitudes toward Consumer Orientation in Making Marketing Decisions," *Pittsburgh Business Review* (June 1977), pp. 7–10; Jack L. Engledow, "Was Consumer Satisfaction a Pig in a Poke?" *Business Horizons* (April 1977), pp. 87–94; and William G. Nickels and Earnestine Hargrove, "A New Societal Marketing Concept," in *Contemporary Marketing Thought*, ed. Barnett A. Greenberg and Danny N. Bellenger (Chicago: American Marketing Association, 1977), p. 541.

[14]Definitive articles on the subject include Philip Kotler and Sidney J. Levy, "Broadening the Concept of Marketing," *Journal of Marketing* (January 1969), pp. 10–15; Leslie M. Dawson, "The Human Concept: New Philosophy for Business," *Business Horizons* (December 1969), pp. 29–38; and Sidney J. Levy and Philip Kotler, "Beyond Marketing: The Furthering Concept," *California Management Review* (Winter 1969), pp. 67–73. See also David J. Luck, "Broadening the Concept of Marketing—Too Far," *Journal of Marketing* (July 1969), pp. 53–55.

[15]The use of marketing by nonprofit organizations is discussed in John D. Claxton, Thomas C. Kinnear, and J. R. Brent Ritchie, "Should Government Programs Have Marketing Managers?" *Michigan Business Review* (May 1978), pp. 10–16; Avraham Shama, "The Marketing of Political Candidates," *Journal of the Academy of Marketing Science* (Fall 1976), pp. 764–777; Leonard L. Berry and Bruce H. Allen, "Marketing's Crucial Role for Institutions of Higher Education," *Atlanta Economic Review* (July–August 1977), pp. 24–31; and Philip Kotler, "Strategies for Introducing Marketing into Nonprofit Organizations," *Journal of Marketing* (January 1979), pp. 37–44.

Introduction to the Marketing Variables

The starting place for effective marketing is the consumer. Part Three is devoted entirely to a thorough treatment of consumer behavior. This coverage is further indication of the importance of consumer analysis in the development of effective marketing programs. Once a particular consumer group has been identified and analyzed, the marketing manager can direct company activities to profitably satisfy that segment.

Although thousands of variables are involved, marketing decision making can be conveniently divided into four strategies: (1) product, (2) pricing, (3) distribution, and (4) promotion.

Product strategy comprises decisions about package design, branding, trademarks, warranties, guarantees, product life cycles, and the development of new products. The marketer's concept of product strategy involves more than the physical product: it also considers the satisfaction of all consumer needs in relation to the good or service. **Pricing strategy,** one of the most difficult areas of marketing decision making, deals with the methods of setting profitable and justified prices. It is closely regulated and subject to considerable public scrutiny. **Distribution strategy** deals with the physical distribution of goods and the selection of marketing channels. **Marketing channels** are the steps a good or service follows from producer to final consumer. Channel decision making deals with establishing and maintaining the institutional structure in marketing channels. It involves retailers, wholesalers, and other channel intermediaries. **Promotional strategy** involves personal selling, advertising, and sales promotion tools. The various as-

Figure 1.2 Elements of the Marketing Mix

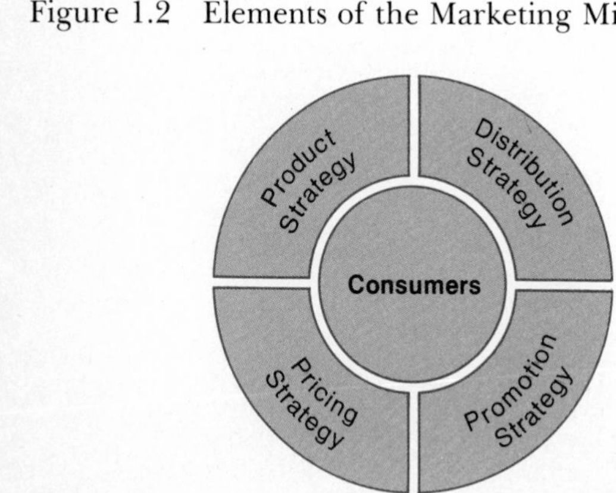

pects of promotional strategy must be blended together in order for the organization to communicate effectively with the marketplace.

The total package forms the **marketing mix**—the blending of the four strategy elements of marketing decision making to satisfy chosen consumer segments. As Figure 1.2 shows, each of the strategies is a variable in the mix. While this four-fold classification is useful in study and analysis, the total package, or mix, determines the degree of marketing success.

Riunite: Developing an Effective Marketing Mix

Riunite wines provide an excellent example of an effective marketing mix.[16] The popular brand is the nation's leading imported table wine, with a 25 percent share of the market. Riunite outsells the second place import by a three to one margin. Villa Banfi, Riunite's importer and marketer, developed the following marketing mix:

Consumer Target *(covered in Chapters 3–9)*

- The mass market consisted of many first-time wine consumers.

Product Strategy *(covered in Chapters 10–12)*

- Riunite is a Lambrusco wine—sweeter, fruitier, fizzier, and with a lower alcohol content than its competitors. It also does not require aging.
- The Villa Banfi product strategy is based on the premise that Americans prefer sweeter and colder drinks.
- The company has also produced a 6.3-ounce bottle in an attempt to reach markets like airlines, fast-food franchises, and sporting events.
- Villa Banfi is also marketing other brands. Bell 'Agio is similar to Riunite and carries a comparable price. A higher-priced vintage label is also being introduced.

Pricing Strategy *(covered in Chapters 13 and 14)*

- Because Riunite does not require aging, Villa Banfi was able to introduce the wine at $1.99 per bottle. It now sells for $3.00—still low by wine industry standards.
- Villa Banfi's Bell 'Agio brand is priced close to Riunite. The importer's vintage wines are priced higher than Riunite.

[16]Bill Abrams, "Selling Wine Like Soda Pop, Riunite Uncorks Huge Market," *Wall Street Journal* (July 2, 1981), Reprinted by permission of *The Wall Street Journal*, © Dow Jones & Company, Inc., 1981.

Distribution Strategy *(covered in Chapters 15–18)*

- The marketing channel for Riunite leads from an Italian grape cooperative to Villa Banfi to wine dealers to the consumer.
- Villa Banfi is soliciting other sales outlets such as airlines, fast-food franchises, sporting events, and restaurant salad bars via the 6.3-ounce bottle.
- The 6.3-ounce bottle is also being promoted through supermarkets, a traditional outlet.

Promotional Strategy *(covered in Chapters 19–21)*

- Villa Banfi's promotional strategy is based primarily on an extensive advertising budget equal to more than 6 percent of annual sales.
- Approximately two thirds of the advertising budget is allocated to television.
- Riunite is now being promoted as a competitor for all drinks, not just wine. Villa Banfi has targeted some of its promotional efforts at soft drinks, beer, and other beverages, in addition to competitive brands of wine.

The Marketing Environment

Marketing decisions are not made in a vacuum. Marketers cannot experiment with single variables while holding other factors constant. Instead, marketing decisions are made on the basis of the constant changes in the mix variables and the dynamic nature of environmental forces. To be successful, these decisions must take into account the five environments—competitive, political and legal, economic, technological, and societal and cultural—in which they operate.

Consider the case of Riunite. Villa Banfi's competition originally came from Cella and Giacobazzi. Later, Coca-Cola's acquisition of Taylor Wines added a new dimension to Riunite's competitive environment. Villa Banfi's political and legal environment is characterized by import regulations and by state and local laws dealing with alcoholic beverages. All of these factors influence marketing decisions.

The economic environment affects all marketers. So Villa Banfi diversified into two other Italian and one California wine ventures. The technological environment is illustrated by package design and product aging requirements. The societal environment has also played a major role in the marketing of Riunite. For instance, many of the brand's customers were first-time wine buyers. And the American preference for sweeter, colder drinks is another societal factor that figured in Riunite's marketing strategy. Environmental influences are the topic of Chapter 2. Consideration of these factors is critical to effective marketing.

The Study of Marketing

Marketing is a pervasive element in contemporary life. In one form or another, it is close to every person. Three of its most important concerns for students are the following:

1. Marketing costs may be the largest item in the personal budget. Numerous attempts have been made to determine these costs, and most estimates have ranged between 40 and 60 percent. Regardless of the exact cost, however, marketing is obviously a key item in any consumer's budget.

   Cost alone, however, does not indicate the value of marketing. If someone says that marketing costs are too high, that person should be asked, "Relative to what?" The standard of living in the United States is in large part a function of the country's efficient marketing system. When considered in this perspective, the costs of the system seem reasonable. For example, marketing expands sales, thereby spreading fixed production costs over more units of output and reducing total output costs. Reduced production costs offset many marketing costs.
2. There is a good chance that individual students will become marketers. Marketing-related occupations account for 25 to 33 percent of the nation's jobs. Indeed, marketing opportunities remained strong even during recent periods when one out of four graduates could not find jobs. History has shown that the demand for effective marketers is not affected by cyclical economic fluctuations.
3. Marketing provides an opportunity to contribute to society as well as to an individual company. Marketing decisions affect everyone's welfare. Furthermore, opportunities to advance to decision-making positions come sooner in marketing than in most occupations. (Societal aspects of marketing will be covered in detail in later chapters.)

Why study marketing? The answer is simple: marketing impacts numerous facets of daily life as well as future careers and economic well-being. The study of marketing is important because it is relevant to students today and tomorrow. It is little wonder that marketing is now one of the most popular fields of academic study.

Summary

The two primary functions of any organization are production and marketing. Traditionally, industry has emphasized production efficiency, often at the expense of marketing. Sometime after World War II, however, the *marketing concept* became the accepted business philosophy. The change was caused by the economy shifting from a seller's market to a buyer's market.

Marketing is the development and efficient distribution of goods, services, ideas, issues, and concepts for chosen consumer segments. It is applicable to both profit-oriented and nonprofit organizations. Marketing decision making can be classified into four strategies: (1) product, (2) pricing, (3) distribution, and (4) promotion. These four variables together form the total marketing mix. Marketing decisions must be made in a dynamic environment determined by competitive, legal, economic, technological, and societal functions.

Three basic reasons for studying marketing are (1) marketing costs may be the largest item in the personal budget; (2) there is a good chance individual students will become marketers; and (3) marketing provides an opportunity to contribute to society as well as to an individual organization.

Key Terms

utility
marketing
exchange process
seller's market
buyer's market
marketing concept
marketing myopia
product strategy
pricing strategy
distribution strategy
promotional strategy
marketing channels
marketing mix

Review Questions

1. What are the four types of utility? With which is marketing concerned?
2. How does the text definition of marketing differ from the definition proposed by the American Marketing Association?
3. Relate the definition of marketing to the concept of the exchange process.
4. Contrast the production era and the sales era.
5. In what ways does the marketing era differ from the previous eras?
6. Explain the concept of marketing myopia. Why is it likely to occur? What steps can be taken to reduce the likelihood of its occurrence?
7. What did the General Electric annual report mean when it said it was introducing the marketer at the beginning rather than at the end of the production cycle?
8. What should be the parameters of the marketing concept?
9. Identify the major variables of the marketing mix.
10. What are the components of the marketing environment? Why are these factors not included as part of the marketing mix?

Discussion Questions and Exercises

1. What types of utility are being created in the following examples?
   - **a.** One-hour cleaners
   - **b.** 7-Eleven convenience food store
   - **c.** Nissan truck assembly plant in Smyrna, Tennessee
   - **d.** Annual boat and sports equipment show in local city auditorium
   - **e.** Regional shopping mall
2. How would you explain marketing and its importance in the U.S. economy to someone not familiar with the subject?
3. Identify the product and the consumer market in each of the following:
   - **a.** Local cable television firm
   - **b.** Milwaukee Brewers baseball club
   - **c.** Planned Parenthood
   - **d.** Dr. Pepper
4. Suggest methods by which the following organizations might avoid marketing myopia by correctly defining their industries:
   - **a.** Atari Computer Division of Warner Communications
   - **b.** United Artists (motion picture company)
   - **c.** Burlington Northern Railroad
   - **d.** Gulf Oil
   - **e.** Bank of America
5. Give two examples of firms you feel are in the following eras:
   - **a.** Production era
   - **b.** Sales era
   - **c.** Marketing era

   Defend your answer.

2

THE ENVIRONMENTS OF MARKETING

Chapter Objectives

1. To identify the five components of the marketing environment.
2. To explain the types of competition faced by marketers and the steps involved in developing a competitive strategy.
3. To identify the three phases of government regulation in the United States.
4. To explain the methods used by the Federal Trade Commission in protecting consumers.
5. To outline the economic factors that affect marketing decisions.
6. To explain the impact of the technological environment on a firm's marketing activities.
7. To explain how the societal/cultural environment influences marketing.

The first call came in around ten on the morning of September 30, 1982. It was from Jim Ritter, a consumer reporter for the Chicago *Sun-Times.* He said he was working on a background story about Tylenol and needed information about its history and current sales. Johnson & Johnson, the $5.4 billion-a-year health-care giant that owns 149 companies in addition to McNeil Consumer Products, the maker of Tylenol, had a reputation for being courteous but close-mouthed about numbers for specific products. So most business journalists and security analysts turned elsewhere to find out what was going on inside the company. Still, a few press calls a day came in from reporters who didn't know better.

James Murray, a public relations deputy, routinely told Ritter he'd check with the people at McNeil and call him back.

"Is that about the terrible thing that happened in Chicago?" asked Elsie Behmer, the director of communications at McNeil, when Murray rang up.

"No," he said, noticing that she sounded out of breath. "What happened in Chicago?"

"We heard some people have been poisoned with Tylenol capsules. I'm going down to a meeting right now to find out more."

Murray started to get up from his desk when his secretary told him the *Sun-Times* reporter was on the phone again and said it was urgent. Ritter told him he hadn't known why his city editor had asked him to call before, but that now he did: the Cook County medical examiner's office had reported that three people had been killed as the result of ingesting cyanide in Tylenol capsules. Did Johnson & Johnson have a comment?

. . . Johnson & Johnson will not be the same again soon. In the weeks that followed, the company went through a trauma from which it still hasn't recovered. In the first phase of its shock, it simply tried to figure out what had happened. In the second phase, it assessed and tried to contain the damage. And in the third phase, J & J prepared to get Tylenol capsules back on the market.

Despite the company's size and wide diversification, the blow to Tylenol will have a huge and direct impact on J & J. Beginning in 1960, McNeil carefully promoted Tylenol among doctors and pharmacists as an alternative pain reliever for people who suffer stomach upset and other side effects from aspirin. In 1975 McNeil began advertising it aggressively to the public, and by 1982 it had an astounding 35 percent share of the $1 billion analgesic market. Tylenol contributed 7 percent of J & J's worldwide sales and 15 to 20 percent of its profits in 1981. Before the poisonings, McNeil executives were confident Tylenol would take over 50 percent of the market by 1986.[1]

As the number of poisoning deaths increased to seven, both J & J officials and government agencies took action. Chicago city officials temporarily banned the sale of all Tylenol products. Johnson & Johnson quickly withdrew all its capsule pain reliever products from the market. It followed its product recall with advertisements offering a $2.50 refund to consumers to replace Tylenol products they had purchased. In a matter of weeks, Johnson & Johnson spent $100 million on the recall and disposal of the products.

Television advertisements featuring McNeil's medical director, Dr. Thomas Gates, asked the consumer public for continued trust in Tylenol. A new triple-sealed tamper-resistant package was developed, and the *new* Tylenol was introduced ten weeks after the poisonings. Early sales reports indicated that these actions were succeeding as Tylenol sales and market share slowly moved toward their previous levels.[2]

[1]Thomas Moore, "The Fight to Save Tylenol," *Fortune* (November 29, 1982), pp. 44–45. Reprinted by permission.

[2]Nancy Giges, "New Tylenol Package in National Press Debut," *Advertising Age* (November 15, 1982), p. 1; Nancy Giges, "Tylenol Tablets Lead Rebound," *Advertising Age* (December 13, 1982), p. 1.

The Conceptual Framework

The tragic Tylenol experience reveals the importance of environmental factors to the success of any organization. Although most marketers will never face the life-and-death issues dealt with by Johnson & Johnson managers, forces outside the control of the decision maker will continue to affect the operations of any firm. These forces must be identified and analyzed; then the marketing decision makers must determine the nature of their impact upon a particular marketing decision. Although they cannot be controlled by the marketing manager, they must be considered together with the controllable variables of the marketing mix in the development of marketing strategies.

Chapter 1 introduced marketing and the elements of the marketing mix used to satisfy chosen market targets. But the blending of a successful marketing mix must be based upon thorough analysis of environmental factors. The marketer's product, distribution, promotion, and pricing strategies must filter through these environmental forces before they reach their goal: the consumers who represent the firm's market target. In this chapter we will examine how each of the environmental variables can affect a firm's marketing strategy.

As Figure 2.1 indicates, the environment for marketing decisions actually consists of five elements: the *competitive* environment, the *political*

Figure 2.1 Elements of the Marketing Mix as They Operate within an Environmental Framework

and legal environment, the *economic* environment, the *technological* environment, and the *societal/cultural* environment. The forces are important because they provide the frame of reference within which marketing decisions are made. However, since they represent outside factors, they are *not* marketing mix components.

In addition to their importance in affecting current marketing decisions, their dynamic nature means that management at every level must continually reevaluate marketing decisions in response to changing environments. Even modest environmental shifts can alter the results of marketing decisions. Polaroid Corporation's failure to recognize the flexibility, ease of use, and rapidly declining prices of videocassette cameras and recorders contributed to disappointing sales for their Polavision instant movies that required users to purchase a display unit and lacked the re-recording features of the videocassette competition.

The Competitive Environment

The interactive process that occurs in the marketplace as competing organizations seek to satisfy markets is known as the **competitive environment.** Marketing decisions by an individual firm influence consumer responses in the marketplace; they also affect the marketing strategies of competitors. As a consequence, marketers must continually monitor the marketing activities of competitors—their products, channels, prices, and promotional efforts.

In a few instances, organizations enjoy a monopoly position in the marketplace. Utilities, such as natural gas, electricity, water, and cable television service, accept considerable regulation from local authorities in such marketing-related activities as rates, service levels, and geographic coverage in exchange for exclusive rights to serve a particular group of consumers. However, such instances are rare. In addition, such traditional monopoly industries as telephone service have been deregulated in recent years, and American Telephone & Telegraph currently faces competition in such areas as the sale of telephone receivers, long-distance telephone service, and installation and maintenance of telephone systems in larger commercial and industrial firms.

Sporting goods provide an illustration of the importance of the competitive environment. Sports and recreation fads result in boom periods for the manufacturers of the equipment involved, and dozens of new competitors enter the market. Bowling boomed in the early 1960s, snowmobiles in 1971, skiing in 1973, tennis in 1975, and aerobic dancing and exercise in 1980. Each of these periods has been followed by a terrific expansion of the related segment of the sporting goods industry. Excess supply soon develops regardless of optimistic predictions in the sport. The net result is that some firms try to compete by cutting prices. Other firms are then forced to make similar reductions to remain competitive. Tensor sold its metal tennis racquets for $25 in 1968 and for $9 by the mid-1970s. Eventually, many of the marginal competitors are forced out of the industry, and production and marketing resume normal patterns.

Jogging and racquetball are among the sports fads today that have given rise to industries serving the participants. Many companies now make running shoes or "training flats" for joggers. Racquetball courts dot the landscape of most suburban areas and smaller cities. Today, supplying racquetball equipment and accessories is a major industry. But there are signs of change: joggers can choose from more than a hundred different models of running shoes, and racquetball courts face increased competition in many major metropolitan areas. The competitive environment is a fact of life even in recreation and leisure activities.

Types of Competition

Marketers actually face three types of competition. The most direct form of competition occurs between marketers of similar products. Xerox photocopiers compete with models offered by Canon, Sharp, and Olivetti. Kubota tractors face competition from Ford Motor Company's farm equipment division, Case, and John Deere.

As Union Oil Company pointed out in the advertisement shown in Figure 2.2, it does not enjoy a monopoly position, as some critics have claimed. It actually competes with 72 leading oil companies, none of which has larger than an 8.5 percent market share.

A second type of competition is competition between products that can be substituted for one another. In the construction industry and in manufacturing, steel products by Bethlehem Steel may compete with similar products made of aluminum by Alcoa or Reynolds Aluminum. Cast-iron pipes compete with pipes made of such synthetic materials as polyvinyl chloride (PVC) in many industries. In instances where a change such as a price increase or an improvement in the strength of a product occurs, demand for substitute products is directly affected.

The final type of competition involves all organizations that compete for the consumer's purchases. Traditional economic analysis views competition as a battle between companies in the same industry or between substitutable products and services. Marketers, however, accept the argument that *all* firms are competing for a limited amount of discretionary buying power. Delco batteries directly compete with the Sears DieHard. U.S. Steel competes with Alcoa with substitutable products. The Mazda GLC competes with a vacation in St. Thomas, and CBS Records competes with an Eddie Murphy movie for the consumer's entertainment dollars.

Figure 2.2 Direct Competition: The U.S. Petroleum Industry

Source: Reprinted by permission of Union Oil Company of California.

Since the competitive environment often determines the success or failure of a product, marketers must continually assess marketing strategies of competitors. New product offerings with technological advances, price reductions, special promotions, or other competitive actions must be monitored in order to adjust the firm's marketing mix in light of such changes. Among the first purchasers of any new product are the product's competitors. Careful analysis of its components—physical components, performance attributes, packaging, retail price, service requirements, and estimated production and marketing costs—allows the marketer to forecast its likely competitive impact. If necessary, adjustments to one or more marketing mix components may take place as a result of the new market entry.

Developing a Competitive Strategy

All marketers must develop an effective strategy for dealing with the competitive environment. Some will compete in a broad range of product markets in many areas of the world. Others prefer to specialize in particular market segments, such as those determined by geographical, age, or income factors. Essentially, the determination of a competitive strategy involves three questions:

1. Should we compete?
2. If so, in what markets should we compete?
3. How should we compete?

The first question—should we compete?—should be answered based on the resources and objectives of the firm and expected profit potential for the firm. In some instances, potentially successful ventures are not considered due to the lack of a match between the venture and the overall organizational objectives. RCA's sale of its Random House division was based upon a poor match between the technologically oriented parent firm and its book publishing subsidiary. Atari sold its Pizza Time Theater outlets due to a perceived mismatch.[3]

The second critical issue in deciding whether to compete is expected profit potential. If the expected profits are insufficient to pay an adequate return on the required investment, then the firm should consider moving into other lines of business. Many organizations have accomplished this switch quite efficiently. This decision should be subject to continual reevaluation so that the firm avoids being tied to traditional markets with declining profit margins. It is also important to anticipate competitive responses.

The second question concerns the markets in which to compete. This decision acknowledges that the marketer has limited resources (sales personnel, advertising budgets, product development capability, and the like) and that these resources must be allocated to the areas of greatest opportunity. Too many marketers have taken a "shotgun" approach to market selection and thus do an ineffective job in many markets rather than a good one in selected markets.

How should we compete? is the third question. It requires the marketer to make the tactical decisions involved in setting up a comprehensive marketing strategy. Product, pricing, distribution, and promotion decisions, of course, are the major elements of this strategy.

The Political and Legal Environment

Before you play the game, learn the rules! It would be absurd to start playing a new game without first understanding the rules, yet some businesspeople exhibit a remarkable lack of knowledge about marketing's **political and legal environment**—the laws and interpretation of laws that require firms to operate under competitive conditions and to

[3]See Michael E. Porter, "How Competitive Forces Shape Strategy," *Harvard Business Review* (March–April 1979), pp. 137–145.

protect consumer rights. Ignorance of laws, ordinances, and regulations could result in fines, embarrassing negative publicity, and possibly expensive civil damage suits.[4]

It requires considerable diligence to develop an understanding of the legal framework for marketing decisions. Numerous laws and regulations, often vague and legislated by a multitude of different authorities, characterize the political and legal environment for marketing decisions. Regulations affecting marketing have been enacted at the federal, state, and local levels, as well as by independent regulatory agencies. Our existing legal framework was constructed on a piecemeal basis, often in response to concerns over current issues.

The United States has tended to follow a public policy of promoting a competitive marketing system. To maintain such a system, competitive practices within the system have been regulated. Traditionally, the pricing and promotion variables have received the most legislative attention.

The Impact of Societal Expectations upon the Political and Legal Framework

We live in and desire a free enterprise society—or do we? The concept of free enterprise is not clear and has been gradually changing. At the turn of the century the prevalent attitude was to let business act quite freely. As a result, it was expected that new products and jobs would be created and the economy would continue to develop and prosper.

This provided great freedom for the scrupulous and unscrupulous. Although most marketers sought to serve their market targets in an equitable fashion, abuses did occur. Figure 2.3 is an example of questionable marketing practices. Such advertisements were not unusual in the late 1800s and the early years of the twentieth century.

In addition, advancing technology resulted in a multitude of products. Considerable expertise was sometimes needed just to choose among them.

With increasing complexity of products, growth of big, impersonal business, and unfair or careless treatment of consumers by a few, the values of society changed. "Government should regulate business more closely," we said. Over time, governments at the federal, state, and local levels have responded, until many laws have been passed to protect consumers and to help maintain a competitive environment for business. Large bureaucracies have been established to accomplish this.

The history of governmental regulation in the United States can be divided into three phases. The first phase was the antimonopoly period

[4]For an excellent reference source on the political and legal environments, see Joe L. Welch, *Marketing Law* (Tulsa, Okla.: PennWell Books, 1980).

Figure 2.3 An Example of Questionable Advertising

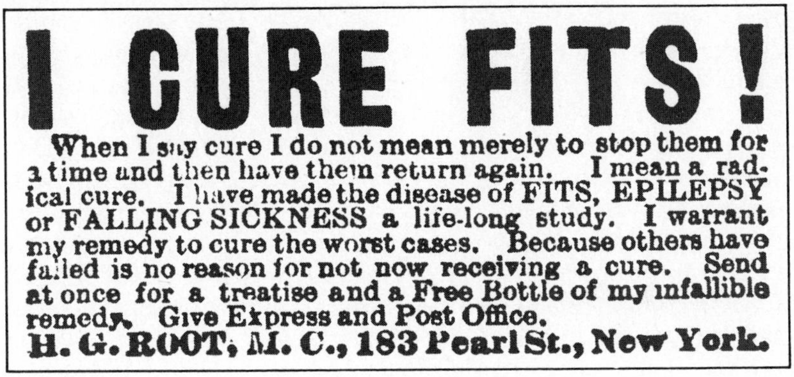

I CURE FITS!

When I say cure I do not mean merely to stop them for a time and then have them return again. I mean a radical cure. I have made the disease of FITS, EPILEPSY or FALLING SICKNESS a life-long study. I warrant my remedy to cure the worst cases. Because others have failed is no reason for not now receiving a cure. Send at once for a treatise and a Free Bottle of my infallible remedy. Give Express and Post Office.

H. G. ROOT, M. C., 183 Pearl St., New York.

Source: S. Watson Dunn and Arnold M. Barban, *Advertising: Its Role in Modern Marketing* (Hinsdale, Ill.: Dryden Press, 1982), p. 84. Reprinted by permission.

of the early twentieth century, when major laws such as the Sherman Act, Clayton Act, and the Federal Trade Commission Act were passed in order to protect competition by reducing the trend toward increasing concentration of industry power in the hands of a small number of competitors. The second phase was aimed at protecting competitors. This phase developed during the Depression era of the 1930s, as independent merchants felt the need for legal protection against competition from larger chain stores. Federal legislation enacted during this era included the Robinson-Patman Act and the Miller-Tydings Resale Price Maintenance Act. The third phase of governmental regulations focused upon protection of consumers. Although consumer protection is an underlying objective of most laws—the Sherman Act, FTC Act, Federal Food and Drug Act, and Meat Inspection Act are good examples—many of the major pro-consumer laws have been enacted during the past 25 years.

The following sections briefly describe the major federal laws affecting marketing. Many of them will be referred to throughout the remainder of the text. In addition, legislation affecting specific marketing practices, such as product warranties or franchise agreements, will be discussed in chapters dealing with these subjects.

Antitrust Legislation

The *Sherman Antitrust Act* (1890) prohibits restraint of trade and monopolization. It subjects violators to civil suits and to criminal prosecution. Although the practices covered by the act were unlawful under common law and under several state acts passed in the previous decade, the Sherman Act was the first piece of federal legislation to clearly delineate the maintenance of a competitive marketing system as national policy.

However, antitrust legislation has not been completely effective in eliminating abuses. A Department of Justice official once estimated that antitrust violations cost U.S. consumers between 3 and 12 percent of the nation's gross national product each year.[5]

The economic philosophy of the Sherman Act contrasts sharply with the philosophies of many foreign countries, where monopolies are openly encouraged by the government. In such cases, governments usually attempt to foster productive efficiency which might be injured by excessive competition. Few nations have antitrust legislation even remotely comparable to that of the United States. As a result, foreign cartels (monopolies) once had a distinct advantage over U.S. companies operating independently in international markets.

Because of this situation, the *Webb-Pomerene Export Trade Act* (1918) exempted voluntary export trade associations from the Sherman Act restrictions—but only in their foreign trade dealings. Exemptions of a similar nature have since been granted on the domestic front for the merger of the National and American Football Leagues and for pollution control research carried out by automobile manufacturers.

The *Clayton Act* (1914) strengthened antitrust legislation by restricting such practices as price discrimination, exclusive dealing, tying contracts, and interlocking boards of directors where the effect "may be to substantially lessen competition or tend to create a monopoly." Later, the *Celler-Kefauver Antimerger Act* (1950) amended the Clayton Act to include the purchase of assets where such purchases would reduce competition.

A third important aspect of the regulation of competition is the *Federal Trade Commission Act,* which also became law in 1914. This act prohibited unfair methods of competition and established the Federal Trade Commission (FTC) as an administrative agency to oversee the various laws dealing with business.

Since its early days, the FTC has assumed a large workload that continues to grow each year. Under the original act, the FTC had to demonstrate injury to competition before a court would declare a marketing practice unfair. The *Wheeler-Lea Act* (1938), however, amended the Federal Trade Commission Act so as to ban deceptive or unfair business practices per se.

[5]S. M. Scherer, *Industrial Market Structure and Economic Performance* (Chicago: Rand McNally, 1980), p. 470.

FTC Activities in Protecting Consumers

Armed with the Wheeler-Lea requirements, the FTC has assumed an activist role in consumer protection. It uses three procedures in carrying out its duties:

1. Conferences with the individuals or industries involved to secure voluntary compliance with its rules.
2. The consent method, under which the FTC secures the agreements of the firm or industry to abandon a practice the FTC deems unfair.
3. Formal legal action. (All FTC decisions can be appealed through the courts.)

The consent order is an FTC favorite for remedying what the agency believes is an undesirable business practice. A few years ago, the commission decided that AMF advertising had depicted children in unsafe bicycling siutations. The resulting consent agreement banned AMF from using commercials showing a variety of dangerous siutations, such as children performing bicycling stunts. AMF was also required to produce two safety messages and distribute them to television stations for use as public service announcements. The consent order specifically required that 5,963,000 children from 6–11 years old see the safety message, or AMF would have to distribute the commercials to a second group of television stations.[6]

Another technique adopted by the FTC during the past two decades is **corrective advertising.**[7] This approach requires firms found to have used deceptive advertising to correct these earlier claims with new promotional messages. In the mid-1970s, STP Corporation advertised that its oil treatment would reduce oil consumption by 20 percent. The FTC ruled that the tests used by the company to base its claims were unreliable, fined the firm $500,000, and required it to spend another $200,000 on corrective advertising in newspapers and magazines. The STP corrective advertisement is shown in Figure 2.4.

Legislation Designed to Regulate Competitors

The *Robinson-Patman Act* (1936) was typical of Depression-era legislation. Known in some circles as the Anti-A&P Act, it was inspired by price competition from the developing grocery-store chains. In fact, the law was originally prepared by the United States Wholesale Grocers Association. The country was in the midst of the Depression, and leg-

[6]"AMF Will Produce TV Ads Featuring Safety in Bicycling," *The Wall Street Journal* (July 9, 1979), p. 5.

[7]Jacob Jacoby, Margaret C. Nelson, and Wayne D. Hoyer, "Corrective Advertising and Affirmative Disclosure Statements: Their Potential for Confusing and Misleading the Consumer," *Journal of Marketing* (Winter 1982), pp. 61–72.

Figure 2.4 An Example of Corrective Advertising

ADVERTISEMENT

FTC NOTICE

As a result of an investigation by the Federal Trade Commission into certain allegedly inaccurate past advertisements for STP's oil additive, STP Corporation has agreed to a $700,000 settlement. With regard to that settlement, STP is making the following statement:

It is the policy of STP to support its advertising with objective information and test data. In 1974 and 1975 an independent laboratory ran tests of the company's oil additive which led to claims of reduced oil consumption. However, these tests cannot be relied on to support the oil consumption reduction claim made by STP.

The FTC has taken the position that, in making that claim, the company violated the terms of a consent order. When STP learned that the test data did not support the claim, it stopped advertising containing that claim. New tests have been undertaken to determine the extent to which the oil additive affects oil consumption. Agreement to this settlement does not constitute an admission by STP that the law has been violated. Rather, STP has agreed to resolve the dispute with the FTC to avoid protracted and prohibitively expensive litigation.

February 13, 1978

islative interest was directed toward saving jobs. The developing chain stores were seen as a threat to traditional retailers and to employment. The Robinson-Patman Act was a government effort to reduce this threat.

The act, which was technically an amendment to the Clayton Act, prohibited price discrimination in sales to wholesalers, retailers, or other producers that was not based on a cost differential. It also disallowed selling at an unreasonably low price in order to eliminate competition. The Clayton Act had applied only to price discrimination by geographic area that injured local sellers. The supporting rationale for the Robinson-Patman legislation was that the chain stores might be able to secure supplier discounts that were not available to the small, independent stores. As one writer expressed it: "The designers of the law, aiming to strengthen the precautionary element in antitrust and to afford greater equality of opportunities, thus gave consideration to the individual competitor as well as to competition in general."[8] The major defenses against charges of price discrimination are that it has been used in an attempt to meet competitors' prices and that it is justified by cost differences.

When a firm asserts that price differentials are used in good faith to meet competition, the logical question is what constitutes good faith pricing behavior? The answer depends on the circumstances of each situation.

When cost differentials are claimed as a defense, the price differences must not exceed the cost differences resulting from selling to different classes of buyers. A major difficulty of the defense is justifying the differences. Indeed, many authorities consider this area one of the most confusing in the Robinson-Patman Act.

The varying interpretations of the act certainly qualify it as one of the vaguest of marketing laws. For the most part, charges brought under the act are handled on an individual basis. Marketers must therefore continually evaluate their pricing actions to avoid potential Robinson-Patman violations.

Unfair Trade Laws Enacted in the 1930s, *unfair trade laws* are state laws requiring sellers to maintain minumum prices for comparable merchandise. These laws were intended to protect small specialty shops, such as dairy stores, from the loss-leader pricing of like products by chain stores. Typically, the retail price floor was set at cost plus some modest markup. Although most of these laws remain on the books, they have become less important in the more prosperous years since the 1930s and are seldom enforced.

Removing Barriers to Competition Fair trade is a concept that affected regulation of competitive activity for decades. In 1931, California became the first state to enact fair trade legislation. Most other states soon followed suit; only Missouri, the District of Columbia, Vermont, and Texas failed to adopt such laws. *Fair trade laws* permitted manufacturers to stipulate a minimum retail price for a product and to require their

[8]Marshall C. Howard, *Legal Aspects of Marketing* (New York: McGraw-Hill, 1964), p. 8.

retail dealers to sign contracts stating that they would abide by such prices.[9]

The basic argument behind the legislation was that a product's image, implied by its price, was a property right of the manufacturer, who should have the authority to protect the asset by requiring retailers to maintain a minimum price. Fair trade legislation can be traced to lobbying by organizations of independent retailers who feared chain-store growth. The economic mania of the Depression years was clearly evident in these statutes.

A U.S. Supreme Court decision holding fair trade contracts illegal in interstate commerce led to passage of the *Miller-Tydings Resale Price Maintenance Act* (1937). This law exempted interstate fair trade contracts from compliance with antitrust requirements. The states were thus authorized to keep these laws on their books if they so desired.

Over the years, fair trade declined in importance as price competition became a more important marketing strategy. These laws became invalid with passage of the *Consumer Goods Pricing Act* (1975). This act halted all interstate use of resale price maintenance, an objective long sought by consumer groups.

Consumer Protection: A Changing Legal Environment

The first activist legislation dealing with a specific marketing practice was the *Pure Food and Drug Act* (1906), which prohibited the adulteration and misbranding of foods and drugs involved in interstate commerce. The bill was enacted because of the unsanitary meat-packing practices of Chicago stockyards. It was strengthened in 1938 by the *Food, Drug, and Cosmetic Act* and in 1962 by the *Kefauver-Harris Drug Amendments* (the latter legislation a response to the thalidomide tragedies). Since that time, the Food and Drug Administration (FDA) has held increased regulatory authority in such matters as product development, branding, and advertising.

Rules governing advertising and labeling constitute another sphere of marketing's legal environment. The *Wool Product Labeling Act* of 1939 (requiring that the kind and percentage of wool in a product be identified), the *Fur Products Labeling Act* of 1951 (requiring identification of the animal from which the fur was derived), and the *Flammable Fabrics Act* of 1953 (prohibiting the interstate sale of flammable fabrics) formed the original legislation in this area. A more recent law—the *Fair Packaging and Labeling Act,* passed in 1967—requires the disclosure of product identity, the name and address of the manufacturer or distributor,

[9]The fair trade concept is reviewed in such articles as James C. Johnson and Louis E. Boone, "Farewell to Fair Trade," *MSU Business Topics* (Spring 1976), pp. 22–30; and L. Louise Luchsinger and Patrick M. Dunne, "Fair Trade Laws—How Fair?" *Journal of Marketing* (January 1978), pp. 50–54.

and information concerning the quality of the contents. In 1971, the *Public Health Cigarette Smoking Act* prohibited tobacco advertising on radio and television.

The truth-in-lending law deserves special attention. Formally known as *Title I of the Consumer Credit Protection Act* (1968), the statute requires disclosure of the annual interest rates on loans and credit purchases. The basic premise is this information will make it easier for consumers to compare sources of credit. Various assessments of the law, however, suggest that many consumers pay relatively little attention to interest rates; furthermore, they often have limited alternative credit sources.

Other laws that may influence marketing practices are the *Fair Credit Reporting Act* and the *Environmental Protection Act*, both of which became law in 1970. The Fair Credit Reporting Act gives individuals access to credit reports prepared about them and permits them to change incorrect information. The Environmental Protection Act established the Environmental Protection Agency (EPA) and gave it the power to deal with major types of pollution. EPA actions, of course, have a profound effect on the marketing system.

The *Consumer Product Safety Act* (1972) also has far-reaching influence on marketing strategy and on the marketing environment. This legislation created the Consumer Product Safety Commission, which has the authority to specify safety standards for most consumer products.

The *Equal Credit Opportunity Act* (1975–1977) banned discrimination in lending practices based on sex, marital status, race, national origin, religion, age, or receipt of payments from public assistance programs. The sex and marital status portions of the act went into effect in 1975, and the remaining portions became effective in 1977.

The *Fair Debt Collection Practices Act* (1978) prohibited harassing, deceptive, or unfair collection practices by debt collecting agencies. In-house debt collectors, such as banks, retailers, and attorneys, are exempt, however. Misrepresentation of the consumer's legal rights is an example of a specific practice that was banned by the act.

Table 2.1 summarizes the major legislative acts affecting marketing and indicates whether a particular law was primarily intended to promote a competitive environment, to assist in regulating competitors, or to regulate marketing practices affecting consumers. The table also lists the elements of marketing strategy affected by the legislation.

Many of the pieces of legislation introduced in this section will be referred to again throughout the text. In summary, the legal framework for marketing decisions is basically a positive environment; it attempts to encourage a competitive marketing system employing fair business practices. What marketing's legal future will be, of course, is open to debate. It appears, however, that future marketing legislation will be more directly concerned with protecting consumer interests and will probably come from three sources: (1) state and local governments,

Table 2.1 Impact of Marketing Legislation on Marketing Decisions

Legislation	Date Enacted	Assists in Maintaining a Competitive Environment	Assists in Regulating Competitors	Regulates Specific Marketing Activities	Impact on the Marketing Mix: Product Strategy	Distribution Strategy	Promotion Strategy	Pricing Strategy
Sherman Antitrust Act	1890	■			■	■	■	■
Clayton Act	1914	■			■	■	■	■
Federal Trade Commission Act	1914	■		■	■	■	■	■
Webb-Pomerene Export Trade Act	1918	■			■	■	■	■
Unfair Trade Laws	1930		■	■				■
Fair Trade Laws	1931		■	■				■
Celler-Kefauver Antimerger Act	1950	■			■	■	■	■
Consumer Goods Pricing Act	1975	■		■				■
Pure Food and Drug Act	1906			■	■			
Robinson-Patman Act	1936		■	■				■
Miller-Tydings Resale Price Maintenance Act	1937		■	■				■
Wheeler-Lea Act	1938			■			■	
Food, Drug, and Cosmetic Act	1938			■	■			
Wool Products Labeling Act	1939			■	■			
Fur Products Labeling Act	1951			■	■			
Flammable Fabrics Act	1953			■	■			
Kefauver-Harris Drug Amendments	1962			■	■			
Fair Packaging and Labeling Act	1967			■	■			
Consumer Credit Protection Act	1968			■	■		■	■
Fair Credit Reporting Act	1970			■	■	■	■	■
National Environmental Protection Act	1970			■	■	■	■	■
Public Health Cigarette Smoking Act	1971			■			■	
Consumer Product Safety Act	1972			■	■			
Equal Credit Opportunity Act	1975–77			■	■	■	■	■
Fair Debt Collection Practices Act	1978			■	■	■	■	■

(2) court decisions, and (3) regulations by such administrative agencies as the Federal Trade Commission and the Food and Drug Administration. These sources, closely tied to consumer affairs, are likely to assume an active role in marketing legislation.

The Economic Environment

In addition to the competitive, political, and legal environments, marketers must understand the **economic environment** and its impact upon their organizations. Three economic subjects of major concern to marketers in recent years have been recession, unemployment, and inflation.

A deteriorating economic environment adversely affects most marketers. However, for some companies, the recent recession was good news. As inflation continues and production declines, with corresponding growth in the level of unemployment, consumer buying patterns shift. Flour millers note that flour sales increase. Automobile repairs and home improvements also increase. Greeting card firms report that consumers buy fewer gifts, but more expensive cards. Hardware stores show higher sales. Decline is of course experienced by many other firms. Clearly, the economic environment has a sizable influence on the way marketers operate.

Stages of the Business Cycle

The economic environment is extremely complex. Operating within it are dynamic business fluctuations that tend to follow a cyclical pattern composed of four stages:

1. Prosperity
2. Recession
3. Depression
4. Recovery[10]

No marketer can disregard the economic climate in which a business functions, for the type, direction, and intensity of a firm's marketing strategy depends upon it. The marketer must also be aware of the economy's relative position in the business cycle and how it will affect the position of the particular firm. This requires the marketer to study forecasts of future economic activity.

Of necessity, marketing activity differs with each stage of the business cycle. During prosperous times, consumers are usually more will-

[10]Many economists argue that society is capable of preventing future depressions through intelligent use of various economic policies. Thus, a recession would be followed by a period of recovery.

ing to buy than when they feel economically threatened. For example, during the recent recession, personal savings climbed to high levels as consumers (fearing possible layoffs and other work force reductions) cut back their expenditures for many products in the nonessential category. Marketers must pay close attention to the consumer's relative willingness to buy. The aggressiveness of one's marketing strategy and tactics is often dependent upon current buying intentions. More aggressive marketing may be called for in periods of lessened buying interest, as when automakers use cash rebate schemes to move inventories.

Inflation Inflation has been a major economic concern to marketers in recent years. **Inflation,** which can occur during any stage of the business cycle, is defined as a rising price level resulting in reduced purchasing power for the consumer. A person's money is devalued in terms of what it can buy. Traditionally, this phenomenon has been more prevalent in countries outside North America. However, during the late 1970s and early 1980s, the United States experienced double-digit inflation. Although the rate of inflation declined considerably during the mid-1980s, the recent experiences led to widespread concern over public policy designed to stabilize price levels and over ways to adjust personally to such reductions in the dollar's spending power.

Stagflation is a word that has been coined to describe a peculiar brand of inflation that characterized some recent economic experiences. It is a situation where an economy has high unemployment and a rising price level at the same time. Formulation of effective strategies is particularly difficult under these circumstances.

Unemployment As the rate of inflation slowed in the mid-1980s, public concerns turned to a second economic problem: *unemployment.* The ranks of the unemployed—officially defined as people actively looking for work who do not have jobs—swelled to 10.8 percent of the U.S. labor force, or 12 million people, by 1983. By contrast, the unemployment rate was 4.5 percent in 1965, 4.9 percent in 1970, and 7 percent in 1980. The 10 percent unemployment rate had not been reached since the Great Depression of the 1930s.

Unemployment results from a number of factors. In some instances, workers in the process of leaving old jobs and finding new ones, or students leaving school and looking for jobs, are unemployed for short periods of time. The estimated 2 to 3 percent of the labor force who are likely to be in the job search phase of their careers are termed *frictionally unemployed.* In other instances, seasonal employees such as farm workers who harvest such crops as citrus fruits and lettuce, construction workers, and added retail clerical workers during holiday periods may vary in number, resulting in *seasonal unemployment.* Still other workers are *structurally unemployed* because they either lack the necessary skills for available jobs or the skills they possess are not demanded by potential employers. Many workers in Minnesota became jobless when the iron ore deposits in the Mesabi Range were exhausted.

Cyclical unemployment, the final type, results from disruptions in overall economic activity. The severe recession of the early 1980s contributed greatly to the ranks of the unemployed. As production slowed and many factories ceased operation entirely, millions of workers found themselves out of work. The consequences of reduced income and uncertainty about future income were reflected in the marketplace.

Government Tools for Combatting Inflation and Unemployment The government can attempt to deal with the twin economic problems of inflation and unemployment by using two basic approaches: fiscal policy and monetary policy. **Fiscal policy** concerns the receipts and expenditures of government. To combat inflation, an economy could reduce government expenditures, raise its revenues (primarily taxes), or try some combination of both. It could also use direct controls, such as wage and price controls. A potential danger of these actions is the possibility of adding to the ranks of the unemployed. **Monetary policy** refers to the manipulation of the money supply and market rates of interest. In periods of rising prices, monetary policy may dictate that the Federal Reserve System take action to decrease the money supply and raise interest rates. These steps would increase the cost of borrowing and discourage additional expenditures. In periods of high unemployment, an increase in the money supply and a resultant decrease in interest rates may serve to stimulate the economy and increase the number of available jobs.

Both fiscal and monetary policy have been used in the recent battles with inflation and unemployment. Their marketing implications are numerous and varied. Higher taxes mean lowered consumer purchasing power, which usually results in sales declines for nonessential goods and services. A lowered money supply means less liquidity is available for potential conversion to purchasing power. High interest rates often lead to a significant slump in the construction and housing industries.

Both unemployment and inflation affect marketing by modifying consumer behavior. Unless unemployment insurance, personal savings, and union supplementary unemployment benefits are sufficient to offset lost earnings, the unemployed individual has less income to spend in the marketplace. Even if the individual is completely compensated for lost earnings, his or her buying behavior is likely to be affected. As consumers become more conscious of inflation, they are likely to become more price conscious in general. This can lead to three possible outcomes, all important to marketers. Consumers can (1) elect to buy now in the belief that prices will be higher later (automobile dealers often use this argument in their commercial messages); (2) decide to alter their purchasing patterns; or (3) postpone certain purchases.

The Technological Environment

The **technological environment** consists of the applications to marketing of knowledge based upon discoveries in science, inventions, and innovations. It results in new products for consumers and improves existing products. It is a frequent source of price reductions through the development of new production methods or new materials. It also can make existing products obsolete virtually overnight—as slide rule manufacturers would attest. Technological innovations are exemplified in the container industry, where glass and tinplate containers have faced intense competition from such innovations as aluminum, fiberfoil, and plastics.

Marketing decision makers must closely monitor the technological environment for a number of reasons. New technology may be the means by which they remain competitive in their industries. It may also be the vehicle for the creation of entirely new industries. Computers, lasers, and xerography all resulted in the development of major industries during the past 25 years.

In addition, marketers must anticipate the effect such technological innovations are likely to have upon the lifestyles of consumers, the products of competitors, the demands of industrial users, and the regulatory actions of government. The advent of videocassette recorders, videodiscs, and lower cost satellite receiving stations may adversely affect concert attendance and movie ticket sales. A longer lasting engine may reduce industrial purchases. A new process may result in reduction of pollution and produce changes in local ordinances.

A major source of technological innovations from government research has been the space program. Hundreds of industrial applications of space technology have been made, and the federal government has encouraged private enterprise to make use of these innovations. Table 2.2 reveals some applications that have already been implemented.

The Energy Crisis

The term *energy crisis* refers to the general realization that our energy resources are not limitless. This realization was first brought on by the 1973–74 Arab oil embargo. Threatened by the cutbacks, much of the industrialized world scrambled for ways of conserving energy. Conservation measures are widespread—for instance, reduced speed limits and inducements to increase insulation usage. A Canadian division of Nashua Corporation even began labeling its promotional material, "Printed in U.S.A. to conserve Canadian raw material and energy."[11]

Several facts have now become evident about the energy crisis of the 1970s. First, the crisis has forced business and society to rethink the

[11] *The Wall Street Journal* (April 11, 1974), p. 1.

Table 2.2 Technological Spinoffs from the U.S. Space Program

Orbiting satellites that can monitor the earth and provide valuable data on crops, weather, and earthquakes.

Carbon fibers used in jet aircraft, golf clubs, and tennis rackets. They are lighter than steel, but they are stronger and stiffer.

Advances in health and medical areas, such as improved splints for broken limbs and more effective cancer detection devices.

New alloys used in tools, kitchenware, and household appliances.

Trajectory and moon landing analyses have resulted in a fully computerized auto traffic control system for a nine-square-mile area in Los Angeles. The system calculates the best traffic light sequence during rush hour traffic. Mobility has been increased by 15 percent during tests, resulting in gas consumption savings and reduced air pollution.

Wind deflectors for trucks have been developed to reduce wind resistance by 24 percent, resulting in a 10 percent fuel savings.

Life rafts equipped with radar reflective canopies greatly increase their visibility from the air.

Orbiting satellites have been responsible for the virtual elimination of the screwworm in the United States. The worm destroys cattle, poultry, and wildlife.

Land surveying satellites can spot 99 percent of the fresh water sources currently not being used in the United States.

Aluminized plastic used to keep fluids cold in space programs is used in lightweight jackets, sleeping bags, and parkas.

Silicone plastic from airplane seats has been used in football helmet liners.

A computer image process used to enhance satellite photos can indicate missing chromosomes in fetuses, thus identifying possible inherited diseases before the infant is born.

Source: Richard T. Hise, Peter L. Gillett, and John K. Ryans, Jr., *Basic Marketing* (Boston, Mass.: Little, Brown & Co., 1979), p. 121. Reprinted by permission.

current allocation of energy resources. Existing sources are being expanded. Traditional resources like coal are being rediscovered. New ones are being sought. Perhaps the most important fact is that attempts are being made to cut waste in energy utilization. The oil embargo of the 1970s forced the industrialized free world to take the necessary steps for its self-preservation.

Marketing has also been affected by the energy crisis. For example, the U.S. tire industry has had to deal with three energy-related setbacks:

1. Reduced levels of driving, causing a reduction in sales.
2. Lower new car sales, reducing the original equipment market (OEM) for tires.
3. Increased costs of petroleum-based raw materials.

Other markets have faced similar problems; the toy industry, for example, depends on a petroleum derivative—plastic. Some plastics have increased substantially in price within a very short time.[12]

[12]A comprehensive discussion of energy prospects and problems appears in Gordon H. G. McDougall, John D. Claxton, J. R. Brent Ritchie and C. Dennis Anderson, "Consumer Energy Research: A Review," *Journal of Consumer Research* (December 1981), pp. 343–354.

Resources and the Average American

One has only to follow a sanitation truck through suburban neighborhoods and apartment complexes to realize the huge amounts of products consumed by the average American. But what about a complete lifetime? The figure below reveals some examples of just how much resources the average American consumes in a lifetime. It also includes the resources used by industry in producing the goods that will ultimately be consumed by our average American.

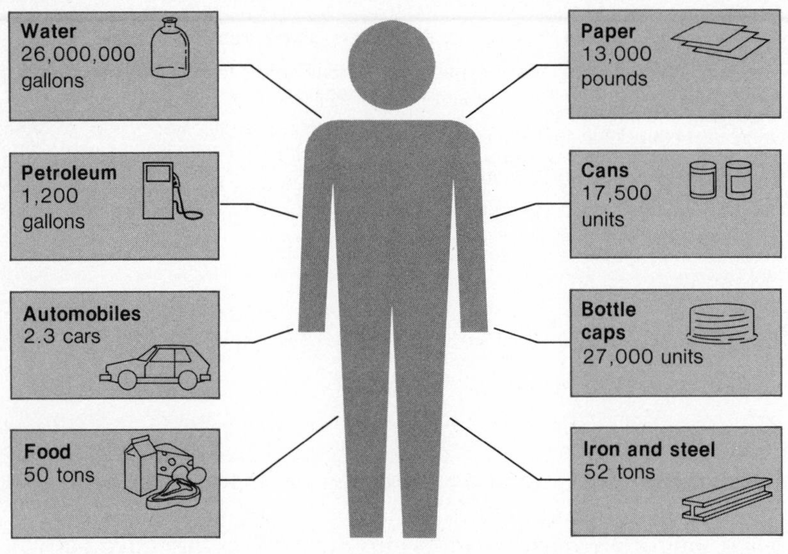

Source: Data reported in G. Tyler Miller, Jr., *Living in the Environment: Concepts, Problems, and Alternatives* (Belmont, Calif.: Wadsworth, 1975), p. 15.

As shortages began to appear in many critical industrial areas, marketers were faced with a relatively strange phenomenon: how should limited supplies be allocated to customers whose demands exceed the quantities available for distribution? Many marketers were not prepared to cope with such a situation. The energy crisis and other shortages have forced marketing to devise a fuller range of strategy alternatives.

Demarketing—Dealing with Shortages

Shortages—temporary or permanent—can be caused by several factors. A brisk demand may exceed manufacturing capacity or outpace the response time required to gear up a production line. Shortages may also be caused by a lack of raw materials, component parts, energy, or labor. Regardless of the cause, shortages require marketers to reorient their thinking.[13]

Demarketing, a term that has come into general use in recent years, refers to the process of cutting consumer demand for a product back to a level that can reasonably be supplied by the firm. Some oil companies, for example, have publicized tips on how to cut gasoline consumption. Utility companies have encouraged homeowners to install more insulation to lower heating bills. Many cities have discouraged central business district traffic by raising parking fees and violation penalities.

Shortages sometimes force marketers to be allocators of limited supplies. This is in sharp contrast to marketing's traditional objective of expanding sales volume. Shortages require marketers to decide whether to spread a limited supply over all customers so that none are satisfied, or to back order some customers so that others may be completely supplied. Shortages certainly present marketers with a unique set of marketing problems.

The Societal/Cultural Environment

The Chevalline Meat Company knows that the societal/cultural environment works against them. When you try to get someone to eat somebody's pony, you've got trouble. Chevalline is trying to induce North Americans to eat more horsemeat, despite an environment that views horses as pets and companions, not livestock for slaughter. U.S. and Canadian consumers eat virtually no horsemeat, although in France and other European countries the meat is well liked.

Chevalline even had some difficulty obtaining a license to open a horsemeat market. Whether the firm will ever change consumer opinion is debatable, but its problems dramatize the importance of understanding and assessing the societal/cultural environment when making marketing decisions.

The **societal/cultural environment** is the marketer's relationship with society and/or its culture. Obviously, there are many different facets of significance. One important category is the general readiness of society to accept a marketing idea, as discussed above.

Another important category is the trust and confidence of the public in business as a whole. Such confidence has been on the decline since

[13]Interesting articles related to this topic include Philip Kotler and Sidney J. Levy, "Demarketing, Yes, Demarketing," *Harvard Business Review* (November–December 1971), pp. 74–80; David W. Cravens, "Marketing Management in an Era of Shortages," *Business Horizons* (February 1974), pp. 79–85; and Sumer C. Aggarwal, "Prepare for Continual Materials Shortages," *Harvard Business Review* (May–June 1982), pp. 6–10.

the mid-1960s. Opinion polls suggest that people have lost confidence in major companies (although they maintain faith in the private enterprise system). These declines should, however, be viewed in perspective. All institutions have lost public confidence to some degree. In fact, some would argue that government and labor unions are even less popular than business.

The societal/cultural environment for marketing decisions has both expanded in scope and increased in importance. Today no marketer can initiate a strategy without taking the societal/cultural environment into account. Marketers must develop an awareness of the manner in which it affects their decisions. The constant flux of societal issues requires that marketing managers place more emphasis on addressing these questions instead of merely concerning themselves with the standard marketing tools. Some firms have created a new position—manager of public policy research—to study the changing societal environment's future impact on the company.

One question facing contemporary marketing is how to measure the accomplishment of socially oriented objectives. A firm that is attuned to its societal environment must develop new ways of evaluating its performance. Traditional income statements and balance sheets are no longer adequate. This issue will be further developed in a later chapter as one of the most important challenges facing contemporary marketing.

Importance in International Marketing Decisions

The cultural context for marketing decision making is often more important in the international sphere than in the domestic. Marketers must be cognizant of cultural differences in the way that business affairs are conducted abroad. Consider the following case:

The stereotype of the American male—hail-fellow-well-met, cordial, friendly, outgoing, and gregarious—does not mesh with the discomfort he feels and often shows in his contacts with Latin Americans and Middle Easterners. These people crowd close to him to talk, and in Latin America his host is likely to greet him with a warm abrazo, *suggesting unfamiliar intimacy. Anyone who has ever attended a party or a reception in Latin America must surely have observed the self-consciousness of the uninitiated stateside visitor, who keeps backing away from his native host, to whom it is natural to carry on a conversation separated by inches. Last year at a businessman's club in Brazil, where many receptions are held for newly arrived executives, the railings on the terrace had to be reinforced because so many businessmen fell into the gardens as they backed away.*[14]

[14]Lawrence Stessin, "Incidents of Culture Shock Among American Businessmen Overseas," *Pittsburgh Business Review* (November–December 1971), p. 3.

Consumer behavior and tastes also differ from place to place, as is suggested by these situations.[15]

1. In Thailand, Helene Curtis Industries switched to black shampoo because Thai women believe it makes their hair look glossier.
2. Nestlé, a Swiss multinational company, now brews more than 40 varieties of instant coffee to satisfy different national tastes.
3. General Foods Corporation entered the British market with its standard powdered Jell-O only to find that British cooks prefer the solid wafer or cake form, even if it takes more time to prepare. After several frustrating years, the company gave up and pulled out of the market.
4. In Italy a company that set up a corn processing plant found that its marketing effort failed because Italians think of corn as pig food.

Many marketers recognize societal differences among countries but assume that a homogeneous societal environment exists domestically. Nothing could be further from the truth! The United States is a mixed society composed of varied submarkets. These submarkets can be classified by age, race, place of residence, sex, and numerous other determinants.

Sex is an increasingly important societal factor. The feminist movement has had a decided effect on marketing, and particularly on promotion. Television commercials now feature women in less stereotyped roles than in previous years.

Since societal variables change constantly, marketers must continually monitor their dynamic environment. What appears to be out of bounds today may be tomorrow's greatest market opportunity. Consider the way subjects that were previously taboo, such as feminine hygiene products, are now commonly advertised.

The societal variables must be recognized by modern business executives since they affect the way consumers react to different products and marketing practices. One of the most tragic—and avoidable—of all marketing mistakes is the failure to appreciate societal differences within our own domestic market.

The rise of consumerism can be partially traced to the growing public concern with making business more responsible to its constituents. Consumerism, which is discussed in detail in a later chapter, is an evolving aspect of marketing's societal environment. Certainly the advent of this movement has influenced the move toward more direct protection of consumer rights in such areas as product safety. This concern will undoubtedly be amplified and expanded in the years ahead.

Source: "Why a Global Market Doesn't Exist," *Business Week* (December 9, 1970), pp. 140, 142, 144.

Figure 2.5 The Marketing Manager and the Marketing Variables—Controllable and Uncontrollable

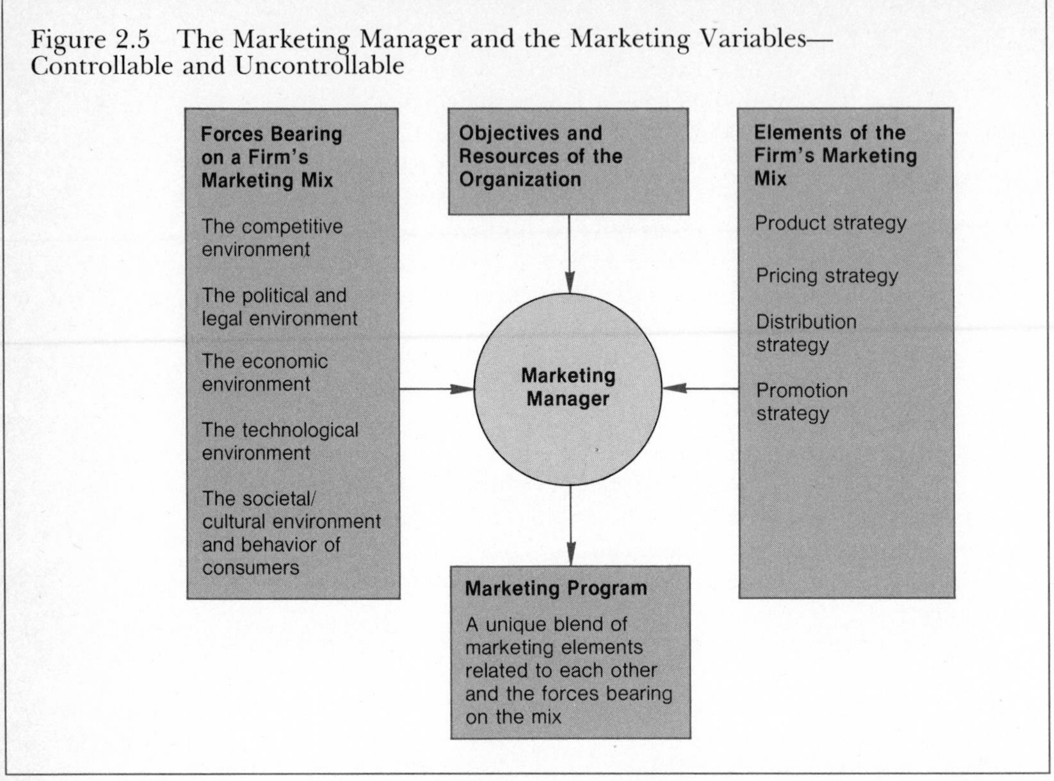

As a conclusion to this look at the marketing environment, Figure 2.5 illustrates how the marketing manager works, controlling marketing elements in relation to the forces bearing on a firm's marketing mix. In light of the opportunities and constraints perceived in the environmental framework, as well as the firm's objectives and resources, the manager develops a marketing program (marketing strategy). The elements or tools of the marketing strategy are product, pricing, distribution, and promotion strategies. These are blended together in a unique manner to make up the marketing mix. The result wins customers, sales, and profits for the firm.

While this concept is simple in itself, it is extremely complicated in practice and difficult to do well. The remainder of this text will elaborate on the process. The next chapters focus upon marketing planning and forecasting as starting points for the ultimate determination of market segments and the design of effective marketing mixes.

Summary

The environment for marketing decisions is the theme of this chapter. Five specific environments are considered: competitive, political and legal, economic, technological, and societal/cultural. These are important to the study of marketing because they provide a framework within which marketing strategies are formulated. Environmental factors are among the most dynamic aspects of contemporary business.

The competitive environment is the interactive process that occurs in the marketplace. Marketing decisions influence the market and are in turn affected by the counterstrategies of competition. The legal segment attempts to maintain a competitive environment and to regulate specific marketing practices. The economic environment often influences the manner in which consumers will behave toward varying marketing appeals. The technological environment generates new and improved products, but may render currently profitable products and services obsolete. Societal aspects, however, may become the most important to marketers. Concern with adapting to a changing societal environment, both domestically and internationally, has advanced to the forefront of marketing thought.

Key Terms

competitive environment
political and legal environment
corrective advertising
economic environment
inflation
stagflation
fiscal policy
monetary policy
technological environment
demarketing
societal/cultural environment

Review Questions

1. Identify and briefly describe the five components of the marketing environment.
2. Explain the types of competition faced by marketers.
3. What are the steps involved in developing a competitive strategy?
4. Government regulation in the United States has evolved in three general phases. Identify each of these phases and give an example of laws enacted during each phase.
5. Explain the methods used by the Federal Trade Commission in protecting consumers.
6. Distinguish between fair trade laws and unfair trade laws.
7. What are the major economic factors affecting marketing decisions?
8. Distinguish between inflation and stagflation. In what ways do they affect marketing?

9. Identify the ways in which the technological environment affects marketing activities.
10. Explain how the societal/cultural environment influences marketing.

Discussion Questions and Exercises

1. Give an example of how each of the environmental variables discussed in this chapter might affect the following firms:
   a. Delta Airlines
   b. Local aerobics exercise center
   c. Pizza Hut
   d. Avon Products
   e. Sears catalog department
   f. Local CATV franchise
2. Comment on the following statement: The legal framework for marketing decisions is basically a positive one.
3. Can the consumerism movement be viewed as a rejection of the competitive marketing system? Defend your answer.
4. As a consumer, do you favor laws permitting resale price maintenance agreements? Would your answer vary if you were the producer of Zenith television sets? If you were the retailer of Zenith television sets? Why or why not?
5. What are the major defenses firms might use if accused of a Robinson-Patman Act violation? Evaluate each defense.

CASES FOR PART 1

Case 1.1
The Electric Feather Pirogue

The Fin and Feather Products Company of Marshall, Texas, produces a line of small, versatile, lightweight boats called the Electric Feather Pirogue (pronounced pē rō). The name *feather* was chosen to emphasize the light weight of the boat, and *electric* because it is propelled by an electric trolling motor. The name *pirogue* refers to the historic small river boats used on the Louisiana bayous. The kayak-shaped boat is 12 feet long, 38 inches wide, and 12 inches deep. It comes complete with motor and has a load capacity of about 540 pounds. Power is provided by a standard 12-volt automotive-type storage battery. The built-in Shakespeare motor is available with 18-pound or 24-pound thrust. The hull is handcrafted fiberglass, sturdily constructed by a hand layup process.

Marketing Strategy

Product

The stable, flat-bottomed Pirogue can operate in very shallow water, so it is ideally suited for fishing, duck hunting, bird watching, or just leisurely stream cruising. The propeller is protected from submerged objects by specially engineered motor guards on each side of the exposed drive unit. A one-and-one-half-inch sheet of polyurethane foam is built into the bottom to provide flotation. The boat is extremely simple to operate. A panel just below the wraparound gunwale contains two control switches—a forward-off-reverse switch and a low-medium-high speed switch.

A horizontal lever just above the panel provides steering control. There is only one moving part in the entire control system. The 3-speed, 18-pound thrust motor has a maximum speed of 10 miles an hour, and the 4-speed, 24-pound thrust motor can attain a speed of 14 miles an hour. The company furnishes a one-year unlimited warranty on the boat, and the Shakespeare Company provides a similar warranty on the motor.

The company produced only one basic model of the boat but offered optional equipment which provided some variation within the product line. Retail prices ranged from approximately $490 to $650 depending on motor size and optional equipment. Although designed to accommodate two people, the stan-

Source: This case was prepared by Robert H. Solomon and Janelle C. Ashley of Stephen F. Austin State University as a basis for class discussion. Reprinted by permission.

dard model has only one molded plastic seat. The second seat, deluxe swivel seats, marine carpeting, and tonneau cover are the major optional items. No trailer is required since the boat fits nicely on the roof of even the smallest car or in the back of a station wagon or pickup truck. Without battery, the Pirogue weighs only about 80 pounds and can easily be handled by one person.

Pricing

In year 1 (the base year), Bill Wadlington purchased controlling interest in, and assumed managerial control of, the seven-year-old Fin and Feather Products Company. One of Wadlington's first moves was to adopt a strict cash-and-carry policy; supplies and equipment were paid for at the time of purchase, and all sales were for cash prior to shipment whether being shipped to a dealer or directly to a customer. All shipments were FOB the factory in Marshall, Texas.

As a result of this policy, the firm had no accounts receivable and virtually no accounts payable. Wadlington anticipated sales of between 800 and 1,000 units in year 1. This volume would approach plant capacity and produce a wholesale dollar volume of approximately $350,000 to $400,000. After only six months of operation Wadlington would not predict an exact annual net profit figure, but he was very optimistic about the first year's profit prospect. It was also difficult to predict exactly what future volume would be, but sales had shown a steady increase throughout the first half of the year. The flow of inquiries from around the United States and from several foreign countries made the future look bright.

Distribution

The company hired no outside salespeople, and Wadlington was the only in-house salesman. There were 15 independent dealers around the country who bought at wholesale and assumed a standard markup. There was no formal agreement or contract between the company and the dealers, but to qualify as a dealer, an individual or firm's initial order had to be for at least five boats. Subsequent orders could be for any quantity desired. Dealers' orders had to be accompanied by a check for the entire amount of the purchase.

In addition to the dealers, the company had 20 agents who were authorized to take orders in areas outside dealer territories. These agents accepted orders for direct shipment to customers and were paid a commission for the boats they sold. Agents were not assigned a specific territory but could not sell in areas assigned to dealers. As with all sales, agent orders had to be prepaid. Direct orders from individuals were accepted at the factory when the customer lived outside a dealer territory. Most direct sales were the result of the company's advertisements in such magazines as *Ducks Unlimited, Outdoor Life, Argosy, Field and Stream,* and *Better Homes and Gardens.*

Promotion

Wadlington had not established a systematic promotional program. The services of an out-of-state advertising agency were used to develop and place ads and to help with brochures and other promotional materials. Almost all negotiations with the agency were handled by phone or mail. The amount of advertising done at any time depended on existing sales volume. As sales declined, advertising was increased; when orders approached plant capacity, advertising was curtailed. Magazines were the primary advertising medium used. Dealers and agents were provided with attractive, professionally prepared brochures. The company had exhibited, or had plans to exhibit, at boat shows in Texas, Ohio, and Illinois. Arrangements had been completed for Pirogues to be used as prizes on one of the more popular network television game shows.

A detailed analysis of sales, in terms of who was buying the boats and for what purpose, had not been made. However, Wadlington did know that one of the most successful ads was in *Better Homes and Gardens*. An examination of orders produced by the ad indicated that they were primarily from women who bought the boat for family use. There had been reports of the boats being used as utility boats for large houseboats and yachts, but the extent of such use was unknown. Although orders had been coming in from all parts of the country, the best sales areas were in the eastern and southeastern parts of the United States. Wadlington attributed this, at least in part, to the fact that the company's past sales efforts had been concentrated almost exclusively in the southern and southwestern areas of the country. After the company began using national media, new markets were tapped. The Pirogue had virtually no direct competition, particularly outside the Texas-Louisiana area.

Discussion Questions

1. Who would be the most likely target groups of customers for boats like the Pirogue?
2. Evaluate the marketing mix elements. Make recommendations concerning:
   a. Product strategy
   b. Distribution strategy
   c. Pricing strategy
   d. Promotional strategy
3. Which environmental variables are most likely to impact the firm's marketing program? Give specific examples.

Case 1.2
QUBE

On December 1, 1977, some consumers in Columbus, Ohio, became active participants in, rather than passive viewers of, the television medium when a new media communication system was marketed by QUBE, a division of Warner Amex Cable Communications, Inc. The system permits two-way communication be-

Source: From *Contemporary Cases in Marketing, Third Edition,* by W. Wayne Talarzyk. Copyright 1983 by Dryden Press, a division of Holt, Rinehart and Winston, Inc. Reprinted by permission of Holt, Rinehart and Winston.

tween subscribers and the company's computer-equipped production studios. By pressing buttons on their QUBE®[1] console (a computer terminal device attached to the home television set), subscribers can receive thirty channels of video entertainment and information. QUBE Cable's[2] two-way communication system offers not only a wide choice of entertainment to its customers but also an interactive capacity which encourages viewers to get involved. For example, subscribers can also take tests, participate in games, register opinions instantly, and actually take part in many programs and events offered by the QUBE interactive service.

Overview of QUBE Cable Service

Warner Amex QUBE Service has set the world's standards for two-way television since it was introduced in Columbus. QUBE service is a sophisticated two-way cable TV system which allows the viewer to actively participate in programming via a home computer console about the size of a desk calculator. QUBE Service is offered by Warner Amex Cable Communications Inc., a jointly owned company of Warner Communications Inc. and the American Express Company. Warner Amex operates 147 cable TV systems in twenty-seven states, serving more than 1,000,000 subscribers. Other Warner Amex systems offering QUBE interactive services are operational in Cincinnati and Pittsburgh and are under construction in Dallas, Houston, suburban St. Louis, and suburban Chicago.

The console, which is slightly larger than a hand calculator and is connected to the set by a twenty-five foot cord, controls selection of channels. Five response buttons on the console allow the subscriber to "touch in" and respond instantly to material appearing on any of the thirty channels. Figure 1 illustrates one version of the QUBE console. Channel descriptions change as new programming is introduced and the console itself varies by city served.

Service Description

Households in the QUBE service area in Columbus are provided with a small, lim-

Figure 1 QUBE Console and Its Operation

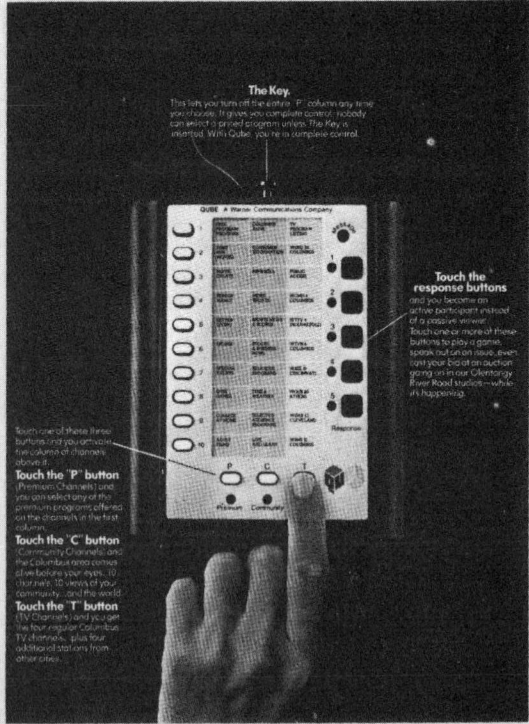

[1]QUBE is a registered service mark of Warner Amex Cable Communications, Inc.

[2]QUBE Cable is a trademark which applies to the system in Columbus, Ohio.

ited-capability channel selector console. The QUBE console makes available thirty channels of entertainment and informational and educational programming. The five response buttons allow the viewer to "touch-in" and anonymously respond to a variety of questions which appear on the screen. In this manner, QUBE asks the questions and viewers "talk back" to their televisions using the response buttons.

This sophisticated response capability is made possible by a computer which regularly polls the QUBE system, gathers information and displays subscribers' responses. These responses are displayed graphically, in percentages, during live programming. The average time it takes for the computer to poll the system and for the results to be displayed on the viewer's screen is under ten seconds.

The computer's constant polling of the QUBE system also makes possible QUBE's unique seven channels of pay-per-view programming. Watching these seven channels, viewers can watch full-length movies in stereo, informational shows ranging from cooking instructions to golf lessons, and special events such as championship boxing. Viewers are allowed a two-minute grace period (accumulated time) to decide whether they want to watch the program. After this two-minute period, viewers are billed for the program by the computer. Viewers receive a monthly bill for all pay-per-view programs, including such details as the name of the movie, the time of day watched, and the length of viewing time. Pursuant to the Warner Amex Code of Privacy, all such subscriber information is kept strictly confidential. Viewers pay only for what they watch on these seven channels.

QUBE system's interactive services are being extended into consumer-oriented services, such as information retrieval, home-shopping, and home banking. Home security (complete burglary, fire, and emergency medical protection) is another important aspect of two-way service. More than 5,000 homes in Columbus already subscribe to Warner Amex Security Systems.

QUBE III, a new-generation home computer console, was introduced on May 18, 1980. Half the size of the earlier console, it can accommodate up to 110 program channels and has data information retrieval or entertainment programming currently available or which may be developed in the next decade. The most advanced system of two-way communication in the United States, QUBE III is being used by QUBE service subscribers in Pittsburgh.

"Touching-in" to QUBE Interactive Service

Individual responses by subscribers using the five response buttons during QUBE polling are not recognized by the computer unless otherwise stated. Viewers normally are anonymous when they "touch-in" to a QUBE question. Announcers on QUBE service's live programs remind viewers "you are no longer anonymous" if individual responses are being recognized. One channel, QUBE T-1, is devoted to local programming not offered by other broadcasters in Columbus. What adds an extra spark to this local programming is QUBE service's unique two-way system of audience involvement. Viewers of QUBE T-1 do not have to be passive TV viewers. With the QUBE console's five response buttons (and a twenty-five-foot cord allowing viewers to hold the console while seated comfortably), viewers are actively involved in programming. Regularly scheduled interactive shows on QUBE T-1 include: "Columbus Alive," the only local talk/variety program in Columbus; "The Magic Touch," an interactive game show in which home viewers are the contestants; "Nuts and Bolts," a weekly show for young teens; and "Soap Scoop," a daily call-in show for soap opera fanatics.

QUBE Stereo Service For a $2 monthly fee, QUBE Cable subscribers can receive a stereo hookup with their cable TV service. Tuning to select positions on the FM dial, viewers can enjoy stereo soundtracks on all four QUBE stereo theatres, Home Box Office, and The Movie Channel. MTV:Music Television also is simulcast in stereo. Diversity of music on the FM band also is increased with imported FM stations from out of town and QUBE's own commercial-free programming of country, soft rock, and album rock music.

Narrowcasting Four of QUBE Cable's thirty channels—P-9, P-10, C-9, C-10—are capable of narrowcasting. Through narrowcasting, a program can be cablecast to a select group of subscribers only. It has been used by several communities in the QUBE Cable service area to conduct town meetings and also is a vehicle for special types of educational programming. Continuing education courses only for lawyers, doctors, and accountants have been narrowcasted by QUBE Cable.

Along the same lines as narrowcasting, QUBE Cable also is capable of "narrowpolling." When the mayor of Gahanna, Ohio (a QUBE franchise town) appears on QUBE Cable for the Gahanna Town Meeting, for example, he can ask interactive questions concerning issues affecting Gahanna and receive feedback only from Gahanna residents. The computer limits the universe of homes "touching-in" to Gahanna residents only.

Pricing and Promotion

Pricing Situation

Present eleven-channel Warner Amex cable subscribers can upgrade to thirty-channel QUBE service by paying a $9.95 installation charge and $14.95 if they want The Movie Channel or Home Box Office as well. New subscribers pay $19.95 for installation of QUBE service and $24.95 for the addition of The Movie Channel or Home Box Office. The monthly charge for QUBE interactive service is $13.95 or $21.90 for QUBE service with The Movie Channel or Home Box Office. Other costs depend on how much the premium channels are used; the prices for individual movies on premium channels are generally $1.50, $2.50, or $3.50 per view. The charges for individual viewings of Live & Learn courses can range from twenty-five cents for karate to $2.50 for preparation for college entrance exams.

QUBE Cable also offers two package plans. The QUBE Entertainment Plan, which includes the full thirty-channel service plus both Home Box Office and The Movie Channel with one QUBE console, costs $31.85 per month. The QUBE Cable Family Plan offers the same features as the Entertainment Plan plus an additional QUBE console. For a monthly charge of $36.85 for the Family Plan, two different QUBE Cable programs can be viewed by various family members at the same time.

Promotional Strategy

Initial promotional efforts were designed simply to create awareness of an interest in QUBE interactive service. Later advertisements focused on more information about QUBE—its advantages and capabilities. Print, radio, and television advertising was used to inform consumers about this new communications phenomenon.

An intensive direct-mail campaign was used to reach Warner Cable's 26,000 subscribers and to encourage them to sign up for QUBE interactive service. Two days later each of these households received a copy of the first month's forty-page QUBE program guide with complete programming and pricing information. The program guide, which had undergone many modifications, was discontinued by QUBE in 1981. QUBE subscribers can get current program listings from an insert in a local Sunday paper, from the program guide on the QUBE system, or from other sources.

Summary Situation

Since the system's inception, QUBE subscribers have participated in a variety of innovative and interactive situations. The following list is illustrative of some of these activities.

"Lulu Smith" was the nation's first major "interactive" television drama when viewers made use of the QUBE interactive service's two-way capability to direct the course of action in the story. The program recounted the adventures of a young girl growing up in an unconventional household and faced with several important decisions in her life. In many cases, the audience decided her fate by making choices on the QUBE console with its five response buttons. Results were immediately coded and processed by QUBE computers. About two-thirds of the show was preproduced. The remainder was live-in-studio, according to the dictates of the viewers. In addition, several preproduced segments reflected different plot options and were aired depending on how the audience wanted the program to proceed.

Immediately following a speech by President Carter, QUBE service subscribers were asked their reactions to the President's remarks by the NBC "Prime Time Saturday" network television program. Subscribers' opinions were immediately tabulated by QUBE computers and flashed on television screens across the nation and Canada.

"The Home Book Club," a new cable television show which enables viewers in the studio audience and at home to participate in discussions on current paperback bestsellers, premiered on QUBE interactive service. The show was the first attempt by the Public Library of Columbus and Franklin County to bring the traditional "book talk" concept into the homes of library users.

In 1978 and again in 1980, QUBE viewers were able to tell the Food and Drug Administration their desires for national policies concerning food labeling and issues relevant to the prescription and over-the-counter drug markets.

The world championship boxing match between Sugar Ray Leonard and Roberto Duran was carried by the QUBE system. QUBE subscribers were able to express their opinions during the live cablecast at the end of each round by pressing buttons on their home QUBE consoles.

When the Columbus Metros semi-professional football team played the Racine Gladiators in the world's first interactive football game, QUBE home subscribers, using their two-way interactive consoles with five response buttons, called all of the offensive and defensive plays for the Metros. The day of the Monday-morning quarterbacks had arrived.

Discussion Questions

1. What marketing strategy do you think QUBE Cable should adopt in attempting to add to its subscriber base?
2. Discuss the alternatives open to QUBE Cable in the area of increasing premium channel usage. What are your recommendations?
3. How would you go about getting more advertisers to avail themselves of QUBE Cable's services?
4. What other services do you think QUBE Cable should offer consumers and businesses?
5. What types of marketing research should QUBE Cable undertake at this point?

Charles Coolidge Parlin

Although the first known research project was conducted more than a century ago by the advertising firm of N.W. Ayer, the individual credited with the creation of marketing research as a profession and a vital aspect of marketing decision making was Charles Coolidge Parlin (1872–1942). The president of Curtis Publishing Company, which published the *Saturday Evening Post,* recognized that the magazine's advertising sales force could be considerably more effective if armed with concrete information abut the magazine's readers and their buying habits. Curtis hired a Wisconsin schoolmaster named Charles Parlin to collect such useful information.

Parlin's first major study focused on the agricultural implements industry and resulted in a 460-page report. His second major report resulted from visits to major U.S. cities and focused on department stores and wholesale and retail dry-goods establishments. In this four-volume report, he made the statement "the consumer is king"—an early summary of the marketing concept. During this period, Parlin organized his activities into a "commercial research" department—the first organized marketing research department.

Parlin's ingenuity in collecting marketing research is illustrated in an example related by Atlanta researcher Kenneth Hollander in the American Marketing Association's *Marketing News*. The Campbell Soup Company refused to advertise in the *Post,* arguing that it was read mainly by working people who were unlikely to pay the sum of ten cents for a prepared can of soup. Parlin turned to the unheard-of technique of "garbagology" to counter Campbell's managers' thesis. He chose a sample of garbage routes in Philadelphia and made arrangements with the sanitation department to dump the garbage at a local National Guard armory. After sifting through the various piles and counting the Campbell's soup cans in each pile, Parlin determined that blue-collar neighborhoods were high-volume purchasers of canned soup, while the more affluent areas depended upon servants to make their soup. The Campbell Soup Company became a regular advertiser in the *Post.*

2

PLANNING THE MARKETING EFFORT

The focus on the four chapters in Part Two is planning—anticipating the future and determining the courses of action designed to achieve organizational objectives. The chapters treat such vital subjects as development of marketing strategies, sales forecasting, use of market segmentation in selecting market targets, and provision of needed, decision-relevant marketing information. This part provides a foundation for the development of appropriate marketing programs for profitably serving chosen market segments.

3

MARKETING PLANNING AND FORECASTING

Chapter Objectives

1. To distinguish between strategic planning and tactical planning.
2. To explain how marketing planning differs at different levels of the organization.
3. To identify the steps in the marketing planning process.
4. To explain the portfolio and the BCG growth-market matrix approaches to marketing planning.
5. To identify the alternative marketing strategies available to marketers.
6. To identify the major types of forecasting methods.
7. To explain the steps involved in the forecasting process.

Most people agreed that David Dixon's plan *could* work. Dixon, a New Orleans art dealer and entrepreneur, felt that a major opportunity was available in the form of a March-to-July football season, and he had spent over two years attempting to make his idea a reality.

First, he wanted to make certain that his own expectations matched those of his would-be markets. Would the U.S. sports public accept the idea of a second professional football league operating during the spring? He commissioned a marketing research survey which revealed not only was there an interest in springtime football, but also a viewer preference for football over any other televised sport. Moreover, the survey reported that three fourths of those surveyed indicated they would watch televised games of the new football league. Although television viewers would not fill stadium seats, Dixon realized that national television coverage was necessary to legitimize the new league and to finance the high-cost franchises. After all, the National Football League had recently signed a $2 billion, five-year contract with the three television networks to be shared equally by the league and its 28 franchises, regardless of a team's record. Dixon planned to follow the same model.

There were some obvious examples of the dangers involved in launching a new league. Although the American Football League was so successful that it eventually merged with the established National Football League, there was the unfortunate experience of the World Football League. The WFL, which folded in its second season, left a legacy of $20 million in debts, a dry cleaner who kept one team's uniforms until bills were paid, Day-Glo footballs, inflated attendance figures, and a decided lack of credibility.

Dixon gained financial stability by locating wealthy individuals who were willing to capitalize teams at an estimated $6 million per team. Investors were also required to deposit a $1.5 million letter of credit to be used should a team be in danger of folding. After Dixon located these individuals, they chose cities for the twelve teams in major markets and secured leases for major stadiums. The map on the next page identifies the three United States Football League (USFL) divisions.

Teams are coached by well-known individuals like Chuck Fairbanks, George Allen, John Ralston, and Red Miller, and games are played in the Pontiac Silverdome, RFK Stadium, the Los Angeles Coliseum, Soldier Field, Giants Stadium outside New York, and other stadiums.

What about the product? As one observer points out, "Football also is unique in the relative anonymity of its players: Helmets mask faces; pads shield bodies. And the turnover of names on the back of jerseys is high. The average professional career lasts four seasons. Indeed, there are stars of considerable celebrity, but many more players work in obscurity." Although a few "name" players such as University of Georgia Heisman Trophy recipient Herschel Walker were signed, USFL teams sought to hold salaries to an average of $40,000, compared with $90,000 for an average player's salary in the NFL. The USFL plan was solid enough to entice ABC to pay $20 million for a two-year television contract for one game a week and play-off coverage. In addition, the league signed a cable television contract with the Entertainment & Sports Programming Network, attracted Miller Brewing Company as a national sponsor, Pan American as its official airlines, and Pony as its official shoe.

In each league city, marketing efforts were designed to develop enthusiasm for the new league and to maximize season ticket sales. The Chicago franchise emphasized the previous successes of coach George Allen and used a name-the-team contest that drew 12,000 entries. Special promotions were designed to lure business groups, who were likely prospects for multiple-ticket sales, and women, who reportedly comprise 40 percent of football's live and television audience. In addition,

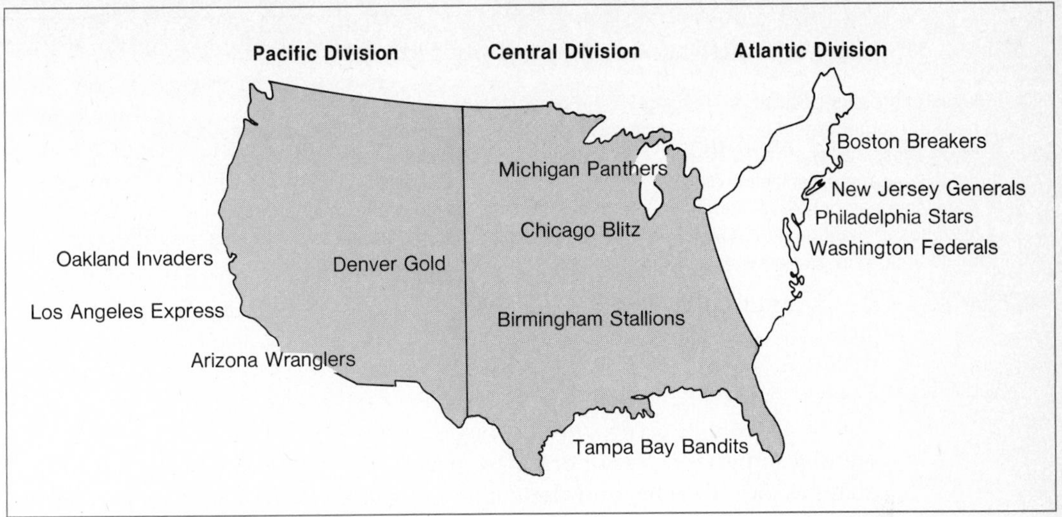

the national sponsors Miller and Pan Am assisted in the launch of the new venture. Season ticket sales grew in each city. David Dixon's marketing plan appeared to be working.[1]

The Conceptual Framework

"Should we grant a license for our new liquid-crystal watch display to a Japanese firm or simply export our models to Japan?"

"Will changing the performance time and date affect concert attendance?"

"Should we utilize company sales personnel or independent agents in the new territory?"

"Should discounts be offered to cash customers? What impact would such a policy have on our credit customers?"

These questions are examples of the thousands of major and minor decisions that the marketing manager regularly faces. Continual changes in the marketplace resulting from changing consumer expectations, technological improvements, competitive actions, economic trends, political and legal changes, as well as product innovations or pressures from distribution channel members, are likely to have sub-

[1]Adapted by permission from Michael Shaprio, "Extolling the Joys of Football in May," *Advertising Age* (January 24, 1983), pp. M–4, M–5, M–46.

Table 3.1 What Planning Can Accomplish for a Firm

1. It leads to a better position or standing for the organization.
2. It helps the organization progress in the ways that its management considers most suitable.
3. It helps every manager think, decide, and act more effectively for progress in the desired direction.
4. It helps keep the organization flexible.
5. It stimulates a cooperative, integrated, enthusiastic approach to organizational problems.
6. It indicates to management how to evaluate and check up on progress toward the planned objectives.
7. It leads to socially and economically useful results.

Source: Subhash C. Jain, *Marketing Planning and Strategy* (Cincinnati: Southwestern Publishing Co., 1981), p. 5.

stantial impact on the operations of any organization. Although these changes are often beyond the control of the marketing manager, effective planning can help the manager anticipate many changes and focus upon possible actions to take. Effective planning is often a major factor in distinguishing between success and failure. Table 3.1 summarizes the major benefits of planning for an organization.

Planning is the process of anticipating the future and determining the courses of action to achieve organizational objectives. As the definition indicates, planning is a continuous process that includes specifying objectives and the actions required to achieve them. The planning process creates a blueprint that not only specifies the means of achieving organization objectives, but also includes checkpoints where actual performance can be compared with expectations in order to determine whether the organizational activities are moving the organization toward its objectives. Such checkpoints are important means of control, which is another critical managerial function and the subject of Chapter 25.

Marketing planning—the implementation of planning activities as they relate to the achievement of marketing objectives—is the basis for all marketing strategies. Product lines, pricing decisions, selection of approximate distribution channels, and decisions relating to promotional campaigns all depend upon plans formulated within the marketing organization.

Strategic Planning versus Tactical Planning

Planning is often classified on the basis of scope or breadth. Some plans are quite broad and long-range, focusing on certain organizational objectives with major impact on the organization for a time period of five or more years. Such plans are typically called strategic plans. **Strategic planning** can be defined as the process of determining the primary objectives of an organization and the adoption of courses of action and

Strategic Planning at Esquire, Inc.

First-time visitors to the headquarters of Esquire, Inc., might believe they have the wrong address. There are no printing presses, no copyeditors, not even a magazine. In fact, only the Esquire name remains from its corporate past as publisher of such notable magazines as *Esquire* and *Gentlemen's Quarterly.* Since 1979, when it sold *GQ* to Condé Nast Publications, Esquire managers have moved into radically different markets by acquiring firms that offer unique products to specific market targets.

The process of diversification into nonpublishing began in 1960 when Esquire purchased Wide-Lite Corporation, a profitable manufacturer of specialty lighting. More recently, the firm purchased Belwin-Mills Publishing Corporation, the dominant publisher of instructional sheet music. Other acquisitions include American Broadcasting Company television stations in El Centro and Palm Springs, California.

Why has this strategic shift proven so successful? *Business Week* recently asked the same question to Bernard Krauss, Esquire's chief executive:

What is common to all of these businesses, contends Krauss, is that they are now leaders in their own small market segments. In educational publishing, Esquire has concentrated on phonics and reading workbooks for slow learners rather than go head to head with industry giants such as SFN, Addison-Wesley Publishing, and Macmillan in basic reading programs. Wide-Lite has continued to grow in a depressed lighting market by ducking the likes of General Electric Company with a product line built around energy-saving, high-intensity discharge lighting and sophisticated electronic lighting-control systems. Similarly, Belwin-Mills has a near-monopoly on instructional band music. . . .

Source: Quotation from "Esquire, Inc.: Finding Profits in Fields Far Beyond Magazines," *Business Week* (February 22, 1982), pp. 78, 83.

the allocation of resources necessary to achieve those objectives.[2] David Dixon's efforts in forming the new United States Football League represent strategic planning.

The word *strategy* is derived from a Greek term meaning "the general's art." Strategic planning has a critical impact on the destiny of the organization since it provides long-run direction for decision makers. At K mart, the nation's second largest retailer, the strategic plan calls for marketers to use low prices on commodity-type items to attract customers who may also buy merchandise with higher margins. In addi-

[2]Alfred D. Chandler, *Strategy and Structure* (Cambridge, Mass.: MIT Press, 1962), p. 13. See also Paul F. Anderson, "Marketing, Strategic Planning and the Theory of the Firm," *Journal of Marketing* (Spring 1982), pp. 15–26.

tion, the plan calls for a store location density in urban markets: each K mart store must be located within three miles of another store in order to reach a larger proportion of the market and to maximize the benefits of local advertising and store image.

By contrast, **tactical planning** focuses on the implementation of those activities specified by the strategic plans. Tactical plans are typically more short-term than strategic plans, focusing more on current and near-term activities that must be completed in order to implement overall strategies. Resource allocation is a common decision area for tactical planning. The decision by Hertz and Avis to counter the premium offers of National Car Rentals with their own premiums were the result of tactical planning.

Planning at Different Levels in the Organization

Planning is a major responsibility for every manager. Although managers at all levels devote some of their work days to planning, the relative proportion of time spent in planning activities and the types of planning vary at different organization levels.

Top management of a corporation—the board of directors, president, and functional vice-presidents, such as the chief marketing officer—spend greater proportions of their time engaged in planning than middle- and supervisory-level managers. In fact, one company president recommends that 30 to 50 percent of a chief executive's time should be spent on strategic planning.[3]

Also, top management is more likely to devote more of their planning activities to longer range strategic planning, while middle-level managers (such as the director of the advertising department, regional sales managers, or the physical distribution manager) tend to focus on narrower, tactical plans for their departments, and supervisory personnel are more likely to engage in developing specific programs to meet the goals for their responsibility areas. Table 3.2 indicates the types of planning engaged in at various organizational levels.

Steps in the Marketing Planning Process

As Figure 3.1 indicates, the basic objectives of the organization are the starting point for marketing planning. The basic goals of the organization are the guideposts from which marketing objectives and plans are

[3]"Strategic Planning Should Occupy 30 to 50 Percent of CEO's Time: Schanck," *Marketing News* (June 1, 1979), p. 1.

Table 3.2 Types of Plans Prepared by Different Levels of Management

Management Level	Type of Plan	General Content
Top		
Board of directors, president, operating division vice-presidents including marketing	Strategic planning	Objectives of organization; fundamental strategies; total budget
Middle		
General sales manager, marketing research director, head of advertising department	Tactical planning	Quarterly and semiannual plans; subdivision of budgets; policies and procedures for each individual's department
Supervisory		
District sales manager, supervisors	Tactical planning derived from planning at higher organization levels	Daily and weekly plans; unit budgets

Source: Adapted from William F. Glueck, *Management,* 2nd ed. (Hinsdale, Ill.: The Dryden Press, 1980), p. 246. Copyright 1980 by Dryden Press, a division of Holt, Rinehart and Winston. Adapted by permission of Holt, Rinehart and Winston.

derived. They provide direction for all phases of the organization and serve as standards in evaluating performance. For Nike, Inc., the overall objective is to be the leading firm in the $1.5 billion quality athletic-shoe market in the United States. Nike's marketing plans—both strategic and tactical—are based on this objective.

Marketing opportunities arise from a number of sources. Marketers at H.B. Reese Candy Company decided to accept the offer to feature their chocolate candy in a Steven Spielberg movie. Millions of moviegoers decided to imitate the candy preference of the tiny traveler from another galaxy in *E.T., The Extra-Terrestrial* and Reese's Pieces enjoyed an unprecedented year of sales and profits as the movie broke all previous attendance records.

The environmental forces described in Chapter 2—competitive, political and legal, economic, technological, and societal/cultural—are forces impacting upon marketing opportunities. For instance, environmental factors have adversely affected the market for afternoon papers. Such papers, frequently called PMs, were very popular when people went to work in the predawn hours and returned home sometime in the afternoon. The PM environment has changed in recent times. The white-collar labor force now reports for work at 9 a.m. rather than 6 a.m. Approximately 60 percent of all married women now work, so that families are more likely to shop during the evening hours, when they used to read PMs. Furthermore, television is rapidly becoming the most popular source of news. The PMs are attempting to counter this trend

Figure 3.1 Steps in the Marketing Planning Process

by improving their suburban, entertainment, and special-interest sections. Some are even beginning to offer morning editions.

Another major influence on a firm's decision to take advantage of marketing opportunities is the resources of the organization. Resources include marketing strengths, production strengths, financial position, research and development capability, and quality of management. Bic, a French manufacturer of inexpensive ballpoint pens, decided to enter the U.S. market, but recognized the problems caused by its lack of an effective distribution system. Its decision was to purchase Waterman, a U.S. firm that manufactured and marketed refillable fountain pens. Although Bic discontinued the Waterman pen line four years later, it had acquired the distribution system it previously lacked.

The Portfolio Approach to Marketing Planning

Marketing objectives and plans result from overall organizational objectives and marketing opportunity analysis. The environmental factors have different impacts upon the organization at different times. Derek Abell has suggested the term **strategic window** to define the limited periods during which the key requirements of a market and the particular competencies of a firm best fit together.[4] Pontiac's decision to develop and market the Fiera in 1983, the first U.S.-built sports car in more than two decades, was in response to its marketers' decision that organizational and environmental factors resulted in a strategic window.

General Electric has made a number of major contributions to the concept of strategic planning. In 1970, General Electric underwent a major reorganization by separating planning- and policy-oriented activity from administration. GE is now regarded as having one of the best long-range planning functions in the United States. Often labeled the world's most diversified company, GE decided in 1971 to reorganize its nine product groups and 48 divisions into a portfolio of businesses labeled **strategic business units** (SBUs). For instance, various GE food preparation appliances had been scattered throughout three separate divisions; they were merged into a housewares SBU. The GE reorganization forced the firm's personnel to focus on customer needs, rather than on internal divisions.

The SBU concept was quickly adopted by such major firms as Union Carbide, Boise Cascade, and International Paper. Although such early experimenters as General Foods have already returned to traditional organizational structure, the SBU concept is utilized currently in about 20 percent of the largest manufacturing corporations in the United States.[5]

The BCG Matrix

The work of the Boston Consulting Group (BCG) is widely known in industry. BCG has developed a four-quadrant matrix, shown in Figure 3.2, that is useful in understanding the strategic planning-marketing strategy interface. The **BCG growth-share matrix** plots *market share,* the percentage of a market controlled by a firm, against market growth potential. All of a firm's various businesses can be plotted in one of the four quadrants. The resulting quadrants are labeled cash cows, stars, dogs, and question marks, and each one has a unique marketing strategy. Marketers employ varying strategies for each category of business.

Cash Cows (high market share, low market growth): Marketers would want to maintain this status for as long as possible since these busi-

[4]Derek F. Abell, "Strategic Windows," *Journal of Marketing* (July 1978), pp. 21–26.

[5]Philippe Haspeslagh, "Portfolio Planning: Uses and Limitations," *Harvard Business Review* (January-February 1982), pp. 58–73.

Figure 3.2 A Matrix for Marketing Planning

	Market Share	
Growth	High	Low
High	**Star**	**Question Mark**
Low	**Cash Cow**	**Dog**

Source: Adapted from "The Product Portfolio," Perspectives No. 66, The Boston Consulting Group, Inc., 1970.

nesses are producing a strong cash flow, which BCG considers to be the basic objective of the firm.

Stars (high market share, high market growth): These businesses show potential for high sales and profits, but marketers must invest heavily in stars to maintain them. Stars often produce a negative cash flow.

Dogs (low market share, low market growth): Marketers minimize their position in these businesses, withdrawing if possible. Cash should be pulled out of these enterprises as quickly as possible.

Question Marks (low market share, high market growth): These situations require that marketers make a basic go/no go decision. Question marks should be converted to stars, or the firm should pull out of these markets.

The BCG matrix highlights the importance of creating a mix that positions the firm to its best advantage. This matrix is largely the result of the firm's pioneering work with the experience curve first identified in 1966. BCG says that the highest market-share competitor will have a cost advantage over others because of the experience curve. The **experience curve** indicates that higher market shares reduce costs because of factors like learning advantages, increased specialization, higher investment, and economies of scale.[6] BCG reports that doubling the experience factor will cut product costs by 25 to 30 percent. The consultants suggest that market share is a better measure of performance than is profitability.

[6]For a critical assessment of the experience curve, see Walter Kiechel III, "The Decline of the Experience Curve," *Fortune* (October 5, 1981), pp. 139–146.

Critics of the BCG approach often point to the tendencies of some marketers to apply it in a largely mechanistic manner. In an attempt to develop a product line of stars, marketers may ignore possible methods of converting products and services labeled as dogs. Or the firm with no stars may be forced to seek means of expanding market and sales opportunities of an existing product regardless of the label attached to it. The advantages of the matrix approach must be balanced against the potential shortcomings by each organization.[7]

The Strategic Planning/Marketing Strategy Interface

The net result of strategic planning is marketing planning designed to achieve corporate objectives. This transaction requires that marketing planning efforts be directed toward establishment of marketing strategies that are resource-efficient, flexible, and adaptable. **Marketing strategy** describes the overall company program for selecting a particular market segment, then satisfying consumers in that segment through careful use of the elements of the marketing mix. Planning is an integral part of marketing strategy formulation and is the basis of effective strategy.

Need for a Comprehensive Marketing Program

A productive marketing strategy requires that all aspects of the marketing mix be considered. The components of an overall marketing strategy are product planning, pricing, distribution, and promotion. An advertising strategy by itself is not a marketing strategy. Marketing mix components are subsets of the overall marketing strategy.

A strategy may emphasize one mix component more than others. For example, a discount store may depend primarily on its pricing strategy, but it must also maintain adequate product selection and efficient distribution and promotion. One industrial goods manufacturer may emphasize its advanced product technology, while a competitor may stress its superior field sales force; neither can totally neglect the other elements of marketing strategy.

Marketers must also be prepared to alter their strategy. When S.C. Johnson introduced Pledge, the first aerosol furniture polish, most competitors were certain it would fail because its quality was believed to be lower than some competitive products, including Johnson's own Old English brand. Pledge proved a major sales success when Johnson

[7]See Walter Kiechel III, "Corporate Strategies Under Fire," *Fortune* (December 27, 1982), pp. 34–39.

carefully positioned it as an easy-to-use dusting product rather than a furniture polish. Johnson succeeded because it adapted its marketing strategy with the "waxed beauty instantly as you dust" advertising theme.[8]

Alternative Marketing Strategies

A number of alternative strategies are available for the marketing manager. The selection of any given strategy is based upon market and product factors, competition, and other environmental influences. In large, multiproduct firms, more than one strategy may be used for different products and services. The five alternative marketing strategies are : (1) balancing strategy, (2) market retention strategy, (3) market development strategy, (4) growth strategy, and (5) new venture strategy.[9] Examples of businesses employing the five strategy positions are given in Table 3.3.

Balancing Strategy The approach used for mature products in established markets where the competition is well known is referred to as the *balancing strategy.* The company seeks to balance revenues and costs and emphasizes control rather than planning. The marketing program is well set and seldom revised extensively.

Market Retention Strategy Established firms usually favor a market retention strategy in their approach to the market. The company seeks to implement product adaptations or expand its markets. Many of the decisions are similar to those employed in a balancing strategy.

Market Development Strategy This strategy requires a major effort on the part of the organization. Resources, personnel, product lines, organizational structure, and the like may have to be altered. The strategy emphasizes new markets and new product requirements.

Growth Strategy A growth strategy is riskier than the alternatives already described. The company offers a new product or enters a new market along with expanding its market or adapting its products. Texas Instruments' decision to move into consumer electronic calculators is an illustration of growth strategy.

[8]Robert S. Wheeler, "Marketing Tales with a Moral," *Product Marketing* (April 1977), p. 43.

[9]The discussion of these strategies is based on David W. Cravens, "Marketing Strategy Positioning," *Business Horizons* (December 1975), pp. 53–61. Cravens notes that other arrays of strategy positions are presented in J. Igor Ansoff, *Corporate Strategy* (New York: McGraw-Hill, 1965), pp. 122–138; John W. Humble, *How to Manage by Objectives* (New York: American Management Association, 1973), p. 75; and David Kollat, Roger Blackwell, and James Robeson, *Strategic Marketing*, 2d ed. (Hinsdale, Ill.: The Dryden Press, 1975), pp. 21–23.

Table 3.3 The Five Alternative Strategy Positions Put to Use

Balancing Strategy

Strategy position occupied by railroads, electric utilities, and various other mature industries.
Holiday Inn's provision of motel services to its existing markets.

Market Retention Strategy

Annual model changes of appliance manufacturers aimed at retaining market share.
Introduction of ribs to the Kentucky Fried Chicken food line.
Modification of styles and models by automobile manufacturers.

Market Development Strategy

Procter & Gamble's development of Pringles potato chips.
Efforts of public transportation firms to lure people away from use of the automobile through modification of services.
Movement of the large aluminum companies into automobile and beverage can markets for their products.

Growth Strategy

Offering first-run movies at a fee on private TV channels in hotels and motels.
Texas Instruments' move into consumer electronic calculator markets.
Designing and marketing a low premium $1 million umbrella personal liability insurance policy for individuals.

New Venture Strategy

Polaroid's introduction of the original Land camera.
Xerox's pioneering development and marketing of copying equipment.
Initial publication and marketing of *Playgirl* magazine.

Source: Adapted from David W. Cravens, "Marketing Strategy Positioning," *Business Horizons* (December 1975), p. 57. Copyright © 1975 by the Foundation for the School of Business at Indiana University. Reprinted by permission.

New Venture Strategy When a firm decides to follow a new venture strategy, it is making an effort in an entirely new area for the company. While risks are high, so are business opportunities because competition is usually limited. The development of an effective marketing program is a difficult aspect of this strategy.

The Importance of Flexibility

Strategic planning should be oriented toward keeping marketing strategies viable in today's competitive environment. Marketers must constantly reassess their plans and revamp their strategies. It is therefore useful to consider some future perspectives for the planning/strategy interface.

The need for adaptable marketing planning is evident in the abundant examples provided by many industries and firms. Toyota's management recognizes the challenge faced by the company in the North

American market. The highly profitable Japanese firm knows that several factors are working against continuation of increased automobile sales for itself and the other makers of imports. Slower domestic sales are one factor. North American firms now offer small cars to compete with the Japanese compacts. A second factor is the rising value of the yen relative to the dollar which forced Toyota to raise its retail prices by more than 20 percent recently.

What has Toyota done to counter the possibility of a slowdown in new car sales? It has begun to produce and market prefabricated houses and commercial buildings through its strong domestic dealer network. Although new products represent a very small percentage of total sales, the move into a completely different industry illustrates Toyota's marketing planning adaptability.

When a Kentucky Fried Chicken franchise opened in Harlan, Kentucky (population 3,300), some customers waited in line 1½ hours to purchase their chicken. Over a ton of fried chicken was sold on the opening day despite the fact that the store did no advertising. Kentucky Fried Chicken's move to a community of 3,300 people illustrates a dramatic change in fast food franchising. KFC Corporation once preferred not to operate in areas of under 35,000 population. Now, 890 of its 4,000 units are located in towns with fewer than 10,000 residents.

Other fast-food franchisers are also revamping their distribution plans. Pizza Hut is considering areas of under 4,000 population, and Burger King has plans for reduced-size units for smaller towns. These fast-food franchisers have found that smaller communities sometimes offer less competition than larger areas. The franchise operators also benefit from changed consumer preferences and national advertising. The move to smaller towns illustrates how fast-food franchisers have modified their marketing planning to cope with the modern business environment.

Potential Influences on Marketing Planning

Various factors will influence marketing planning in the future. Some current trends will likely accelerate in the years ahead and will play a critical role in new marketing strategies. Other anticipated changes will take some factors out of marketing decision making. Many potential influences cluster around a few basic areas: structural changes in the marketing system, public and legal pressures, market changes, and technological changes. Environmental forecasting is an integral component of good strategic marketing planning.

Structural Changes Some structural changes in the marketing system have had a pronounced effect on marketing decisions. The franchise system has altered concepts of small-business ownership. Collective marketing organizations such as OPEC have certainly influenced the world markets for their products, as have Common Market trade practices, which restrict access to historical sales outlets for U.S. exports. Executives must constantly evaluate the changes taking place in the marketing system. Even slight and gradual changes can have a profound effect on sales and profits.

Public and Legal Pressures Future marketing planning could be most affected by public and legal pressures. Actions such as the proposed restructuring of the petroleum industry may shake many of the basic foundations upon which marketers have always operated. Further legislation seems likely as all levels of government strive to fill what some critics see as loopholes in the system. The need for self-regulation in marketing is greater than ever before, if restrictive legislation is to be avoided.

Market Changes Perhaps the most obvious potential influence on strategic plans is market changes. Market potentials for various goods and services shift with changes in geographical patterns of population and income. Lifestyle preferences also influence marketing. Record inflation rates affect marketers of recreational equipment, bank services, and real estate. Often this impact is negative. Monitoring market shifts is vital to successful marketing.

Technological Changes The goods and services that are marketed in the relatively free U.S. competitive system are affected by technological changes. Since technological shifts can make a product obsolete overnight, marketers must be assured of efforts to constantly develop new products. Marketing planning requires that products and services be effectively matched with consumer desires.

Change is inevitable. It is a permanent part of contemporary marketing and must be dealt with constantly. Marketers know that changes in the structure of the marketing system, the public and legal framework, markets, and technology can alter the very foundation of today's marketing discipline. Successful future marketers will be those who are best able to cope with these changes.

Sales Forecasting

The basic building block of marketing planning is the **sales forecast**—the estimate of the firm's sales or income for a specified future period. In addition to its use in marketing planning, the sales forecast also plays an instrumental role in production scheduling, financial planning, inventory planning and procurement, and the determination of personnel needs. An inaccurate forecast will result in incorrect decisions in each of these areas. The sales forecast is also an important tool for marketing control because it produces standards against which actual performance can be measured. Without such standards, no comparisons can be made. If no criterion of success exists, there is also no definition of failure.

Sales forecasts are either short-run or long-run. Short-run forecasts usually include a period up to one year, while long-run forecasts typically cover a longer period. Since both forecasts are developed in basically the same manner, and since more firms forecast sales for the coming year, short-run forecasting will be discussed here.

Types of Forecasting Methods

Although forecasters utilize dozens of techniques of divining the future which range from complex computer simulations to crystal-ball gazing by professional futurists, two broad categories exist. *Quantitative* forecasting methods utilize such statistical techniques as trend extensions based upon past data, computer simulation, and econometrics to produce numerical forecasts of future events. The second type, *qualitative* forecasting techniques, are more subjective in nature. They include surveys of consumer attitudes and intentions, estimates of the field sales force, and predictions of key executives in the firm and in the industry. Since each method has its advantages, most organizations utilize both in their attempts to predict future events.

A survery of forecasting techniques used in 175 firms revealed that qualitative measures such as sales force estimates and the estimates by a jury of executives are most commonly used. The techniques used on a regular basis by the respondent firms are shown in Figure 3.3.

Qualitative Forecasting Techniques[10]

Qualitative techniques include the jury of executive opinion and estimates by the sales force. Both rely upon experience and expectations. The **jury of executive opinion** method consists of combining and averaging the outlook of top executives from such areas as finance, production, marketing, and purchasing. It is particularly effective when top management is experienced and knowledgeable about situations which influence sales, open-minded concerning the future, and aware of the bases for their judgments.

The **sales force composite** is based upon the belief that organizational members closest to the marketplace—those with specialized product, customer, and competitor knowledge—are likely to have better in-

[10]This discussion is adapted from Arthur G. Bedeian and William F. Glueck, *Management,* 3rd ed. (Hinsdale, Ill.: The Dryden Press, 1983), pp. 229–233.

Figure 3.3 Sales Forecasting Methods Used Regularly in 175 Firms

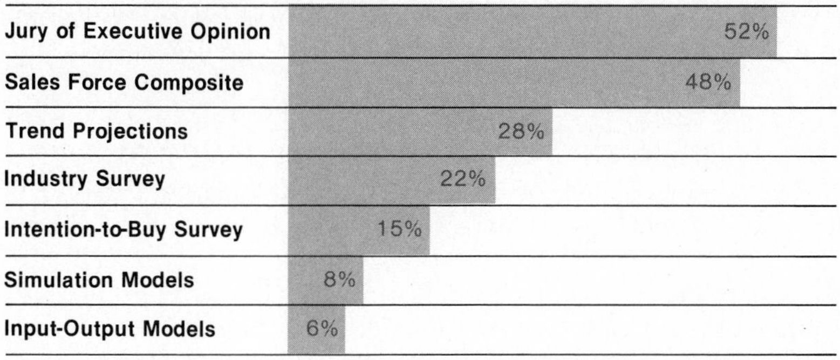
Jury of Executive Opinion
52%
Sales Force Composite
48%
Trend Projections
28%
Industry Survey
22%
Intention-to-Buy Survey
15%
Simulation Models
8%
Input-Output Models
6%

Source: Reported in Douglas J. Dalrymple, "Sales Forecasting Methods and Accuracy," *Business Horizons* (December 1975), p. 71.

sight concerning short-term future sales than any other group. It is typically a bottom up approach, since the salespeoples' estimates are usually combined at the district level, the regional level, and the national level to obtain an aggregate forecast of sales. Few firms rely upon the sales force composite solely, however. Since salespeople recognize the role of the sales forecast in determining expected performance in their territories, they are likely to estimate conservatively. Moreover, their narrow perspectives on their limited geographic territories may prevent them from being knowledgeable about developing trends in other territories, forthcoming technological innovations, or major changes in company marketing strategies. Consequently, the sales force composite is typically combined with other forecasting techniques in developing the final forecast.

A third method of forecasting is through **surveys of buyer intentions.** Mail questionnaires, telephone polls, or personal interviews may be used in attempting to determine the intentions of a representative group of present and potential consumers. This technique is obviously limited to situations where customers are willing to confide their buying intentions. Moreover, customer expectations do not necessarily result in actual purchases.

Quantitative Forecasting Techniques

Quantitative techniques, which make use of past data, attempt to eliminate the guesswork of the qualitative forecasting methods. They include such techniques as market tests, trend projections, and input-output models.

Market tests are frequently used in assessing consumer response to new product offerings. The procedure typically involves establishing a small number of test markets to gauge consumer responses to a new product under actual conditions. Such tests also permit evaluation of different prices, different promotional strategies, and other marketing mix variations through comparisons in different test markets. The primary advantage of market tests is the realism it provides for the marketer. On the other hand, it is an expensive and time-consuming approach that communicates marketing plans to competitors before a product is introduced to the market. Test marketing is discussed in more detail in Chapter 10.

Trend analysis involves forecasting future sales by analyzing the historical relationship between sales and time. It is based upon the assumption that the factors which collectively determined past sales will continue to exert similar influence in the future. If historical data is available, it can be performed quickly and inexpensively.

An example will make this clear. If sales were X last year and have been increasing at Y percent for the past several years, the sales forecast for next year would be calculated as follows:

$$\text{Sales Forecast} = X + XY.$$

In actual numbers, if last year's sales totaled 280,000 units and the average sales growth rate has been 5 percent, the sales forecast would be:

$$\begin{aligned}\text{Sales Forecast} &= 280{,}000 + (280{,}000 \times .05)\\ &= 294{,}000.\end{aligned}$$

The danger of trend analysis lies in its underlying assumption that the future is a continuation of the past. Any variations in the influencing determinants of sales will result in an incorrect forecast. In addition, historical data may not be readily available in some instances, most notably in the case of new products.

During periods of steady growth, the trend extension method of forecasting produces satisfactory results, but it implicitly assumes that the factors contributing to a certain level of output in the past will operate in the same manner in the future. When conditions change, the trend extension method often produces incorrect results. For this reason, forecasters increasingly use more sophisticated techniques and more complex mathematical models.

Input-output models, which depict the interactions of various industries in producing goods, are being developed by the U.S. Department of Commerce and by private agencies. Since outputs (sales) of one industry are the inputs (purchases) of another, a change of outputs in one industry affects the inputs of other industries. Input-output models show the impact on supplier industries of increased production in a given industry and can be used to measure the impact of increased demand in any industry throughout the economy.

Steps in Sales Forecasting

Although sales forecasting methods vary, the most typical method begins with a forecast of general economic conditions which the marketer uses to forecast industry sales and to develop a forecast of company and product sales. This approach can be termed the *top-down method.*

Forecasting General Economic Conditions The most common measure of economic output is *gross national product* (GNP), the market value of all final products produced in a country in a given year. Trend extension is the most frequently used method of forecasting increases in GNP.

Since many federal agencies and other organizations develop regular forecasts of the GNP, a firm may choose to use their estimates. These forecasts are regularly reported in such publications as the *Wall Street Journal* and *Business Week.*

Developing the Industry Sales Forecast Once the economic forecast has been produced, the next step is developing an industry sales forecast. Since industry sales may be related to GNP or some other measure of the national economy, a forecast may begin by measuring the degree of this relationship, then applying the trend extension method to forecast industry sales. More sophisticated techniques, such as input-output analysis or multiple regression analysis, may also be used.

Forecasting Company and Product Sales Once the industry forecast has been done, the company and product forecasts are developed. They begin with a detailed analysis of previous years. The firm's past and present market shares are reviewed, and product managers and regional and district sales managers are consulted about expected sales. Since an accelerated promotional budget or the introduction of new products may stimulate additional demand, the marketing plan for the coming year is also considered.

The product and company forecast must evaluate many aspects of company sales including sales of each product; future trends; sales by customer, territory, salesperson, and order size; financial arrangements; and other aspects. Once a preliminary sales forecast has been developed, it is reviewed by the sales force and by district, regional, and national sales managers.

New Product Sales Forecasting Forecasting sales for new products is an especially hazardous undertaking since no historical data is available. Companies typically employ consumer panels to obtain reactions to the products and probable purchase behavior. Test market data may also be utilized.

Since few products are totally new, forecasters carefully analyze the sales of competing products that may be displaced by the new entry. A new type of fishing reel, for example, will compete in an established market with other reels. This substitute method provides the forecaster with an estimate of market size and potential demand.

Summary

Planning is the process of anticipating the future and determining the courses of action to achieve company objectives, and it is the basis for all strategy decisions. Strategic planning refers to strategy-oriented planning. Marketing planning is the implementation of planning activity as it relates to the achievement of marketing objectives.

The marketing planning process is based upon the overall organizational objectives. Opportunity analysis is a continual process of assessing environmental factors and comparing them with the objectives of the organization and its resources. Marketing objectives are based upon organizational objectives and result in the development of marketing plans. Market target analysis and the development of a marketing mix to satisfy chosen targets make up the marketing strategy of the organization.

The strategic business unit (SBU) concept and the market/growth matrix developed by the Boston Consulting Group are frequently used by marketing planners.

Effective strategic planning is now regarded as a prerequisite to survival. It is an organization-wide responsibility involving chief executive officers, heads of operating units, and corporate strategic planning personnel. Strategic planning provides a basis for marketing planning, which is then translated into the development of marketing strategies.

Five marketing strategies can be identified: (1) balancing strategy, (2) market retention strategy, (3) market development strategy, (4) growth strategy, and (5) new venture strategy. Potential future influences on the planning/strategy interface are the marketing system itself, public and legal pressures, market changes, and technological changes.

Sales forecasting is an important component of both planning and controlling marketing programs. Forecasting techniques may be categorized as quantitative or qualitative. The most common approach to sales forecasting is to begin with a forecast of the national economy and use it to develop an industry sales forecast, which is then used to develop a company and product forecast.

Key Terms

planning
marketing planning
strategic planning
marketing strategy
sales forecast
jury of executive opinion

tactical planning
strategic window
strategic business unit (SBU)
BCG matrix
experience curve
sales force composite
survey of buyer intentions
trend analysis
input-output models

Review Questions

1. Distinguish between strategic planning and tactical planning.
2. Contrast marketing planning at different levels in the organization.
3. Identify the steps in the marketing planning process.
4. Explain the concept of the strategic window. Give an example.
5. Differentiate among *cash cows, dogs, stars,* and *question marks* in the BCG matrix.
6. Outline the five marketing strategies that can be employed by marketers.
7. Identify and discuss the major external and internal influences on marketing strategy.
8. Compare and contrast each of the major types of forecasting methods.
9. Explain the steps involved in the forecasting process.
10. Suggest methods for forecasting sales for newly introduced products.

Discussion Questions and Exercises

1. Give two examples of products in each of the following quadrants of the BCG matrix:
   a. Cash cow **c.** Star
   b. Dog **d.** Question mark
   Suggest marketing strategies for each product.
2. Relate the dicussion of the development of the United States Football League to the model of the marketing planning process shown in Figure 3.1.
3. Discuss the advantages and shortcomings of basing sales forecasts exclusively on estimates developed by the firm's sales force.
4. Assume that growth in industry sales will remain constant for the coming year. Forecast company sales for the coming year based upon the following data:
   Year 1: $320,000
   Year 2: $350,000
   Year 3: $340,000
   Year 4: $380,000
   Year 5: $580,000
   What assumptions have you made in developing your forecast?

5. Which forecasting technique do you feel is most appropriate for each of the following:
   a. Bayer aspirin
   b. Joffrey Ballet
   c. Office supplies retailer
   d. Fender guitars

4

MARKET SEGMENTATION

Chapter Objectives

1. To relate market segmentation to the marketing mix.
2. To explain what is meant by a market.
3. To outline the role of market segmentation in the development of a marketing strategy.
4. To discuss the four bases for segmenting consumer markets.
5. To describe the three bases for segmenting industrial markets.

Back in 1910, American breweries were essentially local businesses that served the particular tastes of nearby consumers. In fact, there were some 1600 breweries operating in the United States in 1910. But only 750 reopened after Prohibition, and their numbers continued to decline in the years that followed. There were only 457 breweries operating after World War II; 78 in the early 1970s; and by 1980, only 43 breweries were left. Brewing became a function of large firms that concentrated on efficient production. As a result, beer prices rose more slowly than other consumer prices; but the nation's diverse array of breweries was lost in the transition.

But now the big breweries are running into some stiff competition. Foreign beers, for example, have become very popular. Imported beer sales rose 27 percent annually between 1975 and 1980, and foreign beer now accounts for 3 percent of the U.S. market.

Other new competitors are the microbrewers—firms that concentrate on producing specialty beers that tend to be heavier than major national brands. Microbrewers now account for about 1 percent of the total U.S. market. Seattle's Red Hook Ale, Albany's Newman's Pale Ale, San Francisco's Anchor Brewing, and other California brewers like Thousand Oaks and Sierra Nevada are examples of microbrewers, sometimes called boutique brewers. These small firms concentrate on producing limited quantities of beer for sophisticated drinkers who refuse to accept the standard domestic brands and think that many of the foreign brands lack freshness.

Microbrewer customers are described as searchers, constantly looking for a special taste in the beer they consume. Several microbrewers have been successful by using benefit segmentation to carve out a unique market niche for their product. In fact, several big breweries are offering their own boutique brands. Coors, for instance, now offers a product called George Killian's Irish Red Ale. Clearly, market segmentation is playing a very important role in the marketing strategies of today's brewers.[1]

The Conceptual Framework

Before a marketing mix strategy can be implemented, the marketer must first identify, evaluate, and select a market target. The starting point is to understand what is meant by a market.

A market is people and institutions, but they alone do not make a market. A real estate salesperson would be unimpressed by news that 50 percent of a marketing class raised their hands in response to the question: "Who wants to buy a condominium in Daytona Beach?" More pertinent would be the answer to this question: "How many of them have $20,000 for the down payment and can qualify for the mortgage loan?" A **market** requires not only people or institutions and the willingness to buy, but also purchasing power and authority to buy.

A successful salesperson quickly learns how to pinpoint which individual in an organization or household has the authority to make particular purchasing decisions. Without this knowledge, too much time can be spent convincing the wrong person that the product or service should be bought.

Types of Markets

Products are often classified as either consumer goods or industrial goods. **Consumer goods** are products purchased by the ultimate consumer for personal use. **Industrial goods** are products purchased for

[1]Liz Roman Gallese, "New Little Breweries Cause Some Ferment in the Beer Business," *The Wall Street Journal* (March 15, 1983), pp. 1, 22.

use either directly or indirectly in the production of other goods or services for resale. A similar dichotomy can also be used for services. Most products purchased by individual consumers—books, records, and clothes, for example—are consumer goods. Rubber and raw cotton, however, are generally purchased by manufacturers and are therefore classfied as industrial goods. Rubber will be used in many products by a producer such as Goodyear Tire & Rubber Company; a manufacturer such as Burlington Industries will convert raw cotton into cloth.

Sometimes the same product is destined for different uses. The spark plugs purchased for the family car constitute a consumer good, but spark plugs purchased by American Motors for use on its American Eagle four-wheel-drive line is an industrial good, since it becomes part of another good destined for resale.[2] The key to proper classification of goods is the determination of the purchaser and the reasons for the purchase.

The Role of Market Segmentation

The world is too large and filled with too many diverse people and firms for any single marketing mix to satisfy everyone. Unless the product or service is an item such as an unbranded, descriptive-label detergent aimed at the mass market, an attempt to satisfy everyone may doom the marketer to failure. Even a seemingly functional product like toothpaste is aimed at specific market segments. Crest focused on tooth-decay prevention; Stripe was developed for children; Close-up hints at enhanced sex appeal; and Aim promises both protection and a taste children like.

The auto manufacturer who decides to produce and market a single model to satisfy everyone will encounter seemingly endless decisions about such variables as the number of doors, type of transmission, color, styling, and engine size. In its attempt to satisfy everyone, the firm may be forced to compromise in each of these areas and, as a result, may discover that it does not satisfy anyone very well. Other firms that appeal to particular segments—the youth market, the high fuel-economy market, the larger family market, and so on—may capture most of the total market by satisfying the specific needs of these smaller market segments. This process of dividing the total market into several relatively homogeneous groups is called **market segmentation.** Marketing mixes are then adjusted to meet the needs of specified market segments. Market segmentation can be used by both profit-oriented and nonprofit organizations.[3]

[2]Some marketers use the term *commercial goods* to refer to industrial goods not directly used in producing other goods.

[3]See Scott M. Smith and Leland L. Beik, "Market Segmentation for Fund Raisers," *Journal of the Academy of Marketing Science* (Summer 1982), pp. 208–216.

Figure 4.1 Segmentation Bases for Consumer Markets

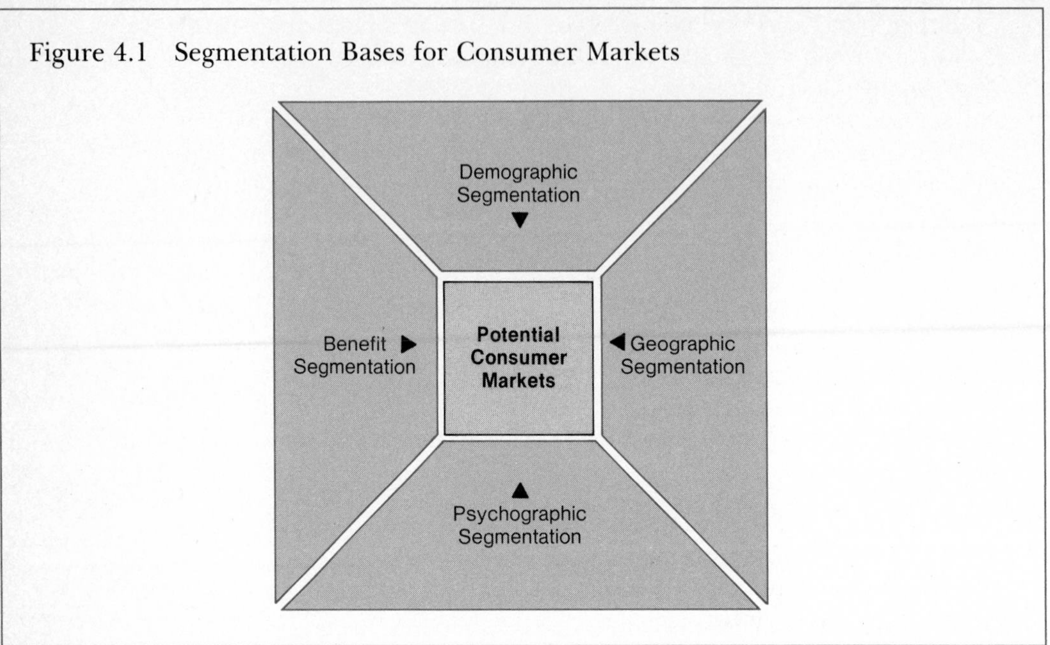

One marketing authority defines market segmentation as follows: "Market segmentation is the subdividing of a market into homogeneous subsets of customers, where any subset may conceivably be selected as a market target to be reached with a distinct marketing mix."[4]

Segmenting Consumer Markets

Market segmentation results from a determination of factors that distinguish a certain group of consumers from the overall market. These characteristics—such as age, sex, geographic location, income and expenditure patterns, and population size and mobility, among others—are vital factors in the success of the overall marketing strategy. Toy manufacturers such as Ideal, Hasbro, Mattel, and Kenner study not only birthrate trends, but also shifts in income and expenditure patterns. Colleges and universities are affected by such factors as the number of high school graduates, changing attitudes toward the value of college educations, and increasing enrollment of older adults. Figure 4.1 identifies four commonly used bases for segmenting consumer markets.

[4]Philip Kotler, *Marketing Management* (Englewood Cliffs, N.J.: Prentice-Hall, 1980), p. 195.

The Tobacco Industry Understands Market Segmentation

Cigarette producers make extensive use of market segmentation. Marlboro is the nation's leading brand, but its maker, Philip Morris, also offers Marlboro Lights, a reduced tar cigarette. This is a form of benefit segmentation designed to attract smokers who worry about the dangers associated with the habit. The Marlboro man theme depicts a macho type of male, thus making use of psychographic segmentation.

Demographic segmentation also plays an important role in the marketing strategies of cigarette producers. While male smokers still outnumber their female counterparts, the number of new female smokers is rising at double the rate for males. During one recent 5-year period, 25 percent of all male teenage smokers quit. By contrast, 40 percent more teenage females began smoking. More, the nation's fastest growing brand of cigarette, has a 75 percent female customer base. Women seem to be the primary market target for many of the new brands.

Even geographical segmentation is used. Lorillard's Heritage brand is being positioned as a regional brand for the South. Heritage advertising features antebellum homes and other Southern scenes. Lorillard's Newport brand already has a regional orientation, selling well in the Northeast and Upper Midwest.

Smokers and nonsmokers alike should be aware that market segmentation is an important element of the marketing strategies designed to attract new smokers and maintain those who have already adopted the habit.

Thought provoker: Could market segmentation be used in nonsmoking campaigns?

Source: "How Cigarette Makers Aim to Fire Up Sales," *Business Week* (December 7, 1981), pp. 65, 68, 70.

Geographic segmentation, the dividing of an overall market into homogeneous groups on the basis of population location, has been used for hundreds of years. The second basis for segmenting markets is *demographic segmentation*—dividing an overall market into homogeneous groups based upon characteristics such as age, sex, and income level. Demographic segmentation is the most commonly used method of subdividing total markets.

The third and fourth bases represent relatively recent developments in market segmentation. *Psychographic segmentation* utilizes behavioral profiles developed from analyses of the activities, opinions, interests, and lifestyles of consumers in identifying market segments. The final basis, *benefit segmentation,* focuses on benefits the consumer expects to derive from a product or service. These segmentation bases can be important to marketing strategies provided they are significantly related to differences in buying behavior.

Geographic Segmentation

A logical starting point in market segmentation is to examine population characteristics. It is not surprising, therefore, that one of the earliest bases for segmentation was geographic.

Although the U.S. population exceeded 235 million by 1984, it is not distributed evenly. Instead, it is concentrated in states with major metropolitan areas. California, Illinois, Florida, Michigan, New York, Ohio, Pennsylvania, and Texas all have more than 9 million residents.

Not only do states vary in population density, but pronounced shifts are also evident. In the 15 months after the 1980 census, more than half of the population growth occurred in only three states—California, Florida, and Texas. During the same period, Indiana, Iowa, Michigan, Ohio, and South Dakota lost population. Census data indicate three major population shifts: (1) shifts to the Sunbelt states of the Southeast and Southwest; (2) continuing shifts from interior states to seacoast states; and (3) shifts to the West.

Population shifts among states are expected to continue. Overall, the U.S. population is expected to grow 16.9 percent from the 1980 census figure to 264.8 million in the year 2000. Wyoming, with a 66.9 percent gain, and Alaska, with a 50.3 percent increase, are expected to lead this growth. Other states with above average projected population increases are Nevada, Utah, Arizona, Texas, Idaho, New Mexico, Colorado, Oklahoma, Tennessee, West Virginia, Florida, Kentucky, Arkansas, North Carolina, South Carolina, Oregon, Alabama, Louisiana, Virginia, Washington, Georgia, Hawaii, New Hampshire, Rhode Island, Mississippi, North Dakota, and Maryland.[5]

Population shifts among states become even more apparent with this fact: 40 percent of the U.S. population was not born in the states where they now reside. In 1900, the figure was 20 percent. The states varied widely on this measure. Only 21 percent of Nevadans were born there, but 81 percent of all Pennsylvanians are natives. Again, the data confirms the movement of people to the South and West.

Such shifts have also occurred within states. Farmers have migrated to urban areas steadily since 1800, and the percentage of farm dwellers has dropped below 4 percent. The 25 largest metropolitan areas listed in Table 4.1 equal about one third of the total U.S. population. Each of these metropolitan areas contains more inhabitants than the entire population of such states as Alaska, Delaware, Hawaii, Idaho, Maine,

[5]Reported in a table from "How the U.S. Will Look in Year 2000," *U.S. News & World Report* (July 26, 1982), p. 8. Regional population shifts are analyzed in Gregory A. Jackson and George S. Masnick, "Take Another Look at Regional U.S. Growth," *Harvard Business Review* (March–April 1983), pp. 76–87.

Table 4.1 The 25 Largest Metropolitan Areas

	1980 Population	Percent Change from 1970
1. New York	9,119,737	−8.6
2. Los Angeles–Long Beach	7,477,657	6.2
3. Chicago	7,102,328	1.8
4. Philadelphia	4,716,818	−2.2
5. Detroit	4,352,762	−1.9
6. San Francisco–Oakland	3,252,721	4.6
7. Washington, D.C.	3,060,240	5.2
8. Dallas–Fort Worth	2,974,878	25.1
9. Houston	2,905,350	45.3
10. Boston	2,763,357	−4.7
11. Nassau–Suffolk, N.Y.	2,605,813	2.0
12. St. Louis	2,355,276	−2.3
13. Pittsburgh	2,263,894	−5.7
14. Baltimore	2,174,023	5.0
15. Minneapolis–St. Paul	2,114,256	7.6
16. Atlanta	2,029,618	27.2
17. Newark	1,965,304	−4.5
18. Anaheim–Santa Ana–Garden Grove, Ca.	1,931,570	35.9
19. Cleveland	1,898,720	−8.0
20. San Diego	1,861,846	37.1
21. Miami	1,625,979	28.3
22. Denver–Boulder	1,619,921	30.7
23. Seattle–Everett, Wa.	1,606,765	12.8
24. Tampa–St. Petersburg	1,569,492	44.2
25. Riverside–San Bernardino–Ontario, Ca.	1,557,080	36.7

Source: U.S. Department of Commerce, Bureau of the Census, Supplemental Report, *1980 Census of Population and Housing,* PC-80-S1-5.

Montana, Nevada, New Hampshire, New Mexico, North Dakota, Rhode Island, South Dakota, Vermont, Wyoming, and Utah.

The United States has traditionally been a very mobile society. Approximately 18 percent of all Americans move each year, but recent data indicates that this movement may be waning. This slowdown is attributed to such factors as poor job prospects elsewhere, two-income families, an aging population, and a heightened concern for one's quality of life.[6] If this trend continues, it would have a decided impact on marketers' use of geographic segmentation. A more stable population would mean marketers could better identify and analyze geographical market segments.

[6]Eugene Carlson, "Americans Don't Seem to be Moving as Much These Days," *The Wall Street Journal* (February 9, 1982), p. 27.

Redefining the City

The movement of the U.S. population from the farm to the city has recently been accompanied by a shift to the suburbs and small towns near metropolitan areas. Recent population statistics report 102 million suburban residents, 34 million more than in central cities and 44 million more than in nonmetropolitan areas. The country's leading suburban areas with the greatest growth rate include Tampa-St. Petersburg (8.1 percent), Houston (7.8 percent), Denver-Boulder (7.4 percent), San Diego (6.7 percent), Riverside-San Bernardino-Ontario, Ca. (6.2 percent), and Anaheim-Santa Ana-Garden Grove, Ca. (5.9 percent).[7]

The Traditional Approach Primarily middle-class families have made the shift to the suburbs. The move has radically changed the cities' traditional patterns of retailing and has led to a disintegration of the downtown shopping areas of many U.S. cities. It has also rendered traditional city boundaries almost meaningless. To accommodate the needs of urban planners and marketing planners, the U.S. Bureau of the Census developed an improved classification system for compiling urban data in 1949. From then until 1981, data was collected on the basis of a Standard Metropolitan Statistical Area (SMSA), which was defined as an integrated economic and social unit containing one city of at least 50,000 inhabitants or twin cities with a combined population of at least 50,000. As of the 1980 Census, there were 323 SMSAs in the United States and Puerto Rico.[8] Later, the government decided they needed a measure for larger urban areas, so a Standard Consolidated Statistical Area (SCSA), defined as an SMSA with a population of at least 1 million and one or more adjoining SMSAs that are related to it by high density population centers and intermetropolitan commuting of workers, was conceived. Fifteen SCSAs were identified.

The Latest Approach In 1983, the SMSA and SCSA categories discussed above were replaced by three new classifications of urban data. An interagency group operating within the U.S. Office of Management and Budget concluded that the old SMSA designation was too general. It was argued that more categories and detailed statistics were needed by urban planners and marketers. The new classifications are:

- **Consolidated Metropolitan Statistical Areas (CMSA)** would include the 25 or so urban giants like New York, Chicago, and Los Angeles.
- **Primary Metropolitan Statistical Areas (PMSA)** are major urban areas with a CMSA—an urbanized county or counties with social

[7]"1982 Survey of Buying Power," *Sales & Marketing Management* (July 26, 1982), p. A 19.

[8]Eugene Carlson, "Small Cities Have a Big Stake in Being Defined as SMSAs," *The Wall Street Journal* (November 17, 1981), p. 25.

and economic ties to nearby areas. PMSAs are identified within areas of one million plus population. Long Island's Nassau and Suffolk counties would be part of the New York CMSA. Aurora-Elgin would be part of the Chicago CMSA. And Oxnard-Ventura would be part of the Los Angeles CMSA.

- **Metropolitan Statistical Areas (MSA)** are freestanding urban areas with an urban center of 50,000 and a total MSA of 100,000 or more. MSAs exhibit social and economic homogeneity. They are usually bordered by non-urbanized counties. Moorhead, Minnesota; Peoria, Illinois; and Sheboygan, Wisconsin are examples.[9]

The Growth Surge of Nonmetropolitan Areas

Although the number of farmers in the United States has been declining for more than a century, the rural areas have been recently repopulated by people moving from central cities and suburban areas. During the past decade, the nonmetropolitan growth rate outpaced that of the urban and suburban areas. Figure 4.2 indicates changes in location of the U.S. population between 1970 and 1980.

A number of factors contribute to the population growth in small towns and rural areas. In some instances, job opportunities have expanded. Growth in such areas as the Rocky Mountains, the Ozark-Ouachita regions of Arkansas and Missouri, and in other resort-retirement developments has been stimulated considerably by the creation and expansion of retirement and recreation communities. Another component of the nonmetropolitan growth rate is urban flight, as some big-city residents seek to escape the overcrowding, crime, pollution, and noise associated with cities. Nearly half of the U.S. cities with populations of 100,000 or more experienced population declines during the 1970s. Finally, for still another group, rural living is simply an extension of the suburbs that is made possible by improved roads to the city.

The growth of the nonmetropolitan population produces more challenges for marketers than market targets in the more densely settled cities and suburban areas. Marketing costs may increase when marketers focus upon nonmetropolitan consumers who, by definition, are less concentrated geographically. On the other hand, the nonmetropolitan population may stimulate development of such communication innovations as cable television and direct-broadcast satellites as a means of serving these growing markets.[10]

[9]The new designations are outlined in "Census Data to Reflect More Precise Geographic Definitions," *Marketing News* (January 21, 1983), p. 20; "Mobile Included in Redrawn MSAs," *Mobile Press Register* (January 15, 1983), p. 9-6; and Eugene Carlson, "Soon MSA, PMSA, and CMSA Will Replace Good Old SMSA," *The Wall Street Journal* (October 12, 1982), p. 31.

[10]The growth of nonmetropolitan areas is discussed in Thayer C. Taylor, "Targeting Sales in a Changing Marketplace," *Sales & Marketing Management* (July 27, 1981), pp. A–6 to A–11.

Figure 4.2 Where the U.S. Population Resides

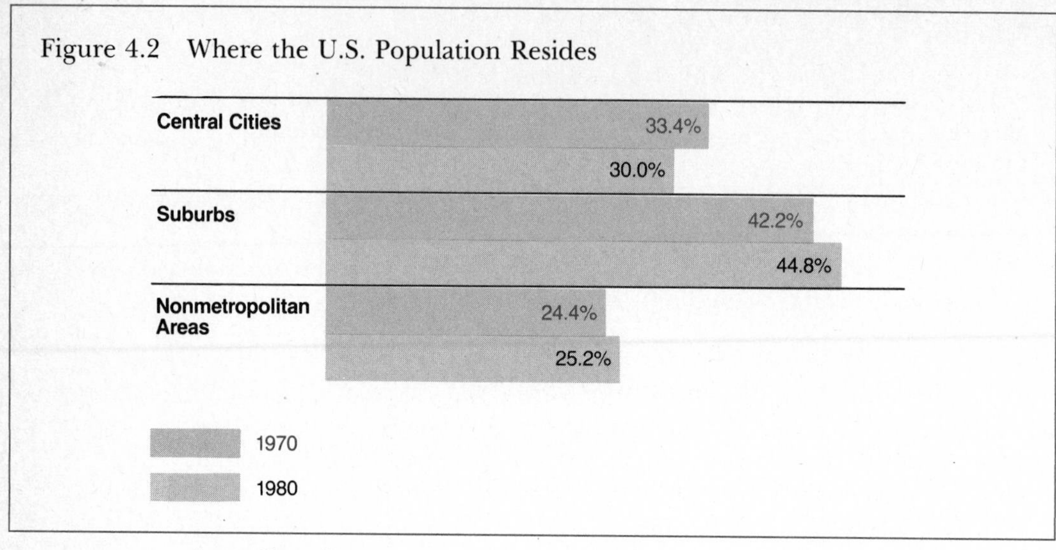

Source: Census Bureau.

Using Geographic Segmentation

There are many instances where markets for products and services may be segmented on a geographic basis. Regional variations in consumer tastes often exist. Per capita consumption of Mexican food, for example, is higher in the Southwest than in New England. Basements, a mainstay in many homes in the North, are relatively rare in the South and Southwest.

Residence location within a geographic area is an important geographic variable. Urban dwellers may have less need for automobiles than their surburban and rural counterparts, while suburban dwellers spend proportionally more on lawn and garden care than people in rural or urban areas. Both rural and suburban dwellers may spend more of their household income on gasoline and automobile needs than urban households.

Climate is another important factor. Snow blowers, snowmobiles, and sleds are popular products in the northern sections of the United States. Residents of the Sunbelt states may spend proportionally less of their total income on heating and heating equipment and more on air conditioning. Climate also affects patterns of clothing purchases.

Geographic segmentation is useful only when differences in preference and purchase patterns for a product emerge along regional lines. Moreover, geographic subdivisions of the overall market tend to be rather large and often too heterogeneous for effective segmentation without careful considerations of additional factors. In such cases, several segmentation variables may need to be utilized.

Demographic Segmentation

The most common approach to market segmentation is to divide consumer groups according to demographic variables. These variables—age, sex, income, occupation, education, household size, and stage in the family life cycle, among others—are typically used to identify market segments and to develop appropriate marketing mixes.[11] Demographic variables are often used in market segmentation for three reasons:

1. They are easy to identify and measure.
2. They are associated with the sale of many products and services.
3. They are typically referred to in describing the audiences of advertising media, so that media buyers and others can easily pinpoint the desired market target.[12]

Vast quantities of data are available to assist the marketing planner in segmenting potential markets on a demographic basis. Sex is an obvious variable for segmenting many markets, since many products are sex-specific. Cigarette manufacturers have utilized sex as a variable in the successful marketing of such brands as Eve, More Light 100s, and Virginia Slims. The development of low-calorie light beer and smaller packaging has led to increased beer consumption among women.[13]

Age, household size, family life cycle stage, and income and expenditure patterns are important factors in determining purchase patterns. The often distinct differences based upon demographic factors justifies their frequent use as a basis for segmentation.

Age—An Important Demographic Segmentation Variable

The bulk of the U.S. population growth during the 1980s will be concentrated in two age groups—young to middle-aged adults between 30 and 45 and persons aged 65 and older. Both markets represent potentially profitable market targets.

The young to middle-aged adult segment includes family households with demands for such goods as homes, furniture, recreation, clothes, toys, and food. The median age of the U.S. population is now 30. This age group is expected to account for two thirds of the population growth during the 1980s. The anticipated configuration of the U.S. population is 1990 is shown in Figure 4.3

[11]An interesting use of demographic segmentation is discussed in Zarrel V. Lambert, "Profiling Demographic Segmentation Characteristics of Alienated Consumers," *Journal of Business Research* (March 1981), pp. 65–86.

[12]Kenneth Runyon, *Consumer Behavior* (Columbus, Ohio: Charles E. Merrill, 1980), p. 35.

[13]George W. Wynn, "Rosebud or Lone Starlet: Is There a Market for Female Beer?" *Proceedings of the Southwestern Marketing Association*, eds. Robert H. Ross, Frederic B. Kraft, and Charles H. Davis, Wichita, Kansas, 1981, pp. 9-12.

Figure 4.3 The Age Distribution of U.S. Population in 1990

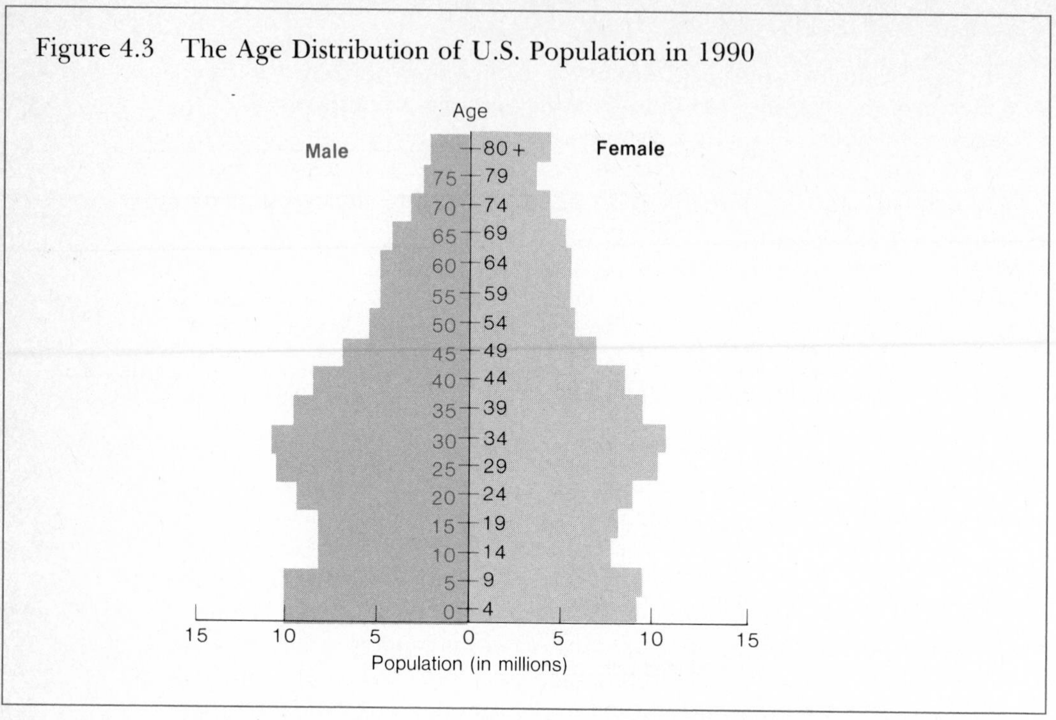

Source: U.S. Bureau of the Census and unpublished tabulations prepared by Leon F. Bowvier for the Select Committee on Immigration and Refugee Policy, 1980. Reprinted from B. G. Yovovich, "Job Hunting: Baby Boomers Battle Mid-Level Bulge," *Advertising Age* (January 4, 1982), p. S-16.

Not so many years ago, there was no such thing as a senior adult market, since few people reached old age. At present, however, over 11 percent of the population is 65 or older. It is comforting to this year's retiree to learn that at age 65 his or her average life expectancy is at least another 16 years. This increase also presents the marketing manager with a unique and potentially profitable market segment.[14]

Each age group represents different consumption patterns, and each serves as the market target for several firms. For instance, Gerber traditionally has been extremely successful in aiming at the infants' and children's market. Table 4.2 lists some of the types of merchandise most often purchased by the various age groups.

[14]Rena Bartos, "Over 49: The Invisible Consumer Market," *Harvard Business Review* (January–February 1980), pp. 140–149; Betsy D. Gelb, "Exploring the Gray Market Segment," *MSU Business Topics* (Spring 1978), pp. 41–46; and Lynn W. Phillips and Brian Sternthal, "Age Differences in Information Processing: A Perspective on the Aged Consumer," *Journal of Marketing Research* (November 1977), pp. 444–457.

Table 4.2 Buying Patterns for Different Age Groups

Age	Name of Age Group	Merchandise
0–5	Young Children	Baby food, toys, nursery furniture, children's wear
6–19	School Children (including teenagers)	Clothing, sports equipment, records, school supplies, food, cosmetics, used cars
20–34	Young Adult	Cars, furniture, houses, clothing, recreational equipment, purchases for younger age segments
35–49	Younger Middle-Aged	Larger homes, better cars, second cars, new furniture, recreational equipment
50–64	Older Middle-Aged	Recreational items, purchases for young marrieds and infants
65 and Over	Senior Adults	Medical services, travel, drugs, purchases for younger age groups

Table 4.3 Family Life Cycle Stages

1. Young Single
2. Young Married without Children
3. Other Young
   a. Young divorced without children
   b. Young married with children
   c. Young divorced with children
4. Middle-Aged
   a. Middle-Aged married without children
   b. Middle-Aged divorced without children
   c. Middle-Aged married with children
   d. Middle-Aged divorced with children
   e. Middle-Aged married without dependent children
   f. Middle-Aged divorced without dependent children
5. Older
   a. Older married
   b. Older unmarried (divorced, widowed)
6. Other
   All adults and children not accounted for by family life cycle stages

Source: Adapted with permission from Patrick E. Murphy and William A. Staples, "A Modernized Family Life Cycle," *Journal of Consumer Research* (June 1979), p. 16.

Segmentation by Family Life Cycle

The **family life cycle** is the process of family formation and dissolution. Using this concept, the marketing planner combines the family characteristics of age, marital status, presence or absence of children, and ages of children in developing a marketing strategy.

Patrick E. Murphy and William A. Staples have proposed a five-stage family life cycle with several subcategories. The stages of the family life cycle are shown in Table 4.3.

The behavioral characteristics and buying patterns of persons in each life cycle stage often vary considerably. Young singles have relatively few financial burdens; tend to be early purchasers of new fashion items; are recreation oriented; and make purchases of basic kitchen

The President Likes His Sliced in Salads. . . .

Avocados appeal to a limited number of market segments. Also known as alligator pears and "poor man's butter," the rough green fruit sells best among households with $40,000 incomes; Californians, who consume 40 percent of the U.S. output; and Mexican-Americans who regard it as a staple. About 80 percent of the U.S. output is produced on the California coast from Santa Barbara south. Avocados are also grown in Florida. Mexico is the world's largest producer.

Because of the tax incentives available to avocado growers, the annual output has escalated tremendously in recent years. Prices have shown a corresponding drop. The industry is beginning to try to reach other geographical and demographic segments. Middle-class consumers in St. Louis, Chicago, Cleveland, Boston, Philadelphia, and Washington, D.C., are being targeted by the California Avocado Commission. The campaign features avocado samplings in supermarkets.

While the ancient Aztecs regarded avocados as an aphrodisiac and confined young Aztec women at harvest time, most non-Californians are unfamiliar with the fruit. About a third of the Midwest and Northeast population have never even tried an avocado. Furthermore, many first-time consumers find the fruit bland. The industry has ample opportunities for increasing avocado sales. One potential market segment may be transplanted Californians. President Reagan, who likes his avocados sliced in salads, receives a case of the fruit each week.

Source: Roy H. Harris, Jr., "A Glut of Avocados Pits Industry Flacks Against Soft Market," *The Wall Street Journal* (April 6, 1982), pp. 1, 25.

equipment, cars, and vacations. By contrast, young marrieds with young children tend to be heavy purchasers of baby products, homes, television sets, toys, and washers and dryers. Their liquid assets tend to be relatively low, and they are more likely to watch television than young singles or young marrieds without children. The empty-nest households in the middle-aged and older categories with no dependent children are more likely to have more disposable income; more time for recreation, self-education, and travel; and more than one member in the labor force than their full-nest counterparts with younger children. Similar differences in behavioral and buying patterns are evident in the other stages of the family life cycle as well.[15]

Analysis of life cycle stages often gives better results than reliance on single variables such as age. The buying patterns of a 25-year-old bach-

[15]These examples are from an earlier life cycle study. See William D. Wells and George Gubar, "Life Cycle Concept in Marketing Research," *Journal of Marketing Research* (November 1966), p. 362. See also Frederick W. Derrick and Alane K. Lehfeld, "The Family Life Cycle: An Alternative Approach," *Journal of Consumer Research* (September 1980), pp. 214–217.

elor are very different from those of a father of the same age. The family of five headed by parents in their forties is a more likely prospect for the World Book Encyclopedia than the childless 40-year-old divorced person.

Marketing planners can use published data such as census reports and divide their markets into more homogeneous segments than would be possible if they were analyzing single variables. Such data is available for each classification of the family life cycle.

The Changing Household

Slightly more than half the households in the United States contain only one or two persons. This development is in marked contrast to households that averaged 5.8 persons when the first census was taken in 1790.

The U.S. Department of Commerce cites serveral reasons for the trend toward smaller households. Among them are lower fertility rates; the tendency of young people to postpone marriage; the increasing tendency among younger couples to limit the number of children; the ease and frequency of divorce; and the ability and desire of many young single adults and the elderly to live alone.

Nearly 18 million people live alone today—about 23 percent of all households. The single-person household has emerged as an important market segment with a special title: **SSWD** (single, separated, widowed, and divorced). SSWDs buy one third of all passenger cars.[16] They are also customers for single-serving food products, such as Campbell's Soup for One and Green Giant's single-serving casseroles.

Today, the average household size is 2.7 persons. While married-couple households continue to dominate, they will probably account for only 55 percent of all 1990 households compared to 70 percent in 1970. The number of individuals living together tripled between 1970 and 1980. As a result, the Census Bureau has listed another category: **POSLSQ**, or people of the opposite sex living in the same quarters.

Segmenting Markets on the Basis of Income and Expenditure Patterns

Markets were defined earlier as people and purchasing power. A common method of segmenting the consumer market is on the basis of income. Fashionable specialty shops stocking designer clothing make most of their sales to high-income shoppers. Other retailers aim their

[16]Ralph Gray, "Ford Puts Two-Seater into Drive," *Advertising Age* (February 23, 1981), p. 10.

appeals at middle-income groups. Still others focus almost exclusively on low-income shoppers.

In most countries income distribution is shaped like a pyramid with a small percentage of households having high incomes and the majority of families earning very low incomes. However, in 1980, nearly 40 percent of all U.S. families earned $25,000 or more. By 1990, over half of all families will be in this category. (See Figure 4.4.)

Household expenditures can be divided into two categories: 1) basic purchases of essential household needs, and 2) other purchases made at the discretion of household members once necessities have been purchased. Total discretionary purchasing power is estimated to have tripled since 1950.

Figure 4.4 Family Income Distribution in 1980 Dollars

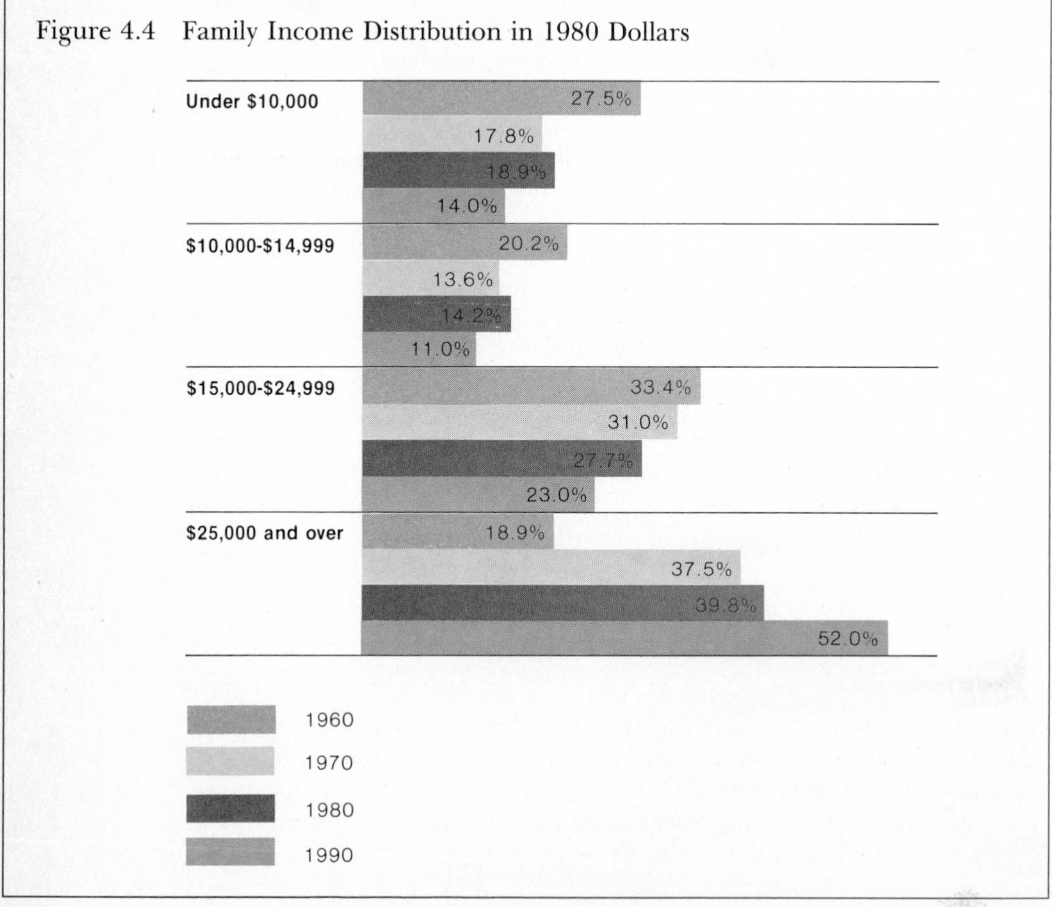

Source: Department of Commerce, The Conference Board.

Engel's Laws

How do expenditure patterns vary with increased income? More than a hundred years ago, Ernst Engel, a German statistician, published what became known as **Engel's laws,** three general statements based on his studies of the impact of household income changes on consumer spending behavior. According to Engel, as family income increases:

1. A smaller percentage of expenditures goes for food.
2. The percentage spent on housing and household operations and clothing remains constant.
3. The percentage spent on other items (such as recreation and education) increases.

Are Engel's laws still valid? Table 4.4 supplies the answers. A steady decline in the percentage of total income spent on food, beverages, and tobacco occurs from low to high incomes. Although high-income families spend a greater absolute amount on food purchases, their purchases represent a smaller percentage of their total expenditures than is true of low-income families. The second law is partly correct, since percentage expenditures for housing and household operations remain relatively unchanged in all but the very lowest income group. The percentage spent on clothing, however, increases with increased income. As Table 4.4 indicates, households which earn less than $10,000 annually spend a smaller percentage of their income on clothing than those who earn more than $10,000. The third law is also true with the exception of medical and personal care, which appear to decline with the increased income.

Table 4.4 Annual Family Income Expenditures by Income Groups

	Family Income			
	Under $10,000	$10,000–$19,999	$20,000–$24,999	$25,000 and Over
Category	Percent of Total Expenditures			
Food, beverages, and tobacco	24	22	20	18
Housing, house furnishings, and equipment	34	30	28	29
Clothing and accessories	7	8	9	11
Other goods and accessories[a]	35	40	43	43

[a]Includes transportation, medical and personal care, recreation and equipment, reading and education, and other goods and services.

Source: Adapted with permission from Helen Axel, ed., *A Guide to Consumer Markets, 1977/1978* (New York: Conference Board, 1977), p. 173.

Engel's laws provide the marketing manager with useful generalizations about the types of consumer demand that evolve with increased income. They can also be useful for the marketer evaluating a foreign country as a potential market target.

Psychographic Segmentation

Although geographic and demographic segmentation traditionally have been the primary bases for dividing consumer and industrial markets into homogeneous segments to serve as market targets, marketers have long recognized the need for fuller, more lifelike portraits of consumers in developing marketing programs. Even though traditionally used variables such as age, sex, family life cycle, income, and population size and location are important in segmentation, lifestyles of potential customers may prove equally important.

Lifestyle refers to the customer's mode of living; it is how an individual lives. Consumers' lifestyles are regarded as a composite of their individual psychological makeups—their needs, motives, perceptions, and attitudes. A lifestyle also bears the mark of many other influences like reference groups, culture, social class, and family members. A frequently used classification system for lifestyle variables is shown in Table 4.5.

Using Psychographics

In recent years, a new technique has been developed which promises to elicit more meaningful bases for segmentation. Although definitions vary among researchers, **psychographics** generally means the psychological profiles of different consumers developed from quantitative research. These profiles are usually developed as a result of asking consumers to agree or disagree with **AIO statements,** which are several hundred statements dealing with activities, interests, and opinions. Some of these dimensions are listed in Table 4.5.

Hundreds of psychographic studies have been conducted on products and services ranging from beer to air travel. A national study of household food buying identified four distinct segments based on psychographic research. Of the 1,800 adults interviewed, 98 percent could be categorized into one of the following groupings:

Hedonists, who represent 20 percent of the population, want the good life—foods that taste good, are convenient, and inexpensive. They aren't worried about sugar, fat, cholesterol, salt, calories, additives, or preservatives. They are most likely young, male, and child-free. Hedo-

Table 4.5 AIO Statement Dimensions

Activities	Interests	Opinions	Demographics
Work	Family	Themselves	Age
Hobbies	Home	Social issues	Education
Social events	Job	Politics	Income
Vacation	Community	Business	Occupation
Entertainment	Recreation	Economics	Family size
Club membership	Fashion	Education	Dwelling
Community	Food	Products	Geography
Shopping	Media	Future	City size
Sports	Advertisements	Culture	Stage in life cycle

Source: Joseph T. Plummer, "The Concept and Application of Life Style Dimensions," *Journal of Marketing* (January 1974), p. 34. Used by permission of the American Marketing Association.

nists are above average consumers of regular soft drinks, beer, margarine, presweetened cereal, candy, and gum.

Don't Wants, another 20 percent of the population, are the mirror image of the Hedonists. They avoid all the "no-no" ingredients in some processed foods. They will sacrifice taste and convenience and will pay more to obtain foods without sugar, artificial ingredients, cholesterol, and fat. They are concerned about calories and nutrition. In effect, their avoidance behavior is more health oriented than diet conscious. This segment is older; more than half are over age 50. They tend to be better educated, live in large urban areas, and don't have children at home. The Don't Wants are major consumers of decaffeinated coffee, fruit juices, wine, unsalted butter, corn oil margarine, nutritionally fortified cereal, yogurt, and sugar-free foods and beverages.

The Weight Conscious, who comprise about one third of the population, are primarily concerned about calories and fat. They like convenience foods, but try to avoid cholesterol, sugar, and salt. They're not particularly nutrition or taste conscious and don't avoid foods simply because they have artificial ingredients or preservatives. Members of this segment tend to have higher incomes and many are women employed full time. Given their concern for calories, the Weight Conscious are above average consumers of iced tea, diet soft drinks, diet margarine, and sugar-free candy and gum.

The Moderates, the final 25 percent of the population, are average in everything. They balance the trade-offs they make in food selection and don't exhibit strong concerns about the avoidance factors. They closely profile the population in demographics, and their consumption levels were average for the foods and beverages listed in the study.[17]

The marketing implications of psychographic segmentations are considerable. Some of these are suggested in a study of heavy users of eye makeup and shortening excerpted in Table 4.6. Psychographic profiles produce a much richer description of a potential market target and should assist promotional decisions in attempting to match the company's image and its product offerings with the type of consumer using the product.

Psychographic segmentation often serves as a component of an overall marketing strategy in which markets are also segmented on the basis of demographic/geographic variables such as age, city size, education, family life cycle stage, and geographic location. These more traditional bases provide the marketer with accessibility to consumer segments through orthodox communications channels like newspapers, radio and television advertising, and other promotional outlets. Psychographic studies may then be implemented to develop lifelike, three-dimensional profiles of the lifestyles of the firm's market target. When combined with demographic/geographic characteristics, psychographics emerges as an important tool in understanding the behavior of present and potential market targets.[18]

Benefit Segmentation

A fourth approach to market segmentation is to focus on such attributes as product usage rates and the benefits derived from the product. These factors may reveal important bases for pinpointing prospective market targets. One analysis of 34 segmentation studies indicated that benefit analysis provided the best predictor of brand use, level of consumption, and product type selected in 51 percent of the cases.[19] Many marketers now consider benefit segmentation the most useful approach to classifying markets.

[17]Reported in "Research on Food Consumption Values Identifies Four Market Segments: Finds 'Good Taste' Still Tops," *Marketing News* (May 15, 1981), p. 17. Used by permission of the American Marketing Association.

[18]For a thorough survey of previous psychographic studies and some case histories of the uses of psychographic research, see William D. Wells, "Psychographics: A Critical Review," *Journal of Marketing Research* (May 1972), pp. 196–213. See also John J. Burnett, "Psychographic and Demographic Characteristics of Blood Donors," *Journal of Consumer Research* (June 1981), pp. 62–86; Mary Ann Lederhaus and Ronald J. Adams, "A Psychographic Profile of the Cosmopolitan Consumers," Robert H. Ross, Frederic B. Kraft, and Charles H. Davis, eds., *Proceedings of the Southwestern Marketing Association*, (Wichita, Kansas: Southwestern Marketing Assoc., 1981), pp. 142–145; and J. Paul Merenski, "Psychographics: Valid by Definition and Reliable by Technique," Venkatakrishna V. Bellur, ed., *Developments in Marketing Science* (Miami Beach: Academy of Marketing Science, 1981), pp. 161–166.

[19]See "Lifestyle Research: A Lot of Hype, Versus Little Performance," *Marketing News* (May 14, 1982), Section 2, p. 5.

Table 4.6 Profile of Heavy Users of Eye Makeup and Shortening

	Heavy User of Eye Makeup	Heavy User of Shortening
Demographic Characteristics	Young, well-educated, lives in metropolitan areas	Middle-aged, medium to large family, lives outside metropolitan areas
Product Use	Also a heavy user of liquid face makeup, lipstick, hair spray, perfume, cigarettes, gasoline	Also a heavy user of flour, sugar, canned lunch meat, cooked pudding, catsup
Media Preferences	Fashion magazines, "The Tonight Show," adventure programs	Reader's Digest, daytime TV serials, family-situation TV comedies
Activities, Interests, and Opinions		
Agrees more than average with	"I often try the latest hairdo styles when they change." "An important part of my life and activities is dressing smartly." "I like to feel attractive to all men." "I want to look a little different from others." "I like what I see when I look in the mirror." "I take good care of my skin." "I would like to spend a year in London or Paris." "I like ballet." "I like to serve unusual dinners." "I really do believe that blondes have more fun."	"I love to bake and frequently do." "I save recipes from newspapers and magazines." "I love to eat." "I enjoy most forms of housework." "Usually I have regular days for washing, cleaning, etc., around the house." "I am uncomfortable when my house is not completely clean." "I try to arrange my home for my children's convenience." "Our family is a close-knit group." "Clothes should be dried in the fresh air and out-of-doors." "I would rather spend a quiet evening at home than go out to a party."
Disagrees more than average with	"I enjoy most forms of housework." "I furnish my home for comfort, not for style." "If it was good enough for my mother, it's good enough for me."	"My idea of housekeeping is once over lightly." "Classical music is more interesting than popular music." "I like ballet." "I'd like to spend a year in London or Paris."

Source: William D. Wells and Arthur D. Beard, "Personality and Consumer Behavior," in Scott Ward and Thomas S. Robertson, eds., *Consumer Behavior: Theoretical Sources*, © 1973, pp. 195–196. Adapted by permission of Prentice-Hall, Inc., Englewood Cliffs, N.J.

Usage Rates

Marketing managers may divide potential segments into two categories: users and nonusers. Users may be further divided into heavy, moderate, and light users.[20]

In some product categories, such as air travel, car rentals, dog food, and hair coloring, less than 20 percent of the population accounts for more than 80 percent of the total purchases. Even for such widely used products as coffee and soft drinks, half of all U.S. households account for almost 90 percent of the total usage.[21]

An early study of usage patterns by Dik Warren Twedt divided users into two categories: light and heavy. Twedt's analysis of consumer-panel data revealed that 29 percent of the sample households could be characterized as heavy users of lemon-lime soft drinks. This group represented 91 percent of sales in the product category.[22] It is, therefore, not surprising that usage rates are important segmentation variables for Coca-Cola, Pepsi-Cola, and 7-Up.

Heavy users often can be identified through analysis of internal records. Retail stores and financial institutions have records of charge-card purchases and other transactions. Warranty records may also be used.[23]

Product Benefits

Market segments may also be identified by the benefits the buyer expects to derive from a product or brand. In a pioneering investigation, Daniel Yankelovich revealed that much of the watch industry operated with little understanding of the benefits watch buyers expect in their purchases. At the time of the study, most watch companies were marketing relatively expensive models through jewelry stores and using prestige appeals. However, Yankelovich's research revealed that about one third of the market reported they purchased the lowest-priced watch and another 46 percent focused on durability and overall product quality. The U.S Time Company decided to focus its product benefits on those two categories and market its Timex watches in drugstores, variety stores, and discount houses. Within a few years of adopting the new segmentation approach, U.S. Time Company became the largest watch company in the world.[24]

[20]An interesting study is reported in Dub Ashton, "Frequent vs. Infrequent Flyers: An Example of Perceptual Segmentation," in Bellur, ed., *Developments in Marketing Science,* pp. 135–138.

[21]Reported in David T. Kollat, Roger D. Blackwell, and James F. Robeson, *Strategic Marketing* (New York: Holt, Rinehart and Winston, 1972), p. 192.

[22]Dik Warren Twedt, "How Important to Marketing Strategy is the 'Heavy User'?" *Journal of Marketing* (January 1964), pp. 71–72.

[23]These methods are suggested in Martin L. Bell, *Marketing: Concepts and Strategy* (Boston: Houghton-Mifflin, 1979), p. 129.

[24]Daniel Yankelovich, "New Criteria for Market Segmentation," *Harvard Business Review* (March–April 1964), pp. 83–90.

Benefit segmentation has also been employed successfully in a number of other consumer markets. One study, for example, revealed seven market segments based on the perceived benefits of drinking liquor. "Mood modification" was the objective of a consumer group that sought to escape stress, boredom, and so forth, while another segment sought "social lubrication," believing that liquor improved social interaction.[25]

Segmenting Industrial Markets

While the bulk of market segmentation research has concentrated on consumer markets, the concept can also be applied to the industrial sector. The overall process is similar. Three industrial market segmentation approaches have been identified: geographic segmentation, product segmentation, and segmentation by end-use application. (See Figure 4.5.)

Geographic Segmentation

Geographic segmentation is useful in industries where the bulk of the customers are concentrated in specific geographical locations. This approach can be used in such instances as the automobile industry, concentrated in the Detroit area, or the tire industry, centered in Akron. It might also be used in cases where the markets are limited to just a few locations. The oil-field equipment market, for example, is largely concentrated in cities like Houston, Dallas, and Tulsa.

Product Segmentation

Product segmentation can be used in the industrial marketplace. Industrial users tend to have much more precise product specifications than ultimate consumers do. Thus, industrial products often fit narrower market segments than consumer products. Designing an industrial good or service to meet specific buyer requirements is a form of market segmentation.

Segmentation by End-Use Applications

A third segmentation base is end-use applications or precisely how the industrial purchaser will use the product. A manufacturer of, say, printing equipment may serve markets ranging from a local utility to a bi-

[25] Alfred E. Goldman, "Market Segmentation Analysis Tells What To Say to Whom," *Marketing News* (January 22, 1982), Section 1, p. 10.

Figure 4.5 Segmentation Bases for Industrial Markets

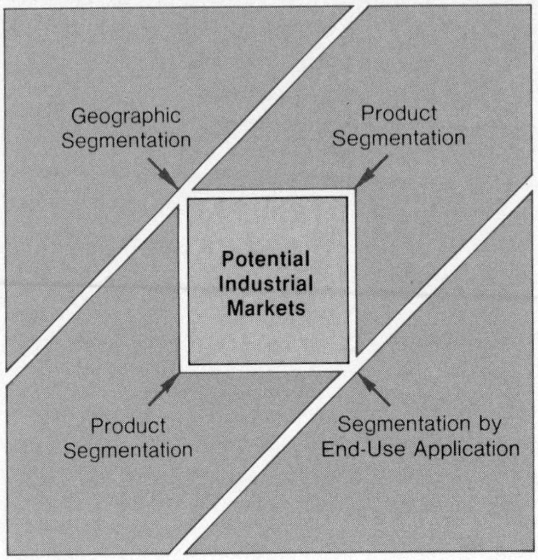

Geographic Segmentation
Product Segmentation
Potential Industrial Markets
Product Segmentation
Segmentation by End-Use Application

cycle manufacturer to the U.S. Department of Defense. Each end-use of the equipment may dictate unique specifications of performance, design, and price. The market for desk-top computers provides a good example. Xerox is targeting its 820-II model to the office market, rather than the home market. Technology Group Inc.'s BMC computer is being offered for end-use applications in accounting and blood diagnostics.[26] Regardless of how it is done, market segmentation is as vital to industrial marketing as it is in consumer markets.

Summary

A market consists of people or organizations with the necessary purchasing power and willingness to buy. The authority to buy must also exist. Markets can be classified by the type of products they handle. Consumer goods are products purchased by the ultimate consumer for personal use. Industrial goods are products purchased for use either

[26]Susan Chace, "Marketing Grows More Vital for Desktop Computer Sales," *The Wall Street Journal* (October 22, 1982), p. 27.

directly or indirectly in the production of other goods and services for resale. Products are typically targeted at specific market segments. The process of dividing the total market into several homogeneous groups is called market segmentation.

Consumer markets can be divided on the bases of geographic, demographic, psychographic, or benefit segmentation. Geographic segmentation is the process of dividing the overall market into homogeneous groups on the basis of population location. It is one of the oldest forms of segmentation. The high mobility of the U.S. population means that considerable effort must go into identifying the various geographical segments. The most commonly used form of segmentation is demographic segmentation, which classifies the overall market into homogeneous groups based upon characteristics such as age, sex, and income levels. Psychographic segmentation is a relatively new approach. It uses behavioral profiles developed from analyses of the activities, opinions, and interests, and lifestyles of consumers to identify market segments. The fourth approach, benefit segmentation, may be the most useful. It segments markets on the basis of the perceived benefits consumers expect to derive from a product or service.

Benefit segmentation is also useful in industrial markets. There are three bases for industrial market segmentation: geographic segmentation, product segmentation, and segmentation by end-use applications. Geographic segmentation is commonly used in concentrated industries. A second industrial market segmentation base is by product. Industrial markets are characterized by precise product specifications, making this approach feasible. Segmentation by end-use applications is the final base. This approach is predicated upon the use that the industrial purchasers will make of the good or service.

This chapter has examined the various bases for segmenting both consumer and industrial markets. Chapter 5 examines how these concepts may be applied to market segmentation strategies. This section concludes with Chapter 6 on marketing research and information systems.

Key Terms

market
consumer goods
industrial goods
market segmentation
Consolidated Metropolitan Statistical Area (CMSA)
Primary Metropolitan Statistical Area (PMSA)
Metropolitan Statistical Area (MSA)
family life cycle
SSWD
POSLSQ
Engel's laws
lifestyle
psychographics
AIO statements

Review Questions

1. Explain why each of the four components of a market is needed for a market to exist.
2. Bicycles are consumer goods; iron ore is an industrial good. What about trucks—are they consumer goods or industrial goods? Defend your answer.
3. Identify and briefly explain the bases for segmenting consumer markets.
4. Identify the major population shifts that have occurred in recent years. How do you account for these shifts?
5. Distinguish among CMSAs, PMSAs, and MSAs.
6. Why is demographic segmentation the most commonly used approach to market segmentation?
7. How can lifestyles be used in market segmentation?
8. Explain the use of product usage rates as a segmentation variable.
9. What market segmentation base would you recommend for the following:
   a. Professional soccer team
   b. Porsche sports car
   c. Columbia Records
   d. Scope mouthwash
10. Identify and briefly explain the bases for segmenting industrial markets.

Discussion Questions and Exercises

1. Match the following bases for market segmentation with the items below:
   a. Geographic segmentation
   b. Demographic segmentation
   c. Psychographic segmentation
   d. Benefit segmentation
   ______1. A government financed study divided U.S. households into five categories of eating patterns: meat eaters; healthy eaters; conscientious eaters; "in a dither" eaters; and on the go eaters.
   ______2. Bamberger's decision to emphasize suburban department stores. (Its only downtown outlet is the original store in Newark, New Jersey.)
   ______3. "7-Up, clear, crisp with no caffeine."
   ______4. Spiegel Inc. targets its catalogs at 25 to 54-year-old working women with household incomes of $34,000.
2. The NFL strike in 1982 caused a major problem for marketers who target their products at affluent younger males. Commercials during National Football League games are a primary method of reaching this group. Substitute broadcasts of Canadian Football

League and small college games produced only about half of the NFL audience. Research also indicated that baseball games tend to draw older, less affluent males. If you were such an advertiser, how would you have dealt with the NFL strike?

3. Prepare a brief report on the future growth prospects of the geographical area in which you live.
4. Explain why the household growth rate is more than double the increase in population.
5. A study by the U.S. Census Bureau dealt with the ancestral background of Americans. Nearly 29 percent of all Americans claim some German ancestry. Over 24 percent of our population is partially Irish; and over 22 percent have some English roots. How could a marketer use this demographic information?

5

MARKET SEGMENTATION STRATEGIES

Chapter Objectives

1. To explain undifferentiated, differentiated, and concentrated marketing strategies.
2. To outline the stages in the market segmentation process.
3. To understand how market target decision analysis can be used in the market segmentation process.
4. To understand how market target decision analysis can be used to assess a product mix.

Metropolitan Life Insurance Co., the nation's leading life insurer, built its century-old reputation on selling to one market segment—lower income consumers. For years, the firm concentrated on writing policies with $5,000 or less face value. This insurance was sold during house calls by agents who went back monthly to pick up the premium. Purchasers were primarily families with modest incomes. The policies they bought were called debit policies because the agent carried a portfolio of accounts called a debit book. Metropolitan's agents were paid a service fee to handle these accounts. Times change, and Metropolitan was forced to reconsider its market target.

Insurance buyers became more sophisticated as family incomes rose. Consumers began to seek alternatives to expensive debit policies. In addition, the firm's selling costs for debit policies were high. Metropolitan decided to move out of the low-income market and target more lucrative middle-income groups. While the company still carries 6.3

million debit policies (out of a total of 47 million policies), it now agressively markets health, homeowners, and automobile insurance along with whole life policies valued at $25,000 and higher. Beginning in 1973, Metropolitan moved its sales force from service fees to just commissions on sales. The changeover was completed in 1981. In the process, the 1970 sales force of 23,400 agents shrunk to 13,000.[1]

The Metropolitan Life Insurance Co. illustration points out the importance of identifying a market target that is viable under current economic and competitive conditions. It also shows the need to monitor market targets and to make even dramatic switches when necessary.

The Conceptual Framework

Chapter 5 furthers the discussion of market segmentation that was introduced in the previous chapter. Chapter 4 dealt with the role of market segmentation in developing a marketing strategy and the bases for segmenting consumer markets (geographic, demographic, psychographic, and benefit segmentation) and industrial markets (geographic, product, and segmentation by end-use application). Here the emphasis shifts to the strategies associated with the concepts of market segmentation.

This chapter looks at three alternative marketing strategies for matching product offerings to specific market segments. These approaches are known as undifferentiated, differentiated, and concentrated marketing. The selection of one of these alternatives is dependent upon a variety of internal and external variables facing the firm.

Next, Chapter 5 outlines the various stages that exist in the segmentation process. The starting point is to identify the dimension that can be used to segment markets. The process ends with the decision on the actual market target segments. Thus, Chapter 5 concludes with a separate section on market target decision analysis, the procedure for selecting targeted market segments.

Alternative Market Matching Strategies

At the very core of the firm's strategies is the objective of matching product offerings with the needs of particular market segments. A successful match is vital to the market success of the firm.

[1]Daniel Hertzberg, "Switching Tactics, Metropolitan Life Aims Its Sales Pitch at Higher Income Prospects," *The Wall Street Journal* (December 30, 1981), p. 9.

Three basic strategies for achieving consumer satisfaction are available. Firms that produce only one product and market it to all customers with a single marketing mix practice **undifferentiated marketing.**[2] This strategy is sometimes called mass marketing. Firms that produce numerous products with different marketing mixes designed to satisfy smaller segments practice **differentiated marketing.** Firms that concentrate all marketing resources on small segments of the total market practice **concentrated marketing.** These market matching strategies are illustrated in Figure 5.1.

Undifferentiated Marketing

The policy of undifferentiated marketing was much more common in the past that it is today. Ignoring the luxury market, Henry Ford built the Model T and sold it for one price to everyone. He agreed to paint the car any color that consumers wanted "as long as it is black."

Although marketing managers recognize the existence of numerous segments in the total market, they generally ignore minor differences and focus on the broad market. To reach the general market, they use mass advertising, mass distribution, and broad themes. One immediate gain from the strategy of undifferentiated marketing is the efficiency resulting from longer production runs. This strategy allowed Henry Ford to mass produce and market a simple, well-designed product. The undifferentiated marketing strategy simplified Ford's production operations. It also minimized inventories, since neither Ford nor its affiliated automobile dealers had to contend with optional equipment and numerous color combinations.

However, there are dangers inherent in the strategy of undifferentiated marketing. A firm that attempts to satisfy everyone in the market faces the threat of competitors who offer specialized products to smaller segments of the total market and better satisfy each of these segments. Indeed, firms implementing a strategy of differentiated marketing or concentrated marketing may enter the market and capture sufficient small segments to make the strategy of undifferentiated marketing unworkable for the competition.

A firm that uses undifferentiated marketing may also encounter problems in foreign markets. The Campbell Soup Company suffered heavy losses in marketing tomato soup in the United Kingdom before the company discovered that the British prefer a more bitter taste. Another U.S. firm, Corn Products Company, discovered real differences

[2]This strategy has also been called product differentiation. See Wendell R. Smith, "Product Differentiation and Market Segmentation as Alternative Marketing Strategies," *Journal of Marketing* (July 1956), pp. 3–8. The terms undifferentiated marketing, differentiated marketing, and concentrated marketing were suggested by Philip Kotler. See his *Marketing Management,* 4th ed. (Englewood Cliffs, N.J.: Prentice-Hall, 1980).

in U.S. and European soup preferences when it failed in an attempt to market Knorr dry soups in the United States. Although dry soups are commonly purchased by Europeans, the U.S. homemaker prefers liquid soup, apparently because of shorter cooking time.

Differentiated Marketing

The company employing a strategy of differentiated marketing is still attempting to satisfy a large part of the total market. Instead of marketing one product with a single marketing program, it markets a number of products designed to appeal to individual parts of the total market. As Figure 5.1 indicates, Ford now offers Lincoln Town Cars, Mustangs, and Escorts to various segments of the new car market. The firm's objective is to produce a greater number of total sales and to develop more product loyalty in each of the submarkets. It does this by providing a marketing mix designed to serve the needs of each market target rather than inducing the consumer segments to purchase one product designed for everyone. Similarly, Cadillac planners noted that import owners tended to trade up to BMWs and Audis, not to traditional Cadillac models. To counteract this the Cimarron was introduced to appeal to younger affluent buyers.[3]

Most firms practice differentiated marketing. Procter & Gamble markets Bold, Bonus, Cheer, Dash, Duz, Gain, Oxydol, Tide, and other detergents to appeal to detergent buyers. Lever Brothers offers two brands of complexion soap, Dove and Lux, and two brands of deodorant soap, Lifebuoy and Phase III.

By providing increased satisfaction for each of numerous market targets, the company with a differentiated marketing strategy can produce more sales than are possible with undifferentiated marketing. In general, however, the costs of a differentiated marketing strategy are greater than those of an undifferentiated strategy. Production costs usually rise because additional products mean shorter production runs and increased set-up time. Inventory costs rise because of added space needs for the products and increases in the necessary record-keeping. Promotional costs also increase as unique promotional mixes are developed for each market segment.

Even though the costs of doing business are typically greater under a differentiated marketing strategy, consumers are usually better served by providing products that are specifically designed to meet the needs of smaller segments. Also, a firm that wants to employ a single marketing strategy for an entire market may be forced to choose a strategy of

[3]Charles G. Burck, "A Small Surprise for Cadillac," *Fortune* (May 4, 1981), pp. 171–172.

Figure 5.1 Alternative Market Matching Strategies

A. Undifferentiated Marketing: Ford Motor Company in 1925

Segment	Market Offering
Urban dwellers	Model T
Small town residents	Model T
Middle income consumers	Model T
Factory workers	Model T
Traveling salespeople	Model T

B. Differentiated Marketing: Ford Motor Company in 1984

Segment	Market Offering
Luxury segment	Lincoln Town Car
Sports car enthusiasts	Mustang GT
Consumers seeking economy and practical performance	Escort
Large families seeking station wagons	Ford
Farm dwellers	Ford trucks

C. Concentrated Marketing: Volkswagen of America in 1955

Segment	Market Offering
Luxury segment	
Sports car enthusiasts	
Consumers seeking economy and practical performance	Volkswagen Beetle
Large families seeking station wagons	
Farm dwellers	

differentiated marketing instead. If competitors appeal to each market target in the total market, the firm must also use this approach to remain competitive.

Concentrated Marketing

Rather than attempting to market its product offerings to the entire market, a firm may choose to focus its entire effort on profitably satisfying a smaller market target. This strategy of concentrated marketing is particularly appealing to new, small firms that lack the financial resources of their competitors.

Perhaps the most famous example of a firm practicing the concentrated marketing strategy is Volkswagen of America. For 20 years, the Volkswagen Beetle was symbolic of a product specifically designed and marketed to buyers wanting economy and practical performance in their transportation. Volkswagen of America concentrated on selling to this segment despite the fact that they sold many other models in Europe. Similarly, Rolls-Royce is known for producing and marketing the ultimate in expensive, luxury automobiles.

Concentration on a segment of the total market often allows a firm to maintain profitable operation. Fisher-Price has developed an enviable image in the toy industry because of its reputation as a high-quality manufacturer and marketer of children's toys.

Concentrated marketing, however, poses dangers as well. Since the firm's growth is tied to a particular segment, changes in the size of the segment or in customer buying patterns may result in severe financial problems. Sales may also drop if new competitors appeal to the same market segment.

Selecting a Strategy[4]

Although most organizations adopt the strategy of differentiated marketing, there is no single best strategy. Any of the three alternatives may prove best in a particular situation. The basic determinants of a market matching strategy are 1) company resources, 2) product homogeneity, 3) stage in the product life cycle, and 4) competitors' strategies.

A concentrated marketing strategy may be a necessity for a firm with limited resources. Small firms, for example, may be forced to select small market targets because of limitations in financing, size of sales force, and promotional budgets.

On the other hand, an undifferentiated marketing strategy should be used for products perceived by consumers as relatively homogeneous. Marketers of grain sell their products on the basis of standardized grades rather than individual brand names. Some petroleum companies use a strategy of undifferentiated marketing in distributing their gasoline to the mass market.

The firm's strategy may also change as the product progresses through the various stages of the life cycle. During the early stages, an undifferentiated marketing strategy might be useful as the firm attempts to develop initial demand for the product. In the later stages, however, competitive pressures may result in modified products and marketing strategies aimed at smaller segments of the total market.

A final factor affecting the choice of a market matching strategy is the strategies used by competitors. A firm may find it difficult to use an undifferentiated strategy if its competitors are actively cultivating smaller segments. In such instances, competition usually forces each firm to adopt a differentiated strategy.[5]

[4]An interesting discussion of market entry strategy appears in Ronald H. King and Arthur A. Thompson, Jr., "Entry and Market Share Success of New Brands in Concentrated Markets," *Journal of Business Research* (September 1982), pp. 371–383.

[5]A similar list is suggested in Kotler, *Marketing Management,* pp. 209–210. Also see R. William Kotrba, "The Strategy Selection Chart," *Journal of Marketing* (July 1966), pp. 22–25.

The Market Segmentation Process[6]

The marketer has a number of potential bases for determining the most appropriate marketing strategy. Geographic, demographic, benefit and psychographic bases are often utilized in converting heterogeneous markets into specific segments that serve as market targets for the consumer-oriented marketer. By contrast, the industrial marketer can segment geographically, by product, or by end-use application. In either case, a systematic five-stage decision process is followed. This framework for market segmentation is shown in Figure 5.2.

Stage I: Select Market Segmentation Bases

Segmentation begins when a firm seeks bases upon which markets can be segmented. These bases are one or more characteristics of potential buyers that allow the marketer to classify them into market segments for further analysis. Segmentation bases should be selected so that each segment contains customers who respond to specific marketing mix alternatives similarly, while customers in different segments respond differently. For example, before Procter & Gamble decides to market Crest to a segment made up of large families, management should be confident that most large families are interested in preventing tooth decay so they will be receptive to the Crest marketing offer. In some cases, this objective is difficult to achieve. Consider the marketer seeking to reach the consumer segment that is over 50 years of age. Saturday evening television commercials can reach this group, but much of the expenditure may be wasted since the other major viewer group is comprised of teenagers.[7]

Stage II: Develop Relevant Profiles for Each Segment

Once segments have been identified, marketers should seek to understand the customer in each segment.

Segmentation bases provide some insight into the nature of customers, but typically not enough to base the kinds of decisions that marketing managers must make. Sufficient description of customers is needed so managers can more pecisely match customer needs with marketing offers. Characteristics that explain the similarities among customers within each segment as well as account for differences among segments

[6]This section is adapted from M. Dale Beckman, David L. Kurtz and Louis E. Boone, *Foundations of Marketing,* 2d ed. (Toronto: Holt Rinehart & Winston, Limited, 1982), pp. 180–182. The materials were originally prepared by Professor J. D. Forbes of the University of British Columbia and are reprinted by permission of the authors and publisher.

[7]Fred Rothenberg, "Saturday-Night Television Isn't What It Used to Be," *The Seattle Times* (July 31, 1982), p. B 8.

must be identified. Thus, the task at this stage is to develop profiles of the typical customer in each segment. For example, profiles for a segment might include lifestyle patterns, attitudes toward product attributes and brands, brand preferences, product use habits, geographic location, and demographic characteristics. For example, the Broadway-Southern California—a leading Los Angeles-based retailer—profiled its female customers as age 25–55; 4 foot 10 inches to 5 foot 3 inches tall; weighing 85–120 pounds; career oriented, and having a $20,000 plus household income. The Broadway used this profile to set up separate petite sections, one of the fastest growing segments of the women's fashion industry.[8]

Stage III: Forecast Market Potentials

In the third stage, market segmentation and market opportunity analysis continue to coincide to produce a forecast of market potential within each segment. Market potential sets the upper limit on the demand that can be expected from a segment and therefore determines maximum sales potential.

This stage should be a preliminary go or no go decision point for management, since it must determine whether the total sales potential in each segment is sufficient to justify further analysis. Some segments will be screened out because they represent insufficient potential demand; others will be sufficiently attractive for the analysis to continue.

Consider the toothbrush segment of the dental supplier and mouthwash market. At present, this segment is a $170 million annual market. It would nearly triple if a marketer could convince the public to replace their toothbrushes when they should be changed. Americans should buy three to four toothbrushes a year at average usage, but the current replacement rate is only 1.3 brushes annually.[9] Obviously, a tremendous market potential exists.

Stage IV: Forecast Probable Market Share

Once market potential has been estimated, the proportion of demand that can be captured by the firm must be determined. This stage requires a forecast of probable market share. Market share forecasts depend upon both an analysis of competitors' positions in target segments and on the specific marketing strategy and tactics designed to serve these segments. These two activities can be performed simultaneously. Moreover, design of marketing strategy and tactics determine the ex-

[8]"Small Clothes Are Selling Big," *Business Week* (November 16, 1981), pp. 152, 156.

[9]Jennifer Alter, "Toothbrush Makers' Lament: Who Notices?" *Advertising Age* (October 4, 1982), p. 66.

pected level of resources—that is, costs that will be necessary to tap the potential demand in each segment.

Colgate once trailed Procter & Gamble in heavy duty detergents, nearly two to one in dishwashing liquids, and also ran behind in soaps. Overall, Colgate trailed Procter & Gamble in half its business, so Colgate diversified its product line. Today, 75 percent of the firm's offerings do not face a directly competitive Procter & Gamble product, or if they do, they compete effectively.[10]

Stage V: Select Specific Market Segments

The information, analysis, and forecasts accumulated through the entire process allows management to assess the potential for the achievement of company goals and to justify the development of one or more segments. For example, demand forecasts, when combined with cost projections, are used to determine the profit and return on investment that can be expected from each segment. Analysis of marketing strategy and tactics will determine the degree of consistency with corporate image and reputation goals as well as with unique organizational capabilities that may be achieved by serving a segment. These assessments will, in turn, help management select specific segments as the market targets.

At this point of the analysis, the costs and benefits to be weighed are not only monetary, but also include many difficult to measure but critical organizational and environmental factors. For example, the firm may not have enough experienced personnel to launch a successful attack on what clearly could be an almost certain monetary success. Similarly, a firm with 80 percent of the market may face legal problems with the Federal Trade Commission if it increases its market concentration. A public utility may not attempt to institute a new increase in electricity consumption because of environmental and political repercussions. The assessment of both financial and nonfinancial factors is a difficult but vital and final stage in the decision process.

There is not, and should not be, any simple answer to the market segmentation decision. The marketing concept's prescription to serve the customer's needs and to earn a profit while so doing implies that the marketer has to evaluate each possible marketing program on how it achieves this goal in the marketplace. By performing the detailed analysis outlined in Figure 5.2, the marketing managers can increase the probability of success in profitably serving consumers' needs.

[10]Philip Kotler and Ravi Singh, "Basic Marketing Strategy for Winning Your Marketing War," *Marketing Times* (November/December 1982), pp. 23–24. This article is reprinted by permission from the *Journal of Business Strategy,* Vol. 1, N. 3, Winter 1981, Copyright © 1981, Warren, Gorham and Lamont, Inc., 210 South St., Boston, Mass. 02111. All rights reserved.

Figure 5.2 The Market Segmentation Decision Process

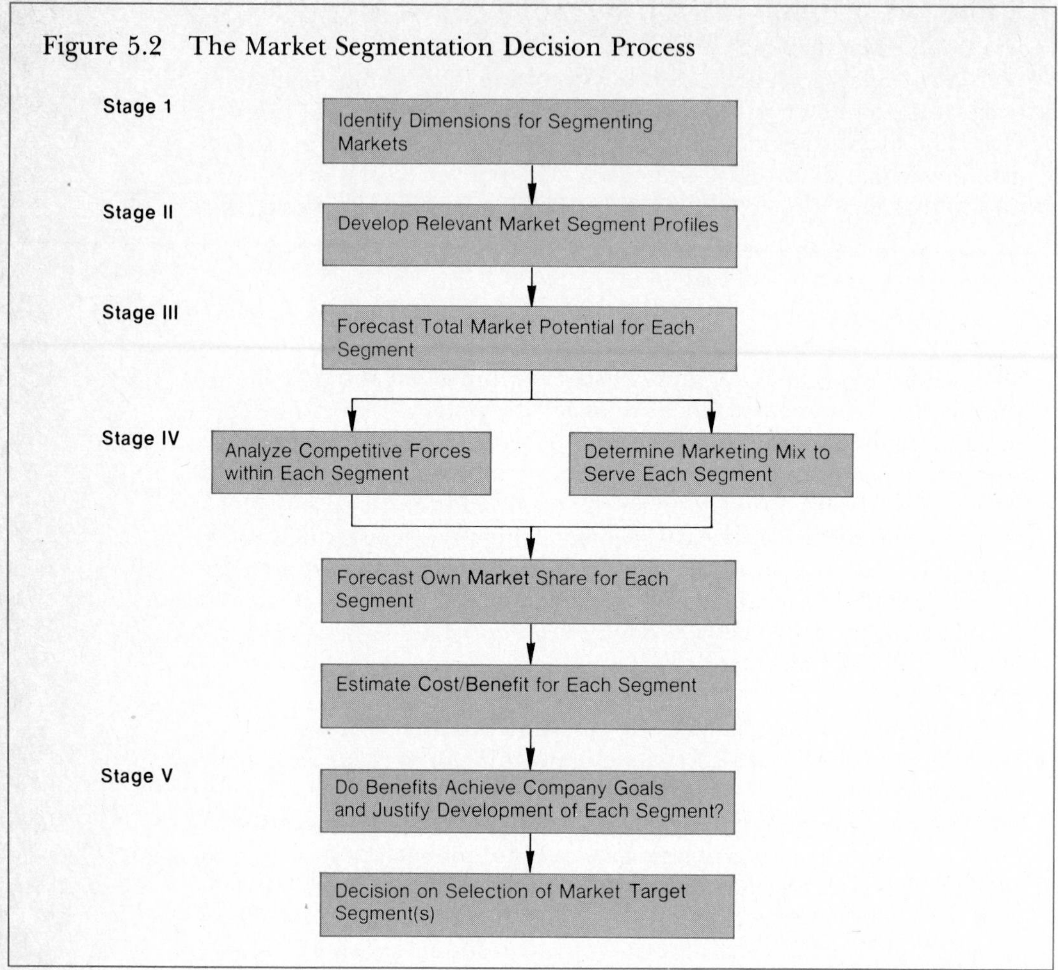

Source: M. Dale Beckman, David L. Kurtz, and Louis E. Boone, *Foundations of Marketing, Second Edition* (Toronto: Holt Rinehart and Winston of Canada, Ltd., 1982), p. 181. The figure was originally prepared by Professor J. D. Forbes and J. B. Warren of the University of British Columbia and is reprinted by permission of the authors and publisher.

Market Target Decision Analysis

Identifying specific market targets is an important aspect of overall marketing strategy. Clearly delineated market targets allow management to effectively employ marketing efforts like advertising. For example, television sports programming attracts a heavily male audience, but not all male audiences are the same. Baseball's audience tends to be older and less affluent than that of NFL games. As a result, the 1982 NFL players strike forced advertisers to shift their expenditures to less

Figure 5.3 Market Target for Typewriters

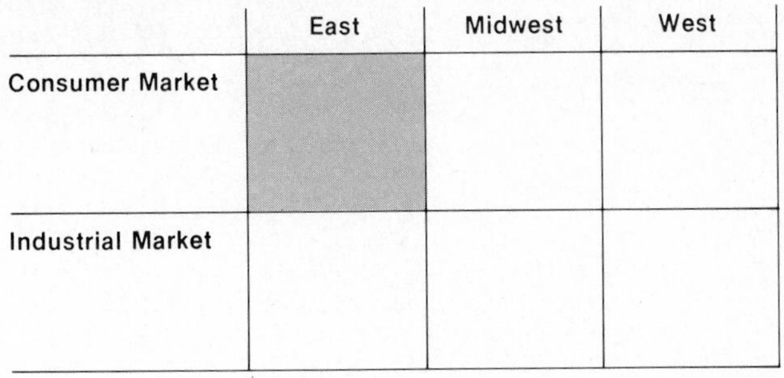

	East	Midwest	West
Consumer Market	(shaded)		
Industrial Market			

expensive programming or other media and caused considerable disruption in the firms' normal marketing strategies.[11]

Market target decision analysis is a useful tool in the market segmentation process. Targets are chosen by segmenting the total market on the basis of any given characteristics (as described in Chapter 4). The example that follows illustrates how market target decision analysis can be applied.[12]

Applying Market Target Decision Analysis

Consider the decisions of a small firm which analyzes the market potential for a proposed line of typewriters. Because of limited financial resources, the company must operate on a regional basis. The grid in Figure 5.3 illustrates the first two decisions for the firm: choosing a geographic area and marketing the typewriters to the ultimate consumers. The typewriter company also could have chosen the industrial market. To have done so would have required a separate marketing strategy, since each of the cells in Figure 5.3 represents unique markets with distinguishing characteristics.

The next steps involve the decision to market the typewriters to high-income households in the young and middle-aged stages of the family life cycle, which in turn involves evaluating the market for typewriters as gifts for school-age children. These decisions are shown in Figure 5.4. Data can be gathered about the size of the market target in the eastern United States and the firm's predicted market share.

[11]"The Football Strike Will Soon Hamstring TV," *Business Week* (October 8, 1982), p. 52.

[12]A similar analysis is suggested in Robert M. Fulmer, *The New Marketing* (New York: Macmillan, 1976), pp. 34–37; Philip Kotler, *Marketing Management* (Englewood Cliffs, N.J.: Prentice-Hall, 1976), pp. 141–151; and E. Jerome McCarthy, *Basic Marketing* (Homewood, Ill.: Richard D. Irwin, 1975), pp. 111–126.

Figure 5.4 Market Target for Typewriters Sold to Consumers in the Eastern United States

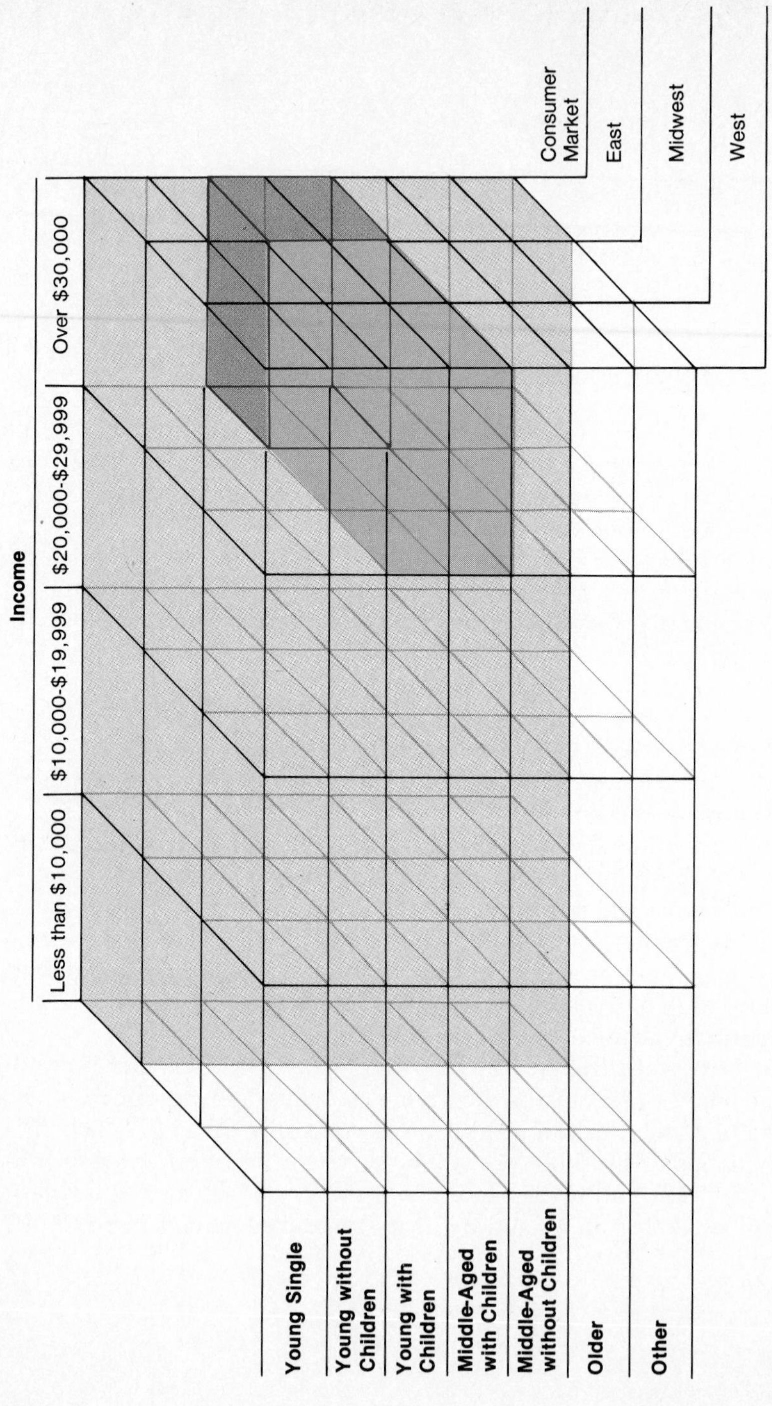

Income

Less than $10,000 | $10,000-$19,999 | $20,000-$29,999 | Over $30,000

Young Single

Young without Children

Young with Children

Middle-Aged with Children

Middle-Aged without Children

Older

Other

Consumer Market

East

Midwest

West

Figure 5.5 Using Market Target Decision Analysis to Evaluate a Product Mix

	Belongers	Achievers	Etc.
Romantic	Phone M Phone A Phone C		
Character		Phone R Phone Y	
Message-Center	Phone T		
Contemporary			

Source: Reprinted from "Properly Applied Psychographics Add Marketing Luster," *Marketing News* (November 12, 1982), p. 10.

The cross-classifications in Figure 5.4 can be further subdivided to gather more specific data about the characteristics of the proposed market target. The potential bases for segmenting markets is virtually limitless. Such divisions are sometimes made intuitively, but usually the decisions are supported by concrete data.[13]

The preceding illustration used geographical and demographical segmentation bases, but it is also possible to use benefit and psychographic segmentation in market target decision analysis. Similarly, geographic, product, and end-use application segmentation bases can be used in targeting industrial market segments.

Using Market Target Decision Analysis in Assessing a Product Mix

Product mix, a concept developed in Chapter 11, refers to the assortment of product lines and individual offerings available from a marketer. Market target decision analysis can be used to assess a firm's product mix and to point up needed modifications. For example, New York Telephone, a firm that serves 5.5 million households, has used the concept to evaluate its product offerings.[14] The company segments the total market by psychographic categories as shown in Figure 5.5.

[13] A good example of this systematic approach to identifying a precise market target appears in Richard P. Carr, Jr., "Developing a New Residential Market for Carpeting: Some Mistakes and Successes," *Journal of Marketing* (July 1977), pp. 101–102.

[14] "Properly Applied Psychographics Add Marketing Luster," *Marketing News* (November 12, 1982), p. 10.

Try Your Hand at Selecting Market Targets

For each of the following situations or products, pick the market target cells for which you would aim. The actual customer profiles are shown below.

Exercise A: Gourmet Food Market Stores that feature higher-priced, top-of-the-line gourmet foods.

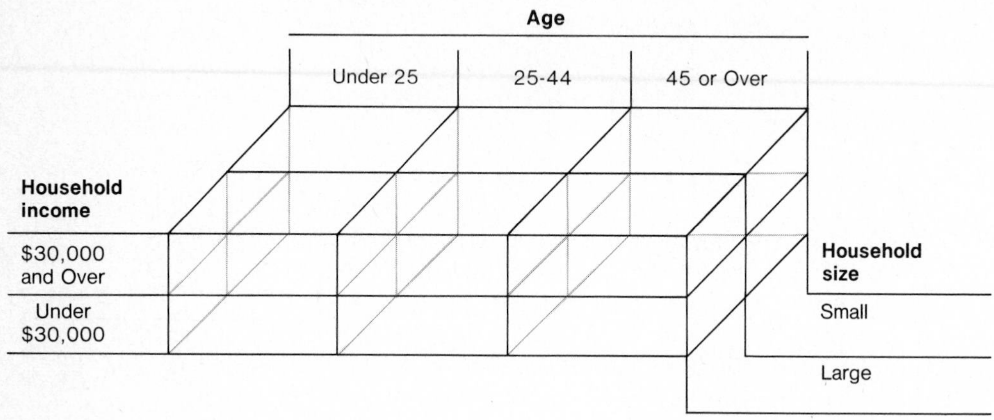

Exercise B: Workbench A 700,000 circulation magazine that is aimed at those who consider craftsmanship their hobby.

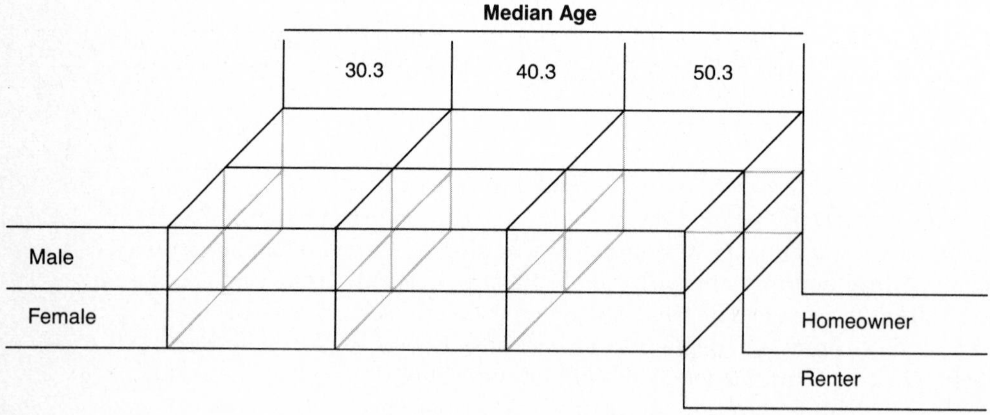

Exercise C: Mercedes-Benz Some models run in the $50,000 range. This exercise refers to American buyers only.

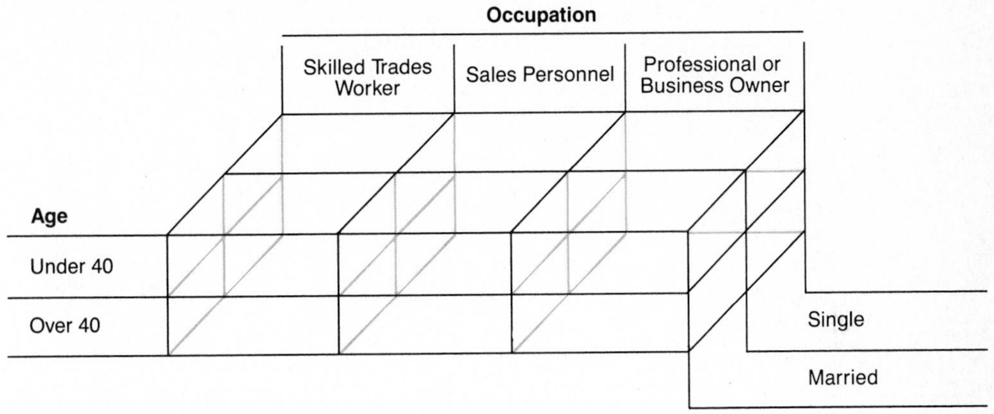

The Solutions

The actual customer profiles of these items is as follows.

Exercise A: Gourmet Food Market

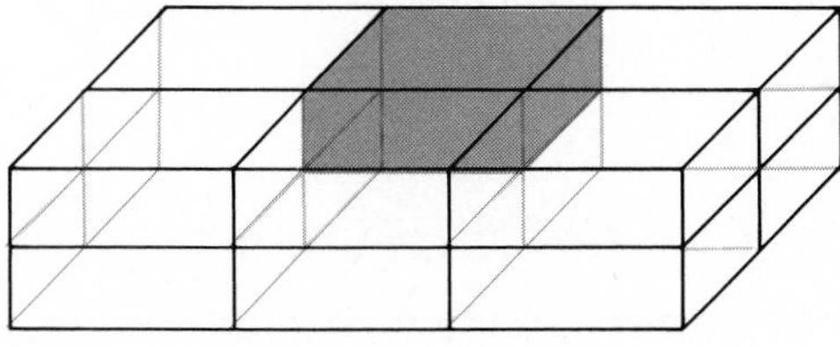

Exercise B: Workbench Magazine

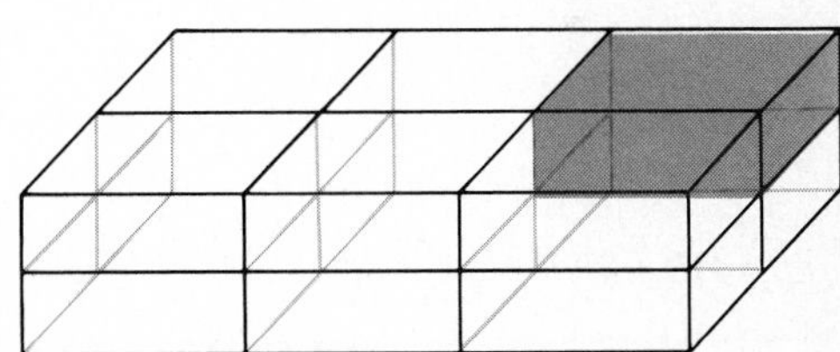

Exercise C: Mercedes-Benz

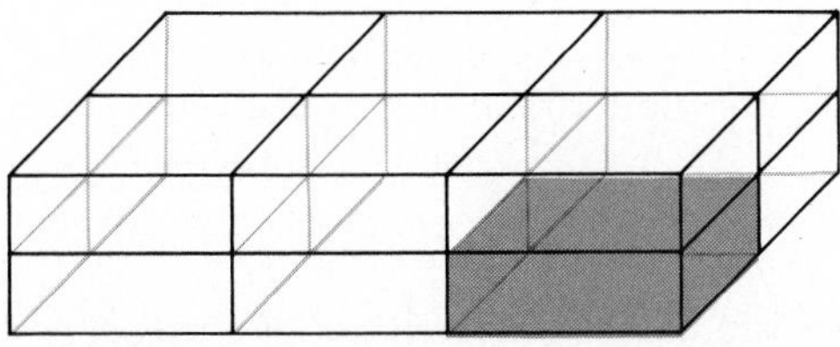

Source: Janet Guyon, "Gourmet-Food Market Grows as Affluent Shoppers Indulge," *The Wall Street Journal* (May 6, 1982), p. 31; "Magazine Publisher Advertisers' Target Growing, 'Overlooked' Empty-Nest Market," *Marketing News* (October 2, 1981), pp. 1, 10; and "Rolling Along," *Fortune* (December 14, 1981), p. 13.

New York Telephone's rule is to offer two and only two telephone sets in a given market segment. Offering three romantic type telephone sets to belongers is inefficient since the three compete with each other. By contrast, a phone model needs a companion product to adequately serve the belonger-message center segment.

The New York Telephone example shows how market target decision analysis can go beyond merely identifying market targets. It can play a cruical role in actually developing marketing strategies such as product mixes.

Summary

This chapter continues the discussion of market segmentation introduced in Chapter 4. Various strategies associated with the market segmentation concept are considered here.

There are three alternative strategies for matching product offerings to specific market segments. Undifferentiated marketing refers to the strategy of firms that produce only one product and market it to all customers with a single marketing mix. By contrast, differentiated marketing is when a firm produces numerous products with different marketing mixes designed to satisfy smaller market segments. The third alternative is concentrated marketing where a firm concentrates all its marketing resources on a small segment of the total market.

Correct strategy decisions are dependent upon a host of situational variables. The basic determinants of market matching strategy are: (1) company resources, (2) degree of product homogeneity, (3) stage in the product life cycle, and (4) competitors' strategies.

The market segmentation process follows a sequential framework consisting of five stages. These stages can be outlined as follows:

- Stage 1. Determine the bases upon which markets can be segmented.
- Stage 2. Develop consumer profiles for the appropriate market segments.
- Stage 3. Assess the overall market potential for the relevant market segments.
- Stage 4. Estimate market share and cost benefit of each market segment given the existing competition and the marketing mix that is selected.
- Stage 5. Select the segments that will become the firm's market targets.

Market target decision analysis is a useful tool in the market segmentation process. A grid is developed that outlines the various market segments by their distinguishing characteristics. All bases for segmentation can be employed in market target decision analysis. In addition to selecting the actual market target segments, the type of analysis can also be used for assessing the firm's current and planned product mix.

Part Two began with a chapter on marketing planning and forecasting. This chapter dealt with the concept of market segmentation. In the next chapter, attention shifts to the research procedures and techniques used to acquire information for building effective marketing strategies. Chapter 6 covers marketing research and information systems and concludes Part Two.

Key Terms

undifferentiated marketing
differentiated marketing
concentrated marketing
market target decision analysis
product mix

Review Questions

1. Outline the basic features of undifferentiated marketing.
2. Outline the basic features of differentiated marketing.
3. Outline the basic features of concentrated marketing.
4. What are the primary determinants of product market strategy selection?
5. List and describe the five stages of the market segmentation process.
6. What is meant by market target decision analysis?
7. Show how market target decision analysis can help select market segments that the firm should attempt to reach.
8. Illustrate how the four consumer-oriented segmentation bases can be used in market target decision analysis.
9. Illustrate how the three industrial market segmentation bases can be used in market target decision analysis.
10. How can market target decision analysis be used to assess a product mix?

Discussion Questions and Exercises

1. What can be learned from the Metropolitan Life Insurance Co. example at the beginning of the chapter? Discuss.
2. Prepare a term paper on an actual firm employing marketing segmentation in the development of its marketing strategy.
3. Match the following strategies with situations below. Which strategy would be most appropriate in each of these situations?
   a. Undifferentiated marketing
   b. Differentiated marketing
   c. Concentrated marketing

_____1. A firm entering the decline phase of the product life cycle.

_____2. Management considers it essential to minimize production and inventory carrying costs.

_____3. A new, small company is trying to gain a foothold in an industry.

_____4. The major competitors are employing a differentiated marketing strategy.

_____5. A firm lacks the financial resources of its major competitors.

_____6. A marketer of a homogeneous product like grain.

_____7. The market is composed of a series of homogeneous market segments, each having its own particular needs and wants.

4. Prepare a report that traces an actual company's experience as it moved through the various market segmentation stages.

5. Assess a firm's actual product mix using market target decision analysis.

Chapter Objectives

1. To relate marketing research and information systems to the elements of the marketing mix.
2. To describe the development and current status of the marketing research function.
3. To list the steps in the marketing research process.
4. To differentiate the types and sources of primary and secondary data.
5. To identify the methods of collecting survey data.
6. To explain the various sampling techniques.
7. To distinguish between marketing research and marketing information systems.
8. To outline the current status of marketing information systems.

MARKETING RESEARCH AND INFORMATION SYSTEMS

Marketing research played a crucial role in Reader's Digest's successful introduction of *Families,* its first new magazine in 60 years in the United States. The magazine is directed toward the nontraditional family situation, which has become the norm in the 1980s.

Author Alvin Toffler notes that the nuclear family consisting of a working husband, homemaking spouse, and two children characterizes only 7 percent of U.S. households today.[1] Reader's Digest saw a market opportunity here. Many existing "family" publications are actually oriented toward young mothers with only a 20 percent editorial content on children. The rest of the content focuses on recipes, beauty aids, and the like. So Reader's Digest decided to target *Families* at the 93 percent non-nuclear segment of the marketplace. Its editorial content

[1]See Alvin Toffler, *The Third Wave* (New York: William Morrow, 1980).

deals with issues like drugs, college financing, cohabitation, and adolescent nutrition.

Reader's Digest personnel developed a prospectus for the magazine complete with sample titles. The research department of the J. Walter Thompson advertising agency was hired to test the sample. The results from interviews in supermarket parking lots—conducted on weekends to get a wider cross-section of the population—were encouraging. Two test issues were developed, and both were received favorably by readers and advertisers.

Some 92 percent of the people who bought the first test issue said they would buy it again. And 86 percent of the readers said they had discussed one of the features with someone; many times with children. The reader demographics of the test issues were also excellent for attracting advertisers. Ninety-four percent of *Families'* audience were college educated, aged 18–49, with household incomes of $25,000 or more. Significantly, 80 percent had children.

Subscription offers were also carefully monitored. Reader's Digest follows up on orders from nonmarket target subscribers. For instance, it changed its headnote "A Reader's Digest Publication" to "A Monthly Magazine from Reader's Digest" because of an order from an elderly bachelor, who thought it was a publication of the Reader's Digest book division.

Families has proved to be a success for Reader's Digest. Its first regular issue contained a record number of advertising pages. Marketing research was a major contributor to that success. A good idea was carefully tested and refined until it became a successful new product entry.[2]

The Conceptual Framework

It has been said that the recipe for effective decisions is 90 percent information and 10 percent inspiration. All marketing strategy decisions depend on the type, quantity, and quality of the information on which they are based. A variety of sources exist for decision-oriented marketing information. Some are well-planned investigations designed to elicit specific information. Other valuable information may be obtained from sales force reports, accounting data, or published reports. Still other information may be obtained from controlled experiments or computer simulations.[3]

[2]The story of *Families* is told in "Test Marketing, Direct Mail Made Families A Winner," *Marketing News* (April 16, 1982), p. 11.

[3]An excellent article on knowledge needs is Calvin P. Duncan and Charles M. Lillis, "Directions for Marketing Knowledge Development: Opinions of Marketing Research Managers," *Journal of the Academy of Marketing Science* (Winter 1982), pp. 2a, 36.

A major source of information takes the form of marketing research. The American Marketing Association defines **marketing research** as the systematic gathering, recording, and analyzing of data about problems relating to the marketing of goods and services.[4] The critical task of the marketing manager is decision making. Managers must make effective decisions that enable their firms to solve problems as they arise and must anticipate and prevent future problems. Many times, though, managers are forced to make decisions without sufficient information. Marketing research aids the decision maker by presenting pertinent facts, analyzing them, and suggesting possible action.

Chapter 6 deals with the marketing research function. Marketing research is closely linked with the other elements of the marketing planning process. All marketing research should be done within the framework of the organization's strategic plan. Research projects should be directed toward the resolution of marketing decisions that conform to an overall corporate strategy. Alfred S. Boote, the marketing research director for the Singer Company, estimates that research costs 50 to 60 percent more for firms that lack a strategic marketing plan because too much useless information is collected.[5]

Much of the material outlined in Chapters 4 and 5 on market segmentation and market target analysis is based on information collected via marketing research efforts. Clearly, the marketing research function is the primary source of the information needed to make effective marketing decisions.

An Overview of the Marketing Research Function

Before looking at how marketing research is actually done, it is important to get an overall perspective of the field. What activities are considered part of the marketing research function? How did the field develop? Who is involved in marketing research?

Marketing Research Activities

All marketing decision areas are candidates for marketing research investigations. As Figure 6.1 indicates, marketing research efforts are commonly centered around determining market and sales potential, de-

[4]Committee on Definitions, *Marketing Definitions: A Glossary of Marketing Terms* (Chicago: American Marketing Association, 1960), p. 17.

[5]"Include Marketing Research in Every Level of Corporate Strategic Planning," *Marketing News* (September 18, 1981), Section 2, p. 8.

Figure 6.1 Marketing Research Activities Conducted by Selected Firms

Measurement of Market Potentials	93%
Sales Analysis	89%
Competitive Product Studies	85%
Short-range Sales Forecasting	85%
New-product Acceptance and Potential	84%
Establishment of Sales Quotas, Territories	75%
Distribution Channel Studies	69%
Studies of Advertising Effectiveness	67%
Packaging Research	60%
Export and International Studies	51%
Social Values and Policies Studies	40%

Source: Data from Dik Warren Twedt, ed., *1978 Survey of Marketing Research* (Chicago: American Marketing Association, 1978), p. 41. Used with permission.

veloping sales forecasts for the firm's products and services, determining appropriate channel strategies, evaluating the effectiveness of the firm's advertising and packaging decisions, and studying export and international marketing potential.

The Evolution of the Marketing Research Function

Marketing research is a relatively new field. Just over a hundred years have passed since N.W. Ayer conducted the first organized research project in 1879. A second important milestone in the development of marketing research occurred in 1911 when Charles C. Parlin organized and became manager of the nation's first commercial research department at the Curtis Publishing Company. A profile of Parlin begins Part Two.

Parlin actually got his start as a marketing researcher by counting soup cans in Philadelphia's garbage! Parlin was employed as a sales representative for advertising space in the *Saturday Evening Post.* He had failed to sell advertising space to the Campbell Soup Company because the firm believed that the magazine reached primarily working-class readers who made their own soup rather than spend 10 cents for a can of prepared soup. Campbell's was targeting its product at higher income people who could afford to pay for convenience. So Parlin began counting the soup cans contained in the garbage of different neighborhoods. To Campbell's surprise, Parlin's research revealed that more canned soup was sold to the working class than the wealthy, who had servants to make soup for them. Campbell's soup quickly became a *Saturday Evening Post* client.[6]

Much of the early research represented little more than written testimonials received from purchasers of the firm's products. Research became more sophisticated during the 1930s as the development of statistical techniques led to refinements in sampling procedures and greater accuracy in research findings.[7] However, mistakes still occurred. The *Literary Digest* conducted a major national study of U.S. households selected at random from lists of telephone numbers and auto registration records and reported that Alf Landon—not Franklin D. Roosevelt—would be elected president. The fiasco resulted from a failure to realize that many voters (most of whom were apparently Democrats) did not have telephones in 1936. The difficulty of predicting human behavior was all too apparent a few years ago when political research organizations called the Carter-Reagan presidential election campaign of 1980 too close to call just days before Reagan won in a landslide.

Participants in the Marketing Research Function

The American Marketing Association reports that 87 percent of the nation's leading manufacturing firms have established their own formal marketing research departments. Although such operations are found mostly in companies manufacturing consumer products, a substantial increase in marketing research departments has occurred recently in financial service firms, such as banks, savings and loan associations, other lending institutions, insurance companies, and major nonprofit organizations.[8] Total expenditures for marketing research in 1983 are estimated at more than $1 billion. Many smaller firms depend on independent marketing research firms to conduct their research studies. Even large firms typically rely on outside agencies to provide interviews, and they often farm out some research studies to independent

[6]This story is told in the following source and elsewhere: Eric Scigliano, "Research Hinges on Human Factors," *Monthly* (October 1981), p. 9.

[7]For a detailed treatment of the historical development of marketing research, see Robert Bartels, *The Development of Marketing Thought* (Homewood, Ill.: Richard D. Irwin, 1962), pp. 106–124.

[8]Dik Warren Twedt, ed., *1978 Survey of Marketing Research* (Chicago: American Marketing Association, 1978), pp. 10–13. See also Rohit Deshpande, "The Usefulness of Marketing Information in Decision Making: An Empirical Study of Marketing Research Projects," in *Evolving Marketing Thought for 1980*, eds., John J. Summey and Ronald D. Taylor (New Orleans: Southern Marketing Association, 1980), pp. 482–485.

Charles C. Parlin Would Probably Like Professor Rathje

Garbage is still an excellent source of marketing information, same as it was in Charles C. Parlin's day. William Rathje of the University of Arizona's anthropology department set up "Le Project de Garbage" to study Tucson's rubbish. His work has been used by the Environmental Protection Agency, General Accounting Office, and the U.S. Senate's Select Committee on Nutrition and Human Needs. Chevron, General Mills, and Alcoa have financed Rathje's work.

The professor and his students analyze the contents of two bags of trash from each of Tucson's census tracts each collection day. Sanitation department employees randomly select the bags. All contents are classified according to 200 product categories, type, weight, volume, cost, container composition, and brand name. Why would anyone spend so much time looking through garbage bags?

Rathje remarks, "Garbage cans don't lie. You are what you throw away." He points out that examining garbage is often a better marketing research technique than surveys. Rathje cites a study in which respondents were asked about their beer consumption. Analysis of their garbage revealed that several people significantly underestimated their use of this product.

Some conclusions from Rathje's own work in Tucson suggest:

- Working-class households drink more imported beer than higher income groups who tend to stick with less costly domestic brands.
- The middle class wastes more food than other income categories, possibly because both spouses work and are too busy to deal with leftovers. Overall, there is a 15 percent (by weight) waste factor in edible food.
- Rathje's garbage also suggests that diet soft drinks and squeezed oranges are a good indication of higher incomes.

Moral of the Story: The University of Arizona is carrying on a proud tradition established by Charles C. Parlin.

Source: Teri Fields, "Garbage Veritas," *PSA Magazine* (May 1982), pp. 84–87.

agencies as well.[9] The decision whether to conduct a study through an outside organization or internally is usually based on cost. Another consideration is the reliability and accuracy of the information collected by the agency.

Research is likely to be contracted to outside groups when the following requirements are met:

1. Problem areas can be defined in terms of specific research projects.

[9]Increased use of such groups in the future is predicted in Linden A. Davis, "What's Ahead in Marketing Research?" *Journal of Advertising Research* (June 1981), pp. 49–51.

Table 6.1 Twenty Largest U.S. Owned Marketing Research Companies

Rank	Organization	Research Revenues (in Millions)
1	A.C. Nielsen	$411.3
2	IMS International	115.2
3	SAMI	72.6
4	Arbitron Ratings Co.	66.4
5	Burke Marketing Services	42.3
6	Market Facts	25.5
7	Audits & Surveys	22.5
8	Marketing & Research Counselors	18.0
9	NPD/HTI	17.9
10	WESTAT, Inc.	15.9
11	Chilton Research Services	15.2
12	Maritz Markets Research	15.0
13	ASI Market Research	14.9
14	Yankelovich, Skelly & White	12.9
15	Walker Research	11.7
16	Ehrhart-Babic Group	11.7
17	Data Development Corp.	11.2
18	Louis Harris & Associates	10.1
19	Erlick & Lavidge	9.3
20	Opinion Research Corp.	8.2

Source: Reprinted from Jack Honomichl, "Nation's 28 Top Market Research Companies See Revenues Jump 13.8% in 1981," *Advertising Age* (May 24, 1982), p. M–7.

2. There is a need for specialized know-how or equipment.
3. Intellectual detachment is a requirement.[10]

A marketing research firm is often able to provide technical assistance and expertise not available within the firm. Also, the use of outside groups helps ensure that the researcher is not conducting the study only to validate the wisdom of a favorite theory or a preferred package design. The most recent survey of marketing research by the American Marketing Association revealed that almost half the total marketing research budget of the responding firms was spent on outside research.[11]

There are 1,023 marketing research companies in the United States.[12] These can range in size from a single owner/manager to a giant firm such as Nielsen with more than $400 million in research revenues. The 20 largest marketing research companies are shown in Table 6.1. A.C. Nielsen is the dominant U.S. marketing research firm.

[10]Bertram Schoner and Kenneth P. Uhl, *Marketing Research: Information Systems and Decision Making* (New York: John Wiley & Sons, Inc., 1975), p. 199.

[11]Twedt, *1978 Survey of Marketing Research,* p. 38.

[12]Scigliano, "Research Hinges on Human Factors," p. 9.

Marketing research companies can be classified as either syndicated services, full-service suppliers, or limited-service suppliers depending upon the primary thrust of the organization.[13] For example, a full service organization might be willing to take on a limited function activity under certain circumstances.

Syndicated Service

A **syndicated service** is an organization that offers to provide a standardized set of data on a regular basis to all who wish to buy it. Market Research Corporation of American (MCRA) gathers information on consumer purchases of food and other household items from a panel of over 7,000 U.S. households. The panel periodically gives MRCA a detailed list of all food and other household products purchased during a particular time. This information can be extremely useful in determining brand preferences, the effects of various promotional activities on retail sales in a particular region or among an age group, and the degree of brand switching that occurs with different products.

One of the most unique syndicated services to be offered in recent years is the Brown-Bag Institute, a Connecticut-based outfit that offers quarterly data on the buying habits of people who take their lunches to school or work.[14] Some 80 million people brown bag it at least part of the time. Approximately 10.7 billion brown-bag meals worth $20 billion are consumed annually. The service will be based on 1,000 quarterly telephone interviews. So far the Brown-Bag Institute has signed up three firms for the $20,000 annual fee: ITT Continental Bakery (Hostess Cupcakes, Twinkies, and Wonder Bread); Nabisco Brands (Planters chips and nuts); King-Seely Thermos (lunch boxes and thermos bottles).

Full-Service Research Suppliers

Full-service research suppliers contract with a client to conduct the complete marketing research project. Full-service research suppliers start at the problem definition or conceptualization stage; work through the research design, data collection, and analysis stages; and prepare the final report to management. Full-service research suppliers literally become the client's marketing research arm.

[13]The classification and definitions of marketing research companies is based on William G. Zikmund, *Exploring Marketing Research* (Hinsdale, Ill.: The Dryden Press, 1982), pp. 79–81.

[14]Bill Abrams, "It Took an Advertising Man to See the Potential in Soggy Brown Bags," *The Wall Street Journal* (January 29, 1982), p. 25.

Limited-Serivce Research Suppliers

Limited-service research suppliers are organizations that specialize in a limited number of marketing research activities. Companies that provide field interviews are the best example. Still others might provide data processing services. Syndicated services can also be considered a limited-service research supplier.

The Marketing Research Process

How is marketing research actually conducted? The starting point, of course, is the need for information to make a marketing decision. This information need can relate to a specific marketing decision or an ongoing set of decisions. If an information need is perceived, the marketing research process can be invoked to produce the needed marketing knowledge.

The marketing research process can be divided into six specific steps: (1) defining the problem; (2) exploratory research; (3) formulating a hypothesis; (4) research design; (5) collecting data; and (6) interpretation and presentation.

Figure 6.2 diagrams the marketing research process from information need to the research-based decision.

Problem Definition

Someone once remarked that well-defined problems are half solved. Problems are barriers that prevent the accomplishment of organizational goals. A clearly defined problem permits the researcher to focus the research process on securing the necessary data to solve the problem. Sometimes it is easy to pinpoint problems. Top executives at Republic Airlines have stood in airport lines in order to spot passenger complaints. The two most common gripes were inadequate flight information and cold in-flight coffee.[15] Once these problems were identified, they were corrected without further research.

However, it is often difficult to determine the specific problem, since the researcher may be confronted with symptoms of an underlying problem. In the late 1970s, Ciba-Geigy was stunned when its newly acquired Airwick Industries suffered a $2 million loss on sales of such products as liquid room fresheners. The parent firm recognized the losses as symptoms of a bitter price war in this market and the need for a more systematic method of developing and introducing product in-

[15]Reported in Priscilla A. La Barbera and Larry J. Rosenberg, "How Marketers Can Better Understand Consumers," *MSU Business Topics* (Winter 1980), p. 29.

Figure 6.2 The Marketing Research Process

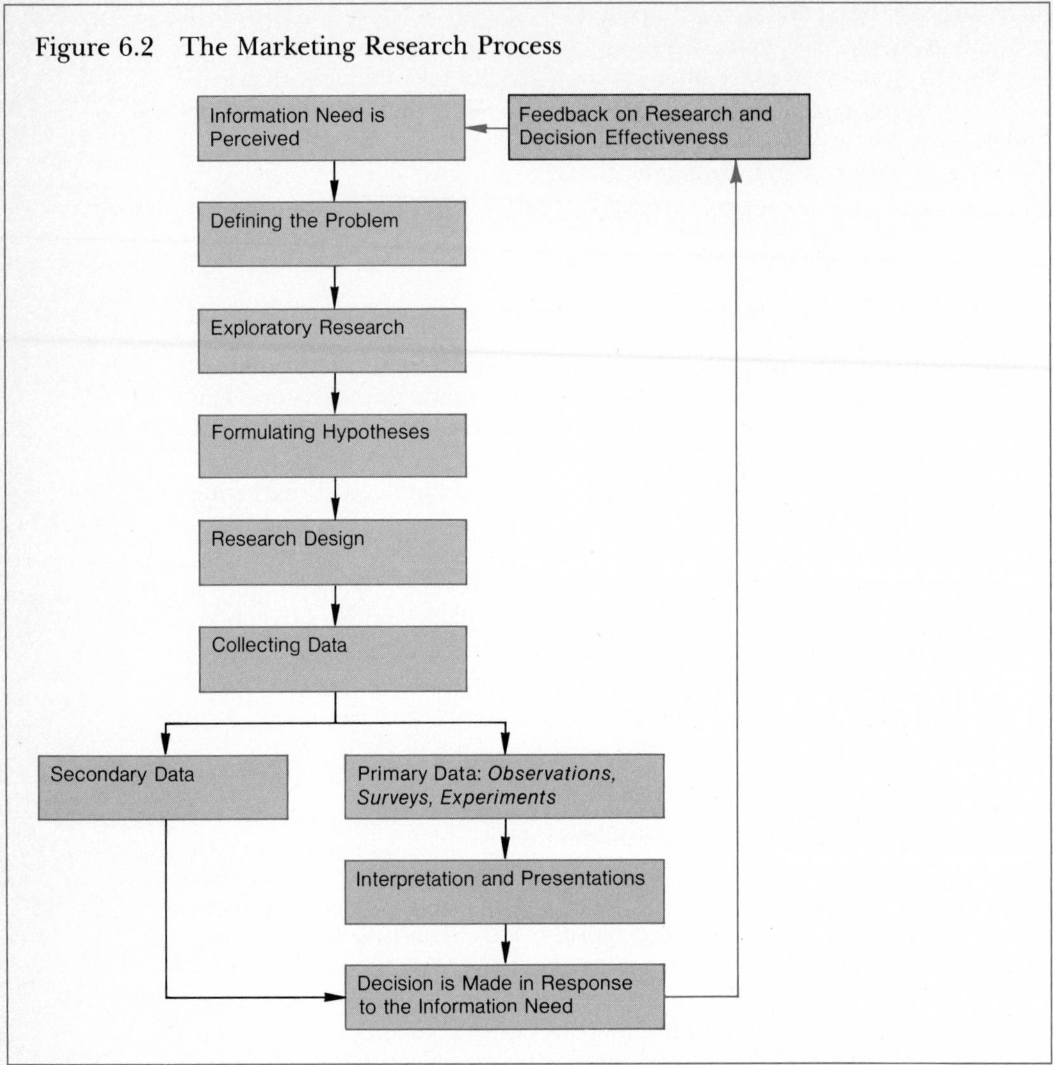

novations to keep pace with competition. In order to solve the problems facing the firm, management had to look beyond the symptoms and search for causes.

Exploratory Research

Searching for the cause of a problem allows the researcher to learn about the problem area and to focus on specific areas for study in seeking solutions. This search, often called **exploratory research,** consists of discussing the problem with informed sources within the firm and with wholesalers, retailers, customers, and others outside the firm and examining secondary sources of information. Marketing researchers often refer to internal data collection as the *situation analysis* and to exploratory interviews with informed persons outside the firm as the *informal investigation.* Exploratory research also involves evaluating company records, such as sales and profit analyses of the company's and its competitors' products. Table 6.2 provides a checklist of questions to be considered in an exploratory analysis.

Formulating Hypotheses

After the problem has been defined and an exploratory investigation conducted, the marketer should be able to formulate a hypothesis, a tentative explanation about some specific event. A **hypothesis** is a statement about the relationship between variables and carries clear implications for testing this relationship.

A marketer of industrial products might formulate the following hypothesis:

Failure to provide 72-hour delivery service will reduce our sales by 20 percent.

Such a statement may prove correct or incorrect. The formulation of this hypothesis does, however, provide a basis for investigation and an eventual determination of its accuracy. Also, it allows the researcher to move to the next step: development of the research design.

Lever Brothers' Pepsodent toothpaste had been on the market since 1944, but by the mid-1960s surveys were indicating that young consumers were dissatisfied with current offerings in two areas: tooth whitening and breath freshening. Lever Brothers began work on its hypothesis that a combination toothpaste and mouthwash could become a successful market entry. The end result of the firm's hypothesis testing was Close-up toothpaste.[16]

Research Design

The research design represents a comprehensive plan for testing the hypothesis formulated about the problem. **Research design** refers to a series of decisions that, taken together, comprise a master plan or model for the conduct of the investigation. Heublin is concerned about environmental factors that might impact its markets so it has set up an environmental monitoring system that scans published data to pick up environmental trends and the like.[17]

[16]"Marketing Oriented Lever Uses Research to Capture Bigger Dentifrice Market Shares," *Marketing News* (February 10, 1978), p. 9.

[17]"Marketing Research Needs Right Organization, People to Fulfill Its Strategic Planning Potential," *Marketing News* (September 18, 1981), Section 1, p. 14.

Table 6.2 Checklist of Factors to Consider in an Exploratory Analysis

Market Considerations

( ) What is the geographical location of the market?
( ) What are the demographic characteristics of the market?
( ) What purchase motivations predominate in this market?
( ) What product use patterns prevail in this market?
( ) What is the nature of demand in this market?

Company and Competitive Considerations

( ) What are the company's objectives?
( ) Who is involved in this industry?
( ) What industry-wide trends exist?
( ) What is the company's market share?
( ) What are the competitors' marketing policies?

Product Considerations

( ) What are the physical characteristics of the products?
( ) What is the degree of consumer acceptance?
( ) How effective is the package as a promotional tool?
( ) What are the relevant manufacturing processes and production capacity?
( ) How close and available are substitute products?

Distribution Channel Considerations

( ) What distribution channels are employed?
( ) What trends impact the distribution channels?
( ) What are the standard reseller margins?

Sales Force Considerations

( ) What market area does the sales force cover?
( ) What does an analysis of sales figures reveal?
( ) What expense ratios exist among the sales force?
( ) How is the sales force compensated?

Promotional Considerations

( ) What advertising media is employed?
( ) How does the firm's promotional expenses compare with the competition?
( ) What sales promotional materials are provided for resellers?
( ) How successful have previous advertising and promotional campaigns been?

Pricing Considerations

( ) What is the elasticity of demand?
( ) Are seasonal or special promotional price cuts helpful?
( ) What profit margins exist for resellers?
( ) What legal restrictions impact pricing decisions?
( ) Is price lining useful?

Sometimes published data is not enough, so the research design must call for a direct test of a hypothesis. Producers at Paramount Pictures were fearful that the planned death of Mr. Spock in *Star Trek II—The Wrath of Khan* would turn "Trekkies" against the movie, so a sample research design was formulated. The movie with Mr. Spock dying was shown to participants at a science-fiction meeting in Kansas City. The audience loved the movie, and Paramount Pictures decided to leave Mr. Spock dead.[18]

Data Collection

A major step in the research design is determining what data is needed to test the hypothesis. Data is classified as primary or secondary. **Primary data** refers to data that is collected for the first time during a marketing research study. The Kansas City screening of *Star Trek II—The Wrath of Khan* would be an example of primary research. **Secondary data** is previously published matter. It serves as an extremely important source of information for marketing researchers such as those at Heublin.

Collecting Secondary Data

Not only is secondary data important to the marketing researcher, it is also very abundant. The overwhelming quantity of secondary data available at little or no cost challenges the researcher to select only pertinent secondary data.

Secondary data consists of two types: internal and external. Internal secondary data includes records of sales, product performances, sales force activities, and marketing costs. External data is obtained from a variety of sources. Governments—local, state, and federal—provide a wide variety of secondary data. Private sources also supply secondary data for the marketing decision maker.

Government Sources The federal government is the nation's most important source of marketing data, and the most frequently used government statistics are census data. Although the U.S. government spent more than $1 billion conducting the 1980 Census of Population, census information is available for use at no charge at local libraries, or it can be purchased on computer tapes for instantaneous access at a nominal charge. In addition to the Census of Population, the Bureau of the Census also conducts a Census of Housing (which is combined with the

[18]"Marquee," *The Seattle Times* (May 16, 1982), p. H 4.

Census of Population), a Census of Business, a Census of Manufactures, a Census of Agriculture, a Census of Minerals, and a Census of Governments.

The 1980 census is so detailed for large cities that breakdowns of population characteristics are available by city block. Local retailers and shopping-center developers can easily gather specific information about customers in the immediate neighborhood without spending the time or money to conduct a comprehensive survey.

So much information is produced by the federal government that marketing researchers often purchase summaries such as the *Monthly Catalog of the United States Government Publications,* the *Statistical Abstract of the United States,* the *Survey of Current Business,* and the *County and City Data Book.* Published annually, the *Statistical Abstract* contains a wealth of current data. The *Survey of Current Business,* updated monthly, focuses on a variety of industrial data. The *County and City Data Book,* typically published every three years, provides a variety of data for each county and each city over 25,000 residents.

State and city governments serve as other important sources of information on employment, production, and sales activities. In addition, university bureaus of business and economic research often collect and disseminate such information.

Private Sources Many private organizations provide information for the marketing executive. For data on activities in a particular industry, trade associations are excellent sources. Advertising agencies continually collect information on the audience reached by various media. A wide range of valuable data is found in the annual "Survey of Buying Power" published by *Sales and Marketing Management* magazine. Figure 6.3 illustrates the detailed information it collects for each state of the United States and the provinces of Canada.[19]

Several national firms also offer information to businesses on a subscription basis. The largest of these, A.C. Nielsen Company, collects data every two months on product sales, retail prices, display space, inventories, and promotional activities of competing brands of food and drug products. Its data sample consists of about 1,600 supermarkets, 750 drugstores, and 150 mass merchandisers.

Secondary Data: Strengths and Weaknesses

The use of secondary data offers two important advantages: (1) the assembly of secondary data is almost always less expensive than the collection of primary data; and (2) less time is involved in locating and

[19]Charles Waldo and Dennis Fuller, "Just How Good Is the 'Survey of Buying Power'?" *Journal of Marketing* (October 1977), pp. 64–66.

Figure 6.3 Sample Data from the *Survey of Buying Power*

CAL. (cont.)
S&MM ESTIMATES

$$ EFFECTIVE BUYING INCOME 1981

METRO AREA / County / City	Total EBI ($000)	Median Hsld. EBI	% of Hslds. by EBI Group: (A) $10,000–$14,999 (B) $15,000–$24,999 (C) $25,000–$49,999 (D) $50,000 & Over A	B	C	D	Buying Power Index
LOS ANGELES - LONG BEACH	**74,740,865**	**23,023**	**10.6**	**23.7**	**36.2**	**9.2**	**3.5402**
Los Angeles	74,740,865	23,023	10.6	23.7	36.2	9.2	3.5402
Alhambra	642,483	21,800	10.8	25.4	36.2	6.0	.0325
Arcadia	684,083	28,878	8.3	19.5	40.5	17.6	.0334
Baldwin Park	310,847	20,379	12.1	32.1	33.6	2.2	.0156
Bellflower	518,195	22,067	11.0	28.8	36.4	4.4	.0262
Burbank	931,033	23,707	11.3	25.6	39.2	7.4	.0411
Carson	669,958	27,806	7.6	24.3	52.8	5.8	.0387
Compton	427,476	18,223	14.5	32.3	25.6	2.0	.0233
Downey	1,001,867	27,730	7.9	23.0	45.5	11.7	.0511
El Monte	500,262	18,510	14.7	30.6	28.6	2.1	.0306
Gardena	463,218	25,672	8.9	23.9	45.6	6.3	.0225
Glendale	1,620,461	22,761	11.1	23.5	35.5	9.7	.0785
Hawthorne	589,324	24,018	11.0	28.2	42.2	4.7	.0294
Inglewood	868,667	21,196	12.6	28.6	35.2	4.4	.0410
Lakewood	776,110	28,700	5.8	22.9	55.7	7.4	.0333
• Long Beach	3,689,018	19,946	11.3	23.3	31.9	6.6	.1690
• Los Angeles	29,422,212	20,645	12.2	23.5	31.5	8.9	1.3874
Lynwood	312,098	20,016	11.9	31.3	31.6	2.7	.0162
Montebello	516,011	24,445	9.9	25.2	39.8	8.8	.0247
Monterey Park	560,007	27,042	8.2	24.1	44.2	10.5	.0241
Norwalk	667,195	25,478	7.1	30.3	48.3	3.4	.0335
Pasadena	1,327,690	20,838	11.7	22.5	29.4	12.0	.0668
Pico Rivera	400,779	24,868	8.5	29.6	45.5	4.1	.0175
Pomona	705,905	20,972	12.3	26.5	35.1	4.1	.0403
Redondo Beach	690,574	26,275	7.9	23.4	46.0	7.6	.0317
Rosemead	286,379	20,241	11.9	28.7	33.8	2.5	.0152
Santa Monica	1,094,342	20,357	12.4	24.2	31.3	8.3	.0523
South Gate	486,028	18,991	14.3	30.1	29.8	2.7	.0237
Torrance	1,591,340	30,735	6.1	19.3	53.5	11.9	.0887
West Covina	911,754	31,181	5.1	19.1	56.6	11.6	.0459
Whittier	826,066	26,570	8.8	21.0	39.3	14.3	.0412
SUBURBAN TOTAL	41,629,635	25,033	9.3	23.8	40.5	9.7	1.9838
LOS ANGELES - LONG BEACH - ANAHEIM CONSOLIDATED AREA	***115,377,373***	***23,430***	***10.5***	***23.8***	***37.4***	***8.8***	***5.5139***
MODESTO	**2,662,793**	**22,381**	**11.7**	**21.8**	**35.3**	**9.1**	**.1271**
Stanislaus	2,662,793	22,381	11.7	21.8	35.3	9.1	.1271
• Modesto	1,217,457	25,627	9.3	20.0	41.0	10.2	.0637
SUBURBAN TOTAL	1,445,336	20,154	13.5	23.2	31.0	8.2	.0634
OXNARD - SIMI VALLEY - VENTURA	**4,589,083**	**22,708**	**10.9**	**28.8**	**38.1**	**4.7**	**.2291**
Ventura	4,589,083	22,708	10.9	28.8	38.1	4.7	.2291
• Oxnard	775,686	19,459	14.5	32.1	30.3	2.5	.0460
• Simi Valley	610,400	25,173	6.6	34.3	48.0	2.7	.0308
• Ventura	769,214	22,561	11.0	26.7	37.1	5.5	.0424
SUBURBAN TOTAL	2,433,783	23,142	10.6	26.7	38.9	5.8	.1099
REDDING	**1,045,471**	**20,377**	**11.5**	**26.3**	**33.2**	**4.5**	**.0561**
Shasta	1,045,471	20,377	11.5	26.3	33.2	4.5	.0561
• Redding	450,075	20,721	11.1	26.9	32.6	4.9	.0302
SUBURBAN TOTAL	595,396	20,126	11.7	25.9	33.7	4.2	.0259

Source: Survey of Buying Power, *Sales & Marketing Management,* July 26, 1982. Reprinted by permission from *Sales & Marketing Management* magazine. © 1982. S&MM Survey of Buying Power.

using secondary data. Table 6.3 shows the estimated time involved in completing a research study requiring primary data. Although the time involved in a marketing research study will vary considerably depending on such factors as the research subject and the scope of the study, an additional time and cost investment is required when primary data is needed.

The researcher, however, must be aware of two potential limitations: the data may be obsolete, or its classifications may not be usable in the proposed research study. Published information can quickly become obsolete. A marketing researcher analyzing the population of the Orlando, Florida, metropolitan market in early 1984 discovers that most of the 1980 census data is obsolete due to the influx of residents to the area. Also, data may have been collected previously on the basis of county or city boundaries, but the marketing manager may require data broken down by city blocks or census tracts. In such cases, the marketing researcher may not be able to rearrange the secondary data in usable form and may have to begin collecting primary data.

Table 6.3 Time Requirements for a Primary Data Research Project

Step	Estimated Time Required For Completion
Problem Definition	Several Days
Development of Methodology	One Week
Questionnaire Design	One Week
Questionnaire Pretest and Evaluation of Pretest Results	Two Weeks
Field Interviews	One to Six Weeks
Coding of Returned Questionnaires	One Week
Data Transfer to Computer Tape	One Week
Data Processing and Statistical Analysis	Seven to Ten Days
Interpretation of Output	One Week
Written Report and Presentation of Findings	Two Weeks
Total Elapsed Time	**12 to 17 Weeks**

Source: Estimates by Alfred S. Boote, Corporate Director of Market Research, The Singer Company. Quoted in "Everyone Benefits from Closer Planning, Research Ties," *Marketing News* (January 9, 1981), p. 30. Used by permission of the American Marketing Association.

Primary Data Collection Alternatives

The marketing researcher has three alternatives in the collection of primary data: observation, survey, or controlled experiment. No single method is best in all circumstances, and any of these methods may prove the most efficient in a particular situation.

The Observation Method

Observational studies are conducted by actually viewing the overt actions of the person being studied. Studies may take the form of a traffic count at a potential location for a fast-food franchise, the use of supermarket scanners to record sales of certain products, or a check of license plates at a shopping center to determine where shoppers live.

The observation method has both advantages and drawbacks. Merits include the fact that observation is often more accurate than questioning techniques like surveys and interviews, and it may be the only way to get competitive information such as prices. The observation method may also be an easier way to get specific data. Limitations to this approach for getting primary data include observer subjectivity and errors in interpretation. For instance, the researchers might incorrectly classify

How Observation Technique Determines Television Program Ratings

The sample size is extremely small; the 1,200 Nielsen households represent a microscopic 0.00164 percent of the millions of homes with TVs. Yet the viewing habits of these persons determine the ratings of television network programs, and the ratings mean their success or cancellation.

More than that, high ratings mean more advertising dollars. A top-rated program like "60 Minutes" may charge $130,000 for a 30-second commercial, while the average 30-second commercial during television's prime time is $75,600.

With so much at stake, it is not surprising that many persons in the entertainment industry criticize the rating system as inaccurately representing the viewing habits of 81.5 million U.S. households. Nielsen executives argue forcefully that they have developed a representative sample. "We select the 1,200 homes based on the U.S. census data," explains Jerry Beman, Nielsen vice-president. "We lay a grid over the entire United States, analyzing the concentration of population and ending up with a scale model of the country. We eventually narrow down our selection to specific homes on specific blocks, and we approach the families. About 80 percent of them agree to cooperate. The entire selection process is very scientific and very expensive."

Each television receiver in the Nielsen households is attached to a recording device called an audimeter. This gadget is connected to the Nielsen computer with special telephone lines and produces a minute-by-minute record of the family's television viewing.

About 45 percent of the sample is changed each year. Five years is the maximum time permitted for participation, but moves reduce the average period to 3.5 years. Nielsen households receive an initial payment of $25, plus $1 a month and 50 percent of their television repair costs.

Nielsen representatives state that their ratings are accurate to within 1.7 percentage points. A program that, according to Nielsen, attracts 35 percent of the viewing audience could actually be attracting from 33.3 to 36.7 percent.

Source: Adapted by permission of Writers Bloc from Richard Trubo, "Who Really Runs TV? An Outfit Called Nielsen," *Detroit News* (March 1, 1978). The 1982 update was provided by A.C. Nielsen Company.

people's economic status because of the way they were dressed at the time of observation.[20]

As an example of the observation method of data collection, the A.C. Nielsen Company uses audimeters to record the times television sets are turned on and which channels are viewed. In a famous study reported

[20]Zikmund, *Exploring Marketing Research*, pp. 216–217.

by Vance Packard, a special camera equipped with a telephoto lens recorded the number of consumer eye blinks per minute and, in some instances, it allegedly indicated the mild hypnotic trance of a person overcome by the complexity of colors and packages on a supermarket shelf.[21]

Eastman Kodak used the observation method in evaluating advertisements it scheduled for the launch of the Ektra camera. Perception Research Service was hired to study patterns of viewer eye movements when looking at advertisements featuring television actor Michael Landon. These eye-tracking tests resulted in Eastman Kodak's moving the headline "Kodak introduces the Ektra pocket camera" from the bottom of the ad to the top, since a majority of eye movements flowed to the top.[22]

The Survey Method

Some information cannot be obtained through observation. The researcher must ask questions in order to obtain information on attitudes, motives, and opinions. The most widely used approach to collecting primary data is the survey method. Three kinds of surveys exist: telephone, mail, and personal interviews.

Telephone Interviews are inexpensive and fast for obtaining small quantities of relatively impersonal information. Since many firms have leased WATS services (telephone company services that allow businesses to make unlimited long-distance calls for a fixed rate per state or region), a call to the most distant state costs no more than an across-town interview.[23]

Telephone interviews account for an estimated 55 to 60 percent of all primary marketing research. A national survey revealed that one woman in five had been interviewed by telephone in 1980 compared with one in seven only two years earlier. The percentage of men who had participated in telephone interviews had grown from one in ten in 1978 to one in seven in 1980.[24] Telephone interviews are, however, limited to simple, clearly worded questions. Also it is extremely difficult to obtain information on respondents' personal characteristics, and the survey may be prejudiced by the omission of households without phones or with unlisted numbers.

[21]Vance Packard, *The Hidden Persuaders* (New York: David McKay, 1957).

[22]John E. Cooney, "In Their Quest for Sure Fire Ads, Marketers Use Psychological Tests to Find Out What Grabs You," *The Wall Street Journal* (April 12, 1979), p. 40.

[23]William Lyons and Robert F. Durant, "Interviewer Costs Associated with the Use of Random Digit Dialing in Large Area Samples," *Journal of Marketing* (Summer 1980), pp. 65–69.

[24]"Marketing Research Industry Survey Finds Increase in Phone Interviewing," *Marketing News* (January 9, 1981), p. 20.

One survey reported that alphabetical listings in telephone directories excluded one third of blacks with telephones and one fourth of large-city dwellers. They underrepresented service workers and separated and divorced persons, too. In addition, the population mobility creates problems in choosing names from telephone directories. As a result, a number of telephone interviewers have resorted to using digits selected at random and matched to telephone prefixes in the geographic area to be sampled. This technique is designed to correct the problem of sampling households having unlisted numbers.[25]

Mail Interviews allow the marketing researcher to conduct national studies at a reasonable cost. Whereas personal interviews with a national sample may be prohibitive in cost, the researcher can contact each potential respondent for the price of a postage stamp. Costs can be misleading, however. For example, returned questionnaires may average only 40 to 50 percent depending on the length of the questionnaire and respondent interest. Also some mail surveys include a coin to gain the reader's attention which further increases costs.[26] Unless additional information is obtained from nonrespondents, the results of mail interviews are likely to be biased, since there may be important differences in the characteristics of respondents and nonrespondents. For this reason, follow-up questionnaires are sometimes mailed to respondents, or telephone interviews are used to gather additional information.[27]

In 1980, the U.S. Bureau of the Census conducted the largest mail survey in history when it mailed census questionnaires to 80 million households. A number of questions were raised, including the difficulties of developing an accurate population count utilizing mail questionnaires. Another sensitive subject concerned confidentiality of answers. The 85 percent response rate was a pleasant surprise to Census Bureau officials and to researchers throughout the world who rely upon mail surveys to obtain research data.[28]

[25]Reported in A. B. Blankenship, "Listed Versus Unlisted Numbers in Telephone-Survey Samples," *Journal of Advertising Research* (February 1977), pp. 39–42. See also Roger Gates, Bob Brobst, and Paul Solomon, "Random Digit Dialing: A Review of Methods," in *Proceedings of the Southern Marketing Association* (New Orleans, November 1977), pp. 163–165; and Donald S. Tull and Gerald M. Albaum, "Bias in Random Digit-Dialed Surveys," *Public Opinion Quarterly* (Fall 1977), pp. 389–395.

[26]Stephen W. McDaniel and C. P. Rao, "The Effect of Monetary Inducement on Mailed Questionnaire Response Quality," *Journal of Marketing Research* (May 1980), pp. 265–268; and Robert A. Hansen, "A Self-Perception Interpretation of the Effect of Monetary and Nonmonetary Incentives on Mail Survey Respondent Behavior," *Journal of Marketing Research* (February 1980), pp. 77–83.

[27]Kevin F. McCrohan and Larry S. Lowe, "A Cost/Benefit Approach to Postage Used on Mail Questionnaires," *Journal of Marketing* (Winter 1981), pp. 130–133; and Jacob Hornik, "Time Cue and Time Perception Effect on Response to Mail Surveys," *Journal of Marketing Research* (May 1981), pp. 243–248.

[28]Mail questionnaire response rate variables have been researched extensively. See recent papers like Julie Yu and Harris Cooper, "A Quantitative Review of Research Design Effects on Response Rates to Questionnaires," *Journal of Marketing Research* (February, 1983), pp. 36–44; and Curt J. Dommeyer, "Will Offering Respondents a Summary of the Results Affect the Responses to a Mail Survey?" Stephen H. Actenhagen (ed.), *Proceedings of the 1982 Western Marketing Educators' Association Conference,* pp. 35–36.

Personal Interviews are typically the best means of obtaining detailed information, since the interviewer has the opportunity to establish rapport with each respondent and can explain confusing or vague questions. Although mail questionnaires are carefully worded and often pretested to eliminate potential misunderstandings, misunderstandings can occur anyway. When an employee of the U.S. Department of Agriculture accidentally ran into and killed a cow with his truck, a department official sent the farmer an apology and a form to be filled out. The form included a space for "disposition of the dead cow." The farmer responded, "kind and gentle."[29]

Personal interviews are slow and the most expensive method of collecting data. However, their flexibility coupled with the detailed information that can be collected often offset these limitations. Recently marketing research firms have rented locations in shopping centers where they have greater access to potential buyers of the products in which they are interested. Downtown retail districts and airports are other on-site locations for marketing research.

Focus Group Interviews have been widely used in recent years as a means of gathering research information. In a **focus group interview,** eight to twelve individuals are brought together in one location to discuss a subject of interest. Although the moderator typically explains the purpose of the meeting and suggests an opening discussion topic, he or she is interested in stimulating interaction among group members in order to develop the discussion of numerous points. Focus groups sessions, which are often one or two hours long, are usually taped so the moderator can devote full attention to the discussion.[30]

The Experimental Method

The final and least-used method of collecting marketing information is that of controlled experiments. An **experiment** is a scientific investigation in which a researcher controls or manipulates a test group or groups and compares the results with that of a control group that did not receive the controls or manipulations. Although such experiments can be conducted in the field or in a laboratory setting, most have been conducted in the field. To date, the most common use of this method

[29]"About That Cow," *The Wall Street Journal* (June 28, 1972), p. 1.

[30]Fred D. Reynolds and Deborah K. Johnson, "Validity of Focus-Group Findings," *Journal of Advertising Research* (June 1978), pp. 21–24; and Bobby J. Calder, "Focus Groups and the Nature of Qualitative Marketing Research," *Journal of Marketing Research* (August 1977), pp. 353–364. Focus groups are also discussed in Edward F. Fern, "The Use of Focus Groups for Idea Generation: The Effects of Group Size, Acquaintanceship, and Moderator on Response Quantity and Quality," *Journal of Marketing Research* (February 1982), pp. 1–13.

by marketers has been in test marketing, a topic that is discussed in detail in Chapter 11.

Marketers often attempt to reduce their risks by **test marketing,** or introducing the product or marketing strategy into an area, then observing its degree of success. Ronald Reagan's 1980 presidential election campaign even test marketed its advertising themes in Lubbock, Texas, and Fresno, California.[31] Marketers usually pick test areas that are reflective of what they envision as the market for their product. Seattle was picked as a test market for Pepsi Free because Pepsi outsells Coca-Cola in the Emerald City, and Seattle and Milwaukee share the lead for the highest per capita consumption of diet soft drinks.[32]

The major problem with controlled experiments is controlling all variables in a real-life situation. The laboratory scientist can rigidly control temperature and humidity. But how can the marketing manager determine the effect of, say, reducing the retail price through refundable coupons when the competition simultaneously issues such coupons? Experimentation will become more common as firms develop sophisticated competitive models for computer analysis. Simulation of market activities promises to be one of the great new developments in marketing.[33]

Sampling Techniques[34]

Sampling is one of the most important aspects of marketing research, because it involves the selection of respondents upon which conclusions will be based. The total group that the researcher wants to study is called the **population** or **universe.** For a political campaign, the population would be all eligible voters. For a new cosmetic line, it might be all women in a certain age bracket.

Information is rarely gathered from the total population during a survey. If all sources are contacted, the results are known as a **census.** Unless the total population is small, the costs will be so great that only the federal government will be able to afford them (and it uses this method only once every ten years). Instead, researchers select a representative group called a sample. Samples can be classified as either probability samples or nonprobability samples. A **probability sample** is

[31]"Reagan's $2 Million Marketing Research Budget Paid Off," *Marketing News* (March 5, 1982), p. 12.

[32]Cathy Reiner, "Seattle-Area Pop Drinkers to Test Decaffeinated Pepsi," *The Seattle Times* (August 3, 1982), p. E 4.

[33]John R. Nevin, "Using Experimental Data to Suggest and Evaluate Alternative Marketing Strategies," in Subhash C. Jain (ed.), *Research Frontiers in Marketing* (Chicago: American Marketing Association, 1978), pp. 207–211; Chem L. Narayana and James F. Harrell, "Evaluation of Quality Factors in Marketing Experiments," *Journal of the Academy of Marketing Science* (Summer 1976), pp. 599–607; and Alan G. Sawyer, Parker M. Worthing, and Paul E. Sendak, "The Role of Laboratory Experiments to Test Marketing Strategies," *Journal of Marketing* (Summer 1979), pp. 60–67.

[34]This discussion follows William G. Zikmund, *Exploring Marketing Research* (Hinsdale, Ill.: The Dryden Press, 1982), pp. 377–393. Used by permission.

one in which every member of the population has an equal chance of being selected. **Nonprobability samples** are arbitrary, and standard statistical tests cannot be applied. Marketing researchers base their studies on probability samples, but it is important to be able to identify all types of samples.[35] Some of the best known sampling plans are outlined below.

Convenience Sample A **convenience sample** is a nonprobability sample based on the selection of readily available respondents. Broadcasting's "on-the-street" interviews are a good example. Marketing researchers sometimes use it in exploratory research, but not in definitive studies.

Judgment Sample Nonprobability samples of people with a specific attribute are called **judgment samples.** Election-night predictions are usually based on polls of "swing voters" and are a type of judgment sample.

Quota Sample A **quota sample** is a nonprobability sample that is divided so that different segments or groups are represented in the total sample. An example would be a survey of auto import owners that included 33 Nissan owners, 31 Toyota owners, 7 BMW owners, and so on.

Referral Sample Sometimes called the snowball sample, the **referral sample** refers to one which is done in waves as more respondents with the characteristics are identified. An industrial goods manufacturer might poll its customer list about a new cutting machine it will introduce. The survey might also seek to identify other businesses who might use such a machine. The referrals would then be the target of a second stage of the research.

Simple Random Sample The basic type of probability sample is the **simple random sample** where every item in the relevant universe has an equal opportunity of being selected. The military draft lottery of more than a decade ago is an example. Each day of the year—and those males born on that day—had an equal opportunity of being selected, thus establishing a conscription list.

Systematic Sample A probability sample that takes every *N*th item on a list, after a random start, is called a **systematic sample.** Sampling from a telephone directory is a common example.

[35]A recent article on sampling is Henry Assael and John Keon, "Nonsampling vs. Sampling Errors in Survey Research," *Journal of Marketing* (Spring 1982), pp. 114–123.

Stratified Sample A **stratified sample** is a probability sample that is constructed so that randomly selected subsamples of different groups are represented in the total sample. It differs from quota sampling because the subsamples are drawn randomly. Stratified samples are an efficient sample methodology in uses like opinion polls, where various groups hold divergent viewpoints.

Cluster Sample A **cluster sample** is a situation where areas or clusters are selected, then all or a sample within each become respondents. This probability sample is very cost-efficient and may be the best option where the population cannot be listed or enumerated. A good example would be a market researcher who identified various U.S. cities then randomly selected supermarkets within those cities to study.

Interpretation and Presentation

A number of marketing research books contain information on how to cope with the many problems involved in surveying the public. Among these problems are designing the questionnaires; selecting, training, and controlling the field interviews; editing, coding, tabulating, and interpreting the data; presenting the results; and following up on the survey.

It is imperative that marketing researchers and research users cooperate at every stage in the research design. Too many studies go unused because marketing management believes the results are too restricted due to lengthy discussions of research limitations or unfamiliar terminology such as "levels of confidence" and "type 1 errors."[36]

Occasional misunderstandings between marketing researchers and the manager-user may lead to friction between the parties and failure to utilize the research findings effectively. Table 6.4 lists several complaints that each party may express about the other. These complaints reflect a lack of understanding of the needs and capabilities of both parties. Such complaints can often be settled by involving both managers and researchers in specifying needed information, developing research designs, and evaluating the research findings. The research report should include recommendations, and whenever possible, an oral

[36]Kenneth Gary McCain, "Business Decision Researchers Can't Afford to Be 'Pure'," *Business and Economic Perspectives* (Spring 1979), pp. 41–46; Jeffry Gandz and Thomas W. Whipple, "Making Marketing Research Accountable," *Journal of Marketing Research* (May 1977), pp. 202–208; and Dwight L. Gentry and John Hoftyzer, "The Misuse of Statistical Techniques in Evaluating Sample Data," *Journal of the Academy of Marketing Science* (Spring 1977), pp. 106–112.

Table 6.4 Common Complaints between Managers and Marketing Researchers

Management Complaints about Marketing Researchers:

Research is not problem-oriented. It tends to provide a plethora of facts, not actionable results or direction.

Researchers are too involved with techniques. They tend to do research for research's sake and they appear to be reluctant to get involved in management "problems."

Research is slow, vague, and of questionable validity. It depends too much on clinical evidence.

Researchers can't communicate; they don't understand, and they don't talk the language of management. In many cases, researchers are inexperienced and not well rounded.

Marketing Researcher Complaints about Management:

Management doesn't include research in discussions of basic fundamental problems. Management tends to ask only for specific information about parts of problems.

Management pays no more than lip service to research and doesn't really understand or appreciate its value. Research isn't given enough corporate status.

Management has a propensity to jump the gun—not allowing enough time for research. Management draws preliminary conclusions based on early or incomplete results.

Management relies more on intuition and judgment than on research. Research is used as a crutch, not a tool. Management tends to "typecast" the marketing researcher.

Source: Reprinted by permission from "Communication Gap Hinders Proper Use of Market Research," *Marketing Insights.* Copyright by Crain Communications, Inc. Reprinted by permission.

report should explain, expand upon, or clarify the written summary. These efforts also increase the likelihood of management's utilizing the research findings.

Marketing Information Systems

Many marketing managers discover that their information problems result from an overabundance—not a paucity—of marketing data. Their sophisticated computer facilities may provide them with daily printouts about sales in 30 market areas, about 100 different products, and about 6,400 customers. Managers sometimes solve the problem of too much information of the wrong kind in the wrong form by sliding the printouts to the edge of the desk, where they quietly fall into the wastebasket. Data and information are not synonymous terms. **Data** refers to statistics, opinions, facts, or predictions categorized on some basis for storage and retrieval. **Information** is data relevant to the marketing manager in making decisions.

Obtaining relevant information appears simple enough. One can establish a systematic approach to information management by installing a planned marketing information system (MIS). The ideal **marketing information system** should be a designed set of procedures and methods for generating an orderly flow of pertinent information for use in making decisions, providing management with the current and future states of the market, and indicating market responses to company and competitor actions.[37] The marketing information system is a subset of the firm's overall management information system (also often called an MIS) that deals specifically with marketing information.

A properly constructed MIS can serve as the nerve center for the company, providing instantaneous information suitable for each level of management. It can act as a thermostat, monitoring the marketplace continuously so that management can adjust actions as conditions change.

The role of marketing information in a firm's marketing system can be illustrated with the analogy of how an automatic heating system works. Once the objective of a particular temperature setting (say 68 degrees Fahrenheit) has been established, information about the actual temperature is collected and compared with the objective, and a decision based on this comparison is made. If the temperature drops below the established figure, the decision is to activate the furnace until the temperature reaches the established level. If the temperature is too high, the decision is to turn off the furnace. Figure 6.4 illustrates a comparison of a marketing system and a heating system.

Deviation from the firm's goals of profitability, improved return on investment, or greater market share may necessitate changes in price structures, promotional expenditures, package design, or other marketing alternatives. The firm's MIS should be capable of revealing such deviations and of suggesting changes that will result in attaining the established goals. Creating an effective MIS, however, is more easily said than done. Several firms' attempts have succeeded only in further complicating their data-retrieval systems.

Marketing Research and the Marketing Information System

Many marketing executives think their organizations are too small to make use of a marketing information system. Others contend that their marketing research departments provide adequate research data for decision making. Such contentions often result from a misconception of the services and functions performed by the marketing research department. Marketing research has already been described as typically focusing on a specific problem or project; its investigations have a definite beginning, middle, and end.

Marketing information systems, on the other hand, are much wider in scope, involving the continual collection and analysis of marketing

[37]Donald F. Cox and Robert E. Good, "How to Build a Marketing Information System," *Harvard Business Review* (May–June 1967), p. 147. See also Charles D. Schewe and William R. Dillon, "Marketing Information Systems Utilization: An Application of Self-Concept Theory," *Journal of Business Research* (January 1978), pp. 67–69.

Figure 6.4 An Analogy—A Marketing Information System and a Heating System

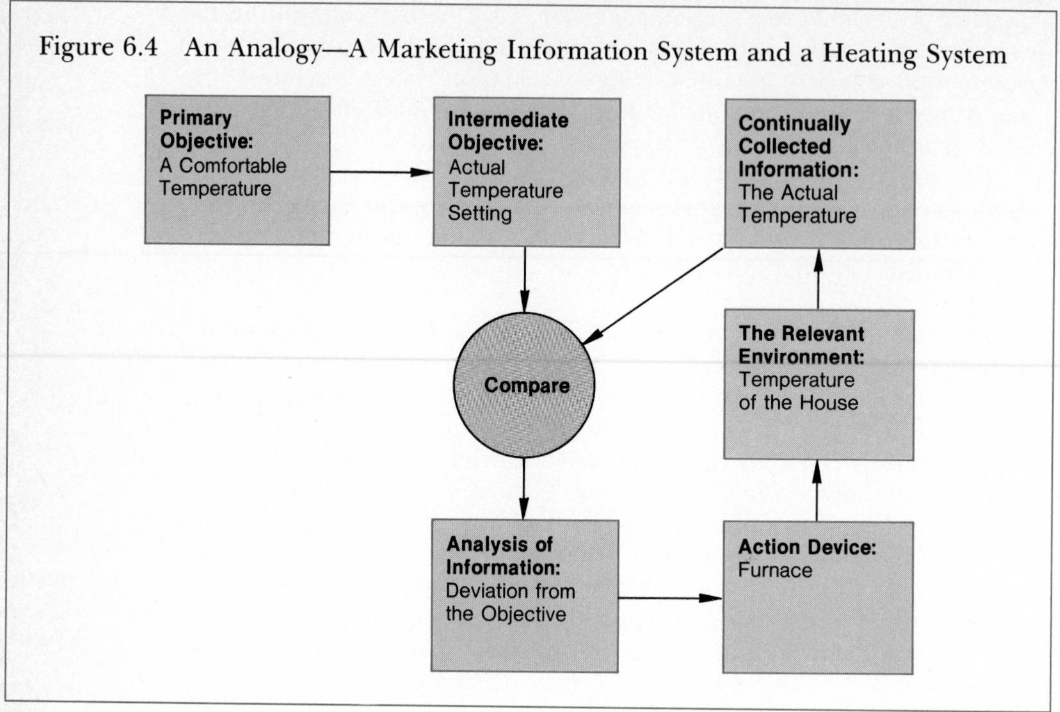

Source: Reprinted by permission from Bertram Schoner and Kenneth P. Uhl, *Marketing Research: Information Systems and Decision Making* (New York: Wiley, 1975), p. 10.

information. Figure 6.5 indicates the various information inputs—including marketing research studies—that serve as components of a firm's MIS.

Robert J. Williams, creator of the first marketing information system, explains the difference:

The difference between marketing research and marketing intelligence is like the difference between a flash bulb and a candle. Let's say you are dancing in the dark. Every 90 seconds you're allowed to set off a flash bulb. You can use those brief intervals of intense light to chart a course, but remember everybody is moving, too. Hopefully, they'll accommodate themselves roughly to your predictions. You may get bumped and you may stumble every so often, but you can dance along.

On the other hand, you can light a candle. It doesn't yield as much light, but it's a steady light. You are continually aware of the movements of other bodies. You can adjust your own course to the courses of the others. The intelligence system is a kind of light. It's no great flash on the immediate state of things, but it provides continuous light as situations shift and change.[38]

[38]"Marketing Intelligence Systems: A DEW Line for Marketing Men," *Business Management* (January 1966), p. 32.

Figure 6.5 Information Components of the Firm's Marketing Information Systems

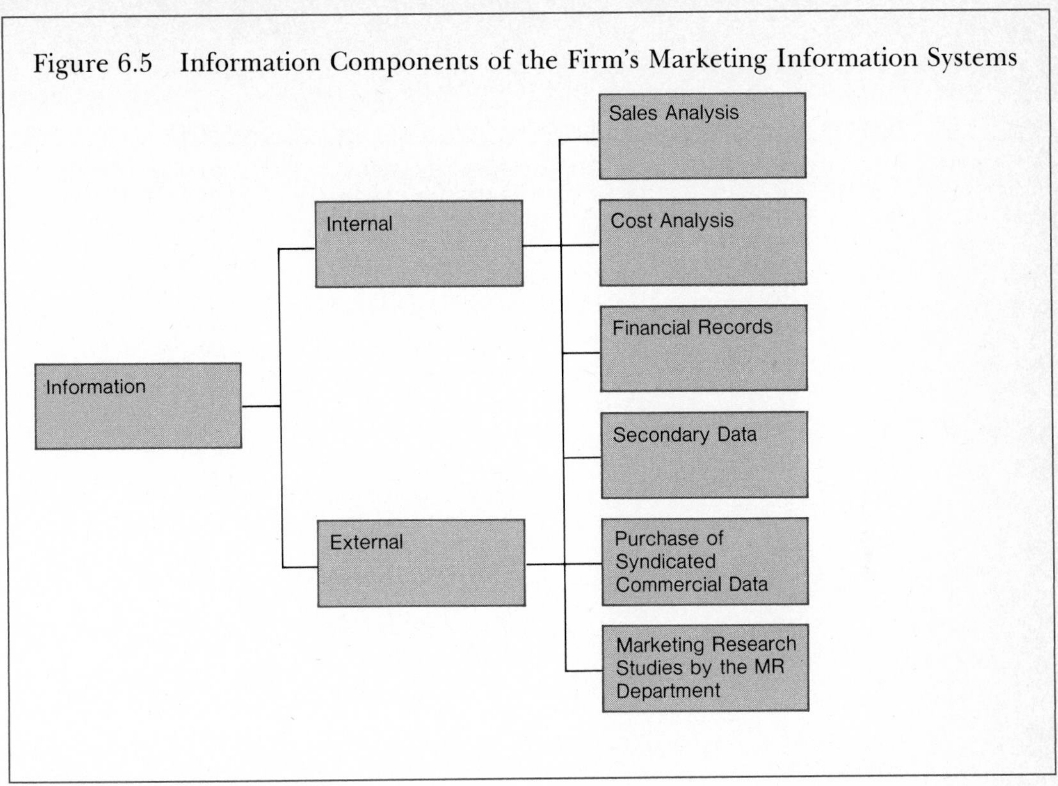

By focusing daily on the marketplace, the MIS provides a continuous systematic and comprehensive study of areas that indicate deviations from established goals. The up-to-the-minute information allows problems to be corrected before they adversely affect operations. Table 6.5 summarizes many of the applications and possible benefits of a sophisticated information system.

Current Status of Marketing Information Systems

Marketing information systems have progressed a long way from the days when they were primarily responsible for clerical activities (and usually at an increased cost over the old method). Today, managers have available special computer programs, remote access consoles, better data banks, direct communication with the computer, and assignment of authority to the computer for review and referral. In some instances, the computer simulates market conditions and makes decisions based on the results of the model. But how does the marketer's information system relate to similar systems for decision makers in other functional areas?

As noted earlier, marketing information systems are major components of the firm's overall management information system—the infor-

Table 6.5 Benefits Possible with an Information System

	Typical Applications	Benefits	Examples
Control Systems	1. Control of marketing costs.	1. More timely computerized reports.	1. Undesirable cost trends are spotted more quickly so that corrective action may be taken sooner.
	2. Diagnosis of poor sales performance.	2. Flexible on-line retrieval of data.	2. Executives can ask supplementary questions of the computer to help pinpoint reasons for a sales decline and reach an action decision more quickly.
	3. Management of fashion goods.	3. Automatic spotting of problems and opportunities.	3. Fast-moving fashion items are reported daily for quick reorder, and slow-moving items are also reported for fast price reductions.
	4. Flexible promotion strategy.	4. Cheaper, more detailed, and more frequent reports.	4. Ongoing evaluation of a promotional campaign permits reallocation of funds to areas behind target.
Planning Systems	1. Forecasting.	1. Automatic translation of terms and classifications between departments.	1. Survey-based forecasts of demand for complex industrial goods can be automatically translated into parts requirements and production schedules.
	2. Promotional planning and corporate long-range planning.	2. Systematic testing of alternative promotional plans and compatibility testing of various divisional plans.	2. Complex simulation models, both developed and operated with the help of data bank information, can be used for promotional planning by product managers and for strategic planning by top management.
	3. Credit management.	3. Programmed executive decision rules can operate on data bank information.	3. Credit decisions are automatically made as each order is processed.
	4. Purchasing.	4. Detailed sales reporting permits automation of management decisions.	4. Computer automatically repurchases standard items on the basis of correlation of sales data with programmed decision rules.

Table 6.5 Benefits Possible with an Information System *(continued)*

	Typical Applications	Benefits	Examples
Research Systems	1. Advertising strategy.	1. Additional manipulation of data is possible when stored for computers in an unaggregated file.	1. Sales analysis is possible by new market segment breakdowns.
	2. Pricing strategy.	2. Improved storage and retrieval capability allows new types of data to be collected and used.	2. Systematic recording of information about past R & D contract bidding situations allows improved bidding strategies.
	3. Evaluation of advertising expenditures.	3. Well-designed data banks permit integration and comparison of different sets of data.	3. Advertising expenditures are compared to shipments by county to provide information about advertising effectiveness.
	4. Continuous experiments.	4. Comprehensive monitoring of input and performance variables yields information when changes are made.	4. Changes in promotional strategy by type of customer are matched against sales results on a continuous basis.

Source: Reprinted by permission of the *Harvard Business Review*. Exhibit from "How to Build a Marketing Information System," by Donald F. Cox and Robert E. Good, *Harvard Business Review* (May–June 1967), p. 146.

mation base for decision making in all functional areas. A recent survey of the 500 largest firms in the United States focused on the allocation of overall management information resources to each of the functional areas. A total of 202 companies responded by indicating the approximate percentage of their total information system resources—including hardware, software, facilities, and personnel—allocated to four organizational functions: administrative, finance, marketing, and production. Figure 6.6 shows their responses and their predictions of relative allocations for the next five years.

Although production and finance currently receive most of the management information system's resources, additional resources are expected to be devoted to marketing during the next five years.

Successful Marketing Information Systems

Although only a few large companies currently have sophisticated computer-based marketing information systems, considerable attention is focused on their contributions. By the end of the decade, most medium-sized companies will have established their own marketing information systems. Monsanto and General Mills are two firms with a successful MIS in operation.

Figure 6.6 Current and Future Allocation of MIS Resources

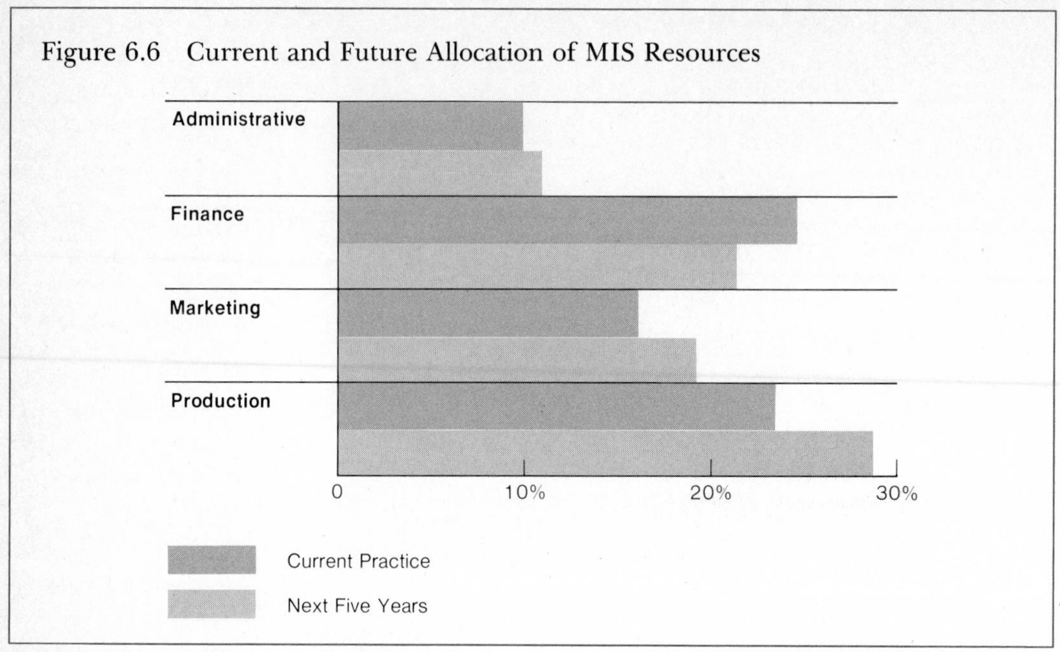

Source: C. Richard Roberts and Louis E. Boone, "MIS Development in American Industry: The Apex," *Journal of Business Strategy* (Spring 1983). Reprinted by permission of the authors.

Monsanto A diversified international industrial company headquartered in St. Louis, Monsanto has designed one of the most advanced marketing information systems in operation. The system provides detailed sales analyses by product, sales district, type of mill, and end use. Consumer analyses for the ultimate use of some Monsanto products (tires, fabrics, and synthetic fibers for carpets, for instance) are obtained from a continuing panel of 7,500 households who represent a cross-section of the national market. Information is collected on purchase patterns by socioeconomic group and is then analyzed to determine current buying trends.

Monsanto also collects survey data to record the actions of competitors. In addition, the system generates short-, medium-, and long-range forecasts for the company and industry. Short-term forecasts are developed for each of 400 individual products.

General Mills The General Mills computer supplies each zone, regional, and district manager with a daily teletype report on (1) the previous day's orders by brand and (2) current projections of monthly sales compared with the monthly total projected the week before. Each of the 1,700 products is analyzed in terms of current profitability and projected annual profitability as compared with target projections made at the beginning of the year. Problem products that require management

Table 6.6 Sample Questionnaire for Determining Marketing Information Needs

1. What types of decisions are you regularly called upon to make?
2. What types of information do you need to make the decision?
3. What types of information do you regularly get?
4. What types of special studies do you periodically request?
5. What types of information would you like to get but are not currently receiving?
6. What information would you like to receive daily? weekly? monthly? yearly?
7. What magazines and trade journals would you like to receive regularly?
8. What types of data analysis programs would you like to receive?
9. What are four improvements you would like to see made in the present marketing information system?

Source: Philip Kotler, "A Design for the Firm's Marketing Nerve Center," *Business Horizons* (Fall 1966), p. 70. Copyright © 1966 by the Foundation for the School of Business at Indiana University. Reprinted by permission.

attention are also listed in the daily report. A similar report looks for problem areas in each region and breaks down each problem by cause.[39]

Developing an MIS

Construction of a marketing information system requires the full support of top management. Management not only must be truly enthusiastic about the potential of the system, but also must believe that it is top management's place to oversee its development. Too often, technical staff are left to build the system without that important management contribution. The next step involves a review and appraisal of the entire marketing organization and the policies that direct it. The marketing managers' responsibilities must be clearly defined. If the system is to measure their performances against company plans, then each person's area of accountability must be specified.

Once the organization is readied for development of the system, its level of sophistication must be determined. Before this can be done, the company's needs and costs of meeting those needs must be carefully considered. The ability of managers to develop and effectively use a sophisticated system must also be considered. Managers must be able to state their specific information needs. A questionnaire, such as the one illustrated in Table 6.6, can be used to pinpoint specific information requirements.

Management must also be able to state explicitly its planning, decision making, and control processes and procedures. An automated ex-

[39]Information from "Marketing Management and the Computer," *Sales Management* (August 20, 1965), pp. 49–60. See also Leon Winer, "Effective Computer Use in Marketing Information Systems and Model Building," in *Marketing: 1776–1976 and Beyond,* (ed.) Kenneth L. Bernhardt (Chicago: American Marketing Association, 1976), pp. 626–629.

A Peek at the Future of Information Systems

The year is 1990. The place is the office of the marketing manager of a medium-sized consumer products manufacturer. The participants in the following discussion are John, the marketing manager; Anne, the director of marketing science; Rod, Anne's assistant, who specializes in marketing research; and Scott, the sales manager for the company. The scene opens as Anne, Rod, and Scott enter John's office.

John: *Good morning. What's on the agenda for this morning?*

Anne: *We want to take a look at the prospects for our new beef substitute.*

John: *What do we have on that new product?*

Rod: *We test marketed it late in 1989 in four cities, so we have those data from last quarter.*

John: *Let's see how it did.*

(All four gather around the remote console video display unit. John activates the console and requests it to display the sales results from the most recent test market. The system retrieves the data and displays the information on the video device.)

John: *That looks good! How does it compare to the first test?*

(The console retrieves and displays the data from the first test on command from John.)

Rod: *Let me check the significance of the sales increase of the most recent test over last year's test.*

(Rod requests that the system test and display the likelihood that the sales increase could be a chance occurrence.)

Rod: *Looks like a solid sales increase.*

Anne: *Good! How did the market respond to our change in price?*

(Anne commands the system to display the graph of the price-quantity response based on the most recent test data.)

John: *Is that about what our other meat substitute products show?*

(John calls up past price-quantity response graphs for similar products.)

John: *Just as I suspected. This new product is a bit more responsive to price. What's the profit estimate?*

(John calls for a profit estimate from the product-planning model within the system.)

John: *Hmm . . . $5,500,000. Looks good. Is that based on the growth model I supplied to the model bank last week?*

Anne: *No. This is based on the market-share progress other food substitutes have shown in the past as well as the*

ception reporting system can be developed for the manager who states: "I always like to know about all situations in which sales, profits, or market shares are running 4 percent or more behind plan. Furthermore, in any exceptional cases I also require the following diagnostic information: prices, distribution levels, advertising, and consumer attitudes."[40]

[40]Cox and Good, "How to Build a Marketing Information System," p. 152.

information we have on the beef substitute from our test markets.

John: *Let's see what mine would do.*

(He reactivates the product-planning model, this time using his growth model. The profit implications are displayed on the console.)

John: *Well, my model predicts $5 million. That's close. Looks like my feelings are close to the statistical results.*

Anne: *Let's see if there's a better marketing strategy for this product. We must remember that these profit estimates are based on the peliminary plan we developed two weeks ago.*

(Anne calls for the marketing mix generator to recommend a marketing program based upon the data and judgmental inputs on file for this product.)

John: *I'm a little worried about our advertising appeals. Can we improve in this area?*

Anne: *Let's see what the response to advertising is.*

(The video unit shows a graph of the predicted sales-advertising response function.)

Anne: *If we changed from a taste appeal to a convenience appeal, what would the results be, John?*

John: *I think it would look like this.*

(John takes a light pen and describes a new relationship on the video unit based upon his judgment of the effectiveness of the new appeal.)

Rod: *Let me check something.*

(Rod calls for a sample of past sales-advertising response curves of similar products using the convenience appeal.)

Rod: *I think you are underestimating the response on the basis of past data.*

John: *Well, this product is different. How much would it cost for a test of this appeal?*

(Rod calls a marketing research evaluation model from the console.)

Rod: *It looks like a meaningful test would cost about $5,000.*

John: *I wonder what risk we'd run if we made a decision to go national with the product right now. What are the chances of a failure with this product as it stands if we include this morning's revisions to the marketing mix?*

(A risk-analysis model is called up on the system.)

John: *Looks like a 35 percent chance of failure. Maybe we'd best run further tests in order to reduce the risk of failure. What's next on the agenda this morning?*

Source: David B. Montgomery and Glen L. Urban, *Management Science in Marketing* (Englewood Cliffs, N.J.: Prentice-Hall, 1969), pp. 1–3. Adapted by permission of Prentice-Hall, Inc., Englewood Cliffs, N.J.

A Futuristic Perspective for MIS

As marketing research becomes increasingly scientific and is combined by a growing number of organizations into fully functional information systems, decision makers benefit by making informed decisions about problems and opportunities. Sophisticated computer simulations make it possible to consider alternative courses of action by posing a number of "what if?" situations. These developments may convert the scenario we imagine in 1990 into reality in a much shorter time.

Summary

Information is vital for marketing decision making. No firm can operate without detailed information of its market. Information may take several forms: one-time marketing research studies, secondary data, internal data, subscriptions to commercial information sources, and the output of a marketing information system.

Marketing research, an important source of information, deals with studies that collect and analyze data relevant to marketing decisions. It involves the specific delineation of problems, research design, collection of secondary and primary data, interpretation of research findings, and presentation of results for management action.

Marketing research started when Charles C. Parlin, an advertising space sales representative for the *Saturday Evening Post,* counted empty soup cans in Philadelphia's trash in an effort to convince the Campbell Soup Company to advertise in the magazine. Today, the most common marketing research activities are determining market potential, developing sales forecasts for the firm's products and services, competitive product analysis, new product estimates, studies related to marketing mix decisions and international trade, and societal and cultural research. Annual expenditures for marketing research now exceed $1 billion, and most large companies have internal market research departments. However, outside suppliers still remain vital to the research function. Some of these outside research suppliers perform the complete research task, while others specialize in limited areas or provide syndicated data services.

The marketing research process can be divided into six specific steps: (1) defining the problem; (2) exploratory research; (3) formulating hypotheses; (4) research design; (5) collecting data; and (6) interpretation and presentation. A clearly defined problem allows the researcher to obtain the relevant decision-oriented information. Exploratory research refers to information gained both outside and inside the firm. Hypotheses—tentative explanations of some specific event—allow the researcher to set out a specific research design, the series of decisions that, taken together, comprise a master plan or model for the conduct of the investigation. The data collection phase of the marketing research process can involve either or both primary data (original data) and secondary data (previously published data). Primary data can be collected by three alternative methods: observation, survey, or experimental. Once the data is collected, it is important that researchers interpret and present it in a way that is meaningful to management.

An increasing number of firms have installed planned marketing information systems. Properly designed, the MIS will generate an orderly flow of decision-oriented information as the marketing executive needs it. The number of firms with planned information systems will grow during the 1980s as more managers recognize their contribution to dealing with the information explosion.

Key Terms

marketing research
syndicated service
full-service research supplier
limited-service research supplier
exploratory research
hypothesis
research design
primary data
secondary data
focus group interview
experiment
test marketing
population
census
probability sample
nonprobability sample
convenience sample
judgment sample
quota sample
referral sample
simple random sample
systematic sample
stratified sample
cluster sample
data
information
marketing information system

Review Questions

1. Outline the development and current status of the marketing research function.
2. Explain the services offered by different types of marketing research suppliers.
3. List and explain the various steps in the marketing research process.
4. Distinguish between primary and secondary data.
5. What advantages does the use of secondary data offer the marketing researcher? What potential limitations exist in using such data?
6. Distinguish among surveys, experiments, and observational methods of data collection.
7. Illustrate each of the three methods for gathering survey data. Under what circumstances should each be used?
8. Explain the differences between probability and nonprobability samples and the various types of each.

9. Distinguish between marketing research and marketing information systems.
10. What is the current status of marketing information systems?

Discussion Questions and Exercises

1. Prepare a brief two to three page report on a syndicated marketing research service. Explain how this data is used by marketing decision makers.
2. Collect from secondary data the following information:
   a. Retail sales in Dayton, Ohio, for last year
   b. Number of persons over 65 in Springfield, Massachusetts
   c. Earnings per share for General Motors last year
   d. Bituminous coal production in the United States in a recent year
   e. Consumer price index for a given month
   f. Number of households earning more than $15,000 in Miami, Florida
3. Look up the "Survey of Buying Power" data for your community or one nearby. What marketing implications can be drawn from these situations?
4. It seems that political predictions often miss their mark. Consider the prediction error made by the *Literary Digest* in the Alf Landon-Franklin D. Roosevelt presidential campaign of 1936; The Truman-Dewey presidential race in 1948; and Reagan's landslide victory over Carter in 1980. What implications do these misses have for marketing researchers?
5. You have been asked to determine the effect on Gillette of Schick's introduction of a revolutionary new blade that is guaranteed to give a hundred nick-free shaves. Outline your approach to the study.

CASES FOR PART 2

Case 2.1
*Star Electronics, Inc.**

Star Electronics is a medium-size manufacturer of electronic components, tools, and repair kits. It enjoyed a sales volume of $27 million in a recent year and employed 540 persons in all phases of its operation. Star Electronics is headquartered in Lincoln, Nebraska. The firm is particularly known for its line of tools, chemicals, and repair kits for the professional and amateur stereo, hi-fi, and television repair people. The amateur or do-it-yourself market appears to be growing in importance.

The professional repair market is reached through several electronics goods wholesalers who call on local electrical supply houses where most repair people and technicians procure their supplies. Up to this point the amateur market has represented less than 10 percent of company sales. This market is reached through Playback and Montgomery Ward retail chain outlets. Star Electronics sells tools, kits, and chemicals to these stores under its own label and also under the retailers' private brands. Products sold under the two labels are generally identical.

*Names of the corporation and its executives are disguised to protect their identity. All material in the case study, however, consists of information obtained from interviews with company executives.

Source: This case was prepared by Professor A. H. Kizilbash, Northern Illinois University, as a basis for class discussion. Reprinted by permission.

Because of the advances made in the design and construction of stereos, hi-fis, and televisions, there is now less need for frequent repairs. When repair is needed, it can be quickly performed by replacing the defective part with a new one, eliminating the need for traditional tools, kits, and chemicals. As a result of these and related developments, Star Electronics sales to the professional repair market has dropped $12 milllion over the past six years.

Recognizing that the professional repair market was shrinking, management of Star Electronics decided to search for a new product line that could strengthen their position in the consumer market. After a careful study by the New Product Development Department, a line of furniture-style stereo speakers was unveiled. The proposed product line consisted of stereo speakers with cabinets made in various furniture styles, such as contemporary, Early American, and Mediterranean. The product developers believed that a majority of stereo speakers sold are of the black box variety and do not blend in well with the decor of a home. It was reasoned that furniture-style speakers would therefore appeal to a vast majority of consumers.

Three months prior to the beginning of full-scale production of the new line of furniture-style stereo speakers, management decided to undertake a marketing study to determine whether a demand for this product existed. David Tanner, a recent college graduate who had been serving as an assistant to the sales manager, was asked to undertake the study. Tanner completed the study in the assigned two months. Excerpts from the report he submitted to the management are reproduced here.

Summary of the Report

Research Method

In order to gain insights into consumer motivation, perceptions, and preferences for stereo speakers, this investigation was conducted in two phases. The first phase of research consisted of a focus group session conducted by a trained psychologist with nine women in Chicago, Illinois. In the second phase 106 personal in-store interviews were conducted with shoppers after demonstrating the product in use. These interviews were conducted in the Chicago area. Two Playback and one Montgomery Ward stores were selected for this purpose. Three identical speakers, each encased in a different style of cabinet were chosen. The three cabinet styles selected were (1) Early American, (2) Mediterranean and (3) black box. Interviewers would ask the respondent to listen to their chosen record on the three speakers. Using a switching system, the respondent had the opportunity to hear the same record on all three speakers. Respondents were *not* forewarned about the similarities and dissimilarities of the three speakers. Interviewees were asked to rate the three speakers on cabinet style, sound quality, and overall preference. They were also asked to state the reasons for their choice.

Focus Group Findings

The following represents hypotheses generated from one exploratory group discussion with nine women from the Chicago area, approximately one half of whom owned console units and one half component stereo units. The statements below, therefore, are intended to be directional and indicative of possible consumer perceptions and behavior and not intended to be definitive.

It would appear that when a family decides to purchase its first stereo set they are young marrieds possibly beginning a family, do not have a great deal of discretionary income, and live in smaller quarters than they anticipate once they begin to establish themselves and earn greater income. Therefore, the first stereo purchase would appear to be a console unit. The console unit, at this point in time, is compact, fits in more appropriately in a small living room, and becomes a piece of furniture.

The middle-aged women participating in this study appeared to be neophytes in stereo sound reproduction when they purchased their first unit. Neither they nor their husbands had a sophisticated understanding of stereo systems. They relied basically on the salesperson for information and at this time in their life cycle appeared to be looking for a satisfactory sound coupled with a good-looking piece of furniture.

A console unit seems to last indefinitely and therefore does not require replacing until the family moves into larger quarters, children become teenagers, and additional music systems are required in the household. The console then may be kept in the living room as a piece of furniture or moved to another room, and a component stereo system is then considered. At this point in time, especially if there are boys in the family and reaching the teenage years, they become music consultants *to their parents. Since these boys are* into music, *they will give advice to their parents, more than likely, to buy a component system and which components to buy.*

While the father accepts the responsibility of paying for it and the mother's input has to do with its acceptability as part of the decor, the son may very well determine the brands and quality of the components. Additional input for upgrading their sets and music quality appears to come from listening to friends' units, assimilating information from Consumer Reports, *and from visiting music stores.*

The comparison between console and component stereo systems seems to be that for consoles you sacrifice sound for style and pay for furniture *versus components which* offer you much better sound, but not much style.

Two major problems appear to surface when discussing components. One is the difficulty in hiding the wires that run from the amplifier, turntable, etc., to the speakers. While some people tape them along shelving, it does pose an unsightly problem for others. The second problem is that stereo component speakers are not attractive *and in some cases are hidden behind furniture or disguised in some way with planters to make them more acceptable as part of the room decor. Therefore, with this frame of reference, the exposure to the test speakers was for the most part quite favorable.*

Women perceived the line of speakers as being highly decorative; depending on whether they preferred Early American or Mediterranean, these speakers would be much preferred over what they term box speakers. *However, it would seem that if these speaker boxes are priced much higher than the plain box speakers there would be resistance to purchasing them simply because they are a* necessity *and not an addition to the room that the woman makes voluntarily. In other words, speakers are more or less forced on her and she must arrange them in her room to accommodate the sound from a stereo. She apparently does this reluctantly, especially if she feels it interferes with her planned decor.*

None of these six speakers, exposed to this group of women, were rejected although the tighter and more heavy grill work seems to be more attractive than the standard type grill work on the market currently. Moreover, they would like to have a choice of colors in the speaker cloth behind the grill work so that they could better integrate it with their color scheme.

On the whole then, while these speakers are more acceptable than the standard box speakers, women would prefer them to be more functional. The use of stereo speakers as end tables seems to be one possibility that is of interest. They could then use the speakers as a table lamp stand, etc. There also appears to be a feeling for an optimum sized *speaker. The 14 × 26 inch speaker seems to approximate a more ideal size than its smaller counterpart but may still be slightly larger than optimum. It also appears that a double door speaker is much preferred over a single door.*

From this initial exploration, it should be kept in mind that ideally these women desire stereo component speakers to be invisible. *Since they obviously cannot be* invisible, *then, they should blend in as much as possible with other decor and be multifunctional in use.*

Additionally, it was interesting to note while women seem to accept two speakers they reject the idea of having to place four speakers in one room for quadraphonic sound. If they must do this, they seem to indicate that the preferable combination would be two sets of different cabinets so that there are not four identical speaker boxes distributed in the same room. Also, it would seem that they would be happy with a three speaker combination. For example, two identical end table speakers and a different speaker at the op-

posite end of the room, which for them would seem to give adequate sound.

Younger married or single women probably feel differently about component stereo units as well might men. But for these middle-aged women and their families the above findings appear to be reasonable.

Survey Findings

Demographic Profile

1. *Respondents were about equally divided for age groups above and below 30. An adequate representation of the age group over 30 was essential in view of the findings from the focus group that mature shoppers may be more receptive towards furniture-style speakers.*
2. *The sample appeared to have a cross-section of various occupational classes, and the distribution of population by sex and marital status was adequate.*
3. *Both homeowners and apartment dwellers were well represented giving us a good fix on both lifestyles.*
4. *Fifty-two percent of the sample population had incomes in excess of $15,000, while 30 percent had incomes in excess of $20,000. This suggests that the bulk of our sample was in the middle and upper-income range which is the target population for stereo and speaker products.*
5. *An overwhelming majority of the respondents were owners of component sets, which is the target populaton for speakers.*
6. *Somewhat different from the findings of the focus group, owners of all styles of stereo sets generally keep sets in the living room of their home or apartments.*
7. *Forty-two percent of the respondents owned ten inch or smaller speakers.*
8. *Most persons surveyed had contemporary or other (generally mix and match) type of furniture in the room in which they kept their stereo equipment.*
9. *Somewhat different from the findings of the focus group interviews, a majority of women did not participate in decisions about stereo purchase. Yet, 42 percent did participate—a significant number.*
10. *Contrary to focus group findings, those women who participated in stereo purchase decisions did* not *appear to have any more influence on the selection of cabinet style over sound quality.*
11. *Subjected to a hypothetical situation ("If you were shopping around for a stereo, which type would you buy?"), a majority (85 percent) would prefer components.*
12. *Out of the three sizes (10, 12, or 15 inch) being tested, a majority (43 percent) would prefer the 12 inch size.*

Store Test and Interview

The study also called for an actual product test for sound, quality, and cabinet style. Interviewees were asked to pick their preferred cabinet size from the three speaker styles being tested (Early American, Mediterranean and black box). Each of these three styles were presented in 10, 12 and 15 inch sizes. Once the respondent chose his or her preferred size, the three speaker styles were played in the preferred size. In this way the respondent was listening to music of his or her choice in the same size speaker of the three cabinet styles. Respondents were told that the three speakers of a given size were of the same price. Hence, all other variables were kept constant, and the respondents were asked to rank the speakers on the basis of sound quality and cabinet style. Data gained from this product test appears in the following tables.

Table 1 Preference for Sound Quality in Three Cabinet Styles

	Rankings		
Cabinet Style	First Choice	Second Choice	Third Choice
Early American	46 (43%)	29 (27%)	29 (27%)
Mediterranean	32 (30%)	39 (37%)	33 (31%)
Black Box	30 (28%)	33 (31%)	41 (39%)

Weighted Averages: Early American = 1.80 Mediterranean = 1.972 Black Box = 2.066

Table 2 Preference for Cabinet Style

	Rankings		
Cabinet Style	First Choice	Second Choice	Third Choice
Early American	45 (43%)	35 (33%)	22 (21%)
Mediterranean	13 (12%)	40 (38%)	49 (46%)
Black Box	46 (43%)	26 (25%)	32 (30%)

Weighted Averages: Early American = 1.708 Mediterranean = 2.264 Black Box = 1.83

Table 3 Overall Preference

	Rankings		
Cabinet Style	First Choice	Second Choice	Third Choice
Early American	51 (48%)	23 (22%)	29 (27%)
Mediterranean	20 (19%)	40 (38%)	43 (41%)
Black Box	35 (33%)	39 (37%)	32 (30%)

Weighted Averages: Early American = 1.736Mediterranean = 2.16 Black Box = 1.972

Table 4 Reasons for First Choice

Reason for First Choice	Respondents
Sound Quality	63 (59%)
Cabinet Style	26 (25%)
Both Sound and Cabinet	17 (16%)

Discussion Questions

1. Describe how the stereo speaker market is affected by life cycle stages of consumers.
2. What recommendations should Tanner make to the Star Electronics sales manager?

Case 2.2 Gistner Funeral Home

Phil Gistner had just returned from the annual convention of his state's association of funeral directors and was reviewing some of his notes from the management sessions:

Death is not as commonplace as it once was. Millions of Americans have never experienced the loss, by death, of someone close to them. Millions of Americans have never been to a funeral, or have even seen a funeral procession, except one which was televised. Millions of Americans have never seen a dead body except on TV, in a movie, on a battlefield, or on a highway. Even where people have been directly involved in the arrangements of a funeral service, there is often confusion or doubt about the role of the funeral director and the cost for his services.

Often the place of the casket in the overall funeral service is unclear or undefined. Historically, the funeral director has been a provider of goods and some services. A casket was purchased and all other services provided free. Today, on the average, the merchandise amounts to only about 20 percent of the total cost of a funeral service.

The casket is not the funeral service, nor is the funeral service the casket. The failure of some funeral directors to accept this fact and explain it to those they serve is in some ways responsible for much of the concern over funeral practices and prices today.

Pricing structures for funeral services at the Gistner Funeral Home had always been based upon a multiple times the wholesale cost of the casket, and Phil was wondering if maybe the time had come to change to a different method of pricing. He was concerned, though, about how customers, the other funeral homes in the area, and his father would react to any such changes.

Background Information

The Gistner Funeral Home was founded in 1906 by George Gistner, Sr., in a small town on the West Coast. George Sr. ran the business with the help of his wife and son until his death in 1947. At that time the funeral home was conducting an average of 75 funeral services a year. Phil joined his father, George Jr., in the operation of business in 1965, at which time the firm was doing about 100 services per year.

Two other funeral homes were operating in the area, one about the same size as Gistner and the other conducting an average of 60 services a year. Both of these homes utilized a pricing system similar to Gistner's, with the price of a funeral service based upon a multiple of the funeral home's cost for the casket. Prices were difficult to compare, since each funeral home represented several different manufacturers of caskets and carried a wide range of casket styles and qualities. Few customers made any attempt to check a competitor's price due to the nature and timing of the purchase decision.

Financial Information for 1982[1]

In 1982, Gistner Funeral Home conducted 170 services at an average price of $1,820. The average wholesale cost of merchandise sold was $420, broken down into $280 for the casket and $140 for the vault. The costs of the casket and vault were multiplied by an average of 5.0 and 3.0, respectively, to arrive at the selling prices. Average variable expenses per funeral were $90. Other relevant financial information for 1982 included: total fixed expenses ($172,000); inventory ($12,500); accounts receivable ($45,000); and fixed assets at market value ($215,000). These figures were relatively consistent with those of the preceding three years. Approximate national operating expenses for funeral firms in the late 1970s are shown in percentages in Figure 1.

Historical Development of Pricing[2]

The pricing policies of the typical funeral firm evolved by historical accident. Funeral directors in the United States were originally casket builders and sellers. Frequently, they were furniture dealers or cabinet makers who began to sell caskets because of their carpentry skills. By 1850, some casket builders had begun to add some services, such as restorative art and livery. Basically, though, they were sellers of caskets until around 1900, when the modern concept of the funeral director became fairly well developed. The funeral director was still judged, however, by the quality of caskets he sold and the breadth of casket selections he offered.

The pricing system used by early funeral directors was obtained by taking three times the cost of the casket. One

Figure 1 Component Breakdown of the Funeral Director's Operations

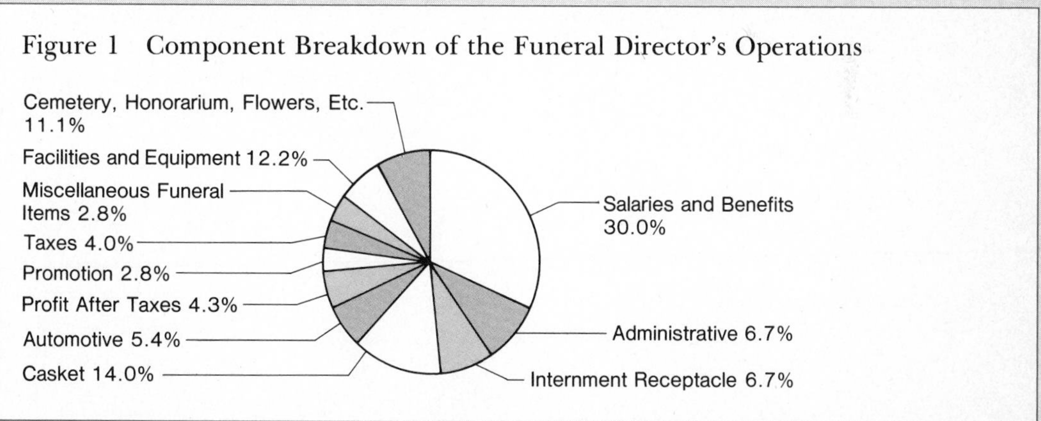

Source: "A Factual Guide to Funeral Costs," published in the public interest by The Ohio Funeral Directors Association.

[1] The figures in this section have been simplified and adjusted somewhat for ease of calculation and analysis and are, therefore, not representative for the typical funeral home.

[2] For a detailed review of the funeral service field, see Roger D. Blackwell, "Price Levels of Funerals: An Analysis of the Effects of Entry Regulation in a Differentiated Oligopoly," unpublished PhD dissertation, Northwestern University, 1966.

third was for the cost of the casket, one third for the extra services offered by the funeral director, and one third for overhead and profit. Although the multiplier has changed, even today funeral directors frequently use a multiple pricing system.

Changing Role of the Funeral Director

In the earlier part of this century, when the church, the family, and the neighborhood were all tightly knit groups, they helped the surviving family members adjust to changes in their lives and relationships brought about by a death. All that was required of funeral directors was an adequate casket and a few simple arrangements.

Today, funeral directors serve the living, and their professional reputation rests upon the ability to assist the survivors in this transition process. They are counselors upon whom the survivor must rely.

To operate successfully within the changing environment, a funeral director must provide comfortable facilities, develop sound technical skill for the restorative process and sanitary control, have legal know-how to cut through government and insurance red tape, and possess the psychological knowledge to instill confidence in his judgment during the adjustment process.

Alternative Pricing Methods

In reviewing alternative pricing systems, Phil compiled the following information on the three widely used methods.[3]

Unit Pricing

In unit pricing, one price covers all the costs of the funeral except cash advances and optional extras. This method, the most widely used at the present time, is frequently based upon some multiple times the funeral director's cost of the casket. Some funeral homes vary the value of the multiple, using a higher multiple for lower cost caskets than for more expensive ones. Other funeral directors actually compute their overhead structure and add this to a reasonable markup on a given casket to arrive at the total price unit. The unit price usually includes such items and services as:

1. Removal of remains to mortuary
2. Complete preparation and dressing of remains
3. Securing of necessary certificates and permits
4. Use of the mortuary staff
5. Assistance of the mortuary staff
6. Transportation of the remains to the cemetary
7. Fixed amount of additional transportation to cemetary
8. Acknowledgement cards and memorial register, and
9. Casket selection.

Complete Itemized Pricing

Complete itemized pricing goes to the other extreme, adding a separate price for each element of the funeral service. Certain states have passed legislation requiring all funeral homes to use this pricing method, thinking that if consum-

[3]Portions of these descriptions are adapted from a study done by the Batesville Casket Company entitled "Funeral Directors' Pricing Methods, a Comprehensive National Survey," 1968.

ers know what they are paying for, they will be better able to select exactly what they need and want.

This system provides a separate price for each of the following:

1. Removal of remains
2. Embalming
3. Dressing, casketing, and cosmetizing
4. Use of chapel
5. Use of other mortuary facilities and equipment
6. Staff assistance
7. Funeral coach
8. Additional vehicles
9. Casket
10. Memorial register, and
11. Acknowledgement cards.

The list then continues with all other items that are considered extras in other pricing methods.

Professional Pricing

The professional pricing system, sometimes called the functional approach, involves charging a separate fee for the professional services of the funeral director rather than just including them with the merchandise he or she sells. Funeral directors charge for their services in the same manner as doctors or lawyers. The casket is then sold separately with a normal markup.

Two to five separate categories may be used with this method. Together, they cover the cost of the funeral except any cash advances or optional extras. Various categories that may be used in different combinations are:

1. Professional services
2. Preparation for burial
3. Use of facilities and equipment
4. Motor vehicles, and
5. Cost of the casket.

Possible Need for Change

Based on a national sample of 1,060 respondents, a recent marketing research study found that the majority of consumers would prefer to have more information concerning funeral prices.[4] When offered a choice of the three common methods of pricing funerals, 33.3 percent stated a preference for unit pricing, 16.5 percent preferred professional pricing, and 50.2 percent voiced a preference for itemized pricing. These responses seem consistent with current consumer concepts which have led to public demand for more information on which consumers can make decisions.

In August 1975, the Federal Trade Commission issued a series of proposed rules for the funeral industry, including a specific approach to price disclosures. While it may be some time before a final decision is made regarding the rules proposed by the federal government, certain states have already enacted legislation which requires funeral directors to disclose more price information in their dealings with consumers.

The specific language of the FTC proposal regarding the price list is as follows:

In connection with the sale or offering for sale of funeral services and/or merchandise to the public, in or affecting commerce as "commerce" is defined in the Federal Trade Commission Act, it is an unfair or deceptive act or practice for any funeral service industry member: To fail to furnish to each customer who inquires in person about the arrangement, purchase, and/or prices of

[4]From Roger D. Blackwell and W. Wayne Talarzyk, *American Attitudes toward Death and Funeral Service* (Evanston, Ill.: The Casket Manufacturers Association, 1974).

funeral goods or services, prior to any agreement on such arrangement or selection by the customer or to any customer who by telephone or letter requests written price information, a printed or typewritten price list, which the customer may retain, containing the prices (either the retail charge or the price per hour, mile or other unit of computation) for at least each of the following items:

(i) *Transfer of remains to funeral home.*
(ii) *Embalming.*
(iii) *Use of facilities for viewing.*
(iv) *Use of facilities for funeral services.*
(v) *Casket (a notation that a separate casket price list will be provided before any sales presentation for caskets is made).*
(vi) *Hearse.*
(vii) *Limousine.*
(viii) *Services of funeral director and staff.*
(ix) *Outer interment receptacles (if outer interment receptacles are sold, a notation that a separate outer interment receptacle price list will be provided before any sales presentation for such items is made.)*[5]

Discussion Questions

1. What is the economic logic behind the unit pricing system?
2. What are the basic advantages and disadvantages of each pricing system?
3. Do you think customers really understand the pricing systems of funeral homes?
4. How would you go about determining the price charged for a director's professional services and facilities?
5. What are the possible advantages to Phil Gistner in switching to a professional pricing system?

[5]Extracted from the *Federal Register*, Vol. 40, No. 169, Friday, August 29, 1975, p. 39903.

John A. Howard

The extent of John A. Howard's contributions is reflected in his selection by the Association of Consumer Research as one of the two first Fellows in Consumer Behavior. Howard (1915–), who holds the George E. Warren Professor of Business Chair at Columbia University, has made numerous contributions to the development of marketing theory during his illustrious career.

Howard's first major work, *Marketing Management: Analysis and Decision* (Richard D. Irwin, 1957), was an analytical, decision-oriented approach to the study of marketing management with considerable emphasis on application of behavioral science research. At about this time, he began to focus his attention on the social sciences. A two-year study of the state of knowledge in marketing, commissioned by the Ford Foundation, began in 1960. Howard described his findings as follows: "When the Ford Foundation, in 1960, asked me to . . . do a study of the state of knowledge in marketing and to make recommendations for improving it, consumer behavior consisted of a few isolated studies. Courses in the field were unknown. Marketing was looked upon as mainly an art with little content to teach. From the Ford Foundation study it was clear, however, that concepts from economics, psychology, and sociology could provide some foundation upon which to build. Today, consumer behavior is a budding, new social science."

The result of Howard's investigation was *Marketing: Executive and Buyer Behavior* (Columbia University Press, 1963). Six years later, he collaborated with Jagdish N. Sheth to produce the widely acclaimed *The Theory of Buyer Behavior* (Wiley, 1969). This theory, described briefly in the Appendix to Chapter 8, has attracted considerable scholarly interest and some empirical testing as marketing theorists attempt to more precisely determine its ability to explain and predict marketplace behavior. The richness and complexity of the theory is further evidence of the coming of age of consumer behavior, and much credit is due to John A. Howard.

3

CONSUMER BEHAVIOR

Understanding consumers and industrial buyers and their behavior is essential to the correct application of the marketing concept. It is also the starting point in the development of an effective marketing strategy. The chapters in Part Three view consumer behavior as a problem-solving function through which individuals make decisions and take actions designed to satisfy felt needs. The chapters focus on the internal factors and external, environmental influences that affect consumer decision making and industrial purchase behavior.

Chapter Objectives

1. To relate interpersonal influences on consumer behavior to the variables of the marketing mix.
2. To explain the classification of behavioral influences.
3. To outline steps in the consumer decision process.
4. To identify the interpersonal determinants of consumer behavior.
5. To explain the role of culture and subculture in consumer behavior.
6. To describe the Asch phenomenon.
7. To know how reference groups impact consumer behavior.
8. To explain the importance of social class in the study of consumer behavior.
9. To outline family influences on consumer behavior and how they are changing.

7

INTERPERSONAL INFLUENCES ON CONSUMER BEHAVIOR

Li Shuang, Ke Ming, Li Yong, and Tan Yun Wei from the People's Republic of China learned a lot about the strange behavior of American consumers in Cleveland. The four accountants were on a six-month assignment with Cleveland-based Ernst & Whinney, a CPA firm. Their visit was part of an agreement whereby one of the firm's partners would go to China, while two teams of Chinese accountants would study U.S. accounting practices in Cleveland and Chicago. But the foursome were probably more shocked by U.S. consumption behavior than the way Americans treat their debits and credits.

On the way from Peking to San Francisco, Li Shuang was puzzled by the cup of salad dressing and glass of water on his airplane tray. So he mixed them together and drank it. Li later remarked in his limited English: "It wasn't very delicious." Similarly, his companion Tan Yun Wei was upset over the "sour oranges" he kept getting when he ordered grapes—which he called grapefruit—for breakfast.

Li Yong admits he had heard a rumor that Americans actually sell dog food in their supermarkets. He was amazed when told the Chinese rumor is true: "Oh, oh, it's true. It's unbelievable. The dogs and cats in America eat better than people in Asian countries." Li points out that most Chinese do not keep dogs as pets, and they are more likely to be eaten than provided for by consumers. Li also did not understand the strange custom of a buyer tipping a seller of a service. He wanted to know why Americans did not tip before performance rather than after the fact, if they wanted better service.

While Ernst & Whinney was renting a suite for the men in a downtown high rise, the rental agent launched into a long discourse on the garbage disposal, dishwasher, and so on. The four clients were oblivious to her spiel. When an Ernst & Whinney employee explained the cultural differences to the rental agent, she gasped: "You mean they don't know what ice cube trays are?"[1]

The four accountants were destined to tell some strange tales about American culture when they got home. One wonders if anyone will believe them.

The Conceptual Framework

Consumer behavior consists of the acts of individuals in obtaining and using goods and services, including the decision processes that precede and determine these acts.[2] This definition includes both the ultimate consumer and the purchaser of industrial products. A major difference in the purchasing behavior of industrial consumers and ultimate consumers is that additional influences from within the organization may be exerted on the industrial purchasing agent.

This chapter assesses interpersonal influences on consumer behavior, while the next chapter explores personal influences. Chapter 9 deals with industrial and organizational buyer behavior.

Classifying Behavioral Influences: Personal and Interpersonal

The field of consumer behavior borrows extensively from other areas like psychology and sociology.[3] The work of Kurt Lewin, for instance, provides an excellent classification of influences on buying behavior.

[1]Dean Rotbart, "Chinese Accountants Find that America Is Hard to Figure," *The Wall Street Journal* (June 5, 1981), pp. 1, 12.

[2]This definition is adapted from James F. Engel and Roger D. Blackwell, *Consumer Behavior,* 4th ed. (Hinsdale, Ill.: The Dryden Press, 1982), p. 9.

[3]See Albert J. Della Bitta, "Consumer Behavior: Some Thoughts on Sheth's Evaluation of the Discipline," *Journal of the Academy of Marketing Science* (Winter 1982), pp. 5–6.

Lewin's work is also used in motivation theory, which is part of the management discipline, because it is a general model of behavior. Lewin's proposition was:

$$B = f(P,E)$$

where behavior *(B)* is a function *(f)* of the interactions of personal influences *(P)* and the pressures exerted upon them by outside forces in the environment *(E)*.[4]

This statement is usually rewritten for consumer behavior as follows:

$$B = f(I,P)$$

where consumer behavior *(B)* is a function *(f)* of the interaction of interpersonal determinants *(I)*, like reference groups and culture, and personal determinants *(P)*, like attitudes, on the consumer. Understanding consumer behavior requires an understanding of both the individual's psychological makeup and the influences of others.

The Consumer Decision Process

Consumer behavior may be viewed as a decision process and the act of purchasing is merely one point in the process. To understand consumer behavior, the events that precede and follow the purchase must be examined. Figure 7.1 identifies the steps in the consumer decision process: problem recognition, search, evaluation of alternatives, purchase decision, purchase act, and postpurchase evaluation. The decision process is utilized by the consumer in solving problems and in taking advantage of opportunities that arise. Such decisions permit consumers to correct differences between their actual and desired states. Feedback from each decision serves as additional experience to rely upon in subsequent decisions.

This process is demonstrated by the young couple whose only television set has been declared irreparable by the service representative. The need to purchase a new set is clearly recognized since it is a primary form of recreation for their young children. The couple questions their friends and acquaintances who have bought televisions recently. They pour over consumer-oriented reports on new models. Once all the necessary information is collected, the couple evaluates the various models on the basis of what is important to them—reliability and price. They decide to buy a new set the next weekend. The actual purchase

[4]See Kurt Lewin, *Field Theory in Social Science* (New York: Harper & Row, 1951), p. 62. See also C. Glenn Walters, "Consumer Behavior: An Appraisal," *Journal of the Academy of Marketing Science* (Fall 1979), pp. 237–284.

Figure 7.1 Steps in the Consumer Decision Process

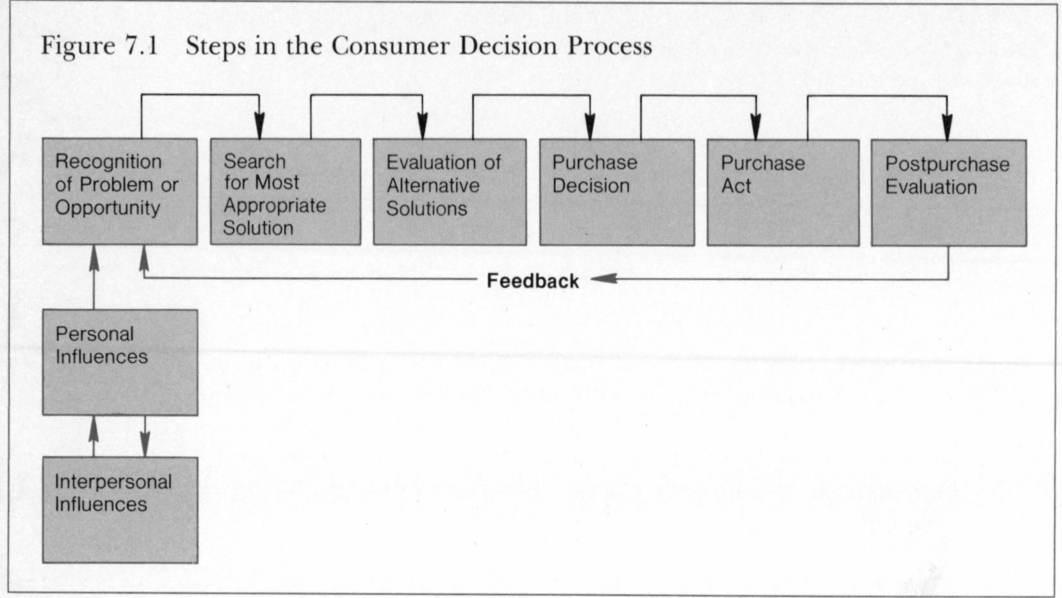

Source: Adapted from C. Glenn Walters and Gordon W. Paul, *Consumer Behavior: An Integrated Framework* (Homewood, Ill.: Richard D. Irwin, Inc., 1970), p. 18 ©1970 by Richard D. Irwin, Inc. and John Dewey, *How We Think* (Boston, Mass.: D. C. Heath, 1910), pp. 101–105. Similar steps are also discussed in Del I. Hawkins, Roger J. Best, and Kenneth A. Coney, *Consumer Behavior: Implications for Marketing Strategy*, revised ed. (Plano, Texas: Business Publications, Inc., 1983), pp. 447–606.

is completed at a local discount store the next Saturday. The new set is hooked up, and the young family sits back to evaluate their purchase.

This process is common to consumer purchase decisions. It is introduced here to provide an advance perspective of the field of consumer behavior. An expanded discussion of the model concludes Chapter 8, after the reader has an overview of the various factors that impact consumer behavior.

Interpersonal Determinants of Consumer Behavior

People are social animals. They often buy products and services that will enable them to project a favorable image to others. These influences may result from the individual's cultural environment, membership or reference groups, and family influences. A general model of the interpersonal (or group) determinants of consumer behavior is shown in Figure 7.2.

The model indicates that there are three categories of interpersonal determinants of consumer behavior: cultural influences, social influences, and family influences. These determinants are described in the remainder of this chapter. The model will be expanded to include personal influences in Chapter 8.

Figure 7.2 Interpersonal Determinants of Consumer Behavior

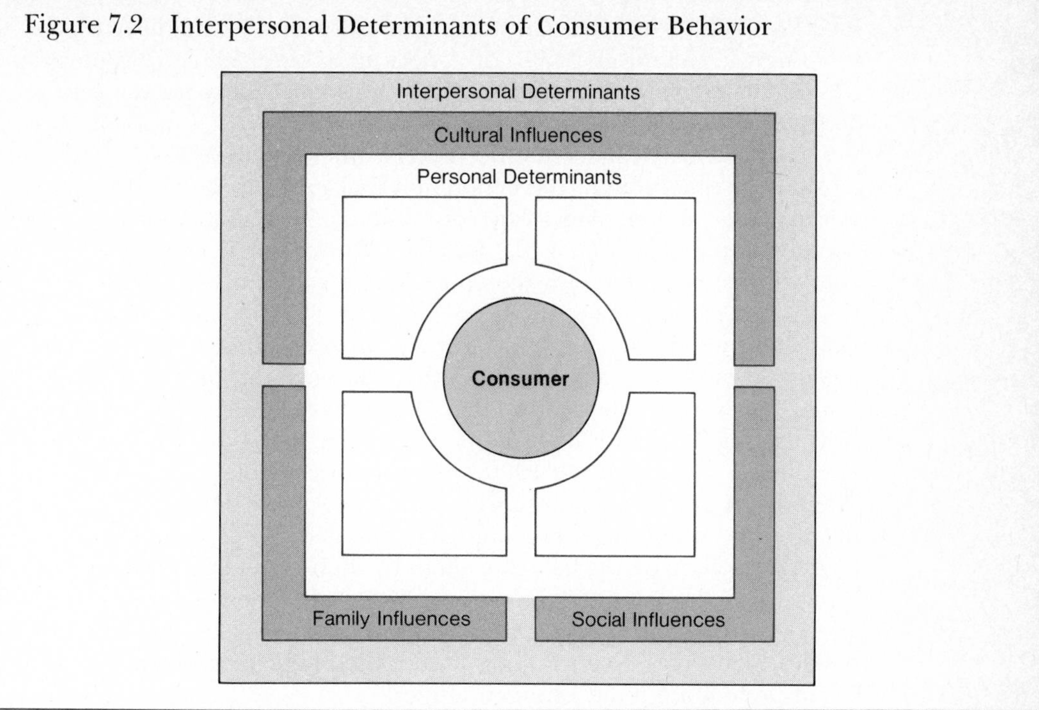

Source: Adapted with permission from C. Glenn Walters and Gordon W. Paul, *Consumer Behavior: An Integrated Framework* (Homewood, Ill.: Richard D. Irwin, 1970), p. 16. © 1970 by Richard D. Irwin, Inc.

Cultural Influences

Culture is the broadest environmental determinant of consumer behavior. Sometimes it is a very elusive concept for marketers to handle. General Mills knew that few Japanese homes had ovens, so it designed a Betty Crocker cake mix that could be made in the widely used electric rice cookers. The product failed because of a cultural factor. Japanese homemakers are very proud of their rice's purity, so they were fearful that a cake flavor would be left in their cookers.[5]

Culture can be defined as "the complex of values, ideas, attitudes, and other meaningful symbols created by people to shape human behavior and the artifacts of that behavior, transmitted from one generation to the next."[6] It is the completely learned and handed-down way of life that gives each society its own peculiar flavor or values.

[5]"Learning How to Please the Baffling Japanese," *Fortune* (October 5, 1981), p. 122.
[6]Engel and Blackwell, *Consumer Behavior*, 4th ed., p. 72.

Core Values in the U.S. Culture

The Protestant work ethic and the accumulation of wealth have played a big part in the development of American culture. While cultural values do change over time, there are always some basic core values that are slow to change. Table 7.1 summarizes some U.S. cultural core values and their particular relevance to consumer behavior.

Many people thought the generation that grew up in the 1960s had permanently altered American core values. This generation was the product of the baby booms that followed World War II and the Korean conflict. It was raised with the conservative values of the 1950s. Free time was spent watching television shows like "Ozzie and Harriet" and "Father Knows Best." As they matured, this generation seemed to rebel against most of the values held by their parents and previous generations. This was the generation that shocked traditional cultural values with its long hair, antiwar protests, marijuana, and Woodstock festival. Despite the turmoil of the 1960s, most American core values survived. What are the flower children of 1960s doing now? They have passed on to early middle age, crossing that dreaded barrier, age 30. They have adopted many of the values held by their parents, including worrying about the younger generation. Most baby boomers are now too concerned with mortgages and receding hair lines to protest anything besides high taxes. Even Rolling Stone Mick Jagger observed: "I can't go on pretending to be 18 much longer."[7]

There are trends and shifts in cultural values, yet traditionally these changes have been gradual not revolutionary like the 1960s generation. Rapid technological shifts may alter this pace in the future, so marketers must constantly assess cultural norms.[8] One of the most recent cultural trends is the search for more interpersonal relationships, rather than the self-centered orientation that characterized recent American value structures. In short, many people are motivated by a desire for increased friendship.[9] This trend has been noted by marketers who now feature more family and friendship groups in their scenarios for commercials. Michelob's restaurant scenes are a good example.

Cultural Influences: An International Perspective

Cultural differences are particularly important for international marketers. This topic is more fully explored in Chapter 22, but it is important to point out that cultural differences do result in different atti-

[7]The discussion of the baby boom generation is adapted from Connie Lauerman, "Where Have All the Flower Children Gone?" *Florida* (November 8, 1981), pp. 6–7.

[8]Daniel Yankelovich, "New Rules," *The Seattle Times* (November 1, 1981), pp. F 1, F 4. Excerpted from the book, *New Rules: Searching for Self-Fulfillment in a World Turned Upside Down* by Daniel Yankelovich. Copyright 1981, Daniel Yankelovich. Distributed by Los Angeles Times Syndicate.

[9]This is noted in Engel and Blackwell, *Consumer Behavior,* 4th ed., p. 75.

Table 7.1 American Core Values

Value	General Features	Relevance to Consumer Behavior
Achievement and Success	Hard work is good; success flows from hard work	Acts as a justification for acquisition of goods ("You deserve it")
Activity	Keeping busy is healthy and natural	Stimulates interest in products that save time and enhance leisure-time activities
Efficiency and Practicality	Admiration of things that solve problems (e.g., save time and effort)	Stimulates purchase of products that function well and save time
Progress	People can improve themselves; tomorrow should be better	Stimulates desire for new products that fulfill unsatisfied needs; acceptance of products that claim to be "new" or "improved"
Material Comfort	"The good life"	Fosters acceptance of convenience and luxury products that make life more enjoyable
Individualism	Being one's self (e.g., self-reliance, self-interest, and self-esteem)	Stimulates acceptance of customized or unique products that enable a person to "express his own personality"
Freedom	Freedom of choice	Fosters interest in wide product lines and differentiated products
External Conformity	Uniformity of observable behavior; desire to be accepted	Stimulates interest in products that are used or owned by others in the same social group
Humanitarianism	Caring for others, particularly the underdog	Stimulates patronage of firms that compete with market leaders
Youthfulness	A state of mind that stresses being young at heart or appearing young	Stimulates acceptance of products that provide the illusion of maintaining or fostering youth

Source: From Leon Schiffman and Leslie Kanuk, *Consumer Behavior*, © 1978, p. 359. Reprinted by permission of Prentice-Hall, Inc., Englewood Cliffs, N.J. 07632.

tudes, mores, and folkways. All have an impact on marketing strategy. Consider the case of the candy company that introduced a new chocolate bar with peanuts in Japan. The candy bar failed because Japanese folklore suggests that eating chocolate with peanuts leads to a nosebleed.[10]

Other examples of cultural influences on marketing strategy are abundant in the international environment. Look at the marketing implications of the following actual situations:

- A Goodyear advertisement demonstrated the strength of its 3T tire cord by showing a steel chain breaking. When the commercial was shown in West Germany, however, it was perceived as an insult to steel chain manufacturers.[11]

[10] "Learning How to Please the Baffling Japanese," p. 122.

[11] *The Wall Street Journal* (March 9, 1977), p. 1.

- Because of inept translation, Schweppes Tonic Water was advertised in Italy as "bathroom water," and in South America, Parker Pen Company unwittingly indicated that its product would prevent unwanted pregnancies.[12]
- Deodorant usage among men ranges from 80 percent in the United States to 55 percent in Sweden, 28 percent in Italy, and 8 percent in the Philippines.[13]
- White is the color of mourning in Japan, and purple is associated with death in many Latin American countries.
- Feet are regarded as despicable in Thailand. Athlete's foot remedies with packages featuring a picture of feet will not be well received.
- In Ethiopia, the time required to make a decision is directly proportional to its importance. This is so much the case that low-level bureaucrats attempt to elevate the prestige of their work by taking a long time to make decisions. Foreigners working in Ethiopia are innocently prone to downgrading their work in the local people's eyes by trying to speed things up.[14]

Marketing strategies that have proven successful in the United States often cannot be applied directly in international markets because of cultural differences. Real differences do exist among different countries, and they must be known and evaluated by the international firm. When Helene Curtis Industries introduced its Every Night Shampoo line in Sweden, it renamed the product Every Day because Swedes usually wash their hair in the morning.[15]

Denture makers are aware of the impact of cultural differences on sales of false teeth. The people of Thailand are extremely fond of betel nuts, which stain their teeth black. For many years, once their original teeth wore out, they were replaced with black dentures. After World War II, however, fashions changed, and the Thais began using abrasives to scrub off black stains. Abrasives are now popular items in Thailand. Scandinavians like greyish false teeth, mostly because the teeth of Scandinavians tend to be naturally grey. The Japanese select false teeth noticeably longer than their natural ones.[16]

World marketers face competition from firms in Germany, France, the Soviet Union, Japan, and several other countries, as well as firms in the host nation. Therefore, they must become familiar with all aspects

[12]Robert Linn, "Americans Turn Deaf Ear to Foreign Tongues," *Orlando Sentinel Star* (November 1, 1981).

[13]"Personal Care Items' Global Outlook Good," *Advertising Age* (April 1, 1974), p. 28.

[14]Edward T. Hall, "The Silent Language of Overseas Business," *Harvard Business Review* (May–June 1960), p. 89.

[15]Patricia L. Layman, "In Any Language, the Beauty Business Spells Success," *Chemical Week* (September 17, 1975), p. 26.

[16]N. R. Kleinsfield, "This Is One Story with Teeth in It—False Ones, that Is," *The Wall Street Journal* (August 18, 1975), p. 1.

of the local population, including its cultural heritage. This can be accomplished by treating each country as having additional market segments that must be thoroughly analyzed before developing a marketing mix to use there.

Subcultures

Cultures are not homogeneous entities with universal values. Within each culture are numerous **subcultures**—subgroups with their own distinguishing modes of behavior. Any culture as heterogeneous as that of the United States is composed of significant subcultures based on factors such as race, nationality, age, rural-urban location, religion, and geographic distribution.[17]

Inhabitants of the Southwest display a lifestyle that emphasizes casual dress, outdoor entertaining, and water recreation. Mormons refrain from buying tobacco and liquor. Blacks may exhibit interest in products and symbols of their African heritage. Orthodox Jews purchase kosher or other traditional foods.

The two largest ethnic subcultures in the United States are blacks and Hispanics. Together, they account for over 41 million of the U.S. population or a little over 18 percent of the total.[18] However, many sources say that the census data undercounts both of these subcultures. Not only are these two ethnic subcultures large, but they also make up a disproportionate part of many important U.S. markets.

Black Consumption Patterns

Blacks represent the largest racial/ethnic subculture in the United States, some 26.5 million strong. They account for about 11.7 percent of the U.S. population, and $140 billion in purchasing power.[19] Several striking differences between the black and white population are present. According to the U.S. Department of Commerce, about 30 percent of blacks are below the poverty level compared to 10 percent of whites. Also, the black population is very young. The median age for blacks in 1985 is expected to be five to seven years younger than for whites.[20]

[17]An interesting discussion of the marketing implication related to one subculture is contained in Elizabeth C. Hirschman, "American Jewish Ethnicity: Its Relationship to Some Selected Aspects of Consumer Behavior," *Journal of Marketing* (Summer 1981), pp. 102–110.

[18]See "Counting Up Blacks and Hispanics," *Sales & Marketing Management* (April 6, 1981), p. 24.

[19]These statistics are from *Ibid,* p. 24; and Theodore J. Gage, "RSVP: An Invitation to Buy," *Advertising Age* (May 18, 1981), Section 2, p. 51.

[20]Engel and Blackwell, *Consumer Behavior,* 4th ed., pp. 85–86.

While marketers recognize that no group of 26.5 million people can be considered a homogeneous market segment for all products, a number of marketing studies have compared consumption patterns of blacks and whites. The major findings are:

- Blacks are very loyal to national brands.
- Blacks save a higher percentage of their income than do whites.
- Blacks spend less on food, housing, medical, and automobile transportation than equivalent whites. They spend more for clothing and nonautomobile transportation. Blacks and whites spend about the same on recreation, leisure, home furnishings, and equipment.
- Blacks tend to buy larger domestic automobiles, rather than foreign-made vehicles.
- Blacks buy more milk, soft drinks, and liquor than whites but less tea and coffee.[21]

The most distinguishing feature of black consumers is their brand loyalty. Blacks have been slow to shift to generic and private brands. In fact, it is estimated that blacks will soon account for 30 to 40 percent of the sales of many national brands. The Wellington Group, a New Jersey-based market research and business development company, found the following to be among the brand favorites of blacks: Listerine, Tide, Pine-Sol, Clorox, S.O.S., Reynolds Wrap, Minute Maid, Maxwell House, Gold Medal, Crisco, Skippy, Kraft mayonnaise, Vaseline Intensive Care, Campbell's baked beans, and Scott towels.[22]

Marketers—whether in majority- or minority-owned firms—must choose their strategies carefully when attempting to reach the growing black market. The product or service must be positioned correctly and the appropriate promotional media selected. S.C. Johnson of Racine, Wisconsin, for instance, was particularly successful in promoting Edge shaving gel to black males. Since the hair follicles of many black men have bumps that lead to nicks, Edge's introductory advertising campaign stressed the theme "Beat the bumps." Edge was a product that met the particular needs of the black marketplace.[23]

Hispanic Consumption Patterns

Hispanics are the nation's second largest subculture. The U.S. Spanish-speaking population is increasing by more than one half million a year and is becoming a very important market segment. This is particularly true in metropolitan Miami, whose Cuban population of 690,000 is ex-

[21]These findings are summarized in Engel and Blackwell, pp. 91–92.

[22]Alphonzia Wellington, "Traditional Brand Loyalty," *Advertising Age* (May 18, 1981), Section 2, p. 52.

[23]Gage, "RSVP: An Invitation to Buy," p. 5–9.

ceeded only by Havana's; Greater Los Angeles, whose 2.1 million Hispanic population is second only to Mexico City's; and New York, whose Puerto Rican population of 1.4 million is greater than San Juan's.

In total, according to the 1980 census, 6.4 percent of the U.S. population, or 14.6 million people, reported they were of Spanish-speaking origin. In the following five states the Hispanic population represented more than 10 percent of the total population: New Mexico (36.6 percent), Texas (21 percent), California (19.2 percent), Arizona (16.2 percent), and Colorado (11.7 percent).[24]

Marketers focus on these markets in several ways. In many communities, the sign *"Aquí se habla español"* (Spanish is spoken here) is displayed in store windows. Approximately 217 television and radio stations now broadcast all or a large portion of the time in Spanish. Procter and Gamble has hired Spanish-speaking salespeople to call on the 5,000 Spanish grocery stores *(bodegas)* and 750 drugstores *(farmacias)* in New York that cater to families of Puerto Rican origin.[25] Overall, the U.S. Spanish-speaking population amounts to a market with $60 billion of purchasing power.[26]

Hispanics are probably a more heterogeneous subculture than blacks due to their variety of national backgrounds. Mexico is identified as the birthplace of 59.4 percent of the U.S. Hispanic population. Other places of origin are: Puerto Rico, 15.1 percent; Central or South America, 7.4 percent; Cuba, 5.9 percent; and other locales, 12.2 percent.[27]

Hispanic consumption of certain products is disproportionate to that of the white majority. Some specific examples are:

- Hispanics purchase 1.5 times as much beer as other population segments.
- Los Angeles Hispanics buy 5 times as much juice, 3.5 times as many baby-food products, 3 times as many cans of spaghetti, 1.8 times as many soft drinks, and 1.5 times as many bottles of shampoo than the rest of the population.

These figures reflect the fact that Hispanics typically have larger families and they dine out less than other population segments.[28] But like blacks, the most noticeable thing about Hispanic consumption patterns is their brand loyalty.[29] The Hispanic subculture, therefore, is of particular importance to marketers of national brands.

[24]U.S. Department of Commerce, Bureau of the Census, *Standard Metropolitan Statistical Areas and Standard Consolidated Statistical Areas: 1980* (PC 80-S1-5) issued October 1981.

[25]"Hispanics Push for Bigger Role in Washington," *U.S. News & World Report* (May 22, 1978), pp. 58–61. See also William G. Zikmund, "A Taxonomy of Black Shopping Behavior," *Journal of Retailing* (Spring 1971), pp. 61–72.

[26]"Learning the Hispanic Hustle," *Newsweek* (May 17, 1982), p. 83.

[27]Reported in a table in "Views from the Inside," *Advertising Age* (April 6, 1981), Section 2, p. 5–8.

[28]These statistics are reported in *U.S. News & World Report* (August 24, 1981), p. 63.

[29]"Learning the Hispanic Hustle," p. 84.

Social Influences

The second interpersonal determinant of consumer behavior is the social influences that impact purchase behavior. Children's earliest awareness is their membership in a very important group, the family. From this group they seek total satisfaction of their physiological and social needs. As they grow older, they join other groups—neighborhood play groups, school groups, Girl Scouts, Little League, and groups of friends, among others—from which they acquire both status and roles.

Status is the relative position of any individual member in the group; **roles** are what the other members of the group expect of the individual who is in any particular position within the group. Some groups (like the Boy Scouts) are formal, and others (like friendship groups) are informal. Groups of either sort supply each member with both status and roles; in doing so, they influence the member's activities.

The Asch Phenomenon

Although most persons view themselves as individuals, groups are often highly influential in purchase decisions. In situations where individuals feel that a particular group or groups are important, they tend to adhere in varying amounts to the general expectations of that group.

The surprising impact that groups and group norms can exhibit on individual behavior has been called the **Asch phenomenon.** The phenomenon was first documented in the following study conducted by psychologist S. E. Asch:

> *Eight subjects are brought into a room and asked to determine which of a set of three unequal lines is closest to the length of a fourth line shown some distance from the other three. The subjects are to announce their judgments publicly. Seven of the subjects are working for the experimenter and they announce incorrect matches. The order of announcement is arranged such that the naive subject responds last. In a control situation, 37 naive subjects performed the task 18 times each without any information about others' choices. Two of the 37 subjects made a total of 3 mistakes. However, when another group of 50 naive subjects responded* after *hearing the unanimous but* incorrect *judgment of the other group members, 37 made a total of 194 errors, all of which were in agreement with the mistake made by the group.*[30]

This widely replicated study illustrates the role of groups upon individual choice making. Marketing applications range from the choice of automobile models and residential locations to the decision to purchase at least one item at a Tupperware party.

[30]Del I. Hawkins, Kenneth A. Coney, and Roger J. Best, *Consumer Behavior: Implications for Marketing Strategy,* rev. ed. (Plano, Texas: Business Publications, 1983), p. 214. The quotation is adapted from S. E. Asch, "Effects of Group Pressure upon the Modification and Distortion of Judgments," in *Readings in Social Psychology,* (ed.) E. E. MacCoby et al. (New York: Holt, Rinehart and Winston, 1958), pp. 174–183.

Reference Groups

In order for groups to exert such influence on individuals, they must be categorized as reference groups. Groups whose value structures and standards influence a person's behavior are said to be **reference groups.** Consumers usually try to keep their purchase behavior in line with what they perceive to be the values of their reference group.

The status of the individual within the reference group produces three subcategories: **membership group,** where the person actually belongs to, say, a country club; **aspirational group,** a situation where a person desires to associate with a group; and a **disassociative group,** one which the individual does not want to be identified with by others.

Although a reference group can be a membership group, it is not essential that the individual be a member in order for the group to serve as a point of reference. This concept helps explain the use of athletes in advertisements. Even though few racing fans possess the skills necessary to power a racing car, all can identify with the Indianapolis 500 winner by injecting their engines with STP.

The extent of reference group influence varies widely. For the influence to be great, two factors must be present:

1. The item must be one that can be seen and identified by others.
2. The item must also be conspicuous; it must stand out, be unusual, and be a brand or product that not everyone owns.

Figure 7.3 shows the influence of reference groups on both the basic decision to purchase a product and the decision to purchase a particular brand. The figure shows that reference groups had a significant impact on both the decision to purchase an automobile and the type or brand that was actually selected. By contrast, reference groups had little impact on the decision to purchase canned peaches or the brand that was chosen. Figure 7.3 was derived from a survey which updated a widely cited 1956 study. The comparison shows that over time the extent of reference group influence can vary for both types of decisions.[31]

Social Classes

Although people prefer to think of the United States as the land of equality, a well-structured class system does exist. Research conducted a number of years ago by W. Lloyd Warner identified a six-class system within the social structure of both small and large cities. A description of the members of each class and an estimate of its population percentage is shown in Table 7.2.

Warner's class rankings are determined by occupation, source of income (not amount), education, family background, and dwelling area.

[31]Francis S. Bourne, *Group Influence in Marketing and Public Relations* (Ann Arbor, Mich.: Foundation for Research on Human Behavior, 1956).

Figure 7.3 Extent of Reference Group Influence on Product and Brand Decision

Weak Product Strong Brand	Strong Product Strong Brand
Magazines Furniture Clothing Instant Coffee Aspirin Air Conditioners Stereos Laundry Detergent Microwave Ovens	Automobiles Color TV
Canned Peaches Toilet Soap Beer Cigarettes Small Cigars	
Weak Product Weak Brand	**Strong Product Weak Brand**

Source: Reprinted from Donald W. Hendon, "A New and Empirical Look at the Influence of Reference Groups on Generic Product Category and Brand Choice: Evidence from Two Nations," *Proceedings of the Academy of International Business: Asia-Pacific Dimensions of International Business* (Honolulu: College of Business Administration, University of Hawaii, December 18–20, 1979), pp. 752–761. Based on Francis S. Bourne, *Group Influence in Marketing and Public Relations* (Foundation for Research on Human Behavior, 1956), p. 8.

Income is not a primary determinant; a pipefitter paid at union scale earns more than many college professors, but his or her purchase behavior may be quite different. Thus the adage "A rich man is a poor man with money" is wrong.

Richard Coleman illustrates the behavior of three families, all earning less than $35,000 a year but all in decidedly different social classes. The upper-middle-class family in this bracket—a young lawyer or college professor and family—is likely to spend its money in a prestige neighborhood, buy expensive furniture from high-quality stores, and join social clubs.

At the same time, the lower-middle-class family—headed by a grocery store owner or a sales representative—will probably purchase a good house in a less expensive neighborhood. It buys more furniture from less expensive stores and typically has a savings account at the local bank.

The lower-class family—headed by a truck driver or welder—spends less money on the house but buys one of the first new cars sold each

Table 7.2 The Warner Social Class Hierarchy

Social Class	Membership	Population Percentage[a]
Upper-upper	Locally prominent families, third- or fourth-generation wealth. Merchants, financiers, or higher-level professionals. Wealth inherited. A great amount of traveling.	1.5
Lower-upper	Newly arrived in upper class—*"nouveau riche."* Not accepted by upper class. Executive elite, founders of large businesses, doctors, lawyers.	1.5
Upper-middle	Moderately successful professionals, owners of medium-sized businesses, and middle management. Status conscious. Child- and home-centered.	10.0
Lower-middle	Top of the average world. Nonmanagerial office workers, small business owners, and blue-collar families. "Striving and respectable." Conservative.	33.0
Upper-lower	Ordinary working class. Semiskilled workers. Income often as high as the next two classes above. Enjoy life. Live from day to day.	38.0
Lower-lower	Unskilled, unemployed, and unassimilated ethnic groups. Fatalistic. Apathetic.	16.0
	Total	100.0

[a]Estimates are based on Warner and Hollings's distributions in rather small communities. However, an estimate of social class structure for the United States approximates these percentages.

Source: Adapted with permission from Charles B. McCann, *Women and Department Store Advertising* (Chicago: Social Research, 1957).

year and owns one of the largest color television sets in town. It stocks its kitchen with appliances—symbols of security.[32]

Use of the same product or service often varies among social classes. A study of commercial bank credit card holders, for example, uncovered class variations in how the cards were used. Lower-class families were more likely to use their credit cards for installment purchases, while upper-class families used them mainly for their convenience as a cash substitute.[33]

[32]See Richard P. Coleman, "The Significance of Social Stratification in Selling," and "Retrospective Comment," in (ed.) Louis E. Boone, *Classics in Consumer Behavior* (Tulsa, Okla.: PPC Books, 1977), pp. 288–302; and Richard P. Coleman and Lee Rainwater, *Social Standing in America: New Dimensions of Class* (New York: Basic Books, 1978).

[33]John W. Slocum, Jr., and H. Lee Mathews, "Social Class and Income as Indicators of Consumer Credit Behavior," *Journal of Marketing* (April 1970), pp. 69–74. See also Gillian Garcia, "Credit Cards: An Interdisciplinary Survey," *Journal of Consumer Research* (May 1980), pp. 327–337; Patrick E. Murphy, "The Effect of Social Class on Brand and Price Consciousness for Supermarket Products," *Journal of Retailing* (Summer 1978), pp. 33–45; and Harold W. Berkman and Christopher C. Gilson, "Social Class and Consumer Behavior: A Review for the 70s," *Journal of the Academy of Marketing Science* (Summer 1976), pp. 644–657.

The role of social class in determining consumer behavior continues to be a source of debate in the field of marketing.[34] Some have argued against using social class as a market segmentation variable. Others disagree as to whether income or social class is the best base for market segmentation. The findings tend to be mixed. One recent study found that social class was the superior segmentation variable for food and nonsoft drink/nonalcoholic beverage markets. Social class also influenced shopping behavior and evening television watching. Income was the superior segmentation variable for major appliances, soft drinks, mixes, and alcoholic beverages. For other categories, like clothing, a combination of the two variables was the best approach.[35]

Opinion Leaders

Each group usually contains a few members who can be considered **opinion leaders** or trend setters. These individuals are likely to purchase new products before others do and to serve as information sources for others in the group.[36]

Generalized opinion leaders are rare; instead, individuals tend to be opinion leaders for specific products and services. Their distinguishing characteristics are considerable knowledge and interest in a particular product or service. Their interest in the product motivates them to seek out information from mass media, manufacturers, and other supply sources; and, in turn, they transmit this information to their nonopinion leader associates through interpersonal communications. Opinion leaders are found within all segments of the population.

Direct, Two-Step, and Multi-Step Communication Flows

Information about products, retail outlets, and ideas flow through a number of channels. In some cases, the flows are from radio, television, and other mass media to opinion leaders, and then from opinion leaders to the masses of the population. Elihu Katz and Paul Lazarsfeld referred to this channel as the two-step process of communication.[37]

In some instances, the information flow is direct. Continuing access to communications channels allows much information to be transmitted

[34]See, for example, Luiz V. Dominquez and Albert L. Page, "Stratification in Consumer Research: A Re-Examination," *Journal of the Academy of Marketing Science* (Summer 1981), pp. 250–271; Paul S. Hugstad, "A Re-Examination of the Concept of Privilege Groups," *Journal of the Academy of Marketing Science* (Fall 1981), pp. 399–408.

[35]Charles M. Schaninger, "Social Class Versus Income Revisited: An Empirical Investigation," *Journal of Marketing Research* (May 1981), pp. 192–208.

[36]See Danny N. Bellenger and Elizabeth C. Hirschman, "Identifying Opinion Leaders by Self-Report," in *Contemporary Marketing Thought,* (eds.) Barnett A. Greenberg and Danny N. Bellenger (Chicago: American Marketing Association, 1977), pp. 341–344.

[37]Elihu Katz and Paul F. Lazarsfeld, *Personal Influence* (New York: Free Press, 1957), p. 32.

Figure 7.4 Direct, Two-Step, and Multi-Step Communication Flows

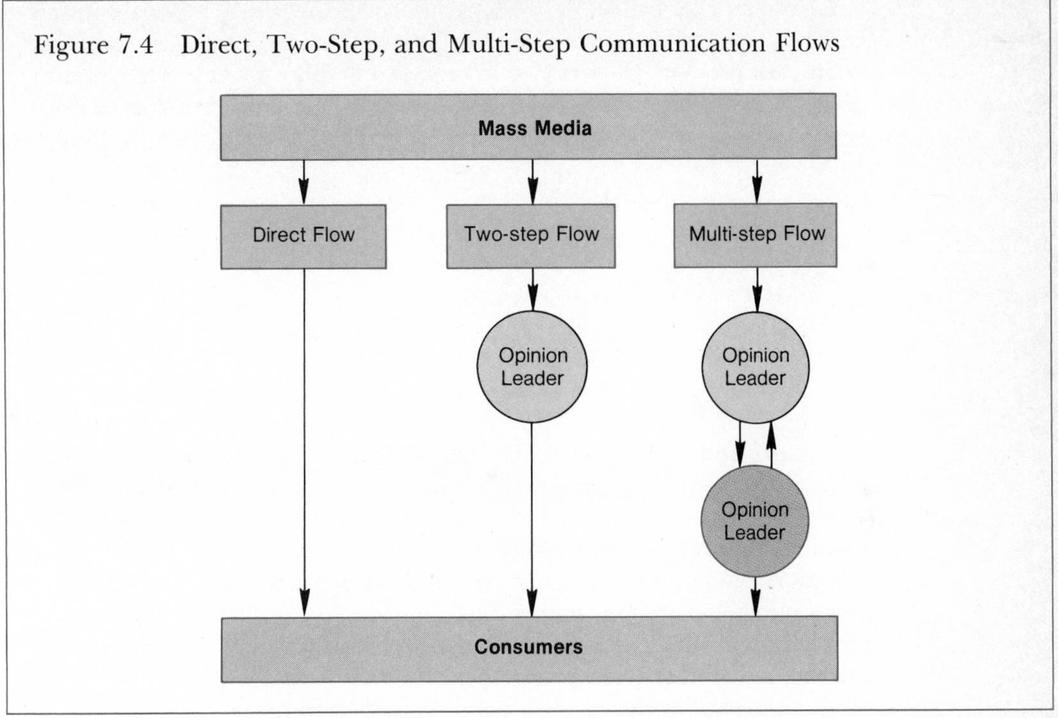

directly to individuals who represent the organization's market target with no intermediaries. Preliminary findings that indicated some success in the use of the experimental drug Interferon in treating certain types of cancer was quickly disseminated to the general public by the mass media. Researchers were forced to utilize the same channels in an attempt to dispel the public's belief that the new drug was a miracle cure.

Another possible channel for information flows is a multi-step flow. In this case, the flows are from mass media to opinion leaders then on to other opinion leaders before being disseminated to the general public. Figure 7.4 illustrates the types of communication flows.

Applying the Opinion Leadership Concept

Opinion leaders play a crucial role in interpersonal communication. The fact that they distribute information and advice to others indicates their potential importance to marketing strategy. Opinion leaders, for instance, can be particularly useful in the launch of new products.

General Motors once provided Chevettes to college marketing classes as a basis for a course project. Rock stations have painted teenagers' cars for them. Of course, the paint job includes the stations' call letters and slogans. Politicians sometimes hold issues forums for community leaders. All of these marketing efforts are directed at the opinion leaders in a particular marketplace. These people play an important role in how successful a new or established product, idea, or political candidacy is communicated to consumers.

Family Influence

One's family is also an interpersonal determinant of consumer behavior. The influence of household members is often significant in the purchase decision process. Because of the close, continuing interactions among family members, the family often represents the strongest source of group influence on the individual.

Most people are members of at least two families during their lifetimes—the family into which they are born and the one they eventually form as they marry and have children. With divorce an increasingly common phenomenon, many people end up involved with three or more families.

The establishment of a new household results in new marketing opportunities. A new household means a new house or apartment and accompanying furniture. The need for refrigerators, vacuum cleaners, and an original oil painting for the living room is dependent not on the number of persons comprising the household but on the number of households themselves.

Less than 60 percent of all U.S. households now include a married couple. The tremendous growth of single and other nonfamily households has caused the average household size to fall to 2.73 persons.[38] In fact, it is estimated that 25 percent of all households will be single-person households by 1990.[39] This suggests a tremendous future opportunity for many marketers.

Another market is established for parents who are left alone when children move away from home. These parents may find themselves with a four-bedroom residence and a half acre of lawn to maintain. Lacking maintenance assistance from their children and no longer needing the large house, they become customers for town houses, condominiums, and high-rise apartments in larger cities. Some become residents of St. Petersburg, Sun City, or other centers for retired persons.

[38] "Marriage Binds Fewer than 60% of U.S. Households," Orlando *Sentinel* (November 16, 1981), p. 6–A.

[39] Carmaron L. Smith and Beverly M. Barry, "Analyze Consumer Behavior, Social Trends to Determine Potential of New Food Products," *Marketing News* (April 6, 1982), p. 6.

Others become market targets for medical insurance, travel, and hearing aids. Designing houses specifically for senior citizens is one effort to reach that market.

Traditional Household Roles

Historically, the wife made the majority of the family purchases, and the husband worked at a paying job most of the day. Even though the preferences of the children or the husband may have influenced her decisions, the wife usually was responsible for food buying and most of the clothing purchases.

Although an infinite variety of roles can be played in household decision making, four role categories are often used: (1) autonomic—an equal number of decisions is made by each partner or the other; (2) male dominant; (3) female dominant; and (4) syncratic—most decisions are jointly made by male and female.[40] Figure 7.5 shows the roles played by household members in the purchase of a number of products.

Shifts in Family Roles

Two forces have changed the female's role as sole purchasing agent for most household items. First, a shorter work week provides each wage-earning household member with more time for shopping. Second, there are a large number of women in the work force. In 1950, only one fourth of married women were also employed outside the home; by 1981, almost 50 percent were working wives. Currently, over half of all married women with school-age children hold jobs outside the home.[41] Studies of family decision making have shown that working wives tend to exert more influence in decision making than nonworking wives. Households with two wage earners also exhibit a large number of joint decisions and an increase in night and weekend shopping.

These changing roles of household members have led many marketers to adjust their marketing programs. Saint Laurie, Ltd., which has specialized in the manufacture of men's suits since 1951, now offers

[40] James F. Engel and Roger D. Blackwell, *Consumer Behavior,* 4th ed., pp. 176–182. See also Wilson Brown, "The Family and Consumer Decision Making," *Journal of the Academy of Marketing Science* (Fall 1979), pp. 335–343.

[41] Charles M. Schaninger and Chris T. Allen, "Wife's Occupational Status as a Consumer Behavior Construct," *Journal of Consumer Research* (September 1981), pp. 189–196; Pierre Filatrault and J. R. Brent Ritchie, "Joint Purchasing Decisions: A Comparison of Influence Structure in Family and Couple Decision-Making Units," *Journal of Consumer Research* (September 1980), pp. 131–140; and Robert M. Cosenza and Duane L. Davis, "The Effect of the Wife's Working Status on Family Dominance Structure," *Journal of the Academy of Marketing Science* (Spring 1980), pp. 73–82.

Figure 7.5 Role Categories in Household Decisions

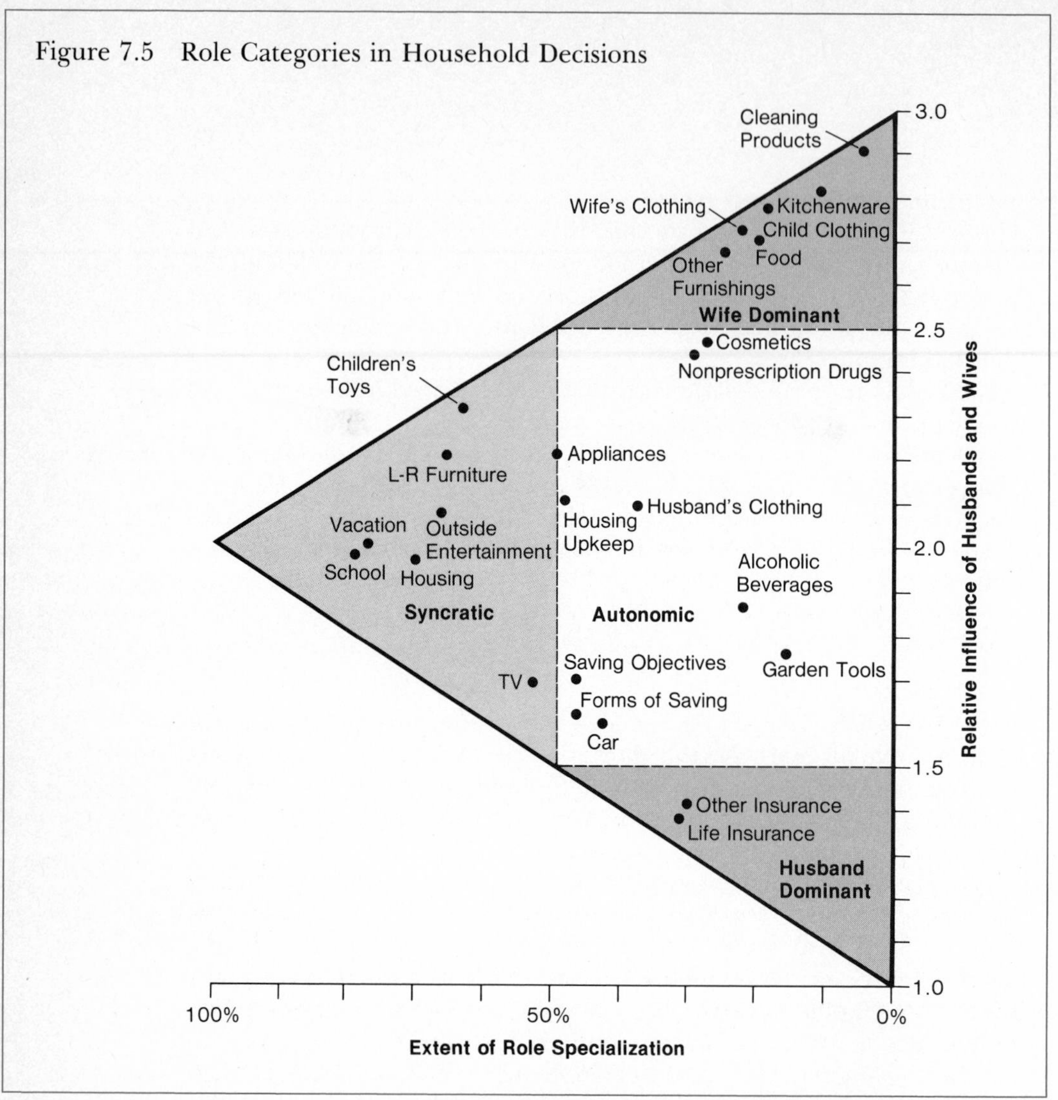

Source: Harry L. Davis and Benny P. Rigaux, "Perception of Marital Roles in Decision Processes," *Journal of Consumer Research* (June 1974), p. 57. Reprinted by permission from the *Journal of Consumer Research* published by the Journal of Consumer Research, Inc.

suits for the career woman. Although nationwide demand for men's suits has been sluggish in recent years, sales of women's suits increased 70 percent in 1980. A survey of 1,000 married men revealed that 77 percent participate in shopping and 70 percent cook. A Del Monte promotional campaign recognized these changes and deemphasized

Teenagers–The Family's New Purchasing Agent

The growing number of married and divorced mothers who work has a decided impact on household purchasing patterns. Recent research shows that both teenage boys and girls play an important role in their families' grocery purchases. According to a recent survey of 1,002 teenagers conducted by the Beta Research Corporation, 64 percent shop for food at one time or another and 36 percent shop at least once a week. Six out of ten of these teens help write the family shopping list. Forty-two percent selected what their families purchased, 18 percent chose both the product and the specific brand, while another 24 percent selected just the brand.

Only slightly more girls than boys did the shopping. The incidence of teenage shopping is nearly equal for various income levels, family makeups and market sizes. Overall, teens spend about 15 percent of the family's total food budget, averaging $24 per shopping trip.

Little advertising has been targeted at these important buyers. Research suggests that radio and magazines, not the traditional newspaper shopping sections, may be the best way to reach this audience. These young shoppers are not only a sizable part of the current market for many products, they are also the future market. Brand loyalties built now may last for decades. For instance, a Yankelovich survey showed that 29 percent of adult women still drank the same coffee they did as a teenager. The growing role of teenage shoppers is certainly an important new development in the study of consumer behavior.

Source: Mark N. Dodosh, "Widely Ignored Teen Market Has a Lot of Spending Power," *The Wall Street Journal* (June 17, 1982), p. 23; Richard Kreisman, "Teens' Role Grows in Family's Grocery Purchases," *Advertising Age* (May 17, 1982), p. 68; and an advertisement for *Seventeen* magazine that appears in *Advertising Age* (May 3, 1982), p. 33.

women as the sole meal preparer. Its theme, "Good things happen when you bring Del Monte home," is applicable to both male and female food shoppers.[42]

Children's Roles in Household Purchasing

The role of the children in purchasing evolves as they grow older. Children's early influence is generally centered around toys to be recommended to Santa Claus and the choice of cereal brands. Younger children are also important to marketers of fast-food restaurants. Even

[42] "Business Shifts Its Sales Pitch for Women," *U.S. News & World Report* (July 9, 1981), p. 46; and Margaret LeRoux, "Exec Claims Most Ads to Women Miss the Mark," *Advertising Age* (May 21, 1979), p. 24.

though the parents may decide when to eat out, the children usually select the restaurant.[43]

According to recent surveys, the country has more than 18 million teenagers who have a total buying power that approaches $35 billion a year. More than 60 percent of all teenagers have either part-time or full-time jobs in which they earn more than $624 million a week. More than 23 percent of the 12 to 19-year-old group earned more than $50 a week, 19 percent earned between $10 and $50, and 19 percent earned under $10. Over 40 percent of all teenagers also receive some form of allowance.[44]

In general, as children gain maturity, they increasingly influence their clothing purchases. One study revealed that teenage boys in the 13 to 15-year age group spend an average of $17.80 a week while teenage girls spend $19.05. Between the ages of 16 to 19, the average weekly expenditure of boys is $37.90 while girls spend $39.50. Thirteen to fifteen-year-old teenage boys spend most of their money on food, snacks, movies, and entertainment. Girls in this same age group buy clothing, food and snacks, tickets for movies and entertainment, and cosmetics and fragrances. Sixteen to nineteen-year-old boys spend most of their money on entertainment, dating, movies, automobiles and gasoline, clothing, food, and snacks while girls of the same age buy clothing, cosmetics, fragrances, automobiles and gasoline, and movie and entertainment tickets.[45]

Summary

Consumer behavior refers to the way people select, obtain, and use goods and services. Both interpersonal and personal factors determine patterns of consumer behavior, but the consumer decision process itself can be divided into six steps: problem recognition, search, evaluation, purchase decision, purchase act, and postpurchase evaluation. The consumer decision process was introduced here to provide an overall perspective. It is explained in detail at the end of Chapter 8.

There are three interpersonal determinants of consumer behavior: cultural influences, social influences, and family influences. Culture is the broadest of these three influences. Culture refers to behavioral values that are created and inherited by a society. The Protestant work ethic and the accumulation of wealth were the original determinants of

[43]George J. Szybillo, Arlene K. Sosanie, and Aaron Tenebein, "Should Children Be Seen but Not Heard?" *Journal of Advertising Research* (December 1977), pp. 7–13.

[44]"Teens with $35 Billion," *Sales & Marketing Management* (October 12, 1981), p. 20.

[45]Lester Rand, *The Rand Youth Poll,* 1981.

American culture. Cultural norms can change over time, although traditionally the pace of change is slow. However, it may occur at a faster pace in the future. An example of a recent shift in values is the desire for expanded friendship rather than self-centered activities.

Cultural influences are particularly significant in international marketing, but it is also a crucial factor in domestic marketing. Increased attention is being devoted to the consumption behavior patterns of U.S. subcultures. The two biggest American subcultures are blacks and Hispanics, both of which are growing market segments.

Social influences concern the nonfamily group influences on consumer behavior. The role that groups play in individual decision making was demonstrated by research conducted by S. E. Asch. If a group's values or standards impact individual behavior, it is said to be a reference group for that person. The importance of reference groups on specific product and brand decision varies.

Social class ranking is another social factor that influences consumer behavior. The existence of a U.S. class system was demonstrated by W. Lloyd Warner years ago. Opinion leaders or trend setters are another important social influence on consumer behavior. The reaction of these people to new products is highly influential in the future success of the good or service. Marketers must make special efforts to appeal to these flagships of consumer behavior.

Family influences are the third interpersonal determinant of consumer behavior. Family purchasing patterns vary. In some cases, the female is dominant; in others, the male. Some purchase decisions are made jointly, while in other situations, the decisions are made separately, but the number of such decisions is roughly equal between male and female. The traditional role for the female was the family's purchasing agent. This situation is now in flux, and more teenagers are doing the shopping for the household.

Chapter 7 introduced the consumer decision process and outlined the interpersonal determinants of consumer behavior. The next chapter considers the personal influences on consumer behavior and develops the earlier discussion of the consumer behavior process. Chapter 9—the last one in this part—discusses industrial and organizational purchasing behavior.

Key Terms

consumer behavior
culture
subculture
status
roles
Asch phenomenon
reference groups
membership groups
aspirational group
disassociative group
opinion leader

Review Questions

1. What are the two primary determinants of behavior according to Lewin?
2. List the steps in the consumer behavior process.
3. Explain the interpersonal determinants of consumer behavior.
4. How does culture impact buying patterns?
5. Identify and discuss the two major subcultures in U.S. society. How do their consumption patterns differ from those of other Americans?
6. Describe the Asch phenomenon.
7. Why are reference groups important in the study of consumer behavior?
8. Relate social class to consumer behavior.
9. Why are opinion leaders important to marketers?
10. Describe family influences on consumer behavior and how they are changing.

Discussion Questions and Exercises

1. Relate a recent purchase you made to the consumer decision process shown in Figure 7.1.
2. Discuss the cultural values or norms that have had the biggest impact on your purchase behavior.
3. For which of the following products is reference-group influence likely to be strong?

   a. Rolex watch
   b. Skis
   c. Shaving lather
   d. 10-speed bicycle
   e. Portable radio
   f. Cigarettes
   g. Electric blanket
   h. Contact lenses

4. Identify the opinion leaders in a group to which you belong. Why are these people the group's opinion leaders?
5. List two products for which the following family members might be most influential:

   a. Mother
   b. 6-year-old child
   c. Father
   d. Teenage son
   e. Teenage daughter
   f. 2-year-old child

8

PERSONAL INFLUENCES ON CONSUMER BEHAVIOR

Chapter Objectives

1. To relate personal influences on consumer behavior to the variables of the marketing mix.
2. To identify the personal determinants of consumer behavior.
3. To distinguish between needs and motives.
4. To explain perception.
5. To describe how attitudes influence consumer behavior.
6. To demonstrate how learning theory can be applied to marketing strategy.
7. To explain the self-concept.
8. To outline the steps in the consumer decision process.
9. To differentiate among routinized response behavior, limited problem solving, and extended problem solving.

It only took "Hackman" 7 blades and 26 minutes and 6 seconds to saw the compact car completely in half. Why did he do it? Hackman was a promotional event run by American Saw & Manufacturing Company to highlight its Lenox hacksaw blades.

The Hackman event was staged on a Saturday afternoon so employees from both shifts and their families could watch it. The company sponsored an employee contest to guess how long it would take Hackman to do his work. The event was covered by local television stations and newspapers. Hackman posters and caps were developed to promote Lenox blades. Smaller bulletins were available to dealers as mailing pieces and point-of-sale handouts.

Hackman was helpful in building employee pride in the products they make. It was also designed to promote Lenox blades to their distribution channels, specifically electrical, plumbing, and construction wholesale trades. To do this, they had to deal with the perceptions of that marketplace.

One American Saw executive put it this way: "There really isn't much excitement about a hacksaw blade. You have to try to build some." This is exactly what Hackman did. He sawed his way through the perceptual filter that buyers erect for this product. The promotion was clearly a success as sales of Lenox hacksaw blades showed a marked increase.[1]

The Conceptual Framework

Chapter 7 defined **consumer behavior** as the acts of individuals in obtaining and using goods and services, including the decision processes that precede and determine these acts.[2] The chapter introduced the concept of the consumer decision process and explained the interpersonal determinants of consumer behavior.

This chapter is a continuation of the discussion of consumer behavior. It concentrates on the personal determinants of consumer behavior such as perception which played such a big part in the Hackman event at American Saw & Manufacturing Company. The chapter concludes by re-introducing and then expanding the discussion of the consumer decision process.

Personal Determinants of Consumer Behavior

Consumer behavior is a function of both interpersonal and personal influences. Figure 8.1 shows that the personal determinants of consumer behavior operate within the framework of interpersonal influences discussed in Chapter 7. The personal determinants of consumer behavior include the individual's needs, motives, perceptions, and attitudes, and self-concept. The interaction of these factors with interpersonal influences cause the individual to act.

Needs and Motives

The starting point in the purchase decision process is the recognition of a felt need. A **need** is simply the lack of something useful. It is an imbalance between the consumer's actual and desired state. The con-

[1]Information provided by American Saw & Manufacturing Company. The quote is from *The Wall Street Journal* (December 31, 1981), p. 31.

[2]This definition is adapted from James F. Engel and Roger D. Blackwell, *Consumer Behavior*, 4th ed. (Hinsdale, Ill.: The Dryden Press, 1982), p. 9.

Figure 8.1 Personal and Interpersonal Determinants of Consumer Behavior

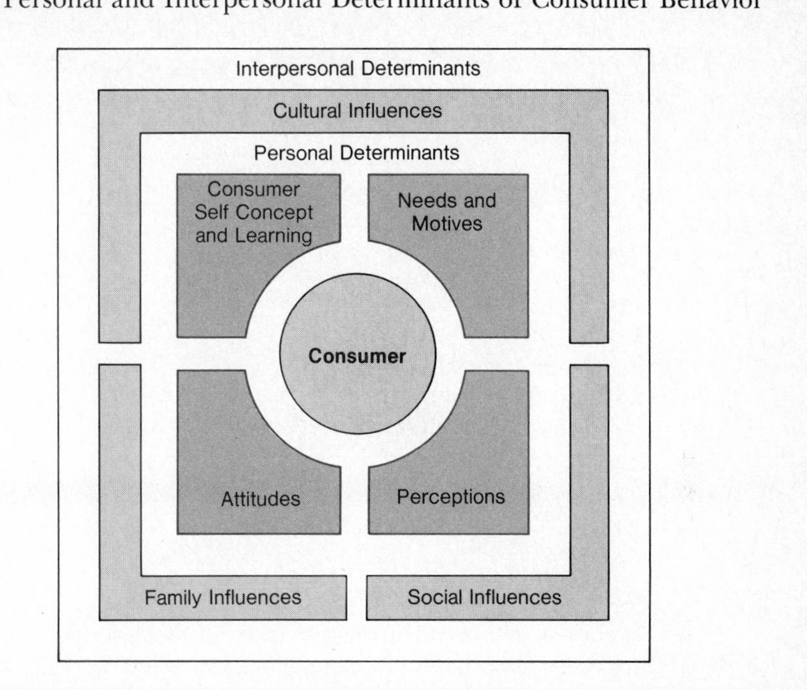

Source: C. Glenn Walters and Gordon W. Paul, *Consumer Behavior: An Integrated Framework* (Homewood, Ill.: Richard D. Irwin, 1970), p. 14 © by Richard D. Irwin, Inc. Reprinted by permission.

sumer is typically confronted with numerous unsatisfied needs, but a need must be sufficiently aroused before it can serve as a motive to buy something.

Motives are inner states that direct people toward the goal of satisfying a felt need. The individual is moved to take action to reduce a state of tension and to return to a condition of equilibrium.

Hierarchy of Needs

Although psychologists disagree on specific classifications, a useful theory of the hierarchy of needs has been developed by A. H. Maslow. Maslow's hierarchy is shown in Figure 8.2. His list is based on two important assumptions:

1. People are wanting animals, whose needs depend on what they already possess. A satisfied need is not a motivator; only those needs that have not been satisfied can influence behavior.

Figure 8.2 Hierarchy of Needs

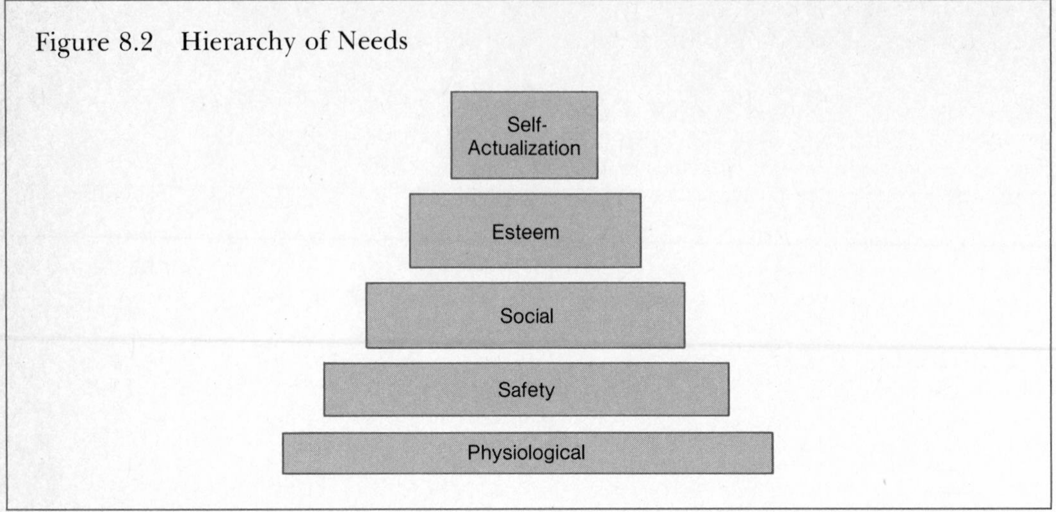

Source: Adapted from A. H. Maslow, "A Theory of Human Motivation," *Psychological Review* (July 1943), pp. 370–396.

2. People's needs are arranged in a hierarchy of importance. Once one need has been at least partially satisfied, another emerges and demands satisfaction.[3]

Physiological Needs The primary needs for food, shelter, and clothing that are present in all humans and must be satisfied before the individual can consider higher-order needs are physiological needs. Once the physiological needs are at least partially satisfied, other needs enter the picture.

Safety Needs The second-level safety needs include security, protection from physical harm, and avoidance of the unexpected. Gratification of these needs may take the form of a savings account, life insurance, the purchase of radial tires, or membership in a local health club. American Express advertisements also target this need.[4]

Social Needs Satisfaction of physiological and safety needs leads to the third level—the desire to be accepted by members of the family and other individuals and groups—the social needs. The individual may be motivated to join various groups, to conform to their standards of dress and behavior, and to become interested in obtaining status as means of

[3]A. H. Maslow, *Motivation and Personality* (New York: Harper & Row, 1954).

[4]See Robert H. Bloom, "Product Redefinition Begins with Consumer," *Advertising Age* (October 26, 1981), p. 51.

fulfilling these needs. Chapter 7 pointed out that social needs are becoming a more important cultural value for today's consumers.

Esteem Needs The higher-order needs are more prevalent in developed countries where a sufficiently high per capita income has allowed most consumers to satisfy the basic needs and to concentrate on the desire for status, esteem, and self-actualization. These needs, which are near the top of the ladder, are more difficult to satisfy. At the esteem level is the need to feel a sense of accomplishment, achievement, and respect from others. The competitive need to excel—to better the performance of others—is almost a universal human trait.

The esteem need is closely related to social needs. At this level, however, the individual desires not just acceptance but also recognition and respect. The person has a desire to stand out from the crowd in some way.

Self-Actualization Needs The top rung of the ladder of human needs is self-actualization, the need for fulfillment, for realizing one's own potential, for using one's talents and capabilities totally. Maslow defines self-actualization this way: "The healthy man is primarily motivated by his needs to develop and actualize his fullest potentialities and capabilities. What man can be, he must be."[5]

Maslow points out that a satisfied need is no longer a motivator. Once the physiological needs are satiated, the individual moves on to the higher-order needs. Consumers are periodically motivated by the need to relieve thirst or hunger, but their interests are most often directed toward satisfaction of safety, social, and other needs in the hierarchy.

Perception

Several years ago, a U.S. pharmaceutical firm developed Analoze, a cherry-flavored combination painkiller and stomach sweetener that could be taken without water. The product failed because consumers associated the ritual of taking pills and a glass of water with pain relief.[6] Analoze was not perceived as an effective remedy because it violated their experience with other pain killers.

Individual behavior resulting from motivation is affected by how stimuli are perceived. **Perception** is the meaning that each person at-

[5]A. H. Maslow, *Motivation and Personality* (New York: Harper & Row, 1954), p. 382. See also George Brooker, "The Self-Actualizing Socially Conscious Consumer," *Journal of Consumer Research* (September 1976), pp. 107–112.

[6]Burt Schorr, "The Mistakes: Many New Products Fail Despite Careful Planning, Publicity," *The Wall Street Journal* (April 5, 1961), pp. 1, 22.

tributes to incoming stimuli received through the five senses (sight, hearing, touch, taste, and smell).

Psychologists once assumed that perception was an objective phenomenon, that the individual perceived only what was there to be perceived. Only recently have researchers come to recognize that what people perceive is as much a result of what they want to perceive as of what is actually there. This does not mean that dogs may be viewed as pigeons or shopping centers as churches. A retail store stocked with well-known brand names and staffed with helpful, knowledgeable sales personnel is perceived differently from a largely self-service discount store. Dodge Colt and the BMW 320 are both automobile imports, yet they carry quite different images.

The perception of an object or event is the result of the interaction of two types of factors:

1. *Stimulus factors:* characteristics of the physical object, such as size, color, weight, or shape.
2. *Individual factors:* characteristics of the individual, including not only sensory processes but also experiences with similar items and basic motivations and expectations.

Perceptual Screens

The individual is continually bombarded with many stimuli, but most are ignored. In order to have time to function, people must respond selectively. The determination of which stimuli they do respond to is the problem of all marketers. How can the consumer's attention be gained so he or she will read the advertisement, listen to the sales representative, or react to the point-of-purchase display?

Even though studies have shown that the average consumer is exposed to more than 500 advertisements daily, most of these ads never break through people's **perceptual screens**—the perceptual filter through which messages must pass. Sometimes breakthroughs are accomplished in the printed media through large ads. Doubling the size of an ad increases its attention value by about 50 percent. Using color in newspaper ads, in contrast to the usual black and white ads, is another effective way of breaking through the reader's perceptual screen. Other methods using contrast include a large amount of white space around the printed area or using white type on a black background.

In general, the marketer seeks to make the message stand out, to make it sufficiently different from other messages that it gains the attention of the prospective customer. Menley & James Laboratories followed the practice of running hay-fever radio commercials for their Contac capsules only on days when the pollen count was above certain minimum levels. Each commercial was preceded by a live announcement of the local pollen count.

Mr. Yuk Corrects a Misperception

Marketers of potentially dangerous products take numerous precautions to keep consumers from accidentally swallowing them—from child-resistant closures to warning labels. Yet it is estimated that of the three million poison exposures that occur each year, 75 to 80 percent involve children under five years of age.

The skull and crossbones shown in the first label is the traditional symbol for poisonous products, but studies indicate that this symbol has lost most of its meaning. In fact, a group of nursery schoolchildren interpreted the label to mean "pirate food."

A new warning symbol is shown in the second label. Mr. Yuk avoids the relationship of the skull and crossbones with pirates while denoting an unpleasant taste. Symbolic representations of danger are especially important in the case of young children, who cannot read written warnings.

Currently, the Mr. Yuk symbol is used by the National Poison Center Network's (NPCN) regional and satellite poison centers in 39 states. These centers provide information and treatment to more than 110 million people and, through their public education activities, reach over 140 million Americans. Realizing that the Mr. Yuk symbol can only be effective if it is understood, the NPCN is engaged in a range of educational activities to teach children and adults exactly what the symbol means.

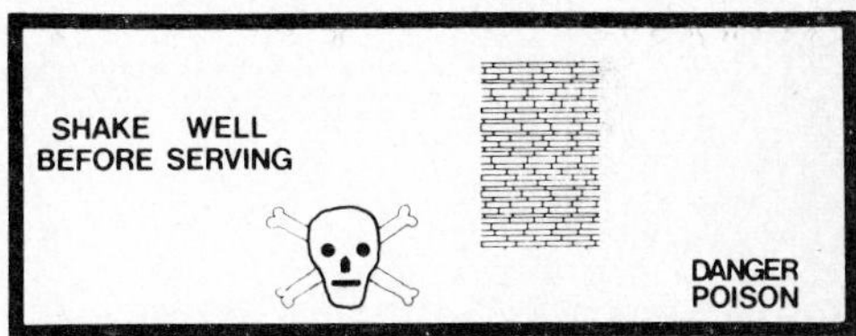

Source: Information provided from Kenneth C. Schneider, "Prevention of Accidental Poisoning Through Package and Label Design," *Journal of Consumer Research* (September 1977), pp. 67–74. The 1982 update was provided by Richard J. Garber of the National Poison Center Network. Labels reprinted by permission from *Journal of Consumer Research* published by the Journal of Consumer Research, Inc.

Selective Perception

Considerable light is shed on selective perception by considering the problem of getting consumers to try a product for the first time. The manufacturer bombards people with television and magazine advertising, sales promotion discounts and premiums, and point-of-purchase displays, often with little change in sales. Follow-up research shows that many consumers have no knowledge of the product or promotion. Why? Because this information simply never penetrated their perceptual filters. Consumers perceive incoming stimuli on a selective basis.

To a large extent they are consciously aware of only those incoming stimuli they wish to perceive.

With such selectivity at work, it is easy to see the importance of the marketer's efforts to obtain a "consumer franchise" in the form of brand loyalty to a product. Satisfied customers are less likely to seek information about competing products. Even when it is forced on them, they are not as likely as others to allow it to pass through their perceptual filters. They simply tune out information that is not in accord with their existing beliefs and expectations.

Weber's Law Impacts Perception

The relationship between the actual physical stimulus, such as size, loudness, or texture, and the corresponding sensation produced in the individual is known as psychophysics. It can be expressed as a mathematical equation:

$$\frac{\Delta I}{I} = k,$$

where

ΔI = the smallest increase in stimulus that will be noticeably different from the previous intensity

I = the intensity of the stimulus at the point where the increase takes place

k = a constant (that varies from one sense to the next).

The higher the initial intensity of a stimulus, the greater the amount of the change in intensity necessary in order for a difference to be noticed. This relationship, known as **Weber's law,** has some obvious implications in marketing. A price increase of $1,000 for a Chevrolet Citation would be readily apparent to prospective buyers; the same $1,000 increase in a Porsche 944 might seem insignificant. A large package requires a much greater increase in size for the change to be noticeable than for a small package. People perceive by exception, and the change in stimuli must be sufficiently great to gain their attention.[7]

Subliminal Perception

Is it possible to communicate with persons without them being aware of the communication? In 1957, the words *eat popcorn* and *drink Coca-Cola* were flashed on the screen of a New Jersey movie theater every

[7]Steuart Henderson Britt, "How Weber's Law Can Be Applied to Marketing," *Business Horizons* (February 1975), pp. 21–29.

five seconds at 1/300th of a second. Researchers reported that these messages, although too short to be recognizable at the conscious level, resulted in a 58 percent increase in popcorn sales and an 18 percent increase in Coca-Cola sales. After these findings were published, advertising agencies and consumer protection groups became intensely interested in **subliminal perception**—the receipt of incoming information at a subconscious level.

Subliminal advertising is aimed at the subconscious level of awareness to avoid viewers' perceptual screens. The goal of the original research was to induce consumer purchasing while keeping consumers unaware of the source of their motivation to buy. Further attempts to duplicate the test findings, however, have invariably been unsuccessful.

Although subliminal advertising has been universally condemned (and declared illegal in California and Canada), it is exceedingly unlikely that it can induce purchasing except in those instances where the person is already inclined to buy. The reasons for this are:

1. Strong stimulus factors are required to even gain attention.
2. Only a very short message can be transmitted.
3. Individuals vary greatly in their thresholds of consciousness.[8] Messages transmitted at the threshold of consciousness for one person will not be perceived at all by some people and will be all too apparent to others. The subliminally exposed message "Drink Coca-Cola" may go unseen by some viewers, while others may read it as "Drink Pepsi-Cola," "Drink Cocoa," or even "Drive Slowly."

Despite early fears, research has shown that subliminal messages cannot force the receiver to purchase goods that he or she would not consciously want.

Attitudes

Perception of incoming stimuli is greatly affected by attitudes about them. In fact, the decision to purchase a product is based on currently held attitudes about the product, the store, or the salesperson. **Attitudes** are a person's enduring favorable or unfavorable evaluations, emotional feelings, or pro or con action tendencies in regard to some object or idea. They are formed over a period of time through individual experiences and group contacts and are highly resistant to change.

[8]See James H. Myers and William H. Reynolds, *Consumer Behavior and Marketing Management* (Boston: Houghton-Mifflin, 1967), p. 14; J. Steven Kelly and Barbara M. Kessler, "Subliminal Seduction: Fact or Fantasy?" in *Proceedings of the Southern Marketing Association* (November 1978), pp. 112–114; and Joel Saegert, "Another Look at Subliminal Perception," *Journal of Advertising Research* (February 1979), pp. 55–57.

Is There a Secret Message Here?

Study the photograph carefully, paying particular attention to the reflections and shadows. Rotate the book clockwise, but stop every few degrees to restudy the drink. Now repeat the procedure by rotating the book counterclockwise. Did you see them—the hidden message, the sexual symbols, the four-letter words?

Is this a flagrant example of unethical marketing? Are hidden messages being secretly transmitted to unwary consumers, or should the secret message theory be added to a mythological category, along with Big Foot and those secret recorded messages of rock stars discernible only when records are played backwards at 16 rpm?

Author Wilson Bryan Key feels that such hidden messages do exist in print advertising. He categorizes them as attempts by unscrupulous marketers to seduce consumers into buying. In his book, *Subliminal Seduction: Secret Ways Ad Men Arouse Your Desires to Sell Their Product,* Key includes several illustrations of such "hidden persuaders" to support his theory.

Marketing authorities Harold W. Berkman and Christopher Gilson offer a much simpler explanation:

Much photography for advertising art is sent to professional retouching studios, where artists set to work correcting photographic imperfections and adding visual effects not captured by the camera. Ice cubes in ads, for example, are usually plastic ice cubes with highlights painted by retouching artists directly on the photos, since real ice cubes would melt under the hot lights of the photographer's studio. Retouchers, like most artistic people in commercial fields, want to add something of their own creativity to their work. Some find it humorous to introduce carefully disguised sexual elements to an ad that must be puritanically strait-laced for the mass market. (One such artist, according to the advertising industry grapevine, has been fired from several retouching studios for that nasty habit, but always managed to find another shop where he can continue his diabolical work.)[a]

Source: Wilson Bryan Key, *Subliminal Seduction: Secret Ways Ad Men Arouse Your Desires to Sell Their Product* (New York: Signet Books, 1975).

[a]Harold W. Berkman and Christopher Gilson, *Consumer Behavior: Concepts and Strategies* (Boston: Kent Publishing Co., 1981), p. 249.

Attitude Components

There are three related components of an attitude: cognitive, affective and behavioral. The cognitive component refers to the individual's information and knowledge about an object or concept. The affective component deals with feelings or emotional reactions. The behavioral component has to do with tendencies to act or to behave in a certain manner. In considering the decision to shop at a warehouse-type food store, the individual would obtain information from advertising, trial visits, and input from family, friends, and associates (cognitive). The consumer would also receive input from others about their acceptance of shopping at this type of store, as well as information about the type of people who shop there (affective). The shopper may ultimately decide to make some purchases of canned goods, cereal, and bakery products there, but continue to rely upon a regular supermarket for major food purchases (behavioral).

All three components exist in a relatively stable and balanced relationship to one another and combine to form an overall attitude about an object or idea. Figure 8.3 illustrates these three components.

Attitude Measurement

Since favorable attitudes are likely to be conducive to brand preferences, marketers are interested in determining consumer attitudes toward their products. Numerous attitude scaling devices have been developed, but the semantic differential is probably the most commonly used technique.[9]

The **semantic differential** is an attitude scaling device that uses bipolar adjectives, such as new-old, reliable-unreliable, sharp-bland, on a seven-point scale. The respondent evaluates the product by checking a point on the scale between the extremes. The average rankings of all respondents then become a profile of the product.

A test comparing three unidentified brands of beer produced the profiles illustrated in Figure 8.4. Brands X and Y dominated the local market and enjoyed generally favorable ratings. Brand Z, a newly introduced beer, was less well-known and received neutral reactions.

Using the information provided by the profiles, weak areas in the brands' images can be noted for remedial action. The semantic differential scale thus provides management with a more detailed picture of both the direction and the intensity of opinions and attitudes about a

[9]C. E. Osgood, G. J. Suci, and P. H. Tannenbaum, *The Measurement of Meaning* (Urbana: University of Illinois Press, 1957). For a comparison of the semantic differential with the Likert Scale and the Stapel Scale, two other widely used attitude scaling formats, see Dennis Menezies and Norbert F. Elbert, "Alternative Semantic Scaling Formats for Measuring Store Image: An Evaluation," *Journal of Marketing Research* (February 1979), pp. 80–87.

Figure 8.3 Attitude Components

Initiator

Stimuli
Products, situations, retail outlets, sales personnel, advertisements, and other attitude objects

Component

Affective

Cognitive

Behavioral

Component Manifestation

Emotions, statements of feelings about specific attributes or overall object

Beliefs, statements of nonevaluative beliefs about specific attributes or overall object

Overt Actions with respect to specific attributes, statements of behavioral intentions with respect to specific attributes or overall object

Attitude

Overall Attitude

Overall orientation toward object

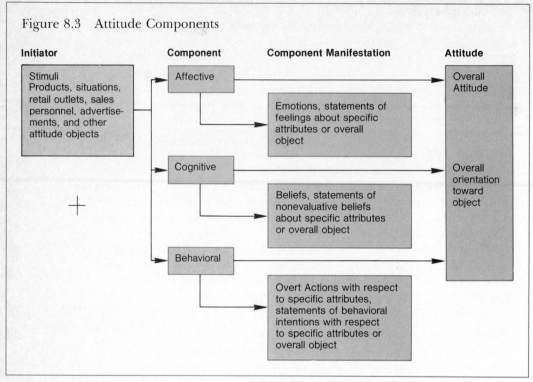

Source: Adapted from M. J. Rosenberg and C. I. Hovland, *Attitude Organization and Change* (New Haven, Conn.: Yale University Press, 1960), p. 3. Reprinted by permission.

Figure 8.4 Using the Semantic Differential to Profile Brand Images

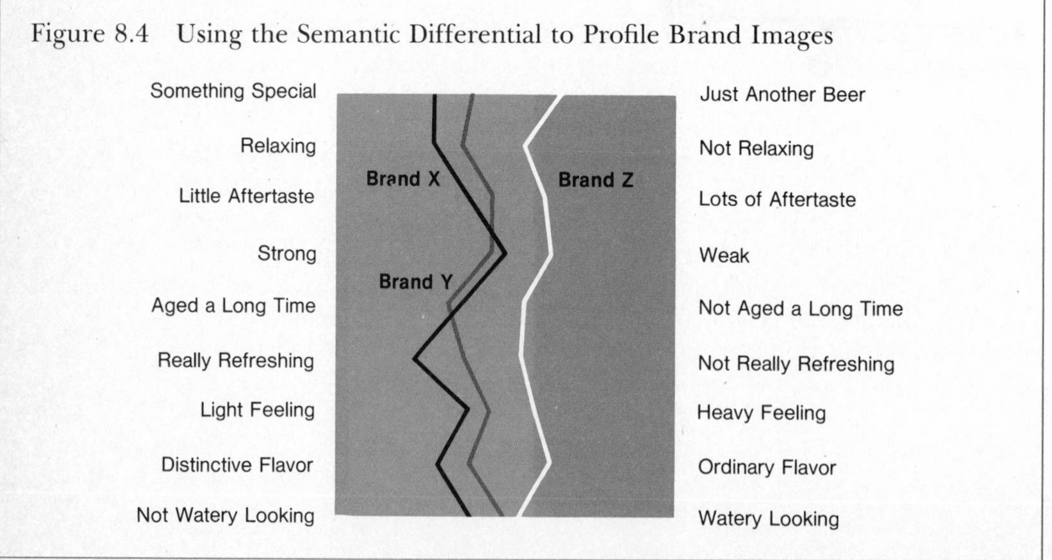

Source: Adapted from William A. Mindak, "Fitting the Semantic Differential to the Marketing Problem," *Journal of Marketing* (April 1961), pp. 28–33. Reprinted from the *Journal of Marketing* published by the American Marketing Association.

product than can be obtained through a typical research questionnaire. It supplies a comprehensive, multidimensional portrait of brand images.

Changing Consumer Attitudes

Given that a favorable consumer attitude is a prerequisite to marketing success, how can a firm lead prospective buyers to adopt this kind of attitude toward its products? The marketer has two choices: to attempt to change consumer attitudes making them consonant with the product, or to first determine consumer attitudes then change the product to match them. If consumers view the product unfavorably, the firm may choose to redesign it to better conform with their desires. It may make styling changes, vary ingredients, change package size, or switch retail stores.

The other course of action—changing consumer attitudes—is much more difficult. A famous study of coffee drinkers revealed surprisingly negative attitudes toward those who serve instant coffee. Two imaginary shopping lists, shown in Table 8.1, were shown to a sample of 100 homemakers. Half were shown List 1 and half List 2. Each respondent was then asked to describe the hypothetical shopper who purchased the groceries. The only difference in the lists was the instant versus the regular coffee.

The woman who bought instant coffee was described as lazy by 48 percent of the women evaluating List 1, but only 24 percent of those evaluating List 2 described the woman who bought regular coffee as lazy. Forty-eight percent described the instant coffee purchaser as failing to plan household purchases and schedules well; only 12 percent described the purchaser of regular coffee this way.

But consumer attitudes often change with time. The shopping list study was repeated 20 years later, and the new study revealed that much of the stigma attached to buying instant coffee had disappeared. Instead of describing the instant coffee purchaser as lazy and a poor planner, most respondents thought she was a working wife.[10] Nonetheless, General Foods took no chances when it introduced its new freeze-dried Maxim as a coffee that "tastes like regular and has the convenience of instant."

[10]Frederick E. Webster, Jr., and Frederick Von Pechmann, "A Replication of the 'Shopping List' Study," *Journal of Marketing* (April 1970), pp. 61–63. See also George S. Lane and Gayne L. Watson, "A Canadian Replication of Mason Haire's 'Shopping List' Study," *Journal of the Academy of Marketing Science* (Winter 1975), pp. 48–59.

Table 8.1 Shopping Lists Used in the Instant Coffee Study

Shopping List 1	Shopping List 2
1½ lbs. of hamburger	1½ lbs. of hamburger
2 loaves of Wonder Bread	2 loaves of Wonder Bread
Bunch of carrots	Bunch of carrots
1 can Rumford's Baking Powder	1 can Rumford's Baking Powder
Nescafé Instant Coffee	1 lb. Maxwell House coffee (drip grind)
2 cans Del Monte peaches	2 cans Del Monte peaches
5 lbs. potatoes	5 lbs. potatoes

Source: Mason Haire, "Projective Techniques in Marketing Research," *Journal of Marketing* (April 1950), pp. 649–656. Reprinted from the *Journal of Marketing* published by the American Marketing Association.

Modifying the Attitudinal Components

Attitude change frequently occurs when inconsistencies among the three attitudinal components are introduced. The most common examples of such inconsistencies are changes to the cognitive component of an attitude as a result of new information. The Pepsi Challenge was launched in an attempt to convince consumers that they preferred the taste of Pepsi, giving them new information that might lead to increased sales. The recent Life Savers advertising campaign built around the theme that a Life Saver contains only ten calories was designed to correct misconceptions in the minds of many consumers about the candy's high caloric content.

The affective component may be altered by relating the use of the new product or service to desirable consequences for the user. The growth of health clubs can be attributed to their success in promoting the benefits of being trim and physically fit.

The third alternative in attempting to change attitudes is to focus upon the behavioral component by inducing the person to engage in behavior that contradicts currently held attitudes. Attitude-discrepant behavior may occur if the consumer is given a free sample of a product. Trying the product may lead to attitude change.

Learning

Marketing is as concerned with the process by which consumer decisions change over time as with describing those decisions at any one point. Thus, the study of how learning takes place is important.[11]

[11]An interesting discussion appears in George P. Moschis, "Patterns of Consumer Learning," *Journal of the Academy of Marketing Science* (Spring 1981), pp. 110–126.

Learning refers to changes in behavior, immediate or expected, as a result of experience.

The learning process includes several components. The first component, **drive,** is any strong stimulus that impels action. Examples of drives are fear, pride, desire for money, thirst, pain avoidance, and rivalry.

The **cue,** the second component of the learning process, is any object existing in the environment that determines the nature of the response to a drive. Examples of cues are a newspaper advertisement for a new French restaurant, an in-store display, and an Exxon sign on a interstate highway. For the hungry person, the shopper seeking a particular item, or the motorist needing gasoline, these cues may result in a specific response to satisfy a drive.

A **response** is the individual's reactions to the cues and drive. Responses might include such reactions as purchasing a package of Gillette Trac II blades, dining at Burger King, or deciding to enroll at a particular college or university.

Reinforcement is the reduction in drive that results from a proper response. The more rewarding the response, the stronger the bond between the drive and the purchase of that particular product becomes. Should the purchase of Trac II blades result in closer shaves through repeated use, the likelihood of their purchase in the future is increased.

Applying Learning Theory to Marketing Decisions[12]

Learning theory has some important implications for marketing strategists. A desired outcome like repeat purchase behavior has to be developed gradually. **Shaping** is the process of applying a series of rewards and reinforcement so that more complex behavior can evolve over time. Both promotional strategy and the product itself play a role in the shaping process.

Figure 8.5 shows the application of learning theory and shaping procedures to a typical marketing scenario. Assume that marketers were attempting to motivate consumers to become regular buyers of a certain product. An initial product trial is induced by a free sample package that includes a substantial discount coupon on a subsequent purchase. This illustrates the use of a cue as a shaping procedure. The purchase response is reinforced by satisfactory product performance and a coupon for the next purchase.

The second stage is to entice the consumer to buy the product with little financial risk. The large discount coupon enclosed in the free sample prompts such an action. The package that is purchased has a

[12]This section is based on Michael L. Rothschild and William C. Gaidis, "Behavioral Learning Theory: Its Relevance to Marketing and Promotion," *Journal of Marketing* (Spring 1981), pp. 70–78.

Figure 8.5 Application of Learning Theory and Shaping Procedure to Marketing

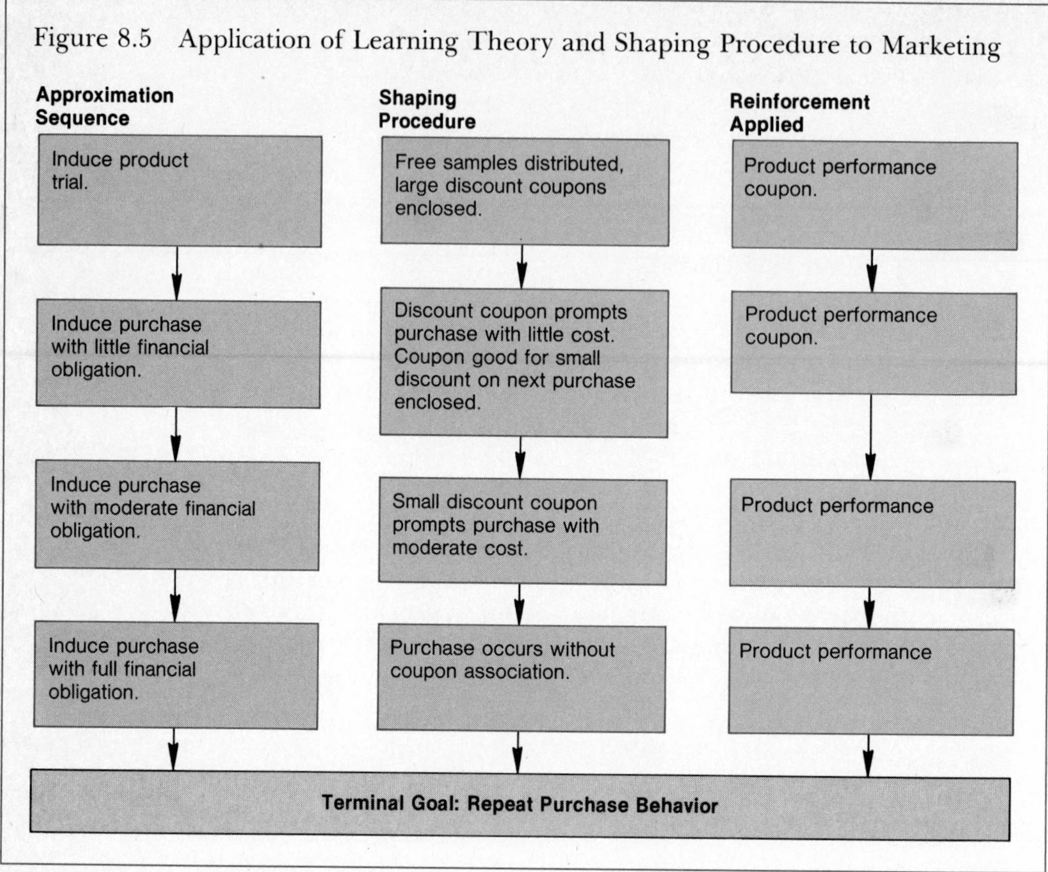
Approximation Sequence
Induce product trial.
Induce purchase with little financial obligation.
Induce purchase with moderate financial obligation.
Induce purchase with full financial obligation.
Shaping Procedure
Free samples distributed, large discount coupons enclosed.
Discount coupon prompts purchase with little cost. Coupon good for small discount on next purchase enclosed.
Small discount coupon prompts purchase with moderate cost.
Purchase occurs without coupon association.
Reinforcement Applied
Product performance coupon.
Product performance coupon.
Product performance
Product performance
Terminal Goal: Repeat Purchase Behavior

Source: Adapted from Michael L. Rothschild and William C. Gaidis, "Behavioral Learning Theory: Its Relevance to Marketing and Promotions," *Journal of Marketing* (Spring 1981), p. 72.

smaller discount coupon enclosed. Again, the reinforcement is satisfactory product performance and the second coupon.

The third step would be to motivate the person to buy the item again at a moderate cost. The discount coupon accomplishes this objective, but this time there is no additional coupon in the package. The only reinforcement is satisfactory product performance.

The final test comes when the consumer is asked to buy the product at its true price without a discount coupon. Satisfaction with product performance is the only continuing reinforcement. Thus, repeat purchase behavior has been literally shaped by effective application of learning theory within a marketing strategy context.

Kellogg's introduction of its Nutri-Grain brand sugarless whole grain cereal illustrates the use of learning theory. Coupons worth 40 cents off—about a third of the product's cost—were distributed to elicit trial purchases by consumers. Inside boxes of the new cereal were additional cents-off coupons of lesser value.[13] Kellogg was clearly trying to shape future purchase behavior.

Self-Concept Theory

The consumer's self-concept plays an important role in consumer behavior. Individuals are physical and mental entities possessing multifaceted pictures of themselves. One young man, for example, may view himself as intellectual, self-assured, moderately talented, and a rising young business executive. People's actions, including their purchase decisions, are related to their mental conception of self—their **self-concept.** The response to direct questions like "Why do you buy Senchal?" is likely to reflect this desired self-image.[14]

The concept of self is the result of the interaction of many of the influences—both personal and interpersonal—affecting buyer behavior. Individual needs, motives, perception, attitudes, and learning lie at the core of an individual's conception of self. So also do the environmental factors of family, social, and cultural influences.

As Figure 8.6 indicates, the self has four components: real self, self-image, looking-glass self, and ideal self. The real self is an objective view of the total person. The self-image, the way individuals view themselves, may distort the objective view. The looking-glass self, the way individuals think others see them, may also be quite different from self-image, since people often choose to project a different image to others. The ideal self serves as a personal set of objectives, since it is the image to which the individual aspires.

In purchasing goods and services, people are likely to choose products that move them closer to their ideal self-image. Those who see themselves as scholars are more likely than others to join literary book clubs. The young woman who views herself as a budding tennis star may become engrossed in evaluating the merits of graphite versus steel rackets and may view any cheaply made imports with disdain. The college graduate on the way up the organization ladder at a bank may hide a love for bowling and instead take up golf, having determined that golf is the sport for bankers.

[13]John Koten, "For Kellogg, the Hardest Part Is Getting People Out of Bed," *The Wall Street Journal* (May 27, 1982), p. 27.

[14]See Corbett Gaulden, "Self and Ideal Self Images and Purchase Intentions," in *Proceedings of the Southern Marketing Association,* (eds.) Robert S. Franz, Robert M. Hopkins and Alfred G. Toma (New Orleans, La., November 1978); and Terrence V. O'Brien, Humberto S. Tapia, and Thomas L. Brown, "The Self Concept in Buyer Behavior," *Business Horizons* (October 1977), pp. 65–74.

Figure 8.6 Self-Concept Theory Components

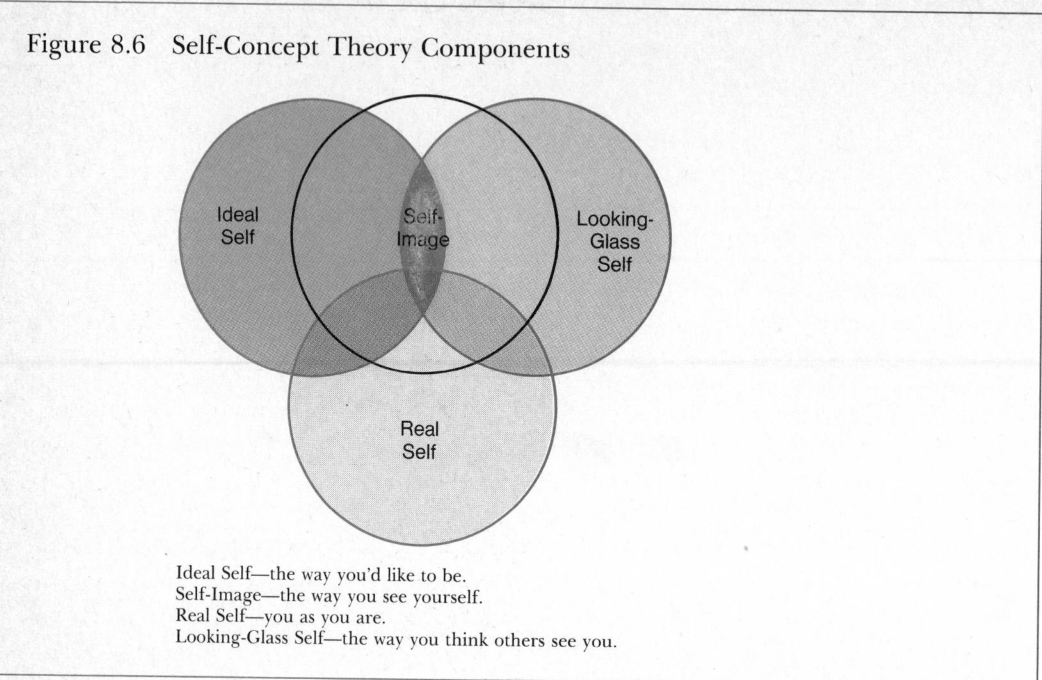

Ideal Self—the way you'd like to be.
Self-Image—the way you see yourself.
Real Self—you as you are.
Looking-Glass Self—the way you think others see you.

Source: John Douglas, George A. Field, and Lawrence X. Tarpey, *Human Behavior in Marketing* (Columbus, Ohio: Charles E. Merrill Publishing Co., 1967), p. 65. Reprinted by permission.

The Consumer Decision Process

Chapter 7 introduced a schematic model of the consumer decision process. It is reproduced here as Figure 8.7. The model contains six stages: problem recognition, search, evaluation of alternatives, the purchase decision, the purchase act, and postpurchase evaluation.

Consumer behavior research traditionally has focused on such specific areas as attitudes, personality, and the influence of reference groups on the individual. To see these fragments in their proper perspective, a model of the entire process is required. This model makes possible the integration of the various components of consumer behavior and assists in understanding the complex relationships among them. It also provides a means of integrating new research findings in the search for a more complete explanation of why consumers behave as they do. The total model approach can be used in major buying situations, such as a first-time purchase of a new product or the purchase of a high-priced, long-lived article. By contrast, it can also be applied to cases of routine purchases handled by the individual in a largely habitual manner, such as the purchase of a newspaper or a particular brand of chewing gum.

Benchwarmer Bob for Twin City Federal Savings & Loan

Many advertisements direct appeals at a person's ideal self or what the individual aspires to in life. But not Benchwarmer Bob! It all started back in 1973 when Twin City Federal Savings & Loan decided to spoof commercials featuring athletes. The savings and loan association believed that some of the Minnesota Vikings were charging excessive fees for work in commercials, so it set out to find an antihero. They looked for an unattractive benchwarmer with a funny name.

A Viking second-stringer, 6-foot 6-inch, 255-pound Bob Lurtsema was selected. In the commercial, Lurtsema plays a not-too-bright character who is always on the losing end of a joke. One of the commercials shows "Bob Lurtsema Day" at an empty stadium. Lurtsema says, "You'd think at least my wife and kids would show up." In another commercial, he lamented the fact that no one knew him with or without his helmet.

The commercials have actually made Lurtsema one of the best-known personalities in Minnesota. The savings and loan even continued the commercials after he was traded to Seattle and later retired. Lurtsema explains his success this way: "So few people truly make it that the majority of people in life are second-stringers."

Maybe so, but Lurtsema, who now gets $50,000 annually for his commercials, probably would not want his fans to know that he was a first-stringer with the Seattle Seahawks and the New York Giants.

Source: Laurence Ingrassia, "Tired of Those Star Athlete Ads? Then Listen to Benchwarmer Bob," *The Wall Street Journal* (January 12, 1982), p. 25.

Both personal and interpersonal influences act on the individual to create a recognition that a consumer behavior exists. This recognition triggers the consumer decision process. The steps of this process are outlined below.

Problem Recognition

The first stage in the decision process occurs when the consumer becomes aware of a discrepancy of sufficient magnitude between the existing state of affairs and a desired state of affairs. Once the problem has been recognized, it must be defined in order that the consumer may seek out methods for its solution. As a consequence of problem recognition, the individual is motivated to achieve the desired state.

Perhaps the most common cause of problem recognition is a routine depletion of the individual's stock of products. A large number of consumer purchases involve the replenishment of items ranging from gasoline to groceries. In other instances, the consumer may possess an inadequate assortment of products. The individual whose hobby is

Figure 8.7 Steps in the Consumer Decision Process

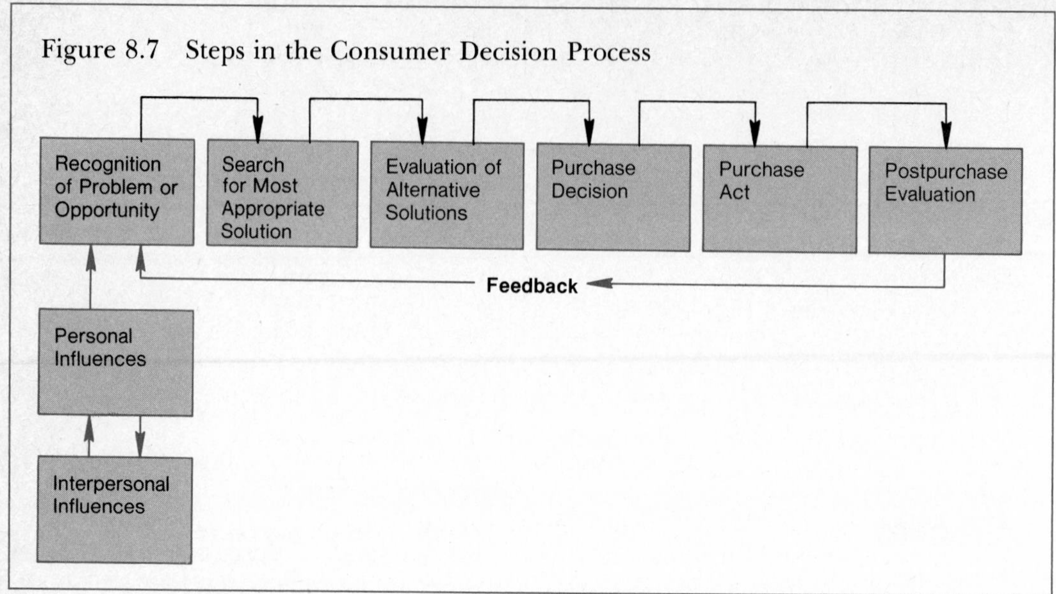

Source: Adapted from C. Glenn Walters and Gordon W. Paul, *Consumer Behavior: An Integrated Framework* (Homewood, Ill.: Richard D. Irwin, Inc., 1970), p. 18 © 1970 by Richard D. Irwin, Inc. and John Dewey, *How We Think* (Boston, Mass.: D. C. Heath, 1910), pp. 101–105. Similar steps are also discussed in Del I. Hawkins, Roger J. Best, and Kenneth A. Coney, *Consumer Behavior: Implications for Marketing Strategy*, revised ed. (Plano, Texas: Business Publications, Inc., 1983), pp. 447–606.

gardening may make regular purchases of different fertilizers, seeds, or gardening tools as the size of the garden grows.

A third cause of problem recognition is dissatisfaction with the consumer's present brand or product type. This situation is common in the purchase of a new automobile, new furniture, or a new fall wardrobe. In many instances, the consumer's boredom with current products and a desire for novelty may be the underlying rationale for the decision process leading to new product purchases.

Another important factor in problem recognition is changed financial status. The infusion of added financial resources from such sources as a salary increase, a second job, or an inheritance may permit the consumer to make purchases that previously had been postponed.

Search

The second step in the decision process is search, the gathering of information related to the attainment of a desired state of affairs. This stage permits the identification of alternative means of problem solution.

Search may be internal or external. Internal search is a mental review of stored information relevant to the problem situation. This includes both actual experiences and observations plus memories of personal communications and exposures to persuasive marketing efforts.

External search is the gathering of information from outside sources by the consumer who is involved in the search process. Outside information sources may include family members, friends and associates, store displays, sales representatives, brochures, and such product-testing publications as *Consumer Reports.*

In many instances, problems are solved by the consumer through internal search. The individual merely relies upon stored information in making a purchase decision. Achieving favorable results using Du Pont's Rain Dance car polish may sufficiently motivate a consumer to repurchase this brand rather than to consider possible alternatives. Since external search involves both time and effort, the consumer will rely upon it only in instances in which adequate information is unavailable in memory.

Alternative brands for consideration and possible purchase are identified during the search process. The number of brands that a consumer actually considers in making a purchase decision is known as the **evoked set.** In some instances, the consumer is aware of the brands worthy of further consideration; in other situations, the external search process involves the acquisition of information necessary to permit the consumer to identify those brands that comprise the evoked set. Not all brands are included in the evoked set. In some instances, the consumer is unaware of certain brands. Other brands are rejected as too costly. Still others have been tried previously and considered unsatisfactory. In other instances, unfavorable word-of-mouth communication or negative reactions to advertising or other marketing efforts result in the elimination of some brands from the evoked set. While the number of brands in the evoked set will vary by product categories, research indicates that the number is likely to be as few as four or five brands.[15]

Evaluation of Alternatives

The third step in the consumer decision process involves the evaluation of alternatives identified during the search process. Actually, it is difficult to completely separate the second and third steps since some evaluation takes place simultaneously with the search process as consumers accept, discount, distort, or reject some incoming information as they receive it.

Since the outcome of the evaluation stage is the choice of a brand or product in the evoked set (or, possibly, the search for additional alternatives should all alternatives identified during the search process prove unsatisfactory), the consumer must develop a set of evaluative criteria for use in making the selection. **Evaluative criteria** may be defined as those features the consumer considers in making a choice

[15]B. M. Campbell, "The Existence of Evoked Set and Determinants of Its Magnitude in Brand Choice Behavior," in *Buyer Behavior: Theoretical and Empirical Foundations,* (eds.) John A. Howard and Lonnie Ostrom (New York: Alfred A. Knopf, Inc., 1973), pp. 243–244.

among alternatives. These criteria can either be objective (federal government automobile engine tests of miles per gallon or comparison of retail prices) or subjective (favorable image of Calvin Klein sportswear). Commonly used evaluative criteria include price, reputation of the brand, perceived quality, packaging, size, performance, durability, and color. Evaluative criteria for detergents include suds level and smell as indicators of cleaning power. Most research studies indicate that consumers utilize six or fewer criteria in the evaluation process.[16]

The Purchase Decision and the Purchase Act

The end result of the search and alternative evaluation stages of the decision process is the actual purchase decision and the act of making the purchase. The consumer has evaluated each of the alternatives in the evoked set utilizing his or her personal set of evaluative criteria and narrowed the alternatives to one.

Another decision facing the consumer is the purchase location. Consumers tend to make store choice decisions by considering such factors as location, prices, assortment, store personnel, store image, physical design, and services provided. In addition, the store selected will be influenced by the product category. In other instances, some consumers will choose the convenience of in-home shopping via telephone or mail order rather than complete the transaction in a retail store.[17]

Postpurchase Evaluation

The purchase act results in satisfaction to the buyer and removal of the discrepancy between the existing state and the desired state or dissatisfaction with the purchase. It is also common for consumers to experience some postpurchase anxieties. Leon Festinger refers to the postpurchase doubt as **cognitive dissonance.**[18]

Dissonance is a psychologically unpleasant state that occurs when an imbalance exists among a person's *cognitions* (knowledge, beliefs, and attitudes). Consumers may, for example, experience dissonance after choosing a particular automobile over several alternative models, when several of the rejected models have some desired features not available with the chosen model.

Dissonance is likely to increase (1) as the dollar value of the purchase increases, (2) when the rejected alternatives have desirable features not present in the chosen alternative, and (3) when the decision is a major one. The consumer may attempt to reduce dissonance in a variety of ways. He or she may seek out advertisements and other information

[16]Engel and Blackwell, *Consumer Behavior,* 4th ed., p. 418.

[17]For a thorough discussion of purchase location, see David L. Loudon and Albert J. Della Bitta, *Consumer Behavior: Concepts and Applications* (New York: McGraw-Hill, 1979), pp. 483–511.

[18]Leon Festinger, *A Theory of Cognitive Dissonance* (Stanford, Calif.: Stanford University Press, 1958), p. 3.

supporting the chosen alternative or seek reassurance from acquaintances who are satisfied purchasers of the product. The individual may also avoid information favoring the unchosen alternative. The Toyota purchaser is likely to read Toyota advertisements and to avoid Nissan and Volkswagen ads. The cigarette smoker may ignore the magazine articles reporting links between smoking and cancer.

Marketers can assist in reducing cognitive dissonance by providing informational support for the chosen alternative. Automobile dealers recognize "buyer's remorse" and often follow up purchases with a warm letter from the president of the dealership, who offers personal handling of any customer problems and includes a description of the product's quality and the availability of convenient, top-quality service.[19]

A final method of dealing with cognitive dissonance is for the consumer to change opinions, thereby restoring the cognitive balance. In this instance, the consumer may ultimately decide that one of the rejected alternatives would have been the best choice and may decide to purchase it in the future.[20]

Should the purchase prove unsatisfactory, the consumer's purchase strategy must be revised to allow need satisfaction to be obtained. Whether satisfactory or not, feedback on the results of the decision process will serve as experience to be called upon in similar buying situations in the future.

Classifying Consumer Problem-Solving Processes

The consumer decision process varies on the basis of the problem-solving effort that is required. There are three categories of problem-solving behavior: routinized response behavior, limited problem solving, and extended problem solving.[21] The classification of a particular purchase according to this framework clearly impacts the consumer decision process.

Routinized Response Behavior Many purchases are made on the basis of a preferred brand or selection from a limited group of acceptable brands. This type of rapid consumer problem solving is referred to as

[19]An interesting discussion appears in Pradeep K. Korgaonkar and Ravi Parameswaran, "Product Involvement, Cognitive Dissonance and Product Satisfaction: An Experimental Study," in *Developments in Marketing Science,* (eds.) Vinay Kothari, Danny Arnold, Tamer Cavusgil, Jay D. Lindquist, Jay Nathan, and Stan Reid, *Proceedings of the Academy of Marketing Science* 1982, pp. 87–91.

[20]See Robert J. Connole, James D. Benson, and Inder P. Khera, "Cognitive Dissonance among Innovators," *Journal of the Academy of Marketing Science* (Winter 1977), pp. 9–20; David R. Lambert, Ronald J. Dornoff, and Jerome B. Kernan, "The Industrial Buyer and Postchoice Evaluation Process," *Journal of Marketing Research* (May 1977), pp. 246–251; and William H. Cummings and M. Venkatesan, "Cognitive Dissonance and Consumer Behavior: A Review of the Evidence," *Journal of Marketing Research* (August 1976), pp. 303–308.

[21]These categories were originally suggested in John A. Howard, *Marketing Management: Analysis and Planning* (Homewood, Ill.: Richard D. Irwin, 1963). The discussion here is based on Donald R. Lehmann, William L. Moore, and Terry Elrod, "The Development of Distinct Choice Process Segments over Time: A Stochastic Modeling Approach," *Journal of Marketing* (Spring 1982), pp. 48–50.

routinized response behavior. The evaluative criteria are set and the available options identified. External search is limited in cases of routinized response behavior. The routine purchase of regular brands of beer, cigarettes, or soft drinks would be examples.

Limited Problem Solving Consider the situation where the consumer has set evaluative criteria but encounters a new, unknown brand. The introduction of a new fragrance line would be an example of a limited problem-solving situation. The consumer knows the evaluative criteria but has not assessed the new brand on the basis of these criteria. A medium amount of time and external search is involved in such situations. Limited problem solving is affected by the multitude of evaluative criteria and brands, the extent of external search, and the process by which preferences are determined.

Extended Problem Solving Analoze, a product described earlier in the chapter, was not clearly classified by consumers. Extended problem solving results from such situations where the brand is difficult to categorize or evaluate. The first step is to compare the item with similar ones such as Analoze was compared to other painkillers. The consumer needs to understand the item itself before evaluating alternatives. In the case of Analoze, the evaluation was negative. Most extended problem-solving efforts are lengthy, involving considerable external search.

Regardless of the type of problem solving, the steps in the basic model of the consumer decision process remain valid. The problem-solving categories described here relate only to the time and effort that is devoted to each step in the process.

Summary

Consumer behavior is a function of both interpersonal and personal influences. Chapter 8 identifies the personal determinants of consumer behavior as needs, motives, perception, attitudes, and self-concept. Learning theory also plays a role in consumer buying processes.

A need is the lack of something useful, while motives are the inner states that direct individuals to satisfy such needs. A. H. Maslow proposed a hierarchy of needs that started with basic physiological needs and proceeded to progressively higher levels of needs—safety, social, esteem and self-actualization. Perception is the meaning that people assign to incoming stimuli received through the five senses. Most of these stimuli are screened or filtered out, so the marketer's task is to break through these screens to effectively present the sales message. Attitudes are a person's evaluations and feelings toward an object or idea. There are three components of attitudes: cognitive (what the person knows), affective (what the person feels about something), and behavioral (how the person tends to act). Learning refers to changes in behavior, immediate or expected, as a result of experience. The learning theory concept can be useful in building a consumer franchise for a particular brand. The self-concept refers to an individual's conception of self. Self-concept theory has important implications for marketing strategy, such as in the case of targeting advertising messages.

The consumer decision process consists of six stages: problem recognition, search, evaluation of alternatives, the purchase decision, the purchase act, and postpurchase evaluation. The process varies on the basis of the problem-solving effort that is required. Routinized response behavior, limited problem solving, and extended problem solving are the three categories of problem-solving behavior.

Chapter 8 was a sequel to the previous chapter. It covered the personal determinants of consumer behavior and completed the discussion of the consumer decision process introduced in Chapter 7. The interpersonal determinants of consumer behavior were also explained in the previous chapter. Part Three concludes with Chapter 9 on industrial and organizational buying behavior.

Key Terms

consumer behavior
need
motives
perception
perceptual screen
Weber's law
subliminal perception
attitudes
semantic differential
learning
drive
cue
response
reinforcement
shaping
self-concept
evoked set
evaluative criteria
cognitive dissonance

Review Questions

1. What are the personal determinants of consumer behavior?
2. How do needs and motives influence consumer behavior?
3. Explain the concept of perception. Consider perceptual screens, selective perception, Weber's Law, and subliminal perception in your explanation.
4. How do attitudes influence consumer behavior? How can negative attitudes be changed?
5. Describe the steps that occur in learning.
6. How can learning theory be applied to marketing strategy?
7. Differentiate among the four components of the self-concept: ideal self, looking-glass self, self-image, and real self.

8. Outline the steps in the consumer decision process.
9. Describe internal and external research.
10. Differentiate among routinized response behavior, limited problem solving, and extended problem solving.

Discussion Questions and Exercises

1. Based on Maslow's hierarchy, which needs are being referred to in the following advertising slogans:
   - "No caffeine. Never had it. Never will." (7-Up)
   - "Where a man belongs." (Camel cigarettes)
   - "The most beautiful summer evenings start with Red." (Johnnie Walker Red Label Scotch)
   - "Don't leave home without it." (American Express Card)
2. Poll your friends about subliminal perception. How many believe that marketers can control consumers at a subconscious level? Report the results of this survey to your marketing class.
3. Find other examples of shaping procedures being used in marketing applications.
4. Outline your own ideal self, looking-glass self, self-image, and real self.
5. Select a recent shopping experience. Then analyze your attitudes related to your consumer behavior in this instance. Be sure your assessment considers all three components of an attitude.

Chapter Objectives

1. To relate buying behavior in industrial and government markets to the variables of the marketing mix.
2. To differentiate among the three types of industrial markets.
3. To identify the three distinctive features of industrial markets.
4. To explain the characteristics of industrial market demand.
5. To identify the basic categories of industrial products.
6. To discuss the nature of the industrial purchase.
7. To outline the classification system for industrial purchasing situations: straight rebuy; modified rebuy; and new task buying.
8. To explain the buying center concept.
9. To explain the steps in the industrial purchasing process.
10. To explain how government markets differ from other markets.

9

BUYER BEHAVIOR IN INDUSTRIAL AND GOVERNMENT MARKETS

"With a name like Smucker's, it has to be good!" This amusing slogan, coupled with a sound marketing program for its jellies and preserves, has made the J.M. Smucker Company a successful, well-known firm to its customers. The firm has been equally successful in the industrial market. Smucker's produces filling bases that are used by other manufacturers in such products as yogurt and bakery items. The tasks involved in marketing strawberry preserves to ultimate consumers is significantly different from the tasks of marketing a related strawberry filling to a yogurt manufacturer.

In marketing its jellies and preserves to the consumer market, the J.M. Smucker Company engages in the classic marketing tasks of identifying market targets and developing an appropriate marketing mix. Each new product to be sold in retail food outlets is carefully developed, tested, and targeted for specifically chosen consumer segments. A company sales force calls on larger accounts, while independent middlemen make calls on retail and wholesale channel members. Promotional programs are designed to stimulate consumer demand and to provide incentives for retailers to handle Smucker's products. Pricing decisions reflect cost, prices of competitors, and consumer demand. All areas of marketing strategy are included in the Smucker's plan.

A radically different marketing program is used in the industrial segment. The market consists of manufacturers who might use Smucker's products in the goods they produce. Smucker's products will lose their identity in the manufacturing process as they are blended into such forms as cakes, cookies, or yogurt.

Once a potential industrial customer is identified, a Smucker's sales representative calls on the account. In some instances, the initial contact is with top management. More typically, the early contacts are with the individual in charge of research and development. Early discussions typically center on specifications for the texture and composition of the required goods.

These specifications are provided to the research and development division at Smucker's and samples are developed. The samples are then supplied to the potential customer who may request further modifications. It is not uncommon for a period of months to pass and a series of modifications to occur before a mixture is finally approved. Next, the attention turns to price, and the salesperson's contact point shifts to the purchasing department. Since large quantities are involved (truckloads or drums rather than jars), a few cents per pound can be significant to both parties. Quality and service are also major criteria in the decision.

Once a contract has been signed, the product is shipped directly from the Smucker's warehouse to the manufacturer's plant. The salesperson follows up frequently with the purchasing agent and the plant manager. The ultimate sales for Smucker's depend upon both the manufacturer's satisfaction with Smucker's products and on the performance of the manufacturer's product in the marketplace.[1]

The Conceptual Framework

Smucker's is a good illustration of a firm that operates in both consumer and industrial markets. Chapter 4 defined the **consumer market** as those individuals who purchase goods and services for personal use. By contrast, the **industrial market** consists of those individuals and or-

[1]Michael D. Hutt and Thomas W. Speh, *Industrial Marketing Management* (Hinsdale, Ill.: The Dryden Press, 1981), pp. 7–8. Copyright © 1981 CBS College Publishing. Adapted by permission of The Dryden Press, CBS College Publishing.

ganizations who acquire goods and services to be used, directly or indirectly, in the production of other goods and services or to be resold to governments, retailers, wholesalers, or other producers. Although industrial marketers face decisions very similar to those of their consumer-market counterparts, important differences do exist in both the characteristics of market targets and in development of appropriate marketing mixes. Professor James D. Hlavacek recognized the differences between the two markets when he noted, "Overall, the strategic and tactical emphasis and elements in the industrial and consumer marketing mixes are as different as silicon chips and potato chips."[2]

The first two chapters in Part Three have dealt with the buying behaviors that exist in consumer markets. Attention now shifts to the industrial market. Chapter 9 examines buying behavior in industrial and government markets. This chapter concludes the section on consumer behavior. The next part of the text considers the product aspect of the marketing mix including a comprehensive classification system for industrial products.

Types of Industrial Markets

The industrial market can be divided into three categories: producers, trade industries (wholesalers and retailers), and governments. **Producers** are industrial customers who purchase goods and services for the production of other goods and services. A United Airlines purchase of the new fuel-efficient Boeing 767 plane, a wheat purchase by General Mills for its cereals, and the purchase of light bulbs and cleaning materials for an Owens-Illinois manufacturing facility all represent industrial purchases by producers. Some products aid in producing another product or service (the new plane); others are physically used up in the production of a product (the wheat); and still others are routinely used in the day-to-day operations of the firm (the maintenance items). Producers include manufacturing firms; farmers and other resource industries; construction contractors; providers of such services as transportation, public utilities, and banks; and nonprofit organizations.

Trade industries are organizations such as retailers and wholesalers that purchase for resale to others. In most instances, resale products, such as clothing, appliances, sports equipment, and automobile parts, are finished goods that are marketed to customers in the selling firm's market area. In other instances, some processing or repackaging may take place. Retail meat markets may make bulk purchases of sides of beef and convert them into individual cuts for their customers. Lumber dealers and carpet retailers may purchase in bulk, then provide quan-

[2]James D. Hlavacek, "Business Schools Need More Industrial Marketing," *Marketing News* (April 4, 1980), p. 1.

tities and sizes to meet customers' specifications. In addition to resale products, trade industries also buy cash registers, computers, display equipment, and other products required to operate their business. These products (as well as maintenance items and the purchase of such specialized services as marketing research studies, accounting services, and consulting) all represent industrial purchases. Retailing and wholesaling activities are discussed in separate chapters later in the text.

Governments at the federal, state, and local level represent the final category of industrial purchasers. This important component of the industrial market purchases a wide variety of products, ranging from highways to education to F–16 fighter aircraft. The primary motivation of government purchasing is to provide some form of public benefit such as national defense, education, or public welfare. Buying behavior in government markets is discussed separately in this chapter because of the immense size and importance of this marketplace.

Scope of Industrial Markets

The scope of the three industrial markets is shown in Table 9.1. Over 16.5 million organizations employ more than 111 million workers. Producers account for approximately 80 percent of the total number of industrial organizations and two thirds of total employment. However, differences may occur among the three categories. For example, there are five times as many retail establishments as manufacturers.

Distinctive Features of the Industrial Markets

The industrial market has three distinctive features: geographic market concentration, a relatively small number of buyers, and a unique classification system called SIC codes.

Geographic Market Concentration

The industrial goods market in the United States is much more concentrated geographically than is the consumer goods market. Figure 9.1 shows the concentration in eastern states like New Jersey, New York, and Pennsylvania; Sunbelt states like California, North Carolina, and Texas; and the Great Lakes states of Illinois, Indiana, Michigan, and Ohio. These ten states accounted for 57 percent of the $1.9 billion in manufacturing shipments during 1981.[3]

[3]Thayer C. Taylor, "Providing the Answers to Market-Planning Problems," *Sales & Marketing Management* (April 26, 1982), p. 8. Data from Sales & Marketing Management's 1982 Survey of Industrial Purchasing Power.

Table 9.1 The Scope of the Three Industrial Markets

Category	Number of Organizations (1979 data)	Number of Employees (1981 data)
Producers		
Agriculture, Forestry, Fisheries	3,970,000	3,518,000
Mining	149,000	1,118,000
Construction	1,422,000	6,060,000
Manufacturing	503,000	21,817,000
Transportation, Communication, and Other Public Utilities	539,000	6,633,000
Finance, Insurance, Real Estate	2,106,000	6,133,000
Services	4,496,000	29,360,000
Total	13,185,000	74,639,000
Trade Industries		
Wholesaling Establishments	613,000	4,016,000
Retailers	2,664,000	16,508,000
Total	3,277,000	20,524,000
Governments		
Federal Government	1	2,772,000
State and Local Governments	82,687*	13,253,000
Total	82,688	16,025,000
Overall Totals	16,544,688	111,188,000

*1982 data.

Source: U.S. Bureau of the Census, *Statistical Abstract of the United States: 1982–1983*, 103d ed. (Washington, D.C.: U.S. Government Printing Office, 1982), pp. 273, 390, 398, 529.

Small Number of Buyers

In addition to geographic concentration, the industrial market has a limited number of buyers. Even though factories with 20 or more employees represent one third of the total number of U.S. manufacturing establishments, they produce 95 percent of total industry output.[4] Figure 9.2 shows the number of production facilities in each region according to the most recent Census of Manufactures. The industrial growth of the Sunbelt region is reflected in the fact that the Southeast, with 69,558 industrial prospects (plants) leads the Great Lakes region. Only the Mideast contains a greater number of manufacturing facilities than this emerging industrial market. The Rocky Mountain and Far West regions experienced the largest increases in new plants during the five-year period since the last census with gains of 32.4 percent and

[4]*Ibid*, p. 8.

Figure 9.1 The Geographical Location of U.S. Manufacturers

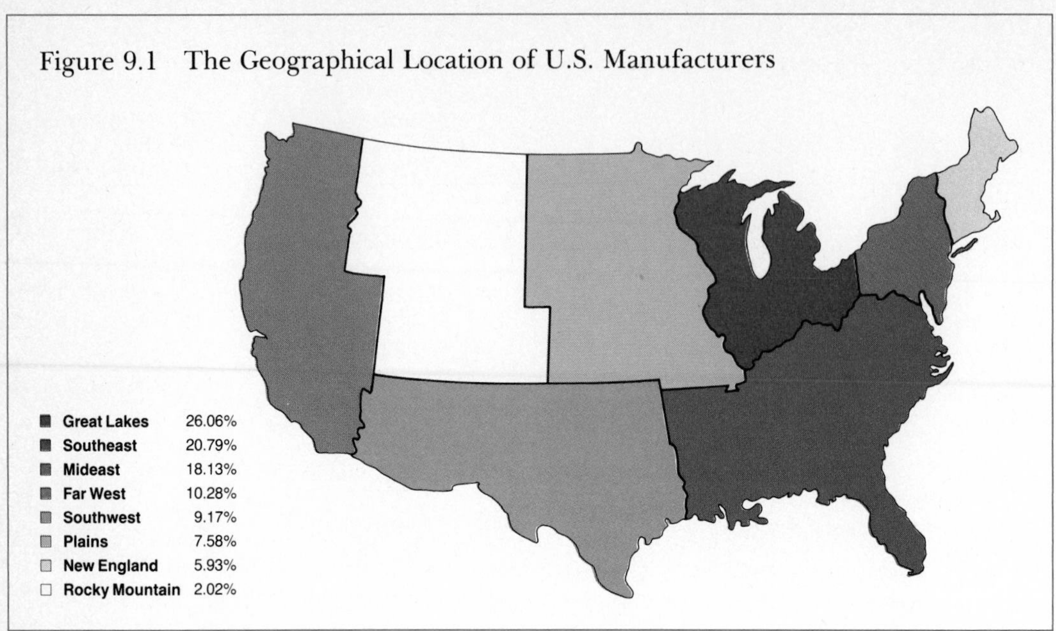

Source: Thayer C. Taylor, "Providing the Answer to Market-Planning Problems," *Sales & Marketing Management* (April 26, 1982), p. 9. Data source: Sales & Marketing Management's 1982 Survey of Industrial Purchasing Power. © Sales & Marketing Management.

26.6 percent, respectively. The Mideast region posted a slight decline in the number of production facilities.

Individual industries also have a limited number of buyers. Four companies produce the U.S. automobile output. The aircraft industry is concentrated in Seattle, Wichita, Kansas, Burbank, California, and Marietta, Georgia; it is comprised of only 119 manufacturing facilities. All U.S. production of cigarettes takes place in only 12 plants.[5]

The concentration of the industrial market greatly influences the marketing strategy used in serving it. Industrial marketers usually can make profitable use of a sales force to provide regular personal contacts with a small, geographically concentrated market. Wholesalers are less frequently used, and the marketing channel for industrial goods is typically much shorter than for consumer goods. Advertising also plays a much smaller role in the industrial goods market. It is used primarily as an aid to personal selling and to enhance the reputation of the firm and its products and services.

Standard Industrial Classification (SIC) Codes

Marketers are aided in their efforts to reach these geographically concentrated and limited number of industrial buyers by a wealth of statis-

[5]Some of this data is from *Ibid,* p. 12.

Figure 9.2 Regional Differences and Growth Rates in Production Facilities

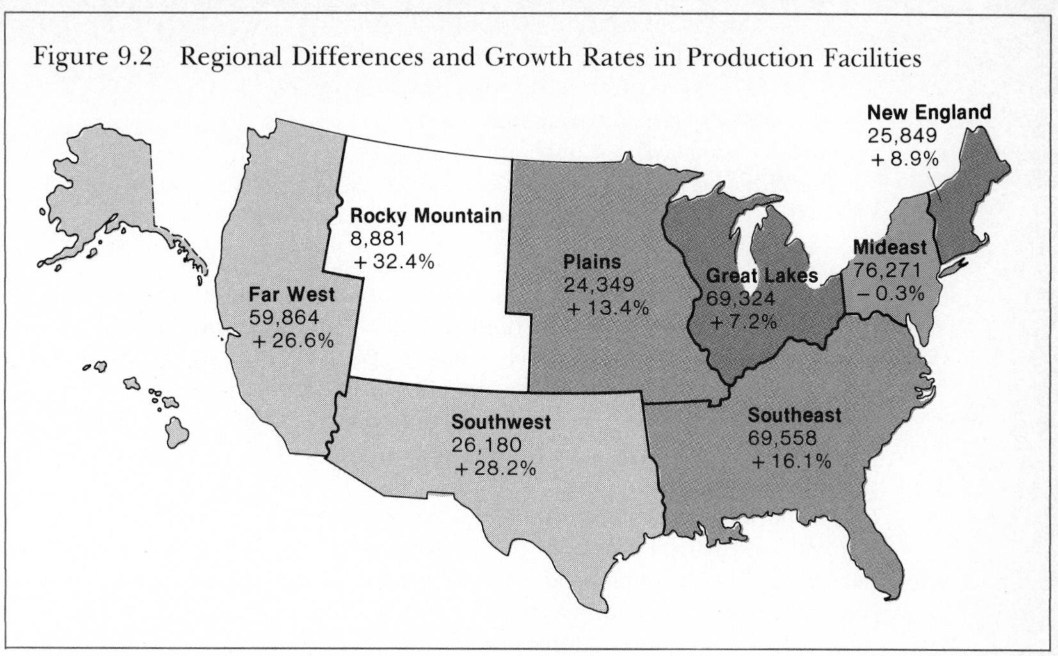

Note: Figures indicate the number of plants in each region and the percentage change in total number of plants for the five-year period between the 1972 and 1977 Census of Manufactures.

Source: Sales & Marketing Management calculations; Census Bureau, *1977 Census of Manufactures: Selected Statistics for States: MC77-S-2 (P),* and individual state reports in the geographic area series. Used by permission of Sales & Marketing Management.

tical information. The federal government is the largest single source of information. Every five years it conducts a Census of Manufactures as well as a Census of Retailing and Wholesaling, which provide detailed information on industrial establishments, output, and employment. Specific industry studies are summarized in the annual U.S. Industrial Outlook, a government publication providing statistical data and discussing industry trends.

Trade associations and business publications provide additional information on the industrial market. Private firms such as Dun & Bradstreet publish detailed reports on individual firms. These data serve as useful starting points for analyzing industrial markets.

The federal government's **Standard Industrial Classification (SIC)** system greatly simplifies the process of focusing on an industrial market target. This numerical system subdivides the industrial marketplace into more detailed product/service industries or market segments. The SIC codes are divided into ten broad industry groups, into which all types of organizations can be classified:

01–09 Agriculture, Forestry, Fishing
10–14 Mining

15–17 Contract Construction
20–39 Manufacturing
40–49 Transportation and Other Public Utilities
50–59 Wholesale and Retail Trade
60–67 Finance, Insurance, and Real Estate
70–89 Services
91–97 Government—Federal, State, Local, International
99 Others

Each major industry within these classifications is assigned its own two-digit number; three and four-digit numbers subdivide the industry into smaller segments. For example, a major group such as the food industry is assigned SIC 20. A specific three-digit industry such as dairy products is SIC 202. The next category, specific industries, would use the fourth digit. Creamery butter, for example, is SIC 2021 and fluid milk is SIC 2026.[6]

In the most recent Census of Manufactures, the Census Bureau assembled industrial data at two additional levels: five-digit product classes and seven-digit product or commodity categories. Figure 9.3 illustrates the classification system and the detail in which data is available. The detailed breakdowns that are possible with the SIC codes provide an excellent base for industrial market segmentation. The SIC categories can be used in market target decision analysis to select targeted segments of the industrial market.

Since most published data on industrial markets utilize the SIC system, the SIC codes are invaluable tools in analyzing the industrial marketplace. The information for each market segment provides the marketer with a comprehensive description of the activities of his or her potential customers on both a geographical and a specific industry basis.

Industrial Market Demand Characteristics

Considerable differences exist in the marketing of consumer and industrial products. Gillette's Paper Mate division had long been a successful provider of medium-priced ball-point pens to consumer markets, but this market is increasingly divided into low and premium-priced segments. Paper Mate decided to come out with new offerings at both ends of the price spectrum.

The firm also decided to enter the office supplies field—an industrial market. It established a special commercial sales force to promote its

[6]"What Is This Thing Called SIC?" *Sales & Marketing Management* (April 27, 1981), pp. 26–27.

Figure 9.3 The Standard Industrial Classification

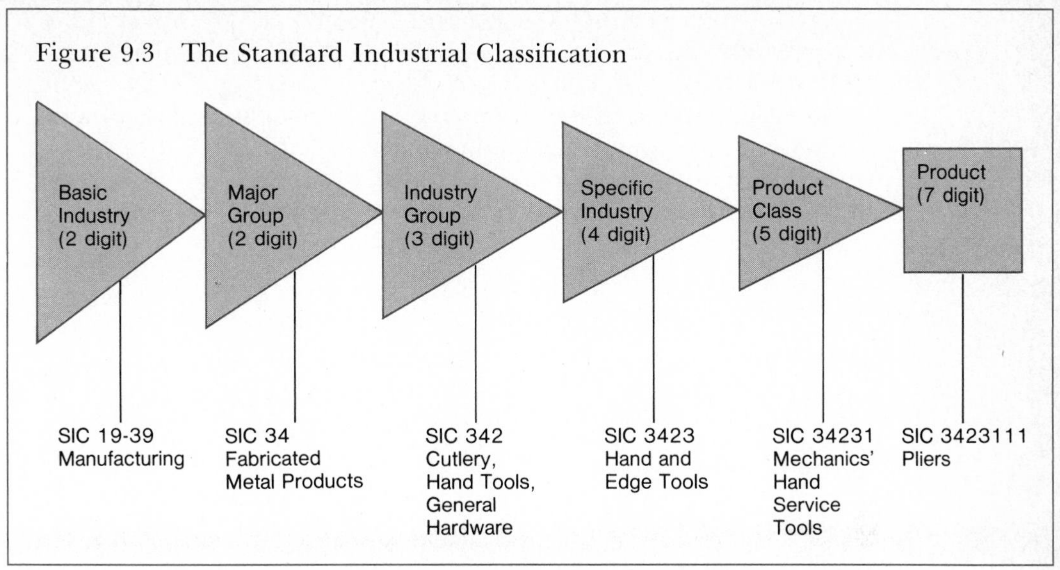

Source: Michael D. Hutt and Thomas W. Speh, *Industrial Marketing Management* (Hinsdale, Ill.: The Dryden Press, 1981), p. 105. Copyright © 1981 CBS College Publishing. Reprinted by permission of The Dryden Press, CBS College Publishing.

pens to industrial buyers. Paper Mate also acquired Liquid Paper Corp., an established name in the office-supplier field. Liquid Paper's industrial marketing strengths are seen as complementing the consumer market in which Paper Mate has specialized.[7] Gillette marketers clearly recognized that the industrial marketplace was different from the consumer markets in which they had traditionally competed. The unique characteristics of industrial settings require that marketing strategies be tailored to the special requirements of this marketplace.

What are the primary characteristics of industrial market demand? Most lists would include the following: derived demand, joint demand, inventory adjustments, and demand variability.[8]

Derived Demand

The term **derived demand** refers to the linkage between desires to make industrial purchases and the desires of customers for the firm's output. For example, the demand for cash registers (an industrial good)

[7] "Paper Mate's Broader Outlook," *Business Week* (January 28, 1980), p. 69.

[8] These characteristics are suggested in Robert W. Haas, *Industrial Marketing Management* (New York: Petrocelli/Charter, 1976), pp. 21–26; and Richard M. Hill, Ralph S. Alexander, and James S. Cross, *Industrial Marketing*, 4th ed. (Homewood, Ill.: Richard D. Irwin, 1975), pp. 46–47.

is partially derived from demand at the retail level (consumer products). Increased retail sales may ultimately result in greater demand for cash registers.

On the other hand, the "down-sizing" of automobile engines by auto manufacturers in an attempt to develop smaller, fuel-efficient cars adversely affects spark-plug manufacturers like Champion. Since the four-cylinder engines use half as many plugs as V-8s, Champion's total sales may decline drastically unless total auto sales increase dramatically, or unless Champion can increase its share of the total market.

Joint Demand

The demand for some industrial products is related to the demand for other industrial goods to be used jointly with the first item, a concept known as **joint demand.** Coke and iron ore are required to make pig iron. If the coke supply is reduced, there will be an immediate effect on the demand for iron ore. Petroleum

Inventory Adjustments

Changes in inventory policy can have an impact on industrial demand. A two-month supply of raw materials is often considered the optimal inventory in some manufacturing industries.[9] Suppose economic conditions or other factors dictate that this level be increased to a 90-day supply. The raw materials supplier would then be bombarded with a tremendous increase in new orders. Thus, inventory adjustments can be a major determinant of industrial demand.

Demand Variability

Derived demand in the industrial market is linked to immense variability in industrial demand. Assume the demand for Industrial Product A is derived from the demand for Consumer Product B—an item whose sales volume has been growing at an annual rate of 10 percent. Now suppose that the demand for Product B slowed to a 5 percent annual increase. Management might decide to delay further purchases of Product A, using existing inventory until market conditions were clarified. Therefore, even modest shifts in the demand for Product B greatly affect Product A's demand. The disproportionate impact that changes in consumer demand has upon industrial market demand is called the *accelerator principle.*

[9]The 60-day figure is suggested in Bob Luke, "Purchasing Agents: Supply Sergeants to the Business World," *Detroit News* (May 20, 1979), p. 2–E.

Basic Categories of Industrial Products

There are two general categories of industrial products: capital items and expense items. **Capital items** are long-lived business assets that must be depreciated over time. *Depreciation* is the accounting concept of charging a portion of a capital item as a deduction against the company's annual revenue for purposes of determining its net income. Examples of capital items include major installations like new plants and office buildings as well as equipment. The Economic Recovery Tax Act of 1981 divided capital items into four groups with depreciation periods of three, five, ten, and fifteen years respectively. Machinery, for example, is in the five-year category, meaning that its cost is depreciated over a five-year period.[10]

Expense items, by contrast, are products and services that are used within a short period of time. For the most part, they are charged against income in the year of purchase. Examples of expense items include the supplies that are used in operating the business, ranging from paper clips to machine lubricants.

Chapter 10 presents a comprehensive classification of industrial products. The initial breakdown of capital and expense items is useful because buying behavior varies significantly depending upon how a purchase is treated from an accounting viewpoint. Expense items may be bought routinely and with minimal delay, while capital items involve major fund commitments and are thus subject to considerable review by the purchaser's personnel. Differences in industrial purchasing behavior are discussed in the sections that follow.

The Nature of the Industrial Purchase

Industrial purchase behavior tends to be more complex than the consumer decision process described in Chapters 7 and 8. There are several reasons for this increased complexity:

1. Many persons may exert influence in industrial purchases, and considerable time may be spent in obtaining the input and approval of various organizational members.
2. Organizational purchasing may be handled by committees with greater time requirements for majority or unanimous approval.
3. Many organizations attempt to utilize several sources of supply as a type of insurance against shortages.

[10]See Stuart A. Smith and Janet R. Spragens, *How You Can Get the Most from the New Tax Law* (New York: Bantam Books, 1981), pp. 99–100.

Most industrial firms have attempted to systematize their purchases by employing a professional consumer—the industrial purchasing manager. These technically qualified professional buyers are responsible for handling most of the organization's purchases and for securing needed products at the best possible price. Unlike the ultimate consumer who makes periodic purchase decisions, a firm's purchasing department devotes all its time and effort to determining needs, locating and evaluating alternative sources of supply, and making purchase decisions.

The Complexity of Industrial Purchases

Where major purchases are involved, negotiations may take several weeks or even months, and the buying decisions may rest with a number of persons in the organization. The choice of a supplier for industrial drill presses, for example, may be made jointly by the purchasing agent and the company's production, engineering, and maintenance departments. Each of these principals may have a different point of view to be taken into account in making a purchase decision. As a result, representatives of the selling firm must be well versed in the technical aspects of the product or service and be capable of interacting with managers of the various departments involved in the purchase decision. In the transportation equipment industry, for instance, it takes an average of 4.9 face-to-face presentations to make a sale. The average cost of closing the sale—including salesperson compensation and travel and entertainment expenses—is $1,121.02. Table 9.2 shows the average number of sales calls required to complete a sale in several industries and the average cost of each sale.

Many industrial products are purchased for long periods of time on a contractual basis. Manufacturing operations require a continuous supply of materials, and one- or two-year contracts with suppliers ensure this steady supply. Other industrial goods, such as conveyors, forklifts, and typewriters, generally last several years before replacement is necessary.[11]

Purchase decisions frequently are made on the basis of service, certainty of supply, and efficiency of the supplied products. These factors must be considered along with the prices quoted for the products.

Automobile manufacturers purchase batteries, glass windows, spark plugs, and steel as ingredients for their output. Since demand for these items is derived from the demand for consumer goods, most price changes do not substantially affect their sale. For example, price in-

[11]Alvin J. Williams, "Fast Complaint Response Should Help Develop Long-Term Marketing Issue," *Marketing News* (May 1, 1981), Section 2, p. 8.

Table 9.2 Calls and Costs Needed to Close a Sale

Industry	Average Number of Calls to Close a Sale	Average Cost to Close a Sale[a]
Food and Kindred Products	2.6	$ 229.16
Furniture and Fixtures	3.8	388.20
Paper and Allied Products	4.7	597.22
Petroleum/Refining and Related Industries	4.0	360.56
Primary Metal Industries	3.9	465.89
Transportation Equipment	4.9	1,121.02
Transportation by Air	4.1	265.68
Business Services	5.6	800.01
Automotive Repair, Services and Garages	5.0	488.00

[a]Determined by multiplying the average number of calls to close a sale by the average cost per sales call for each industry.

Source: "Industrial Sales Call Tops $137, but New 'Cost to Close' Hits $589," *Marketing News* (May 1, 1981), p. 1. Used by permission of the American Marketing Association.

creases for paint have little effect on auto sales at Ford because paint represents only a minute portion of an automobile's total cost of manufacture.

The Scenario for a Typical Industrial Purchase of a Capital Item

The manufacturer of a reinforced fiberglass utility light pole faced a complicated decision process that involved the members of several departments and months of negotiations before a sale could be made. The new pole has several advantages over the traditional steel, wood, or aluminum pole: lightweight, nonelectrical conducting and noncorrosive properties, and the fact that it never needs painting while meeting strength requirements. Its major disadvantage, other than purchaser unfamiliarity, is its high initial purchase price compared to the metal alternatives. The decision process began with the manager of the utility company. Next, the utility's purchasing department manager was contacted who, in turn, contacted the engineering head. After a list of alternative suppliers and materials was prepared by purchasing and approved by engineering, the purchasing manager then discussed the organization's needs with salespeople representing three suppliers. The salespeople met with the managers of the stores department, the marketing department, and the engineering department. After a series of meetings with the salespeople and numerous discussions among the utility's various department heads, a decision was made to submit the new fiberglass pole to a test conducted by the engineering department. The results of the test were reported to the various department heads. Bids were then requested from Suppliers A, B, and C. These bids were reviewed by the department heads, who ultimately decided to select the new fiberglass pole offered by Supplier B. This complex decision process is diagrammed in Figure 9.4.[12]

Classifying Industrial Purchasing Situations

Industrial buying behavior is affected by situational variables. Industrial purchase decisions vary in terms of the degree of effort and involvement by different levels within the organization. There are three generally recognized industrial purchasing situations: straight rebuy, modified rebuy, and new task buying.[13]

Straight Rebuy

A **straight rebuy** is a recurring purchase decision where an item that has performed satisfactorily is purchased again by a customer. This industrial buying situation occurs when a purchaser is pleased with the good or service and the terms of sale are acceptable. The buyer sees little reason to assess other options, so the purchaser follows some routine buying format.

Low-cost products like paper clips and number 2 pencils for an office would be typical examples. If the purchaser is pleased with the products and their prices and terms, future purchases will probably be treated as a straight rebuy from the current vendor. Even expensive items especially designed for a customer's needs can be treated as a straight rebuy in some cases. For example, the Department of Defense is committed to buying about 7000 M–1 Abrams tanks from General Dynamics. This is an expensive product specifically designed to replace the M–60 as the main U.S. battle tank.

Marketers facing straight rebuy situations should concentrate on maintaining good relations with the buyer by maintaining adequate service and the like. Competitors are faced with the difficult task of presenting a unique sales proposal that will break this chain of repurchases.

[12]The development of the new type of pole and the problems involved in its adoption are described in Arch G. Woodside, "Marketing Anatomy of Buying Process Can Help Improve Industrial Strategy," *Marketing News* (May 1, 1981), Section 2, p. 11.

[13]These are suggested in Patrick J. Robinson, Charles W. Farris, and Yoram Wind, *Industrial Buying and Creative Marketing* (Boston: Allyn and Bacon, 1967), Chapter 1. The discussion here follows Hutt and Speh, *Industrial Marketing Management*, pp. 51–55.

Figure 9.4 The Decision to Purchase a New Type of Utility Pole

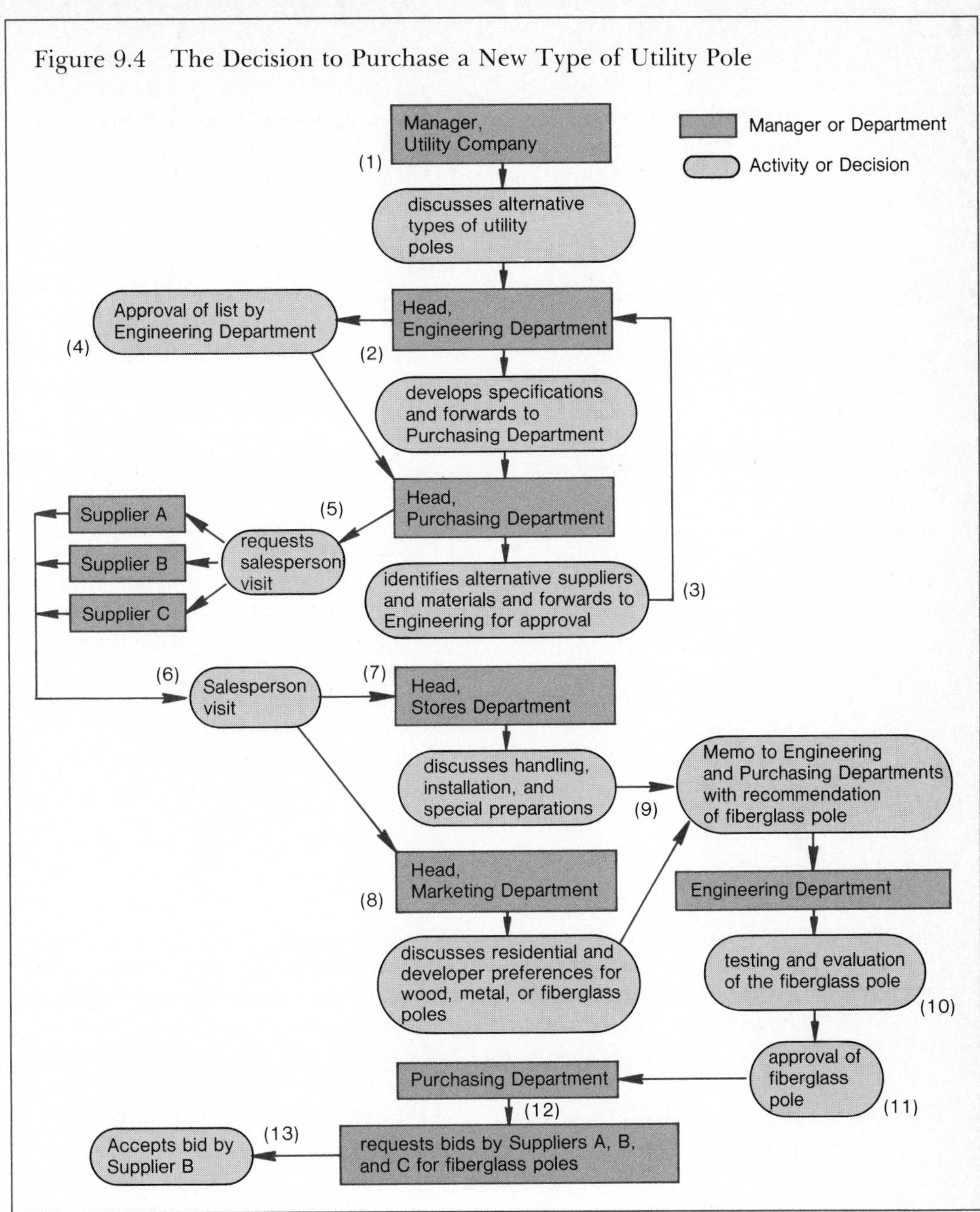

Source: Adapted from Arch G. Woodside, "Marketing Anatomy of Buying Process Can Help Improve Industrial Strategy," *Marketing News* (May 1, 1981), Section 2, p. 11. Used by permission of the American Marketing Association.

Modified Rebuy

A **modified rebuy** is a situation where purchasers are willing to re-evaluate their available options. The appropriate decision makers feel that it may be to their advantage to look at alternative product offerings using established purchasing guidelines. This might occur if a marketer allows a straight rebuy situation to deteriorate because of poor service or delivery. Perceived quality and cost differences can also create a modified rebuy situation.

Industrial marketers want to move purchasers into a straight rebuy position by responding to all of their product and service needs. Competitors, on the other hand, try to move buyers into a modified rebuy situation by correctly assessing the factors that would make buyers reconsider their decisions.

New Task Buying

New task buying refers to first-time or unique purchase situations that require considerable effort on the part of the decision makers. Once such a need has been identified, evaluative criteria can be established and an extensive search launched. Alternative product and service offerings and vendors are considered. An example might occur when a firm enters a new field and has to seek out suppliers of component parts that have not previously been purchased.

Industrial marketers should work closely with the purchaser in the case of new task buying situations. This will allow them to study the factors the purchaser considers important and to design their marketing proposal to match the needs of the industrial buyer.

The Buying Center Concept

The buying center is a vital concept to understanding industrial purchase behavior.[14] The **buying center** simply refers to everyone who participates in some fashion in an industrial buying action. For example, a buying center can include the architect who designs a new research laboratory; the scientist who will use the facility; the purchasing manager who screens contractor proposals; the chief executive officer who makes the final decision; and the vice-president for research who signs the formal contracts for the project.[15]

[14]This section is based on Hutt and Speh, *Industrial Marketing Management*, pp. 80–85.

[15]Buying centers are discussed in two articles in the July 1982 issue of the *Journal of Business Research*. See Gloria P. Thomas and John F. Grashof, "Impact of Internal and External Environments' Stability on the Existence of Determinant Buying Roles," pp. 159–168; and Yoram Wind and Thomas S. Robertson, "The Linking Pin Role in Organizational Buying Centers," pp. 169–184. Also see Earl Naumann, Robert McWilliams, and Douglas J. Lincoln, "How Different Buying Center Members Influence Different Purchasing Phases," in *Developments in Marketing Science*, (eds.) Vinay Kothari, Danny R. Arnold, James Cavusgil, Jay D. Lindquist, Jay Nathan, and Stan Reid *(Proceedings of the Academy of Marketing Science*, 1982), pp. 186–190.

Buying centers are not part of the firm's formal organizational structure. They are informal groups whose composition will vary from one purchase situation to another. Buying centers typically include anywhere from 4 to 20 participants.[16] Buying centers tend to evolve as the purchasing process moves through its various stages. They also vary from one firm to the next.

Buying center participants play different roles in the purchasing process. These roles are generally recognized as users, gatekeepers, influencers, deciders, and buyers. Each of these is defined in Table 9.3.

The critical task for the industrial marketer is to be able to determine the specific role and the relative buying influence of each buying center participant. Sales presentations and information can then be tailored to the appropriate role that the individual plays at each step in the purchase process. Industrial marketers have also found that while their initial, and in many cases most extensive, contacts are all with the purchasing department, the buying center participants having the greatest influence often are not in the purchasing department.[17]

The Process of Buying Industrial Goods and Services[18]

The exact procedures that are used in buying industrial goods and services vary according to the buying situation confronted: straight rebuy, modified rebuy, or new task buying. Most industrial purchases follow the same general process. Research by Agarwal, Burger, and Venkatesh suggested the model presented in Figure 9.5. While this model was formulated for industrial machinery purchases, it has general application to the industrial buying process.

Dissecting the Model

According to the conceptualization in Figure 9.5, there are two primary stages in the industrial buying process. Feasible suppliers are determined in the initial stage. Then there is a second stage involving a more

[16]Hutt and Speh, *Industrial Marketing Management,* p. 80, cite the following sources for their statistics: "Industrial Salespeople Report 4.1 Buying Influences in Average Company," *LAP Report* 1042.2 (McGraw-Hill Research, October 1977); and G. van der Most, "Purchasing Process: Researching Influences Is Basic to Marketing Plan," *Industrial Marketing* (October 1976), p. 120.

[17]An interesting discussion of influences is found in Robert J. Thomas, "Correlates of Interpersonal Purchase Influence in Organizations," *Journal of Consumer Research* (September 1982), pp. 171–182. Also see Robert E. Krapfel, Jr., "An Extended Influence Model of Organizational Buyer Behavior," *Journal of Business Research* (June 1982), pp. 147–157.

[18]This section is based on Manoj K. Agarwal, Philip C. Burger, and Alladi Venkatesh, "Industrial Consumer Behavior: Toward An Improved Model," in *Developments in Marketing Science,* (eds.) Venkatakrishna V. Bellur, Thomas R. Baird, Paul T. Hertz, Roger L. Jenkins, Jay D. Lindquist, and Stephen W. Miller (Miami Beach: Academy of Marketing Science, 1981), pp. 68–73.

Table 9.3 Definitions of Buying Center Roles

Role	Description
Users	As the role name implies, these are the personnel who will be using the product in question. Users may have anywhere from inconsequential to an extremely important influence on the purchase decision. In some cases, the users initiate the purchase action by requesting the product. They may even develop the product specifications.
Gatekeepers	Gatekeepers control information to be reviewed by other members of the buying center. The control of information may be in terms of disseminating printed information or advertisements or through controlling which salesperson will speak to which individuals in the buying center. To illustrate, the purchasing agent might perform this screening role by opening the gate to the buying center for some sales personnel and closing it to others.
Influencers	These individuals affect the purchasing decision by supplying information for the evaluation of alternatives or by setting buying specifications. Typically, technical personnel such as engineers, quality control personnel, and research and development personnel are significant influences to the purchase decision. Sometimes individuals outside of the buying organization can assume this role (e.g., an engineering consultant or an architect who writes very tight building specifications).
Deciders	Deciders are the individuals who actually make the buying decision, whether or not they have the formal authority to do so. The identity of the decider is the most difficult role to determine: buyers may have formal authority to buy, but the president of the firm may actually make the decision. A decider could be a design engineer who develops a set of specifications that only one vendor can meet.
Buyers	The buyer has *formal* authority for selecting a supplier and implementing all procedures connected with securing the product. The power of the buyer is often usurped by more powerful members of the organization. Often the buyer's role is assumed by the purchasing agent, who executes the clerical functions associated with a purchase order.

Source: Adapted from Frederick E. Webster, Jr. and Yoram Wind, *Organizational Buying Behavior* (Englewood Cliffs, N.J.: Prentice-Hall, 1972), pp. 77–80. This adaptation is reprinted from Michael D. Hutt and Thomas W. Speh, *Industrial Marketing Management* (Hinsdale, Ill.: The Dryden Press, 1981), p. 83.

detailed analysis of potential suppliers and resulting in an eventual purchase decision. The specific steps are outlined below.

Need Recognition A triggering event such as an equipment failure stimulates recognition of a perceived need for an industrial purchase.

Information Search Buying center members begin to collect information on potential suppliers. This information is obtained from sales personnel, advertisements, word of mouth, pamphlets, and other sources. The net result of this stage is to delineate the technical nature of the purchase.

Delineation of Suppliers Given the specifications established in the previous step, potential suppliers are then determined. Budget considerations can also be a factor in this step.

Figure 9.5 A Model of the Industrial Buying Process

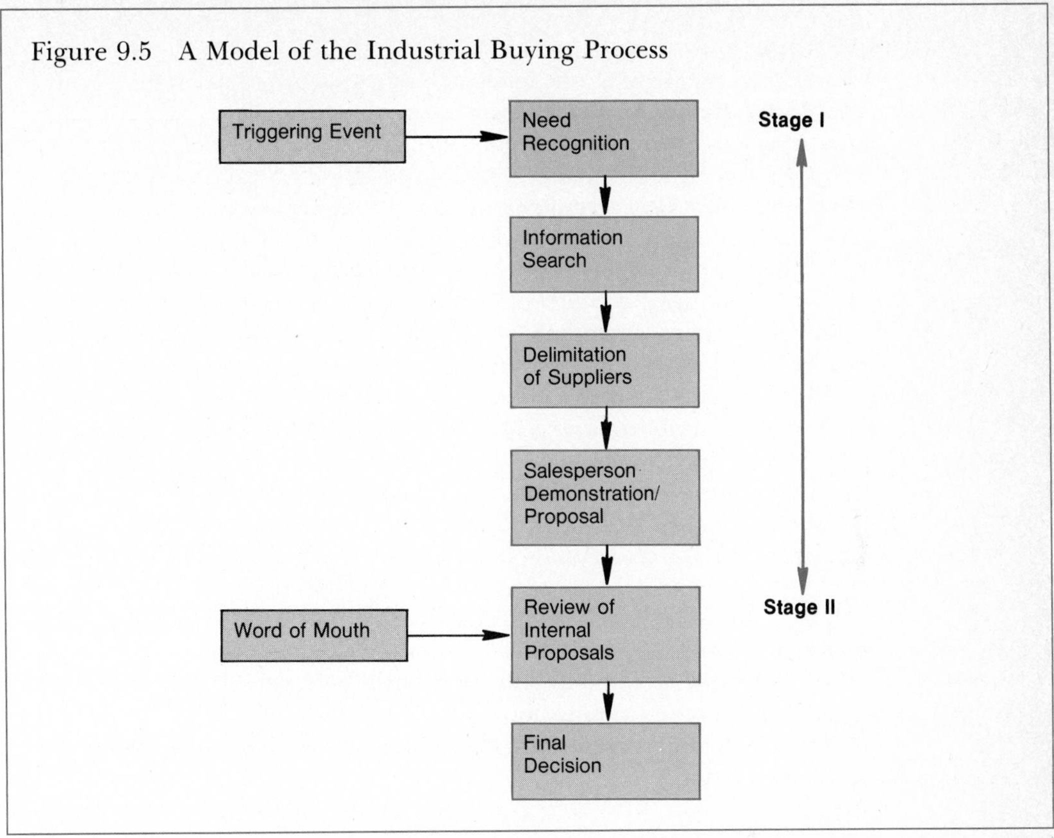

Source: Reprinted from Manoj K. Agarwal, Philip C. Burger, and Alladi Venkatesh, "Industrial Consumer Behavior: Toward an Improved Model," in *Developments in Marketing Science*, (eds.) Venkatakrishna V. Bellur, Thomas R. Baird, Paul T. Hertz, Roger L. Jenkins, Jay D. Lindquist, and Stephen W. Miller (Miami Beach: Academy of Marketing Science, 1981), p. 72.

Sales Demonstration/Proposal Vendor sales representatives are then invited to provide demonstrations and sales proposals. These proposals typically include technical and economic options as well as prices.

Word of Mouth Buying center members may then contact current users of the product for their evaluations of its performance. Reliability, costs, and operational abilities are explored. Some vendors are eliminated because of negative information.

Final Decision Eventually a purchase decision is made. In many cases, this extensive buying process leads to a consensus decision, but some buying center members are more important than others in this final decision stage.

Reciprocity

A highly controversial practice in a number of industrial purchasing situations is **reciprocity,** the extension of purchasing preference to suppliers who are also customers. For example, an office-equipment manufacturer may favor a particular supplier of component parts if the supplier has recently made a major purchase of the manufacturer's products. Reciprocal arrangements were traditionally used in industries with homogeneous products with similar prices, such as the chemical, paint, petroleum, rubber, and steel industries.

Two other forms of reciprocity have been used. **Reverse reciprocity** is the practice of extending supply privileges to firms who provide needed supplies. In times of shortages, reverse reciprocity occasionally emerges as firms attempt to obtain raw materials and parts to continue operations. A more recent reciprocity spinoff is the voluntary price rollback, where purchasers request vendors to agree to temporary price cuts or freezes. While no threats are made, it is difficult for a supplier to refuse a request from a major purchaser. This sometimes forces the vendor to ask for concessions from its own work force and/or employees.[19]

The various forms of reciprocity suggest the close links that exist between the various elements of the industrial marketplace. Although some reciprocal agreements still exist, both the Justice Department and the Federal Trade Commission view them as attempts to reduce competition. Federal intervention is common in cases where agreements are used systematically.[20]

Government Markets

Government markets can be considered another aspect in the marketing of industrial products. There are many similarities between other industrial markets and the government market. Both seek to purchase many similar goods and services. However, there are differences in the way items are procured primarily due to the numerous regulations that affect government markets.

[19]These price cuts are described in Thomas F. O'Boyle, "Price Cutting Being Forced on Suppliers," *The Wall Street Journal* (May 14, 1982), p. 27.

[20]The history and current status of reciprocal agreements is summarized in E. Robert Finney, "Reciprocity: Gone but Not Forgotten," *Journal of Marketing* (January 1978), pp. 54–59. See also William J. Kehoe and Byron D. Hewett, "Reciprocity and Reverse Reciprocity: A Literature Review and Research Design," in *Proceedings of the Southern Marketing Association,* (eds.) Robert S. Franz, Robert M. Hopkins, and Al Toma (New Orleans, La., November 1978), pp. 481–483; and Monroe M. Bird, "Reverse Reciprocity: A New Twist to Industrial Buyers," *Atlanta Economic Review* (January–February 1976), pp. 11–13.

The Importance of the Government Market

At all levels the government is a sizable segment of the industrial market. Total spending for goods and services by all three levels of government—federal, state, and local—amounted to about $650 billion in 1982, an increase of 10 percent over the previous year. Although total federal expenditures rose modestly from previous years, defense expenditures and overall purchases by state and local governments sharply increased.[21]

Organization of Government Markets

By law most government purchases must be made on the basis of **bids,** or written sales proposals, from vendors. As a result, government buyers develop **specifications:** specific descriptions of needed items for prospective bidders. An example of government specifications is shown in Figure 9.6.

The federal government buys most branded items through the General Services Administration (GSA), specifically the organization's Federal Supply Service. About 500 other federal entities maintain procurement functions, including military purchases.[22] In fact, there are some 15,000 government procurement offices.[23] State governments often have offices comparable to the General Service Administration at the federal level.

Prospective government suppliers can learn of opportunities for sales by contacting the various government agencies. Most contracts are advertised by each agency, and information on bidding procedures can be obtained directly from the agency. Directories explaining procedures involved in selling to the federal government are available from the Government Printing Office, and most states provide similar information.[24]

Government Markets—Marketing Opportunities and Problems

The GSA was once unable to find three bidders for a $50,000 order of facial tissue, filing cabinets, garbage cans, and table napkins. Despite its immense size, the government market is often viewed as unprofitable by many suppliers. A survey conducted by *Sales & Marketing Management* reported that industrial marketers registered a variety of complaints about government purchasing procedures. These included ex-

[21]"Business at Midyear: Turn for Better Ahead," *U.S. News & World Report* (July 6, 1981), pp. 26–27.

[22]"Out of the Maze," *Sales & Marketing Management* (April 9, 1979), p. 45.

[23]David E. Gumpert and Jeffrey A. Timmons, "Penetrating the Government Procurement Maze," *Harvard Business Review* (May–June 1982), p. 18.

[24]Information sources on federal purchasing are described in *Ibid,* pp. 14–16, 18, 20.

Figure 9.6 An Example of Government Specifications

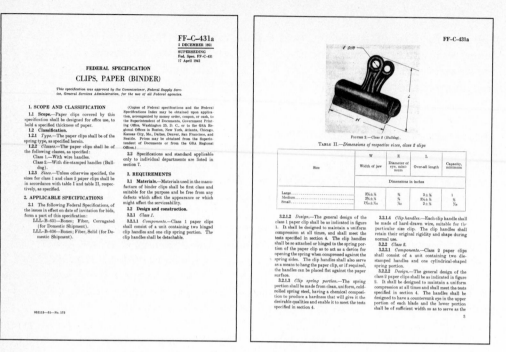

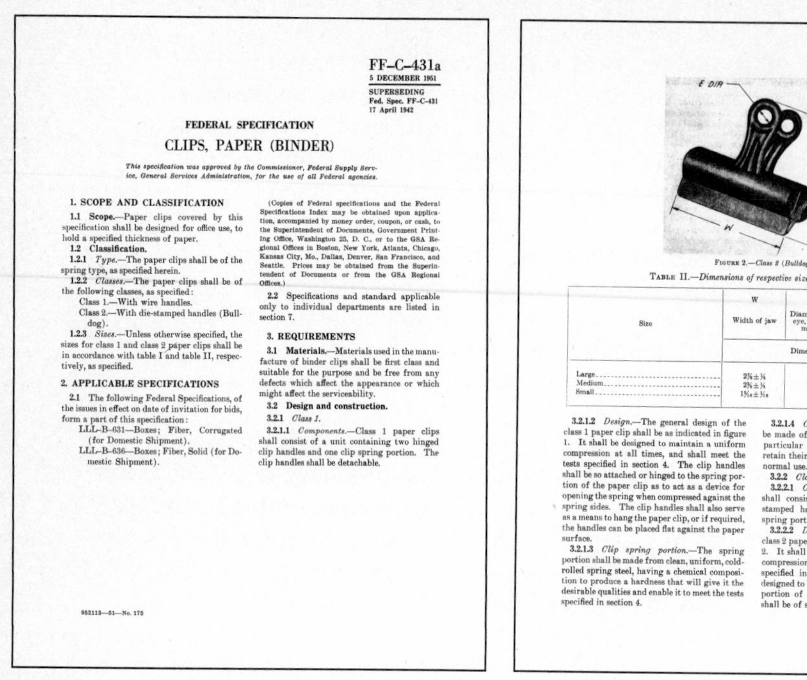

FF-C-431a
5 DECEMBER 1951
SUPERSEDING
Fed. Spec. FF-C-431
17 April 1942

FEDERAL SPECIFICATION

CLIPS, PAPER (BINDER)

This specification was approved by the Commissioner, Federal Supply Service, General Services Administration, for the use of all Federal agencies.

1. SCOPE AND CLASSIFICATION

1.1 **Scope.**—Paper clips covered by this specification shall be designed for office use, to hold a specified thickness of paper.

1.2 **Classification.**

1.2.1 *Type.*—The paper clips shall be of the spring type, as specified herein.

1.2.2 *Classes.*—The paper clips shall be of the following classes, as specified:

Class 1.—With wire handles.
Class 2.—With die-stamped handles (Bulldog).

1.2.3 *Sizes.*—Unless otherwise specified, the sizes for class 1 and class 2 paper clips shall be in accordance with table I and table II, respectively, as specified.

2. APPLICABLE SPECIFICATIONS

2.1 The following Federal Specifications, of the issues in effect on date of invitation for bids, form a part of this specification:

LLL-B-631—Boxes; Fiber, Corrugated (for Domestic Shipment).
LLL-B-636—Boxes; Fiber, Solid (for Domestic Shipment).

(Copies of Federal specifications and the Federal Specifications Index may be obtained upon application, accompanied by money order, coupon, or cash, to the Superintendent of Documents, Government Printing Office, Washington 25, D. C., or to the GSA Regional Offices in Boston, New York, Atlanta, Chicago, Kansas City, Mo., Dallas, Denver, San Francisco, and Seattle. Prices may be obtained from the Superintendent of Documents or from the GSA Regional Offices.)

2.2 Specifications and standard applicable only to individual departments are listed in section 7.

3. REQUIREMENTS

3.1 **Materials.**—Materials used in the manufacture of binder clips shall be first class and suitable for the purpose and be free from any defects which affect the appearance or which might affect the serviceability.

3.2 **Design and construction.**

3.2.1 *Class 1.*

3.2.1.1 *Components.*—Class 1 paper clips shall consist of a unit containing two hinged clip handles and one clip spring portion. The clip handles shall be detachable.

952113—51—No. 175

FF-C-431a

FIGURE 2.—*Class 2 (Bulldog).*

TABLE II.—*Dimensions of respective sizes, class 2 clips*

Size	W Width of jaw	E Diameter of eye, minimum	L Over-all length	Capacity, minimum
	Dimensions in inches			
Large	$2\frac{5}{8} \pm \frac{1}{8}$	$\frac{3}{8}$	$3 \pm \frac{1}{8}$	1
Medium	$2\frac{3}{8} \pm \frac{1}{8}$	$\frac{3}{8}$	$2\frac{1}{2} \pm \frac{1}{8}$	$\frac{1}{2}$
Small	$1\frac{5}{16} \pm \frac{1}{16}$	$\frac{7}{32}$	$2 \pm \frac{1}{8}$	$\frac{5}{16}$

3.2.1.2 *Design.*—The general design of the class 1 paper clip shall be as indicated in figure 1. It shall be designed to maintain a uniform compression at all times, and shall meet the tests specified in section 4. The clip handles shall be so attached or hinged to the spring portion of the paper clip as to act as a device for opening the spring when compressed against the spring sides. The clip handles shall also serve as a means to hang the paper clip, or if required, the handles can be placed flat against the paper surface.

3.2.1.3 *Clip spring portion.*—The spring portion shall be made from clean, uniform, cold-rolled spring steel, having a chemical composition to produce a hardness that will give it the desirable qualities and enable it to meet the tests specified in section 4.

3.2.1.4 *Clip handles.*—Each clip handle shall be made of hard-drawn wire, suitable for the particular size clip. The clip handles shall retain their original rigidity and shape during normal use.

3.2.2 *Class 2.*

3.2.2.1 *Components.*—Class 2 paper clips shall consist of a unit containing two die-stamped handles and one cylindrical-shaped spring portion.

3.2.2.2 *Design.*—The general design of the class 2 paper clips shall be as indicated in figure 2. It shall be designed to maintain a uniform compression at all times and shall meet the tests specified in section 4. The handles shall be designed to have a countersunk eye in the upper portion of each blade and the lower portion shall be of sufficient width so as to serve as the

3

cessive paperwork, bureaucracy, needless regulations, emphasis on low-bid prices, decision-making delays, frequent shifts in procurement personnel, and excessive policy changes.[25]

On the other hand, marketers generally credit the government with being a relatively stable market. Once an item is purchased by the government, the probability of additional sales is good. Other marketers cite such advantages as the instant credibility established by sales to the federal government, timely payment, excise tax and sales tax exemptions, acceptance of new ideas, and reduced competition.

Although one survey reported that 68 percent of its industrial respondents did not maintain a separate government sales manager or sales force, many firms report success with specialized government marketing efforts. J.I. Case, Goodyear, Eastman Kodak, and Sony are examples. There are also specialist distributors, such as Government Marketing Services of Rockville, Maryland, that sell small orders of

[25]This information is based on "Out of the Maze," *Sales & Marketing Management* (October 12, 1981), pp. 44–46 ff.

New York's Metropolitan Transportation Authority Can Be Very Picky. . . .

The Board of New York City's Metropolitan Transportation authority has among its diverse responsibilities the provision of toilet paper for the system's 1,100 restrooms. When it was asked to approve a $168,840 toilet-paper purchase over three lower bids, the authority asked the obvious question: why did management reject the lower bids?

The MTA president replied that one supplier was rejected because there was not enough tissue on the rolls. The other two bids were denied because the paper was not soft enough. In fact, the executive compared the tissue to sandpaper. With this explanation, the board concluded this unique purchasing process by approving the requested allocation.

Source: "For 1,100 Restrooms, It Should Be Soft," *The Seattle Times* (May 16, 1982), p. A 6. Reprinted by permission of United Press International.

branded, off-the-shelf items to government buyers for manufacturers like Texas Instruments and General Electric.

Improving the Government Procurement Function

Both the Carter and Reagan administrations attempted to make the government procurement function more effective. Four recent developments are worth noting at the federal level. Similar developments have influenced some state and local governments.[26]

- There is movement toward uniform procurement regulations so that all government buyers operate by a standard set of requirements.
- The Pentagon, GSA, and other government buyers, in an attempt to reduce spending, are turning to more off-the-shelf goods rather than issuing special-order contracts.
- *Life-cycle costing*—the cost of using a product over its lifetime, not just the initial bid price—is now accepted by the GSA. Potential energy savings are part of this new policy in granting government contracts.[27]
- A variety of reforms are being implemented in the GSA itself. Most of these involve streamlining its organization, increasing procurement efficiency, and improving its counseling of would-be suppliers.

[26]"Out of the Maze," pp. 46, 48, 50, 52, and "Reagan and the Procurement Elephant," *Sales & Marketing Management* (October 12, 1981), p. 16.

[27]For a discussion of the application of life-cycle costing to energy-related products, see R. Bruce Hutton and William L. Wilkie, "Life Cycle Cost: A New Form of Consumer Information," *Journal of Consumer Research* (March 1980), pp. 349–360.

Summary

The industrial market consists of those individuals and organizations who acquire goods and services to be used, directly or indirectly, in the production of other goods and services or to be resold to governments, retailers and wholesalers, and producers. The three types of industrial markets are: producers (industrial customers who purchase goods and services for production of other goods and services); trade industries (organizations such as retailers and wholesalers who purchase for resale to others); and government (at federal, state, and local levels). The industrial marketplace is a significant portion of the U.S. economy.

The industrial market has three distinctive features: geographic market concentration, a relatively small number of buyers, and a unique classification system called SIC codes. The Standard Industrial Classification (SIC) subdivides the industrial marketplace into ten broad industry categories. These groups are further subdivided by a numbering system that now goes to seven digits.

There are four major characteristics of industrial market demand. Derived demand means that the demand for industrial goods is linked to the demand for consumer goods. Joint demand refers to the fact that the demand for some industrial products is related to the demand for other industrial goods which are used jointly with the first item. Changes in inventory policy can also have a significant effect on industrial demand. The fourth characteristic of industrial market demand involves the accelerator principle, which indicates that even modest changes in consumer demand can have a disproportionate impact on industrial demand.

There are two basic categories of industrial products: capital items and expense items. Capital items are long-lived business assets that must be depreciated for a period ranging from 3 to 15 years. Depreciation is the accounting concept of charging a portion of a capital item as a deduction against the company's annual revenue for purposes of determining its net income. Expense items, by contrast, are products and services that are used within a short period of time. For the most part, they are charged against income in the year of purchase. A more elaborate classification of industrial products is developed in the next chapter.

Industrial buyer behavior tends to be more complex than the consumer behavior of individuals. More people and time are involved, and buyers often seek several supply sources. There are three generally recognized industrial purchasing situations: straight rebuy, modified rebuy, and new task buying. A straight rebuy is a recurring purchase decision where an item that has performed satisfactorily is purchased again. A modified rebuy is a situation where purchasers are willing to re-evaluate their available options. New task buying refers to first-time or unique purchase situations that require considerable effort on the part of the decision makers.

Industrial buying behavior is also characterized by the concept of a buying center. The buying center simply refers to everyone that participates in some fashion in an industrial buying action. Buying centers include users, decision makers, influencers, gatekeepers who control information, and buyers who actually consummate the transaction. The actual process of buying an industrial product or service consists of need recognition; a search for information; delineation of vendors; solicitation of sales proposals; review of proposals; and the actual purchase decision. A controversial practice that comes into play for some industrial purchasing situations is reciprocity, the extension of purchasing preference to suppliers who are also customers.

Government markets are a sizable segment of the U.S. economy. Government differs from other industrial markets because of the numerous regulations that impact procurement practices. For instance, most government purchases, by law, must be made on the basis of bids or written sales proposals from vendors. Government buyers usually develop specific descriptions of needed items for prospective buyers, called specifications. Numerous changes are underway in the government procurement function in an attempt to streamline the buying process.

Key Terms

consumer market
industrial market
producers
trade industries
Standard Industrial Classification (SIC)
derived demand
joint demand
capital item
expense item
straight rebuy
modified rebuy
new task buying
buying center
reciprocity
reverse reciprocity
bids
specifications

Review Questions

1. What are the three major types of industrial markets?
2. Describe the three distinctive features of industrial markets.
3. Explain the characteristics of industrial market demand.
4. Differentiate between capital items and expense items.
5. Why is industrial purchase behavior so complex?
6. Differentiate among straight rebuy, modified rebuy, and new task buying.
7. Explain the concept of a buying center.
8. Outline the general process for buying goods and services.
9. Discuss the issue of reciprocity.
10. Explain how government markets differ from other industrial markets.

Discussion Questions and Exercises

1. Prepare a brief report on the market opportunity that exists in some specific industrial market. Be sure to consult all of the standard reference sources on the industrial marketplace.
2. How could an industrial marketer use the SIC codes?
3. Find some actual examples of where derived demand, joint demand, inventory adjustments, and the accelerator principle affected industrial market demand. Report your findings to the class.
4. Prepare a report on a recent purchase by a local organizational buyer. What can be learned from this exercise?
5. Prepare a brief report on the market opportunity that exists in a specific government market. Identify all of the information sources that are available for such an assessment.

CASES FOR PART 3

Case 3.1
Gerber Products Company

Daniel Gerber pioneered the baby food market when he introduced strained applesauce in 1928. Gerber now has 170 baby food varieties and claims roughly 65 percent of the baby food market. As a result of a severe drop in births and rugged competition, Gerber's sales for 1973 showed an increase of only 2.5 percent to $285.4 million. What was more important, its profits dropped 27.9 percent to $11,100,000. The previous year, sales had slipped for the first time in history, by 1.5 percent, and profits fell 23.9 percent. Although it had diversified somewhat, Gerber looked to baby food for 88 percent of its sales and most of its profits. The Gerber name is seen in food stores and has some exposure in discount houses, drugstores, and specialty stores. Its baby food line is augmented by a limited line of nonfood baby items. Gerber also entered the child-care field and the insurance industry, but both of these sidelines were disappointing. Its day-care centers were money losers, although later solution of local management problems led the company to expect profits in 1974. The insurance branch performance was even worse, suffering continuing losses.

Gerber management has blamed most of its problems on the declining birth rate. The company therefore expressed a desire to reduce its dependence on the baby food line. It saw diversification (day-care centers and insurance) and entrance into the adult food market as possible solutions.

Gerber and other "baby industry" firms were the first to feel the crunch of birth decline. The end of the population explosion was expected to have a tremendous effect on the entire marketplace for at least a full generation. After birth rates of 4.2 million in 1956 and 3.7 million as recently as 1970, the 1973 birth rate slid to only 3.1 million.

Organizational Objectives

The management at Gerber realized that decisive action was needed in the face of problems over which it had little control. Plans to overcome the losses called for introduction of new organizational objectives. Gerber management seemed to be dedicated to the accomplishment of the new objectives, designed to remove the

Source: "Reaction to Demographic Change: Gerber" (pp. 409–413), in *Marketing* by Donald P. Robin. Harper & Row, publishers.

company's dependence on a single product category. Since the baby market was shrinking, Gerber felt it had to capture a larger share of the total dollar spent on babies. Since baby food has a very low markup—often 2 to 5 percent—volume had to remain high and distribution broad. Gerber saw the need to expand its product lines to encompass all of a baby's needs. This and entrance into the adult food market were seen as the means of relieving Gerber's dependence on baby food. A consolidation of sales operations and a broadening of distribution into discount houses, drug chains, department stores, and specialty stores were to help provide the volume for the low-margin baby food line.

The Marketing Environment

Competition

Gerber's stiffest competition came from Heinz and Beechnut, which controlled roughly 35 percent of the baby food market. Their aggressiveness was seen in a damaging price war that began in 1969 and lasted until 1973. Gerber's market share dropped to 60 percent as price spreads reached three to four cents per jar of baby food. Gerber retaliated by reducing its prices and regained its previous market share, but the federal price controls of 1971 caught the company with low prices. Both Gerber and its competition suffered considerably as a result of this price war.

The price war was promoted by the fact that the various baby foods are very similar. There is little product differentiation except in brand name. The target for Gerber was the same as for Heinz and Beechnut, but these competitors lacked the volume and widespread distribution that Gerber had. Thus, the price war was at least partly motivated by the desire of Gerber's competitors to take a bigger share of the market.

Gerber's entrance into the adult food market would bring it into competition with several strong firms. For example, in the market for catsup, Gerber would face such sales leaders as Heinz, Del Monte, and Hunt-Wesson. Its entrance into the peanut butter market was opposed by such brands as Skippy, Peter Pan, and Jif.

Gerber developed a Marketing Auditing Report System (MARS)—a computerized system covering 50,000 food stores (85–90 percent of all retail food stores)—to give instant information on its products in a particular store, chain, or area. The reports detailed shelf space, position, mixture, and sales as compared to the competition. The information was gathered by 1,000 salespeople, who filled out forms that could be read by a central computer's scanner.

Internal Organizational Environment

To increase its effectiveness, the management at Gerber had created its own marketing research team after finding consumer research to be scarce in the "baby field." It also established a venture group for new-product development. This group screened five potential products per week and made recommendations to a seven-person management committee. Promising products were then referred to a management task force for additional research or product development.

Social and Cultural Factors

The reduction in births was not the only cultural factor that interested Gerber and affected its strategy. While the birth rate may have been the main influence in producing a more prosperous middle class, other changes in the American family also had a great effect on Gerber's marketing. The family no longer fit the traditional mold on which its retail strategy had been based. Child-care centers seemed logical in a society where both parents desired to pursue careers. These changes in the American family were results of people's desires for careers, increased mobility, and greater independence, and the availability of the "pill" for ready birth control.

The Marketing Strategy

Target Customers

Gerber saw its target customers as families with babies, working mothers, and a new young adult market. It hoped to accomplish its objectives by using the proper marketing mix for these three groups of buyers.

Product

The company wanted to expand its product line to include toiletries, disposable diapers, disposable nurser bags and bottles, vaporizers, humidifiers, sterilizers, a complete line of baby wear, and any other products recommended by the venture group.

Gerber's products for the adult food market were varied. It proposed to market baby food fruits and desserts to adults as snack foods and as ingredients in a special line of recipes. It planned to introduce catsup and peanut butter products. The most innovative product idea was a line of single-serving, prepackaged foods for adults, especially single adults and couples.

Price

The recent price war had shown Gerber that the price of baby food could be 1 to 1.5 cents per jar above the competition without losing sales. Therefore, a small premium could be expected from this product line. However, new product prices would probably have to be competitive.

Promotion

Promotion of the new products and objectives was vitally important. As an indication of Gerber's changing attitudes, the slogan "Babies are our only business" was first shortened to "Babies are our business" and then dropped altogether. Substantial television and print advertising programs were used to make potential customers aware of the new product lines.

Channels

Gerber's channel outlets were largely food stores where the company had considerable influence. It hoped to create entire "baby needs" departments alongside its baby food shelves. Inclusion of the nonfood items was expected to be beneficial for Gerber and the retailer alike. Food—especially baby food—is a low margin item (2- to 5-percent markup), while nonfood items have a considerably higher margin, even though the turnover is much lower. As a strategy to gain new channels, Gerber planned to offer its nonfood products with a 30- to 40-percent margin that would be very attractive to retailers.

The new "singles" line (single-serving foods for adults) was planned to have a promotional bonus to retailers—an introductory margin of 41 percent before moving down to a standard margin of 24 to 26 percent. These larger-than-average margins and a "Rediscover Gerber" campaign were expected to establish broader distribution of the nonfood baby items and the "singles" line. The traditional products to be introduced—catsup and peanut butter—were to undergo additional market testing before an expensive full-market entry was made. Expansion of distribution into new outlets, such as discount houses, drug chains, department stores, and specialty stores (because of the promotional margin strategy), was expected to bring Gerber increased revenue and profits.

Discussion Questions

1. Why was a strategy of diversification so important to Gerber?
2. In pursuing diversification, how was Gerber attempting to exploit its name and position in the market?
3. What benefits were expected from each of the new products Gerber tried? In each case, were buyer reactions adequately considered?

Case 3.2
Aqua-Craft Corporation

Aqua-Craft manufactures a broad line of boats designed for the mass market. The fifty models in the line include cruisers, runabouts, canoes, sailboats, and utility and fishing boats. The company follows a competitive pricing policy with specific prices ranging from $149 for a nine-foot flat bottom to $4,495 for an inboard or outboard cruiser. The boats are distributed by the company's own sales force and by the salespersons of 45 independent distributors to more than 1,500 dealers located throughout the United States.

The company has enjoyed a remarkable rate of growth. Sales increased from $5.2 million in 1950 to $10.2 million in 1960. Despite a leveling-off trend in industry sales in the 1960s, Aqua-Craft continued to grow, and by 1971 sales reached an all-time high of $21.7 million.

By the summer of 1971, however, management was becoming increasingly concerned over the ability of the company to sustain its past rate of growth. Management felt that their past differential advantages were likely to become less effective in the future.

The company had pioneered numerous technological innovations in boat construction and was generally regarded

Source: From *Contemporary Cases in Consumer Behavior* by Roger D. Blackwell, James F. Engel, and David T. Kollat. Copyright 1977 by The Dryden Press, a division of Holt, Rinehart and Winston, Inc. Reprinted by permission of Holt, Rinehart and Winston.

by dealers and boat owners as a quality builder. However, it was becoming apparent, particularly in recent years, that competitors could match the company's manufacturing expertise. As a consequence, management wondered how long it could rely on its quality image to stimulate increased sales.

The company's other major differential advantage—a strong dealer organization—also showed signs of decaying. In recent years many of the company's independent distributors began carrying two or three other lines of boats. Because there were minimal differences in the profitability of these lines, many distributors were not pushing the Aqua-Craft line to the degree that they had in the past. Although the company was finding it more and more difficult to exert the desired degree of control over distributors, it had decided, at least for the time being, that it would have to accept the system because the investment required to establish company-owned distribution facilities was considered prohibitive.

The growing number of competitors, particularly large firms like Chrysler, was also a source of concern. If a large competitor decided to get into the boat business in a major way, management feared that the company's sales and market share would decline precipitously.

Current Use of Consumer Behavior Information

In the past, the company has made only minimal use of information on consumer attitudes and behavior. Product strategies have been formulated largely on the basis of materials availabilities and prices, metals technology, and production-run considerations. The company has always depended on executive insights and hunches about what consumers want in boats. In the company's early years, this seemed to be a workable strategy because the company manufactured only fishing boats and because many executives—particularly Hull and Claude Whipple, the company's founders—were, as sporting enthusiasts, intimately familiar with the desirable attributes of this type of boat.

Several developments in recent years had convinced many executives that executive intuition about consumer attitudes was a risky approach to product strategy considerations. The company had expanded into other lines of boats, and company executives knew less about what consumers were looking for. Moreover, most competitors were producing boats with nearly identical functional features. As a result, product competition was shifting to other product dimensions: styling, color, trim configurations, and so on. It was becoming increasingly difficult to estimate which of these dimensions would be most effective in establishing brand preference. And the cost of estimating incorrectly was increasing because of the dramatic increase in inventory investment resulting from product-line proliferation.

Pricing decisions were also made almost completely independently of consumer considerations. The company balanced cost and competitive price considerations in setting prices. All models were priced in order to make the maximum contribution to overhead and profit and to still be reasonably close to competitors' prices. In the past, the models not making any contribution to overhead and profit were dropped from the line. The company has done little experimenting with price variations, and executives admit that they did not really know how important price was when consumers were deciding between different brands.

The company has relied mainly on the judgment of the independent distributors in selecting dealers to handle Aqua-Craft boats. In the past, distributors have been fairly successful in achieving broad distribution for the line. In the last few years, however, problems have arisen, as the growing number of boat manufacturers have caused many distributors to become brand indifferent, and many dealers have reduced the number of brands carried in order to minimize their investment in inventory. Management was wondering about such things as whether or not the importance of various types of dealers was changing, whether the company had distribution with the right types of dealers, and how intense distribution should be.

The amount to be spent on advertising is determined by applying a fixed percentage of forecasted sales (1.5 percent). Readership studies of boat owners conducted by boating magazines are used to select advertising media and vehicles.

Sources of Consumer Behavior Information Currently Being Used

Aqua-Craft utilizes several sources of information about the behavior of boat owners. Distributor invoices are used to tabulate boat sales by model, price, color, style, and geographic location. This information is used along with comparable data for the entire industry to predict sales and schedule production and inventory requirements.

The company collects similar information from its warranty program. The company guarantees its boats against defects in workmanship and in materials, providing certain conditions are met. The information from the warranty card is used by management to analyze the movement of boats by model, color, price and geographic location.

Occasionally, the company's advertising agency conducts studies dealing with various dimensions of consumer behavior. The agency has determined how sales vary by occupation, and the reasons people buy boats.

First, it was found that sales to various occupational groups followed the experience of their segment of the industry. Skilled workers accounted for 23.6 percent of sales followed by semiskilled workers with 19.3 percent and professionals with 16.9 percent. In addition, the following were the reasons stated as to why people buy boats (figures exceed 100 percent because of multiple mention):

Cruising	53 percent
Fishing	41 percent
Hunting	8 percent
Skiing	62 percent
All other	6 percent

These are the only internal sources of information about consumer behavior presently available to management. Information from external sources is limited to publicly circulated industry reports. Typically, these deal with industry sales patterns by manufacturer and model and with the reasons people are buying boats.

Current Problems

By spring 1971 management was growing increasingly concerned about the lack of information pertaining to the market they were attempting to penetrate. This came to a head when the media schedule was being finalized. The advertising agency proposed that the company follow the same schedule with the same publications as used in the past, including *Field and Stream, Yachting, Popular Science, Popular Mechanics,* and *Motor Boating.* Past advertisements have shown boating as a quiet, restful sport—especially fishing and cruising—or as a social activity involving water skiing and young women.

Management's greatest concerns were motivated by the increasing role of teenagers in the decision to purchase a boat. Also, it was felt that the homemaker has a significant say as well, especially in view of the major expenditure required. Therefore, the advertising agency was directed to undertake a study that shows the relative influence of various members of the family in the purchase of a boat.

Discussion Questions

1. Has management focused on the most important research question? Are there other types of information about the decision process that would be of greater priority?
2. Outline the way in which the agency should proceed in determining the roles of family members in the purchase of a boat. What types of questions should be asked? Who should be interviewed?
3. Indicate the specific ways that the results of the family decision-making study could be used in designing a marketing strategy.

Melvin T. Copeland

The need to develop a product classification system to explain the differences in marketing various goods has been addressed by such marketing theorists and practitioners as Charles C. Parlin, Leo Aspinwall, Richard H. Holton, and Louis P. Bucklin. The earliest and best-known classification schema was proposed by a Harvard professor named Melvin T. Copeland (1884–1975). Copeland's classification of convenience, shopping, and specialty goods, based upon Parlin's earlier mention of convenience, emergency, and shopping goods, has been widely disseminated and is used by the American Marketing Association as the official classification for consumer goods (Chicago: American Marketing Association, 1960, pp. 11, 21–22).

Copeland, known affectionately to generations of colleagues and students at Harvard as "Doc," earned his A.B. at Bowdoin College and his A.M. and Ph.D. at Harvard. He taught economics for a year at New York University before returning permanently to Harvard in 1912. In 1915, he coined the term *marketing* for the title of a course he was teaching.

Copeland was a pioneer in the case approach to the teaching of business. His book *Problems in Marketing* was the first casebook ever published in business. It has been revised many times since its initial publication in 1920, and it continues to be widely used today. Another of Copeland's six books, *Principles of Merchandising* (Chicago: A. W. Shaw, 1924), proved a major contribution to the general study of marketing in colleges and universities.

Throughout his career at Harvard, Copeland was active in the Bureau of Business Research, and he served as its director from 1942 to 1953. He retired in 1953 as George Fisher Baker Professor Emeritus. Copeland died on March 27, 1975, at Annisquam, Massachusetts.

4

PRODUCTS AND SERVICES

This part focuses on the problems, activities, and decisions involved in developing the most appropriate products and services for the firm's chosen market target. A separate chapter is devoted to the important topic of marketing of services. Other subjects include the product lifecycle concept, new product development, product line planning, product identification, packaging, labeling, and product safety.

10

Chapter Objectives

1. To relate product strategy concepts to the other variables of the marketing mix.
2. To explain the concept of the product life cycle.
3. To identify the determinants of the speed of the adoption process.
4. To explain the methods for accelerating the speed of adoption.
5. To identify the classifications of consumer goods and to describe each category.
6. To identify the types of industrial goods.

PRODUCT STRATEGY

It took Searle Pharmaceuticals Inc. over a decade to introduce what *Fortune* magazine labeled a product of the year. The lengthy period before the 1982 launch of Aspartame illustrates why product development and management is such an important element of the marketing mix, even if it is a trying aspect. Searle executives estimate that the artificial sweetener may soon account for $500 million of the company's sales, nearly half the current total.

The story of Aspartame began when a Searle chemist, James Schlatter, spilled some amino acids. When he licked his fingers, Schlatter discovered the spill was sweet. Aspartame had been synthesized earlier by a British firm, but Searle secured the *patent* (the exclusive use of an invention for 17 years) on the product as a sweetener.

The Skokie, Illinois, company then asked the Food and Drug Administration for approval to put Aspartame on the market. The FDA granted the product approval as a low-calorie sweetener until a Missouri doctor complained that Aspartame might cause brain damage in youngsters. The FDA withheld Aspartame from the market for seven years while it debated this contention. Searle eventually sued to force the government agency to make a decision.

Aspartame is marketed as a table-top sweetener under the brand name Equal. It is also sold as a drink mix sweetener under the NutraSweet label. Aspartame has several advantages over sugar and saccharin, the widely used artificial sweetener. A four-calorie packet of Equal contains the sweet taste of two teaspoons of sugar but not the 32 calories. The cost is about the same as sugar.

Saccharin became the dominant artificial sweetener when the FDA banned cyclamates in 1970, fearing they caused cancer. Cyclamates were better tasting than saccharin and had achieved annual revenues of $1 billion before they were prohibited. In 1977 the FDA decided saccharin might also cause cancer so it, too, was banned. However, there was no other approved artificial sweetener, so the FDA postponed the saccharin ban. Even today a health warning is carried on saccharin much like the one on cigarette packages.

Unlike saccharin, Aspartame is now considered completely safe, and it does not have the aftertaste associated with saccharin. The only disadvantage of the Searle product is that Equal sells for more than its leading saccharin competitor. Searle does not yet have approval to sell Aspartame as a soft drink sweetener. Currently, diet soft drinks are a $3 billion market for saccharin.

For several years, no diet soft drinks were available in Canada because of a ban on saccharin. In 1981, however, Canadian health officials approved the use of Aspartame in soft drinks. The new diet products already command 12 percent of the Canadian market. The Canadian experience also indicated another advantage of Aspartame which is a longer shelf life for this type of diet soft drink.

Searle's battle to introduce a quality product raises some of the issues and concepts marketers must deal with today. In Searle's case, the 17-year patent that protects Aspartame has only six years to run, and competitors are no doubt waiting to enter the latest phase of the battle for the $12 billion artificial sweetener market.[1]

The Conceptual Framework

Part Four examines products and services—the first element of the marketing mix. Chapter 10 looks at product concepts, and Chapter 11, the product mix and new product planning. Part Four concludes with a separate chapter on services, Chapter 12.

[1]Gene Bylinsky, "The Battle for America's Sweet Tooth," *Fortune* (July 26, 1982), pp. 28–32; Andrew C. Brown, "Products of the Year," *Fortune* (December 28, 1981), p. 66.

The other elements of the marketing mix—pricing structures, distribution channels, and promotional strategies—must be based on the products and services the organization provides. However, products and services are similarly dependent on these other marketing variables. For example, General Electric has developed a new light bulb, the Halarc, that lasts considerably longer and uses less energy than conventional bulbs, but GE is still trying to determine if consumers will pay over $10 for their new product.[2]

A narrow definition of the word *product* would focus on the physical or functional characteristics of a good or service offered to consumers. For example, a videocassette recorder is a rectangular container of metal and plastic wires connecting it to a television set, accompanied by a series of special tapes for recording and viewing. But the purchaser has a much broader view of the recorder. He bought the convenience of viewing television programs at his leisure, the warranty and service of the manufacturer, the prestige of owning this relatively new product innovation, and the ability to rent or purchase recently released movies for home viewing. Marketing decision makers must have this broader conception of product in mind and realize that people are buying want satisfaction.

The shopper's conception of a product may be altered by such features as packaging, labeling, or even the retail outlet at which the product is purchased. An image of high quality has been created for Maytag appliances by virtue of the advertising campaign that features the Maytag repairer as the loneliest person in town. Maytag's standard of high quality is responsible for its strong consumer franchise.

Some products have few or no physical attributes. A haircut and blow dry by the local hairdresser produces only well-groomed hair. A tax counselor produces only advice. Therefore, a broader view of products must include services. Consequently, a **product** is a bundle of physical, service, and symbolic attributes designed to produce consumer want satisfaction. Figure 10.1 reflects this broader definition by identifying the various components of the total product.

Brands, packages, and labels are discussed in Chapter 11. Product image is discussed throughout Part Four. In addition, these three elements are usually supported by a warranty and service program. A **warranty** is a guarantee to the buyer that the producer will replace the product or refund its purchase price if it proves defective during a specified period of time.

The Magnuson-Moss Warranty Act (1975) gives the Federal Trade Commission the power to develop regulations affecting warranty practices for any product costing more than $15 that is covered by a written warranty. While the act does not require firms to give warranties, it is

[2]Jacques Neher, "Halarc Prospects Dim, but GE Puts Up a Brave Front," *Advertising Age* (March 22, 1982), pp. 68–69.

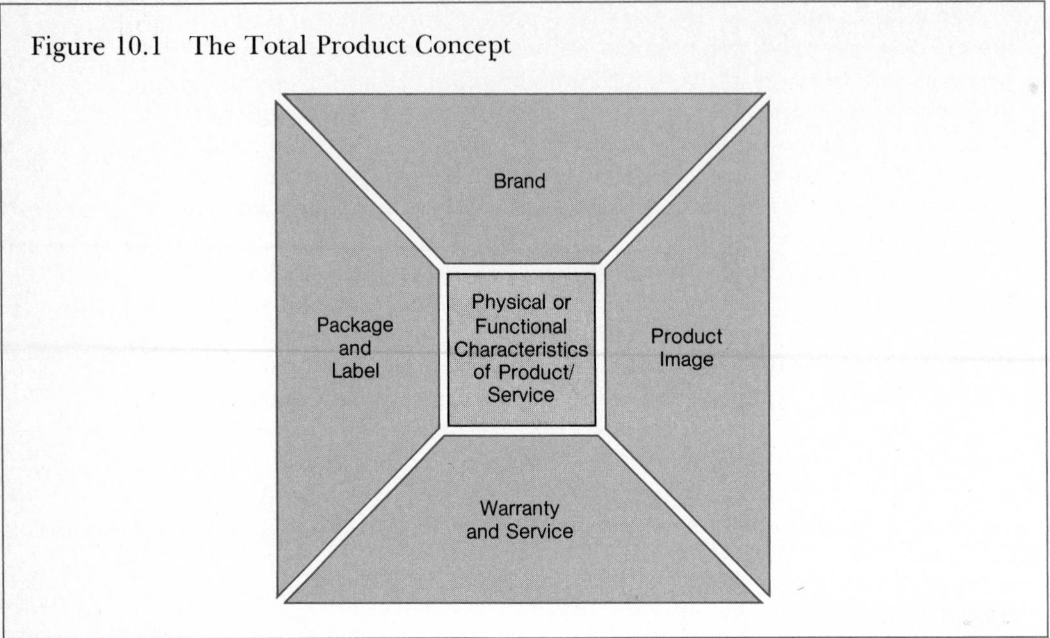

Figure 10.1 The Total Product Concept

designed to assist the consumer in comparison shopping. Warranties must be easy to read and understand, and firms offering them must also establish informal mechanisms for processing consumer complaints.[3]

The Product Life Cycle

Products, like individuals, pass through a series of stages. While humans progress from infancy to childhood to adulthood to retirement to death, successful products progress through four stages—introduction, growth, maturity, and decline—before their death. This progression is known as the **product life cycle.** The cycle is depicted in Figure 10.2, with examples of products currently at each stage of development.[4]

[3]Janet Marr, "The Magnuson-Moss Warranty Act," *Family Economics Review* (Summer 1978), p. 307.

[4]A good summary of the product life-cycle concept is contained in George S. Day, "The Product Life Cycle: Analysis and Applications Issues," *Journal of Marketing* (Fall 1981), pp. 60–67. Also see Gerald J. Tellis and C. Merle Crawford, "An Evolutionary Approach to Product Growth Theory," *Journal of Marketing* (Fall 1981), pp. 125–132.

Figure 10.2 The Product Life Cycle Concept

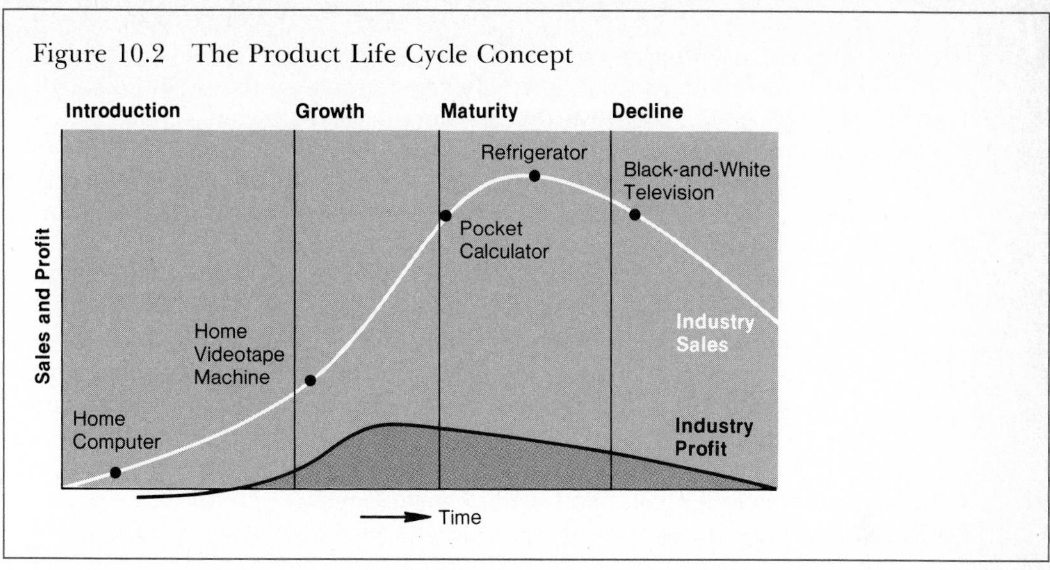

Introductory Stage

The firm's objective in the early stages of the product life cycle is to stimulate demand for the new market entry. Since the product is not known to the public, promotional campaigns stress information about its features. They also may be directed toward middlemen in the distribution channel to induce them to carry the product. In this phase, the public becomes acquainted with the merits of the product and begins to accept it.

As Figure 10.2 indicates, losses are common during the introductory stage due to heavy promotion and extensive research and development expenditures. The groundwork is being laid for future profits. Firms expect to recover their costs and to begin earning profits when the new product moves into the second phase of its life cycle—the growth stage.

Pressdent is an example of a product that entered the introductory stage recently. Pressdent is a pump-dispensed toothpaste that was originally discovered by a 10-year-old who dumped water and toothpaste into a liquid-soap container. The child's father decided to set up a company to market the new product. Pressdent was first introduced in Canada, then Southern California. The eventual goal is 3.5 percent of the American dentifrice market. Whether Pressdent ever makes it out of the introductory stage remains to be seen, but the small company remains confident. The entrepreneurial father, Nathalie Goulet, remarked, "Eventually toothpaste in a tube will go the way of shaving cream in a tube."[5]

[5]Alan Freeman, "Will People Buy Toothpaste that Doesn't Come in a Tube?" *The Wall Street Journal* (June 3, 1982), p. 25.

Growth Stage

Sales volume rises rapidly during the growth stage as new customers make initial purchases and early buyers repurchase the product. Word-of-mouth and mass advertising induce hesitant buyers to make trial purchases. Approximately 750,000 videotape machines were sold in the United States in 1980, six times the number sold in 1977. These machines, a product that is currently in the growth stage, are in one out of every 45 homes with a television set.[6]

As the firm begins to realize substantial profits from its investment during the growth stage, it attracts competitors. Success breeds imitation, and other firms inevitably rush into the market with competitive products in search of profit. Royal Crown provides a good example of this situation. Royal Crown has developed more new products than any of its competitors like Coca-Cola, PepsiCo, Dr. Pepper, and 7-Up. It was the first to sell soft drinks in cans, use 16-ounce returnable bottles, and offer a diet cola. Still Royal Crown remains only the fifth largest firm in the industry. Royal Crown vice-president Arnold Belasco observed: "At each stage, the industry pooh-poohs what we consider a breakthrough, then follows our lead."[7]

Maturity Stage

Industry sales continue to grow during the early part of the maturity stage, but eventually they reach a plateau as the backlog of potential customers is exhausted. By this time, a large number of competitors have entered the market, and profits decline as competition intensifies. Levi Strauss & Co. is an example of a firm affected by a maturing marketplace. An aging U.S. population and newer trends like the "preppy" and "dress up" look have had a decided impact on the jeans business. Levi Strauss—well known for its marketing expertise—is now taking steps to deal with the market stage that confronts it.[8]

In the maturity stage, differences among competing products diminish as competitors discover the product features and promotional characteristics most desired by the market. Heavy promotional outlays emphasize subtle differences among competing products, and brand competition intensifies. For the first time, available products exceed industry demand. Companies attempting to increase their sales and market share must do so at the expense of competitors. As competition intensifies, the competitors often cut prices in an attempt to attract new buyers. Even though a price reduction may be the easiest method of

[6]Kathleen K. Wayne, "Video Fever," *Forbes* (September 1, 1980), p. 36.

[7]Margaret Loeb, "Royal Crown Shakes Soft-Drink Business with Changes but Never Quite Gets Ahead," *The Wall Street Journal* (May 24, 1982), p. 21.

[8]Victor F. Zonana, "Levi Tries to Revive Sagging Jeans Business Amid Predictions of Denim Look's Demise," *The Wall Street Journal* (November 11, 1981), p. 33.

Figure 10.3 Product Life Cycle Overlap

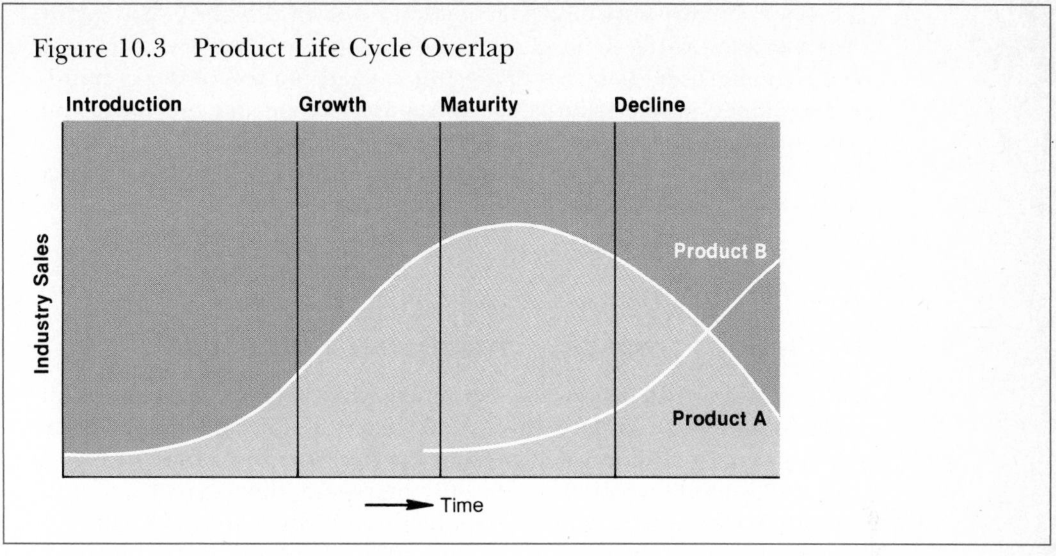

inducing additional purchases, it is also one of the simplest moves for competitors to duplicate. Reduced prices result in decreased revenues for all firms in the industry unless the price cuts produce enough increased purchases to offset the loss in revenue on each item sold.[9]

Decline Stage

In the final stage of the product's life, innovations or shifting consumer preferences bring about an absolute decline in industry sales. The safety razor and electric shaver replace the straight razor. Pac-Man replaces Rubik's Cube as the latest fad, and the black-and-white television is exchanged for a color set. As Figure 10.3 indicates, the decline stage of the old product doubles as the growth stage for a new product entry.

Industry profits decline and in some cases actually become negative as sales fall and firms cut prices in a bid for the dwindling market. Manufacturers gradually begin to leave the industry in search of more profitable products.

Robert Mac Donald, the President of ITT Life Insurance Corp., did just that in 1982, when he withdrew from the whole life insurance business. Whole life insurance, which combines protection with a savings aspect paying about 4 percent interest, accounted for 96 percent of the insurer's new business in 1981. But Mac Donald noted that term insur-

[9]Students of economics will recognize this situation as exemplifying price elasticity of demand. For a discussion of the concept of elasticity, see Edwin G. Dolan, *Basic Economics,* 3d ed. (Hinsdale, Ill.: The Dryden Press, 1983).

ance, policies that provide protection but no savings feature, had grown over 50 times faster than whole life over a five-year period. ITT now sells a combination plan that divests the savings portion of the premium into a money market fund. Mac Donald's decision did not make him popular with some members of the insurance community: ". . . no one says I am wrong. They just insist that whole life is a durable product. Well, so are buggy whips."[10]

Departures from the Traditional PLC Model

The preceding discussion has examined what is considered the traditional product life cycle with its four clearly delineated stages. Some sources suggest additional stages, but the four identified here in Figure 10.2 are generally accepted within the marketing discipline.

Considerable controversy surrounds the format and usefulness of product life-cycle theory, despite the multitude of writings on the subject. These issues concern: (1) the length of each product life-cycle stage; (2) the existence of product life-cycle variants; and (3) the current role of product and service fashions and fads.

Length of Cycle Stages

Research now suggests that product life cycles may be getting shorter, specifically in the introductory and growth stages.[11] While definitive conclusions are not yet available, most marketers do accept the fact that product life cycles and their stages show considerable variation in length.

Professor John O. King has argued that the PLC models should reflect the reality that products and services move through product life cycles at varying speeds. King correctly suggests redrawing the model in Figure 10.2 to show a broken horizontal axis, reflecting the varying lengths of the PLC stages. (See Figure 10.4.)

Alternative Product Life Cycles

Research by the Marketing Science Institute reported that few products actually had life cycles resembling the traditional model. The study dealt with 100 categories of food, health, and personal care products. The traditional model was applicable for only 17 percent of the general

[10]Lisa Gross, "Good Bye, Whole Life," *Forbes* (March 29, 1982), p. 133.

[11]William Qualls, Richard W. Olshavsky, and Ronald E. Michaels, "Shortening the PLC—An Empirical Test," *Journal of Marketing* (Fall 1981), pp. 76–80.

Figure 10.4 The King Adaptation of the PLC Concept

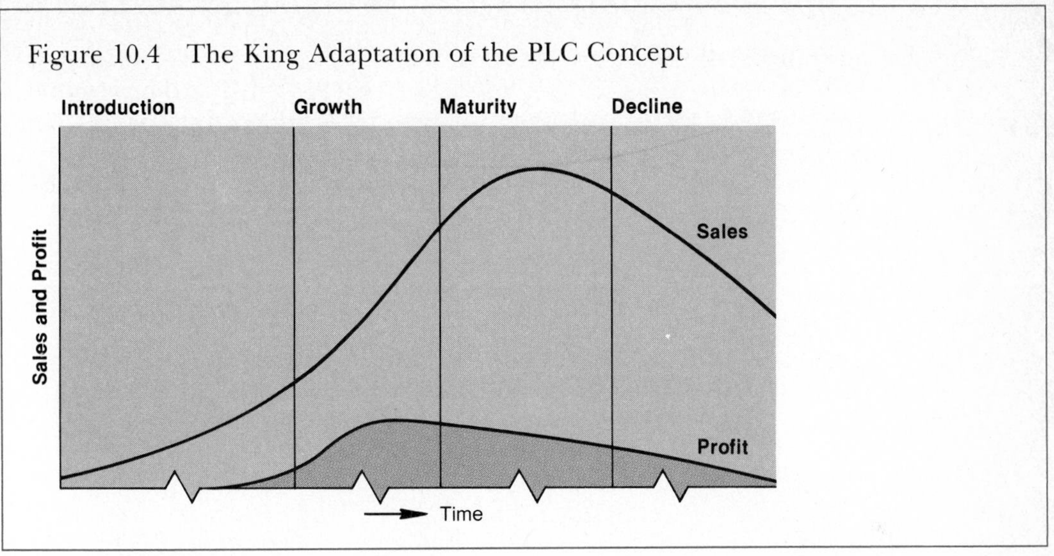

Source: John O. King, "Revised Graph of Product Life Cycle Theory Could Eliminate Confusion in Marketing Texts." Reprinted with permission from *Marketing News* (July 24, 1981), p. 26. Published by the American Marketing Association.

categories and 20 percent of the specific brands.[12] This research supports the argument that alternative product life cycles exist. Variants to the traditional model are shown in Figure 10.5.

As shown in Figure 10.5, some products simply do not make it. These can be labeled the "instant busts"; a failure simply does not go through the four steps of the traditional model. Still other products are introduced and then have to be modified in some way, such as design, packaging, promotional strategy, before the introduction is continued. Information derived from test market situations can indicate that changes are necessary if the product launch is to be successful. (Test markets are described in Chapter 11.) This type of start-up, start-again launch is labeled the "aborted introduction" in Figure 10.5.

Still other products become market speciality items (discussed later in the chapter) thus providing long and stable maturity stages. A common variant is the "pyramided cycle," where the product is adapted via additional technological or marketing inputs. This variant is characterized by a series of regrowth periods and will also be discussed later in the chapter.

[12]Rolando Pilli and Victor J. Cook, "A Test of the Product Life Cycle as a Model of Sales Behavior," *Marketing Science Institute Working Paper* (November 1967) and "Validity of the Product Life Cycle," *The Journal of Business* (October 1969), pp. 385–400. This research is reviewed in William S. Sachs and George Benson, *Product Planning and Management* (Tulsa, Okla.: PennWell Books, 1981), p. 80.

Figure 10.5 Alternative Product Life Cycles

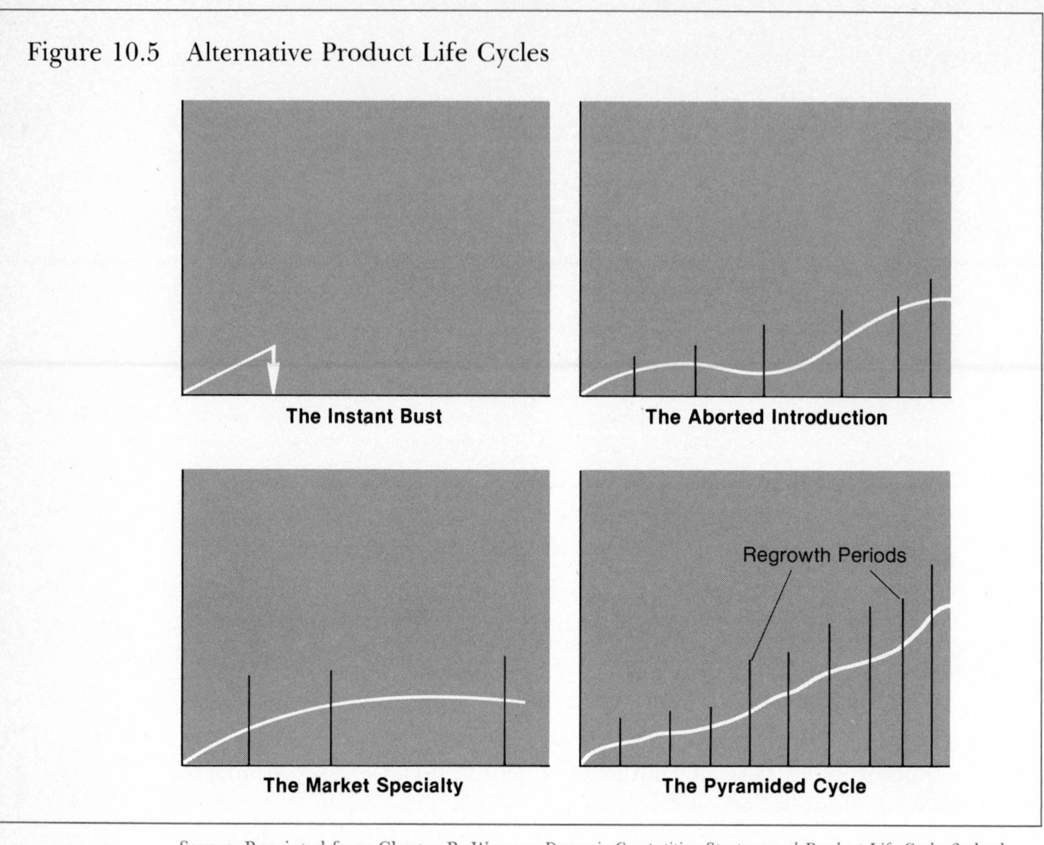

Source: Reprinted from Chester R. Wasson, *Dynamic Competitive Strategy and Product Life Cycle,* 3rd ed. (Austin, Texas: Austin Press, 1978), p. 13.

Fashions and Fads

Fashions and fads are also important to marketers. **Fashions** are currently popular products that tend to follow recurring life cycles (see Figure 10.6).[13] Women's apparel fashions provide the best examples. The miniskirt was reintroduced in 1982 after being out of fashion for over a decade.

By contrast, **fads** are fashions with abbreviated life cycles. Consider the case of popular music for teenagers. Disco gave way to punk and new wave, which has since been replaced by the *new music,* a takeoff on

[13]Fashion cycles are discussed in Raymond A. Marquardt, James C. Makens, and Robert G. Roe, *Retail Management,* 3d ed. (Hinsdale, Ill.: The Dryden Press, 1983), pp. 98–99. Also see George B. Sproles, "Analyzing Fashion Life Cycles—Principles and Perspectives," *Journal of Marketing* (Fall 1981), pp. 116–124.

Figure 10.6 Fad Cycles

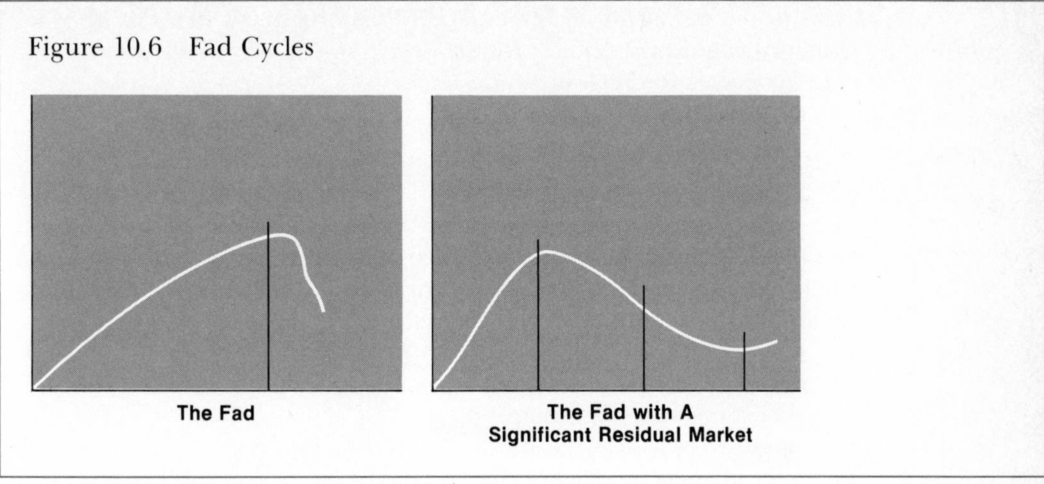

Source: Reprinted from Chester R. Wasson, *Dynamic Competitive Strategy and Product Life Cycle,* 3rd ed. (Austin, Texas: Austin Press, 1978), p. 13.

rock-and-roll.[14] Most fads experience short-lived popularity and then fade quickly. However, there are some that maintain a residual market among certain market segments. Both of these fad cycles are shown in Figure 10.6.

Product Life Cycles Considerations in Marketing Strategy

The product life cycle—with all its variants—is a useful tool in marketing strategy decision making. For instance, the knowledge that profits assume a predictable pattern through the stages and that promotional emphasis must shift from product information in the early stages to brand promotion in the later ones should allow the marketing decision maker to improve conditions that exist in each stage of the product life cycle through appropriate marketing efforts.

A firm's marketing efforts should emphasize stimulating demand at the introductory stage. The emphasis shifts to cultivating selective demand in the growth period. Market segmentation should be used extensively in the maturity period. During the decline, the emphasis again

[14]Stephen Grover, "Record Business Slumps as Taping and Video Games Take Away Sales," *The Wall Street Journal* (February 18, 1982), p. 25.

shifts to increasing primary demand. Table 10.1 also suggests appropriate pricing, distribution, product development, and service and warranty strategies for each life-cycle stage.

Extending the Product Life Cycle

One marketing strategy is to extend the product life cycle as long as possible. Marketing managers can accomplish this objective if they take action early in the maturity stage. Product life cycles can be extended indefinitely by actions designed to:

1. Increase the frequency of use by present customers.
2. Add new users.
3. Find new uses for the product.
4. Change package sizes, labels, or product quality.[15]

Examples of such actions are cited below.

Increasing the Frequency of Use Noxzema was originally an occasional-use skin medicine that was intended to be a routine-use, beauty-care item. Similarly, Underwood Deviled Ham started as a hor d'oeuvres topping but research indicated that heavy users treated it as a sandwich spread. Underwood quickly made it into just that—a sandwich spread.[16]

Add New Users Cadillac introduced its Cimarron to attract non-Cadillac buyers who usually purchased cars like BMW. Crest and Colgate were re-introduced as sweeter-tasting gels to appeal to younger consumers further extending the life cycles of these well-known brands.[17] Finding new users is sometimes difficult. Gerber Products failed in attempts to sell its products to the 15 to 22 age group as desserts and snacks. Many still regarded Gerber as baby food.[18]

Find New Uses Q-tips cotton swabs were originally sold as a baby-care item, but Chesebrough-Pond's Inc.'s marketers found a new use for them as makeup applicators. Arm & Hammer's baking soda was used primarily in cooking until its product life cycle was extended by finding

[15]See David R. Rink and John E. Swan, "Product Life Cycle Research: A Literature Review," *Journal of Business Research* (September 1979), pp. 219–242.

[16]Theodore Karger, "5 Ways to Find New Uses—Re-Evaluate Your Old Products," *Marketing Times* (July/August 1981), p. 17.

[17]Bill Abrams, "Warring Toothpaste Makers Spend Millions Luring Buyers to Slightly Altered Products," *The Wall Street Journal* (September 9, 1981), p. 33.

[18]Gail Bronson, "Baby Food It Is, but Gerber Wants Teen-Agers to Think of It as Dessert," *The Wall Street Journal* (July 17, 1981), p. 29.

Table 10.1 Organizational and Environmental Conditions with Appropriate Marketing Efforts for Various Life Cycle Stages

	Introduction	Growth	Maturity: Early Maturity	Maturity: Late Maturity	Decline
Organizational Conditions	High costs Inefficient production levels Cash demands	Smoothing production Lowering costs Operation efficiencies Product improvement work	Efficient scale of operation Product modification work Decreasing profits	Low profits Standardized production	
Environmental Conditions	Few or no competitors Limited product awareness and knowledge Limited demand	Expanding markets Expanded distribution Competition strengthens Prices soften a bit	Slowing growth Strong competition Expanded market Heightened competition	Faltering demand Fierce competition Shrinking number of competitors Established distribution patterns	Permanently declining demand Reduction of competitors Limited product offerings Price stabilization
Marketing Efforts	Stimulate demand Establish high price Offer limited product variety Increase distribution	Cultivate selective demand Product improvement Strengthen distribution Price flexibility	Emphasize market segmentation Improve service and warranty Reduce prices	Ultimate in market segmentation Competitive pricing Retain distribution	Increase primary demand Profit opportunity pricing Prune and strengthen distribution

Source: Adapted from Burton H. Marcus and Edward M. Tauber, *Marketing Analysis and Decision Making* (Boston: Little, Brown & Co., 1979), pp. 115–116. Copyright © 1979 by Burton H. Marcus and Edward M. Tauber. Reprinted by permission of Little, Brown and Company.

new uses as a denture cleaner, swimming pool pH adjuster, cleaning agent, flame extinguisher, first-aid remedy, and refrigerator freshener.[19]

Change the Package Size, Label, or Product Quality Levi Strauss Canada Inc. has introduced a limited edition jean called 555. The straight-leg jean uses details of the original jean that Levi Strauss made during the California Gold Rush of 1849. Each pair carries a five-digit serial number. A postage-paid card is used to register each pair of the $33.95 jeans.[20]

Consumer Adoption Process

Once the product is launched, consumers begin a process of evaluating the new item. This evaluation is known as the **adoption process,** whereby potential consumers go through a series of stages from learning of the new product to trying it and deciding to purchase it regularly or to reject it. These stages in the consumer adoption process can be classified as:

1. Awareness: individuals first learn of the new product but lack information about it.
2. Interest: they begin to seek out information about it.
3. Evaluation: they consider whether the product is beneficial.
4. Trial: they make a trial purchase in order to determine its usefulness.
5. Adoption/Rejection: if the trial purchase is satisfactory, they decide to make regular use of the product.[21]

The marketing manager needs to understand the adoption process so that he or she can move potential consumers to the adoption stage. Once the manager is aware of a large number of consumers at the interest stage, steps can be taken to stimulate sales. For example, Gillette introduced Aapri Apricot Facial Scrub by mailing 15 million samples to households in the United States and Canada. Total sample costs for the new skin product designed to compete with Noxzema, Pond's, and Oil of Olay were $4.1 million.[22] Sampling is a technique that reduces the risk of evaluation and trial, moving the consumer quickly to the adoption stage.

[19]Karger, "5 Ways to Find New Uses—Re-Evaluate Your Old Products," p. 18.

[20]Alan Freeman, "Levi Unit Tries to Give Jeans Limited Appeal," *The Wall Street Journal* (August 11, 1981), p. 25.

[21]Everett M. Rogers and F. Floyd Shoemaker, *Communication of Innovations* (New York: The Free Press, 1971), pp. 135–157.

[22]"Gillette Spends $17.4 Million to Introduce Aapri, Gain Foothold in Skin Care Market," *Marketing News* (May 29, 1981), p. 6. For a discussion of the use of marketing techniques to facilitate trial purchases, see James W. Taylor and Paul S. Hugstad, "Add-On Purchasing: Consumer Behavior in the Trial of New Products," *Journal of the Academy of Marketing Science* (Winter 1980), pp. 294–299.

Adopter Categories

Some people purchase a new product almost as soon as it is placed on the market. Others wait for additional information and rely on the experiences of the first purchasers before making trial purchases. *Consumer innovators*—first purchasers—comprise the initial buyers in the beginning of a product's life cycle. Some families were first in their communities to buy color television sets. Some doctors are first to prescribe new drugs, and some farmers planted hybrid seeds much earlier than their neighbors. Some people are quick to adopt new fashions, and some drivers made early use of automobile diagnostic centers.

A number of investigations analyzing the adoption of new products has resulted in the identification of five categories of purchasers based on relative time of adoption. These categories, shown in Figure 10.7, are innovators, early adopters, early majority, late majority, and laggards.

The **diffusion process** is the acceptance of new products and services by the members of the community or social system. Figure 10.7 shows this process follows a normal distribution. A few people adopt at first, then the number of adopters increases rapidly as the value of the innovation is apparent. The rate finally diminishes as fewer potential consumers remain in the nonadopter category.

Since the categories are based on the normal distribution, standard deviations are used to partition them. Innovators are the first 2.5 percent to adopt the new product; laggards are the last 16 percent to do so. Excluded from Figure 10.7 are the nonadopters, those who never adopt the innovation.

Identifying the First Adopters

Locating first buyers of new products represents a challenge for the marketing manager. If first buyers can be reached early in the product's development or introduction, they can serve as a test market, evaluating the product and making suggestions for modifications. Since early purchasers are often opinion leaders from whom others seek advice, their attitudes toward new products are quickly communicated to others. Acceptance or rejection of the innovation by these purchasers can help forecast the expected success of the new product.

Unfortunately, first adopters of one new product are not necessarily first adopters of other products or services. A large number of research studies has, however, established some general characteristics of most first adopters.

First adopters tend to be younger, to have a higher social status, to be better educated, and to enjoy a higher income than others. They are more mobile than later adopters and change both their jobs and home addresses more often. They are also more likely to rely on impersonal

Figure 10.7 Categories of Adopters on the Basis of Relative Time of Adoption

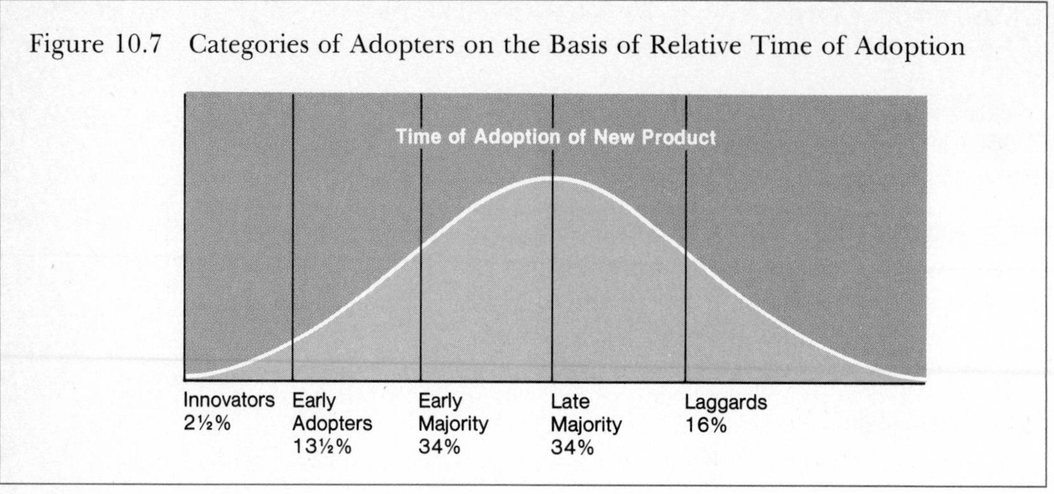

Source: Reprinted by permission of Macmillan Publishing Company, Inc., from *Communication of Innovations: A Cross Cultural Approach*, by Everett M. Rogers and F. Floyd Shoemaker. Copyright © 1971 by the Free Press, a Division of Macmillan Publishing Company, Inc.

information sources than are later adopters, who depend more on promotional information from the company and word-of-mouth communication.[23]

Rate of Adoption Determinants

Frisbees progressed from the product introduction stage to the market maturity stage in a period of six months, but it took the U.S. Department of Agriculture 13 years to convince corn farmers to use hybrid seed corn, an innovation capable of doubling corn yields. The adoption rate is influenced by five characteristics of the innovation:

Relative Advantage: the degree to which the innovation appears superior to previous ideas or products. The greater the relative advantage—in terms of lower price, physical movements, or ease of use—the faster the adoption rate.

Compatibility: the degree to which the innovation is consistent with the values and experiences of potential adopters. The failure of Analoze, the waterless pain remedy discussed earlier, resulted largely from con-

[23]Ronald Marks and Eugene Hughes, "Profiling the Consumer Innovator," in *Evolving Marketing Thought for 1980,* (eds.) John H. Summey and Ronald D. Taylor (New Orleans: Southern Marketing Association, 1980), pp. 115–118; Elizabeth Hirschman, "Innovativeness, Novelty Seeking and Consumer Creativity," *Journal of Consumer Research* (December 1980), pp. 283–295; and Richard W. Olshavsky, "Time and the Rate of Adoption of Innovations," *Journal of Consumer Research* (March 1980), pp. 425–428.

sumers' unwillingness to accept a product whose directions for use conflicted drastically with consumer custom.

Complexity: the relative difficulty of understanding the innovation. The more difficult the new product is to understand or to use, the longer it will take to be generally accepted in most cases.

Divisibility: the degree to which the innovation can be used on a limited basis. First adopters face two types of risk, financial losses and ridicule by others if the new product proves unsatisfactory. The option of sampling the innovation on a limited basis allows these risks to be reduced and generally accelerates the rate of adoption.

Communicability: the degree to which the results of using the product are observable or communicable to others. If the superiority of the innovation can be displayed in a tangible form, the adoption rate will be increased.[24]

These five characteristics can be implemented to some extent by the marketing manager in accelerating the rate of adoption. Product complexity must be overcome by informative promotional messages. Products should be designed to emphasize their relative advantages and, whenever possible, should be divisible for sample purchases. If divisibility is impossible, in-home demonstrations or trial placements in the home can be used. Positive attempts must also be made to ensure compatibility of the innovation with the adopters' value systems.

These actions are based on extensive research studies of innovators in agriculture, medicine, and consumer goods. They should pay off in increased sales by accelerating the rate of adoption in each of the adopter categories.

Defining Consumer and Industrial Goods

How a firm markets its product depends largely on the product itself. For example, Chanel stresses subtle promotions in prestige media such as *The New Yorker* and *Vogue* magazines and markets its perfumes through department stores and specialty shops. Hershey Chocolate Company markets its candy products through candy wholesalers to thousands of supermarkets, variety stores, discount houses, and vending machine companies. A firm manufacturing and marketing forklifts may use sales representatives to call on industrial buyers and ship its product either directly from the factory or from regional warehouses.

[24]For a more thorough discussion of the speed of the adoption process, see Rogers and Shoemaker, *Communication of Innovations,* pp. 135–157.

Product strategy differs for consumer goods and industrial goods. As defined earlier, consumer goods are products destined for use by the ultimate consumer, and industrial goods are products used directly or indirectly in producing other goods for resale. These two major categories can be broken down further.

Classifying Consumer Goods

Although a number of classification systems have been suggested, the system most often used is based on consumer buying habits. The three categories of consumer goods are convenience goods, shopping goods, and specialty goods.[25]

Convenience Goods

The products that the consumer wants to purchase frequently, immediately, and with a minimum of effort are called **convenience goods.** Milk, bread, butter, eggs, and beer (the staples of most 24-hour convenience food stores) are all convenience goods; so are newspapers, chewing gum, magazines, M&M's and the items found in most vending machines.

Convenience goods are usually sold by brand name and are low priced. Many of them, such as bread, milk, and gasoline, are staple items and the consumer's supply must be constantly replenished. In most cases, the buyer has already decided to purchase a particular brand of gasoline or candy or to buy at a particular store, and spends little time deliberating about the purchase decision. Products purchased on the spur of the moment and out of habit when the supply is low are referred to as *impulse goods.*

The consumer rarely visits competing stores or compares price and quality in purchasing convenience goods. The possible gains to be made from such comparisons are outweighed by the costs of acquiring the additional information. This does not mean, however, that the consumer is destined to remain permanently loyal to one brand of beer, candy, or cigarettes. People continually receive new information from radio and television advertisements, billboards, and word-of-mouth communication. Since the price of most convenience goods is low, trial

[25]This three-way classification of consumer goods was first proposed by Melvin T. Copeland. See his *Principles of Merchandising* (New York: McGraw-Hill, 1924), chapters 2–4. For a more recent discussion of this classification scheme, see Marvin A. Jolson and Stephen L. Proia, "Classification of Consumer Goods—A Subjective Measure?" in *Marketing: 1776–1976 and Beyond* (Chicago: American Marketing Association, 1976), pp. 71–75.

purchases of competing brands or products are made with little financial risk, and often new habits are developed.

Since the consumer is unwilling to spend much effort in purchasing convenience goods, the manufacturer must strive to make them as convenient as possible. Candy, cigarettes, and newspapers are sold in almost every supermarket, service station, and restaurant. Where retail outlets are physically separated from a large number of consumers, the manufacturer constructs small "stores" in the form of vending machines and places them in spots that are convenient for its customers, such as office buildings and factories. Coca-Cola distributors know that most of their customers will not leave the building in search of a Coke if the vending machine is completely stocked with Pepsi even if they prefer Coca-Cola. Coca-Cola distributors must protect their brand loyalty by ensuring that their product is equally available.

Retailers usually carry several competing brands of convenience products and are unlikely to promote any particular one. The promotional burden, therefore, falls on the manufacturer, who must advertise extensively to develop consumer acceptance of the product. The Coca-Cola promotional program consists of radio and television commercials, magazine ads, billboards, and point-of-purchase displays in stores. These efforts to motivate the consumer to choose Coke over competing brands are a good example of a manufacturer's promotion designed to stimulate consumer demand.

Shopping Goods

In contrast with convenience goods, **shopping goods** are purchased only after the consumer has made comparisons of competing goods in competing stores on bases such as price, quality, style, and color. The purchaser of shopping goods lacks complete information prior to the shopping trip and gathers information during it.

A woman intent on adding a new dress to her wardrobe may visit many stores, try on a number of dresses, and spend days making the final choice. She may follow a regular route from store to store in surveying competing offerings and ultimately will select the dress that most appeals to her. New stores carrying assortments of shopping goods must ensure that they are located near other shopping goods stores so that they will be included in shopping expeditions.

Shopping goods are typically more expensive than convenience goods and are most often purchased by women. In addition to women's apparel, shopping goods include such items as appliances, furniture, jewelry, shoes, and used automobiles.

Some shopping goods, such as children's shoes, are considered homogeneous; that is, the consumer views them as essentially the same. Others, such as furniture and clothing, are considered heterogeneous or essentially different. Price is an important factor in the purchasing of homogeneous shopping goods, while quality and styling are relatively more important in the purchase of heterogeneous goods.[26]

Important features of shopping goods are the physical attributes of the product, its price and styling, and even the retail store that handles it. The brand is often of lesser importance, in spite of the large amounts of money manufacturers often spend promoting their brands.

Since buyers of shopping goods expend some effort in making their purchases, manufacturers of shopping goods utilize fewer retail stores than for convenience goods. Retailers and manufacturers work closely in promoting shopping goods, and retail purchases are often made directly from the manufacturer or its representative rather than the wholesaler. Fashion merchandise buyers for department stores and specialty shops make regular buying trips to regional and national markets in New York, Dallas, and Los Angeles. Buyers for furniture retailers often go directly to the factories of furniture manufacturers or visit furniture trade shows.

Specialty Goods

The specialty goods purchaser is well aware of what he or she wants and is willing to make a special effort to obtain it. The nearest Cartier dealer may be 100 miles away, for example, but the watch purchaser willing to spend several thousand dollars will go there to buy a prestigious watch.

Specialty goods possess some unique characteristics that cause the buyer to prize that particular brand. For these products, the buyer has complete information prior to the shopping trip and is unwilling to accept substitutes.

Specialty goods are typically high priced and are frequently branded. Since consumers are willing to exert considerable effort to obtain them, fewer retail outlets are required. Mercury outboard motors and Porsche sports cars may be handled by only one or two retailers for each 100,000 people.

Relating the Consumer Goods Classification to Marketing Mix Factors

The three-way consumer goods classification allows the marketing manager to gain additional information for use in developing a marketing strategy. Consumer behavior patterns differ for each class of consumer goods. For example, once a new food product has been classified as a

[26]For an early discussion of the distinctions between homogeneous and heterogeneous shopping goods, see E. J. McCarthy, *Basic Marketing* (Homewood, Ill.: Richard D. Irwin, 1964), pp. 398–400. See also Harry A. Lipson and John R. Darling, *Marketing Fundamentals* (New York: John Wiley and Sons, 1974), p. 244.

Table 10.2 The Marketing Impact of the Consumer Goods Classification

Factor	Convenience Goods	Shopping Goods	Specialty Goods
Consumer Factors			
Planning time involved in purchase	Very little	Considerable	Extensive
Purchase frequency	Frequent	Less frequent	Infrequent
Importance of convenient location	Critical importance	Important	Unimportant
Comparison of price and quality	Very little	Considerable	Very little
Marketing Mix Factors			
Price	Low	Relatively high	High
Advertising	By manufacturer	Both	Both
Channel length	Long	Relatively short	Very short
Number of retail outlets	Many	Few	Very small number; often one per market area
Store image	Unimportant	Very important	Important

convenience good, insights are gained about marketing needs in branding, promotion, pricing, and distribution methods. The impact of the goods classifications and their associated consumer factors are related to marketing mix variables in Table 10.2.

Problems in Applying the Consumer Goods Classification

The consumer goods classification also poses some problems. The major problem is that it suggests a circumscribed, three-way series of demarcations into which all products easily fit. Some products do fit neatly into one of the classifications, but others fall into the grey areas between each category.

How, for example, should a new automobile be classified? It is expensive, sold by brand, and handled by a few exclusive dealers in each city. Before classifying it as a specialty good, other characteristics must be considered. Most new-car buyers shop extensively among competing models and auto dealers before deciding on the best deal. A more effective way to utilize the classification is to consider it a continuum representing degrees of effort expended by the consumer.[27] If this is done,

[27]A similar classification scheme has been proposed by Leo Aspinwall, who considers five product characteristics in classifying consumer goods: replacement rate, gross margin (the difference between cost and selling price), adjustment (the necessary changes made in a goal to satisfy precisely the consumer's needs), time of consumption (the time interval during which the product provides satisfaction), and length of consumer searching time. See Leo V. Aspinwall, "The Characteristics of Goods Theory," in *Four Marketing Theories* (Boulder: Bureau of Business Research, University of Colorado, 1961).

the new-car purchase can be located between the categories of shopping and specialty goods, but nearer the specialty-goods end of the continuum.

A second problem with the classification system is that consumers differ in their buying patterns. One person will make an unplanned purchase of a new Chevy Citation, while others will shop extensively before purchasing a car. One buyer's impulse purchase does not make the Citation a convenience good. Goods are classified by the purchase patterns of the majority of buyers.

Classifying Industrial Goods

Industrial goods can be subdivided into five categories: installations, accessory equipment, fabricated parts and materials, raw materials, and industrial supplies. Industrial buyers are professional consumers; their job is to make effective purchase decisions. The purchase decision process involved in buying supplies of flour for General Mills, for example, is much the same as that used in buying the same commodity for Pillsbury. Thus the classification system for industrial goods must be based on product uses rather than on consumer buying patterns.

Installations

Installations are major capital assets like factories and heavy machinery used to produce products and services. Installations are the specialty goods of the industrial market. New planes for United Airlines or locomotives for Burlington Northern are examples of installations.

Since installations are relatively long-lived and involve large sums of money, their purchase represents a major decision for an organization. Negotiations often extend over a period of several months and involve the participation of numerous decision makers. In many cases, the selling company must provide technical expertise. When custom-made equipment is involved, representatives of the selling firm work closely with the buyer's engineers and production personnel to design the most feasible product for the buying firm.

Price is almost never the deciding factor in the purchase of installations. The purchasing firm is interested in the product's efficiency and performance over its useful life. The firm also wants a minimum of breakdowns. "Down time" is expensive because employees are nonproductive (but still are paid) while the machinery is repaired.

Since most of the factories of firms purchasing installations are geographically concentrated, the selling firm places its promotional emphasis on well-trained salespeople who often have a technical background.

Most installations are marketed directly on a manufacturer-to-user basis. Even though a sale may be a one-time transaction, contracts often call for regular product servicing. In the case of extremely expensive installations, such as computer and electronic equipment, some firms lease the installations rather than sell them outright and assign personnel directly to the lessee to operate or to maintain the equipment.

Accessory Equipment

Fewer decision makers are usually involved in purchasing **accessory equipment**—second-level capital items that are used in the production of products and services but are usually less expensive and shorter-lived than installations. Although quality and service still remain important criteria in purchasing accessory equipment, the firm is likely to be much more price conscious. Accessory equipment includes such products as desk calculators, hand tools, portable drills, small lathes, and typewriters. Although these goods are considered capital items and are depreciated over several years, their useful life is generally much shorter than that of an installation.

Because of the need for continuous representation and the more widespread geographic dispersion of accessory equipment purchasers, a wholesaler, often called an **industrial distributor,** may be used to contact potential customers in each geographic area. Technical assistance is usually not necessary, and the manufacturer of accessory equipment often can effectively utilize such wholesalers in marketing the firm's products. Manufacturers also use advertising more than do installation producers.

Component Parts and Materials

While installations and accessory equipment are used in producing the final product, **component parts and materials** are the finished industrial goods that actually become part of the final product. Champion spark plugs make a new Chevrolet complete; batteries are often added to Mattel toys; tires are included with a Dodge pickup truck. Some materials, such as flour, undergo further processing before producing a finished product.

Purchasers of component parts and materials need a regular continuous supply of uniform quality goods. These goods are generally purchased on contract for a period of one year or more. Direct sale is common, and satisfied customers often become permanent buyers. Wholesalers sometimes are used for fill-in purchases and in handling sales to smaller purchasers.

The Ordeal of Becoming a McDonald's French Fry

French fries are a big deal at McDonald's. They account for $1 billion annually, about one fifth of total sales. Except for breakfast sales, 70 percent of McDonald's customers order them. As a result, McDonald's pays particular attention to the raw materials used in their popular product.

McDonald's uses only russet Burbanks which have a unique taste and make crispier french fries because of a high solid to water ratio. Their primary supplier is J.R. Simplot of Caldwell, Idaho, who processes the potatoes into frozen french fries. McDonald's has exacting standards for its fries. McDonald's fries are:

- Steamed, not blanched or quick-scalded
- Dried at higher than normal heat levels, and
- Sprayed with sugar, not dipped.

The company believes this process produces better fries. Even the length has to be just right. Only 20 percent of McDonald's fries can be less than 2 inches long; 40 percent have to be 2 to 3 inches long; and another 40 percent must exceed 3 inches.

McDonald's ran into some problems with its raw materials standards when it expanded overseas. Russet Burbanks are not grown in Europe, and potato imports are prohibited. McDonald's considers European-grown potatoes unacceptable, so it tried some unique approaches to getting russet Burbanks into Europe. The Dutch agreed to admit five potatoes after an eight-month quarantine, but they were destroyed by a potato virus. McDonald's planted russet Burbanks in Spain under the theory that they would be acceptable throughout Europe when Spain joined the Common Market in 1983, but this effort also failed. However, McDonald's did get its potatoes to grow in Tasmania, so they can now supply Australian outlets with the proper type of french fries. In any case, it is clear that McDonald's regards russet Burbanks an important raw material in their business.

Source: Meg Cox, "A French-Fry Diary: From Idaho Furrow to Golden Arches," *The Wall Street Journal* (February 8, 1982), pp. 1, 23.

Raw Materials

Farm products, such as cattle, cotton, eggs, milk, pigs, and soybeans, and natural products, such as coal, copper, iron ore, and lumber, constitute **raw materials.** They are similar to component parts and materials in that they become part of the final products.

Since most raw materials are graded, the purchaser is assured of standardized products with uniform quality. As with component parts and materials, direct sale of raw materials is common, and sales are typically made on a contractual basis. Wholesalers are increasingly involved in the purchase of raw materials from foreign suppliers.

Price is seldom a deciding factor in the purchase of raw materials, since it is often quoted at a central market and is virtually identical among competing sellers. Purchasers buy raw materials from the firms they consider most able to deliver in the quantity and the quality required.

Supplies

If installations represent the specialty goods of the industrial market, then operating supplies are the convenience goods. **Supplies** are regular expense items necessary in the daily operation of the firm, but not part of the final product.

Supplies are sometimes called **MRO items** because they can be divided into three categories: (1) maintenance items, such as brooms, floor-cleaning compounds, and light bulbs; (2) repair items, such as nuts and bolts used in repairing equipment; and (3) operating supplies, such as heating fuel, lubricating oil, and office stationery.

The regular purchase of operating supplies is a routine aspect of the purchasing agent's job. Wholesalers are very often used in the sale of supplies due to the items' low unit prices, small sales, and large number of potential buyers. Since supplies are relatively standardized, price competition is frequently heavy. However, the purchasing agent spends little time in making purchase decisions. He or she frequently places telephone orders or mail orders, or makes regular purchases from the sales representative of the local office-supply wholesaler.

Summary

A critical variable in the firm's marketing mix is the product it plans to offer its market target. The best price, most efficient distribution channel, and most effective promotional campaign cannot gain continuing purchases of an inferior product.

Consumers view products not only in physical terms but more often in terms of expected want satisfaction. The broad marketing conception of a product encompasses a bundle of physical, service, and symbolic attributes designed to produce this want satisfaction. The total product concept consists of the product image, brand, package and label, and warranty and service.

Most successful products pass through the four stages of the product life cycle: introduction, growth, maturity and decline. Several departures from the traditional product life-cycle model are noted in Chapter 10. First, there is evidence that product life cycles may be getting shorter, particularly in the introductory and growth stages. Second, research shows that few products actually conform to the standard PLC model, so several alternative product life cycles are outlined. Finally, there is the matter of fashions and fads. Fashions are currently popular products that tend to have recurring life cycles. By contrast, fads are fashions with abbreviated life cycles.

The product life-cycle concept has a significant impact on marketing strategy. Pricing, distribution, and promotion strategies, as well as product strategy, must vary in accordance with the product life-cycle stage. Marketers should also attempt to extend the life cycles of successful products for as long as possible.

Consumers also go through a series of stages in adopting new product offerings: initial product awareness, interest, evaluation, trial purchase, and adoption or rejection of the new product.

Although first adopters of new products vary among product classes, several common characteristics have been isolated. First adopters are often younger, better educated, and more mobile, and they have higher incomes and higher social status than later adopters.

The rate of adoption for new products depends on five characteristics: (1) relative advantage, the degree of superiority of the innovation over the previous product; (2) compatibility, the degree to which the new product or idea is consistent with the value system of potential purchasers; (3) complexity of the new product; (4) divisibility, the degree to which trial purchases on a small scale are possible; and (5) communicability, the degree to which the superiority of the innovation can be transmitted to other potential buyers.

Products are classified as either consumer or industrial goods. Consumer goods are used by the ultimate consumer and are not intended for resale or further use in producing other products. Industrial goods are used either directly or indirectly in producing other products for resale.

Differences in consumer buying habits can be used to further classify consumer goods into three categories: convenience goods, shopping goods, and specialty goods. Industrial goods are classified on the basis of product uses. The five categories in the industrial goods classification are installations, accessory equipment, component parts and materials, raw materials, and industrial supplies.

Chapter 10 examined some basic concepts applicable to products and services. In the next chapter, attention shifts to product mix decisions and new product planning. The section concludes with a separate chapter on services.

Key Terms

product
warranty
product life cycle
fashions
fads
adoption process
diffusion process
convenience goods
shopping goods
specialty goods
installations
accessory equipment

industrial distributor
component parts and materials
raw materials
supplies
MRO items

Review Questions

1. Describe the total product concept.
2. Draw and explain the product life-cycle concept.
3. Outline the various departures from the traditional PLC model.
4. Suggest several means by which the life cycle of a product (such as Scotch tape) can be extended.
5. Identify and briefly explain the stages in the consumer adoption process.
6. Describe each of the determinants of the rate of adoption.
7. Why is the basis used for categorizing industrial goods different from that used for categorizing consumer goods?
8. Compare a typical marketing mix for convenience goods with a mix for specialty goods.
9. Outline the typical marketing mix for a shopping good.
10. Discuss the marketing mix for the various types of industrial goods.

Discussion Questions and Exercises

1. Select a specific product in each stage of the product life cycle (other than those shown in the text). Explain how the marketing strategies vary by life-cycle stage for each product.
2. Trace the life cycle of a recent fad. What marketing strategy implications can you draw from your study?
3. Home burglar alarm systems using microwaves are the fastest-growing product in the home-security market. Such systems operate by filling rooms with microwave beams, which set off alarms when an intruder intercepts one of them. What suggestions can you make to accelerate the rate of adoption for this product?
4. Classify the following consumer goods:
   - **a.** Furniture
   - **b.** Puma running shoes
   - **c.** Felt-tip pen
   - **d.** Swimsuit
   - **e.** Datsun sports car
   - **f.** Binaca breath freshener
   - **g.** *Sports Illustrated* magazine
   - **h.** Original oil painting
5. Classify the following products into the appropriate industrial goods category. Briefly explain your choice for each product.
   - **a.** Calculators
   - **b.** Land
   - **c.** Light bulbs
   - **d.** Wool
   - **e.** Paper towels
   - **f.** Nylon
   - **g.** Airplanes
   - **h.** Tires

Chapter Objectives

1. *To relate product mix decisions and new product planning to the other variables of the marketing mix.*
2. *To explain the various product mix decisions that must be made by marketers.*
3. *To explain the reasons most firms develop a line of related products rather than a single product.*
4. *To outline alternative new product strategies and determinants of their success.*
5. *To identify and explain the various organizational arrangements for new product development.*
6. *To list the stages in the product development process.*
7. *To explain the role of brands, brand names, and trademarks.*
8. *To describe the major functions of the package.*
9. *To explain the functions of the Consumer Product Safety Commission and the concept of product liability.*

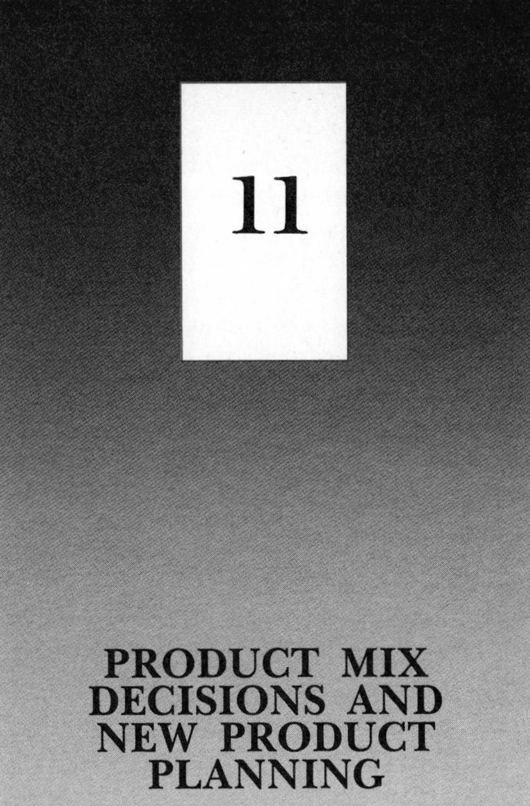

11

PRODUCT MIX DECISIONS AND NEW PRODUCT PLANNING

The $2.8 billion Camden, New Jersey, company started at the beginning of this century with a new idea: water was drained from a can of soup in order to cut shipping and storage costs so the product could be sold for 10 cents rather than the standard 30 cents. Over the years, the Campbell Soup Company has introduced a lot of new products. The firm now dominates the soup business, and offers other products including Vlasic pickles and relishes, V–8 cocktail vegetable juice, Pepperidge Farm products, Godiva chocolates, the Franco-American line, and Swanson frozen dinners.

During the 1970s, Campbell's product development efforts fell off. While it averaged 18 new products each year, many failed, often because of inadequate market tests. Sometimes the consumer testing program consisted of simple taste tests by Campbell's management personnel. Some items in Campbell's oriental soup line may have suffered because of limited testing.

Things are now different at Campbell's. Gordon McGovern, the chief executive officer, is pushing new product development as a means of reaching his goals of 15 percent annual growth in revenues and profits. One new product that resulted from this effort is Prego, a home-style spaghetti sauce. Campbell is also working on upgraded frozen dinners to go head on with Stouffer's and a revised Franco-American line targeted at Chef Boy-ar-dee.

The company has also invested $10 million in DNA Plant Technology Corp., a biotechnology outfit that is trying to produce the perfect tomato. According to Campbell sources, the perfect tomato would resist disease, rot, and worms. It would not be damaged by the weight of other tomatoes during storage, and would produce a flavorful, rich, red catsup.

Not all of Campbell's new products will come from such exotic laboratory efforts. Consider the case of Swanson which produced 100,000 pounds of surplus chicken thighs a week because they are not used in frozen dinners. Some were sold via tailgate sales in the company parking lot, but a more reliable outlet was needed. The chicken thighs were added to the product line of Pepperidge Farm Thrift Stores. Pepperidge Farm's "new product" is now bringing in $4,000 weekly to Campbell's coffers.[1]

The Conceptual Framework

Chapter 10 considered several basic product concepts. This chapter expands the discussion of products and services by examining the product mix and new product planning. A starting point is to consider the concept of a product mix.

A **product mix** is the assortment of product lines and individual offerings available from a marketer. Its two primary components are **product line,** a series of related products, and **individual offerings,** single products.

Product mixes are typically measured by width of assortment and depth of assortment. Width of assortment refers to the number of product lines that the firm offers, while depth of assortment refers to the extension of a particular product line.[2] Philip Morris Incorporated offers an assortment of consumer product lines—cigarettes, beer, and soft drinks. These product lines would be considered the width of the

[1]New product development at Campbell is described in Betsy Morris, "After a Long Simmer, the Pot Boils Again at Campbell Soup Co.," *The Wall Street Journal* (July 16, 1982), pp. 1, 8; and "Campbell Soup's Looking for 'Super Tomato'," *The Wall Street Journal* (April 2, 1982), pp. 25, 36.

[2]The width and depth of assortment is described in Raymond A. Marquardt, James C. Makens, and Robert G. Roe, *Retail Management,* 3d ed. (Hinsdale, Ill.: The Dryden Press, 1983), pp. 95–96.

Figure 11.1 The Phillip Morris Product Mix

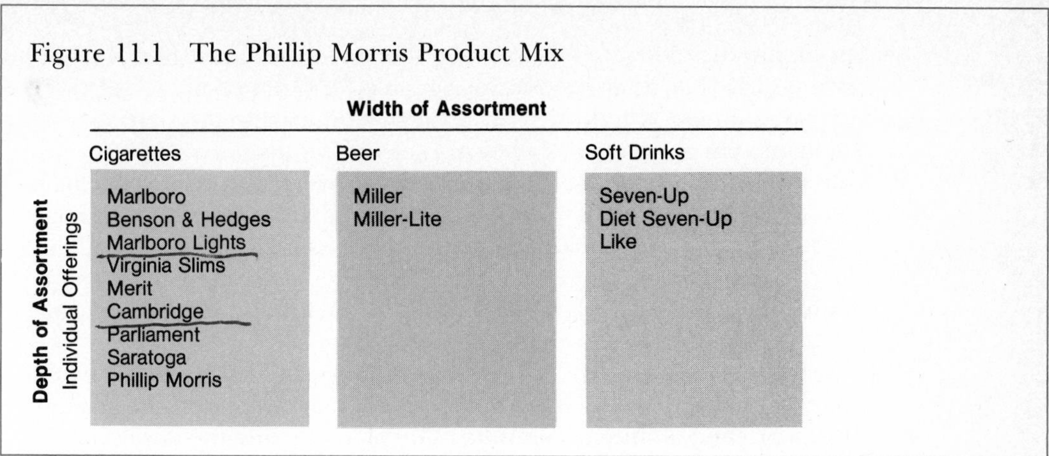

Philip Morris product mix. The depth is determined by the number of individual offerings within each product line. For example, their soft drink line consists of 7-Up, Diet 7-Up, and Like. The cigarette line is headed by Marlboro and the beer line by Miller and Miller Lite. (See Figure 11.1.)

The Existing Product Mix

The starting point in any product planning effort is to assess the firm's current product mix. What product lines does it now offer? How deep are the offerings within each of the product lines? The marketer wants to look for gaps in the assortment that can be filled by new products or modified versions of existing products.

Cannibalization

The firm wants to avoid a costly new product introduction that will adversely affect sales of one of its existing products. A product that takes sales from another offering in a product line is said to be **cannibalizing** the line. Such was the case back in 1964 when Maxim instant coffee was introduced. Marketers at General Foods hoped that the popularity of the Maxwell House name would help Maxim. It did, but it also took millions of sales dollars from the established offering.[3] Marketing research should ensure that any cannibalization mistakes are minimized or at least anticipated.

[3]"Name Game," *Time* (August 31, 1981), p. 42.

Line Extension

An important rationale for assessing the current product mix is to determine whether line extension is feasible. A **line extension** refers to the development of individual offerings that appeal to different market segments, but are closely related to the existing product line. If cannibalization can be minimized, line extension provides a relatively cheap way of increasing sales revenues at minimal risk. Hershey's Krackel candy bar was outsold about four to one by Nestle's Crunch, but Hershey's addition of a larger bar—the Big Block—allowed it to nearly double the sales of Krackel.[4] This situation illustrates the line extension of an existing Hershey product.

Once the assessment of the existing product mix has been made and the appropriate line extensions considered, marketing decision makers must turn their attention to product line planning and the development of new products.

The Importance of Product Lines

Firms who market only one product are rare today. Most offer their customers a product line—a series of related products. Polaroid Corporation, for example, began operations with a single product, a polarized screen for sunglasses and other products. Then, in 1948, it introduced the world's first instant camera. For the next 30 years, these products proved to be sufficient for annual sales and profit growth. By 1983, however, instant cameras accounted for only about two thirds of Polaroid's sales. The company had added hundreds of products in both industrial and consumer markets, ranging from nearly 40 different types of instant films for various industrial, medical, and other technical operations, to batteries, sonar devices, and machine tools.[5] Several factors account for the inclination of firms such as Polaroid to develop a complete line rather than concentrate on a single product.

Desire to Grow A company places definite limitations on its growth potential when it concentrates on a single product. In a single 12-month period, Lever Brothers introduced 21 new products in its search for market growth and increased profits. A study by Booz, Allen & Hamilton management consultants revealed that firms expect newly developed products to account for 37 percent of their sales and 51 percent of their profits over the next five years.[6]

[4]Nancy Giges, "Nestle's Chief's Mission: Pick Winners, Ax Losers," *Advertising Age* (September 7, 1981), p. 64.

[5]Polaroid's product development strategies are described in "Polaroid: Turning Away from Land's One Product Strategy," *Business Week* (March 2, 1981), pp. 108–112.

[6]Bill Abrams, "Despite Mixed Record, Firms Still Pushing for New Products," *The Wall Street Journal* (November 12, 1981), p. 25.

Firms often introduce new products to offset seasonal variations in the sales of their current products. Since the majority of soup purchases are made during the winter months, Campbell Soup Company has made attempts to tap the warm-weather soup market. A line of fruit soups to be served chilled was test-marketed, but results showed that U.S. consumers were not yet ready for fruit soups. The firm continued to search for warm-weather soups, however, and in the early 1980s, it added gazpacho and other varieties to be served chilled to its product line.

Optimal Use of Company Resources By spreading the costs of company operations over a series of products, it may be possible to reduce the average costs of all products. Texize Chemicals Company started with a single household cleaner and learned painful lessons about marketing costs when a firm has only one major product. Management rapidly added the products K2r and Fantastik to the line. The company's sales representatives can now call on middlemen with a series of products at little more than the cost of a single product. In addition, Texize's advertising produces benefits for all products in the line. Similarly, production facilities can be used economically in producing related products. For example, Chrysler has designed a convertible, van, and sports car from the K car design.[7] Finally, the expertise of all the firm's personnel can be applied more widely to a line of products than to a single one.

Increasing Company Importance in the Market Consumers and middlemen often expect a firm that manufactures and markets small appliances to also offer related products under its brand name. The Maytag Company offers not only washing machines but also dryers, since consumers often demand matching appliances. Gillette markets not only razors and blades but also a full range of grooming aids, including Foamy shave cream, Right Guard deodorant, Gillette Dry Look hair spray and Super Max hair dryers.

The company with a line of products is often more important to both the consumer and the retailer than the company with only one product. Shoppers who purchase a tent often buy related items, such as tent heaters, sleeping bags and air mattresses, camping stoves, and special cookware. Recognizing this tendency, the Coleman Company now includes in its product line dozens of items associated with camping. The firm would be little known if its only product were lanterns. Similarly, new cameras from Eastman Kodak help the firm sell more film—a product that carries a 60 percent profit margin.[8]

[7]Douglas R. Scase, "Chrysler Is Upbeat as Market Share Rises, but Some Doubt It Can Maintain Success," *The Wall Street Journal* (April 22, 1982), p. 33.

[8]Howard Rudnitakey, "Snap Judgments Can Be Wrong," *Forbes* (April 12, 1982).

Exploiting the Product Life Cycle

As its output enters the maturity and decline stages of the product life cycle, the firm must add new products if it is to prosper. The regular addition of new products to the firm's line helps ensure that it will not become a victim of product obsolescence. The development of stereophonic sound in the 1950s shifted high-fidelity phonographs from the maturity stage to the decline stage, and companies such as RCA, Magnavox, and Zenith began to develop new products utilizing stereo.[9]

New Product Planning

The product development effort requires considerable advance planning. New products are the lifeblood of any business firm, and a steady flow of new entries must be available if the firm is to survive. Some new products would be major technological breakthroughs. For instance, Procter & Gamble has filed patent applications for a male baldness cure, a margarine that cuts cholesterol in the blood, and a plaque-eliminating dental product.[10] Other new products are simple product-line extensions. In other words a new product is simply a product new to either the company or the customer. A Booz, Allen & Hamilton survey found that for products introduced since 1976, about 85 percent were line extensions, and only 15 percent were truly new products.[11]

The Product Decay Curve

New product development is risky and expensive. A Conference Board study of 148 medium and large American manufacturing companies revealed that one out of three new industrial and consumer products introduced within the past five years has failed. The leading cause of new product failure was insufficient and poor marketing research.[12]

Dozens of new product ideas are required to produce even one successful product. Booz, Allen & Hamilton surveyed 51 companies and reported its findings in the form of the product decay curve depicted in Figure 11.2. Of every 58 ideas produced in these firms, only 12 passed the preliminary screening test designed to determine whether they were compatible with company resources and objectives. Of these 12, only 7 showed sufficient profit potential in the business analysis phase. Three survived the development phase, two made it through the

[9]Roger Leigh Lawton and A. Parasuraman, "So You Want Your New Product Planning to Be Productive," *Business Horizons* (December 1980), pp. 29–34; and Roger Calantone and Robert G. Cooper, "New Product Scenarios: Prospects for Success," *Journal of Marketing* (Spring 1981), pp. 48–60.

[10]Carol J. Loomis, "P & G Up Against Its Wall," *Fortune* (February 23, 1981), pp. 49–54.

[11]Abrams, "Despite Mixed Record, Firms Still Pushing for Products," p. 25.

[12]David S. Hopkins, *New Product Winners and Losers* (New York: The Conference Board, Inc., 1980). See also "Booz Allen Looks at New Products' Role," *The Wall Street Journal* (March 26, 1981), p. 25.

Figure 11.2 The Decay Curve for New Product Ideas

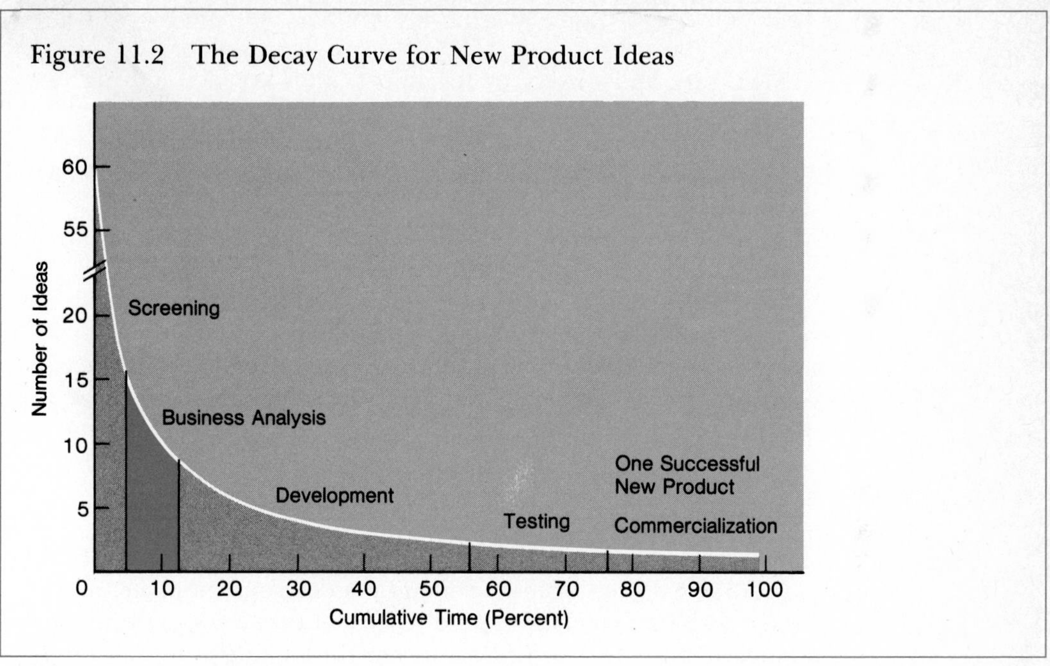

Source: Adapted by permission from *Management of New Products* (New York: Booz, Allen & Hamilton, 1968), p. 9.

test marketing stage, and only one, on the average, was commercially successful. Thus, of 58 ideas, less than 2 percent resulted in a successful product.

A 1981 follow-up study by Booz, Allen reported that while the success rate may be no better today, new product development is becoming more cost effective. According to the new Booz, Allen data, only seven new product ideas are given serious consideration. Furthermore, some 54 percent of total new product expenditures are going to successes, compared with 30 percent in 1968. Capital investment in new products has fallen from 46 percent to 26 percent of total new product spending.[13] These figures suggest that new product development is now more efficient.

Determinants of Success for New Products

What determines the success or failure of a new product? A research effort known as Project New Product suggests the following six categories as determinants of new product outcomes:[14]

[13]Abrams, "Despite Mixed Record, Firms Still Pushing for Products," p. 25.

[14]This list is adapted from Rogert Calantone and Robert G. Cooper, "New Product Scenarios: Prospects for Success," *Journal of Marketing* (Spring 1981), p. 49.

- The relative strengths of the new product and its marketplace launch.
- The nature and quality of the information available during the product development process.
- The relative proficiency of new product development efforts.
- The characteristics of the marketplace at which the new product is aimed.
- The fit or compatibility of the new product and the firm's resource base.
- The specific characteristics of the new product effort.

These hypothetical variables allowed researchers at McGill University to classify various types of new products. These generalizations are valuable because they suggest the variables which must be considered in the new product development effort.

Product Development Strategies

The firm's strategy for new product development should vary in accordance with the existing product mix and the determinants cited above. Marketing decision makers also need to look at the firm's present market position. Figure 11.3 provides a means for looking at overall product developmental strategy. Four forms of product development are suggested: product improvement, market development, product development, and product diversification.

A *product improvement strategy* refers to modification in existing products. Product positioning often plays a major role in such strategy. **Product positioning** refers to the consumer's perception of a product's attributes, use, quality, and advantages and disadvantages in relation to competing brands. A good example is Philip Morris's recent effort to reposition 7-Up as a caffeine-free soft drink. The company had earlier been successful in positioning its Miller Lite beer in the diet-conscious segment of beer buyers.[15]

A market development strategy concentrates on finding new markets for existing products. Market segmentation (discussed in Chapters 4 and 5) is a useful tool in such an effort. Arm & Hammer's penetration of new markets with an established product is illustrative of this strategy.

Product development strategy, as it is defined here, refers to the introduction of new products into identifiable or established markets. Sometimes, the new product is the firm's first entry in this particular marketplace. In other cases, firms choose to introduce new products into markets in which they have already established positions in an attempt to increase overall market share. These new offerings are called *flanker*

[15] "Seven-Up Uncaps a Cola—And an Industry Feud," *Business Week* (March 22, 1982), pp. 98, 100. Also see "Seven-Up's Caffeine War," *Newsweek* (April 9, 1982), p. 73.

Figure 11.3 Forms of Product Development

	Old Product	New Product
Old Market	Product Improvement	Product Development
New Market	Market Development	Product Diversification

Source: Charles E. Meisch, "Marketers, Engineers Should Work Together in 'New Product' Development Departments," *Marketing News* (November 13, 1981), p. 10. Earlier discussion of these strategies is credited to H. Igor Ansoff, "Strategies for Diversification," *Harvard Business Review* (September-October 1957), pp. 113–124. See Philip Kotler, *Principles of Marketing*, 2nd ed. (Englewood Cliffs, N.J.: Prentice-Hall, Inc., 1983), pp. 34, 52.

Does the World Really Want a . . .?

Here are some new products and services that may or may not make it in today's competitive marketplace. What do you think about their chances of success?

- *Career Guard.* John Lorriman was a $40,000-a-year executive who fought with his boss constantly. Eventually he was fired, and a new product idea was generated. Lorriman began developing an insurance policy that pays a person's salary for two years if they are laid off or fired because of personality conflicts, takeover, and bankruptcies. Career Guard, which is designed for executives earning $25,000 or more, also provides legal help and employment assistance. The cost is 1.3 percent of the person's salary. Career Guard is now offered in Canada.
- *Pick Point Enterprises.* A small Mirror Lake, New Hampshire, firm, Pick Point Enterprises, is now offering lighted tennis balls. This new product is made of translucent plastic and contains a chemical that radiates light, much like a firefly.
- *Juicie Treat.* Rosebud Products has introduced just the thing for Fido. Juicie Treat is a drink for dogs that is made of vitamin-enriched sugar water but has the smell of beef bouillon. It can also be mixed with dog food and sells for 99 cents per quart. An initial launch in New York's Sloan's Supermarket indicated little interest by pet owners.

Source: Peggy Berkowitz, "These Days, You Don't Have to Be the Boss's Kid to Get Job Insurance," *The Wall Street Journal* (April 7, 1982), p. 29; "Business Bulletin," *The Wall Street Journal* (January 28, 1982), p. 1; and, "Arf! Gimme a Virgin Bullshot," *Newsweek* (April 12, 1982), p. 64.

brands. Butcher's Blend Dry Dog Food is Ralston Purina's flanker to their Dog Chow line.[16]

Product diversification strategy refers to the development of new products for new markets. In some cases, the new market targets are complimentary to existing markets; in others, they are not.

Booz, Allen & Hamilton management consultants point out the need for new products to be consistent with the firm's overall strategic orientation. A beverage firm, for instance, has set four strategic requirements for a new product:

- It must appeal to the under-21 age segment.
- It must utilize off-season or excess capacity.
- It must successfully penetrate a new product category for the firm.
- Alternatively, it could become a cash cow that funds other new products.[17]

As the above section indicates, new product planning is a complex area. The critical nature of product planning decisions requires an effective organizational structure to make them.

The Organizational Structure for New Product Development

A prerequisite for efficient product innovations is an organizational structure designed to stimulate and coordinate new product development. New product development is a specialized task and requires the expertise of many departments.[18] A company that delegates new product development responsibility to the engineering department often discovers that engineers sometimes design good products from a design standpoint but bad ones in terms of consumer needs. Most successful medium and large companies assign new product development to one or more of the following alternatives: new product committees, new product departments, product managers, or venture teams.

[16]Edward M. Tauber, "New Roles for Old Items," (An MT Forum) *Marketing Times* (July–August 1981), p. 40.

[17]Abrams, "Despite Mixed Record, Firms Still Pushing for Products," p. 25.

[18]David Gordon and E. Edward Blevins, "Organizing for Effective New-Product Development," *Journal of Business* (December 1978), pp. 21–26; and James Rothe, Michael Harvey, and Walden Rhines, "New Product Development under Conditions of Scarcity and Inflation," *Michigan Business Review* (May 1977), pp. 16–22.

New Product Committees

The most common organizational arrangement for new product development is the new product development committee. It is typically composed of representatives of top management in such areas as marketing, finance, manufacturing, engineering, research, and accounting. Committee members are less concerned with the conception and development of new product ideas than with reviewing and approving new product plans. Publishing houses, for instance, often have editorial review committees that must approve new project ideas before an editor can work with an author in developing a new book.

Since the members of new product committees are key executives in the functional areas, their support for any new product plan is likely to result in its approval for further development. However, new product committees tend to be slow in making decisions and conservative in their views, and sometimes they compromise so members can get back to their regular company responsibilities.

New Product Departments

Many companies establish a separate, formally organized new product department. The organization of a department overcomes the limitations of the new product committee system and makes new product development a permanent, full-time activity. The department is responsible for all phases of the product's development within the firm, including screening decisions, development of product specifications, and coordinating product testing. The head of the department has substantial authority and typically reports to the president or to the top marketing officer.

Product Managers

Product managers (also called brand managers) are individuals assigned one product or product line and given responsibility for determining its objectives and marketing strategies. Procter & Gamble assigned the first product manager back in 1927 when they made one person responsible for Camay soap.[19] The product manager is now widely accepted by marketers. Johnson & Johnson, Richardson-Vicks, and General Mills are examples of firms employing these marketers.

Product managers set prices, develop advertising and sales promotion programs, and work with sales representatives in the field. Although product managers have no line authority over the field sales

[19]Reported in Ann M. Morrison, "The General Mills Brand of Manager," *Fortune* (January 12, 1981), pp. 99–107. Another interesting discussion appears in "Brand Management System Is Best, but Refinements Needed," *Marketing News* (July 9, 1982), p. 12.

force, the objective of increasing sales for the brand is the same, and managers attempt to help salespeople accomplish their task. In multi-product companies, product managers are key people in the marketing department. They provide individual attention to each product, while the firm as a whole has a single sales force, marketing research department, and advertising department that all product managers can utilize.

In addition to having primary responsibility for marketing a particular product or product line, the product manager is often responsible for new product development, the creation of new product ideas, and recommendations for improving existing products. These suggestions become the basis for proposals submitted to top management.

The product manager system is open to one of the same criticisms as the new product committee: new product development may get secondary treatment because of the manager's time commitments for existing products. Although a number of extremely successful new products have resulted from ideas submitted by product managers, it cannot be assumed that the skills required for marketing an existing product line are the same as those required for successfully developing new products.[20]

Venture Teams

Another technique for organizing new product development is the use of venture teams. One third of the 100 largest U.S. industrial firms utilize venture teams, and at least 20 of these teams have been established within the last 15 years.

The **venture team** concept is an organizational strategy for developing new product areas by combining the management resources of technological innovations, capital, management, and marketing expertise. Like new product committees, venture teams are composed of specialists from different areas of the organization: engineering representatives for expertise in product design and the development of prototypes; marketing staff members for development of product concept tests, test marketing, sales forecasts, pricing, and promotion; and financial accounting representatives for detailed cost analyses and decisions concerning the concept's probable return on investment.

Unlike committees, venture teams do not disband after every meeting. Team members are assigned the project as a major responsibil-

[20]Jacob M. Duker and Michael V. Laric, "The Product Manager: No Longer on Trial," in *The Changing Marketing Environment: New Theories and Applications,* (eds.) Kenneth Bernhardt, Ira Dolich, Michael Etzel, William Kehoe, Thomas Kinnear, William Perrault, Jr., and Kenneth Roering (Chicago: American Marketing Association, 1981), pp. 93–96; and Peter S. Howsam and G. David Hughes, "Product Management System Suffers from Insufficient Experience, Poor Communication," *Marketing News* (June 26, 1981), Section 2, p. 8.

ity, and teams possess the necessary authority to both plan and carry out a course of action. Some sources also differentiate venture teams from task forces. A *new product task force* is an interdisciplinary group on temporary assignment that works through functional departments. Their basic task is to coordinate and integrate the work of the functional departments on some specific project. By contrast, venture teams work independently and are not tied to functional departments.[21]

As a means of stimulating product innovation, the venture team is typically separated from the permanent organization and linked directly with top management. The Cudahy Packing Company moved its three-member venture team from the Phoenix headquarters to a suite of offices in New York City. Since the venture team manager reports to the division head or the chief administrative officer, communication problems are minimized and high-level support is assured.

The venture team must meet such criteria as prospective return on investment, uniqueness of the product, existence of a well-defined need, degree of the product's compatibility with existing technology, and strength of patent protection. Although the organization is considered temporary, the actual life span of venture teams is flexible, often extending over a number of years. When the commercial potential of new products has been demonstrated, the product may be assigned to an existing division, become a division within the company, or serve as the nucleus of a new company.

The flexibility and authority of the venture team allows large firms to develop the maneuverability of smaller companies. Venture teams established by Colgate-Palmolive have already broadened the base of the toiletries and detergents manufacturer into such products as freeze-dried flowers. The teams also serve as an outlet for innovative marketing by providing a mechanism for translating research and development ideas into viable products.

The venture team with its single mission, unstructured relationships, insulation from the daily routine, and entrepreneurial thrust is an organizational concept uniquely suited to the task of product innovation. For many companies whose future depends as much on the successful launching of new products as the successful marketing of existing ones, the venture-team concept offers a promising mechanism for more innovative marketing and the growth which it makes possible.[22]

[21]William S. Sachs and George Benson, *Product Planning and Management* (Tulsa, Okla.: PennWell Books, 1981), p. 164.

[22]Richard M. Hill and James D. Hlavacek, "The Venture Team: A New Concept in Marketing," *Journal of Marketing* (July 1972), p. 50. See also Dan T. Dunn, Jr., "The Rise and Fall of Ten Venture Groups," *Business Horizons* (October 1977), pp. 32–41; and William W. George, "Task Teams for Rapid Growth," *Harvard Business Review* (March–April 1977), pp. 71–80.

The Pillsbury Bake-Off

When it was started in 1949, the Pillsbury Bake-Off contest was viewed as a way to get publicity for Pillsbury flour and bakery products. Contestants are asked to submit recipes for selected baked goods, and these are then judged. Prizes are awarded to the winners, and their recipes are published. Tens of thousands enter the Pillsbury program each year.

Aside from the public relations aspects of the contest, the Pillsbury Bake-Off has been an excellent source of new products for the company. Some of Pillsbury's cake mix lines and several parts of another one are the direct result of the Bake-Off.

Source: Eric von Hippel, "Get New Products from Customers," *Harvard Business Review* (March–April 1982), p. 118.

Stages in the New Product Development Process

Once the firm has organized for new product development, it can establish procedures for evaluating new product ideas. The new product development process involves six stages: (1) idea generation, (2) screening, (3) business analysis, (4) product development, (5) test marketing, and (6) commercialization. At each stage, management faces the decision to abandon the project, continue to the next stage, or seek additional information before proceeding further.[23]

Idea Generation

New product development begins with ideas that emanate from many sources: the sales force, customers who write letters asking, "Why don't you . . . ," marketing employees, research and development specialists, competitive products, retailers, and inventors outside the company. It is important for the firm to develop a system for stimulating new ideas and for rewarding persons who develop them.[24]

[23]For an excellent treatment of the product development process, see Robert D. Hisrich and Michael P. Peters, *Marketing a New Product* (Menlo Park, Calif.: Benjamin/Cummings Publishing, 1978); Richard T. Hise, *Product/Service Strategy* (New York: Mason/Charter Publishers, 1977); A. Edward Spitz, *Product Planning*, 2d ed. (New York: Mason/Charter Publishers, 1977); and William S. Sachs and George Benson, *Product Planning and Management* (Tulsa, Okla.: PennWell Books, 1981).

[24]See Eric von Hippel, "Successful Industrial Products from Customer Ideas," *Journal of Marketing* (January 1978), pp. 34–49; and James L. Ginter and W. Wayne Talarzyk, "Applying the Marketing Concept to Design New Products," *Journal of Business Research* (January 1978), pp. 51–66.

Table 11.1 Basic Criteria for Preliminary Screening

1. The item should be in a field of activity in which the corporation is engaged.
2. If the idea involves a companion product to others already being manufactured, it should be made from materials to which the corporation is accustomed.
3. The item should be capable of being produced on the type and kind of equipment that the corporation normally operates.
4. The item should be easily handled by the corporation's existing sales force through the established distribution pattern.
5. The potential market for the product should be at least $______.
6. The market over the next five years should be expected to grow at a faster rate than GNP.
7. Return on investment, after taxes, must reach a minimum level of ______ percent.

Source: Reprinted from William S. Sachs and George Benson, *Product Planning and Management* (Tulsa, Okla.: PennWell Books, 1981), p. 231.

Screening

This critical stage involves separating ideas with potential from those incapable of meeting company objectives. Some organizations use checklists to determine whether product ideas should be eliminated or subjected to further consideration. These checklists typically include such factors as product uniqueness, availability of raw materials, and compatibility of the proposed product with current product offerings, existing facilities, and capabilities. In other instances the screening stage consists of open discussions of new product ideas among representatives of different functional areas in the organization. Screening is an important stage in the developmental process, since any product ideas that proceed beyond this stage will cost the firm time and money.[25] Table 11.1 presents some basic criteria for the screening process.

Business Analysis

Product ideas surviving the initial screening are subjected to a thorough business analysis. The analysis involves an assessment of the potential market, its growth rate, and the likely competitive strengths of the new product. Decisions must be made about the compatibility of the proposed product with such company resources as financial support for necessary promotion, production capabilities, and distribution facilities.

Concept testing, or the consideration of the product idea prior to its actual development, is an important aspect of the business analysis stage. **Concept testing** is a marketing research project that attempts to

[25]See William B. Locander and Richard W. Scamell, "Screening New Product Ideas—A Two-Phase Approach," *Research Management* (March 1976), pp. 14–18.

measure consumer attitudes and perceptions relevant to the new product idea. Focus groups (see Chapter 6) and in-store polling can be effective methods for assessing a new product concept.

Product Development

Those product ideas with profit potential are converted into a physical product. The conversion process is the joint responsibility of the development engineering department, which turns the original concept into a product, and the marketing department, which provides feedback on consumer reactions to product designs, packages, colors, and other physical features. Numerous changes may be necessary before the original mock-up is converted into the final product.

The series of tests, revisions, and refinements should result ultimately in the introduction of a product with great likelihood of success. Some firms obtain the reactions of their own employees to proposed new product offerings. Employees at Levi Strauss test new styles by wearing them and reporting on the various features. Thom McAn asks its workers to report regularly over an eight-week testing period on shoe wear and fit.

Occasionally attempts to be the first with a new product result in the product's premature introduction. Kellogg's and several other cereal makers experienced this problem several years ago when they all failed in their attempts to introduce freeze-dried fruit cereal. In the rush to be first on the market with the new offering, they did not perfect the product. The small, hard pellets of real fruit took too long to reconstitute in the bowl, and millions of bowls of cereal went into garbage cans.[26]

Test Marketing

To determine consumer reactions to its product under normal conditions, many firms test market their new product offerings. Up to this point, consumer information has been obtained by submitting free products to consumers, who then give their reactions. Other information may come from shoppers asked to evaluate competitive products. Test marketing is the first stage at which the product or service must perform in a real-life environment.

Test marketing is the process of selecting a specific city or television-coverage area considered reasonably typical of the total market and introducing the product or service with a total marketing campaign in this area. A carefully designed and controlled test allows management

[26]Reported in Edward Buxton, *Promise Them Anything* (New York: Stein & Day, 1972), p. 101.

Figure 11.4 Recommended Test Markets

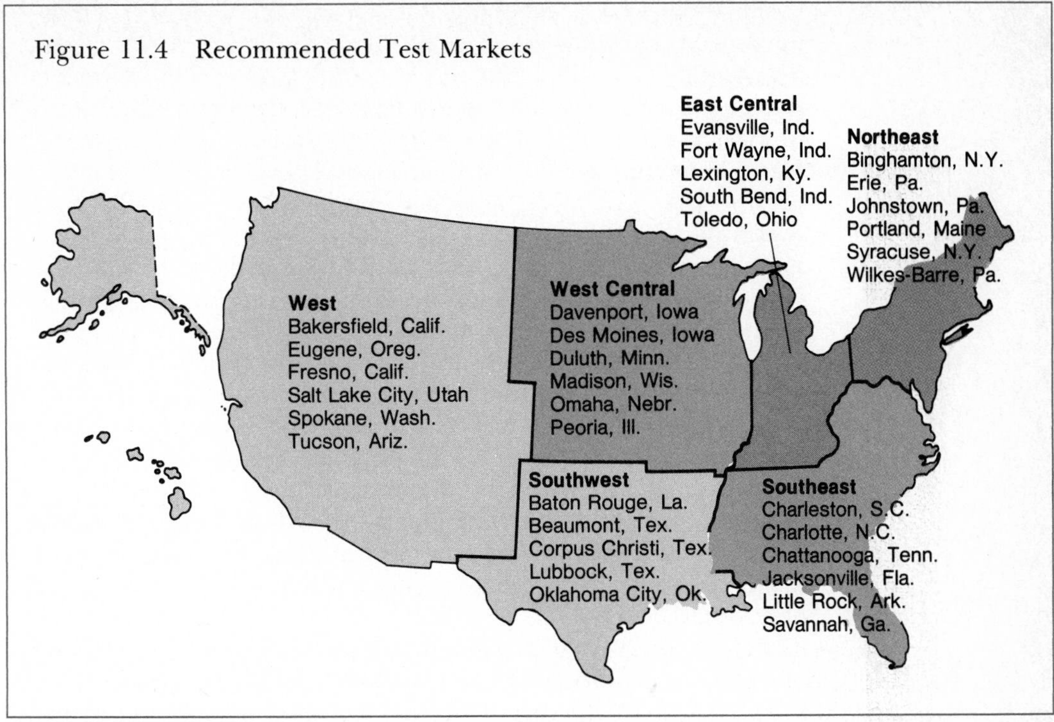

Source: Reported in Janet Neiman, "Grocers Look Beyond Data," *Advertising Age* (February 9, 1981), p. s-12. Copyright 1981 by Crain Communications, Inc. Reprinted by permission.

to estimate what sales will be for a full-scale introduction. Figure 11.4 indicates U.S. test-market cities frequently used by marketers.

Some firms omit the test marketing stage and move directly from product development to full-scale production. They cite four problems with test marketing:

1. Test marketing is expensive. As one marketing executive at Ralston Purina pointed out:

   It's very difficult to run a little [test market] for six months or a year in three or four markets across the United States and then project what your sales volume is going to be two or three years in the future, mainly because you're testing in such small localities, generally to keep your costs down.

   You simply can't afford to test your product in markets like New York, Philadelphia, Los Angeles. So you run your test in Tucson, Arizona, Fort Wayne, Indiana, Fresno, California. And your test costs are over $1 million even in places like that.[27]

[27]Quoted in Mary McCabe English, "Marketers: Better than a Coin Flip," *Advertising Age* (February 9, 1981), p. S–15. Copyright 1981 by Crain Communications, Inc. Reprinted by permission.

2. Competitors who learn about the test market often disrupt the findings by reducing the price of their products in the test area, distributing cents-off coupons, installing attractive in-store displays, or giving additional discounts to retailers to induce them to display more of their products. In a recent court settlement, Hartz Mountain agreed not to engage in advertising designed to disrupt the test of a new pet product by a subsidiary of A.H. Robins.
3. Long-lived durable goods, such as dishwashers, hair dryers, and videodisc players, are seldom test marketed due to the major financial investment required for the development, the need to develop a network of dealers to distribute the products, and the parts and servicing required. A company such as Whirlpool invests from $1 million to $33 million in the development of a new refrigerator. To develop each silicon chip that performs a single function in an Apple microcomputer costs approximately $1 million and takes from one to 15 months. Producing a prototype for a test market is simply too expensive, so the "go/no go" decision for the new durable product is typically made without the benefit of test market results.[28]
4. Test marketing a new product or service communicates company plans to competitors prior to its introduction. Kellogg's discovered a new product with suspected sales potential by learning of the test marketing of a new fruit-filled tart designed to be heated in the toaster and served for breakfast. Kellogg's rushed a similar product into full-scale production and became the first national marketer of the product Pop Tarts. Other test-marketed products beaten into the national market by competitors include Helene Curtis' Arm in Arm deodorant (preempted by Church & Dwight's Arm & Hammer deodorant); General Foods' Maxim (Nestle's Taster's Choice); Hills Brothers High Yield Coffee (Procter & Gamble's Folger's Flakes); and Hunt-Wesson's Prima Salsa tomato sauce (Chesebrough-Ponds' Ragu Extra Thick & Zesty).[29]

The decision to skip the test-marketing stage should be based on the conclusion that the new product or service has an extremely high likelihood of success. The cost of developing a new detergent, for example, from idea generation to national marketing has been estimated at $25 million! Even if a company experiences losses on a product or service that fails at the test-marketing stage, the firm saves itself from incurring even greater losses and embarrassment in the total market. Otherwise, the product or service may join the ranks of such monumental failures

[28] Dylan Landis, "Durable Goods for a Test?" *Advertising Age* (February 9, 1981), pp. S–18, S–19.
[29] B. G. Yovovich, "Competition Jumps the Gun," *Advertising Age* (February 9, 1981), pp. S–18, S–19.

as du Pont's Corfam synthetic leather with losses of more than $100 million, or Polaroid's ill-fated Polavision instant movie system, whose development and production costs were estimated at between $200 million and $500 million.[30]

Commercialization

The few product ideas that survive all the steps in the development process are ready for full-scale marketing. Marketing programs must be established, outlays for necessary production facilities must be made, and the sales force, middlemen, and potential customers must be acquainted with the new product. A systematic approach to new product development is essential.

Systematic planning of all phases of new product development and introduction can be accomplished through the use of such scheduling methods as the Program Evaluation and Review Technique (PERT) and the Critical Path Method (CPM). These techniques, developed originally by the U.S. Navy in connection with construction of the Polaris missile and submarine, map out the sequence in which each step must be taken and show the time allotments for each activity. Detailed PERT and CPM flowcharts coordinate all activities involved in the development and introduction of new products.

As Table 11.2 indicates, new product development and introduction can take many years. A study of the elapsed time between initial development and full-scale introduction of 42 products revealed a time lag ranging from 1 year for Gerber strained baby food to 55 years for television. Since the time needed for orderly development of new products can be longer than expected, the planning horizon for new product ideas may have to be extended five to ten years into the future.[31]

Product Deletion Decisions

Although many firms devote a great deal of time and resources to the development of new products, the thought of eliminating old ones is painful for many executives. Often, sentimental attachments to marginal products with declining sales prevent objective decisions to drop them.

[30]Reported in "Polaroid: Turning Away from Land's One-Product Strategy," *Business Week* (March 2, 1981), p. 111.

[31]Lee Adler, "Time Lag in New-Product Development," *Journal of Marketing* (January 1966), p. 17.

Table 11.2 Elapsed Time between Initial Development and Full-Scale Introduction

Product	Years	Product	Years
Strained baby food	1	Fluoride toothpaste	10
Filter cigarettes	2	Freeze-dried instant coffee	10
Frozen orange juice	2	Penicillin	15
Polaroid Land camera	2	Polaroid color-pack camera	15
Dry dog food	4	Xerox electrostatic copier	15
Electric toothbrush	4	Transistors	16
Plastic tile	6	Minute rice	18
Roll-on deodorant	6	Instant coffee	22
Stripe toothpaste	6	Zippers	30
Liquid shampoo	8	Television	55

Source: Adapted from Lee Adler, "Time Lag in New Product Development," *Journal of Marketing* (January 1966), pp. 17–21. Used by permission of the American Marketing Association.

To avoid waste, product lines must be pruned and old, marginal products must eventually be eliminated. Marketers typically face this decision during the late maturity and early decline stages of the product life cycle. Periodic reviews of weak products should be conducted in order to eliminate them or to justify retaining them.

In some instances, a firm will continue to carry an unprofitable product to provide a complete line of goods for its customers. Even though most grocery stores lose money on bulky, low unit-value items such as salt, they continue to carry them to meet shopper demand.

Shortages of raw materials have prompted some companies to discontinue the production and marketing of previously profitable items. Due to such shortages, du Pont dropped Zerex antifreeze from its product line and Alcoa discontinued its Alcoa aluminum foil.

In other cases, profitable products are dropped because they fail to fit into the firm's existing product line. The introduction of automatic washing machines necessitated the development of low-sudsing detergents. Monsanto produced the world's first detergent of this sort, All, in the 1950s. All was an instant success, and Monsanto was swamped with orders from supermarkets throughout the nation. The Monsanto sales force was primarily involved in marketing industrial chemicals to large-scale buyers, and the company would have needed a completely new sales force to handle the product. Nine months after the introduction of All, Procter & Gamble introduced the world's second low-sudsing detergent, Dash. The Procter & Gamble sales force handled hundreds of products and could spread the cost of contacting dealers over all of them. Monsanto had only All. Rather than attempt to compete, Monsanto sold All in 1958 to Lever Brothers, a Procter & Gamble competitor that had a marketing organization capable of handling the product.

Product Identification

Manufacturers identify their products with brand names, symbols, and distinctive packaging; so do certain large retailers, such as J.C. Penney and Sears. Almost every product that is distinguishable from another contains a means of identification for the buyer. Aspiring "preppies" immediately know that they have found the right brand when they see the Izod alligator. The California Fruit Growers Exchange literally brands its oranges with the name Sunkist. The purchasing agent for a construction firm can turn over a sheet of aluminum and find the name and symbol for Alcoa. Choosing the means of identifying the firm's output represents a major decision for the marketing manager.

Brands, Brand Names, and Trademarks

A **brand** is a name, term, sign, symbol, design, or some combination used to identify the products of one firm and to differentiate them from competitive offerings. A **brand name** is that part of the brand consisting of words or letters that comprise a name used to identify and distinguish the firm's offerings from those of competitors.[32] It is, therefore, that part of the brand which can be vocalized. A **trademark** is a brand that has been given legal protection; the protection is granted solely to the brand's owner. The term *trademark* includes not only the pictorial design, but also the brand name. More than 500,000 trademarks are currently registered in the United States.[33]

For the consumer, the process of branding allows repeat purchases of the same product, since the product is identified with the name of the firm producing it. The purchaser thus can associate the satisfaction derived from a hot dog, for example, with the brand name Corn King Franks. For the marketing manager, the brand serves as the cornerstone of the product's image. Once consumers have been made aware

[32]Committee on Definitions, *Marketing Definitions: A Glossary of Marketing Terms* (Chicago: American Marketing Association, 1960), pp. 9–10.

[33]The registration of trademarks and related issues are discussed in Louis E. Boone and James C. Johnson, "Trademark Protection: What's in a Name?" *Business* (April–June 1982), pp. 12–17.

of a particular brand, its appearance becomes further advertising for the firm. Shell Oil's symbol of a seashell is instant advertising to motorists who view it while driving.

Well-known brands also allow the firm to escape some of the rigors of price competition. Although any chemist will confirm that all brands of aspirin contain the same amount of the chemical acetylsalicylic acid, Bayer has developed so strong a reputation that it can successfully market its aspirin at a higher price than competitive products. Well-known gasoline brands typically sell at slightly higher prices than independent brands because many purchasers feel that they are buying higher-quality gasoline.

What Constitutes a Good Brand Name? Effective brand names are easy to pronounce, recognize, and remember. Short names like Busch, Gleem, Klear, and Off! meet these requirements. Multinational marketing firms face a particularly acute problem in selecting brand names; an excellent brand name in one country may prove disastrous in another. When Standard Oil decided to reduce its number of gasoline brands from three (Esso, Enco, and Humble) to one, company officials ruled out Enco, because in Japanese the word means stalled car. The ultimate choice was Exxon—a unique, distinctive name.

Every language has *o* and *k* sounds, and *okay* has become an international word. Every language also has a short *a* so that Coca-Cola and Texaco are effective brands in any country. An advertisement campaign for E-Z washing machines failed in the United Kingdom, however, because the British pronounce *z* as zed.

For 21 years, Nissan Motor Corporation marketers struggled with an easily mispronounced brand name for its Datsun cars and trucks. Datsun encountered difficulty in the United States and other English-speaking nations where some people pronounced the *a* like the *a* in *hat,* while others pronounced it like the *o* in *got.* Finally, Nissan marketers decided to change the name of all of its automobile products to Nissan beginning with its Stanza model in 1982. Total costs of the change—to be effected in more than 135 countries—are estimated as high as $150 million.[34]

The brand name should give the buyer the right connotation. The Tru-Test name used on True Value Hardware line of paints produces the desired image. Accutron suggests the quality of the high-priced and accurate timepiece sold by Bulova. Sometimes, though, brand names are ineffective. Research conducted several years ago by the Cities Service Company revealed that a large number of gasoline buyers vaguely associated the brand name Cities Service with some type of public utility. In addition, the name was too long to display on billboards. Cities

[34]"A Worldwide Brand for Nissan," *Business Week* (August 24, 1981), p. 104.

Service decided to change its name to a five-letter word beginning with CIT. After considering several hundred possibilities, its management selected the name of CITGO and enclosed it in a new three-tone red triangle. The total cost of changing the brand name was approximately $20 million. Cities Service sales increased 11 percent the following year compared with an industry average of 6 percent. Credit for the marked sales improvement was given to a revitalized marketing program, but the new, modern brand CITGO was the visible symbol of the changing company.

The brand name must also be legally protectable. The Lanham Act (1946) states that registered trademarks must not contain words in general use, such as automobile or suntan lotion. These generic words actually describe a particular type of product and thus cannot be granted exclusively to any company.

When a unique product becomes generally known by its original brand name, the brand name may be ruled as a descriptive **generic name;** if this occurs, the original owner loses exclusive claim to it. For example, in 1983 the U.S. Supreme Court ruled that the trademark for Parker Brothers' "Monopoly" was invalid because it had become a general term for such games. The case involved Parker Brothers, who first produced "Monopoly" in 1935, and a San Francisco State University economics professor who developed a game called "Anti-Monopoly."[35] The generic names *nylon, aspirin, escalator, kerosene,* and *zipper* were also once brand names. Other generic names that were once brand names include cola, yo-yo, linoleum, and shredded wheat.

There is a difference between brand names that are legally generic and those that are generic in the eyes of many consumers. Jell-O is a brand name owned exclusively by General Foods, but to most consumers the name Jell-O is the descriptive name for gelatin desserts. Legal brand names like Jell-O are often used by consumers as descriptive names. Xerox is such a well-known brand name that it is frequently and incorrectly used as a verb. Many English and Australian consumers use the brand name Hoover as a verb for vacuuming.

To prevent their brand names from being ruled descriptive and available for general use, most owners take steps to inform the public of their exclusive ownership of the name. Coca-Cola uses the ® symbol for registration immediately after the name *Coca-Cola* and *Coke* and sends letters to newspapers, novelists, and others who use Coke with a lower-case letter informing them that the name is owned by Coca-Cola.[36] These companies face the dilemma of attempting to retain ex-

[35]"No More Monopoly on Monopoly," *The Seattle Times* (February 22, 1983), p. A6.

[36]John Koten, "Mixing with Coke over Trademarks is Always a Fizzle," *The Wall Street Journal* (March 9, 1978). For a thorough discussion of the brand name decision, see James U. McNeal and Linda M. Zeren, "Brand Name Selection for Consumer Products," *MSU Business Topics* (Spring 1981), pp. 35–39.

clusive rights to a brand name when it is generic to a large part of the market.

Since any dictionary name may eventually be ruled generic, some companies create new words for their brand names. Names such as Tylenol, Keds, Rinso, and Kodak have been created by their owners.

Measuring Brand Loyalty Brands vary widely in consumer familiarity and acceptance.[37] While a boating enthusiast may insist on a Johnson outboard motor, one study revealed that 40 percent of U.S. homemakers could not indentify the brands of furniture in their own homes. Brand loyalty can be measured in three stages: brand recognition, brand preference, and brand insistence.

Brand recognition is a company's first objective for its newly introduced products—to make them familiar to the consuming public. Often, this is achieved through offers of free samples or discount coupons for purchases. Several new brands of toothpaste have been introduced on college campuses in free sample kits called Campus Pacs. Once consumers have used a product, it moves from the unknown to the known category, and the probability of its being repurchased is increased provided the consumer was satisfied with the trial sample.

Brand preference is the second stage of brand loyalty. In this stage, consumers, relying on previous experience with the product, will choose it over its competitors if it is available. A college student who prefers Stroh's will usually switch to another brand if it is not available at the tavern where he or she is to meet friends after an evening class. Companies with products at the brand preference stage are in a favorable position for competing in their industry.

Brand insistence, the ultimate stage in brand loyalty, is that situation in which consumers will accept no alternatives and will search extensively for the product. A product at this stage has achieved a monopoly position with that particular group of consumers. Although brand insistence is the goal of many firms, it is seldom achieved. Only the most exclusive specialty goods attain this position with a large segment of the total market.

The Importance of Brand Loyalty A study of 12 patented drugs illustrates the importance of brand acceptance. The sample included well-known drugs like Librium and Darvon. The research indicated that patent expiration had minimal effect on the drugs' market shares or price levels. This resiliency was credited to the brand loyalty for the pioneer product in the field.[38] Another measure of the importance of brand

[37]The question of brand choice is pursued in articles like J. Morgan Jones and Fred S. Ziefryden, "An Approach for Assessing Demographic and Price Influences on Brand Purchase Behavior," *Journal of Marketing* (Winter 1982), pp. 36–46.

[38]Meir Statman and Tyzoon T. Tyebjee, "Trademarks, Patents, and Innovation in the Ethical Drug Industry," *Journal of Marketing* (Summer 1981), pp. 71–81.

Formica versus the Federal Trade Commission

An excellent example of a manufacturer's brand name that was challenged as generic is Formica. Formica Corporation owns this trademark, which it uses to identify its product lines in the decorative plastic laminate industry.

In 1978 the Federal Trade Commission, in an effort to protect consumers from what it viewed as a monopoly position resulting from Formica Corporation's exclusive rights to a name that the FTC considered to be generic, petitioned the Patent and Trademark Office to cancel the United States registration of the Formica trademark. (This trademark is also registered by the company in numerous other countries, which registrations were not involved in this case.) The case received more than the usual publicity surrounding a trademark dispute, since it marked the first time that the FTC had sued to cancel a trademark registration on the grounds that the trademark had become generic. Suits between competing firms on this ground have been relatively commonplace.

In the legal proceedings, Formica Corporation questioned the FTC's authority on technical grounds under the trademark law, but the Court of Customs and Patent Appeals, again on technical grounds unrelated to the merits of the question, ruled that the case should continue. But before it proceeded further, Congress resolved the question in an appropriations bill by withdrawing funding for any FTC challenge of famous trademarks as generics. The FTC's petition concerning the Formica trademark was subsequently dismissed with prejudice.

Formica Corporation officials had argued to the FTC and the press that the FTC action was unwarranted and reflected considerable ignorance of the decorative plastic laminate industry. In the first place, they argued that most purchases are made by fabricators of furniture and new or remodeled kitchen equipment and bathrooms, and by wholesalers, all of whom are aware of competing brands. Direct purchases by consumers account for only about one dollar of every fourteen dollars of the brand's sales. Second, Formica officials estimated that its share of the overall market was less than 40 percent—down from 100 percent when they pioneered the product—which is much less than the two-thirds share often considered indicative of a monopoly. Finally, and perhaps equally significant, is the fact that Formica Corporation's present competitors stated that none of them would use the Formica name in place of their own trademark were the name ruled generic.

The Formica case provides insight into the operating philosophy of the Federal Trade Commission, at least in the 1978–1980 era. In this case it may also illustrate an instance of a government agency failing to understand the relevant market as well as buying practices in this industry

loyalty is found in the Brand Utility Yardstick used by J. Walter Thompson advertising agency. These ratings measure the percentage of buyers who remain brand loyal even if a 50-percent cost savings was available from generic products. Beer consumers were very loyal with 48 percent refusing to switch. Sinus-remedy buyers were also brand loyal with a 44 percent rating. By contrast, only 13 percent of the aluminum-foil buyers would not switch to the generic product.[39]

Some brands are so popular that they are carried over to unrelated products because of their marketing advantages. The decision to use a popular brand name for a new product entry in an unrelated product category is known as **brand extension.** It should not be confused with line extension, which refers to new sizes, styles, or related products. Brand extension, by contrast, refers only to carrying over the brand name.

Examples of brand extension are abundant in contemporary marketing. Deere & Co.'s insurance line prominently features the John Deere brand made famous in the farm machinery business. In fact, John Deere Insurance proudly notes: "Our name is the best insurance you can buy." Similarly, General Foods is extending its Jell-O brand. The company now has Jell-O Pudding Pops, Jell-O Slice Creme, and Jell-O Gelatin Pops. Despite the fact that most people associate the Mrs. Paul's brand with fish sticks, it has now been extended to a frozen fried-chicken line.[40]

Family Brands and Individual Brands Brands can be classified as family brands or individual brands. A **family brand** is a single brand name used for several related products. Norton Simon markets hundreds of food products under the Hunt brand. General Electric has a complete line of kitchen appliances under the GE name. Johnson & Johnson offers a line of baby powder, lotions, disposable diapers, plastic pants, and baby shampoo under one name.

On the other hand, a manufacturer may choose to utilize **individual brands,** items known by their own brand names rather than by the names of the companies producing them or by an umbrella name covering similar items. Lever Brothers, for example, markets Aim, Close-Up and Pepsodent toothpastes; All and Wisk laundry detergents; Imperial margarine; Caress, Dove, Lifebuoy, and Lux bath soaps; and Shield deodorant soap. Individual brands are more expensive to market because a new promotional program must be developed to introduce each new product to its market target.

When family brands are used, any promotional outlay benefits all the products in the line. For instance, a new addition to the Heinz line

[39]Bill Abrams, "Brand Loyalty Rises Slightly, but Increase Could Be Fluke," *The Wall Street Journal* (February 7, 1982), p. 21.

[40] "Name Game," *Time* (August 31, 1981), p. 41.

gains immediate recognition because the family brand is well known. Use of family brands also makes it easier to introduce the product to the customer and to the retailer. Since grocery stores stock an average of more than 10,000 items, they are reluctant to add new products unless they are convinced of potential demand. A marketer of a new brand of turtle soup would have to promise the grocery-store buyer huge advertising outlays for promotion and evidence of consumer buying intent before getting the product into the stores. With its dominant share of the U.S. soup market, the Campbell Soup Company could merely add turtle soup to its existing line and secure store placements more easily than could another company with individual brand names.

Family brands should be used only when the products are of similar quality, or the firm will risk harming its product image. Using the Mercedes-Benz name on a new, less-expensive auto might severely tarnish the image of the other models in the Mercedes-Benz product line.

Also, individual brand names should be used for dissimilar products. Campbell Soup Company once marketed a line of dry soups under the brand name Red Kettle. Large marketers of grocery products, such as Procter & Gamble, General Foods, and Lever Brothers, employ individual brands to appeal to unique market segments. These brands also enable the firm to stimulate competition within the organization and to increase total company sales. Consumers who do not want Tide can choose Cheer, Dash, or Oxydol rather than purchase a competitor's brand.

National Brands or Private Brands?

Most of the brands mentioned in this chapter have been brands offered by manufacturers, commonly termed **national brands.** But to an increasing extent, large wholesalers and retailers operating over a regional or national market are placing their own brands on the products they market. The brands offered by wholesalers and retailers are usually called **private brands.**[41] Sears, the nation's largest retailer, sells its own brands—Kenmore, Craftsman, DieHard and Harmony House. Safeway shelves are filled with such company brands as Lucerne, Mrs. Wright's, Town House, Bel Air, White Magic and Edwards. In total, these private brands represent 31 percent of the total retail sales in all U.S. Safeway stores. The growth of private brands and generic products (discussed in the section that follows) has greatly expanded the number of alternatives available to consumers. There are now some 28,000 nationally advertised brands in the United States.[42]

[41]See E. B. Weiss, "Private Label? No It's Now Presold—Wave of Future," *Advertising Age* (September 30, 1974), p. 27.

[42]Bill Abrams, "Shoppers Are Often Confused by All the Competing Brands," *The Wall Street Journal* (April 22, 1982), p. 33.

Private brands allow large retailers such as Bloomingdale's, Neiman-Marcus, Safeway, and Sears to establish an image and to maintain control over the products they handle. Neiman-Marcus estimates total annual sales of $10 million with its Red River brand of cowboy hats, women's clothing, and western wear. Retailers or wholesalers who develop their own line of private brands assume the responsibility for product image, quality, price, and availability.

Even though the manufacturer's brands are largely presold through national promotional efforts, the wholesaler and retailer can easily lose customers when the same products are available in competing stores. Exclusive retailers, such as Saks Fifth Avenue, Lord & Taylor, and Neiman-Marcus, have problems maintaining their image of exclusivity when hundreds of department stores and specialty shops stock Calvin Klein shirts and Pierre Cardin neckties, so a fashion store such as Bloomingdale's offers designer pants with the store's name on the rear pocket. By eliminating the promotion costs of the manufacturer's brands, the dealer can usually offer a private brand at prices lower than that of the competing national brands. In Bloomingdale's case, a best-selling pair of Bloomingdale's women's pants retails at $26 as compared with about $40 for such competing designer brands as Calvin Klein or Liz Claiborne.[43]

Generic Products Food and household staples characterized by plain labels, little or no advertising, and no brand names are called **generic products.** These "no-name" products were first sold in Europe, where their prices were as much as 30 percent below brand name products. They now capture about 40 percent of total volume in European supermarkets.

Jewel Food Stores first brought generics to the United States in 1977. Today, generic items sell for about 49 percent less than national brands and 36 percent less than private brands.[44]

Generics account for between 5 and 15 percent of selected food and nonfood sales and are found in over 60 percent of all U.S. supermarkets throughout the country. The most popular generic products in U.S. supermarkets include canned green beans and corn, jams, jellies and preserves, peanut butter, teabags, plastic household bags, light and heavy duty detergents, paper towels, and toilet tissue.[45]

[43]Jeffrey H. Birnbaum, "Chic Stores Will Push Their Own Labels," *The Wall Street Journal* (April 23, 1981).

[44]Bill Abrams, "Reports of Generics' Success May Be Greatly Exaggerated," *The Wall Street Journal* (May 7, 1981), p. 29.

[45]Norman Seigle, "Generic Foods—A Further Report," *Nargus Merchandising Letter* (May 1980); Robert Dietrich, "Still Rooted in the Basics, Generics Sprout New Buds Too," *Progressive Grocer* (May 1980), p. 119. Generics are also discussed in Robert H. Ross and Frederic B. Kraft, "Creating Low Consumer Product Expectations," *Journal of Business Research* (March 1983), pp. 1–9; Betsy Gelb, " 'No-Name' Products: A Step towards 'No-Name' Retailing," *Business Horizons* (June 1980), pp. 9–13; and Joseph A. Bellizzi, Harry F. Krueckelbert, and John R. Hamilton, "A Factor Analysis of National, Private, and Generic Brand Attributes," in *1981 Proceedings of the Southwestern Marketing Association,* (eds.) Robert H. Ross, Frederic B. Kraft, and Charles H. Davis, pp. 208–210.

Battle of the Brands Competition between manufacturers' brands and the private brands offered by wholesalers and large retailers has been called the battle of the brands.[46] Although the battle appears to be intensifying, the marketing impact varies widely among industries. One survey showed that private brands represented 36 percent of the market in replacement tires but only 7 percent in portable appliances. Private brands account for 52 percent of shoe sales but only 15 percent of gasoline sales.

The growth of private brands has paralleled the growth of chain stores in the United States, most of which has occurred since the 1930s. Chains that market their own brands become customers of the manufacturer, which places the chains' private brand names on the products it produces.

Such leading manufacturers as Westinghouse, Armstrong Rubber, and Heinz are obtaining larger and larger percentages of their total income through selling private label goods. Private label sales to Sears and other major customers account for two thirds of Whirlpool's sales.

Polaroid recently began manufacturing private label instant cameras for Sears. Witco Chemical Company, the nation's largest producer of private brand detergents, recently introduced its own brand, Active. This brand now competes with Witco brands sold by Safeway, Jewel, and other grocery chains, which places Witco in the position of competing with its own customers. Although some manufacturers refuse to produce private brand goods, most regard such production as reaching another segment of the total market.

Great inroads have been made into the dominance of the manufacturers' national brands. Private brands and generics have proven that they can compete with national brands and have often succeeded in causing price reductions on the national brands to make them more competitive.

Packaging

Procter & Gamble thought it had resolved a traditional problem in the packaging of skin lotions. Their Wondra brand had the spigot cap at the bottom of the bottle so consumers could get every drop of lotion they paid for. But the brand experienced a marked decline in market share, and perhaps part of it was attributable to the Wondra package. A competitor's test found that the new design caused some anxiety for

[46]An interesting discussion appears in Jon M. Hawes, Stephen P. Hutchens, and John Thanopoulos, "Quality and Value Perception of Arkansas Consumers for National, Private and Generic Brand Grocery Products," *Arkansas Business and Economic Review*, vol. 15, no. 1, pp. 4–10.

consumers because it forced them to modify their long-established habits in applying skin lotions.[47]

Packaging represents a vital component of the total product concept. Its importance can be inferred from the size of the packaging industry. Approximately $50 billion is spent annually on packaging in the United States, and the industry is comparable in size with the automobile and meat-packing industries. With about a million workers, the package-making industry is one of the nation's largest industrial employers.

The package has several objectives. These can be classified under three general goals:

1. Protect against damage, spoilage, and pilferage.
2. Assist in marketing the product.
3. Be cost effective.

Protection Against Damage, Spoilage, and Pilferage

The original packaging objective was to offer physical protection. The typical product is handled several times between manufacture and consumer purchase, and its package must protect the contents against damage. Further, perishable products must be protected against spoilage in transit, storage, or awaiting consumer selection.

Another important role provided by many packages for the retailer is in preventing pilferage. At the retail level, pilferage is estimated to cost retailers $9 million each day. Many products are packaged with oversized cardboard backing too large to fit into a shoplifter's pocket or purse. Large plastic packages are used in a similar manner on such products as eight-track and cassette tapes.

Assist in Marketing the Product

The package designers of the 1980s frequently use marketing research in testing alternative designs. Increasingly scientific approaches are utilized in designing a package that is attractive, safe, and esthetically appealing. Kellogg's, for instance, tested Nutri-Grain's package as well as the product itself.[48]

In a grocery store containing as many as 15,000 different items, a product must capture the shopper's attention. Walter Margulies, chairman of Lippincott & Margulies advertising, summarizes the importance of first impressions in the retail store: "Consumers are more intelligent, but they don't read as much. They relate to pictures." Margulies also cites another factor: one of every six shoppers who needs eyeglasses does not wear them while shopping. Consequently, many marketers of-

[47]Bill Abrams, "Packaging Often Irks Buyers, but Firms Are Slow to Change," *The Wall Street Journal* (January 28, 1981), p. 25.

[48]"Packaging Linked to Ad's Effect," *Advertising Age* (May 3, 1982), p. 63.

fering product lines are adopting similar package designs in order to create more visual impact in the store. Packaging Stouffer's frozen foods in orange boxes and the adoption of common package designs by such product lines as Weight Watchers foods and Planter's nuts represent attempts to dominate larger sections of retail stores as Campbell's does.[49]

Packages can also offer the consumer convenience. Pump dispenser cans facilitate the use of products ranging from mustard to insect repellent. Pop-top cans provide added convenience for soft drinks, beer, and other food products. The six-pack carton, first introduced by Coca-Cola in the 1930s, can be carried with minimal effort by the food shopper.

A growing number of firms provide increased consumer utility with packages designed for reuse. Peanut butter jars and jelly jars have long been used as drinking glasses. Bubble bath can be purchased in plastic bottles shaped like animals and suitable for bathtub play. Packaging is a major component in Avon's overall marketing strategy. The firm's decorative reusable bottles have even become collectibles.

Cost Effective Packaging

Although packaging must perform a number of functions for the producer, marketer, and consumer, it must accomplish them at a reasonable cost. Packaging currently represents the single largest item in the cost of producing a can of beer. It also accounts for 70 percent of the total cost of the single-serving packets of sugar found in restaurants.

An excellent illustration of how packaging can be cost effective is provided by the large Swedish firm, Tetro-Pak. They pioneered aseptic packaging for products like milk and juice. Aseptic packaging wraps a laminated paper around a sterilized product and seals it off. The big advantage of the packaging technology is that products can be kept unrefrigerated for months. Aseptically packed milk, for instance, will keep its nutritional qualities and flavor for six months. With 60 percent of a supermarket's energy bill going for refrigerations, aseptic packaging is certainly cost effective. The paper packaging is also cheaper than the cans and bottles used for unrefrigerated fruit juices. Handling cost can also be reduced in many cases.[50]

The Metric Revolution in Packaging and Product Development

Marketers in the United States are increasingly adopting the metric system in their packaging and product development decisions. Metrics is a standard of weights and measures used throughout most of the world.

[49]Bill Abrams and David P. Garino, "Package Design Gains Stature as Visual Competition Grows," *The Wall Street Journal* (August 6, 1981).

[50]Robert Ball, "Warm Milk Wakes Up the Packaging Industry," *Fortune* (August 7, 1982), pp. 78–82.

Seven-Up now comes in half-liter bottles as a substitute for pints and quarts. Some canned and packaged foods list metric equivalents to ounces and pounds on their labels. Mustangs equipped with 2.3-liter engines are being powered by motors designed entirely in metric measurements.

The metric revolution has clearly affected the development of new products and their packaging. One survey found that 34 percent of all new products were designed in metrics, while 16 percent of the firms studied reported losing some sales because they did not offer a metric product.[51]

U.S. marketers must make the switch to metrics if they are to continue to compete in the world marketplace. Such firms as Caterpillar Tractor, John Deere, International Harvester, and IBM have been using metrics for years in their foreign trade. The switch to metrics should increase export sales by small U.S. firms that cannot afford to produce two sets of products for different markets.

Labeling

Although in the past the label was often a separate item applied to the package, most of today's plastic packages contain it as an integral part of the package. Labels perform both promotional and informational functions. A **label** in most instances contains the brand name or symbol, the name and address of the manufacturer or distributor, the product composition and size, and recommended uses for the product.

Consumer confusion and dissatisfaction over such incomprehensible sizes as giant economy size, king size, and family size led to passage of the **Fair Packaging and Labeling Act** (1966). The act requires a label to offer adequate information concerning the package contents and a package design that facilitates value comparisons among competitive products.

Food and Drug Administration regulations require that the nutritional contents be listed on the label of any food product to which a nutrient has been added or for which a nutritional claim has been made. Figure 11.5 shows a label listing the nutritional ingredients.

Voluntary packaging and labeling standards have also been developed in a number of industries. As a result, the number of toothpaste sizes was reduced from 57 to 5 and the number of dry detergent sizes from 24 to 6. In other industries, such as drug, food, fur, and clothing, federal legislation has been enacted to force companies to provide information and to prevent branding that misleads the consumer. The marketing manager in such industries must be fully acquainted with these laws and must design packages and labels in compliance with them.

[51] "Shift to Metrics Moving Ahead in Millimeters," *U.S. News & World Report* (June 7, 1982), p. 77.

Figure 11.5 Product Label with Specified Nutritional Contents

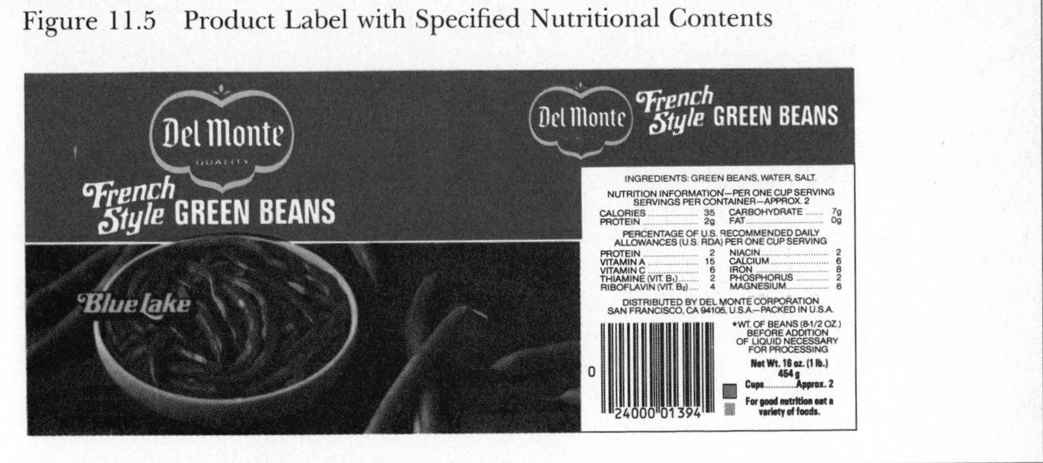

Source: Reprinted by permission of Del Monte Corporation.

Universal Product Code (UPC) The Universal Product Code (UPC) designation is another very important point of a label or package. Figure 11.5 shows the zebra-stripe UPC on the Del Monte French-style green beans label. In other cases, the code lines are printed right into the package, such as on a can of Tab.

The **Universal Product Code,** introduced in 1974 as an attempt to cut expenses in the supermarket industry, are codes read by optical scanners that print the item and its price on the cash register receipt. Some 95 percent of all package grocery items contain the UPC lines.

While the cost of UPC scanners is high—about $125,000 for a four-lane supermarket—they do permit considerable cost savings. The advantages include:

1. Labor savings because products are no longer individually priced.
2. Faster customer check-out times.
3. Better inventory control since the scanners can be tied to inventory records.
4. Similarly, the Universal Product Code is a major asset to marketing research in the industries involved with it.
5. Fewer errors in entering purchases at the check-out counter.

Despite these and other advantages, UPC still faces several obstacles. Many consumers still do not understand the purpose and advantages of the UPC scanners. In some localities, regulations specifically require individually priced items, thus negating the labor savings advantage of UPC scanners. Overall, it is obvious that the Universal Product Code is going to play an even greater role in product management in the coming decade. Lew Norwood, a spokesperson for the National Association of Retail Grocers, remarked: "We told our members that if they weren't into the computer age by 1986, they'd be in big trouble."[52]

Product Safety

If the product is to fulfill its mission of satisfying consumer needs, it must, above all, be safe. Manufacturers must design their products in such a way as to protect the consumers who use them. Packaging plays an important role in product safety. Aspirin bottle tops have been made child-proof (and virtually parent-proof) by St. Joseph's and Bayer since 1968. This safety issue is estimated to have reduced by two thirds the number of children under five years of age who have swallowed accidental doses of aspirin.

Prominently placed safety warnings on the labels of such potentially hazardous products as cleaning fluids and drain cleaners inform users of the dangers of these products and urge them to store the products out of the reach of children. Change in product design have reduced the dangers involved in the use of such products as lawn mowers, hedge trimmers, and toys.

The Consumer Product Safety Commission

Federal and state legislation has long played a major role in promoting product safety. Many of the piecemeal federal laws passed over a period of 50 years were unified by the **Consumer Product Safety Act** (1972), which created a powerful regulatory agency—the Consumer Product Safety Commission (CPSC). The new agency has assumed jurisdiction over every consumer product except food, automobiles, and a few other products already regulated by other agencies.

The CPSC has the authority to ban products without a court hearing, order the recall or redesign of products, and inspect production facilities; and it can charge managers of accused companies with criminal offenses. It has a national toll-free "hot-line" (800-638-8326) to receive consumer inquiries and complaints. Research on consumer accidents produced the twenty common dangers list shown in Table 11.3.

The Consumer Product Safety Commission has been active in developing and enforcing rules designed to reduce the 36 million product-related injuries that occur each year. Recent concerns have been

[52]This section is based on Raymond A. Marquardt, James C. Makens, and Robert G. Roe, *Retail Management,* 3d ed. (Hinsdale, Ill.: The Dryden Press, 1983), pp. 280–283; Edward M. Cooper and Harvey H. Sundel, "Attitudes of Users and Non-users of Scanner Equipped Retail Food Stores: An Empirical Study," in *Progress in Marketing Theory and Practice,* (eds.) Ronald D. Taylor, John S. Summey, and Blaise J. Bergiel (Proceedings of the Southern Marketing Association), pp. 186–190; and, "Store Scanners: Not a Super Market," *Newsweek* (June 22, 1981), p. 14. The Norwood quote is from the *Newsweek* article.

Table 11.3 Twenty Common Dangers to Consumers

Rank	Item	National Estimates of Injuries Requiring Emergency Room Treatment (in thousands)
1	Stairs, steps, ramps, and landings	763
2	Bicycles and bicycle accessories	518
3	Baseball	478
4	Football	470
5	Basketball	434
6	Nails, carpet tacks, screws, and thumbtacks	244
7	Chairs, sofas, and sofa beds	236
8	Skating	225
9	Non-glass tables	225
10	Glass doors, windows, and panels	208
11	Beds	199
12	Playground equipment	165
13	Lumber	151
14	Cutlery and knives	140
15	Glass bottles and jars	140
16	Desks, cabinets, shelves, bookcases, magazine racks, and footlockers	126
17	Swimming	126
18	Drinking glasses	111
19	Ladders and stools	99
20	Fences	99

Note that estimates represent product involvement in injuries and may not indicate causality.
Source: U.S. Consumer Product Safety Commission, "Estimated Number of Injuries Associated with Consumer Products Requiring Emergency Room Treatment," (July 1, 1980–June 30, 1981.)

wood-burning stoves, kerosene heaters, chain saws, lawn mowers, baby equipment and toys, chemical hazards, upholstered furniture, power tools, children's products, formaldehyde, benzidine dyes, and asbestos products.

The Concept of Product Liability

Product liability refers to the concept that manufacturers and marketers are responsible for injuries and damages caused by their products. There has been a tremendous increase in product liability suits in recent years. Over 100,000 such cases are filed annually.[53] Although

[53] "Product Safety: A New Hot Potato for Congress," *U.S. News & World Report* (June 14, 1982), p. 62. A good review of product liability law appears in Mary Jane Scheffet, "Market Share Liability: A New Doctrine of Causation in Product Liability," *Journal of Marketing* (Winter 1983), pp. 35–43.

many of these claims are settled out of court, others are decided by juries who have sometimes awarded multimillion dollar settlements. In 1978, a jury awarded a judgment of $128.5 million against Ford Motor Company in an accident case involving a Pinto. A judge later reduced the total to $6.1 million.

Not only have marketers stepped up effort to ensure product safety, but product liability insurance has become an essential ingredient in any new or existing product strategy. Premiums for this insurance have risen at an alarming rate, and in some cases, coverage is almost impossible to obtain. A Detroit producer of components for pleasure boats discovered that its liability insurance premiums had increased from $2,500 to $160,000 in a two-year period even though the insurance company had never paid a claim on the firm's behalf. Several manufacturers of football helmets discontinued production in recent years due to the unavailability of the insurance.[54] The seriousness of the product liability insurance situation prompted passage of the *Product Liability Risk Retention Act of 1981* which authorized producers to set up their own insurance firms.

Efforts are underway in several states to exempt companies from liability for injuries or property loss resulting from misuse of the products or from customer negligence. Such an exemption would have protected the retailer who paid damages to two men hurt by a lawn mower they lifted off the ground to trim a hedge.

CPSC activities and the increased number of liability claims have prompted companies to improve their safety standards voluntarily. For many companies, safety has become a vital ingredient of the broad definition of product.

Summary

A product mix is the assortment of product lines and individual offerings available from a marketer. The two primary components are product line, a series of related products, and individual offerings, or single products. Product mixes are assessed in terms of width and depth of assortment. Width of assortment refers to the variety of product lines offered, while depth refers to the number of individual offerings. Firms usually produce several related products rather than a single product in order to achieve the objectives of growth, optimal use of company resources, and increased company importance in the market.

New products experience a decay curve from idea generation to commercialization. Only one of 58 new product ideas typically make it

[54]*The Product Liability Crisis* (Lansing, Mich.: Michigan Product Liability Council, 1978); and "Liability Lawsuits Could Drive Product Prices through the Roof," *Marketing News* (January 23, 1981), p. 12.

all the way to commercialization. The success of a new product depends on a host of factors and can be the result of four alternative product development strategies: product improvement, market development, product development, and product diversification.

New product organizational responsibility in most large firms is assigned to new product committees, new product departments, product managers, or venture teams. New product ideas evolve through six stages before their market introduction: (1) idea generation, (2) screening, (3) business analysis, (4) product development, (5) test marketing, and (6) commercialization.

While new products are added to the line, old ones may face deletion from it. The typical causes for product eliminations are unprofitable sales and failure to fit into the existing product line.

Product identification may take the form of brand names, symbols, distinctive packaging, labeling, and the Universal Product Code. Effective brand names should be easy to pronounce, recognize, and remember; they should give the right connotation to the buyer; and they should be legally protectable. Brand loyalty can be measured in three stages: brand recognition, brand preference, and finally, brand insistence. Marketing managers must decide whether to use a single family brand for their product line or to use an individual brand for each product. Retailers have to decide the relative mix of national and private brands as well as generic products that they will carry.

Modern packaging is designed to: (1) protect against damage, spoilage, and pilferage; (2) assist in marketing the product; and (3) be cost effective. The metric revolution is also having a significant impact on U.S. packaging. Labels identify the product, producer, content, size, and uses of a packaged product. Most products also contain a Universal Product Code designation so that optical check-out scanners can be used.

Product safety has become an increasingly important component of the total product concept. This change has occurred through voluntary attempts by product designers to reduce hazards, through various pieces of legislation, and through establishment of the Consumer Product Safety Commission. The concept of product liability, or the legal responsibility of a producer or marketer for injuries or damages caused by a defective product, is also becoming increasingly important.

Chapter 10 introduced some basic product concepts. This chapter significantly expanded the discussion of products and services by looking at product mix decisions and new product planning. In the next chapter, attention shifts to the services sector.

Key Terms

product mix
product line
individual offerings
cannibalizing
line extension
product positioning

product managers
venture team
concept testing
test marketing
brand
brand name
trademark
generic name
brand recognition
brand preference
brand insistence
brand extension
family brand
individual brands
national brands
private brands
generic products
label
Fair Packaging and Labeling Acts
Universal Product Code
Consumer Product Safety Act
product liability

Review Questions

1. What is meant by a product mix? How is the concept used in making effective marketing decisions?
2. Why do most business firms market a line of related products rather than a single product?
3. Explain the product decay curve.
4. Outline the alternative organizational structures for new product development.
5. Identify the steps in the new product development process.
6. What is the chief purpose of test marketing? What potential problems are involved in it?
7. List the characteristics of an effective brand name. Illustrate each characteristic with an appropriate brand name.
8. Identify and briefly explain each of the three stages of brand loyalty.
9. What are the objectives of modern packaging?
10. Explain the chief functions of the Consumer Product Safety Commission. What steps can it take to protect consumers from defective and hazardous products?

Discussion Questions and Exercises

1. General Foods gave up on Lean Strips, a textured vegetable protein strip designed as a bacon substitute, after eight years of test marketing. Lean Strips sold well when bacon prices were high, but poorly when they were low. General Foods hoped to offer a protein analog product line that also included Crispy Strips, a snack and salad dressing item. Consumers liked the taste of Crispy Strips, but it was too expensive for repeat purchases, and the product was abandoned before Lean Strip's demise. General Foods said that it would concentrate on new product categories instead of concentrating on individual items like Lean Strips.

What can be learned from General Food's experience with Lean Strips?

2. **Trademark Infringement Quiz**
The Lanham Act grants exclusive usage of specified trademarks to their owners. Such marks assist consumers by allowing them to distinguish between a preferred product and those of competitors. Yet many trademarks are quite similar in sound, color, or appearance. In instances of possible trademark infringement, a legal decision must be made. The following examples are actual trademark cases in which decisions have been reached. In which of these instances would you have ruled that trademark infringement has occurred? (Answers are printed upside down below.)

Court Case	(Circle Your Choice) A Case of Trademark Infringement?	
1. *Jockey* men's underwear and hosiery vs. *Jockey* shoe polish	YES	NO
2. *Mustang* automobiles vs. *Mustang* mobile homes	YES	NO
3. *All* detergent vs. *All Out* rust remover	YES	NO
4. Miller *Lite* beer vs. Budweiser *Light*	YES	NO
5. *Space Saver* clothes drying racks vs. *Space Server* belt and tie hangers	YES	NO
6. *Pepsi* soft drinks vs. *Pepsup* barbecue sauce	YES	NO
7. *Triox* insecticides vs. *Tri-X* fertilizer	YES	NO
8. *Dial* soap vs. *Di-All* insecticide (with clock dial on label)	YES	NO
9. *English Leather* toiletries vs. *London Leather* toiletries	YES	NO
10. *Pepsodent* dentifrice vs. *Pearlident* dentifrice	YES	NO

Answers: (1) Yes; (2) No; (3) No; (4) No; (5) Yes; (6) No; (7) Yes; (8) No; (9) Yes; (10) Yes.

Source: Adapted from Richard H. Buskirk, *Principles of Marketing* (Hinsdale, Ill.: The Dryden Press, 1975), pp. 268–271. Used by permission of the author.

3. Campbell Soup Company's Belgian candy company, Godiva Chocolates, introduced a designer line called "Bill Blass Chocolates." The premium chocolates sold for $14 per pound. Relate this action to the material discussed in Chapter 11.

4. Exxene, a $1 million manufacturer of antifog coatings for goggles, was sued for trademark infringement by Exxon Corp. The oil company giant claimed that it had nearly exclusive rights to the letters *EXX* regardless of what followed it. Four and a half years later, a jury awarded Exxene $250,000 in damages instead. Exxon filed an appeal. Relate this case to the textbook discussion of trademarks.

5. Although implementation has been delayed, Congress has voted to require passive restraint systems in all automobiles sold in the United States. It was estimated that automatic seat belts would add up to $150 to a cost of a car, and air bags could carry a $1,100 price tag. What does this requirement suggest about the relationship between product safety and cost-effective product development? Discuss.

Chapter Objectives

1. To relate services to other elements of the marketing mix.
2. To distinguish between products and services.
3. To explain the nature and role of the service sector.
4. To identify the distinguishing features of services.
5. To discuss buyer behavior as it relates to services.
6. To outline the similarities and differences in the environment for service firms.
7. To describe the marketing mix for service firms.
8. To suggest methods for increasing productivity for services.

12

SERVICES

It all began in Douglas, Arizona, back in 1913, when the city decided to put up a half-dozen board shacks for travelers. Few students today could imagine what automobile travel was like in the early decades of this century. For east-to-west travelers, the paved roads ended in Omaha. Most overnight accommodations were in hotels that were located in city centers to serve railroad passengers, not along roadsides. Furthermore, motorists were usually filthy from road dust and frequent breakdowns, so many were reluctant to use stylish hotels.

Early twentieth century motorists often chose to camp along the roadside at night. As this trend developed, many communities offered municipal auto camps for travelers. Some, like Douglas, Arizona, even erected crude shelters.

Sensing an opportunity, entrepreneurs began to compete against the municipalities. Eventually cabins were built, and the motel industry established itself on the American landscape. By 1926, it was estimated that there were 2,000 cabin camps in the United States. They were called by a variety of names: cabin camp, tourist camp, tourist court, auto court, motor court, and autel. But in 1925, a San Luis Obispo, California, camp owner came up with the name that prevailed—motel. The new service industry was growing rapidly. *Business Week* estimated that there were 15,000 motels in 1935 and 20,000 in 1940; still the industry was not without its problems.

Hotel associations lobbied legislatures to strictly regulate the new competitive threat. In some places, the legislation that was passed forced the motels to upgrade their offerings. Eventually this hurt hotels even more.

The early motels also suffered from some negative public opinion. FBI Director J. Edgar Hoover argued that they were often hide-outs for criminals. One of the most famous shootouts of the 1930s occurred at the Red Crown Cabin Camp near Platte City, Missouri, when Bonnie Parker and Clyde Barrow temporarily escaped from police in a blaze of gunfire. The cabins or motels were also criticized as rendevous for romantic interludes. A 1935 study by Southern Methodist University did not help the image of the developing industry. It found that the average Saturday turnover was 1.5.

Despite the bad publicity, the motel industry continued to prosper. By 1960, there were 60,000 motels. A new trend had also developed. Chains of motels began to dominate the industry by replacing the independent owner/operators. Quality Courts and Travel Lodge were set up in the 1940s. Holiday Inn opened its first motel in 1952 in Memphis. The motel chains standardized the service offerings and began to offer many of the amenities that used to characterize hotels. Recently, no-frills motels have become a major competitive factor. They offer less ambiance and services for a lower price. One wonders if the next wave of innovation in the motel industry will be cabin camps?[1]

The Conceptual Framework

The first two chapters in the section on product/service strategy dealt with the basic concepts of this aspect of marketing. Product lines, product life cycles, branding, and classification systems are examples of some of these concepts.

[1]Source: Paul Lancaster, "The Great American Motel," *American Heritage Magazine,* Copyright © 1982 by American Heritage Publishing Co., Inc. Reprinted in *Review* (August 1982), pp. 34–37 ff.

Chapter 12 deals with services. In a fundamental sense, marketers approach the development of marketing programs for both products and services in the same manner. Such programs begin with an investigation, analysis, and selection of a particular market target and follow with the development of a marketing mix designed to satisfy the chosen target. Although tangible products and intangible services are similar in that both provide consumer benefits, there are significant differences in the marketing of each. Both the similarities and differences are examined in this chapter. Services are treated in a special chapter because of two factors:

1. The immense size of the service industry market sector.
2. The differences between marketing strategies for services and for tangible products.

Services are troublesome to define. It is difficult to distinguish between certain kinds of goods and services. Personal services, such as hair styling and dry cleaning, are easily recognized as services, but they represent only a small part of the total service industry.

Some firms provide a combination of goods and services to their customers. Wackenhut Corporation, a protection specialist, markets alarms and closed-circuit TVs (goods) in addition to uniformed guards and trained dogs (services). An optometrist may give eye examinations (a service) and sell contact lenses and eyeglasses (goods). Some services represent an integral part of the marketing of physical goods. For example, a Burroughs sales representative may emphasize the firm's service capabilities at minimizing machine down-time. These examples suggest that some method of alleviating definitional ambiguity is needed.

Defining Services

One useful method is the utilization of a product spectrum, which shows that most products have both goods and services components. Figure 12.1 presents a **goods-services continuum**—a method for visualizing the differences and similarities of goods and services.[2] A tire is a pure good, although the service of balancing it may be sold along with it or included in the total price. Hair styling is a pure service. In the middle ranges of the continuum are products with both goods and services components. The satisfaction that results from dining in an exclusive restaurant like Denver's Cafe Giovanni, Philadelphia's La Traffe, or Washington's Maison Blanche is derived not only from the food and drink, but also from the services rendered by the establishment's personnel.[3]

[2]A goods-services continuum is suggested in G. Lynn Shostack, "Breaking Free from Product Marketing," *Journal of Marketing* (April 1977), p. 77. See also John M. Rathmell, "What Is Meant by Services?" *Journal of Marketing* (October 1966), pp. 32–36.

[3]The restaurant list is suggested by Carol Lalle, "125 Restaurants You Can Rely on," *Esquire* (August 1982), pp. 41–50, 52, 55–56.

Figure 12.1 The Goods-Services Continuum

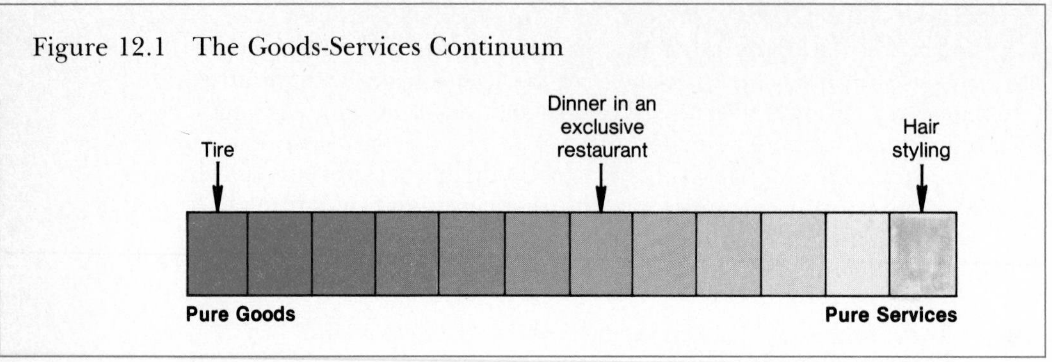

Although it is difficult, if not impossible, to describe all the services available to consumer and industrial purchasers, a general definition can be developed. **Services** are intangible tasks that satisfy consumer and industrial user needs when efficiently developed and distributed to chosen market segments.

The Nature of the Service Sector

There has been a considerable increase in the expenditures for consumer services during the previous decade. Services—ranging from such necessities as electric power and medical care to such luxuries as foreign travel, backpacking guides, ski resorts, and tennis schools—now account for almost 50 percent of the average consumer's total expenditures. Services also provide 70 percent of all jobs and account for two thirds of the U.S. gross national product.[4]

The distribution of consumer service expenditures is shown in Table 12.1. Over a third of the consumer service dollar went to housing-related expenditures. Medical care placed second. In fact, the rapid escalation of medical care expense has led to a host of proposals to cap these costs in the future. At this point, there is still no concensus on how to best restrain these cost increases.

The increasing complexity of modern business has also provided substantial opportunities for such business service firms as Arthur Andersen and Company (certified public accountants), A.C. Nielsen (marketing research), and Brinks, Inc. (protection). For most consumer and business service firms, marketing is an emerging activity for two reasons: (1) the growth potential of the service market represents a vast

[4]James Cook, "You Mean We've Been Speaking Prose All These Years," *Forbes* (April 11, 1983), p. 143.

Table 12.1 Percentage Distribution of Consumer Service Expenditures

Service	Percent of Total Expenditure
Shelter	34.6%
Medical care	18.3
Household operations	14.2
Personal business	11.6
Transportation	8.2
Recreation	4.5
Education	3.2
Foreign travel	1.8
Other	3.6

Source: Department of Commerce and Conference Board. Used by permission.

marketing opportunity, and (2) increased competition is forcing traditional service industries to emphasize marketing in order to compete in the marketplace.

Features of Services

The preceding discussion suggests that services are varied and complex. Following are the four key features of services that have major marketing implications:

1. Services are intangible.
2. Services are perishable.
3. The standardization of services is difficult.
4. Buyers are often involved in the development and distribution of services.

Intangibility Services do not have tangible features that appeal to consumers' senses of sight, hearing, smell, taste, and touch. They are therefore difficult to demonstrate at trade fairs, to display in retail stores, to illustrate in magazine advertisements, and to sample. Consequently, imaginative personal selling is usually an essential ingredient in the marketing of services.

Furthermore, buyers are often unable to judge the quality of a service prior to purchase. Because of this, the reputation of the service's vendor is often a key factor in the buying decision. Consumers are literally buying a promise, so it is important to "tangibilize" services. A good example is an architect's rendering of an office building that shows contented workers enjoying a casual lunch in a beautiful courtyard.[5]

Perishability The utility of most services is short-lived; therefore, they cannot be produced ahead of time and stored for periods of peak demand. Vacant seats on an airplane, idle dance instructors, and unused electrical generating capacity represent economic losses that can never be recovered. Sometimes, however, idle facilities during slack periods must be tolerated so the firm will have sufficient capacity for peak periods. Such industries as electric and natural gas utilities, resort hotels, telephone companies, and airlines all face the problem of perishability.

Some service firms are able to overcome this problem with off-peak pricing. Resorts feature high and low season pricing schemes, the telephone company grants reduced rates on Saturday, and baseball teams offer low-priced general admission seats.

Difficulty of Standardization It is often impossible to standardize offerings among sellers of the same service or even to assure consistency in the services provided by one seller. Carol Brothers, a Youngstown, Ohio, interior decorator, spent two years attempting to achieve standardization by developing the Speed Team Cleaning System whereby a team of two maids clean houses in five hours at a typical fee of $35 per visit. Brothers has sold 32 Pop-Ins maid service franchises primarily in the Midwest.[6]

Involvement of Buyers Buyers often play major roles in the marketing and production of services. The hair stylist's customer may describe the desired style and make suggestions at several stages during the styling process. Different firms often require unique blends of insurance coverage, and the final policy may be developed after several meetings between the purchaser and the insurance agent. Although purchaser specifications also play a role in the creation of major products such as installations, the interaction of buyer and seller at both the production and distribution stages is a common feature of services.

Classifying Consumer and Industrial Services

Literally thousands of services are available to consumer and industrial users. In some instances, they are provided by specialized machinery with almost no personal assistance (such as an automated car wash). In

[5]Theodore Levitt, "Marketing Intangible Products and Product Intangibles," *Harvard Business Review* (May–June 1981), pp. 94–102. The example is from pp. 96–97.

[6]Marlys Harris, "Opportunities in Franchising's New Wave," *Money* (February 1982), pp. 77–78.

other cases, the services are provided by skilled professionals with little reliance on specialized equipment (such as accountants and management consultants). Figure 12.2 provides a means of classifying services based on the following two factors: the degree of reliance on equipment in providing the service, and the degree of skill possessed by the people who provide the service. The initial classification is based on whether the service is equipment based or people based. The second level of classification is in accordance with the skill levels of the performance.

Buyer Behavior

Important elements of buyer behavior were discussed earlier in the text. Many similarities exist between buyer behavior for goods and for services, yet there are some important differences. These may be grouped into three categories: (1) attitudes, (2) needs and motives, and (3) purchase behavior. In most of these, the personal element of the

Figure 12.2 Types of Service Businesses

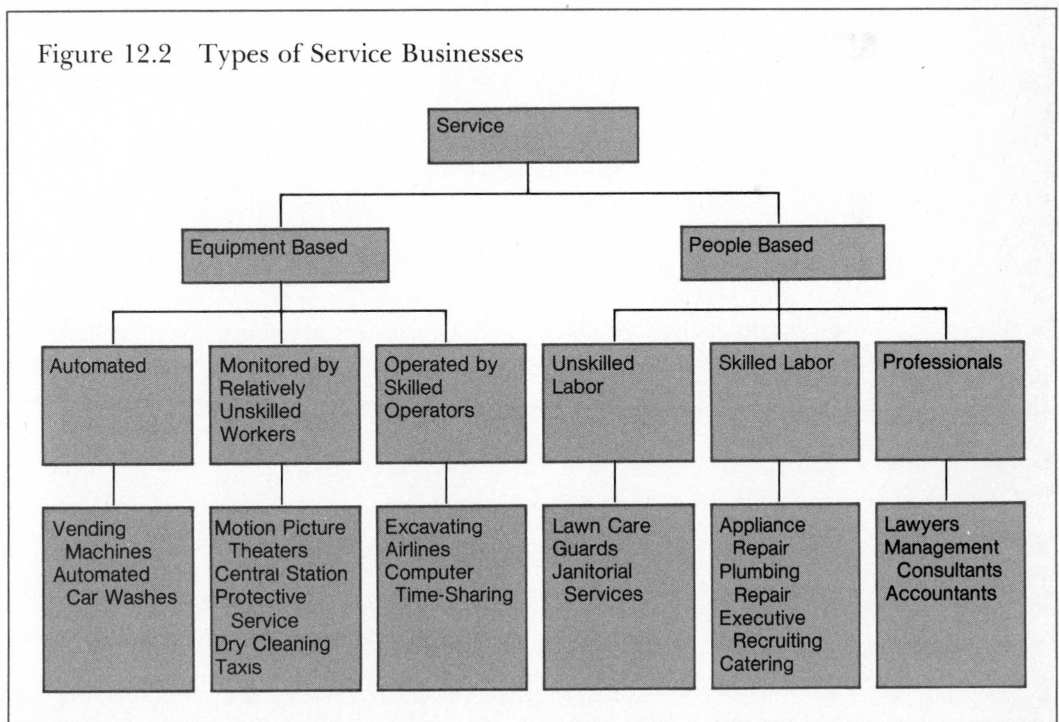

Source: Dan R. E. Thomas, "Strategy Is Different in Service Businesses," *Harvard Business Review* (July–August 1978), p. 161. Reprinted by permission of the *Harvard Business Review*.

services is the key to the consumer's decision on which services to purchase.[7]

Service marketers are sometimes perceived as more personal, friendlier, and more cooperative than goods marketers. These and other distinctive personal elements often differentiate service marketers from goods marketers and thus provide the service marketer with a unique marketing opportunity.

Personal contact between salespeople and customers occurs in the marketing of goods as well as services; however, service representatives play an even more important role. One writer described it in this way:

> *With service retailing there is a change in the sequence of events that occur—the sale must be made before production and consumption take place. Thus the truism that all customer contact employees are engaged in personal selling is much more real for the service firm than for the goods firm. With goods, the physical object can carry some of the selling burden. With services, contact personnel* are *the service. Customers, in effect, perceive them to be "the product." They become the physical representation of the offering. The service firm employees are both factory workers* and *salespersons because of the simultaneous production and consumption of most services.*[8]

Attitudes

A consumer's attitudes will directly influence his or her buying decision for almost any product or service. Because of the intangible quality of services, attitudes seem to be especially important in the marketing of them. It is likely that the characteristic of intangibility causes buyers to rely on subjective impressions of a service and its seller when purchasing a service. This reliance on subjective impressions is less apparent in the purchase of tangible goods. Two important distinctions between goods and services are relevant: (1) services are perceived as being more personal than goods, and (2) consumers are sometimes less satisfied with purchases of services. Dissatisfaction with the personal ele-

[7]This section is based on Eugene M. Johnson, "Are Goods and Services Different?—An Exercise in Marketing Theory," unpublished DBA dissertation, Washington University, 1969, pp. 83–205. Used by permission. See also Leonard L. Berry, "Services Marketing Is Different," *Business* (May–June 1980), pp. 24–29; Joseph L. Orsini, "Strategic Implications of Differences between Goods and Services: An Empirical Analysis of Information Source Importance," in *Proceedings of the 1982 Conference of the Western Marketing Educators,* (ed.) Stephen H. Achtenhagen, pp. 61–62; and Duane L. Davis and Robert M. Cosenza, "Identifying Search Prone Segments in the Service Sector: A Test of Taxonometric Research," in *Developments in Marketing Science,* (eds.) Vinay Kothari, Danny R. Arnold, James Cavusgil, Jay D. Lindquist, Jay Nathan, and Stan Reid (Las Vegas, Nevada: Proceedings of the Sixth Annual Conference of the Academy of Marketing Science, 1982), pp. 301–305.

[8]William R. George, "The Retailing of Services—A Challenging Future," *Journal of Retailing* (Fall 1977), pp. 89–90. See also Richard B. Chase, "Where Does the Customer Fit in a Service Operation?" *Harvard Business Review* (November–December 1978), pp. 137–142.

ments of a service, such as an unfriendly flight attendant or impolite bank teller, can be the antecedent of a negative attitude toward the entire service.

Needs and Motives

A comparison of needs and buying motives for goods and services suggests that similarities dominate. Essentially the same types of needs are satisfied whether a person buys the materials for home repair or hires a service organization to perform the task. Although service needs have increased in importance, these needs usually can be satisfied by new or modified goods as well as by services.

A need that often does stand out is the consumer's desire for personal attention. By appealing to this need, the stylist, the banker, or the insurance agent provides a form of satisfaction that the seller of a good cannot easily match. The desire for personal attention is often the dominant need satisfied by a service.

Purchase Behavior

Research suggests that differences between goods and services are most noticeable in the case of purchase behavior. Goods-selection decisions are normally concerned more with the question of whether to purchase, while services-selection decisions emphasize proper timing and selection of a source.[9] This situation suggests several distinctions between purchase behavior for goods and services. The degree of prepurchase planning may differ; influences on the buyer may vary; and the buyer may be more personally involved in a service purchase.

Consumers are influenced more by others—friends, neighbors, and salespeople—when buying services than when buying goods. Because services are intangible, it is difficult for the buyer to judge quality and value. Buyers are usually unable to inspect or sample a service prior to its purchase, so they may depend on the experiences and observations of others.

The dominant role of personal influence in the selection of services has two principal implications for services marketing: (1) added emphasis must be placed upon developing a professional relationship between

[9]Sidney P. Feldman and Merline C. Spencer, "The Effect of Personal Influence in the Selection of Consumer Services," in *Marketing and Economic Development,* (ed.) Peter D. Bennett (Chicago: American Marketing Association, 1967), p. 440. See also Richard B. Chase, "Where Does the Customer Fit in a Service Organization?" *Harvard Business Review* (November–December 1978), pp. 137–142; and Duane Davis, "Alternative Predictors of Consumer Search Propensities in the Service Sector," in *Marketing in the 80s,* (eds.) Richard P. Bagozzi, Kenneth L. Bernhardt, Paul S. Busch, David W. Cravens, Joseph F. Hair, Jr., and Carol A. Scott (Chicago: American Marketing Association, 1980), pp. 160–163.

service suppliers and their customers, and (2) promotional efforts must be aimed toward exploiting word-of-mouth promotion.

The Status of Marketing in Service Firms

The service sector has traditionally been a cottage-type industry consisting of many small, independent firms. Some aspects still are, like American Sports Advisors, Inc. with sales of $2.7 million. The Hicksville, N.Y., firm provides weekly odds on football, basketball, and baseball games and is partially owned by a former accounting professor.[10] Other service firms have become giant organizations. Philbro, an international mineral trading and investment banking firm, is the nation's largest diversified service firm. Philbro's annual revenues are in excess of $25 billion.[11]

Although spending for services has increased substantially, the development of marketing as a major business activity has come slowly to most service industries. This is largely due to what Theodore Levitt has called **marketing myopia,** a topic discussed in Chapter 1.[12] Levitt's thesis is that top executives in many industries have failed to recognize the scope of their businesses. Future growth is endangered because management is product-oriented rather than customer-oriented. Levitt specifically mentions certain service industries in his examples—namely, the dry cleaning, motion picture, railroad, and electric utilities industries. The film studio president, for example, who defines the firm's activities as "making movies" instead of as "marketing entertainment" is suffering from marketing myopia, according to Levitt.

Indicative of the low status of marketing in many service industries are the findings of a survey of manufacturing and service firms. Research concluded that "the marketing function appears to be less structured in service companies than in manufacturing firms." Service organizations often lack the equivalent of a marketing vice-president. The following major findings were reported:

In comparison to manufacturing firms, service firms appear to be (1) generally less likely to have marketing mix activities carried out in the marketing department, (2) less likely to perform analysis in the offering area, (3) more likely to handle their advertising internally rather than go to outside agencies, (4) less likely to have an overall sales plan, (5) less likely to develop sales training programs, (6) less likely to use marketing research firms and market-

[10]Jon Schriber, "Nicely-Nicely Computer," *Forbes* (December 7, 1981), p. 150.

[11]See *Fortune* (July 12, 1982), p. 132.

[12]Theodore Levitt, "Marketing Myopia," *Harvard Business Review* (July–August 1961), pp. 45–56.

ing consultants, and (7) less likely to spend as much on marketing when expressed as a percentage of gross sales.[13]

Marketing research might have helped WLS, a Chicago TV station, better direct the advertising campaign it used to launch a new news anchor team. In an effort to catch up to WBBM, Chicago's audience leader, WLS decided to appeal more strongly to younger viewers by introducing what it called "The New Generation" news team. The anchors, both under 40 and supported by a colorful sportscaster and a podiatrist turned weatherman, replaced an older anchor team. WLS launched "The New Generation" advertising campaign without any testing. The campaign featured extensive broadcast, print, and outdoor advertising. One spot showed the new female anchor telling the retiring 66-year-old anchor: "It's important we tell the truth." The viewer reaction was negative, and the advertising campaign was described as condescending by some. The advertising campaign was promptly halted.[14]

Similarities and Differences in the Environment for Service Firms

The environmental framework for marketing decisions was discussed in Chapter 2. In many ways, the economic, societal/cultural, legal, technological, and competitive forces exert the same types of pressures on service firms as they exert on goods producers. However, certain features of the environment for service marketing must be highlighted.

Economic Environment

The growth of consumer expenditures for services has been accompanied by further expansion of business and government services to keep pace with the increasing complexity of the American economy. The sharp increase in spending for services and the development of service industries as the major employer of labor has been one of the most significant economic trends in our post-World War II economy. Most explanations of this trend are predicated on the changes associated with a maturing economy and the by-products of rapid economic growth. A theory developed by economist Colin Clark describes the growth of service industries.[15] In the first (and most primitive) stage, the vast major-

[13]William R. George and Hiram C. Barksdale, "Marketing Activities in the Service Industries," *Journal of Marketing* (October 1974), pp. 69, 75.

[14]Kevin Higgins, "TV Stations Rely on Research, Marketing Tactics to Improve Quality of News Shows," *Marketing News* (March 5, 1982), pp. 1, 4.

[15]Colin Clark, *The Conditions of Economic Progress,* 3d ed. (London: Macmillan, 1957), pp. 490–491.

ity of an economy's population is engaged in farming, hunting, fishing, and forestry. As the society becomes more advanced, the emphasis shifts from an agrarian economy to one based on manufacturing activities. The final (and the most advanced) stage occurs when the majority of labor is engaged in the so-called **tertiary industries,** the production of services.

Technological advances, population shifts, and changes in consumer needs have also contributed to increased spending for consumer services. The evolution of science and technology has altered productivity trends, and higher productivity in the manufacturing industries has brought about the shift of workers to service industries. Technological advances have helped create a higher standard of living for the average person, who currently spends a larger portion of his or her increased discretionary income for services. In addition, population changes—particularly increased urbanization—have widened the demand for personal and public services. Changes in consumer needs, such as an increased demand for convenience, has led to greater spending for consumer services.

Even more marked than the growth of consumer expenditures for services has been the increased spending for business services. The servicing of business has become very profitable, and companies in this field range from suppliers of temporary help to highly specialized consultation services. Two reasons exist for the rapid growth of business services. First, business service firms frequently are able to perform a specialized function more cheaply than the purchasing company can do itself. Enterprises providing maintenance, cleaning, and protection services to office buildings and industrial plants are common examples.

Societal/Cultural Environment

The societal/cultural environment has a significant impact on the marketing of services. Consumers are offered a wide array of services; some are accepted, others rejected. Tastes also can shift over time. For instance, the increased use of counselors and consultants affects many aspects of modern personal, family, and work lives. A few years ago some of these services were not even available, let alone influential. Now there are even leisure consultants to advise consumers on what to do with their spare time.

A variety of societal/cultural trends are relevant to the increased marketing of services. For example, there is evidence that the American consumer's tastes are shifting to a preference for services as status symbols. Travel, culture, health and beauty, and higher education have partially replaced durable goods as status symbols in the minds of many consumers. Other trends include a growing emphasis on security, which has widened the market for insurance, banking, and investment services; greater concern for health, which has led to a greater demand for dental, medical, and hospital services; and the changing attitude toward credit, which has expanded the demand for the services of banks and other lending agencies.

Attitudes toward some services change slowly, however. One study of the attitudes of homemakers toward the use of personal services observed a continuing resistance to using some services due to perceived conflict with a homemaker's lifestyle. Although they recognized the time and effort saved by purchasing personal services, these homemakers still believed that purchasing services violated the virtues of hard work and self-reliance which are part of the homemaker's traditional image.[16]

Political and Legal Environment

Service businesses are more closely regulated than most other forms of private enterprise. Nearly all service firms are subject to government regulation in addition to the usual taxes, antitrust legislation, and restrictions on promotion and price discrimination. For example, a local bus company must have the approval of the public service commission before adding or dropping a route, and a hair stylist must comply with state licensing requirements.

Marketers of services must recognize the impact of governmental regulation on their competitive strategies. Regulation affects the marketing of services in three significant ways:

1. It generally reduces the range of competition; if competition remains, its intensity usually increases.
2. It reduces a marketer's array of options and introduces certain rigidities into the marketing process.
3. Because the decisions of the regulatory agency are binding, part of the marketing decision process must be to predict the actions of the regulatory agency.[17]

Many service industries are regulated at the national level by such government agencies as the Federal Power Commission, the Interstate Commerce Commission, the Federal Trade Commission, the Federal Communications Commission, and the Securities and Exchange Commission. Other service industries—insurance, banking, and real estate—are traditionally regulated at state and local levels. In addition, many personal and business services are restricted at state and local levels by special fees or taxes, certification, and licensing. Often included in this category are members of the legal and medical professions, funeral directors, accountants, engineers, and members of similar professions.

[16]William R. Darden and Warren A. French, "Selected Personal Services: Consumer Reactions," *Journal of Retailing* (Fall 1972), pp. 42–48.

[17]Blaine Cooke, "Analyzing Markets for Services," in *Handbook of Modern Marketing,* (ed.) Victor P. Buell (New York: McGraw-Hill, 1970), pp. 2–44.

Technological Environment: Productivity Remains a Problem

Historically, two thirds of the economic growth in the United States has resulted from increases in **productivity**—the output produced by each worker. Technological developments accounted for significant increases in productivity in the past. Cyrus H. McCormick was able to almost triple the output of the average wheat farmer, and Henry Ford's innovations made it possible to reduce the cost of an average car by 50 percent. How are increases in productivity accomplished in a service economy?

Theodore Levitt argues that service marketers should assume a "manufacturing" attitude. "Instead of looking to the service workers to improve results by greater exertion of animal energy, managers must see what kinds of organizations, incentives, technology, and skills could improve overall productivity."[18]

Levitt cites McDonald's as the ultimate example of how service can be industrialized:

Each variety of McDonald's hamburger is in a color-coded wrapper. Parking lots are sprinkled with brightly painted, omnivorous trash cans that even the most chronic litterer finds difficult to ignore. A special scoop has been devised for French fries so that each customer will believe he is getting an over-flowing portion, while actually receiving a uniform ration. Employee discretion is eliminated; everything is organized so that nothing can go wrong.[19]

The manufacturing attitude is already evident in many service firms. Conversion of such businesses as dry cleaners and car washes from hand labor to automatic equipment has increased output per worker. The introduction of wide-bodied jets by the airlines enables them to fly twice as many passengers with the same number of high-salaried pilots and flight engineers. The development of multiple-unit motion picture theaters with a single refreshment stand, ticket-selling booth, and projection room reduced necessary floor space and the number of people needed to operate them.[20] For small personal loans, some banks have shifted from analysis by loan officers to a simple "scorecard" to evaluate prospective borrowers (one point for having a telephone, five points for home ownership, five points for several years of steady employment, and so on). The challenge to service marketers is to produce gains in productivity while not sacrificing the quality of service.

[18]"The 'Big Mac' Theory of Economic Progress," *Forbes* (April 15, 1977), p. 137. See also Theodore Levitt, "The Industrialization of Service," *Harvard Business Review* (September–October 1976), pp. 63–75.

[19]Levitt, "The Industrialization of Service," p. 70.

[20]Dan R. E. Thomas, "Strategy Is Different in Service Business," *Harvard Business Review* (July–August 1978), p. 160. See also Donald J. Hempel and Michael V. Laric, "A Total Performance System for Evaluating Marketing Productivity in Service Industries," in *Marketing Looks Outward,* (ed.) William Locander (Chicago: American Marketing Association, 1977), pp. 73–79.

In some ways the service industries represent a new frontier in marketing.[21] Many service firms have remained very production-oriented, even in the face of a changing business environment. But even these companies are beginning to realize the value of an effective marketing strategy.

Services will be a major growth sector of our economy during the coming decade. Consumers will spend more for services, and significant employment gains will evolve in this area. These advances can be achieved only if service industries improve their productivity record, and this will most likely occur through improved marketing.

Competitive Environment

The competitive environment for services represents a paradox. For many service industries, competition comes not from other services but from goods manufacturers or from government services. Internal competition is almost nonexistent in some service industries. Price competition is often limited in such services as communication and legal and medical services. Moreover, many important service producers like hospitals, educational institutions, and religious and welfare agencies are nonprofit organizations. Finally, many service industries are difficult to enter and may require a major financial investment, special education or training, or may be restricted by government regulations.

Competition from Goods Direct competition between goods and services is inevitable since competing goods and services often provide the same basic satisfactions. Consumers may satisfy their service requirements by substituting goods. Competition has increased because manufacturers, recognizing the changing needs of consumers, are building services and added conveniences into their products. Wash-and-wear clothing has affected laundry services; improved appliances have reduced the need for domestic employees; and television competes with motion pictures and other forms of entertainment. Consumers often have a choice between goods and services that perform the same general function.

Competition from Retailers and Manufacturers The entry of retailers and manufacturers into consumer and service markets also increases the intensity of competition for the service dollar. Large retailers, such as Sears, J.C. Penny, and Montgomery Ward, are providing services such as optical centers, insurance, dental offices, legal services, and automobile repairs. Sears has been a leader in the trend to diversify into ser-

[21]New service opportunities are discussed in Donna Iven Queshi, "Service Marketing: An Empirical Study," in *Proceedings of the 1982 Conference of the Western Marketing Educators,* (ed.) Stephen H. Achtenhagen, pp. 59–60.

vices with its entry into insurance (Allstate Insurance), real estate (Coldwell Banker) and investments (Dean Witter Reynolds Inc.). These large retailers have apparently decided that the mass merchandising of consumer services is possible and profitable.

Competition from Government Many services are provided by government. Some services can be provided only by government agencies, but others compete with privately produced goods and services. Often the consumption of government services is mandatory, such as social security and compulsory education. Current public debates concern how to pay for these services and what level of government is responsible for providing them.

The Marketing Mix for Service Firms

Satisfying the service needs of buyers requires the development of an effective marketing mix. Service policies and pricing, distribution, and promotional strategies must be combined in an integrated marketing program.[22] The section that follows introduces the marketing mix for service firms. Detailed discussions of the marketing mix are presented in Chapters 10 to 21.

Service Policies

As with tangible products, services may be classified according to their intended use. All services are either consumer services or industrial services. Even when the same service (telephone, gas, or electric services, for example) is sold to both consumer and industrial buyers, the service firm often maintains separate marketing groups for each market segment.

Consumer services may be classified as convenience, shopping, and specialty services. Dry cleaning, shoe repairs, and similar personal services are commonly purchased on a convenience basis. Auto repairs and insurance are services that usually involve some shopping effort to compare price and quality. Specialty services may include professional services, such as financial, legal, and medical assistance.

Some service firms have developed new services or diversified their service mix in an attempt to boost sales. Insurance policies for homeowners, vacation package tours, and air-travel family plans all represent

[22]An interesting illustration is the marketing mix for legal services. This is discussed in Donna K. Darden, William R. Darden, and G. E. Kiser, "The Marketing of Legal Services," *Journal of Marketing* (Spring 1981), pp. 123–134.

Table 12.2 Examples of Service Product Innovations

Nature of Service	New Service Product	Service Product Improvement
Communications	Communication satellite	Free-standing public telephone
Consulting and business facilitating	Equipment leasing	Overnight TV rating service
Educational	Three-year degrees	New curricula
Financial	Bank credit cards	"Bank by mail"
Health	Treatment with lasers	Intensive care
Household operations	Laundromat	Fuel budget accounts
Housing	Housing for the elderly	Motel swimming pool
Insurance	National health insurance	No-fault insurance
Personal	Physical fitness facilities	
Recreational	Dual cinema	New play
Transportation	Unit train	Flight reservation system

Source: Adapted from *Marketing in the Service Sector* by John M. Rathmell. Copyright © 1974. Reprinted by permission of Winthrop Publishers Inc., Cambridge, Massachusetts.

examples of expanded service offerings that have received favorable consumer response.

New services are often an improved method of delivering an existing service. Table 12.2 presents a list of service product innovations.

Some important differences between service policies and product policies should be noted. First, because services are intangible, packaging and labeling decisions are very limited. Service marketers are rarely able to use the package to promote their services. Second, the lack of a tangible product limits the use of sampling as a means of introducing a new service to the market.

Pricing Strategy

In service industries, pricing practices are not substantially different from those in goods industries. In developing a pricing strategy, the service marketer must consider the demand for the service; production, marketing, and administrative costs; and the influence of competition.[23] However, for many services price competition has been limited. The prices charged by most utilities are closely regulated by federal, state, and local government agencies. For many other service firms, such as advertising agencies, there is a traditional pricing structure that is followed within the industry.

[23]See Martin R. Schlissel, "Pricing in a Service Industry," *MSU Business Topics* (Spring 1977), pp. 37–48.

Price negotiation forms an important part of many professional service transactions. Consumer services that sometimes may involve price negotiation include auto repairs, foreign travel, and financial, legal, or medical assistance. Specialized business services, such as equipment rental, market research, insurance, and maintenance and protection services, are also priced through direct negotiation. Many firms use variable pricing to overcome the problems associated with the perishable nature of services. For example, deregulation has permitted airlines to offer discounted fares on many highly competitive routes.

Distribution Strategy

Distribution channels for services are usually simpler and more direct than channels of distribution for products. In part, this is due to the intangibility of services. The marketer of services is often less concerned with storage, transportation, and inventory control, and shorter channels of distribution are typically employed.[24] Another consideration is the need for continuing, personal relationships between performers and users of many services. Consumers will remain clients of the same insurance agent, bank, or travel agent if they are reasonably satisfied. Likewise, public accounting firms and lawyers are retained on a relatively permanent basis by industrial buyers.

If marketing intermediaries are used by service firms, they are usually agents or brokers. In the travel industry, for instance, retail agents often sell vacation packages developed by travel brokers. These packages typically combine travel, hotel, and restaurant services.

Promotional Strategy

Promotion is an important aspect of the marketing mix for most services. For instance, the advertising of services is somewhat more challenging than the advertising of products since it is more difficult to illustrate intangible services. A variety of strategies may be implemented. One is to make the service seem more tangible by personalizing it. This may be accomplished by featuring employees, celebrities, or sports personalities in the advertising.

A second strategy is to attempt to create a favorable image for the service or the service company.[25] Some of the themes used by service organizations are efficiency, progressiveness, status, and friendliness.

[24]Some insights into the distribution of services are offered in James H. Donnelly, Jr., "Marketing Intermediaries in Channels of Distribution for Services," *Journal of Marketing* (January 1976), pp. 55–57; and Dean E. Allmon and Michael T. Troncalli, "Concepts of a Channel of Distribution for Services," in *Proceedings of the Southern Marketing Association,* (eds.) Robert S. Franz, Robert M. Hopkins, and Alfred G. Toma (New Orleans, La., November 1978), pp. 209–210.

[25]See Eugene M. Johnson, *An Introduction to the Problems of Service Marketing* (Newark: University of Delaware, 1964), pp. 61–87.

The Unique Distribution Strategy of a Utah Pediatrician

Glen C. Griffin, a Utah pediatrician, has developed a unique distribution strategy for his service. Patients arriving at Griffin's office find a motel-style building with signs that say:

- Appointments—brown doors
- Accidents—orange doors
- Business—glass doors

Patients enter directly into waiting rooms through doors with green lights over them. Closed-circuit cameras note their arrival, and the time is recorded.

Each examining room is exactly alike; it is equipped with a sofa, stuffed chair, and chest of drawers, which serves as a medical cabinet for Griffin. The rooms are linked to a long hallway by which the pediatrician makes his rounds. Hallway door lights indicate the occupied rooms, and timers show how long they have been at the office. Taped messages are played in the examining rooms reporting that the doctor is on schedule or has been delayed by an emergency.

Griffin's office complex also has its own laboratory to facilitate his diagnoses. The office opens at 7 a.m. six days a week so patients can call for same-day appointments. Griffin's efficient delivery system allows him to average 40 patients per day, compared to 30 for others in this field. During peak periods he can handle up to 50 patients daily. It seems reasonable to speculate that Glen Griffin could have been as good a marketer as he is a pediatrician.

Source: Ray Vicker, "A Doctor's Drive-In: Pediatrician in Utah Isn't Kidding Around," *The Wall Street Journal* (January 27, 1982), pp. 1, 18.

For example, advertisements for American Express show its card being used by well-known personalities.

A third advertising strategy shows the tangible benefits of purchasing an intangible service. A local bank shows a retired couple relaxing in Florida because of an Individual Retirement Account (IRA) they had established years ago. These and many similar themes help buyers relate to the benefits of the particular service they may be otherwise unable to visualize.

The desire of many service buyers for a personal relationship with a service seller increases the importance of personal selling. In fact, unless a very simple or highly standardized service is sold, personal selling is usually the backbone of service marketing. Life insurance marketing provides a good illustration of the key role of the sales representative. Because insurance is a confusing, complex subject for the average buyer, an agent must be a professional financial advisor who develops a close personal relationship with the client. Life insurance companies and other service firms must develop a well-trained, highly motivated sales force to provide the high-quality, personalized service that customers require.

Sales promotion is difficult because services are intangible. Sampling, demonstrations, and physical displays are limited, but service firms often do use premiums and contests. Publicity is also important for many services, especially for entertainment and sports events. Television and radio reports, newspaper articles, and magazine features inform the public of events and stimulate interest. Contributions to charitable causes, employees' service to nonprofit organizations, sponsorship of public events, and similar activities are also publicized to influence the public's opinion of the service firm.[26]

Summary

Almost 50 percent of all personal consumption spending goes for the purchase of services. Services can be defined as intangible tasks that satisfy consumer and industrial user needs when efficiently developed and distributed to chosen market segments. Shelter is the biggest consumer service expenditure followed by medical care.

The marketing of services displays many similarities to the marketing of goods, but there are also some significant differences. Four key elements of services have marketing implications:

1. Services are intangible.
2. Services are perishable.
3. Standardization of services is difficult.
4. Buyers are often involved in the development and distribution of services.

Important aspects of buyer behavior are also different for services as contrasted to goods. These differences may be grouped into three categories: attitudes, needs and motives, and purchase behavior.

Although service industries have grown substantially, their development of effective marketing programs has been slow. Many service firms have not adopted the marketing concept; others, such as insurance companies, have become very efficient marketers.

Environmental factors affect service industries just as they influence goods producers. Marketers of services must be continually aware of changes in the economic, societal/cultural, political and legal, technological, and competitive environments.

An effective marketing mix is mandatory in the service industries. Service policies (service industries' versions of product planning) and pricing, distribution, and promotional strategies must all be combined into a coordinated marketing mix if the service marketer is to succeed.

[26]The use of promotions in service industries is discussed in Christopher H. Lovelock and John A. Quelch, "Consumer Promotions in Service Marketing," *Business Horizons* (May–June 1983), pp. 66–75.

Service industries will need to improve their marketing effectiveness if they are to increase productivity and attain the maximum profit from growing demands.

The discussion of services in Chapter 12 concludes the section on product/service strategy. Attention now turns to the pricing of products and services in Part Five.

Key Terms

good-services continuum
services
marketing myopia
tertiary industries
productivity

Review Questions

1. Explain why services are difficult to define.
2. How is a goods-services continuum useful in defining the term *service*?
3. Outline the distribution of the consumer service dollar.
4. Describe the evolution of the service sector.
5. Explain the classification of services on the bases of reliance on equipment and relative skills of service personnel.
6. Identify and outline the key features of services.
7. How does Levitt's marketing myopia thesis relate to service industries?
8. What is the status of the marketing concept in service industries?
9. Explain how Colin Clark's concept describes the growth of service industries.
10. Cite major differences in the marketing strategies of firms producing goods and firms producing services.

Discussion Questions and Exercises

1. Prepare a brief report on the marketing activities conducted by a local health-care practitioner such as a hospital, health maintenance organization, medical or dental practice, or laboratory. What generalization can be reached from your study?
2. Describe the last service you purchased. What was your impression of the way in which the service was marketed? How could the firm's marketing effort have been improved?
3. Holiday Inn, Inc., has tried to overcome the problems of a service industry by stressing consistency in their product offering. The slogan "The best surprise is no surprise" is an illustration of Holiday Inn's effort to provide a service of consistently reliable quality. What is your opinion of Holiday Inn's approach to the consistency problem faced by all varieties of services?

4. Outline a marketing mix for the following service firms:
   a. Local radio station
   b. Independent insurance agency
   c. Janitorial service
   d. Funeral home
5. Identify three or four service firms and propose methods by which their productivity can be improved. Point out any potential problems with your proposal.

CASES FOR PART 4

Case 4.1
Muncie Manufacturing Company

On October 3, 1979, William R. Nelson, division manager of Muncie Manufacturing Company and vice-president of its billion-dollar conglomerate parent company, called a meeting of the division's top echelon to expedite the launch of a new line of pipes and tubing. He is chagrined that, according to Production Manager Ian McMichaels, the scheduled commercialization date of July 1, 1981, cannot be met.

This impatience is shared by Dale N. Schroder, Ph.D. (chemical engineering), director of research and development, who personally contributed much to the new line. Also attending is Controller Frank B. Abt, CPA, an enthusiastic advocate of formal planning. The final participant is J. Robertson (Bob) Hellas, sales manager. All of these executives, now in their 50s, have been with the division a long time.

Sales Department

A major producer of plastic pipes and tubes, Muncie Manufacturing Company has a functional organization. (See Figure 1, p. 361.) In the sales department, executives reporting to Bob Hellas include four regional industrial sales managers (corresponding to Muncie's four factories), an advertising manager, and a consumer-goods product manager. The regional sales managers supervise 35 salespersons. The sales force obtains leads and exhortations from headquarters and from regional sales managers, but, by and large, the salespeople make up their own schedules. In addition to prospecting for orders, following up customers, and so on, an important part of their job is verifying that distributors are well stocked with Muncie's wares.

Compensation of the sales force is salary plus ten percent commission on total dollar sales above individual quota. On the average, salespersons' earnings derive 50 percent from salary and 50 percent from commission. Muncie also reimburses each salesperson for travel and entertainment in accordance with the company's policy manual.

Muncie confines its industrial advertising to reminder-type messages in specialized industry periodicals serving the division's markets. An advertising manager, Peter Munn, was hired in 1979. A

Source: This case was prepared by Harold W. Fox, George A. Ball Distinguished Professor in Marketing at Ball State University in Muncie, Indiana. Names and data of the cooperating firms have been altered to preserve anonymity. Reprinted by permission.

former lobbyist, he deals with Muncie's industrial advertising agency; plans industrial sales promotion campaigns; designs collateral materials such as catalogs, brochures, point-of-purchase displays, and booklets; books space at trade shows; releases publicity; and relieves the sales manager of other nonselling promotional tasks.

Consumer goods, mainly garden hose and sprinklers, are under the jurisdiction of Tony Pasco. Determination of consumer goods' brand names, prices, advertisements and sales promotions, and distribution channels is separate from the industrial unit. Hellas is very satisfied with the profit and progress of this subdivision, and lets Product Manager Pasco run it almost autonomously on a modest budget. According to the controller, this business could and should be tripled, even at the risk of losing some commodity business; i.e., sales of plastic piping and tubing to lawn equipment manufacturers.

Product Lines

In 1978, sales of Muncie plastic tubes and pipes amounted to $53 million—about the same as in 1976 and 1977. The burgeoning department of consumer goods registered a new high of $3.4 million in 1978.

On tubes and pipes up to 10 inches in diameter, plastics are in many uses more flexible, more durable, and more economical than conventional materials. The main resins are polyvinyl chloride and styrene. Lately, supply of these resins has occasionally been interrupted or threatened because of feedstock shortages and dangers to the health of suppliers' employees. The general consensus is that during the 1980s these supply problems will become worse.

Over the past two years, the research and development department of Muncie Manufacturing Company has developed a patented energy-efficient formulation. Proved workable in the laboratory, this new formulation substitutes readily available synthetics for petroleum-based inputs. Muncie pins its hopes for the 1980s on this forthcoming line to recapture leadership in its established markets and to penetrate hitherto closed applications.

End Uses

All industrial distributors and most end users of plastic pipe and tubing divide their purchases among several competing vendors. Muncie's market share has slipped from number 1 to number 2.

A major end use of polyvinyl chloride pipes and components is irrigation for farms and turfs. Plastics are superior to metal and open-ditch water transportation systems. Due to consolidations and industrialization, much of agriculture buys on a rational basis. The faster-growing turf irrigation market is comprised of municipal park districts and manufacturers of lawn watering installations.

Another important end use is residential and commerical construction. Sales to large buyers, such as electrical and mechanical contractors and mobile home manufacturers, are direct, often on a bid basis; so are most sales of electrical conduits to public utilities and large construction companies for the protection and insulation of electric power lines and telephone lines. Smaller users buy from various distributors.

In the 1970s, acceptance of plastic pipe had been more rapid in public than in private systems. Many local building codes specify copper, aluminum, steel, or iron, thus excluding plastic pipe from home systems. This exclusion was strongly advocated by plumbing unions, which pointed to the traditional materials' superior strength and resistance to thermal expansion, melting, and crushing. Where plastic pipe has been allowed, it proved to generate substantial labor savings because both installation and maintenance are much simpler.

Plastic pipe and tubing are also used in the production operations of various industries. Sales potential seems to be smaller than in the forementioned uses, but business can be much more profitable.

Technical and commercial services must satisfy the particular needs of these industries. Aerospace, for example, insists on the highest quality and is willing to trade off cost for highest performance. The medical equipment industry is similarly disposed. Muncie Manufacturing Company is still number 1 in aerospace. With its effective reliability and quality assurance procedures, Muncie is in a superior position to serve these customers.

Electronics manufacturers and copper mines, on the other hand, are price conscious. In between these extremes are food processors and paper companies. These last two industries are especially concerned about contamination of their raw materials from migrating plastic ingredients.

A recent study ranked growth prospects in the 1980s as follows, from highest to lowest: electronics, medical equipment, aerospace, copper mining, food processing, paper manufacture. Muncie Manufacturing Company is very strong with aerospace, paper mills, and food processors, but relatively weak in the other fields.

Besides price and quality, an important consideration for most buyers is delivery. Except for some specialties, plastic tubes and pipes from different manufacturers are interchangeable. Buyers often switch from one source to another based on earliest availability.

List prices FOB factory on competing plastic pipes and tubes are the same. Price shading leads to immediate retaliation. Muncie's four geographically dispersed plants have low freight rates and speedy transit to all buyers. This capability is an important competitive advantage.

Altogether, Muncie's success rests largely on the momentum from early aggressive entry into this field, large size, high quality, and excellent physical distribution. Moreover, when reciprocity was a sales factor, the division could apply influence on its huge parent's purchases, although, in practice, assistance was rare.

Physical Status of the New Line

After the top-echelon meeting on the stalled innovation convened, the discussion turned quickly to the production department. "The new formulation works perfectly in the lab," the R&D director noted. "I see no reason why we don't proceed with full-scale production now."

Ian McMichaels, the production manager, was still irate over the loss of production and the cost of extruder repairs charged to his department when R&D personnel experimented with the new formulation on the production floor last month. The new formulation works only within very narrow tolerances. Slight deviations in the mix proportions can clog the dies and cause the electrical system to overheat. Apparently this is what had occurred. Nothing like this had ever happened before.

McMichaels explained calmly that factory operations are not controllable to the same extent as laboratory trials. Small batches in the lab are not necessarily indicative of long runs in the plant. Jobs will have to be redesigned and machine surveillance tightened. Quality control has advised him that standard grades of raw material vary more widely than R&D specifications for the new formulation allow. As of now, the new formulation is not producible. Another difficulty is post extrusion bath.

The controller interrupted, "What does the union say about job redesign?"

"That's a good question," replied McMichaels. "As I was saying, the present single bath. . ."

"Hold it!" This time it was Nelson, the division manager, who broke in. "Rather than go over technical details that we can figure out for ourselves, you may be better served by a systematic approach. I suggest that you and Dale (the R&D director) get together this week and work out a practical method for speedy and smooth transition from R&D to production.

"Could the three of us meet on Monday in my office at 10:00 a.m. to discuss your plan? Let's go over all feasible options and your reasons for recommending one particular approach." The two executives nodded, signifying acquiescence.

Marketing Status

"This brings us to the second point," resumed William Nelson, "our entry marketing strategy." Nelson looked at Hellas. The sales manager conceded that he lacked detailed knowledge about the new line. "I guess I've been too busy producing profitable business. No apologies needed for that, eh?"

Somewhat defensively, Hellas explained that the new line did not pose any new marketing problems. When the new formulation has been debugged, Muncie will simply ship it instead of the old. Customers would, of course, receive notice. None should object. No price increase will be necessary, according to the accounting department. And the last he had heard, the R&D department had proved performance of the new was identical with the old.

Schroder, the R&D director, confirmed this reasoning. Total discontinuation of the old formulation will be necessary. Changeovers between old and new are too expensive and time consuming. The sensitivity of the new formulation requires perfect purification of the machines before a run starts. This entails first producing scrap from the residues of the old then running an industrial cleanser until all vestiges are removed. Extra tests are needed to assure that the new formulation is properly balanced. All of this applies only to changes from old to new formulation. There is no difficulty other than minor setup for adjustments *within* either formulation. Product mix changes per se are simple.

In the opinion of Abt, the controller, the unfurling challenges call for formal planning. There are things to be done between now and the time when shipments begin, but this suggestion did not sit well with the other functional managers.

At this point, an urgent telephone call for Nelson from the corporate president required the division manager to adjourn the meeting. The functional managers decided to break for lunch and resume the meeting at 2 p.m.

Discussion Question

1. What recommendations would you make to the division manager?

Figure 1 Organization of Muncie Manufacturing Company

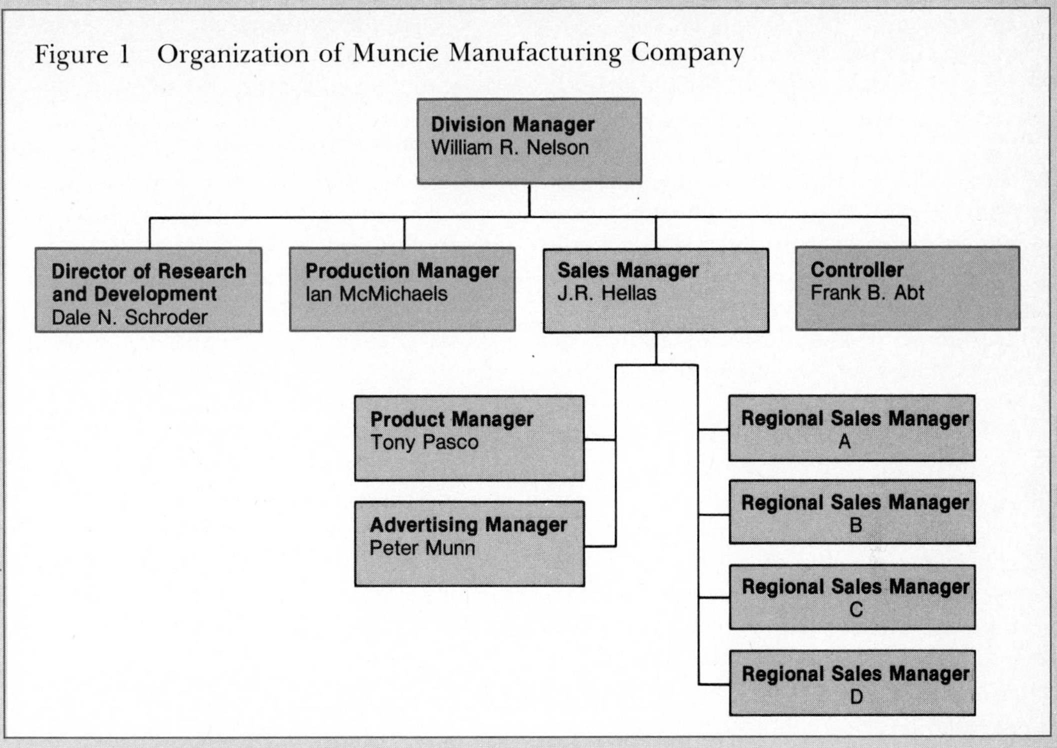

Case 4.2
Robitussin

The Company

A. H. Robins, Inc., has evolved from a small community pharmacy opened in 1866 in Richmond, Virginia, by Albert Hartley Robins to a diversified multinational corporation operating in more than 100 countries. The corporate headquarters, which houses both corporate and pharmaceutical division offices, is located in the Richmond area, with branch offices in Dallas; Los Angeles; and Des Plaines, Illinois. The research center opened in 1963 with more than 325 scientists and technicians engaged in research in many product areas.

The A. H. Robins Company is engaged principally in the manufacture of finished-dosage forms of pharmaceutical products. Finished products are manufactured and packaged from raw materials purchased from suppliers of phar-

Source: Reprinted by permission of Ian Stewart, A. H. Robins, Inc., and Professors Thomas D. Giese and Thomas J. Cosse, University of Richmond.

maceutical grade chemicals. The company's principal products are ethical prescribed and ethical over-the-counter drug products which are promoted nationally by 1,350 field representatives to physicians, dentists, and pharmacists. Some of Robins' best-known brand names are Robitussin, a cough and cold syrup; Donnatal, an antispasmodic drug; and Robaxin, a skeletal muscle relaxant.

Robins' products are distributed to drug wholesalers which sell to retail drug stores and to hospitals. This distribution system has proven successful in the past. But, in the current drug market the chains do more than half the industry volume. If the large chains do buy direct from a manufacturer (at a lower price), they give those brands in-store marketing support, such as end aisle displays, extra shelf facings, and co-op advertising.

While maintaining its major position as manufacturer and researcher of pharmaceuticals, A. H. Robins has diversified into consumer products. In 1963, Robins acquired Morton Manufacturing in Lynchburg, Virginia, the producer of Chap Stick lip balm. In 1967, Robins acquired Polk Miller Products of Richmond, Virginia, producers of the Sergeant's line of pet care products. These two companies later formed Miller-Morton Company in an effort to consolidate consumer product activities. Robins enjoyed further success in the consumer goods area with the introduction of Lip Quencher, a lipstick utilizing the moisturizing qualities of Chap Stick. In 1967, it continued its entry into the consumer field with the acquisition of Parfums Caron, a leading producer of French fragrance products. Consumer products are advertised nationally and marketed through department stores, specialty shops, and drug outlets.

A. H. Robins entered the international markets in the 1960s by establishing manufacturing and distribution centers in Australia, Colombia, England, and Mexico. Foreign expansion was precipitated by both a demand for Robins products abroad and increasing foreign government regulation which restricted imports into these countries. Subsidiaries in Australia, Brazil, Canada, Colombia, France, Mexico, the Philippines, South Africa, the United Kingdom, Venezuela and West Germany provided a base for the company's growing international operations. In recent years, 33 percent of net sales and 34 percent earning before tax, interest, and amortization expenses have been applicable to international operations.

The Product

Robitussin, a cough and cold syrup, is marketed in five forms, one of which is an ethical prescribed form; the other four are ethical over-the-counter forms. The product to date has been marketed only through wholesalers and directly to nonproprietary hospitals. Demand is stimulated by detailers calling on members of the medical profession and "detailing" the drug—describing its advantages and features so that physicians would either prescribe or recommend the product.

Promotion is complemented by sampling, trade deals, and trade and medical profession journal advertising. However, demand for the product is now static as it has reached the mature state in its present market segment.

The cough syrup market grew 5 percent the previous year. Within the overall market, the largest growth was in food stores.

Sales in food stores, which accounted for 24 percent of total sales, are increasing at a faster rate than drug-store sales. The sales in drug stores are polarizing towards the chains and large independents who want to purchase directly from the manufacturer rather than through the wholesaler, which results in lower margins for retail outlets.

While the ethical segment of the cough syrup market was still trending up slightly in dollars, the proprietary brands in food and drug outlets exhibited a healthy 10 percent increase in dollar terms as compared with a 2 percent increase for the ethical segment.

In unit terms, the cough syrup market was not growing; but within the segments, food store sales were moving up in importance while drug store units were declining. One study showed that the average homemaker visited the grocery store about three times a week and the drug store twice a month. In the drug stores the ethical brands were holding their share while proprietary brands were declining.

By way of comparison with other cold-remedy products, the cough syrup market is 12 percent larger than the cold-tablet market and more than three times larger than the nasal-spray market.

The heavy users of cough syrup preparations differ from most categories of cold products since the heaviest users usually do not purchase their own product because half the actual users are under eighteen years of age. The prime prospect households can be described as follows:

- Female head of household 25-49 years old
- Households with children 2-17 years old and with 5 or more persons
- Household annual income of $15,000 or lower
- Less educated
- Heavy usage among nonwhites

The breakdown of unit sales by brand is as follows: Robitussin has a 21.6 percent share of unit sales in drugstores compared to Vicks' 16 percent. In food and drug stores combined, Robitussin has an estimated 14 percent share versus Vicks' 27 percent. Based on an earlier survey, the leading brands of cough syrup used were Formula 44, doctor's prescription, and Nyquil.

Towards the end of the financial year, as the planning stage for the following year was being finalized, George Mancini, Robitussin's product manager, had noted that over the past several years the line had only been growing in the 1 to 2 percent range in comparison with the 6 to 8 percent growth of the overall cough syrup market. Robitussin was becoming a mature product in its present segment of ethical over-the-counter drugs.[1]

Discussion Questions

1. Relate this case to the product life cycle concept.
2. What action should A. H. Robins take with respect to Robitussin?

[1]Drug industry practice was to classify products as either "ethical" or "proprietary" depending on the marketing method employed. Ethical products were marketed by promotion directly to the medical profession. The ethical classification was further subdivided into those drugs which required prescription and those which could be purchased without a prescription called "over-the-counter" (OTC) drugs. Proprietary products were promoted directly to the consumer.

Alfred R. Oxenfeldt

Alfred R. Oxenfeldt (1917–), the author of the multi-stage approach to pricing, possesses a broad range of experience in both the academic and business worlds. His experience has led Oxenfeldt to conclude that little similarity exists between the largely intuitive or cost-oriented pricing practices of most business executives and the often unrealistic microeconomic theory he has studied. From his attempts to reconcile the cost-oriented approaches, the microeconomic approaches of economic theorists, and the pragmatic approach of marketing specialists, the multi-stage explanation was born. Oxenfeldt described this approach in his book *Executive Action in Marketing* (Wadsworth, 1966):

The multi-stage approach to pricing sorts the major elements in most price decisions into successive steps. The particular sequence of the steps is an essential part of the method, for each one is calculated to simplify the succeeding one and to reduce the likelihood of error. Thus, this method attempts to divide the price decision into manageable parts, each one logically antecedent to the next, so that the decision at every stage facilitates all subsequent decisions. The major emphasis in this approach to pricing is on long-range policy considerations that should govern the selection of price; it thereby should eliminate the danger that a pricing decision will be opportunistic, gaining slight profit in the present while creating difficulties to be overcome in the future (p. 292).

Oxenfeldt's sequential framework for improved pricing behavior consists of six stages:

(1) *Selection of market targets;* (2) *Selection of brand image;* (3) *Composition of the marketing mix;* (4) *Selection of a specific price policy;* (5) *Choice of a price strategy;* and (6) *Selection of a specific price.* The six-step framework is richly described in Oxenfeldt's widely reprinted article "Multi-stage Approach to Pricing" in the July-August 1960 issue of the *Harvard Business Review,* an article that continues to be included in anthologies more than two decades after its initial publication.

Oxenfeldt serves as professor of marketing at Columbia University, where he has taught since 1956.

5

PRICE

Recent empirical data indicates that pricing strategy plays an increasingly important role in marketing. Part Five includes two chapters on this critical element of the marketing mix. Chapter 13 examines the role of prices as well as price determination in both theory and practice. Chapter 14 examines how the pricing structure is set and the overall management of this function.

Chapter Objectives

1. *To identify the major categories of pricing objectives.*
2. *To explain the concept of elasticity and the determinants of the degree of price elasticity for a product or service.*
3. *To identify the practical problems involved in applying price theory concepts to actual pricing decisions.*
4. *To explain the major cost-plus approaches to price setting.*
5. *To list the major advantages and shortcomings of using breakeven analysis in pricing decisions.*
6. *To explain the superiority of modified breakeven analysis over the basic breakeven model.*

13

PRICE DETERMINATION

The firm's headquarters is furnished in a style favored by more prosperous county jails. The building, located at Newark Airport's old North Terminal, houses three-year-old People Express Airlines, perhaps the greatest rate-cutter of the industry.

The firm's services compare with those of a no-frills food store. Passengers carry their own luggage with them onto the plane (unless they want to pay $3 a bag). In-flight coffee costs 50 cents. First-class seating is not available, since People Express engineers and technicians ripped out both galleys and first-class seating to increase capacity on the firm's Boeing 737–100 jets by 30 percent. Even the purchase of the jets from Lufthansa was designed to minimize costs. By buying ten-year-old jets and then refitting them, People Express paid $4.5 million per plane, as compared with $13 million for new models.

The results are some of the lowest airfares in the United States. Recent examples include $40 peak-hour fares between Newark and Pittsburgh and $23 during off-peak hours, as compared with the previous industry standard of $123. The 820 air-mile flight between Newark and Jacksonville was initially priced at $59.

While pricing strategy is a critical ingredient of the marketing mix employed by People Express, retaliatory moves by carriers who compete on the same routes are always possible. People Express chairman Donald C. Burr does not feel that his firm's pricing strategy is detrimental to competition. "We believe our competitors are beginning to recognize what happens when we move into a market. We don't take market share from them, we make the market bigger for everybody. Don't worry, we'll be here ten years from now."[1]

The Conceptual Framework

The chapters in Part Four examined the first critical element of a firm's marketing mix: the determination of the products and services to offer the market target. The two chapters in Part Five focus upon price—the second marketing mix element. Determination of profitable and justified prices is the result of considering such factors as pricing objectives and alternative approaches to setting prices. These topics are discussed in this chapter. The following chapter focuses upon management of the pricing function and discusses pricing strategies, price-quality relationships, and both industrial pricing and pricing in the public sector. The starting place for examining pricing strategy is to understand the meaning of the term *price.*

Price is the exchange value of a good or service; and the value of an item is what it can be exchanged for in the marketplace. In earlier times, the price of an acre of land might have been twenty bushels of wheat, three cattle, or a boat. Price is a measure of what one must exchange in order to obtain a desired good or service. When the barter process was abandoned in favor of a monetary system, price became the amount of funds required to purchase an item. As David Schwartz has pointed out, contemporary society uses a number of names to refer to price:

Price is all around us. You pay rent *for your apartment,* tuition *for your education, and a* fee *to your physician or dentist.*

The airline, railway, taxi, and bus companies charge you a fare; *the local utilities call their price a* rate; *and the local bank charges you* interest *for the money you borrow.*

[1]Stanley W. Angrist, "Up with People," *Forbes* (May 10, 1982), p. 182.

The price for driving your car on Florida's Sunshine Parkway is a toll, *and the company that insures your car charges you a* premium.

The guest lecturer charges an honorarium *to tell you about a government official who took a* bribe *to help a shady character steal* dues *collected by a trade association.*

Clubs or societies to which you belong may make a special assessment *to pay unusual expenses. Your regular lawyer may ask for a* retainer *to cover her services.*

The "price" of an executive is a salary; *the price of a salesperson may be a* commission; *and the price of a worker is a* wage.

Finally, although economists would disagree, many of us feel that income taxes *are the price we pay for the privilege of making money!*[2]

All products and services possess some degree of utility or want-satisfying power. An individual might be willing to exchange the utility derived from a Windsurfer for that of a component sound system. In the marketplace of the 1980s, prices are translated into monetary terms. Consumers evaluate the potential satisfaction to be derived from a range of possible purchases and then allocate their exchange power (in monetary terms) to obtain the greatest possible satisfaction.

Importance of Price as a Marketing Mix Element

Ancient philosophers recognized the importance of price to the functioning of an economic system. Some of their early written accounts refer to attempts to determine a fair or just price. However, their limited understanding of time, place, and possession utilities thwarted such efforts.

Price continues to serve as a means of regulating economic activity. Employment of any or all of the four factors of production (land, capital, human resources, and entrepreneurship) depends upon the prices received by each factor. For an individual firm, prices and the corresponding quantity to be purchased by its customers represent the revenue to be received. Prices therefore influence a firm's profit as well as its employment of the factors of production.

How Marketing Executives Rank the Price Variable

Two decades ago, marketing professor Jon G. Udell conducted a survey of marketing executives to determine the relative importance of price as an element of their firms' marketing mixes. When the various factors

[2]Adapted from *Marketing Today* by David J. Schwartz, copyright © 1981 by Harcourt Brace Jovanovich, Inc. Reprinted by permission of the publisher.

Figure 13.1 Relative Importance of Marketing Variables: A Comparison of the Udell Study and the Boone and Kurtz Study

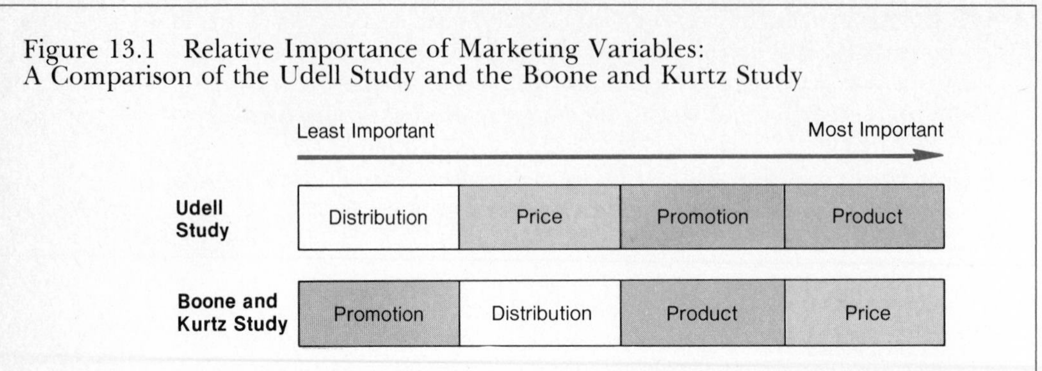

Sources: Udell rankings from Jon G. Udell, "How Important Is Pricing in Competitive Strategy?" *Journal of Marketing* (January 1964), pp. 44–48. Boone and Kurtz rankings from Louis E. Boone and David L. Kurtz, *Pricing Objectives and Practices in American Industry: A Research Report.*

included on the questionnaire were reorganized into the four major mix variables, price was ranked third—ahead only of distribution.[3]

But times have changed. A recent study of marketing executives revealed that price currently ranks as the single most important marketing mix variable.[4] Product planning and management is a close second, and distribution and promotion rank third and fourth, respectively. Figure 13.1 compares the Udell findings to those of the later study.

Pricing Objectives

Just as price is a component in the total marketing mix, so are pricing objectives a component of the overall objectives of the organization. As Chapter 3 explained, marketing objectives represent the desired outcomes that executives hope to attain eventually. These objectives are based upon the overall objectives of the organization. Pricing objectives are also a critical component of the means-end chain extending from overall aims of the firm. The objectives of the firm and the marketing organization provide the basis for the development of pricing objectives, which are then utilized for development and implementation of more specific pricing policies and procedures.

[3]Jon G. Udell, "How Important Is Pricing in Competitive Strategy?" *Journal of Marketing* (January 1964), pp. 44–48.

[4]Louis E. Boone and David L. Kurtz, *Pricing Objectives and Practices in American Industry: A Research Report.* All rights reserved. These findings are consistent with those of Professor Robert A. Robicheaux. See "How Important Is Pricing in Competitive Strategy? Circa 1975," in *Proceedings of the Southern Marketing Association,* (eds.) Henry W. Nash and Donald Robin (Atlanta: November 1976), pp. 55–57.

Figure 13.2 Pricing Objectives of Eight Large Companies

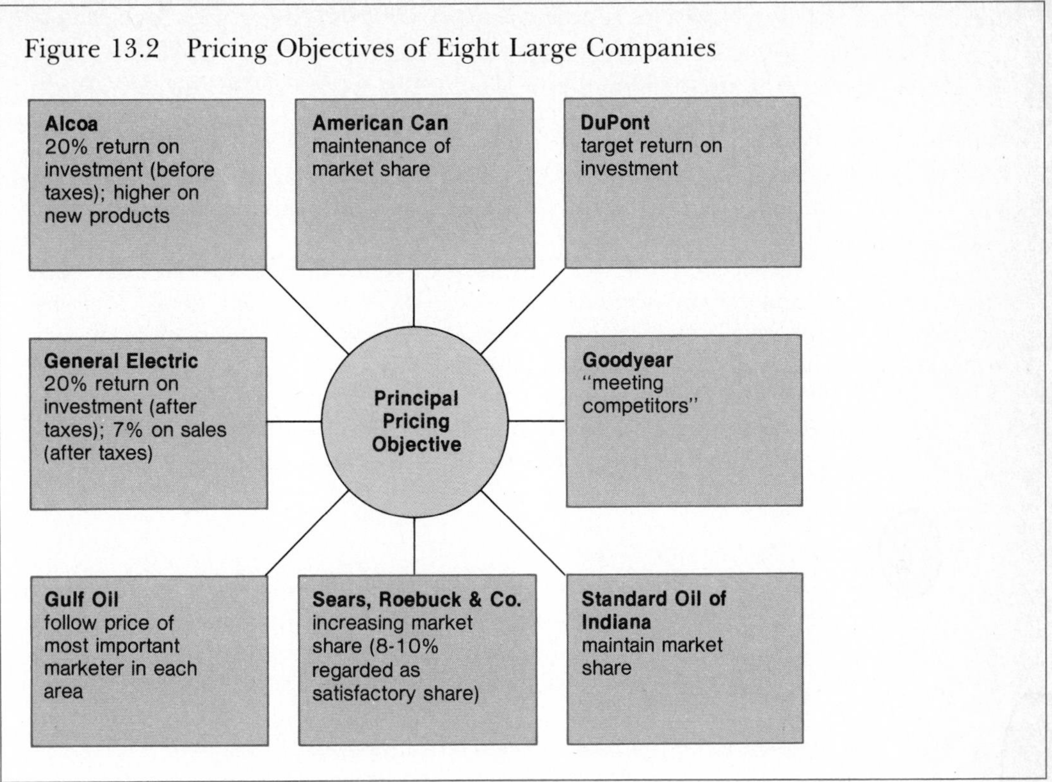

Source: Robert F. Lanzillotti, "Pricing Objectives in Large Companies," *American Economic Review* (December 1958), pp. 924–26.

A firm's major overall objective may be to become the dominant factor in the domestic market. Its marketing objective might then be to achieve maximum sales penetrations in each region. The related pricing objective would be sales maximization. This means-end chain might lead to the adoption of a low-price policy implemented by the highest price discounts to channel members of any firm in the industry.

Pricing objectives vary from firm to firm. In a pioneering study of pricing objectives of major U.S. corporations, economist Robert F. Lanzillotti identified the primary pricing objectives of each firm.[5] As Figure 13.2 indicates, satisfactory return on investment, attainment of specified market shares, and meeting the actions of competitors are common objectives.

[5]Robert F. Lanzillotti, "Pricing Objectives in Large Companies," *American Economic Review* (December 1958), pp. 921–940.

Pricing objectives can be classified into four major groups: (1) profitability objectives; (2) volume objectives; (3) meeting competition objectives; and (4) prestige objectives. Profitability objectives include profit maximization and target return goals. As Figure 13.2 indicates, Alcoa, du Pont, and General Electric specify profitability objectives. Volume objectives can be categorized as either sales maximization or market share goals. The objectives of American Can, Sears, and Standard Oil (Indiana) fall into this category.

A recent study of U.S. businesses asked marketers to identify both the primary and secondary pricing objectives of their firms. Meeting competitive prices was most often mentioned as a primary or secondary pricing objective. It was followed closely by two profitability-oriented objectives: a specified return on investment and specified total profit levels. These two objectives ranked first and second, respectively, as primary pricing objectives.[6] The findings are shown in Table 13.1.

Profitability Objectives

In classical economic theory, the traditional pricing objective has been to maximize profits. The study of microeconomics is based on certain assumptions—that buyers and sellers are rational and that rational behavior constitutes an effort to maximize gains and to minimize losses. In terms of actual business practice, this means that profit maximization is assumed to be the basic objective of individual firms.

Profits are a function of revenue and expenses:

$$\text{Profits} = \text{Revenues} - \text{Expenses.}$$

Revenue is determined by the selling price and quantity sold:

$$\text{Total Revenue} = \text{Price} \times \text{Quantity Sold.}$$

Price should therefore be increased to the point where it causes a disproportionate decrease in the number of units sold. A 10 percent price increase that results in only an 8 percent cut in volume adds to the firm's revenues. However, a 10 percent hike that results in an 11 percent sales decline reduces revenues.

Economists refer to this approach as *marginal analysis.* They identify **profit maximization** as the point where the addition to total revenue is just balanced by the increase in total cost. The basic problem is how to achieve this delicate balance between marginal revenue and marginal cost. Relatively few firms actually achieve the objective of profit max-

[6]Research by Saeed Samiee ranked "satisfactory return on investment" first among a similar list of objectives. Samiee correctly points out the difficulties in making the "meeting competition" objective operational. See "Pricing Objectives of U.S. Manufacturing Firms," in *Proceedings of the Southern Marketing Association,* (eds.) Robert S. Franz, Robert M. Hopkins, and Alfred G. Toma (New Orleans, 1978), pp. 445–447.

Table 13.1 Primary and Secondary Pricing Objectives of U.S. Firms

Pricing Objective	As Primary Objective	As Secondary Objective	As Either Primary or Secondary Objective
	Percentage of Respondents Ranking the Item		
Profitability Objectives			
Specified rate of return on investment	60.9	17.2	78.1
Specified total profit level	60.2	17.2	77.4
Increased total profits above previous levels	34.4	37.5	71.9
Specified rate of return on sales	47.7	23.4	71.1
Volume Objectives			
Increased market share	31.3	42.2	73.5
Retaining of existing market share	31.3	35.9	67.2
Serving of selected market segments	26.6	39.1	65.7
Specified market share	15.6	40.6	56.2
Meeting Competition Objectives			
Meeting of competitive price level	38.3	43.0	81.3
Prestige Objectives			
Creation of a readily identifiable image for the firm and/or its products	21.9	41.4	63.3

Source: Louis E. Boone and David L. Kurtz, *Pricing Objectives and Practices in American Industry: A Research Report.*

imization. A significantly larger number prefer to direct their efforts toward goals that are more reasonably implemented and measured.

Consequently, target return objectives have become common in industry, particularly among the larger firms, where public pressure typically prohibits consideration of the profit maximization objective.[7] Automobile companies are an example of this phenomenon. **Target return objectives** are either short-run or long-run goals usually stated as a percentage of sales or investment. A company may, for instance, seek a 15 percent annual rate of return on investment or an 8 percent

[7]Target rate-of-return pricing is discussed in Douglas G. Brooks, "Cost-Oriented Pricing: A Realistic Solution to a Complicated Problem," *Journal of Marketing* (April 1975), pp. 72–74.

rate of return on sales. A specified rate of return on investment was the most commonly reported primary pricing objective in Table 13.1. Goals of this nature also serve as useful guidelines in evaluating corporate activity. As one writer has aptly expressed it: "For management consciously accepting less than maximum profits, the target rate can provide a measure of the amount of restraint. For firms making very low profits, the target rate can serve as a standard for judging improvement."[8]

Target return objectives offer several benefits to the marketer. As noted above, they serve as a means for evaluating performance. They also are designed to generate a "fair" profit, as judged by management, stockholders, and the general public as well.

Volume Objectives

Many business executives argue that a more accurate explanation of actual pricing behavior is economics professor William J. Baumol's belief that firms strive for **sales maximization** within a given profit constraint.[9] In other words, they set a minimum at what they consider the lowest acceptable profit level and then seek to maximize sales (subject to this profit constraint) in the belief that the increased sales are more important than immediate high profits to the long-run competitive picture. The companies continue to expand sales as long as their total profits do not drop below the minimum return acceptable to management.

Another volume-related pricing objective is the market share objective—the goal set for the control of a portion of the market for a firm's product or service. The company's specific goal can be to maintain or increase its share of a particular market, say, from 10 percent to 20 percent.[10]

In Figure 13.2, Sears expressed its pricing objective as a market share growth rate of 8 to 10 percent annually. As Table 13.1 indicates, almost two thirds of all responding firms list volume objectives as either a primary or secondary pricing objective.

Although *growth* is typically the end result of volume objectives, some firms with relatively high market shares may even prefer to reduce their share of specific markets at times due to possible government ac-

[8]Robert A. Lynn, *Price Policies and Marketing Management* (Homewood, Ill.: Richard D. Irwin, 1967), p. 99. See also Stuart U. Rich, "Firms in Some Industries Should Use Both Target Return and Marginal Cost Pricing," *Marketing News* (June 25, 1982), Section 2, p. 11.

[9]William J. Baumol, "On the Theory of Oligopoly," *Economica* (August 1958), pp. 187–198. See also William J. Baumol, *Business Behavior, Value and Growth* (New York: Macmillan, 1959).

[10]An interesting discussion appears in Carl R. Frear and John E. Swan, "Marketing Managers' Motivation to Revise Their Market Share Goals: An Expectancy Theory Analysis," in *1981 Southwestern Marketing Proceedings*, (eds.) Robert H. Ross, Frederic B. Kraft, and Charles H. Davis (Wichita, Kansas), pp. 13–16.

tion in the area of monopoly control. Market share is a frequently used indicator in court evaluations of cases involving alleged monopolistic practices.

The PIMS Studies Market share objectives may prove critical in the achievement of other organizational objectives. High sales, for example, often mean more profits. The extensive **Profit Impact of Market Strategies (PIMS) project** conducted by the Marketing Science Institute analyzed more than 2,000 firms and revealed that two of the most important factors influencing profitability were product quality and market share.

The linkage between market share and profitability is dramatically expressed by Figure 13.3. For firms enjoying more than 40 percent of a market, their pretax return on investment averages 32.3 percent. By contrast, firms with a minor, less than 10 percent, market share generate pretax investment returns of 13.2 percent.

The underlying factor in explaining the positive relationship between profitability and market share appears to be the operating expe-

Figure 13.3 Relationship of Market Share to Return on Investment

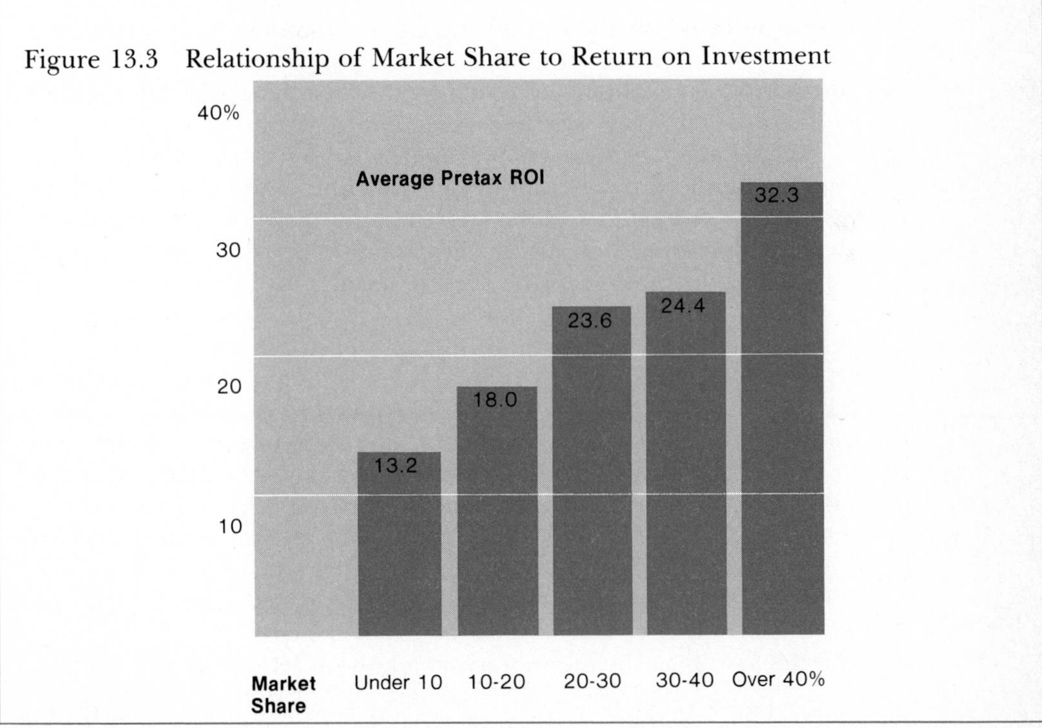

Source: Reprinted by permission of the *Harvard Business Review*. An exhibit from "Successful Share Building Strategies" by Robert D. Buzzell and Frederik D. Wiersma (January/February 1981), p. 137.

rience and lower overall costs of high-market-share firms as compared with competitors who possess smaller shares of the market. Accordingly, the segmentation strategies for astute marketers may involve focusing upon obtaining large shares of smaller markets and less on smaller shares of a larger market. The financial returns may be enhanced by being a major competitor in several smaller market segments than being a relatively minor factor in a larger market.[11]

Meeting Competition as a Pricing Objective

This third pricing objective is much less aggressive than profitability or volume objectives. Competing firms operationalize this pricing objective by simply matching the prices of the established industry price leader. In the Lanzillotti study of pricing objectives, Goodyear, Gulf, and National Steel specified meeting competitive prices as a primary pricing objective. As Table 13.1 indicates, four of every five respondent firms listed this as a primary or secondary objective, the pricing objective most often mentioned.

Frequently, the net result of this pricing objective is to deemphasize the price element of the marketing mix and focus more strongly on nonprice competition. Although price is a highly visible mix component and an effective method of obtaining a differential advantage over competitors, a price reduction is also an easily duplicated move. The airline price competition of recent years exemplifies the actions and reactions of competitors for passenger and freight business. Because of the direct impact of such price changes on overall profitability, many firms attempt to promote stable prices by utilizing the objective of simply meeting competition and competing for market share by focusing upon product/service strategies, promotional decisions, and distribution—the nonprice elements of the marketing mix.

Prestige Objectives

A final category of pricing objectives unrelated to either profitability or sales volume is prestige objectives. Prestige objectives involve establishment of relatively high prices in order to develop and maintain an image of quality and exclusiveness. Such objectives reflect marketers' recognition of the role of price in the creation of an overall image for the firm and its products and services.

For years Curtis Mathes used price as a surrogate indicator of quality for its television sets. The Curtis Mathes advertisements made the point with the line ". . . the highest-priced television set in America; and it's

[11]Robert D. Buzzell and Frederik D. Wiersema, "Successful Share-Building Strategies," *Harvard Business Review* (January–February 1981), pp. 135–144.

worth it." Neiman-Marcus, the prestigious Dallas-based retailer, annually issues a catalogue of luxuries for Christmas gift-giving. Recent examples of its offerings include a 24-piece set of custom linens, costing $900, to match customers' china; a $1.2 million condominium on the island of Kauai, Hawaii; a 9½-inch disk of cut and engraved crystal for $900; and a $200 Iglu-Maker. While some marketers set relatively high prices in order to maintain a prestige image with their consumers, others prefer the opposite approach of developing a low-price image among customers.

Price Determination

The determination of price may be viewed in two ways: the theoretical concepts of supply and demand and the cost-oriented approach that characterizes current business practice. During the first part of this century, most considerations of price determination emphasized the classical concepts of supply and demand. Since World War II, however, the emphasis has shifted to a cost-oriented approach. Hindsight allows us to see that both concepts have certain flaws.

Another concept of price determination is often overlooked. **Customary prices** are retail prices that consumers expect as a result of custom, tradition, and social habit. The candy makers' attempt to hold the line on the traditional ten-cent candy bar led to considerable reduction in the product size. Similar practices have prevailed in the marketing of soft drinks as bottlers attempt to balance consumer expectations of customary prices with the realities of inflation.

Hershey Foods Corporation approached the dilemma of rising product costs for a snack item by simultaneously increasing the product size and price. In 1982, Hershey increased the weight of its milk chocolate bar and Reese's Peanut Butter Cups between 33 and 38 percent to accompany a wholesale price increase of 20 percent. Even though the cost per candy bar increased, Hershey's marketers emphasized that the cost per ounce was actually less than in 1969.[12]

The division of the U.S. beer market into premium and popular price levels provides another example of a traditional pricing system. In the 1930s, several major brewers were faced with excess capacity that could not be absorbed by their local markets. These brewers began to ship their product to distant markets. The freight charges were covered by charging retail prices higher than those charged for local beers. The higher prices were justified by the marketers' claims that their beers were of higher quality than the local beers. The "imports," classified as

[12]Hershey Foods Corporation Press Release (March 9, 1982).

premium by their marketers, often actually were better than the numerous local brands. Today, any difference in quality among beers is probably negligible, and there is little difference in the production costs of premium and popular beers. However, the traditional pricing system continues to exist.[13]

At some point in time, someone has to set initial prices for products. Sustained inflation has also created a need for periodically reviewing firms' price structures. The remainder of this chapter discusses the traditional and current concepts of price determination. It also considers how best to integrate the concepts in order to develop a realistic approach to pricing.

Price Determination in Economic Theory

The microeconomic approach to price determination assumes a profit maximization objective and leads to the derivation of correct equilibrium prices in the marketplace. This approach considers both supply and demand factors, and therefore provides a more complete analysis than that typically utilized by business firms.

Demand refers to a schedule of the amounts of a firm's product or service that consumers will purchase at different prices during a specific period. *Supply* refers to a schedule of the amounts of a product or service that will be offered for sale at different prices during a specified time period. These schedules may vary for different types of market structures. Four types of market structures exist: pure competition, monopolistic competition, oligopoly, and monopoly. **Pure competition** is a market structure in which there are such a large number of buyers and sellers that none of them has a significant influence on price. Other characteristics of pure competition are a homogeneous product and ease of entry for sellers that results from low start-up costs.

This marketing structure is largely theoretical in contemporary society; however, the agricultural sector exhibits many of the characteristics of a purely competitive market and provides the closest example of this marketing structure.

Monopolistic competition, which typifies most retailing, is a market structure with large numbers of buyers and sellers. However, it involves a heterogeneous product and product differentiation, which allow the marketer some degree of control over prices. An **oligopoly** is a market structure in which there are relatively few sellers. Each seller may affect the market, but no one seller controls it. Because of high start-up costs, new competitors encounter significant barriers to entry. The demand curve facing each individual firm in an oligopolistic market contains a

[13]Charles G. Burck, "While the Big Brewers Quaff, the Little Ones Thirst," *Fortune* (November 1972), p. 106.

unique "kink" at the current market price. Because of the impact of a single competitor upon total industry sales, any attempt by one firm to reduce prices in an effort to generate additional sales is likely to be matched by competitors. The result of total industry price cutting is a reduction in total industry revenues. Oligopolies occur frequently in the steel, petroleum-refining, automobile, and tobacco industries.

A **monopoly** is a market structure with only one seller of a product and no close substitutes for it. Antitrust legislation has nearly eliminated all but temporary monopolies (such as those provided by patent protection) and regulated monopolies such as the public service utilities—telephone, electric, cable television—and natural gas companies. The government allows regulated monopolies in markets where competition would lead to an uneconomic duplication of services. In return for this license, government reserves the right to regulate the monopoly's rate of return.

The demand side of price theory is concerned with revenue curves. Average revenue *(AR)* is obtained by dividing total revenue *(TR)* by the quantity *(Q)* associated with these revenues:

$$AR = \frac{TR}{Q}$$

The average revenue is actually the demand curve facing the firm. Marginal revenue *(MR)* is the change in total revenue (ΔTR) that results from selling an additional unit of output (ΔQ):

$$MR = \frac{\Delta TR}{\Delta Q}$$

The demand curves—average revenue lines—and marginal revenue curves for each market are shown later in Figure 13.5. Average variable cost *(AVC)* is simply the total variable costs *(TVC)* divided by the related quantity *(Q)*:

$$AVC = \frac{TVC}{Q}$$

Similarly, average fixed cost *(AFC)* is determined by dividing total fixed costs *(TFC)* by the related quantity *(Q)*:

$$AFC = \frac{TFC}{Q}$$

Marginal cost *(MC)* is the change in total cost (ΔTC) that results from producing an additional unit of output (ΔQ):

$$MC = \frac{\Delta TC}{\Delta Q}$$

Marginal costs are therefore similar to marginal revenue—the change in total revenue resulting from the sale of an incremental unit. The point of profit maximization is where marginal costs are equal to marginal revenues. The cost curves of the equations shown above appear in Figure 13.4. The marginal cost *(MC)* curve intersects the average variable cost *(AVC)* curve and average cost *(AC)* curve at their minimum points.

In the short run, a firm will continue to operate even if the price falls below AC, provided it remains above AVC. Why does this constitute rational market behavior? If the firm were to cease operations after the price fell below AC, it would still have some fixed costs, but it would have *no* revenue. Any amount received above AVC can be used to cover at least part of the fixed costs. The manager is acting rationally by continuing to produce as long as price exceeds AVC, since this minimizes losses. If price falls below AVC, the manager should cease operations because continued operation would *increase* the amount of losses. The supply curve, therefore, is the marginal cost curve above its intersection with AVC, since this is the area of rational pricing behavior for the firm.

How are the prices set in each of the product market situations? Figure 13.5 shows how prices are determined in each of the four product markets. The point of profit maximization ($MC = MR$) sets the equilibrium output (Point A), which is extended to the AR line to set the equilibrium price (Point B). In the case of pure competition, $AR = MR$, so price is a predetermined variable in this product market.

The Concept of Elasticity in Pricing Strategy

Although the intersection of demand and supply curves determine the equilibrium price for each of the market structures shown in Figure 13.5, the specific curves vary. In order to understand why they vary, it is necessary to understand the concept of elasticity.[14]

Elasticity is a measure of responsiveness of purchasers and suppliers to changes in price. The *price elasticity of demand* (or elasticity of demand) is the percentage change in the quantity of a product or service demanded, divided by the percentage change in its price. A 10 percent increase in the price of eggs that results in a 5 percent decrease in the quantity of eggs demanded yields a price elasticity of demand for eggs of 0.5.

The *price elasticity of supply* of a good is the percentage change in the quantity of a product or service supplied, divided by the percentage change in its price. A 10 percent increase in the price of shampoo that brought about a 25 percent increase in the quantity supplied yields a price elasticity of supply for shampoo of 2.5.

[14]This section is adapted from Edwin G. Dolan, *Basic Economics*, 3d ed. (Hinsdale, Ill.: The Dryden Press, 1983); and Richard H. Leftwich, *The Price System and Resource Allocation* (Hinsdale, Ill.: The Dryden Press, 1979), pp. 55–56. Reprinted by permission of Holt, Rinehart & Winston.

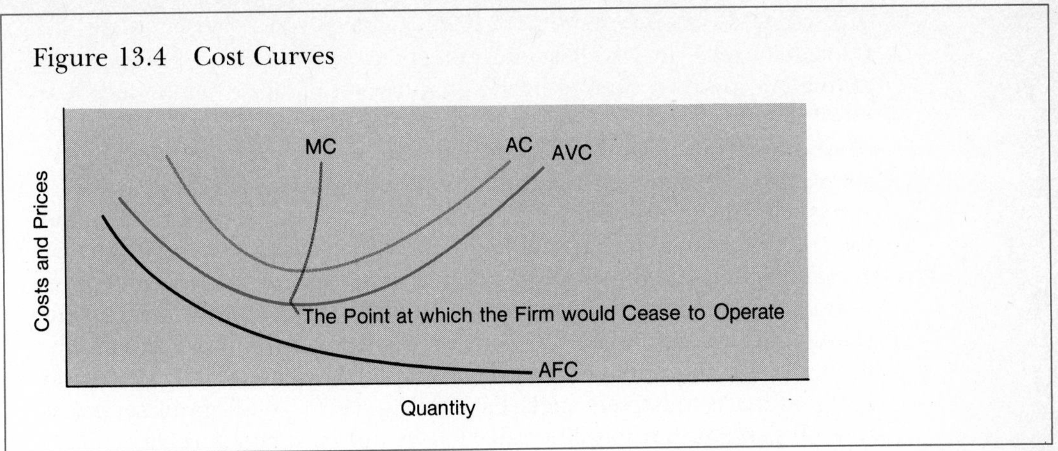

Figure 13.4 Cost Curves

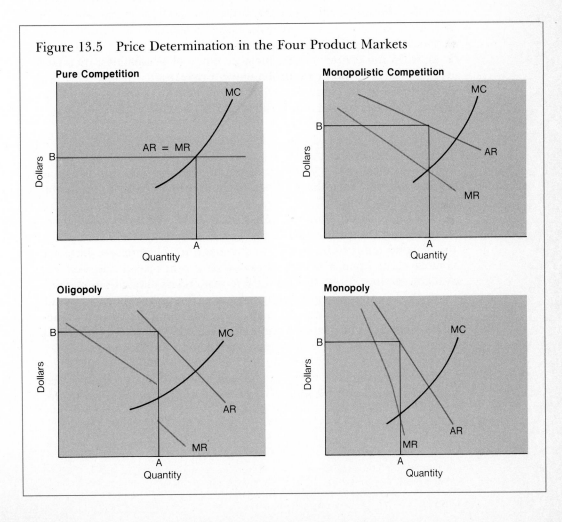

Figure 13.5 Price Determination in the Four Product Markets

Pure Competition

MC
AR = MR
B
Dollars
A
Quantity

Monopolistic Competition

MC
B
AR
Dollars
MR
A
Quantity

Oligopoly

B
MC
Dollars
AR
MR
A
Quantity

Monopoly

MC
B
Dollars
AR
MR
A
Quantity

Elasticity Terminology

Consider a case in which a one percent change in price causes more than a one percent change in the quantity supplied or demanded. Numerically, that means an elasticity greater than one. When the elasticity of demand or supply is greater than one, it is termed *elastic.* An extreme case occurs when the quantity of a good supplied or demanded varies with no change in the price. In this case, the supply or demand for the good is said to be perfectly elastic. Perfectly elastic supply or demand is illustrated by a perfectly horizontal supply or demand curve.

If a one percent change in price results in less than a one percent change in quantity, a good's elasticity of supply or demand will be numerically less than one and is called *inelastic.* For example, the demand for gasoline is relatively inelastic. During 1979, retail gasoline prices rose 50 percent, but gasoline sales fell by only about 8 percent.

An extreme case occurs when the quantity supplied or demanded does not change at all when the price changes. Then the supply or demand is called perfectly inelastic. Perfect inelasticity of supply or demand means a perfectly vertical supply or demand curve.

Between the elastic and the inelastic range of possibilities, there is a case in which a one percent change in price results in exactly a one percent change in quantity. When the numerical elasticity is equal to one, that supply or demand is called *unit* (or *unitary*) *elastic.*

Determinants of Elasticity

Why is the elasticity of supply or demand high for some products and services and low for others? What constitute the specific determinants of demand elasticity?[15]

One factor determining the elasticity of demand is the availability of substitutes or complements. If a product or service has close substitutes, the demand tends to be elastic. The demand for olive oil, for instance, is more elastic than it would otherwise be if other salad oils were not available as substitutes. The demand for cars is less elastic than it would be if good public transportation were available everywhere. If something is a minor complement to an important good, its demand tends to be inelastic. The demand for motor oil, for example, tends to be inelastic, because it is a complement to the more important good, gasoline.

Elasticity of demand is also influenced by whether a product or service is a necessity or a luxury. For example, dining out is a luxury for

[15]For a discussion of the application of price elasticity to a consumer service, see Steven J. Skinner, Terry L. Childers, and Wesley H. Jones, "Consumer Responsiveness to Price Differentials: A Case for Insurance Industry Deregulation," *Journal of Business Research* (December 1981), pp. 381–396.

most people. If restaurant prices increase, most people can respond by eating at home instead. By contrast, medical or dental care are considered necessities, so price changes will have little effect on the frequency of people's medical or dental visits.

Elasticity is further influenced by the portion of a person's budget that is spent on a product or service. Matches, for example, are no longer really a necessity, and good substitutes exist. Nonetheless, the demand for matches is thought to be very inelastic because people spend so little on them that they hardly notice a price change. However, the demand for housing and transportation is not perfectly inelastic even though they are necessities. Both occupy a large part of people's budgets, so a change in price cannot be ignored.

Elasticity of demand is also affected by the time perspective under consideration. Demand is often less elastic in the short run than in the long run. Consider the demand for home heating fuel. In the short run, when the price goes up, people find it difficult to cut back on the quantity they use. They are accustomed to living at a certain temperature, dressing a certain way, and so forth. Given time, though, they may find ways to economize. They can better insulate their homes, form new habits of dressing more warmly, or even move to a warmer climate.

All the factors mentioned here are only tendencies; yet often the tendencies reinforce one another. The classic case of inelastic demand is salt, which has no good substitute, is a nutritional necessity, and uses a very small part of one's budget. Sometimes, though, the rules just do not seem to fit. Alcohol and tobacco, which are not necessities and do occupy a large share of some personal budgets, also are subject to notoriously inelastic demand.

Elasticity and Revenue

There is an important relationship between the elasticity of demand and the way that total revenue changes as the price of a product or service changes. Suppose New York City wants to find a way to raise more money for the city budget. One possible fund-raising method is to change the subway fare, but should it be raised or lowered? The correct answer depends on the elasticity of demand for subway rides. A 10 percent decrease in fares is sure to attract more riders, but unless there is more than a 10 percent increase in riders, total revenue will fall. A 10 percent increase in fares will bring in more money per rider, but if more than 10 percent of the riders are lost, revenue will fall. A price cut will increase revenue only if demand is elastic, and a price increase will raise revenue only if demand is inelastic. New York City officials seem to believe that the demand for subway rides is inelastic; they raise fares every time they need more money for the city budget.

Practical Problems of Price Theory

From the viewpoint of the marketer, price theory concepts are sometimes difficult to apply in practice. What, then, are their practical limitations?

1. *Many firms do not attempt to maximize profits.* Economic analysis is subject to the same limitations as the assumptions on which it is based—for example, the proposition that all firms attempt to maximize profits.
2. *It is difficult to estimate demand curves.* Modern accounting procedures provide managers with a clear understanding of cost structures. The managers can therefore readily comprehend the supply side of the pricing equation, but it is difficult to estimate demand at various price levels. Demand curves must be based on market research estimates that often are not as exact as cost figures. Over time, however, these problems may be eliminated by the use of advanced research methodology. Although the demand element can be identified, it is often difficult to measure in the real-world setting.[16]
3. *Inadequate training and communication hinder price theory in the real world.* Many managers lack the formal training in economics to be able to apply its concepts to their own pricing decisions. On the other hand, many economists remain essentially theorists, devoting little interest or effort to real-world pricing situations. This dual problem significantly hinders the use of economic theory in actual pricing practice.

Price Determination in Practice

The practical limitations inherent in price theory have forced practitioners to turn to other techniques. The cost-plus approach is the most commonly used method of setting prices today. For many years, government contracts with suppliers called for payments of all expenses plus a set profit usually stated as a percentage of the cost of the project. These cost-plus contracts, as they were known, have been abandoned in favor of competitive bidding or specifically negotiated prices.

Cost-plus pricing takes some base cost figure per unit and adds a markup to cover unassigned costs and to provide a profit. The only real difference in the multitude of cost-plus techniques is the relative sophistication of the costing procedures employed. For example, a local apparel shop may set prices by adding a 40 percent markup to the

[16]Some problems of using economic models in practice are discussed in Kent B. Monroe and Albert J. Della Bitta, "Models for Pricing Decisions," *Journal of Marketing Research* (August 1978), pp. 413–428. Also see Robert J. Dolan and Abel P. Jeuland, "Experience Curves and Dynamic Models: Implications for Optional Pricing Strategies," *Journal of Marketing* (Winter 1981), pp. 52–62.

invoice price charged by the supplier. The markup is expected to cover all other expenses and permit the owner to earn a reasonable return on the sale of the clothes.

In contrast to this rather simple pricing mechanism, a large manufacturer may employ a pricing formula that requires a computer to handle the necessary calculations. But advanced calculations are reserved for a sophisticated costing procedure. In the end, the formula still requires someone to make a decision about the markup. The apparel shop and the large manufacturer may be vastly different with respect to the cost aspect, but they are remarkably similar when it comes to the markup side of the equation.

This discussion demonstrates one of the problems associated with cost-oriented pricing: "Costs do not determine prices, since the proper function of cost in pricing is to determine the profit consequences of pricing alternatives."[17] Unfortunately, this point is not always understood by marketers.

The two most common cost-oriented pricing procedures are the full cost method and the incremental cost method. *Full cost pricing* uses all relevant variable costs in setting a product's price. In addition, it allocates the fixed costs that cannot be directly attributed to the production of the specific item being priced. Under the full cost method, if job order 515 in a printing plant amounts to 0.000127 percent of the plant's total output, then 0.000127 percent of the firm's overhead expenses are charged to that job. This approach allows the marketer to recover all costs plus the amount added as a profit margin.

The full cost approach has two basic deficiencies. First, there is no consideration of the competition or of the demand for the item. Perhaps no one wants to pay the price the firm has calculated! Second, any method of allocating overhead (fixed expenses) is arbitrary and may be unrealistic. In manufacturing, overhead allocations are often tied to direct labor hours. In retailing, the square footage of each profit center is sometimes the factor used in computations. Regardless of the technique, it is difficult to show a cause-effect relationship between the allocated cost and most products.

One way to overcome the arbitrary allocation of fixed expenses is by *incremental cost pricing*, which attempts to use only those costs directly attributable to a specific output in setting prices. Consider a small manufacturer with the following income statement:

Sales (10,000 units at $10)		$100,000
Expenses:		
Variable	$50,000	
Fixed	40,000	90,000
Net profit		$ 10,000

[17]Theodore E. Wentz, "Realism in Pricing Analysis," *Journal of Marketing* (April 1966), p. 26.

Why Detroit Can't Cut Prices

Probably nothing Detroit does today makes less sense to consumers than the way it sets car prices. If Detroit persists in its contention that its pricing structure is a function of the need to calculate costs five years before production, it is unlikely that the Byzantine pricing structure will change much. However, consumer rebellion is forcing auto makers to take a new look at their manufacturing costs and marketing assumptions before affixing a model's price. Two factors complicate the search for a solution to the problem of reducing car prices: persistent inflation and the domestic auto makers' need to pay for an $80 billion retooling switch to small vehicles.

Traditionally, the domestic auto makers keyed their prices to General Motors Corporation, because that company controls more than 60 percent of the market for U.S.-built cars. The process got more complicated when imports, mainly from Japan, began infiltrating the United States. Foreign auto makers pay different labor rates, make different assumptions about investment paybacks for new tooling, and even manage their factories differently. Several studies say the difference in production costs between U.S. and Japanese auto makers is at least $1,500 per car. That difference would give Japanese companies a huge cushion from which to react to permanent price cuts from Detroit. Robert J. Orsini, vice-president for strategic management consulting with William C. Roney & Co., estimates that domestic car makers must find a way to cut production costs a staggering $2,200 per car if they expect to compete fully with the Japanese. Analysts suggest Detroit could give up its determination to break even on a new car model within four or five years and stretch the payback period to perhaps eight years as the Japanese do. This would reduce costs per year by altering the way the auto makers account for such expenses.

But LeRoy H. Lindgren, a vice-presi-

Suppose the firm is offered a contract for an additional 5,000 units. Since the peak season is over, these items can be produced at the same average variable cost. Assume that the labor force would be idle otherwise. In order to get the contract, how low could the firm price its product?

Under the full cost approach, the lowest price would be $9 per unit. This figure is obtained by dividing the $90,000 in expenses by an output of 10,000 units.

The incremental approach, on the other hand, could permit a price of $5.10 which would significantly increase the possibility of securing the additional contract. This price would be composed of the $5 variable cost related to each unit of production plus a 10 cents-per-unit contribution to fixed expenses and overhead. The income statement now looks like this:

dent and industrial cost consultant with Rath & Strong, Inc., believes that much of the $1,500 difference comes from the production snags that accompany Detroit's conversion to front-wheel drive and brand-new body designs. "We're going through a tremendous conversion, and the Japanese aren't," he says. Lindgren figures it takes a plant about two years after such sweeping changes in tooling and manufacturing methods to achieve output efficiencies. In the meantime, he says, many U.S. auto plants are running up costs per car two or three times their eventual levels.

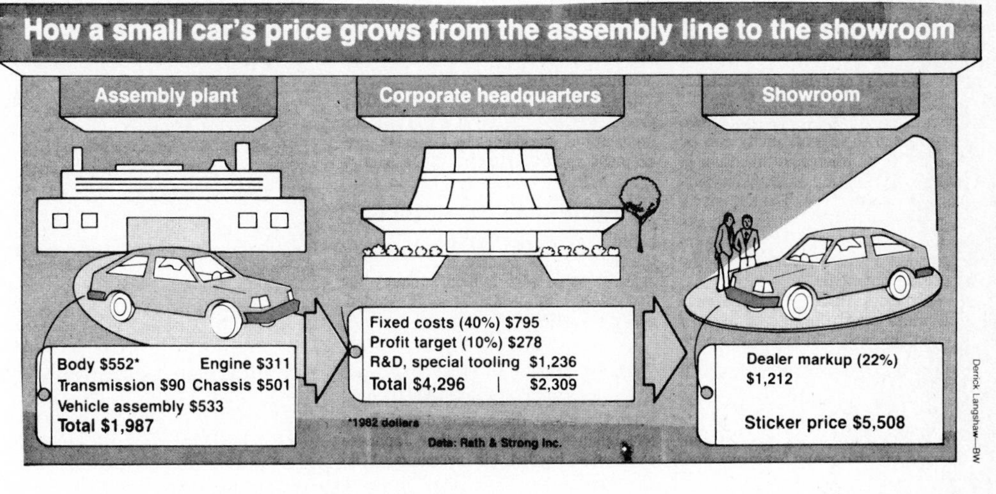

Source: "Why Detroit Can't Cut Prices," *Business Week* (March 1, 1982), pp. 110–111. Drawing by Derrick Langshaw. Reprinted by permission.

Sales (10,000 at $10; 5,000 at $5.10)		$125,500
Expenses:		
Variable (15,000 × $5)	$75,000	
Fixed	40,000	115,000
Net profit		$ 10,500

Profits are increased under the incremental approach. Admittedly, the illustration is based on two assumptions: (1) the ability to isolate markets so that selling at the lower price will not affect the price received in other markets; and (2) the absence of legal restrictions on the firm. The example, however, does illustrate that profits can sometimes be enhanced by using the incremental approach.

Markups, Markdowns, and Turnover

A frequent criticism of pricing practices is that decision makers have consistently attempted to develop rigid procedures by which prices can be derived in a largely mechanical fashion. These efforts often produce inappropriate prices for specific market situations because they ignore the creative aspects of pricing. Markup policies are an example of this problem. A **markup** is the amount a producer or channel member adds to cost in order to determine the selling price. It is typically stated as either a percentage of the selling price or cost. The formulas used in calculating markup percentages are as follows:

$$\text{Markup Percentage on Selling Price} = \frac{\text{Amount Added to Cost (the Markup)}}{\text{Price}}$$

$$\text{Markup Percentage on Cost} = \frac{\text{Amount Added to Cost (the Markup)}}{\text{Cost}}$$

Consider an example from retailing. Suppose an item selling for $1 has an invoice cost of $.50. The total markup is $.50. The two markup percentages would be calculated as follows:

$$\text{Markup Percentage on Selling Price} = \frac{.50}{\$1.00} = 50\%$$

$$\text{Markup Percentage on Cost} = \frac{\$.50}{\$.50} = 100\%$$

To determine selling price when only cost and markup percentage on selling price are known, the following formula is utilized:

$$\text{Price} = \frac{\text{Cost in Dollars}}{100\% - \text{Markup Percentage on Selling Price}}$$

In the example cited above, price could be determined as $1.00:

$$\text{Price} = \frac{\$.50}{100\% - 50\%} = \frac{.50}{50\%} = \$1.00.$$

Similarly, the markup percentage can be converted from one basis (selling price or cost) to the other by using the following formula:

$$\text{Markup Percentage on Selling Price} = \frac{\text{Markup Percentage on Cost}}{100\% + \text{Markup Percentage on Cost}}$$

$$\text{Markup Percentage on Cost} = \frac{\text{Markup Percentage on Selling Price}}{100\% - \text{Markup Percentage on Selling Price}}$$

Again, using the data from the example above, the following conversions can be made:

$$\text{Markup Percentage on Selling Price} = \frac{100\%}{100\% + 100\%} = \frac{100\%}{200\%} = 50\%$$

$$\text{Markup Percentage on Cost} = \frac{50\%}{100\% - 50\%} = \frac{50\%}{50\%} = 100\%$$

Markdowns A related pricing issue that is particularly important to retailers is markdowns. Markups are based partially on executive judgments about the prices consumers are likely to pay for a given product or service. If buyers refuse to pay the price, however, the marketer must determine whether to take a **markdown,** a reduction in the price of the item. The markdown percentage—the actual figure that is typically advertised—for the sale item can be computed as follows:

$$\text{Markdown Percentage} = \frac{\text{Markdown}}{\text{"Sale" (New) Price}}$$

Suppose no one was willing to pay $1.00 for an item and the marketer decided to reduce the price to $.75. Advertisements for the special sale item might note that it had been marked down one third.

$$\text{Markdown Percentage} = \frac{\$.25}{\$.75} = 33\tfrac{1}{3}\%$$

Markdowns are also used for evaluative purposes. For instance, department managers or buyers in a large department store could be evaluated partially on the basis of the average markdown percentage on the product lines for which they are responsible.

Turnover All too often, traditional markup and markdown percentages lead to competitive inertia within an industry. Standard percentages are too frequently applied to all items in a given category regardless of factors such as demand.

A method for avoiding competitive inertia is to use flexible markups that vary with the **stock turnover rate**—the number of times the average inventory is sold annually. The figure can be calculated by one of the following formulas. When inventory is recorded at retail:

$$\text{Stock Turnover} = \frac{\text{Sales}}{\text{Average Inventory}}$$

When inventory is recorded at cost:

$$\text{Stock Turnover} = \frac{\text{Cost of Goods Sold}}{\text{Average Inventory}}$$

Store A, with $100,000 in sales and an average inventory of $20,000 (at retail), would have a stock turnover of 5. Store B, with $200,000 in sales, a 40 percent markup rate, and an average inventory of $30,000 (at cost), would have a stock turnover of 4.

Table 13.2 Relationship between Markup Percentage and Stock Turnover Rate

Stock Turnover Rate in Relation to the Industry Average	Markup Percentage in Relation to the Industry Average
High	Low
Average	Average
Low	High

Store A

$$\text{Stock Turnover} = \frac{\$100{,}000}{\$20{,}000} = 5$$

Store B

$200,000 Sales
−80,000 Markup (40 percent)
$120,000 Cost of Goods Sold

$$\text{Stock Turnover} = \frac{\$120{,}000}{\$30{,}000} = 4$$

While most marketers recognize the importance of turnover, they often use it more as a measure of sales effectiveness than as a pricing tool. However, it can be particularly useful in setting markup percentages if some consideration is given to consumer demand.

Table 13.2 indicates the relationship between stock turnover rates and markup. Above average turnover rates, such as for grocery products, are generally associated with relatively low markup percentages. On the other hand, higher markup percentages typically exist in such product lines as jewelry and furniture where relatively lower annual stock turnover rates are common.

Breakeven Analysis

The technique of **breakeven analysis** is a means of determining the number of products or services that must be sold at a given price in order to generate sufficient revenue to cover total costs. Figure 13.6 presents a graphical depiction of the breakeven point. The total cost curve includes both fixed and variable segments, and total fixed cost is represented by a horizontal line. Average variable cost is assumed to be constant per unit as it was in the earlier example for incremental pricing.

The breakeven point is the point at which total revenue *(TR)* just equals total cost *(TC)*. It can be found by using the following formulas:

$$\text{Breakeven Point (in Units)} = \frac{\text{Total Fixed Cost}}{\text{Per Unit Contribution to Fixed Cost}}$$

$$\text{Breakeven Point (in Dollars)} = \frac{\text{Total Fixed Cost}}{1 - \dfrac{\text{Variable Cost per Unit}}{\text{Price}}}$$

Figure 13.6 Breakeven Chart

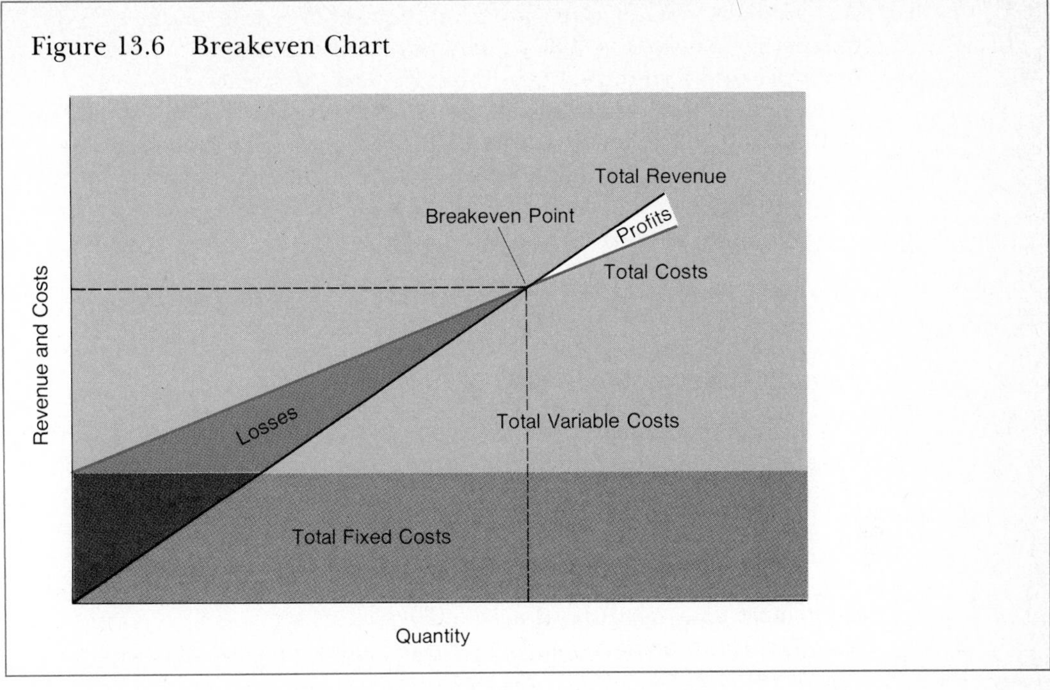

In our earlier example, a selling price of $10 and an average variable cost of $5 resulted in a per unit contribution to fixed costs of $5. This figure can be divided into total fixed costs of $40,000 to obtain a breakeven point of 8,000 units, or $80,000 in total sales revenue:

$$\text{Breakeven Point (in Units)} = \frac{\$40{,}000}{\$5} = 8{,}000 \text{ units}$$

$$\text{Breakeven Point (in Dollars)} = \frac{\$40{,}000}{1 - \dfrac{\$5}{\$10}} = \frac{\$40{,}000}{.5} = \$80{,}000$$

Breakeven analysis is an effective tool for marketers in assessing the required sales in order to cover costs and achieve specified profit levels. It is easily understood by both marketing and nonmarketing executives and may assist in deciding whether required sales levels for a certain price are in fact realistic goals. However, it is not without shortcomings.

First, the model assumes that costs can be divided into fixed and variable categories. Some costs, such as salaries and advertising outlays, may be either fixed or variable depending upon the particular situation. In addition, the model assumes that per unit variable costs do not change at different levels of operation. However, these may vary as a result of quantity discounts, more efficient utilization of the work force, or other economies resulting from increased levels of production and sales. Finally, the basic breakeven model does not consider demand. It is a cost-based model and does not directly address the crucial question of whether consumers will actually purchase the product at the specified price and in required quantities necessary to break even or to generate profits. The challenge of the marketer is to modify breakeven analysis and the other cost-oriented approaches to pricing in order to introduce demand analysis. Pricing must be examined from the buyer's perspective. Such decisions cannot be made in a management vacuum in which only cost factors are considered.

Toward Realistic Pricing

Traditional economic theory considers both costs and demand in the determination of an equilibrium price. The dual elements of supply and demand are balanced at the point of equilibrium. In actual industry practice, however, most pricing approaches are largely cost-oriented. Since purely cost-oriented approaches to pricing violate the marketing concept, modifications are required in order to add demand analysis to the pricing decision.

Consumer research of such issues as degree of price elasticity, consumer price expectations, existence and size of specific market segments, and perceptions of strengths and weaknesses of substitute products is necessary for developing sales estimates at different prices. Since much of the resultant data involves perceptions, attitudes, and future expectations, such estimates are likely to be less precise than cost estimates.

The Modified Breakeven Concept

In Figure 13.6, the breakeven analysis was based upon the assumption of a constant $10 retail price regardless of quantity. What happens when different retail prices are considered? **Modified breakeven anal-**

Table 13.3 Revenue and Cost Data for Modified Breakeven Analysis

	Revenues		Costs			
Price	Quantity Demanded	Total Revenue	Total Fixed Cost	Total Variable Cost	Total Cost	Total Profit (or Loss)
$14	3,000	$ 42,000	$ 40,000	$ 15,000	$ 55,000	($13,000)
12	6,000	72,000	40,000	30,000	70,000	2,000
10	10,000	100,000	40,000	50,000	90,000	10,000
8	14,000	112,000	40,000	70,000	110,000	2,000
6	26,000	156,000	40,000	130,000	170,000	(14,000)

Figure 13.7 Modified Breakeven Chart Reflecting Costs and Consumer Demand

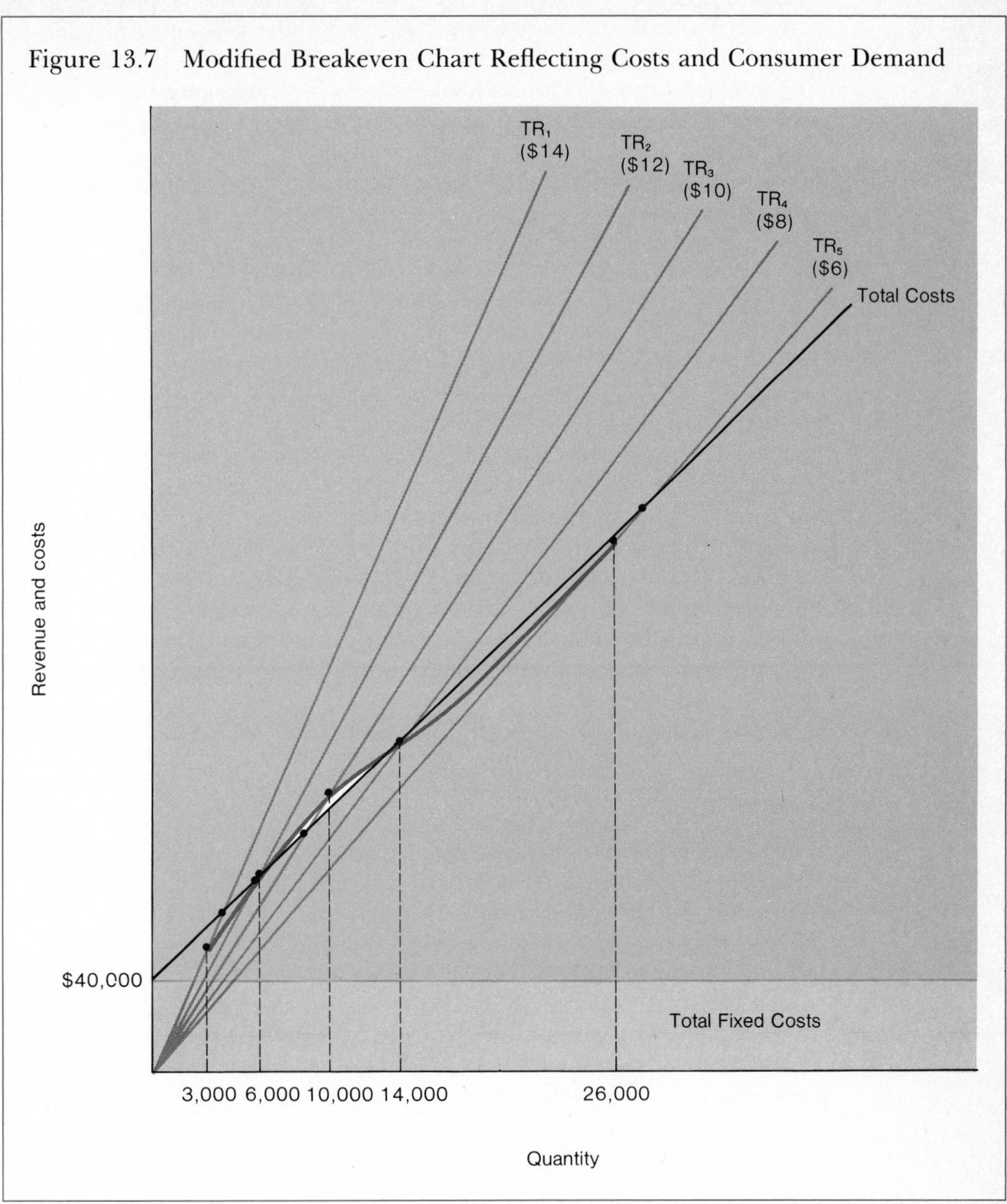

ysis combines the traditional breakeven analysis model with an evaluation of consumer demand.

Table 13.3 summarizes both the cost and revenue aspects of a number of alternative retail prices. The cost data are based upon the costs utilized earlier in the basic breakeven model. The expected unit sales for each specified retail price are obtained from consumer research. The data in the first two columns of Table 13.3 represent a demand schedule by indicating the number of units consumers are expected to purchase at each of a series of retail prices. This data can be superimposed onto a breakeven chart in order to identify the range of feasible prices for consideration by the marketing decision maker. This is shown in Figure 13.7.

As Figure 13.7 indicates, the range of profitable prices exists from a low of approximately $8 ($TR_4$) to a high of $12 ($TR_2$), with a price of $10 ($TR_3$) generating the greatest projected profits. Changing the retail price produces a new breakeven point. At a relatively high $14 retail price, the breakeven point is 4,445 units; at a $10 retail price the breakeven point is 8,000 units; and at a $6 price, 40,000 units must be sold in order to break even.

The contribution of modified breakeven analysis is that it forces the pricing decision maker to consider whether the consumer is likely to purchase the required number of units of a product or service in order to achieve breakeven at a given price. It demonstrates that a larger number of units sold does not necessarily produce added profits, since—other things equal—lower prices are necessary to stimulate added sales. Consequently, it necessitates careful consideration of both costs and consumer demand in determining the most appropriate price.

Summary

Price—the exchange value of a good or service—is important because it regulates economic activity as well as determines the revenue to be received by an individual firm. As a marketing mix element, pricing is one of those gray areas where marketers struggle to develop a theory, technique, or rule of thumb on which they can depend. It is a complex variable because it contains both objective and subjective aspects. It is an area where precise decision tools and executive judgment meet.

Pricing objectives should be the natural consequence of overall organizational goals and more specific marketing goals. They can be classified into four major groupings: (1) profitability objectives, including profit maximization and target return; (2) volume objectives, including sales maximization and market share; (3) meeting competition objectives; and (4) prestige objectives.

Prices can be determined by theoretical or cost-oriented approaches. Economic theorists attempt to equate marginal revenue and marginal cost. Elasticity is an important element in price determination. The degree of consumer responsiveness to changes in price is affected by such factors as availability of substitute or complementary goods, whether a product or service is a necessity or a luxury, the portion of a person's budget being spent, and the time perspective under consideration.

Price determination in actual practice frequently emphasizes costs. Both breakeven analysis and the use of markups are essentially cost-plus approaches to pricing.

A more realistic approach to effective price decisions is to integrate both buyer demand and costs. Modified breakeven analysis is a method for accomplishing this task.

In Chapter 14, the discussion of pricing continues by examining the development of pricing strategies and the use of decision models in pricing. The concepts of price-quality relationships, price quotations, industrial pricing, and pricing in the public sector are discussed in the chapter.

Key Terms

price
profit maximization
target return objectives
sales maximization
Profit Impact of Market Strategies (PIMS) project
customary prices
pure competition
monopolistic competition
oligopoly
monopoly
elasticity
cost-plus pricing
markup
markdown
stock turnover
breakeven analysis
modified breakeven analysis

Review Questions

1. Identify the four major categories of pricing objectives.
2. Categorize each of the following into a specific type of pricing objective:
   a. 8 percent increase in market share
   b. 5 percent increase in profits over previous year
   c. Prices no more than 5 percent higher than prices quoted by independent dealers
   d. 20 percent return on investment (before taxes)
   e. Highest prices in product category to maintain favorable brand image
   f. Follow price of most important competitor in each market segment
3. What are the major price implications of the PIMS studies? Suggest possible explanations for the relationships discovered by the studies.
4. What market situations exist for the following products:
   a. Telephone service
   b. U.S.-made cigars
   c. Golf clubs
   d. Steel
   e. Soybeans
   f. Dishwashers
   g. Tape recorders
   h. Skis

5. Explain the concept of elasticity. What are the determinants of the degree of price elasticity for a product or service?
6. What are the practical problems involved in attempting to apply price theory concepts to actual pricing decisions?
7. Explain the advantages of using incremental cost pricing rather than full cost pricing. What potential drawbacks exist?
8. Explain the relationship between markups and stock turnover rates.
9. Explain the primary benefits of using breakeven analysis in price determination. What are the shortcomings of the basic breakeven model?
10. In what ways is modified breakeven analysis superior to the basic model?

Discussion Questions and Exercises

1. A retailer has just received a new kitchen appliance invoiced at $28. The retailer decides to follow industry practice for such items and adds a 40 percent markup percentage on selling price. What retail price should the retailer assign to the appliance?
2. If a product has a markup percentage on selling price of 28 percent, what is its markup percentage on cost?
3. An economic downturn in the local area has seriously affected sales of a retailer's line of $150 dresses. The store manager decides to mark these dresses down to $125. What markdown percentage should be featured in advertising this sale item?
4. A store with an average inventory of $50,000 (at cost) operates on a 40 percent markup percentage on selling price. Annual sales total $750,000. What is the stock turnover rate?
5. What is the breakeven point in dollars and units for a product with a selling price of $25, related fixed costs of $126,000, and per unit variable costs of $16?

Chapter Objectives

1. To explain the organization for pricing decisions.
2. To describe how prices are quoted.
3. To identify the various pricing policy decisions that must be made by marketers.
4. To compare skimming and penetration pricing and explain when each approach should be used.
5. To relate price to consumer perceptions of quality.
6. To contrast negotiated prices and competitive bidding.
7. To explain the importance of transfer pricing.
8. To describe pricing in the public sector.

14

MANAGING THE PRICING FUNCTION

Ralston Purina Company turned to a simple attention-getter in early 1982 when it wanted to stimulate its sales of canned cat food. The company lowered the wholesale price by about four cents a can. That sort of action has been almost unheard of among packaged-goods marketers until recently. Their typical sales blandishments are cents-off coupons, bigger advertising budgets, sweepstakes, refunds, temporary price discounts, or minor product changes resulting in claims that brands are new and improved.

"We're paying a lot more attention to price now," says Blair Gensamer, marketing director for Ralston's grocery products division, which also has lowered prices of its Mainstay and Moist & Chunky dog foods. "It's a tool that's being neglected."

That view apparently is shared by such leading consumer products marketers as Procter & Gamble, Kellogg's, Coca-Cola, Scott Paper Co., Mobil, Union Carbide, and Lever Brothers Company. For various reasons, all recently have cut their prices on certain brands. Some of the companies are fighting private brands and generic products, while others want to reduce temporary discounts or to revive lagging products.

Whatever their motives, manufacturers that reduce list prices are being praised by retailers. "Consumers are getting fed up with the hocus-pocus of coupons, refunds, and price specials," says Thomas Stemberg, senior vice-president of First National Supermarkets. "They're looking for everyday basic value." James Henson, president of Jewel Food Stores, urges manufacturers to "attack and justify every penny spent in non-ingredient costs."[1]

The Conceptual Framework

The Ralston Purina experience suggests that the pricing variable can significantly affect the success of any firm's marketing program. The previous chapter introduced the concept of price and its role in the economic system and in marketing strategy. This chapter considers who should be responsible for the pricing decision and the sequential approach to such decisions. It examines alternative pricing strategies and administering price structures. Finally, other pricing practices such as negotiated prices, competitive bidding, and pricing in the public sector are considered.

Organization for Pricing Decisions

In translating pricing objectives into pricing decisions, there are two major steps to follow. First, someone must be assigned responsibility for making pricing decisions and administering the pricing structure. Then the overall pricing structure—that is, the selected price and the appropriate discounts for channel members as well as for various quantities and for geographic and promotional considerations—must be set.

A recent survey of marketing executives found that the people or groups most commonly chosen to set price structures were (1) a pricing committee composed of top executives, (2) the president of the company, and (3) the chief marketing officer. According to the same survey, the pricing structure is administered most often by marketers. As

[1]Bill Abrams, "Consumer-Goods Firms Turn to Price Cuts to Increase Sales," *The Wall Street Journal* (May 13, 1982), p. 29. Reprinted by permission.

Figure 14.1 Executives Responsible for Setting and Administering Price Structures

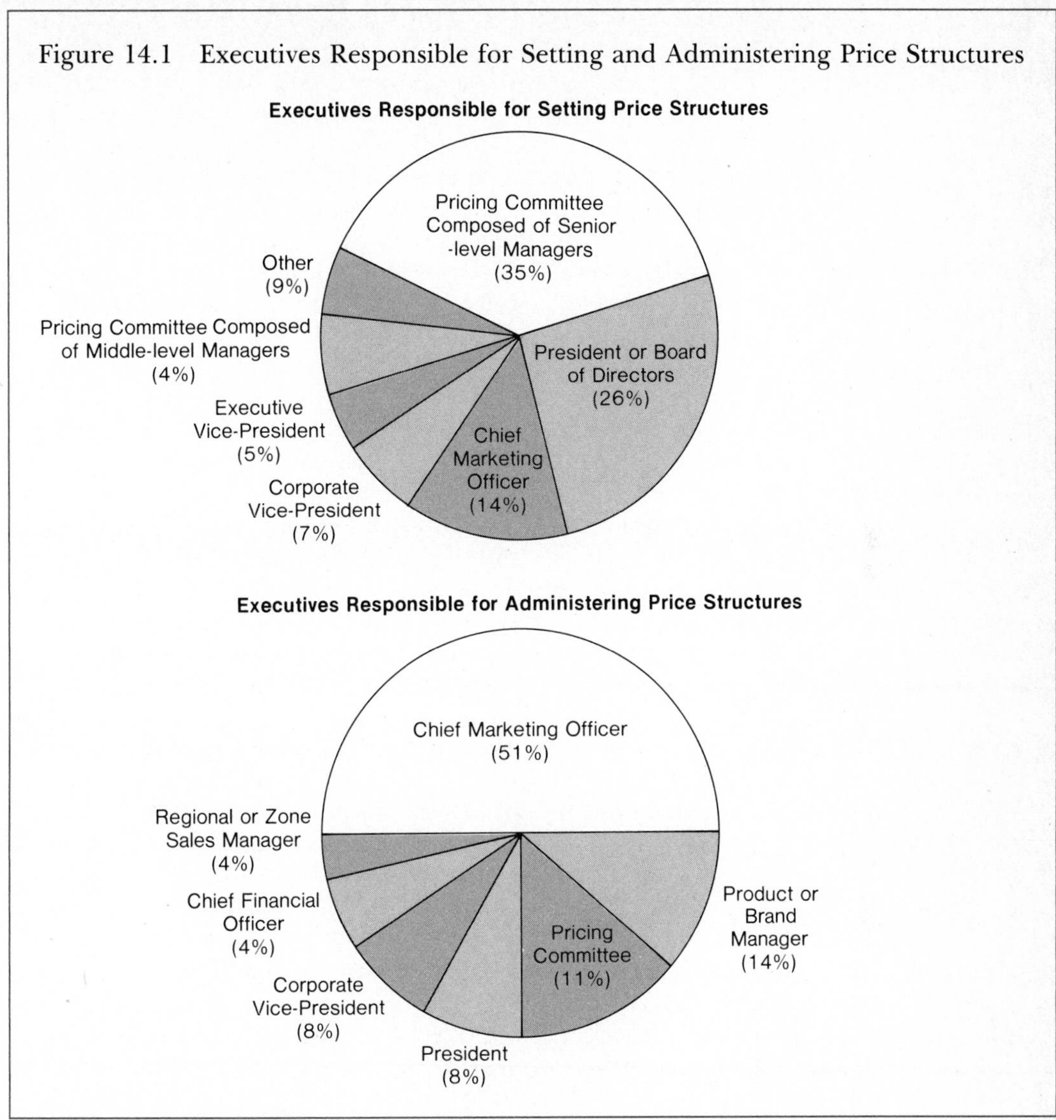

Source: *Pricing Objectives and Practices in American Industry: A Research Report* by Louis E. Boone and David L. Kurtz.

Figure 14.1 indicates, the chief marketing officer was the responsible person in 51 percent of the firms surveyed. In all, marketers administered the pricing structure in over 68 percent of the companies. These results seem consistent with industry's attempt to implement the marketing concept.

Setting Prices at Humbolt Electric

The management of Humbolt Electric Company, the world's third largest manufacturer of small appliances, was considering the introduction of its newest product, a battery-driven household blender. One of the company's greatest concerns was how to price the blender. Here is how Humbolt went about solving its pricing quandary.

With the help of the market research department, the blender's market target was defined as younger couples who the firm believed were more inclined to purchase a new appliance innovation. Management decided to retain its existing brand image as a quality, higher-priced product line. The composition of the marketing mix was announced by Allan R. Ferzacurri, the director of marketing, after consultation with market research, sales, and advertising personnel in the organization. They decided the blender would be custom-packaged and distributed through leading department stores in line with Humbolt's existing brand image. Since the battery-driven blender would carry a price tag somewhat higher than conventional blenders, Ferzacurri decided to employ substantial promotional expenditures to support the new appliance entry.

Humbolt elected to follow its existing price policy of maintaining its suggested retail price. The firm did not offer discounts, promotional allowances, or other price reductions to its dealers. Ferzacurri's pricing strategy was one of skimming the cream off the market rather than trying to gain consumer acceptance through low introductory prices. Finally, the specific price of the new item was set at 15 percent above that of standard plug-in blenders after the marketing staff compared profit consequences of alternative prices by using breakeven analysis and evaluated varying markup percentages in relation to expected stock turnover.

The Humbolt approach to pricing implies that selection of the final price is really the natural consequence of a series of other considerations. Pricing strategy should be oriented toward long-run considerations, and related decision making should be sequential rather than mechanistic. The arithmetic of pricing should not overwhelm broader factors in such a process.

Source: M. Dale Beckman, David L. Kurtz, and Louis E. Boone, *Foundations of Marketing*, 2d ed. (Toronto: Holt, Rinehart and Winston of Canada, Ltd., 1982), p. 392.

Price Quotations

The method for quoting prices depends on many factors, such as cost structures, traditional practices in the particular industry, and the policies of individual firms. In this section we examine the reasoning and methodology behind price quotations.

Movie-goers accustomed to a $3 ticket price have been paying more in recent years—$4 and even $5 for new movies. The decision of how much to charge ticket buyers is affected by many variables: prices at competing theaters; prices at alternative entertainment outlets, such as concerts; consumer price elasticity of demand; and costs. Consider the case of the movie *Summer Lovers.* The movie, a story of R-rated romance set in Greece, cost $5.3 million to produce. As Figure 14.2 reveals, finance and marketing expenses add another $15 million, requiring $20 million in box-office income to break even. For this film, a price must be selected that is most likely to generate revenues of greater than the overall $20 million cost.

The basis upon which most price structures is built is the **list price,** the rate normally quoted to potential buyers. List price is usually determined by one or a combination of the methods discussed in Chapter 13. The sticker prices on new automobiles are good examples: they show the list price for the basic model then add the list price for the options that are included.

Discounts, Allowances, and Rebates

The amount that a consumer pays—the **market price**—may or may not be the same as the list price. In some cases discounts or allowances reduce the list price. List price is often used as the starting point from which discounts that set the market price are taken. Discounts can be classified as cash, quantity, or trade.

Cash discounts are reductions in price that are given for prompt payment of a bill. They are probably the most commonly used variety. Cash discounts usually specify an exact time period, such as 2/10, net 30. This means that the bill is due within 30 days, but if it is paid in 10 days, the customer may subtract 2 percent from the amount due. Cash discounts have become traditional pricing practice in many industries. They are legal provided that they are granted all customers on the same terms. Such discounts were originally instituted to improve the liquidity position of sellers, lower bad-debt losses, and reduce the expenses associated with the collection of bills. Whether these advantages outweigh the relatively high cost of capital involved in cash discounts depends upon the seller's need for liquidity as well as alternative sources (and costs) of funds.

Trade discounts, which are also called *functional discounts,* are payments to channel members or buyers for performing some marketing function normally required of the manufacturer. These are legitimate as long as all buyers in the same category, such as wholesalers and retailers, receive the some discount privilege. Trade discounts were initially based on the operating expenses of each trade category, but they have now become more of a matter of custom in some industries. An example of a trade discount would be "40 percent, 10 percent off list price" for wholesalers. In other words, the wholesaler passes the 40 percent discount on to his or her customers (retailers) and keeps the 10

Figure 14.2 Cost Components of the Movie "Summer Lovers"

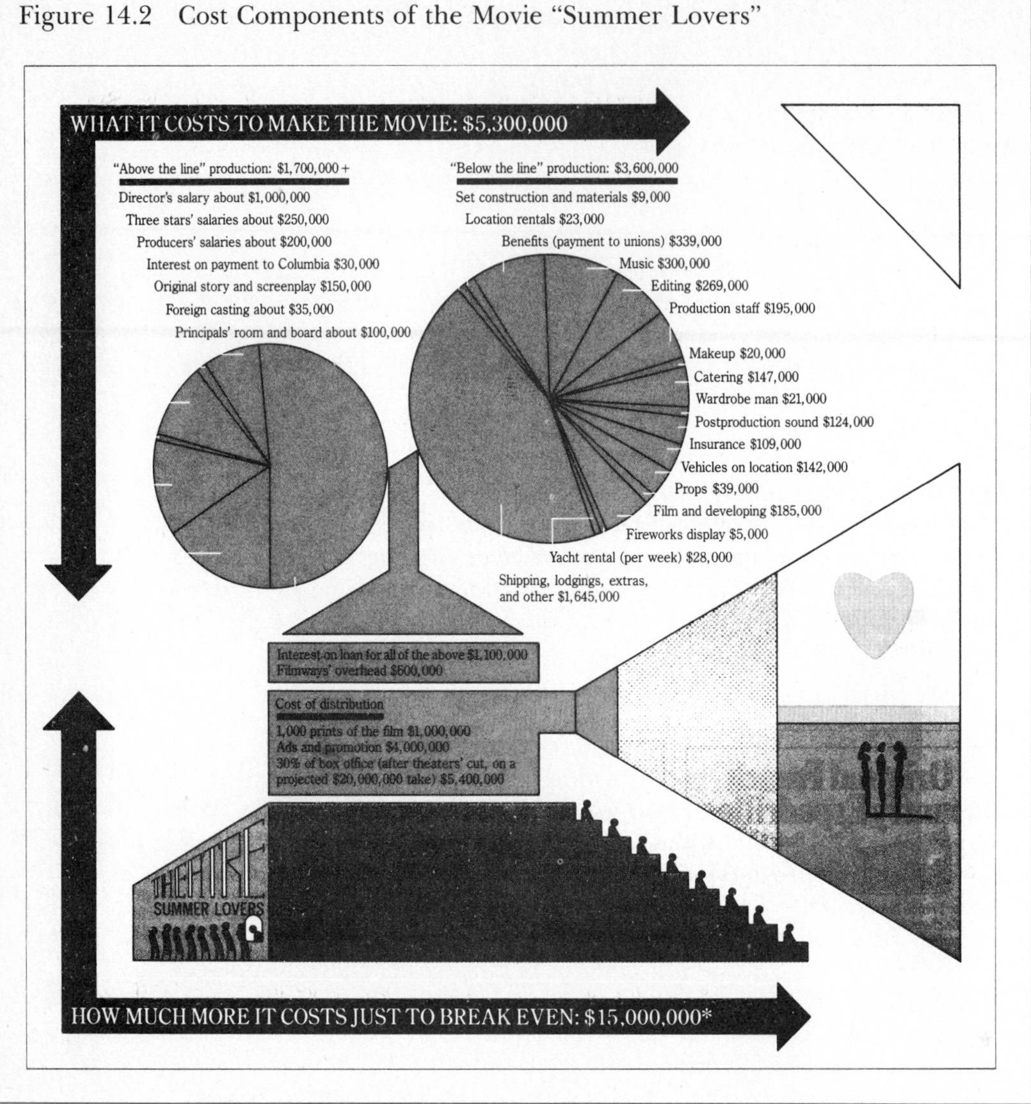

*Theater's take: 10% of box office or $2,000,000

Source: Stan Berkowitz and David Lees, "What Price Romance?" *Esquire* (July 1982), p. 107. Illustration by Nigel Holmes. Reprinted by permission of Nigel Holmes.

percent discount as payment for such activities as storing and transporting.

Quantity discounts are price reductions granted because of large purchases. These discounts are justified on the grounds that large-volume purchases reduce selling expenses and may shift a part of the storing, transporting, and financing functions to the buyer. Quantity dis-

Table 14.1 A Noncumulative Quantity Discount Schedule

Units Purchased	Price
1	List price
2–5	List price less 10 percent
5–10	List price less 20 percent
Over 10	List price less 25 percent

counts are lawful provided they are offered on the same basis to all customers.[2]

Quantity discounts may be either noncumulative or cumulative. *Noncumulative quantity discounts* are one-time reductions in list price. For instance, a firm might offer the discount schedule in Table 14.1. *Cumulative quantity discounts* are reductions determined by purchases over a stated time period. Annual purchases of $25,000 might entitle the buyer to an 8 percent rebate, while purchases exceeding $50,000 would mean a 15 percent refund. These reductions are really patronage discounts since they tend to bind the customer to one source of supply.

Allowances are similar to discounts in that they are deductions from the price the purchaser must pay. The major categories of allowances are trade-ins and promotional allowances. **Trade-ins** are often used in the sale of durable goods such as automobiles. They preserve the basic list price of the new item while reducing the amount the customer has to pay by allowing credit on a used object, usually of the kind being purchased. **Promotional allowances** are attempts to integrate promotional strategy in the channel. For example, manufacturers often provide advertising and sales-support allowances for other channel members. Automobile manufacturers have offered allowances to retail dealers several times in recent years so the dealers could reduce prices in order to stimulate sales.

Rebates are refunds by the seller of a portion of the purchase price. They have been used most prominently by automobile manufacturers eager to move models during periods of slow sales. Faced with intense competition in the home computer market, Texas Instruments reduced the price of its lowest-priced computer by one third with a $100 rebate offer.

In 1982, General Electric held the title of the leading rebater in the United States. The firm, which began using rebates in 1974 with offers

[2]See Asho K. Rao, "Quantity Discounts in Today's Market," *Journal of Marketing* (Fall 1980), pp. 44–51.

on radios and tape recorders, offered shoppers rebates on 62 small appliances, 23 refrigerators and ovens, 4 lighting fixtures, and some televisions and stereos. However, the extensive use of rebates by other firms and the problems involved in processing rebates led GE marketers to reduce rebates to about 30 items. As GE's vice-president in charge of hard goods pointed out, "The novelty and freshness have worn off. I don't think any product was ever rebated into a No. 1 position or into consumer recognition."[3]

Geographical Considerations

Geographical considerations are important in pricing when the shipment of heavy, bulky, low-unit-cost materials is involved. Prices may be quoted where either the buyer or seller pays all transportation charges or there is some type of expense sharing.

The way in which this problem is handled can greatly influence the success of a firm's marketing program by helping to determine the scope of the geographic market area the firm is able to serve, the vulnerability of the firm to price competition in areas located near its production facilities, the net margins earned on individual sales of the product, the ability of the firm to control or influence resale prices of distributors, and how difficult it is for sales people in the field to quote accurate prices and delivery terms to their potential customers.[4]

The seller has several alternatives in handling transportation costs.

FOB plant or *FOB origin* pricing provides a price that does not include any shipping charges. The buyer must pay all the freight charges. The seller pays only the cost of loading the merchandise aboard the carrier selected by the buyer. The abbreviation FOB means "free on board." Legal title and responsibility pass to the buyer once the purchase is loaded and a receipt is obtained from the representative of the common carrier.

Prices may also be shown as FOB origin—freight allowed. The seller permits the buyer to subtract transportation expenses from the bill. The amount the seller receives varies with the freight charges charged against the invoice. This alternative, called **freight absorption,** is commonly used by firms with high fixed costs because it permits a considerable expansion of their market since the same price is quoted regardless of shipping expenses.

The same price (including transportation expenses) is quoted to all buyers when a **uniform delivered price** is the firm's policy. Such pricing is the exact opposite of FOB prices. This system is often compared

[3]Robert Johnson, "Rebating Rises, but Unhappy Firms Can't Think of a Good Alternative," *The Wall Street Journal* (December 9, 1982), p. 31.

[4]Donald V. Harper, *Price Policy and Procedure* (New York: Harcourt Brace Jovanovich, 1966), p. 204.

Figure 14.3 Zone Pricing for a Chicago Firm

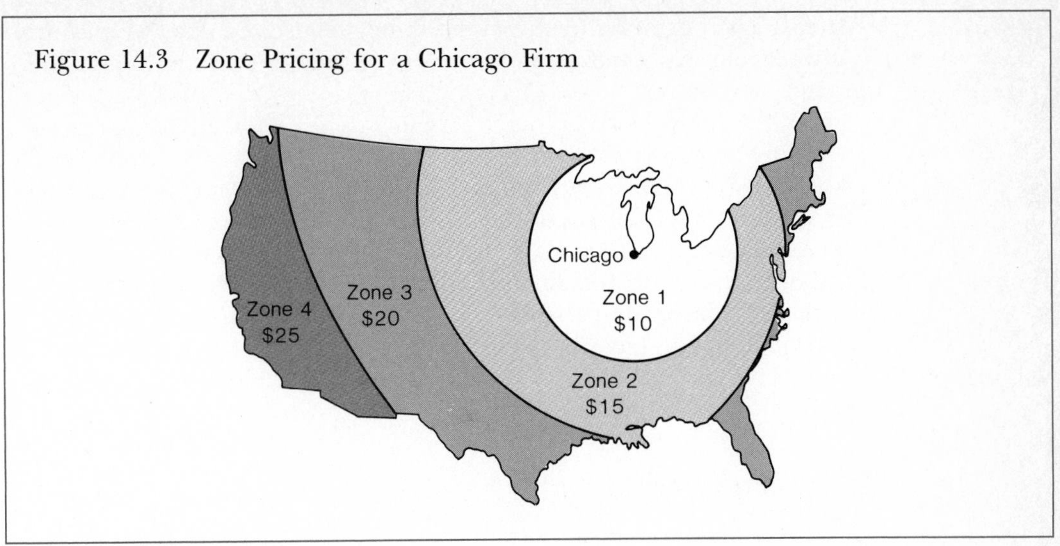

to the pricing of mail service. Hence, it is sometimes called *postage-stamp pricing.* The price that is quoted includes an average transportation charge per customer, which means that distant customers are actually paying a lesser share of selling costs while customers near the supply source pay what is known as *phantom freight* (the average transportation charge exceeds the actual cost of shipping).

In **zone pricing,** which is simply a modification of a uniform delivered pricing system, the market is divided into different zones and a price is established within each. By including average transportation costs for shipments within each zone as part of the delivered price of goods sold within the zone, phantom freight is reduced (but not eliminated). The U.S. Postal Service's package rates depend upon zone pricing. The primary advantage of this pricing policy is that it is easy to administer and enables the seller to be more competitive in distant markets. Figure 14.3 shows how a marketer located in Chicago might divide its market into geographic segments. All customers in Zone 1 would be charged $10 per unit freight while more distant customers would pay freight costs based upon the zone in which they are located.

In a **basing point system,** the price to the customer includes the price at the factory plus freight charges from the basing point nearest the buyer. The basing point is the point from which freight charges are determined; it is not necessarily the point from which the goods are shipped. Both single and multiple basing point systems are used. In either case, the actual shipping point is not considered in the price quotation.

During the 1940s, several legal cases involving the steel, glucose, and cement industries were brought against users of basing point pricing systems. The outcomes of the proceedings themselves were confusing, but the result was a reduction in the use of these systems as a basis for pricing.

The best-known basing point system was the *Pittsburgh-plus pricing* procedure that was used in the steel industry for many years. Steel price quotations contained freight charges from Pittsburgh regardless of where the steel was produced. As the industry matured, other steel centers, such as Chicago, Gary, Cleveland, and Birmingham, emerged. Pittsburgh, however, remained the basing point for steel pricing. This meant that a buyer in Terre Haute, Indiana, who purchased steel from a Gary mill had to pay phantom freight from Pittsburgh.

Price Policies

Price policies are an important ingredient in the firm's total image. They provide the overall framework and consistency needed in pricing decisions. A **pricing policy** is a general guideline based upon pricing objectives that is intended for use in specific pricing decisions.

Decisions concerning price structure generally tend to be more technical than decisions concerning price policies. Price structure decisions take the selected price policy as a given and use it to specify the discount structure details. Price policies have a greater strategic importance, though, particularly in relation to competitive considerations. They are the bases on which pricing decisions are made.

Many businesses would be well advised to spend more managerial effort in the establishment and periodic review of their pricing policies. Some years ago, a top executive aptly referred to the study and determination of prices as "creative pricing":

Few businesspersons, I am sure, would deny that every well-run business should have a price policy. We give a great deal of thought and planning to our engineering, manufacturing, advertising and sales promotion policies. Certainly the same kind of careful study and planning should be directed toward the formulation of those price policies that will best serve the various long-run objectives of our businesses. I call pricing based on such a well-formulated policy "creative pricing." There are probably better ways of saying it, but this term comes pretty close to describing what I believe to be the true function of pricing.[5]

Pricing policies must deal with varied competitive situations. The type of pricing policy used depends upon the environment within which the pricing decision must be made. The types of policies to con-

[5]Fred C. Foy, "Management's Part in Achieving Price Respectability," *Competitive Pricing* (New York: American Management Association, 1958), pp. 7–8.

The High-Class Nickel Discount

When the proprietor of a restaurant runs a newspaper ad for a meal costing less than $7, the price usually ends in 9—$5.99, for example—to imply a discount. A price in the $7 to $10 range usually ends in 5.

We owe the discovery of these facts of restaurant life to Lee Kreul, a professor at Purdue's School of Consumer and Family Sciences, who analyzed 467 prices from 242 restaurants advertised in 24 newspapers around the country. Restaurateurs switch from 9 to 5 as prices go up, he thinks, because at higher price levels "it takes more than 1 cent to create the discount illusion" and because patrons interested in paying more than $7 for a meal might think a price ending in 9 suggests "discounts, low quality, or hurried service."

Source: Jack C. Horn, "The High-Class Nickel Discount," *Psychology Today Magazine* (September 1982). Reprinted by permission.

sider are new product pricing, price flexibility, relative price levels, price lining, and promotional prices. They should all be calculated by using a pricing procedure similar to the ones described in Chapter 13.

Psychological Pricing

Psychological pricing is based upon the belief that certain prices or price ranges are more appealing to buyers than others. There is, however, no consistent research foundation for such thinking, and studies often report mixed findings.[6] Prestige pricing, mentioned in Chapter 13, is one of many forms of psychological pricing.

Odd pricing is a good example of the application of psychological pricing. Prices are set ending in numbers not commonly used for price quotations. A price of $16.99 is assumed to be more appealing than $17, supposedly because it is a lower figure.

Originally odd pricing was used to force clerks to make change, thus serving as a cash-control device within the firm.[7] Now it has become a customary feature of contemporary price quotations. For instance, one discounter uses prices ending in 3 and 7 rather than 5, 8, or 9, because

[6]See, for example, Zarrel V. Lambert, "Perceived Prices as Related to Odd and Even Price Findings," *Journal of Retailing* (Fall 1975), pp. 13–22, 78.

[7]See David M. Georgoff, "Price Illusion and the Effect of Odd-Even Retail Pricing," *Southern Journal of Business* (April 1969), pp. 95–103. See also Dik W. Twedt, "Does the 9 Fixation in Retailing Really Promote Sales?" *Journal of Marketing* (October 1965), pp. 54–55; Benson P. Shapiro, "The Psychology of Pricing," *Harvard Business Review* (July–August 1968), pp. 14–16; and David M. Georgoff, *Odd-Even Retail Price Endings: Their Effects on Value Determination, Product Perception, and Buying Propensities* (East Lansing: Michigan State University, 1972).

of a belief that customers regard price tags of $5.95, $6.98, $7.99 as *regular* retail prices, while $5.97 and $6.93 are considered *discount* prices.

Unit Pricing

Consumer advocates have often pointed out the difficulty of comparing consumer products that are available in different size packages or containers. Is a 28-ounce can selling for 75 cents a better buy than two 16-ounce cans priced at 81 cents or another brand that sells three 16-ounce cans for 89 cents? The critics argue that there should be a common way to price consumer products.

Unit pricing is a response to this problem. Under **unit pricing** all prices are stated in terms of some recognized unit of measurement (such as grams and liters) or a standard numerical count. There has been considerable discussion about legislating mandatory unit pricing. The American Marketing Association's board of directors has endorsed unit pricing, and many of the major food chains have adopted it.

Some supermarket chains have come to regard the adoption of unit pricing as a competitive tool upon which to base extensive advertising. However, unit pricing has not been particularly effective in improving the shopping habits of the urban poor. Others argue that unit pricing significantly increases retail operating costs.

The real question, of course, is whether unit pricing improves consumer decisions. One study found that the availability of unit prices resulted in consumer savings and that retailers also benefited when unit pricing led to greater purchases of store brands. The study concluded that unit pricing was valuable to both buyer and seller and that it merited full-scale usage.[8] Unit pricing is a major pricing policy issue that must be faced by many firms.

New Product Pricing

The pricing of new products presents a peculiar problem to marketers. The initial price that is quoted for an item may determine whether or not the product will eventually be accepted in the marketplace. The initial price also may affect the amount of competition that emerges.

Consider the options available to a company pricing a new product. While many choose to price at the level of comparable products, some select other alternatives (see Figure 14.4). A **skimming pricing** policy chooses a *relatively high* entry price. The name is derived from the expression "skimming the cream." One purpose of this strategy is to

[8]J. Edward Russo, "The Value of Unit Price Information," *Journal of Marketing Research* (May 1977), pp. 193–201.

allow the firm to recover its research and development costs quickly. The assumption is that competition will eventually drive the price to a lower level. Such was the case with electric toothbrushes. A skimming policy, therefore, attempts to maximize the revenue received from the sale of a new product before the entry of competition.

A skimming strategy is also useful in segmenting the overall market on a price basis. In the case of new products that represent significant innovations, relatively high prices convey an image of distinction and appeal to buyers who are less sensitive to price. Ball-point pens were introduced shortly after World War II at a price of about $20. Today the best-selling ball-point pens are priced at less than $1. Other examples of products that were introduced using a skimming strategy include television sets, Polaroid cameras, videocassette recorders, home computers, and pocket calculators. Subsequent price reductions allowed the marketers of these products to appeal to additional market segments that are more price sensitive.

A third advantage of a skimming strategy is that it permits the marketer to control demand in the introductory stages of the product's life cycle and adjust its productive capacity to match demand. A danger of low initial price for a new product is that demand may outstrip the firm's production capacity, resulting in consumer and middlemen complaints and possibly permanent damage to the product's image. Excess demand occasionally results in poor quality products as the firm strives to satisfy consumer desires with inadequate production facilities.

During the late growth and early maturity stages of the product life cycle, the price is typically reduced for two reasons: (1) the pressure of competition and (2) the desire to expand the product's market. Figure 14.4 shows that 10 percent of the market for Product X would buy the item at $10, while another 20 percent would buy at $8.75. Successive price declines will expand the firm's market as well as meet new competition.

A skimming policy has one chief disadvantage: it attracts competition. Potential competitors see that the innovating firms make large returns and also enter the market. This forces the price even lower than where it might be under a sequential skimming procedure. However, if a firm has a patent protection, as Polaroid had, or a proprietory ability to exclude competition, it may use a skimming policy for a relatively long period. Figure 14.5 indicates that 14.4 percent of the respondents in a recent pricing study used a skimming policy. Skimming also appears to be more common in industrial markets than in consumer markets.

Penetration pricing is the opposite policy in new product pricing. With this policy, an entry price for a product is lower than what is intended as the long-term price. The pricing study shown in Figure 14.5 suggests that penetration pricing is used more often in consumer

Figure 14.4 The Market for Product X

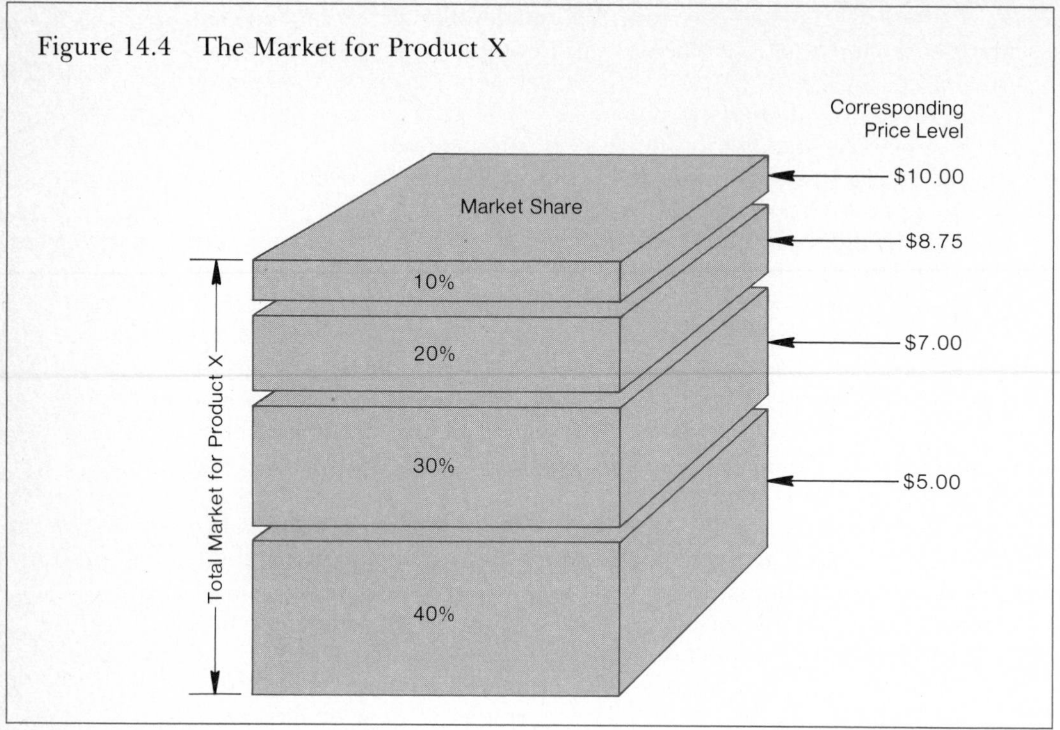

markets. Soaps and toothpastes are good examples of this kind of pricing.

The premise of penetration pricing is that an initially lower price will help secure market acceptance. Since the firm later intends to increase the price, brand popularity is critical to the success of a penetration policy. One advantage of such a policy is that it discourages competition, since the prevailing low price does not suggest the attractive returns associated with a skimming policy.

Penetration pricing is likely to be used in instances where demand for the new product or service is highly elastic. In such instances, large numbers of consumers are highly price sensitive. In addition, it is more likely to be used in instances where large scale operations and long production runs result in substantial reductions in the firm's production and marketing costs. Finally, penetration pricing may be appropriate in instances where the new product is likely to attract strong competitors when it is introduced. Such a strategy may allow it to reach the mass market quickly and capture a large share of the market prior to entry by competitors.

MCI Telecommunications competes with American Telephone & Telegraph with a penetration pricing strategy designed to attract long-distance telephone users. As Figure 14.6 shows, MCI's advertisements

Figure 14.5 Use of New Product Pricing Strategies

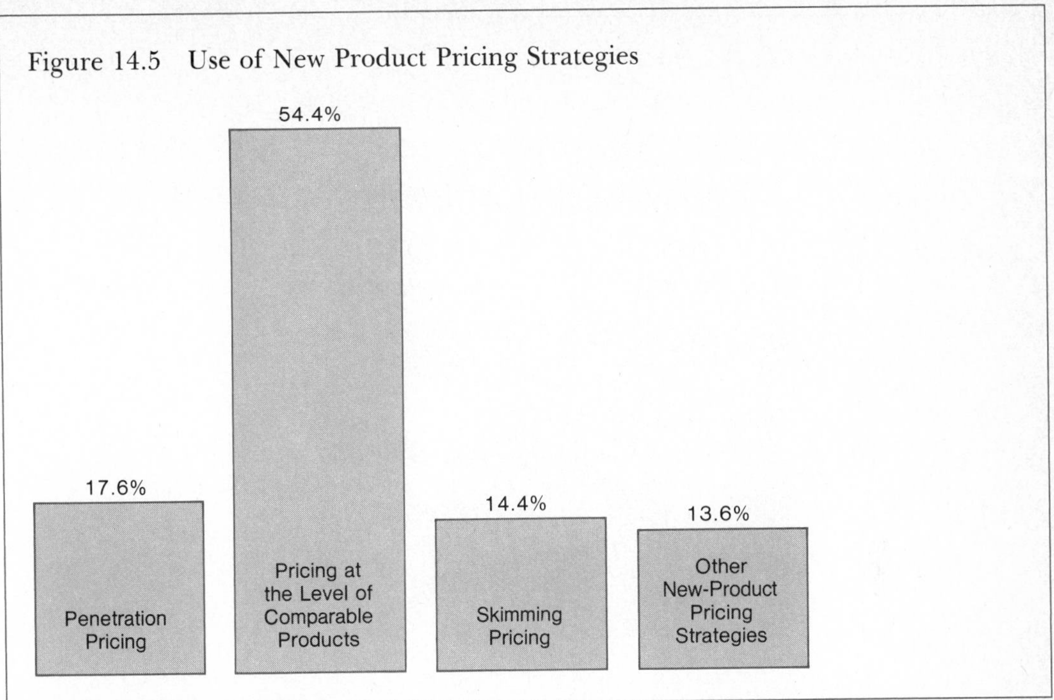

Source: *Pricing Objectives and Practices in American Industry: A Research Report* by Louis E. Boone and David L. Kurtz.

use AT&T's "Reach out and touch someone" headline, but they emphasize their price advantages with the statement, "You haven't been talking too much. You've just been paying too much."

The key decision, of course, is when to move the price to its intended level. Consumers tend to resist price increases; therefore, correct timing is essential. The solution depends upon the degree of brand loyalty that is achieved. Brand loyalty must be at the point where a price increase does not cause a disproportionate decrease in customers. A series of modest price changes, rather than a single large hike, also can retain customers.

A firm may, of course, decide to use neither a skimming nor a penetration price. It may try to price a new product at the point where it is intended to sell in the long run. All three new product pricing strategies are common.

Price Flexibility

Marketing executives must also determine company policy with respect to **flexible pricing.** Is the firm going to have just one price or pursue a variable price policy in the market? Generally, *one-price policies* charac-

Figure 14.6 Example of Penetration Pricing

Source: Reprinted by permission of MCI Telecommunications Corporation, Washington, D.C.

terize situations where mass selling is employed, while *variable pricing* is more common where individual bargaining typifies market transactions.

A one-price policy is common in retailing since it facilitates mass merchandising. For the most part, once the price is set, the manager can direct his or her attention to other aspects of the marketing mix. Flexible prices, by contrast, are found more in wholesaling and industrial markets. This does not mean that price flexibility exists only in manufacturing industries. A study of the retail home-appliance market concluded that persons who purchased identical products from the same dealer often paid different prices for them. The primary reasons for the differences were customer knowledge and bargaining strength.[9]

While variable pricing has the advantage of flexibility in selling situations, it may conflict with the Robinson-Patman Act provisions. It may also lead to retaliatory pricing by competitors, and it is not well received by those who have paid the higher prices.

Relative Price Levels

Another important pricing policy decision concerns the relative price level. Are the firm's prices to be set above, below, or at the prevailing market price? In economic theory this question would be answered by supply and demand analysis. However, from a practical viewpoint, marketing managers *administer* prices. Cost-oriented pricing allows them the option of subjectively setting the markup percentages.[10] Chapter 13 provided a framework for determining markups, but the decision maker must still develop a basic policy in regard to relative price levels.

Following the competition is one method of negating the price variable in marketing strategy, since it forces competitors to concentrate on other factors. Some firms choose to price below or above competition. These decisions are usally based on a firm's cost structure, overall marketing strategy, and pricing objectives.

Price Lining

Most companies sell a varied line of products. An effective pricing strategy considers the relationship among the firm's products rather than viewing each in isolation. Specifically, **price lining** is the practice of marketing merchandise at a limited number of prices.[11] For example, a clothier might have a $150 line of men's suits and a $225 line. Price lining is used extensively in retail selling; the old five-and-ten-cent stores were run this way. It can be an advantage to both retailer and customer. Customers can choose the price range they wish to pay, then concentrate on all the other variables, such as color, style, and material. The retailer can purchase and offer specific lines rather than a more general assortment.

[9]Walter J. Primeaux, Jr., "The Effect of Consumer Knowledge and Bargaining Strength on Final Selling Price: A Case Study," *Journal of Business* (October 1970), pp. 419–426. Another excellent article is James R. Krum, "Variable Pricing as a Promotional Tool," *Atlanta Economic Review* (November–December 1977), pp. 47–50.

[10]A technique for testing price levels above and below current levels is described in D. Frank Jones, "A Survey Technique to Measure Demand under Various Pricing Strategies," *Journal of Marketing* (July 1975), pp. 75–77.

[11]See Alfred R. Oxenfeldt, "Product Line Pricing," *Harvard Business Review* (July–August 1966), pp. 137–144. Also, an article by Kent B. Monroe and Andris A. Zoltners discusses some other interesting aspects of product line pricing. See "Pricing the Product Line during Periods of Scarcity," *Journal of Marketing* (Summer 1979), pp. 49–59.

Price lining requires that one identify the market segment or segments to which the firm is appealing. For example, "Samsonite sees its market not as all luggage, but as the 'medium-priced, hard-side' portion of the luggage trade."[12] The firm must decide how to line its product prices. A dress manufacturer might have lines priced at $39.95, $59.95, and $89.95. Price lining not only simplifies the administration of the pricing structure, but it also alleviates the confusion that can occur when all products are priced separately. Price lining is really a combined product/price strategy.

One problem with a price-line decision is that once it is made, retailers and manufacturers have difficulty in adjusting it. Rising costs, therefore, put the seller in the position of either changing the price lines, with the resulting confusion, or reducing costs by production adjustments, which opens the firm to the complaint that "XYZ Company's merchandise certainly isn't what it used to be!"

Promotional Prices

A **promotional price** is a lower-than-normal price used as an ingredient in a firm's selling strategy. In some cases promotional prices are recurrent, such as the annual shoe store "buy one pair of shoes, get the second pair for one cent" sale. Another such instance is a new pizza restaurant which has an opening special to attract customers. In other situations a firm may introduce a promotional model or brand to allow it to compete in another market.

Most promotional pricing is done at the retail level. One type is **loss leaders,** goods priced below cost to attract customers who, the retailer hopes, will then buy other regularly priced merchandise. The use of loss leaders can be effective. However, loss-leader pricing is not permitted in those states with unfair trade practices acts (see Chapter 2).

Probably one of the best innovators of this pricing method was Cal Mayne. He was one of the first marketers to systematically price specials and to evaluate their effect on gross margins and sales. Mayne increased sales substantially by featuring coffee, butter, and margarine at 10 percent below cost. Ten other demand items were priced competitively and at a loss when necessary to undersell competition. Still another group of so-called secondary demand items were priced in line with competition. Mayne based his pricing policy on the theory that a customer can only remember about 30 prices. Keep prices down on these items and the customer will stay with you.[13]

(The ethical or moral implications of this practice are not being considered here.)

[12]Robert A. Lynn, *Price Policies and Marketing Management* (Homewood, Ill.: Richard D. Irwin, 1967), p. 143.

[13]Bernie Faust, William Gorman, Eric Oesterle, and Larry Buchta, "Effective Retail Pricing Policy," *Purdue Retailer* (Lafayette, Ind.: Department of Agricultural Economics, 1963), p. 2.

Some studies, however, have reported considerable price confusion on the part of consumers. One study of consumer price recall reported that average shoppers misquoted the price they last paid for coffee by over 12 percent, toothpaste by over 20 percent, and green beans by 24 percent. While some people named the prices exactly, others missed by several hundred percent.[14]

Three potential pitfalls should be considered when one faces a promotional pricing decision:

1. Promotional prices may violate unfair trade practices acts in some states.
2. Some consumers are little influenced by price appeals, so promotional pricing will have little effect on them.
3. Continuous use of an artificially low rate may result in it being accepted as customary for the product. For example, poultry, which was used as a loss leader during the 1930s and 1940s, has suffered from such a phenomenon in the United States.

The Price-Quality Concept

One of the most researched aspects of pricing is the relationship between price and the consumer's perception of the product's quality. In the absence of other cues, price is an important indication of the way that the consumer perceives the product's quality.[15] The higher the price, the better the buyer believes the quality of the product to be. One study asked 400 people what terms they associated with the word *expensive.* Two thirds of the replies were related to high quality, words such as *best* and *superior*. The relationship between price and perceived quality is a well-documented fact in contemporary marketing.

Probably the best price-quality conceptualization is the idea of *price limits.*[16] It is argued that consumers have limits within which product quality perception varies directly with price. A price below the lower limit is regarded as too cheap, while one above the higher limit means it is too expensive.

[14]Karl A. Shilliff, "Determinants of Consumer Price Sensitivity for Selected Supermarket Products: An Empirical Investigation," *Akron Business & Economic Review* (Spring 1975), pp. 26–32.

[15]J. Douglass McConnell, "An Experimental Examination of the Price-Quality Relationship," *Journal of Business* (October 1968), pp. 439–444. A recent exchange on this issue appears in the May 1980 issue of the *Journal of Marketing Research*. See Peter C. Riesz, "A Major Price-Perceived Quality Study Re-Examined," pp. 259–262; and J. Douglass McConnell, "Comment on a Major Price-Perceived Quality Study Re-Examined," pp. 263–264.

[16]Kent B. Monroe and M. Venkatesan, "The Concepts of Price Limits and Psychophysical Measurement: A Laboratory Experiment," in *Marketing in Society and the Economy: Proceedings of the American Marketing Association,* (ed.) Phillip R. McDonald (Cincinnati: American Marketing Association, 1969), pp. 345–351.

This concept provides a reasonable explanation of the price-quality relationship. Most consumers do tend to set an acceptable price range when purchasing goods and services. The range, of course, varies among consumers depending upon their socioeconomic characteristics and buying dispositions. Consumers, nonetheless, should be aware that price is not necessarily an indicator of quality. In Canada the Alberta Department of Consumer and Corporate Affairs summarized seven price-quality research studies, six covering *Consumer Reports* analyses of 932 products between 1940 and 1977, and one for 43 products tested by *Canadian Consumer* between 1973 and 1977. Findings indicated that while there was a positive relationship between price and quality, the correlation was low (Spearman rank correlation = .25). About 25 percent of the products tested had a negative price-quality relation; that is, products which were ranked lower in performance had higher prices than products deemed superior by the U.S. and Canadian consumer testing organizations.[17]

Negotiated Prices and Competitive Bidding

Many situations involving government and industrial procurement are not characterized by set prices, particularly for nonrecurring purchases, such as a defense system for the armed forces. Markets such as these are growing at a fast pace. In the United States, government purchases now exceed 20 percent of the nation's gross national product; in Canada, the various government units spend almost one-half of the total GNP.

Competitive bidding is a process by which buyers request potential suppliers to make price quotations on a proposed purchase or contract. *Specifications* give a description of the item (or job) that the government or industrial firm wishes to acquire. One of the most important tasks in modern purchasing management is to describe adequately what the organization seeks to buy. This generally requires the assistance of the firm's technical personnel, such as engineers, designers, and chemists.

Competitive bidding strategy should employ the concept of *expected net profit,* which can be stated as:

$$\text{Expected Net Profit} = P\,(\text{Bid} - \text{Costs})$$

where P = the probability of the buyer accepting the bid.

Consider the following example. A firm is contemplating submission of a bid for a job that is estimated to cost \$23,000. One executive has proposed a bid of \$60,000; another, \$50,000. It is estimated that there

[17]*Market Spotlight* (Edmonton: Alberta Department of Consumer and Corporate Affairs, March 1979).

is a 40 percent chance of the buyer accepting Bid 1 ($60,000) and a 60 percent change that Bid 2 ($50,000) will be accepted. The expected net profit formula indicates that bid 2 would be best since its expected net profit is the higher.

Bid 1	Bid 2
ENP = 0.40 ($60,000 − $23,000)	ENP = 0.60 ($50,000 − $23,000)
= 0.40 ($37,000)	= 0.60 ($27,000)
= $14,800	= $16,200

The most difficult task in applying this concept is estimating the probability that a certain bid will be accepted. But this is not a valid reason for failing to quantify one's estimate. Experience can provide the foundation for such estimates.

In some cases industrial and governmental purchasers use *negotiated contracts* instead of inviting competitive bidding for a project. In these situations, the terms of the contract are set through talks between the buyer and a seller.

Where there is only one available supplier or where contracts require extensive research and development work, negotiated contracts are likely to be employed. For example, some state and local governments permit their agencies to negotiate purchases under a certain limit, say, $500 or $1,000. This policy is an attempt to eliminate the economic waste involved in obtaining bids for relatively minor purchases.

One response to inflation has been the use of escalator pricing.[18] An **escalator clause** allows the seller to adjust the final price based upon changes in the costs of the product's ingredients between the placement of the order and the completion of construction or delivery of the product. Such clauses typically base the adjustment calculation on the cost-of-living index or a similar indicator. While an estimated one third of all industrial marketers use escalator clauses in some of their bids, they are most commonly used with major projects involving long time periods and complex operations.

The Transfer Pricing Dilemma

One pricing problem peculiar to large-scale enterprises is that of determining an internal **transfer price**—the price for sending goods from one company profit center to another.[19] As companies expand, they

[18]See Mary Louise Hatten, "Don't Get Caught with Your Prices Down: Pricing in Inflationary Times," *Business Horizons* (March/April 1982), pp. 23–28.

[19]See Sylvain R. F. Plasschaert, *Transfer Pricing and Multinational Corporations* (New York: Praeger, 1979); and Roger Y. W. Tang, *Transfer Pricing Practices in the United States and Japan* (New York: Praeger, 1979).

tend to decentralize management. Profit centers are set up as a control device in the new decentralized operation. **Profit centers** are any part of the organization to which revenue and controllable costs can be assigned, such as a department.

In large companies, the centers can secure many of their resource requirements from within the corporate structure. The pricing problem becomes: what rate should Profit Center A (maintenance department) charge Profit Center B (sales department) for the cleaning compound used on B's floors? Should the price be the same as it would be if A did the work for an outside party? Should B receive a discount? The answer to these questions depends upon the philosophy of the firm involved.

The transfer pricing dilemma is an example of the variations that a firm's pricing policy must deal with. Consider the case of UDC-Europe, a Universal Data Corporation subsidiary that itself has ten subsidiaries. Each of the ten is organized on a geographic basis, and each is treated as a separate profit center. Intercompany transfer prices are set at the annual budget meeting. Special situations, like unexpected volume, are handled through negotiations by the subsidiary managers. If complex tax problems arise, UDC-Europe's top management may set the transfer price.[20]

Pricing in the Public Sector

The pricing of public services has also become an interesting, and sometimes troublesome, aspect of contemporary marketing. Traditionally, government services were very low cost or were priced using the full-cost approach: users paid all costs associated with the service. In more recent years, there has been a move toward incremental or marginal pricing, which considers only those expenses specifically associated with a particular activity. However, it is often difficult to determine the costs that should be assigned to a particular activity or service. Governmental accounting problems are often more complex than those of private enterprise.

Another problem in pricing public services is that taxes act as an *indirect* price of a public service. Someone must decide the relationship between the direct and indirect prices of such a service. A shift toward indirect tax charges (where an income or earnings tax exists) is charging on the *ability-to-pay* rather than the *use* principle.

[20]M. Edgar Bennett, "Case of the Tangled Transfer Price," *Harvard Business Review* (May–June 1977), p. 22.

The pricing of any public service involves a basic policy decision as to whether the price is an instrument to recover costs or a technique for accomplishing some other social or civic objective. For example, public health services may be priced near zero so as to encourage their use. On the other hand, parking fines in some cities are high to discourage use of private automobiles in the central business district. Pricing decisions in the public sector are difficult because political and social considerations often outweigh the economic aspects.

Summary

The main elements to consider in setting a price strategy are the organization for pricing decisions, pricing policies, price-quality relationships, negotiated prices, competitive bidding, transfer pricing, and pricing in the public sector. Methods for quoting prices depend on factors such as cost structures, traditional practices in a particular industry, and policies of individual firms. Prices quoted can involve list prices, market prices, cash discounts, trade discounts, quantity discounts, and allowances such as trade-ins, promotional allowances, and rebates.

Shipping costs often figure heavily in the pricing of goods. A number of alternatives exist for dealing with these costs: FOB plant, when the price does not include any shipping charges; freight absorption, when the buyer can deduct transportation expenses from the bill; uniform delivered price, when the same price—including shipping expenses—is charged to all buyers; and zone pricing, when a set price exists within each region.

Pricing policies vary among firms. Among the most common are psychological pricing; unit pricing; new product pricing, which includes skimming pricing and penetration pricing; price flexibility; relative pricing; price lining; and promotional pricing.

The relationship between price and consumer perception of quality has been the subject of much research. A well-known and accepted concept is that of price limits—limits within which the perception of product quality varies directly with price.

Sometimes, prices are negotiated through competitive bidding, a situation in which several buyers quote prices on the same service or good. At other times, prices depend on negotiated contracts, a situation in which the terms of the contract are set through talks between a particular buyer and seller.

A phenomenon of large corporations is transfer pricing, in which a company sets prices for transferring goods or services from one company profit center to another.

Pricing in the public sector has become a troublesome aspect of marketing. It involves decisions on whether the price of a public service serves as an instrument to recover costs or as a technique for accomplishing some other social or civic purpose.

The discussion of pricing decisions in Chapters 13 and 14 dealt with the second element of the firm's marketing mix. Chapters 15 through 18 examine the third component: marketing channels. In this section we analyze the activities, institutions, and problems involved in linking marketers with the consumer and user groups who constitute their market target.

Key Terms

list price
market price
cash discount
trade discount
quantity discount
trade-in
promotional allowance
rebate
FOB plant
freight absorption
uniform delivered price
zone pricing
basing point system
pricing policy
psychological pricing
odd pricing
unit pricing
skimming pricing
penetration pricing
price flexibility
price lining
promotional pricing
loss leader
escalator clause
transfer price
profit center

Review Questions

1. Who in the organization is most likely to be responsible for setting a price structure? Who is most likely to administer a price structure?
2. How are prices likely to be quoted?
3. Contrast the freight absorption and uniform delivered pricing systems.
4. List and discuss the reasons for establishing price policies.
5. What are the benefits derived from utilizing a skimming approach to pricing?
6. Under what circumstances is penetration pricing most likely to be used?
7. When does a price become a promotional price? What are the pitfalls in promotional pricing?
8. What is the relationship between prices and consumer perceptions of quality?
9. Contrast negotiated prices and competitive bidding.
10. What types of decisions must be made in the pricing of public services? What role could escalator clauses play in this area?

Discussion Questions and Exercises

1. What type of new product pricing would be appropriate for the following items:
   a. A new deodorant
   b. A fuel additive that increases mileage by 50 percent
   c. A new pattern of fine china
   d. A new ultrasensitive burglar, smoke, and fire alarm
   e. A new video game
2. How are prices quoted for each of the following:
   a. An American Airlines ticket to Montreal
   b. An aluminum siding installation by a local contractor
   c. A new jogging suit from a sportswear retailer
   d. A new Nissan Stanza
3. Comment on the following statement: Unit pricing is ridiculous because everyone ignores it.
4. Prepare a list of arguments that might be used in justifying a basing point pricing system.
5. What criteria should be considered for transfer pricing in a large corporation like Westinghouse Electric?

CASES FOR PART 5

Case 5.1
Jai Lai Restaurant

The Jai Lai Restaurant is a large, high-quality, "cloth tablecloth and napkins" establishment. Its colorful history dates back to 1933, when Jasper E. Wottring founded the original cafe. He conceived the name from the game jai alai, which he observed being played while visiting Florida. The *a* was removed from *alai* in the belief it would make the name easier to recognize and remember.

In the early 1950s, the Jai Lai was moved to a new building with a seating capacity of 600. The large dining area was separated into five rooms by Spanish-style open arches and the interior included such interesting touches as a large bar dating back to pre-Prohibition days and exotic fish in lighted aquariums mounted in the perimeter walls.

The present owner and president of the corporation, Ted Girves, bought out one of the partners in 1963 and became a 50 percent stockholder. Mr. Wottring had died in the late 1950s. His son Dave is general manager. This new management team has been responsible for several changes, including hiring more waitresses instead of waiters and expanding the menu.

Slow Business during the Week

In early 1975, mangement decided to tackle a problem which seems to plague the restaurant business in general—how to generate more business on the slow weekdays (Monday–Thursday). The Jai Lai had no trouble drawing turn-away crowds on the weekends, yet weekday patronage was disappointing. Whereas they would typically serve 1,200–1,300 people on Saturday night, the average Monday crowd would total only 350–400 people.

Management examined certain approaches, such as outright discounting and coupons, which had been adopted by competitors, and concluded that such programs might harm the restaurant's quality image and convey the impression that they were "hurting" for business. Any program they adopted would have to be distinctive and effective, yet not jeopardize the quality image they had worked so long and hard to achieve.

Proposal—A Rebate Program

The automotive rebate programs then in progress inspired the idea of a similar

Source: From *Cases for Analysis in Marketing*, 2d ed. by W. Wayne Talarzyk. Copyright 1980 by The Dryden Press, a division of Holt, Rinehart and Winston, Inc. Reprinted by permission.

"rebate" on selected dinners. Customers purchasing the selected dinners on Monday through Thursday evenings would receive the rebate in the form of silver dollars at the time the bill was paid.

There was a certain logic behind the rebate format:

- *A silver dollar rebate, as opposed to a simple discount or paper-money rebate, would be much more distinctive, stimulating conversation and recall.*
- *While other programs such as coupons or discounts actually reduced the amount of the bill and thus tended to reduce tip income and hurt employee morale, a rebate would have but a limited effect in this direction.*
- *By getting a full-priced check, the customer would see that prices were not high normally.*
- *Management could vary the dinners eligible for rebate and observe the resulting customer behavior.*

It was decided that the program would have the following objectives:

1. To better utilize the restaurant's capacity during the week
2. To increase profitability[1]
3. To broaden its customer base, i.e., to attract new, regular customers.

The last objective was considered particularly important. The mangement felt that even if the restaurant only broke even on the incremental weekday business, the program would still be worthwhile if it attracted new, regular clientele. Such people might return on a weekend or on a weekday (ordering a dinner not eligible for rebate) and thus improve overall profitability. The management felt particularly confident that the restaurant's quality food and atmosphere would induce many of the first-time visitors to return.

Implementation of the Program

The rebate program was initiated in early March, coupled with Sunday newspaper advertising to build awareness of the program. Examples of the newspaper advertising are shown in Exhibit 1.

After seven months, management decided to see if the size of the rebate influenced sales. In October, therefore, the rebate was changed from $2.00 to $1.00 on selected items.

Although dollar value per check decreased slightly, revenue overall rose substantially. The restaurant was able to handle the increased number of patrons with only a 20 percent increase in the weekday work force.

Review of the Program

Management, although encouraged by the response to the rebate program, had several misgivings at the end of the program's first three months. First, weekend business had hardly been affected by the program. Second, management had noted that as soon as a dinner was no longer eligible for rebate, its sales immediately plummeted to pre-rebate levels. (Of course, sales of dinners newly placed on rebate immediately rose.) Third, the incremental sales of a dinner placed on rebate seemed to be greatly affected by the original price of the dinner.

[1] In order to increase profitability, there would have to be a substantial sales increase of relatively expensive dinners. Jai Lai's total direct costs amounted to about 67–75 percent of the menu price with 40–50 percent being direct food costs and 27–30 percent being direct labor costs.

Inexpensive dinners placed on rebate suddenly became extremely popular, whereas expensive dinners experienced relatively modest increases. The Club Steak Dinner ($4.95) went from average Monday–Thursday sales of 45 weekly to 600–700 weekly within two weeks of being made eligible for rebate. After four weeks, the Porterhouse Steak Dinner ($8.50) replaced the Club Steak Dinner on the list of eligible rebate dinners. The result: Club Steak sales immediately slipped to Monday–Thursday sales of 50 weekly; Portherhouse sales increased, but not so dramatically—from Monday–Thursday sales of 20 weekly to about 210 weekly.

In conclusion, management began to view their new Monday–Thursday trade not as new, regular customers, but more as bargain hunting "opportunists" who would not patronize the restaurant except as induced by the rebate. At this point in time they are trying to evaluate the merits of continuing the rebate program.

Discussion Questions

1. Should the rebate program continue?
2. What other options are available to management in its attempts to increase Monday–Thursday business?

Exhibit 1 Examples of Newspaper Advertisements for Rebate Program

Case 5.2
Executive Inns, Inc.

Early in 1979, Charles Rabb, manager of the Executive Inn, had just completed reading a new book on pricing. As he leaned back in his chair, he pondered some pricing principles that the book's author had expounded. To be sure that he had the principles correctly in his mind, he reopened the book and reread the principles.

The correct pricing of a product line should follow three principles:

1. *Each product should be priced correctly in relation to all other products in the line. Specifically, perceptively*

Source: This case was prepared by Kent B. Monroe, Virginia Polytechnic Institute and State University. Reprinted by permission.

noticeable differences in the products should be equivalent to perceived value differences.

2. *The highest and lowest prices in the product line have a special complementary relation to other products in the line and should be priced so as to facilitate desired buyer perceptions.*
3. *Price differentials between products in the product line should get wider as price increases over the product line. This principle follows the behavioral findings that price perception follows a logarithmic scale rather than an arithmetic or linear scale.*[1]

Rabb realized that his director of marketing and sales had completed a study of room sales several weeks ago, and he asked his secretary to get a copy of the report for him to read that evening.

History of the Hotel

The Executive Inn is a 900-room hotel located in a major city in the southeastern United States. The hotel first opened for business in the spring of 1969, and since that time has had an average room occupancy of 80 percent. Room occupancy had peaked at 87 percent in 1976. Part of the decline in the succeeding two years was due to a number of new hotels that had been opened in the past few years. Indeed, about 1,500 new hotel rooms had become available in 1977. Another 500-room hotel was under construction three blocks away with an expected occupancy date of mid-1980.

Over the past seven years, the hotel had successfully attracted a major portion of its room business from traveling business and salespeople. The hotel was located close to the downtown business district, and travelers had immediate access to the airport expressway. The drive to the airport took about 15 minutes in normal traffic. Also, the hotel was about five blocks away from the state university. Parents, alumni, and friends of the university have found the hotel a convenient place to stay when coming to sports, cultural, and other campus events. Although its location was not as attractive for tourists, many tourists stayed in the hotel when visiting the city.

The Marketing and Sales Director's Report

That evening Rabb read the report of the marketing and sales director. The report was organized in three parts: analysis of room demand, comparison of the supply of rooms with demand, and ranking rooms according to noticeable physical attributes.

The first exhibit shows that the hotel had 900 rooms and 21 different single and double occupancy room rates (see Table 1). The director had taken two samples of 14 days each, recording the number of persons paying each single room rate on each day. These data were converted into the average percentage of persons paying each rate, as shown in Table 2.

The director then assumed that if 5 percent of the guests occupied a $16 room, then 5 percent of 900, or 45 rooms, was the demand for a $16 room. Using this reasoning, he developed Figure 1.

Finally, all of the rooms in the hotel were evaluated according to factors of noticeable differences. The noticeable attributes were room size, location in terms of room floor and view, and facilities

[1]Kent B. Monroe, *Pricing: Making Profitable Decisions* (New York: McGraw-Hill, 1979).

Table 1
Price and Room Classification Schedule

Room Price		
Single Occupancy	Double Occupancy	Number of Rooms
$16.00	$19.50	30
16.50	20.00	40
17.00	20.50	30
17.50	21.00	300
18.00	21.50	200
18.50	22.00	50
19.00	22.50	30
19.50	23.00	30
20.00	23.50	60
21.00	24.50	10
22.00	25.50	10
24.00	27.50	25
26.00	29.50	10
27.00	30.50	5
27.50	31.00	5
28.00	31.50	10
29.00	32.50	5
29.50	33.00	20
30.00	33.50	5
32.00	35.50	15
35.00	38.50	10

Table 2
Sample Occupancy Data (Single Rate)

Room Price	Average Percentage Paying Price	Cumulative Percentage
$16.00	5.0%	5.0%
16.50	4.0	9.0
17.00	8.0	17.0
17.50	8.0	25.0
18.00	10.0	35.0
18.50	20.0	55.0
19.00	10.0	65.0
19.50	8.0	73.0
20.00	7.0	80.0
21.00	5.0	85.0
22.00	5.0	90.0
24.00	3.0	93.0
26.00	1.0	94.0
27.00	1.0	95.0
27.50	0.5	95.5
28.00	0.5	96.0
29.00	1.0	97.0
29.50	1.0	98.0
30.00	0.5	98.5
32.00	1.0	99.5
35.00	0.5	100.0

available such as television, air conditioning, refrigerator, and size of bedding. This part of the study revealed that the hotel had nine noticeably different types of rooms.

Room Prices

Rabb believed that the Executive Inn was not following the pricing principles he had just read about, and he decided to ask the marketing and sales director to recommend a new pricing schedule. Currently, the prices were competitive with other hotels in the city, but Rabb was concerned that the current pricing schedule was too complex and probably was not correct for his market.

Discussion Questions

1. What is wrong with the current pricing scheme used by Executive Inn, Inc.? Explain.
2. Using the pricing principles discussed in the case, develop a pricing strategy for Executive Inn.
3. How will the opening of additional rooms among competitors affect Executive Inn's pricing strategy? Explain.

Figure 1 Room Demand at Current Prices

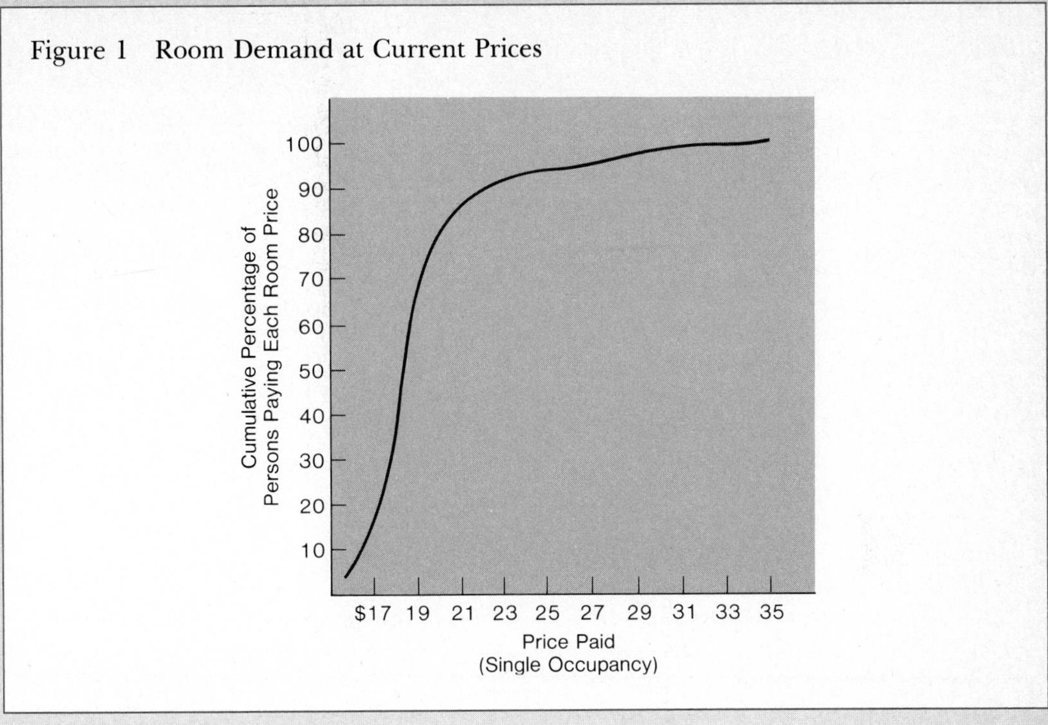

Wroe Alderson

Perhaps the foremost theorist among marketing scholars during the twentieth century was Wroe Alderson (1898–1965). Although Alderson's varied career included government, private business, private consulting, and academe, his intellect and curiosity led him to read widely in such diverse areas as cybernetics, economics, management, sociology, and psychology, and to draw heavily from these fields in constructing his own theory of marketing. In 1959, he became a professor of marketing at the Wharton School of Finance and Commerce at the University of Pennsylvania, a post he held until his death in 1965.

Alderson's concern for the advancement of science in marketing was attested in the pioneering article he coauthored with Reavis Cox, entitled "Toward a Theory of Marketing," in the October 1948 issue of the *Journal of Marketing*. That year he also served as president of the American Marketing Association. Two years later, he and Cox collected a symposium of essays with the title *Theory in Marketing* (Irwin, 1950). His first extended theory of marketing appeared in his landmark book *Marketing Behavior and Executive Action* (Irwin, 1957). In it he presented his functional theory of marketing.

Robert Bartels, in his book, *The History of Marketing Thought* (Grid, 1976), summarized Wroe Alderson's contributions as follows:

(The functional theory) represented an effort to show the relationships of marketing thought to knowledge developed in the other social sciences. His analysis proceeded from a concept of market behavior as group behavior and of individuals seeking to achieve their purposes through organized behavior systems. He regarded their market behavior as problem-solving action. Marketing organizations were seen as behavior systems developed to serve the market, their operations governed by principles of action that he called functionalism (p. 158).

Alderson completed the manuscript for his book *Dynamic Marketing Behavior* (Irwin, 1965) shortly before his death.

6

DISTRIBUTION

This section deals with the third element of the marketing mix and focuses on the problems, activities, and institutions involved in moving the appropriate products and services to the firm's chosen market target. Channel selection and strategy are the subject of Chapter 15, while Chapters 16 and 17 analyze wholesalers and retailers—the marketing institutions that comprise many marketing channels. Chapter 18 focuses on physical distribution—the physical movement of products from producer to consumer or industrial user.

15

Chapter Objectives

1. To relate channel strategy to the other variables of the marketing mix.
2. To explain the role of distribution channels in marketing strategy.
3. To describe the various types of distribution channels.
4. To explain the concept of power in the distribution channel.
5. To outline the major channel strategy decisions.
6. To discuss conflict and cooperation in the distribution channel.

CHANNEL STRATEGY

How can a firm with an 80 percent market share have problems? That is exactly the situation which faced Binney & Smith Inc., the makers of Crayola crayons. The firm had continued to show sales increases over the years because of the strong market position and population growth. Binney & Smith remained complacent even after its market target—children—began to decline in numbers.

The company continued to concentrate on the education market and selling through school-supply distributors. Binney & Smith largely ignored mass merchandisers like K mart and Woolworth, spending 60 percent of its marketing dollars on their traditional market. Yet the firm's education market was only yielding 30 percent of its sales.

Binney & Smith acquired a poor reputation with mass merchandisers. They turned down requests for extended payment terms which were common practice among toy manufacturers who also sold to these large retailers. In addition, Binney & Smith's promotions were timed wrong because they had traditionally regarded their product as nonseasonal.

Since then, new management has drastically altered the crayon producer's distribution strategy. Binney & Smith now concentrates on mass merchandisers. Its sales force has distributed Crayola Fun Centers, an in-store display for 37 Crayola products. The company also puts substantial monies into a cooperative advertising program, whereby it shares promotional costs with retailers.

The success of their new distribution strategy is quite evident. Binney & Smith's Easton, Pennsylvania plant is running three shifts a day. In fact, the company has decided to spend $15 million expanding its capacity. In the meantime, Binney & Smith's sales force has stopped distributing new Fun Center racks, a subtle bit of demarketing necessitated by its successful new distribution strategy.[1]

The Conceptual Framework

Basic channel strategy—such as the decisions reached by Binney & Smith—are the beginning focus for a discussion of the distribution function and its role in the marketing mix. Part Four considered product development, strategy, and decisions. Part Five considered the pricing function of marketing.

Channel strategy is the focus of the opening chapter in Part Six, which deals with the distribution function. This chapter covers such basic issues as the role and types of distribution channels; power in the distribution channel; channel strategy decisions; and conflict and cooperation in the channel of distribution. Later Chapters 16 and 17 deal with wholesaling and retailing, the marketing institutions in the distribution channel. Chapter 18 ends Part Six with a discussion of physical distribution. The starting point of this section is to look at what marketers call distribution channels.[2]

Although Dresser Industries' gasoline pumps are made in Salisbury, Maryland, they are sold all over the United States. Boeing aircraft made in the state of Washington is marketed to numerous overseas airlines. The Volkswagen bought by someone in Dallas was probably made in New Stanton, Pennsylvania. In each case, methods must be devised to bridge the geographic gap between producer and consumer. Distribution channels are used to provide consumers with a convenient means of obtaining the products and services they desire. **Distribution chan-**

[1]Steven F. Lax, "The Greening of Crayola," *Forbes* (April 12, 1982), pp. 190, 192.

[2]An interesting discussion appears in Michael M. Pearson, "Ten Distribution Myths," *Business Horizons* (May–June 1981), pp. 17–23.

nels refer to the various marketing institutions and the interrelationships responsible for the physical and title flow of goods and services from producer to consumer or industrial user. Middlemen are the marketing institutions in the distribution channel. A **middleman** is a business firm operating between the producer and the consumer or industrial purchaser. The term therefore includes both wholesalers and retailers.

Wholesaling is the activities of persons or firms who sell to retailers, other wholesalers, and industrial users but do not sell in significant amounts to ultimate consumers. The terms *jobber* and *distributor* are considered synonymous with wholesaler in this book.

Confusion can result from the practices of some firms that operate both wholesaling and retailing operations. Sporting goods stores, for example, often maintain a wholesaling operation in marketing a line of goods to high schools and colleges as well as operating retail stores. For the purposes of this text, it is simpler to conceive of such operations as two separate institutions.

A second source of confusion is the misleading practice of some retailers who claim to be wholesalers. Such stores may actually sell at wholesale prices and can validly claim to do so. However, stores that sell products purchased by individuals for their own use and not for resale are by definition **retailers,** not wholesalers.

The Role of Distribution Channels in Marketing Strategy

Distribution channels play a key role in marketing strategy since they provide the means by which goods and services are conveyed from their producers to consumers and users. The importance of distribution channels can be explained in terms of the utility that is created and the functions that are performed.

The Creation of Utility

Distribution channels create three types of utility for consumers. *Time utility* is created when distribution channels have products and services available for sale when the consumer wants to purchase them. *Place utility* is created when goods and services are available in a convenient location. *Possession utility* is created when title to the goods passes from the producer or intermediary to the purchaser.

Swimwear provides a good illustration of the distribution channel creating time utility. Swimwear for the coming spring and summer has already been produced in the months of December and January and is en route to retail stores throughout the nation. Swimwear manufacturers' success or failure depends on consumer reactions to new colors, styles, and fabrics that are decided on months earlier. But the swimsuits are ready in the store for the first warm day in March or April that customers decide to shop for them.

The provision of place utility is illustrated by flight insurance vending machines in airport terminals or a stock of *TV Guides* near a supermarket checkout counter. Similarly, the offices of a real estate broker, escrow company, or lending institution are often used to create possession utility. Legal title and possession of a new home is often transferred to a buyer in these settings.

The Functions Performed by Distribution Channels[3]

The distribution channel performs several functions in the overall marketing system. These include facilitating the exchange process; sorting to alleviate discrepancies in assortment; standardizing transactions; and the search process.[4]

Facilitating the Exchange Process The evolution of distribution channels began with the exchange process described in Chapter 1. As market economies grew, the exchange process itself became complicated. There were more producers and potential buyers, so middlemen came into existence to facilitate transactions by cutting the number of marketplace contacts. For example, if ten orchards in eastern Washington each sell to six supermarket chains, there are a total of 60 transactions. If the producers set up and market their apples through a cooperative, the number of contacts declines to 16. This process is described in detail in Chapter 16.

Sorting to Alleviate Discrepancies in Assortment Another essential function of the distribution channel is to adjust discrepancies in assortment via a process known as sorting. A producer tends to maximize the quantity of a limited line of products while the buyer needs a minimum quantity of a wide selection of alternatives. **Sorting** is the process that alleviates such discrepancies by adjusting the buyer's and the producer's needs.

Figure 15.1 shows an example of the sorting process. First, an individual producer's output is divided into separate homogeneous categories such as the various types and grades of apples. These apples are then combined with the similar crops of other orchards, a process

[3]This section is adapted by permission from Louis W. Stern and Adel I. El-Ansary, *Marketing Channels*, 2d ed. (Englewood Cliffs, N.J.: Prentice-Hall, Inc., 1982), pp. 6–11.

[4]These functions were developed in Wroe Alderson, "Factors Governing the Development of Marketing Channels," in *Marketing Channels for Manufactured Products*, (ed.) Richard M. Clewitt (Homewood, Ill.: Richard D. Irwin, 1954), pp. 5–22.

Figure 15.1 The Sorting Process

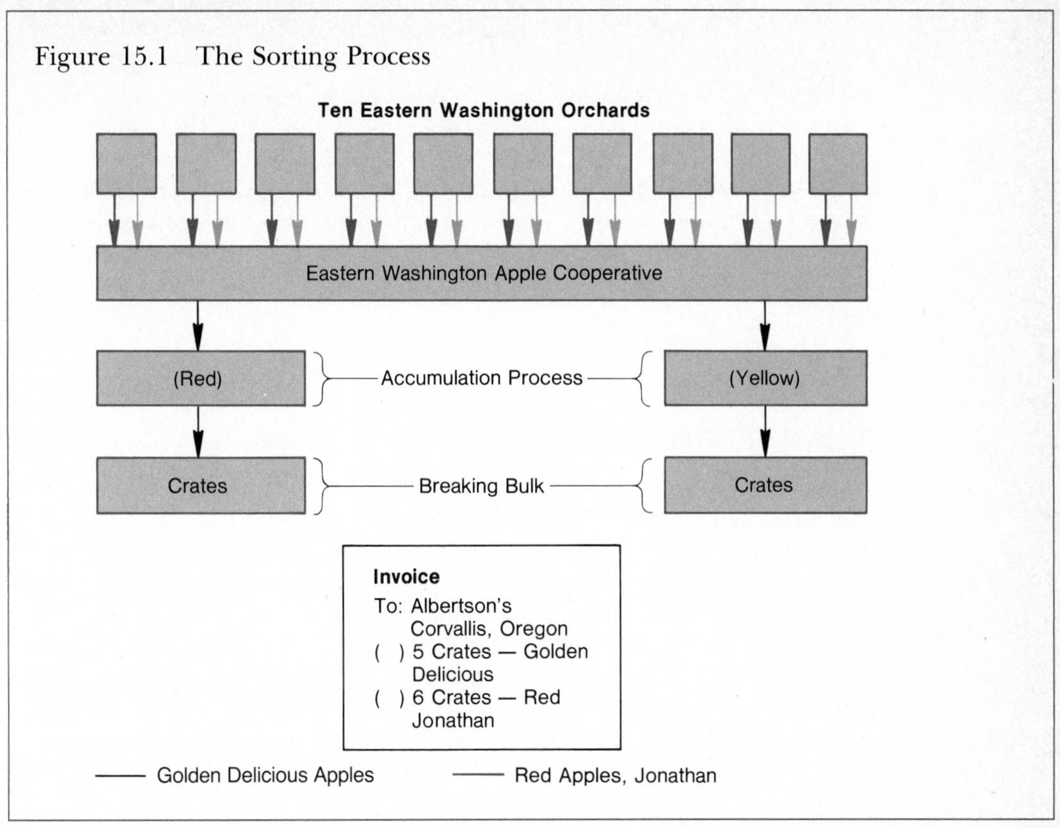

known as accumulation. These accumulations are broken down into smaller units or divisions, such as crates of apples. This is often called "breaking bulk" in marketing literature. Finally, an assortment is built for the next level in the distribution channel. For example, the eastern Washington cooperative might prepare an assortment of four crates of Golden Delicious and six crates of Red Jonathan apples for an Albertson's supermarket in Corvallis, Oregon.

Standardizing the Transaction If each transaction in a complex market economy was subject to negotiation, the exchange process would be chaotic. Distribution channels standardize exchange transactions in terms of the product, such as the grading of apples into types and grades, and the transfer process itself. Order points, prices, payment terms, delivery schedules, and purchase lots tend to be standardized by distribution channel members. For example, supermarket buyers might have on-line communications links with the cooperative cited in Figure 15.1. Once a certain stock position is reached, more apples would automatically be ordered from either current output or cold storage.

The Search Process Distribution channels also accommodate the search behavior for both buyers and sellers. (Search behavior was discussed earlier in Chapter 7.) Buyers are searching for specific products and services to fill their needs, while sellers are attempting to find what consumers want. A college student looking for some Golden Delicious apples might go to the fruit section of Albertson's in Corvallis, Oregon. Similarly, the manager of that department would be able to provide the Washington cooperative with information about sales trends in his or her marketplace.

Types of Distribution Channels

Literally hundreds of marketing channels exist today, and it is obvious that there is no such thing as one best distribution channel. The best channel for Electrolux vacuum cleaners may be directly from manufacturer to consumer through a sales force of 15,000 to 20,000 people. The best channel for frozen french fries may be from food processor to agent middleman to merchant wholesaler to supermarket to consumer. Instead of searching for the best channel for all products, the marketing manager must analyze alternative channels in light of consumer needs to determine the most appropriate channel (or channels) for the firm's products and services.[5]

Even when the proper channels have been chosen and established, the marketing manager's channel decisions have not ceased. Channels, like so many marketing variables, change, and today's ideal channel may prove disastrous in a few years. For example, Ocean Spray Cranberries, Inc. uses its regular sales force to sell its cranapple, grapefruit, and tomato-vegetable juices and products. However, in 25 to 30 percent of the United States, it is testing a commission program that pays H.J. Heinz Co. sales representatives to sell its food-service product line to restaurants.[6]

Until the 1960s, the typical channel for beer was from brewery to local distributor (wholesaler) to local pubs, since most beer was consumed in these retail outlets. The majority of the beer purchases in the 1980s are made at local supermarkets, and the channel for Busch, Tuborg, Stroh's, Heineken, and Miller Lite must reflect these changes in consumer buying patterns.

[5]Wilke English, Dale M. Lewison, and M. Wayne DeLozier, "Evolution in Channel Management: What Will Be Next?" in *Proceedings of the Southwestern Marketing Association,* (eds.) Robert H. Ross, Frederic B. Kraft, and Charles H. Davis (Wichita, Kansas: 1981), pp. 78–81.

[6]"Ocean Spray's Juicy Future," *Business Week* (November 23, 1981), pp. 71, 74.

Figure 15.2 Alternative Distribution Channels

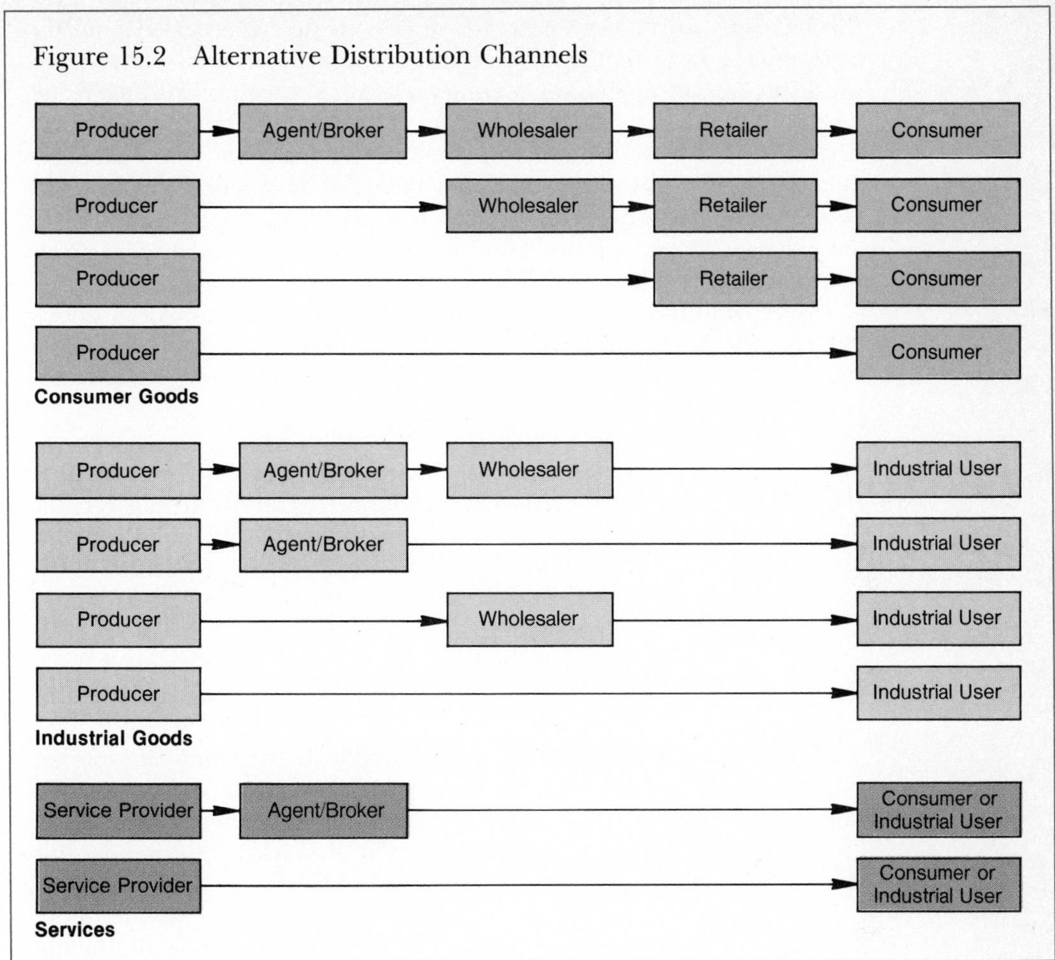

Alternative Distribution Channels

Figure 15.2 depicts the major channels available for marketers of consumer and industrial products and services. In general, industrial products channels tend to be shorter than consumer goods channels due to geographic concentrations of industrial buyers and a relatively limited number of purchasers. In addition, retail sales are characteristic only of consumer goods purchases; therefore, the retailer is not found in industrial channels. Service channels also tend to be short. This is due to the intangibility of services and the need to maintain personal relationships in the channel.

Producer to Consumer or Industrial User The simplest, most direct distribution channel is not necessarily the most popular, as evidenced by the relatively small percentage of dollar volume of sales that moves along this route. Less than 5 percent of all consumer goods move from producer to consumer. For a company like Mary Kay Cosmetics, the direct producer to consumer channel is very effective. Mary Kay Ash began her firm with nine sales representatives. She now employs 122,000 beauty consultants, and her company has annual revenues of $250 million.[7] Tupperware, Avon, and numerous mail-order houses are other examples of the firms whose products move directly from manufacturer to ultimate consumer.

Direct channels are much more important to the industrial goods market. Most major installations, accessory equipment, and even fabricated parts and raw materials are marketed through direct contacts between seller and buyer.

Producer to Wholesaler to Retailer to Consumer The traditional channel for consumer goods proceeds from producer to wholesaler to retailer to user. It is the method used by small retailers and by literally thousands of small producers that make limited lines of products. Small companies with limited financial resources utilize wholesalers as immediate sources of funds and as a means to reach the hundreds of retailers who will stock their products. Small retailers rely on wholesalers as buying specialists who ensure a balanced inventory of goods produced in various regions of the world.

The wholesaler's sales force is responsible for reaching the market with the producer's output. Many manufacturers also use specialized sales representatives, who call on retailers and help merchandise their line. These representatives serve as sources of market information, but they do not actually sell the product.

Producer to Wholesaler to Industrial User Similar characteristics in the industrial market often lead to the utilization of middlemen between the producer and industrial purchaser. The term *industrial distributor* is commonly utilized in the industrial market to refer to those wholesalers who take title to the goods they handle. Office equipment is a good example of this channel. In an effort to orient its own sales force toward high-priced computer products, IBM has turned to industrial distributors. The IBM industrial distributors sell only two products: a moderately priced display terminal and a desk-top printer. IBM continues to sell its entire product line, but it concentrates on high-priced items.[8]

[7]Marcia Froelke Coburn, "Direct's Sleeker Sell," *Advertising Age* (March 1, 1982), p. m–18.

[8]James A. White, "IBM Expands Outside Its Sales Channel," *The Wall Street Journal* (October 7, 1981), p. 2. Industrial distributors are also discussed in James D. Hlavacek and Tommy J. McCusition, "Industrial Distributors—When, Who, and How?" *Harvard Business Review* (March–April 1983), pp. 96–101.

Producer to Agent to Wholesaler to Retailer to Consumer Where products are produced by a large number of small companies, a unique middleman—the agent—performs the basic function of bringing buyer and seller together. The agent is, in fact, a wholesaling middleman who does not take title to the goods. The agent merely represents the producer or the regular wholesaler (who does take title to the goods) in seeking a market for the manufacturer's output or in locating a source of supply for the buyer. Chapter 16 describes two types of wholesaling middlemen—merchant wholesalers, who take title to the goods they handle, and agent wholesaling middlemen, who do not take title to the goods.

Agents are used in such industries as canning and frozen food packing. In these industries, many producers supply a large number of geographically scattered wholesalers. The agent wholesaling middleman performs the service of bringing buyers and sellers together.

Producer to Agent to Wholesaler to Industrial User Similar conditions often exist in the industrial market, where small producers attempt to market their offerings to large wholesalers. The agent wholesaling middleman, often called a *manufacturers' representative,* serves as an independent sales force in contacting the wholesaler buyers.

Producer to Agent to Industrial User Where the unit sale is small, merchant wholesalers must be used to cover the market economically. By maintaining regional inventories, they achieve transportation economies by stockpiling goods and making the final small shipment over a short distance. Where the unit sale is large and transportation accounts for a small percentage of the total product cost, the producer to agent to industrial user channel is usually employed. The agent wholesaling middlemen become, in effect, the company's sales force.

Service Provider to Consumer or Industrial User Distribution of services to both consumers and industrial users is usually simpler and more direct than for industrial and consumer goods. In part, this is due to the intangibility of services. The marketer of services is often less concerned with storage, transportation, and inventory control; shorter channels are typically used.

Another consideration is the need for continuing, personal relationships between performers and users of many services. Consumers will remain clients of the same insurance agent, bank, or travel agent as long as they are reasonably satisfied. Likewise, public accounting firms and attorneys are retained on a relatively permanent basis by industrial buyers.

Service Provider to Agent to Consumer or Industrial User When marketing intermediaries are used by service firms, they are usually agents or brokers. Common examples include insurance agents, securities brokers, travel agents, and entertainment agents.

For instance, travel and hotel packages are sometimes created by intermediaries and then marketed at the retail level by travel agents to both vacationers and firms wanting to offer employee incentive awards.

A Special Note on Channel Strategy for Consumer Services A dominant patronage motive for many consumer services, such as banks, motels, and auto rental agencies, is convenient locations. It is absolutely essential that careful consideration be given to retail site selection. Banks in particular have been sensitive to locating branches in suburban shopping centers and malls to meet the needs of customers in those areas. The wide acceptance of retail banking has led to the installation of automated electronic tellers that enable customers to withdraw funds and to make deposits when a bank's offices are closed. The U.S. Postal Service has set up similar vending machines in shopping malls.

Multiple Distribution Channels

The use of more than one channel for similar products is increasingly commonplace. In some instances, multiple channels (or dual distribution) are utilized when the same product is marketed both to the ultimate consumer and to industrial users. Dial soap, for example, is distributed to grocery wholesalers, who deliver it to food stores, which market it to consumers. But a second distribution channel also exists; large retail chains and motels purchase the soap directly from the manufacturer.

In other cases, the same product is marketed through a variety of types of retail outlets. A basic product such as a paint brush is carried in inventory by the traditional hardware store; it is also handled by such nontraditional retail outlets as auto accessory stores, building-supply outlets, department stores, discount houses, mail-order houses, supermarkets, and variety stores. Each retail store may utilize different distribution channels.

Firestone automobile tires are marketed through several channels. They are distributed to General Motors, where they serve as a component part for new Chevrolets; to Firestone-owned retail outlets; to tire wholesalers, who sell them to retail gas stations; and to franchised Firestone outlets. Each channel enables the manufacturer to serve a different market.

Reverse Channels

While the traditional concept of marketing channels involves movement of products and services from producer to consumer or industrial user, there is increasing interest in reverse channels. **Reverse,** or backward, **channels** refer to the various marketing institutions and the

A Multiple Channel Problem in the Miniblind Business

Rainbow Window Fashions, Inc., a successful small manufacturer of venetian blinds, was organized by Louis Sterner when he realized that the growing market for one-inch miniblinds was not being satisfied. About 90 percent of miniblind sales were custom-made orders, which typically took up to five weeks to fill.

Sterner decided to produce and stock quality miniblinds that would be available for immediate installation. However, his new enterprise had a distribution problem. Small, independent stores sold the most miniblinds, but brand recognition came from acceptance by department stores. Sterner felt he needed this recognition to establish Rainbow's position in the marketplace. His dilemma was complicated by the fact that department store buyers were reluctant to accept brands sold by the smaller stores.

Sterner decided to offer two brands: the Rainbow label went to department stores, while smaller retailers got stripped down versions of the miniblind under the Streamline brand. The firm's small sales force was able to penetrate both of these distribution channels successfully. Today, Rainbow Window Fashions is growing by about $2 to $3 million annually.

Source: Sanford L. Jacobs, "How Entrepreneur Exploited Chance the Big Firms Ignored," *The Wall Street Journal* (March 1, 1982), p. 23.

paths goods follow from consumer or industrial user to producer or marketing intermediaries. William G. Zikmund and William J. Stanton point out several problems in developing reverse channels in the recycling process:

The recycling of solid wastes is a major ecological goal. Although recycling is technologically feasible, reversing the flow of materials in the channel of distribution—marketing trash through a "backward" channel—presents a challenge. Existing backward channels are primitive, and financial incentives are inadequate. The consumer must be motivated to undergo a role change and become a producer—the initiating force in the reverse distribution process.[9]

Reverse channels will increase in importance as raw materials become more expensive and as additional laws are passed to control litter and the disposition of packaging materials, such as soft-drink bottles. In order for recycling to succeed, four basic conditions must be satisfied:

1. A technology must be available that can efficiently process the material being recycled.

[9]William Zikmund and William J. Stanton, "Recycling Solid Wastes: A Channels-of-Distribution Problem," *Journal of Marketing* (July 1971), p. 34.

2. A market must be available for the end product—the reclaimed material.
3. A substantial and continuing quantity of secondary product (recycled aluminum, reclaimed steel from automobiles, recycled paper) must be available.
4. A marketing system must be developed that can bridge the gap between suppliers of secondary products and end users on a profitable basis.

In some instances, the reverse channel consists of traditional marketing intermediaries. In the soft-drink industry, retailers and local bottlers perform these functions. In other cases, manufacturers take the initiative by establishing redemption centers. A concentrated attempt by the Reynolds Metals Company in Florida permitted the company to recycle an amount of aluminum equivalent to 60 percent of the total containers marketed in the state.[10] Other reverse channel participants may include community groups which organize "clean-up" days and develop systems for rechanneling paper products for recycling and specialized organizations developed for waste disposal and recycling.

Reverse Channels for Product Recalls and Repairs Reverse channels are also used for product recalls and repairs. Ownership of some products (like tires) is registered so that proper notification can be sent in case of recalls. For example, in the case of automobile recalls, owners are advised to have the problem corrected at their dealership. Similarly, reverse channels have been used for repairs to some products. The warranty for a small appliance might specify that if repairs were needed in the first 90 days, the item should be returned to the dealer. After that period, the product should be returned to the factory. Such reverse channels are a vital element of product recalls and repair procedures.

Facilitating Agencies in the Distribution Channel

A **facilitating agency** provides specialized assistance for regular channel members (such as producers, wholesalers, and retailers) in moving products from producer to consumer. Included in the definition of facilitating agencies are transportation companies, warehousing firms, financial institutions, insurance companies, and marketing research companies.

Facilitating agencies perform a number of special services. Insurance companies assume some of the risks involved in transporting the goods; marketing research firms supply information; financial institutions provide the necessary financing; advertising agencies help sell the goods;

[10]Donald A. Fuller, "Aluminum Beverage Container Recycling in Florida: A Commentary," *Atlanta Economic Review* (January–February 1977), p. 41.

and transportation and storage firms store and physically move the goods. In some instances, the major channel members perform these services. Facilitating agencies are not, however, involved in directing the flow of goods and services through the channel.

Power in the Distribution Channel

Some marketing institutions must exercise leadership in the distribution channel if it is to be an effective aspect of marketing strategy. Decisions must be made and conflicts among channel members resolved. Channel leadership is a function of one's power within the distribution channel.[11]

Bases of Power

There are five bases of power: reward power, coercive power, legitimate power, referent power, and expert power.[12] All of these bases can be used to establish a position of channel leadership.[13]

Reward Power If channel members can offer some type of reward to another member, then they possess reward power. The granting of an exclusive sales territory or franchise would be examples.

Coercive Power The threat of economic punishment is known as coercive power. A manufacturer might threaten an uncooperative retailer with loss of its dealership. Another example of coercive power would be Sears' strength with its suppliers. The giant retailer's market size is a significant base of power in its distribution channel.

Legitimate Power Distribution channels that are linked contractually provide examples of legitimate power. A franchise might be contractually required to perform such activities as maintaining a common type of outlet, contributing to general advertising, and remaining open during specified time periods.

Referent Power Referent power stems from an agreement among channel members as to what is in their mutual best interests. For in-

[11]Interesting discussions of power appear in F. Robert Dwyer and Orville C. Walker, Jr., "Bargaining in an Asymmetrical Power Structure," *Journal of Marketing* (Winter 1981), pp. 104–115.

[12]These bases were identified in John R. P. French, Jr., and Bertram Raven, "The Bases of Social Power," in *Group Dynamics: Research and Theory,* 2d ed., (eds.) Darwin Cartwright and Alvin Zandler (Evanston, Ill.: Row, Putnam, 1960), pp. 607–623. The list originally came from *Studies in Social Power,* (ed.) Darwin Cartwright (Ann Arbor: University of Michigan, 1959), pp. 612–613.

[13]The discussion that follows is based on Bert Rosenbloom, *Marketing Channels: A Management Overview,* 2d ed. (Hinsdale, Ill.: The Dryden Press, 1983).

stance, many manufacturers maintain dealer councils to help resolve potential problems in distribution of a product or service. Both parties have a mutual interest in maintaining effective channel relationships.

Expert Power Knowledge is the determinant of expert power. For instance, a manufacturer might assist a retailer with store layout or advertising based on its marketing expertise with the product line.

Channel Captains

The dominant and controlling member of the channel is called the **channel captain.**[14] Historically, the channel leadership role was performed by the producer or wholesaler, since retailers tend to be both small and localized. However, retailers are increasingly taking on the role of channel captain as large chains assume traditional wholesaling functions and even dictate product design specifications to the manufacturer.

Producers as Channel Captains Since producers and service providers typically create new product and service offerings and enjoy the benefits of large-scale operations, they fill the role of channel captain in many marketing channels. Examples of such manufacturers include Armstrong Cork, General Electric, Magnavox, Sealy Mattress, and Western Auto Stores.

Retailers as Channel Captains Retailers are often powerful enough to serve as channel captains in many industries. Larger chain operations may bypass independent wholesalers and utilize manufacturers as suppliers in producing the retailers' private brands at quality levels specified by the chains. Major retailers, such as K mart, Sears, J.C. Penney, and Montgomery Ward, serve as leaders in many of the marketing channels with which they are associated.

Wholesalers as Channel Captains Although the relative influence of wholesalers has declined since 1900, they continue to serve as vital members of many marketing channels. Large-scale wholesalers, such as the Independent Grocers' Association (IGA), serve as channel captains as they assist independent retailers in competing with chain outlets.

[14]Bruce J. Walker and Donald W. Jackson, Jr., "The Channels Manager: A Needed New Position," in *Proceedings of the Southern Marketing Association,* (eds.) Robert S. Franz, Robert M. Hopkins, and Al Toma (New Orleans, La.: November 1978), pp. 325–328. See also R. Kenneth Teas and Stanley D. Sibley, "An Examination of the Moderating Effect on Channel Member Size of Perceptions of Preferred Channel Linkages," *Journal of the Academy of Marketing Science* (Summer 1980), pp. 277–293.

Channel Strategy Decisions

Marketers face several channel strategy decisions. The selection of a specific distribution channel is the most basic of these decisions, but the level of distribution intensity must also be determined. Channel decision makers must also address the issue of vertical marketing systems.

Selection of a Distribution Channel

What makes a franchised retail dealer network best for the Ford Motor Company? Why do operating supplies often go through both agents and merchant wholesalers before being purchased by the industrial firm? Why do some firms employ multiple channels for the same product? The firm must answer many such questions in choosing distribution channels. The choice is based on an analysis of market, product, producer, and competitive factors. Each factor can be of critical importance, and the factors are often interrelated.

Market Factors

A major determinant of channel structure is whether the product is intended for the consumer or the industrial market. Industrial purchasers usually prefer to deal directly with the manufacturer (except for supplies or small accessory items), but most consumers make their purchases from retail stores. Often, products for both industrial users and consumers are sold through more than one channel.

The needs and geographic location of the firm's market affect channel choice. Direct sales are possible where the firm's potential market is concentrated. A small number of potential buyers also increases the feasibility of direct channels. Consumer goods are purchased by households everywhere. Since these households are numerous and geographically dispersed, and since they purchase a small volume at a given time, middlemen must be employed to market products to them.

A good illustration of how market factors influence distribution is provided by Jostens, which has been able to capture 40 percent of the market for high-school class rings and yearbooks by using a 1,000-member sales force of former high-school teachers and coaches. This direct channel, served by a highly educated sales force that averages $50,000 per year in commissions, has proven extremely successful. When gold prices soared, Jostens diversified into the wholesale market with a line of engagement and other fine rings. However, the sales force was largely unsuccessful in serving a new type of customer (the retail jeweler) and a new channel had to be devised.[15]

[15] "Jostens: A School Supplier Stays with Basics as Enrollment Declines," *Business Week* (April 21, 1980), pp. 124, 129.

Order size will also affect the channel decision. Producers are likely to use shorter, more direct channels in cases where retail customers or industrial buyers place relatively small numbers of large orders. Retailers often employ buying offices to negotiate directly with manufacturers for large-scale purchases. Wholesalers may be used to contact smaller retailers.

Shifts in consumer buying patterns also influence channel decisions. The desire for credit, the growth of self-service, the increased use of mail-order houses, and the greater willingness to purchase from door-to-door salespeople all affect a firm's marketing channel.

Product Factors

Product factors also play a role in determining optimal distribution channels. Perishable products, such as fresh produce and fruit, and fashion products with short life cycles, typically move through relatively short channels directly to the retailer or the ultimate consumer. For instance, Nabisco Brands Inc. distributes its cookies and crackers from the bakery to retail shelves. Fig Newtons, Oreos, Ritz crackers, and other Nabisco brands that command 40 percent of the U.S. market are delivered to retail customers by a fleet of 1,200 company-owned trucks and a 3,000-member sales force.[16] As another example, each year Hines & Smart Corporation ships some 5 million pounds of live lobsters in specially designed styrofoam containers directly to restaurants and hotels throughout North America.

Complex products, such as custom-made installations or computer equipment, are typically sold by the producer to the buyer. As a general rule, the more standardized the product, the longer the channel. Standardized goods usually are marketed by wholesalers. Also, products that require regular service or specialized repair service usually are not distributed through channels employing independent wholesalers. Automobiles are marketed through a franchised network of retail dealers whose employees receive training on how to properly service their cars.

Another generalization about distribution channels is that the lower the unit value of the product, the longer the channel. Convenience goods and industrial supplies with typically low unit prices are frequently marketed through relatively long channels. Installations and more expensive industrial and consumer goods employ shorter, more direct channels.

Producer Factors

Companies with adequate financial, managerial, and marketing resources are less compelled to utilize middlemen in marketing their products. A financially strong manufacturer can hire its own sales force,

[16]"Nabisco: Diversifying Again, but This Time Wholeheartedly," *Business Week* (October 20, 1980), p. 71.

warehouse its own products, and grant credit to retailers or consumers. A weaker firm must rely on middlemen for these services (although some large retail chains purchase all of the manufacturer's output, thereby bypassing the independent wholesaler). Production-oriented firms may be forced to utilize the marketing expertise of middlemen to replace the lack of finances and management in their organization.

A firm with a broad product line is usually able to market its products directly to retailers or industrial users since its sales force can offer a variety of products. Larger total sales permit the selling costs to be spread over a number of products and make direct sales feasible. The single-product firm often discovers that direct selling is an unaffordable luxury.

The manufacturer's need for control over the product also influences channel selection. If aggressive promotion is desired at the retail level, the producer chooses the shortest available channel. For new products, the producer may be forced to implement an introductory advertising campaign before independent wholesalers will handle the items.

Competitive Factors

Some firms are forced to develop unique distribution channels because of inadequate promotion of their products by independent middlemen. Avon's famous shift to house-to-house selling was prompted by intense competition with similar lines of cosmetics. Similarly, when Honeywell discovered that its Concept 70 home security system was being inadequately marketed by the traditional channel of wholesaler to retailer, it switched to a direct-to-home sales force.

Table 15.1 summarizes the factors affecting the selection of a distribution channel and examines the effect of each factor upon the overall length of the channel.

Determining Distribution Intensity

Adequate market coverage for some products could mean one dealer for 50,000 people. American Home Products defines adequate coverage for Anacin and Dristan headache and cold remedies at almost every supermarket, discount store, drugstore, and variety store, plus many vending machines. The degree of distribution intensity can be viewed as a continuum with three general categories: intensive distribution, selective distribution, and exclusive distribution.

Intensive Distribution Producers of convenience goods practice **intensive distribution** when they provide saturation coverage of the market, enabling the purchaser to buy the product with a minimum of effort. Examples of goods distributed in this way include soft drinks, candy, gum, and cigarettes.

Table 15.1 Factors Affecting the Selection of a Distribution Channel

Factor	Channels Tend to Be Shorter When:
Market Factors	
Consumer market or industrial market	Industrial users
Geographic location of market target	Geographically concentrated customers
Customer service needs	Specialized knowledge, technical knowhow, and regular service needs are present
Order size	Customers place relatively large orders
Product Factors	
Perishability	Products are perishable, either because of fashion changes or physical perishability
Technical complexity of product	Highly technical products
Unit value	High unit value products
Producer Factors	
Producer resources—financial, managerial, and marketing	Manufacturer possesses adequate resources to perform channel functions
Product line	Manufacturer has broad product line to spread distribution costs
Need for control over the channel	Manufacturer desires to control the channel
Competitive Factors	
Need for promotion to channel members	Manufacturer feels that independent middlemen are inadequately promoting products

Bic pens can be purchased in more than 200,000 retail outlets in the United States. The American Time Company uses an intensive distribution strategy for its Timex watches. Consumers can buy a Timex in many jewelry stores, the traditional retail outlet for watches. In addition, they can find Timex watches in department stores, discount stores, drugstores, hardware stores, and variety stores.

Mass coverage and low unit prices make the use of wholesalers almost mandatory for such distribution. An important exception to this generalization is Avon Products, which sells directly to the consumer through a nationwide network of neighborhood sales personnel. These representatives purchase directly from the manufacturer at 60 percent of the retail price and service a limited area of about 100 households with cosmetics, toiletries, jewelry, and toys.

Selective Distribution **Selective distribution** involves the selection of a small number of retailers in a market area to handle the firm's product line. By limiting the number of retailers, the firm can reduce its total marketing costs while establishing better working relationships within the channel. Cooperative advertising (in which the manufacturer pays a percentage of the retailer's advertising expenditures and the retailer prominently displays the firm's products) can be utilized for mutual benefit, and marginal retailers can be avoided. Where product service is important, the manufacturer usually provides dealer training and assistance. Price cutting is less likely, since fewer dealers are handling the firm's line. For example, Massachusetts-based Epicure Products, Inc. requires its dealers to be technically proficient in marketing and servicing the firm's high fidelity speakers. Dealers are also required to maintain listening rooms for the convenience of customers.[17]

Exclusive Distribution When producers grant exclusive rights to a wholesaler or retailer to sell in a geographic region, they are practicing **exclusive distribution**—an extreme form of selective distribution. The best example of exclusive distribution is within the automobile industry. For example, a city of 100,000 population will have a single Honda dealer or one Pontiac agency. Exclusive dealership agreements also occur in the marketing of some major appliances and in fashion apparel.

Some market coverage may be sacrificed through a policy of exclusive distribution, but this loss is often offset by the development and maintenance of an image of quality and prestige for the products and the reduced marketing costs associated with a small number of accounts. Producers and retailers cooperate closely in decisions concerning advertising and promotion, inventory to be carried by the retailers, and prices.

The Legal Problems of Exclusive Distribution The use of exclusive distribution presents a number of potential legal problems in three areas—exclusive dealing agreements, closed sales territories, and tying agreements. While none of these practices is illegal per se, all may be ruled illegal if they reduce competition or tend to create a monopoly situation.

Exclusive Dealing Agreements. An **exclusive dealing agreement** prohibits a middleman (either a wholesaler or, more typically, a retailer) from handling competing products. Producers of high-priced shopping goods, specialty goods, and accessory equipment often require such agreements as assurance by the middleman of total concentration on the firm's product line. These contracts are considered violations of the Clayton Act if the producer's or the dealer's sales volume represents a substantial percentage of total sales in the market or sales area. The courts have ruled that sellers who are initially entering the market can use exclusive dealing agreements as a means of strengthening their

[17]Paul A. Allen, "Why Distributors Sue Manufacturers," *Inc.* (November 1981), p. 157.

competitive position. But the same agreements are considered violations of the Clayton Act when used by firms with sizable market shares, since competitors may be barred from the market because of the agreements.

Closed Sales Territories. Producers with **closed sales territories** restrict the geographic territories for each of their distributors. Although the distributors may be granted exclusive territories, they are prohibited from opening new facilities or marketing such products outside their assigned territories. The legality of closed sales territories depends on whether the restrictions decrease competition. If competition is lessened, closed sales territories are considered to be in violation of the Federal Trade Commission Act and of provisions of the Sherman Act and the Clayton Act.

The legality of closed sales territories is also determined by whether they are horizontal or vertical. Horizontal territorial restrictions involve agreements by retailers or wholesalers to avoid competition among products from the same producer. Such agreements have consistently been declared illegal. However, the U.S. Supreme Court recently ruled that vertical territorial restrictions—those between the producer and the wholesaler or retailer—may be legal. While the ruling was not entirely clear-cut, such agreements are likely to be legal in cases where the manufacturer occupies a relatively small part of the market. In such cases, the restrictions may actually increase competition among competing brands. The wholesaler or retailer faces no competition from other dealers carrying the manufacturer's brand and can therefore concentrate on effectively competing with other brands.[18]

Tying Agreements. The third legal question of exclusive dealing involves the use of a **tying agreement,** an agreement that requires a dealer who wishes to become the exclusive dealer for a producer's products to also carry other products by the producer in inventory. In the clothing industry, for example, such an agreement may require the dealer to carry a line of less popular clothing in addition to the fast-moving items.

Tying agreements violate the Sherman Act and the Clayton Act when they lessen competition or create monopoly situations by keeping competitors out of major markets. For this reason, the International Salt Company was prohibited from selling salt as a tying product with the lease of its patented salt-dispensing machines for snow and ice removal. The Supreme Court ruled that such an agreement unreasonably eliminated competition among sellers of salt.

[18]Michael B. Metzger, "Schwinn's Swan Song," *Business Horizons* (April 1978), pp. 52–56.

Tying agreements continue to proliferate in franchising operations. One study estimated that over 70 percent of all franchises are required to purchase at least some of their operating supplies from the franchisors.[19]

Vertical Marketing Systems

The traditional marketing channel has been described as a "highly fragmented network in which vertically aligned firms bargain with each other at arm's length, terminate relationships with impunity, and otherwise behave autonomously."[20] This potentially inefficient system of distributing goods is gradually being replaced by **vertical marketing systems (VMS)**—"professionally managed and centrally programmed networks preengineered to achieve operating economies and maximum impact."[21] VMS produce economies of scale through their size and by eliminating duplicated services. As Table 15.2 indicates, three types prevail—corporate, administered, and contractual.

Corporate System Where there is single ownership of each stage of the marketing channel, a corporate vertical marketing system exists. A reported 50 percent of all Sears products are purchased from manufacturers in which the nation's largest retailer has an equity interest. Holiday Inn owns a furniture manufacturer and a carpet mill. Hartmarx (formerly Hart, Schaffner & Marx) markets its Hickey-Freeman, Christian Dior, and Playboy suits through its company-owned chain of 275 men's clothing stores. Both IBM and Xerox have opened retail outlets.

In 1970, Genesco ranked first among U.S. apparel manufacturers with $1.2 billion in sales. Although sales of its Jarman and Johnston & Murphy brands through its own Flagg and Hardy shoe retailers accounted for one third of total sales, Genesco managers were convinced that the key to further growth in shoe sales was to emphasize the sale of low-cost, unbranded shoes to such mass merchandisers as Sears. This proved to be a painful move, however, as it left the manufacturer at the whim of the giant retail chains. In addition, competitively priced imported shoes succeeded in capturing 53 percent of the U.S. shoe market by 1980, complicating Genesco's problems. New management

[19]Shelby D. Hunt and John R. Nevin, "Tying Agreements in Franchising," *Journal of Marketing* (July 1975), pp. 20–26.

[20]This section is based on Bert C. McCammon, Jr., "The Emergence and Growth of Contractually Integrated Channels in the American Economy," in *Marketing and Economic Development* (Chicago: American Marketing Association, 1965), pp. 496–515. Used by permission.

[21]*Ibid,* p. 496.

Table 15.2 Vertical Marketing Systems

Type of System	Description	Examples
Corporate	Channel owned and operated by a single organization	Hartmarx Firestone Sherwin-Williams
Administered	Channel dominated by one powerful member who acts as channel captain	Magnavox General Electric Kraftco Corning Glass
Contractual	Channel coordinated through contractual agreements among channel members	*Wholesaler Sponsored Voluntary Chain:* IGA Western Auto Stores Associated Druggists Sentry Hardware *Retail Cooperative:* Associated Grocers *Franchise Systems:* H & R Block 7-Eleven Stores Century 21 Real Estate AAMCO Transmissions Coca-Cola bottlers

sought a solution to these problems through further development of a corporate VMS. Genesco decided to double the 960 company-owned shoe outlets by 1985. Although Genesco ranked third out of 325 U.S. shoe manufacturers, their strategy for overtaking market leaders Thom McAn and Kinney Shoes was to develop an integrated, manufacturer-owned VMS.[22]

Administered System Channel coordination is achieved through the exercise of power by a dominant channel member in an administered vertical marketing system. Magnavox obtains agressive promotional support from its retailers because of the strong reputation of its brand. Although the retailers are independently owned and operated, they cooperate with the manufacturer because of the effective working relationships built up over the years.

Contractual System The most significant form of vertical marketing systems is the contractual vertical marketing system, which accounts for nearly 40 percent of all retail sales. Instead of the common ownership

[22]"Genesco: An Apparel Empire Returns to its Retailing Base—Shoes," *Business Week* (June 23, 1980), pp. 90–99.

of channel components that characterized the corporate VMS or the relative power of a component of an administered system, the contractual VMS is characterized by formal agreements among channel members. In practice, there are three types of agreements: the wholesaler-sponsored voluntary chain, the retail cooperative, and the franchise.

Wholesaler-Sponsored Chain. The wholesaler-sponsored voluntary chain represents an attempt by the independent wholesaler to preserve a market for the firm's products by strengthening the firm's retailer customers. In order to enable the independent retailers to compete with the chains, the wholesaler enters into a formal agreement with a group of retailers wherein the retailers agree to use a common name, have standardized facilities, and purchase the wholesaler's products. Often, the wholesaler develops a line of private brands to be stocked by the members of the voluntary chain.

A common store name and similar inventory allows the retailers to achieve cost savings on advertising, since a single newspaper ad promotes all the retailers in the trading area. IGA Food Stores, with a membership of approximately 5,000 stores, is a good example of a voluntary chain. McKesson & Robbins Drug Company has established a large voluntary chain in the retail drug industry.

Retail Cooperatives. A second type of contractual VMS is the retail cooperative, which is established by a group of retailers who set up a wholesaling operation to better compete with the chains. The retailers purchase shares of stock in the wholesaling operation and agree to buy a minimum percentage of their inventory from the firm. The members may also choose to use a common store name and to develop their own private brands in order to carry out cooperative advertising. Retail cooperatives have been extremely successful in the grocery industry, accounting for one fifth of all retail grocery sales.

Franchising. A third type of contractual VMS is the **franchise**—a contractual arrangement in which dealers (franchisees) agree to meet the operating requirements of a manufacturer or other franchisor. The dealers typically receive a variety of marketing, management, technical, and financial services in exchange for a specified fee.

Although franchising has attracted considerable interest since the late 1960s, the concept actually began 100 years earlier when the Singer Company established franchised sewing machine outlets following the Civil War. Early impetus for the franchising concept came after 1900 in the automobile industry. Increasing automobile travel created demands for nationwide distribution of gasoline, oil, and tires, for which franchising was also used.[23] The soft-drink industry is another example

[23]Thomas G. Marx, "Distribution Efficiency in Franchising," *MSU Business Topics* (Winter 1980), p. 5.

of a franchise: a contractual arrangement exists between the syrup manufacturer and the wholesaler bottler.

The franchising format that has created the most excitement in retailing during the past 20 years has been the retailer franchise system sponsored by the service firm. McDonald's is an excellent example of such a franchise operation. The company brings together suppliers and a chain of hamburger outlets. It provides a proven system of retail operation (the operations manual for each outlet weighs several pounds) and lower prices through its purchasing power on meat, buns, napkins and necessary supplies. In return, the franchisee pays a fee of about $350,000 for the use of the McDonald's name and a percentage of gross sales. Other familiar examples are Hertz, Century 21 and Red Carpet real estate agencies, Tantrific tanning salons, Pizza Hut, Howard Johnson's, and Weight Watchers.

McDonald's has almost 7,000 restaurants in operation. The early McDonald's outlets offered a severely restricted menu and little or no seating. Their 1984 counterparts provide an expanded breakfast and luncheon selection and often afford seating capacity of 100 to 300 diners. These efforts are aimed at obtaining even more of the $116 billion spent annually in U.S. restaurants. The average person eats out 3.5 times a week with the result that over 77 million customers patronize the nation's restaurants each day. According to a 1981 Gallup survey, four out of ten adults would like to eat out more often but are restricted by a tight budget. Because of price and convenience, the nation's fast-food restaurants attract consumers from almost all demographic groups.[24] Table 15.3 lists the five largest fast-food restaurants in the United States.

Fast-food franchising has already proven itself in the international market. McDonald's hamburgers are consumed daily in Tokyo, London, Rome, and Paris. Kentucky Fried Chicken has opened more than 500 restaurants outside the United States in locations as diverse as Manila, Munich, Nairobi, and Nice. In some countries, adjustments to U.S. marketing plans have been made to accommodate local needs. Although their menu is rigidly standardized in the United States, McDonald's executives approved the addition of wine to the menu in French outlets. Also, Kentucky Fried Chicken substituted french fries for mashed potatoes to satisfy its Japanese customers.[25]

The infatuation with the franchising concept and the market performance of franchise stocks lured dozens of newcomers into the market. Lacking experience and often armed with a well-known name as their sole asset, many of these firms (among them Broadway Joe's, Chicken Delight, and Minnie Pearl's) quickly disappeared.

[24]National Restaurant Association Food Service Trends, December 1981.

[25]See Donald W. Hackett, "U.S. Franchise Systems Abroad—The Second Boom," in *Marketing: 1776–1976 and Beyond,* (ed.) Kenneth L. Bernhardt (Chicago: American Marketing Association, 1976), pp. 253–256.

Table 15.3 The Nation's Largest Fast-Food Firms

Rank	Company	Food Service Volume in Millions	Food Service Units
1	McDonald's	$6,226	6,739
2	Kentucky Fried Chicken	2,298	5,958
3	Wendy's International	1,209	2,229
4	International Dairy Queen	1,020	4,805
5	Hardee's	920	1,408

Source: "The '400' Ranking," *Restaurants and Institutions* (July 1, 1982), p. 77.

The median investment for a franchise varies tremendously from one business area to another. For example, the investment required for a company-owned restaurant franchise recently averaged $260,000. Similarly, automotive products and services franchises required a $75,000 investment and tax preparation services franchises averaged $8,000. The popularity of franchising has caused the number of franchise establishments to mushroom to 476,000, up 80,000 from a decade ago. The great bulk of the nation's franchises are in gasoline service stations, restaurants, business aids and services, automotive products and services, nonfood retailing, and automobile and truck dealers.[26]

Since 1971, the Federal Trade Commission has been engaged in a concentrated attempt to minimize potential abuses of the franchise system. Abuses uncovered by the FTC included the following:

One battery company, recently tripped up by the Federal Trade Commission, promised a return of more than $10,000 a year on an investment of $1,695. Another company, an electronics equipment marketer, blandly assured its franchisees that they could make over $400 per month on a total investment of $1,895. A Dallas credit card company told its franchisees, who were required to invest between $3,500 and $10,000, that they could not help but make over $125,000 per year. Within two years this organization had fleeced would-be franchisees out of more than $200,000.[27]

The FTC has a rule called *Disclosure Requirements and Prohibitions Concerning Franchising and Business Opportunities,* designed to protect would-be investors by requiring disclosure of factual information concerning franchisor claims, guarantees, franchising experience, occurrence of any bankruptcy, and evidence of the moral character of the key person-

[26]U.S. Department of Commerce, Bureau of Industrial Economics, *Franchising in the Economy, 1980–1982,* Tables 1 and 23; and "More Than You Ever Wanted to Know," *U.S. News & World Report* (April 12, 1982), p. 14.

[27]Quoted in John R. Nevin, Shelby D. Hunt, and Michael G. Levas, "Legal Remedies for Deceptive and Unfair Practices in Franchising," *Journal of Macromarketing* (Spring 1981), p. 24. Used by permission.

nel in the franchise. Also specified are services to be provided by each party and the specific terms of the franchising agreement, including all costs involved.

Whether corporate, administered, or contractual, vertical marketing systems are already a dominant factor in the consumer goods sector of the U.S. economy. An estimated 64 percent of the available market is currently in the hands of retail components of VMS.

Overcoming Conflict in the Distribution Channel

Distribution channels must be organized and regarded as a systematic cooperative effort if operating efficiencies are to be achieved. Yet channel members often perform as separate, independent, and even competitive forces. Too often, marketing institutions within the channel believe it extends only one step forward or backward. They think in terms of suppliers and customers rather than of vital links in the total channel.[28]

Channel conflict can evolve from a number of sources:

A manufacturer may wish to promote a product in one manner . . . while his retailers oppose this. Another manufacturer may wish to get information from his retailers on a certain aspect relating to his product, but his retailers may refuse to provide this information. A producer may want to distribute his product extensively, but his retailers may demand exclusives. A supplier may force a product onto its retailers, who dare not oppose, but who retaliate in other ways, such as using it as a loss leader. Large manufacturers may try to dictate the resale price of their merchandise; this may be less or more than the price at which the retailers wish to sell it. Occasionally a local market may be more competitive for a retailer than is true nationally. The manufacturer may not recognize the difference in competition and refuse to help this channel member. There is also conflict because of the desire of both manufacturers and retailers to eliminate the wholesaler.[29]

Types of Conflict

Two types of conflict—horizontal or vertical—may occur. Horizontal conflict may occur between channel members at the same level, such as two or more wholesalers or two or more retailers, or between middlemen of the same type, such as two competing discount stores or several

[28]Channel conflict is examined in James R. Brown and Ralph L. Day, "Measures of Manifest Conflict in Distribution Channels," *Journal of Marketing Research* (August 1981), pp. 263–274.

[29]Bruce Mallen, "A Theory of Retailer-Supplier Conflict, Control, and Cooperation," *Journal of Retailing* (Summer 1963), p. 26. Reprinted with permission. See also F. Robert Dwyer, "Channel-Member Satisfaction: Laboratory Insights," *Journal of Retailing* (Summer 1980), pp. 45–65.

A Case of Channel Conflict: Mitsubishi and Chrysler

Mitsubishi Motors Corp. gained access to Chrysler's dealer network when the Detroit firm purchased 15 percent of the Japanese company in 1971. The Dodge Colt and Plymouth Champ are examples of Mitsubishi products now sold by Chrysler dealers. Chrysler typically sold one sixth of all Mitsubishi cars. This business relationship continued for about a decade until Mitsubishi renegotiated its agreement with Chrysler.

Conditions had changed drastically for the two firms by 1981. The American economy was in a recession and foreign car imports to the United States were restricted. The revised agreement called for the Japanese to continue to provide cars to Chrysler until 1990, but it also allowed Mitsubishi to set up its own dealer network in the United States.

Since the agreement was revised, the Japanese auto maker has set up 70 dealers in 16 states on the West, East, and Gulf Coasts. The channel conflict between Chrysler dealers and the new Mitsubishi dealers is readily apparent. Both will be selling Mitsubishi cars and trucks. Furthermore, import restrictions may require Mitsubishi to cut its allotment to Chrysler dealers because of the number of units sold through its own U.S. dealers.

The long-term resolution of this conflict is uncertain, but the current Mitsubishi–Chrysler agreement calls for cooperation in production and technological efforts until 1990. Some think that the Japanese firm may assume an equity position in Chrysler because the U.S. government's loan guarantee for Chrysler requires the manufacturer to look for a merger partner.

Source: "Mitsubishi Revs Up to Go Solo," *Business Week* (May 3, 1982), pp. 129, 132.

retail florists. More often, however, horizontal conflict occurs between different types of middlemen who handle similar products. The retail druggist competes with variety stores, discount houses, department stores, convenience stores, and mail-order houses, all of which may be supplied by the producer with identically branded products. Consumer desires for convenient, one-stop shopping have led to multiple channels and the use of numerous outlets for many products.

Vertical conflict occurs between channel members at different levels—between wholesalers and retailer or between producers and wholesalers or retailers. Vertical conflict occurs frequently and is often the more severe form of conflict in the channel. Conflict may occur between producers and retailers when retailers develop private brands to compete with the producers' brands, or when producers establish their own retail stores or create a mail-order operation which competes with retailers. Conflict between producers and wholesalers may occur in cases where the producer attempts to bypass the wholesaler and make direct sales to retailers or industrial users. In other instances, wholesalers may promote competitive products.

A recent instance of vertical conflict occurred between the Coca-Cola Company and its 550 wholesale bottlers who bottle, warehouse, distribute, sell, and merchandise Coca-Cola made from syrup provided by the Atlanta-based parent. Over a ten-year period during the 1960s and 1970s, the makers of Dr. Pepper expanded from regional distribution in the Midwest and Southwest to national coverage. This was accomplished by convincing 25 percent of the nation's Coca-Cola bottlers to also bottle Dr. Pepper. Even the Atlanta bottler became a Dr. Pepper distributor. However, the parent firm exercised its power in the soft-drink channel and succeeded in convincing many of its franchised bottlers to drop Dr. Pepper in favor of Mr. Pibb, Coca-Cola's own pepper-type soda. Even though many Coke bottlers followed Coke's lead, the shift was only temporary. Between 1973 and 1977, 53 Coke bottlers changed from Mr. Pibb to Dr. Pepper, including the bottler in Knoxville, Tennessee, who had been the first to bottle Mr. Pibb. Currently, approximately 200 Coke bottlers also bottle Dr. Pepper.[30]

A third type of vertical conflict may occur between wholesalers and retailers. Retailers may believe that wholesalers fail to offer credit or to allow returns on the same basis as they provide for other types of retail outlets. Wholesalers may complain that retailers are making sales to institutions that previously dealt directly with the wholesaler. A wholesaler in the sporting goods field, for example, may argue that sales by retail sporting goods outlets directly to local schools systems are unfairly competing with its own sales force.[31]

Cooperation in the Distribution Channel

The basic antidote to channel conflict is effective cooperation among channel members. However, channels usually have more harmonious relationships than conflicting ones; if they did not, the channels would have ceased to exist long ago. Cooperation is best achieved by considering all channel members as part of the same organization. Achieving cooperation is the prime responsibility of the dominant member of the channel, the channel captain, who must provide the leadership necessary to ensure efficient functioning of the channel. The channel captains' power bases determine their relative effectiveness.

[30]"Dr. Pepper: Pitted Against the Soft-Drink Giants," *Business Week* (October 6, 1975), p. 70. For a discussion of Coca-Cola's relationships with its bottlers, see Peter W. Bernstein, "Coke Strikes Back," *Fortune* (June 1, 1981), pp. 30–36. Update provided by the Dr. Pepper Company, July 3, 1982.

[31]*Educators Conference Proceedings,* (eds.) Neil Beckwith, Michael Houston, Robert Mittelstaedt, Kent B. Monroe, and Scott Ward (Chicago: American Marketing Association, 1970), pp. 495–499; Michael Etgar, "Sources and Types of Intra Channel Conflict," *Journal of Retailing* (Spring 1979), pp. 61–78; and Louis W. Stern and Torger Reve, "Distribution Channels as Political Economies," *Journal of Marketing* (Summer 1980), pp. 52–64.

Summary

Distribution channels refer to the various marketing institutions and the interrelationships responsible for the physical and title flow of goods and services from producer to consumer or industrial user. Wholesaling and retailing middlemen are the marketing institutions in the distribution channel.

Distribution channels bridge the gap between producer and consumer. By making products and services available when and where the consumer wants to buy, and by arranging for transfer of title, marketing channels create time, place, and possession utility.

Distribution channels also perform such specific functions as (1) facilitating the exchange process; (2) sorting to alleviate discrepancies in assortment; (3) standardizing the transaction; and (4) accommodating the search process.

A host of alternative distribution channels are available for makers of consumer products, industrial products, and services. They range from contacting the consumer or industrial user directly to using a variety of middlemen. Multiple channels are also increasingly commonplace today. The chapter also discussed a unique distribution system—the reverse channel that is used in recycling, product recalls, and in some service situations.

Channel leadership is primarily a matter of relative power within the channel. Five bases for power are examined: reward power, coercive power, legitimate power, referent power, and expert power. The channel leader that emerges is called the channel captain.

Basic channel strategy decisions involve channel selection, the level of distribution intensity, and the use of vertical marketing systems. The selection of a distribution channel is based on market, product, producer, and competitive factors. The decision on distribution intensity involves choosing from among intensive distribution, selective distribution, or exclusive distribution. The issue of vertical marketing systems also has to be explored by the marketing manager. There are three major types of vertical marketing systems: corporate, administered, and contractual, which includes wholesaler-sponsored chains, retail cooperatives, and franchises.

Channel conflict is a problem in distribution channels. There are two types of conflict: horizontal, between the channel members at the same level; and vertical, between channel members at different levels. Marketers should work toward cooperation among all channel members as the remedy for channel conflict.

Chapter 15 has set the stage for discussion of marketing's distribution functions by examining the basic issues in channel strategy. The next two chapters look at wholesaling and retailing middlemen. Chapter 18 deals with physical distribution and concludes the section on distribution.

Key Terms

distribution channel
middlemen
wholesaling
retailer
sorting
reverse channels
facilitating agencies
channel captain
intensive distribution
selective distribution
exclusive distribution
exclusive dealing agreement
closed sales territories
tying agreements
vertical marketing systems (VMS)
franchise

Review Questions

1. What types of products are most likely to be distributed through direct channels?
2. Which marketing channel is the traditional channel? Give some reasons for its frequent use.
3. Why would manufacturers choose more than one channel for their products?
4. Explain the concept of power in the distribution channel.
5. Under what circumstances is the retailer likely to assume a channel leadership role?
6. Explain and illustrate the major factors affecting distribution channel selection.
7. Why would any manufacturer deliberately choose to limit market coverage through a policy of exclusive coverage?
8. Explain and illustrate each type of vertical marketing system.
9. What advantages does franchising offer the small retailer?
10. In what ways could the use of multiple channels produce channel conflict?

Discussion Questions and Exercises

1. Chipwich, an ice cream and chocolate-chip cookie snack, is marketed via vendor carts as well as supermarkets. Relate Chipwich's distribution strategy to the material presented in Chapter 15.
2. Which degree of distribution intensity is appropriate for each of the following:

   a. *People* magazine
   b. Ocean Pacific (OP) swimwear
   c. Irish Spring soap
   d. McCulloch chain saws
   e. Cuisinart food processors
   f. Honda motorcycles
   g. Waterford crystal
3. Outline the distribution channels used by a local firm. Why were these particular channels selected by the company?

4. Prepare a brief report on the dealer requirements for a franchise that has units in your area.
5. One generalization of channel selection mentioned in the chapter was that low unit value products require long channels. How can you explain the success of a firm (such as Avon) that has a direct channel for its relatively low unit value products?

Chapter Objectives

1. To relate wholesaling to the other variables of the marketing mix.
2. To identify the functions performed by wholesaling middlemen.
3. To explain the channel options available to a manufacturer who desires to bypass independent wholesaling middlemen.
4. To identify the conditions under which a manufacturer is likely to assume wholesaling functions rather than use independents.
5. To distinguish between merchant wholesalers and agents and brokers.
6. To identify the major types of merchant wholesalers and instances where each type might be used.
7. To describe the major types of agents and brokers.

16

WHOLESALING

At 9:15 a.m., George Ferriso enters the A & P Supermarket on Le Moine Avenue in Fort Lee, New Jersey. He introduces himself to the store manager, then registers in a sign-in notebook located near the loading dock. Ferriso goes first to the deli section where he finds that a label from an Otto Roth cheese has fallen off. He heats it with a lighter and sticks it back on the package. Ferriso then deals with a damaged package of Sau-Sea shrimp cocktail and out-of-stock situations with King onion dip and Minute Maid orange juice.

The rest of Ferriso's day is similar. He issues a credit for a spoiled package of Celebrity ham at Fort Lee's Food Line. At the Shop Rite, the dairy manager complains that Best Kosher Sausage has been shipping its low-fat frankfurters, salami, and knockwurst too near the dates they are coded to be removed from sale. Later at the Shop Rite in Emerson, New Jersey, he meets with the manager of a dairy section that has limited refrigerated space. Ferriso worries that the manager is upset with him because some Minute Maid fruit punch was shipped with defective seals.

What does George Ferriso do for a living? He is a retail sales supervisor for Boerner Co., a $300 million food broker that represents many national brands. Food brokers, who account for about 50 percent of all food items sold to retailers, are classified as wholesaling middlemen.[1] And wholesaling is the focus of this chapter.

Wholesaling is the initial marketing institution in most channels of distribution from manufacturers to consumer or industrial user. Chapter 15 introduced the basic concepts of channel strategy, primarily from the point of view of the manufacturer. Attention now shifts to the institutions within the distribution channel.

Wholesaling middlemen are a critical element of the marketing mixes of many products, but many middlemen are also separate business entities with their own marketing mixes. A good starting point for the discussion is to look at the terminology used in wholesaling.

The Conceptual Framework

Wholesaling involves the activities of persons or firms who sell to retailers and other wholesalers or to industrial users, but not in significant amounts to ultimate consumers. The term **wholesaler** is applied only to wholesaling middlemen who take title to the products they handle. **Wholesaling middlemen** is a broader term that describes not only middlemen who assume title to the goods they handle, but also agents and brokers who perform important wholesaling activities without taking title to the goods. Under this definition, then, a wholesaler is a merchant middleman.

The most recent Census of Wholesale Trade lists nearly 383,000 wholesaling establishments with a total sales volume of $1.26 trillion. Wholesaling middlemen are concentrated in the Middle Atlantic and East North Central states. The New York City metropolitan area alone accounts for 11 percent of all wholesale trade.

Wholesaling Functions

The route that goods follow on the way to the consumer or industrial user is actually a chain of marketing institutions. Goods that bypass the marketing intermediaries in the chain and move directly from producer

[1]Steven Mintz, "S&MM Spends a Day in the Field with a Food Broker," *Sales & Marketing Management* (June 7, 1982), pp. 54–56.

to consumer constitute only 3 percent of the total in the consumer goods market. Unprecedented increases in the prices of goods and services in the 1980s have led to rising complaints about middlemen who allegedly drive prices up because of their high profits and questionable services. Many discount retailers claim lower prices as a result of direct purchases from producers. Chain stores often assume wholesaling functions and bypass the independent wholesalers.

Are these complaints and claims valid? Are wholesaling middlemen the dinosaurs of the 1980s? Answers to these questions can be discerned by considering the functions and costs of these marketing intermediaries.

Wholesaling Middlemen Provide a Variety of Services

A marketing institution can continue to exist only so long as it performs a service that fulfills a need. Its demise may be slow but inevitable once other channel members discover they can survive without it. Table 16.1 examines a number of possible services provided by wholesaling middlemen. Numerous types of wholesaling middlemen exist and not all of them provide every service listed in Table 16.1. Producers-suppliers and their customers, who rely on wholesaling middlemen for distribution, select those intermediaries providing the desired combination of services.

The listing of possible services provided by wholesaling middlemen clearly indicates the provision of marketing utility—time, place, and ownership or possession—by these intermediaries. The services also reflect the provision of the basic marketing functions of buying, selling, storing, transporting, risk taking, financing, and supplying market information.

The critical marketing functions—transportation and convenient product storage, reduced costs of buying and selling through reduced contacts, marketing information, and financing—form the basis of evaluating the efficiency of any marketing intermediary. The risk-taking function is present in each of the services provided by the wholesaling middleman.

Transporting and Storing Products

Wholesalers transport and store products at locations convenient to customers. Manufacturers ship products from their warehouse to numerous wholesalers, who then ship smaller quantities to retail outlets in locations convenient to purchasers. A large number of wholesalers assume the inventory function (cost) for the manufacturer. They benefit through the convenience afforded by local inventories. The manufacturer benefits through reduced cash needs, since its products are sold directly to the retailer or wholesaler.

Table 16.1 Possible Wholesaling Services for Customers and Producers-Suppliers

Service	Services Provided for: Customers	Services Provided for: Producer-Suppliers
Buying Anticipates customer demands and possesses knowledge of alternative sources of supply; acts as purchasing agent for their customers.	■	
Selling Provides a sales force to call upon customers thereby providing a low-cost method of servicing smaller retailers and industrial users.		■
Storing Provides a warehousing function at lower cost than most individual producers or retailers could provide. Reduces the risk and cost of maintaining inventory for producers, and provides customers with prompt delivery services.	■	■
Transporting Customers receive prompt delivery in response to their demands, reducing their inventory investments. Wholesalers also break-bulk by purchasing in economical carload or truckload lots, then reselling in smaller quantities to their customers, thereby reducing overall transportation costs.	■	■
Providing Market Information Serves as important marketing research input for producers through regular contacts with retail and industrial buyers. Provides customers with information about new products, technical information about product lines, reports on activities of competitors, industry trends, and advisory information concerning pricing changes, legal changes, and so forth.	■	■
Financing Aids customers by granting credit that might not be available were the customers to purchase directly from manufacturers. Provides financial assistance to producers by purchasing goods in advance of sale and through prompt payment of bills.	■	■
Risk-Taking Assists producers by evaluating credit risks of numerous distant retail customers and small industrial users. Extension of credit to these customers is another form of risk-taking. In addition, the wholesaler responsible for transportation and stocking goods in inventory assumes risk of possible spoilage, theft, or obsolesence.	■	■

Costs are reduced at the wholesale level by making large purchases from the manufacturer. The wholesaler receives quantity discounts from the manufacturer and incurs lower transportation costs because economical carload or truckload shipments are made to the wholesaler's warehouses. At the warehouse, the wholesaler divides the goods into smaller quantities and ships them to the retailer over a shorter distance (but at a higher rate) than would be the case if the manufacturer filled the retailer's order directly from a central warehouse.

Cutting Transactions Cuts Costs

When wholesaling middlemen represent numerous manufacturers to a single customer, the costs involved in buying and selling often decrease. The transaction economies are shown by the example in Figure 16.1. In this illustration, five manufacturers are marketing their outputs to four different retail outlets. A total of 20 transactions result if no intermediary is utilized. By adding a wholesaling middleman, the number of transactions is reduced to nine.

An Information Source

Because of their central position between the manufacturer and retailers or industrial buyers, wholesalers serve as important information links. Wholesalers provide their retail customers with useful information about new products. In addition, they supply manufacturers with information about the market acceptance of their product offerings.

A Financing Source

Wholesalers also perform a financing function. They often provide retailers with goods on credit, allowing the retailers to minimize their cash investment in inventory and pay for most of the goods as they are sold. This allows them to benefit from the principle of leverage, whereby a minimum amount spent on goods in inventory inflates the return on invested funds. A retailer with an investment of $1 million and profits of $100,000 will realize a return of 10 percent. If the necessary invested capital can be reduced to $800,000 through credit from the wholesaler, and if the $100,000 profits can be maintained, the retailer's return increases to 12.5 percent.

Wholesalers of industrial goods provide similar services for the purchasers of their goods. In the steel industry, middlemen (referred to as metal service centers) currently market one fifth of all steel shipped by U.S. mills. One such center, the Earle M. Jorgensen Company in Los Angeles, stocks 6,500 items for sale to many of the 50,000 major metal users who buy in large quantities directly from the steel mills but who turn to service centers for quick delivery of special orders.

Figure 16.1 Achieving Transaction Economy with Wholesaling Middlemen

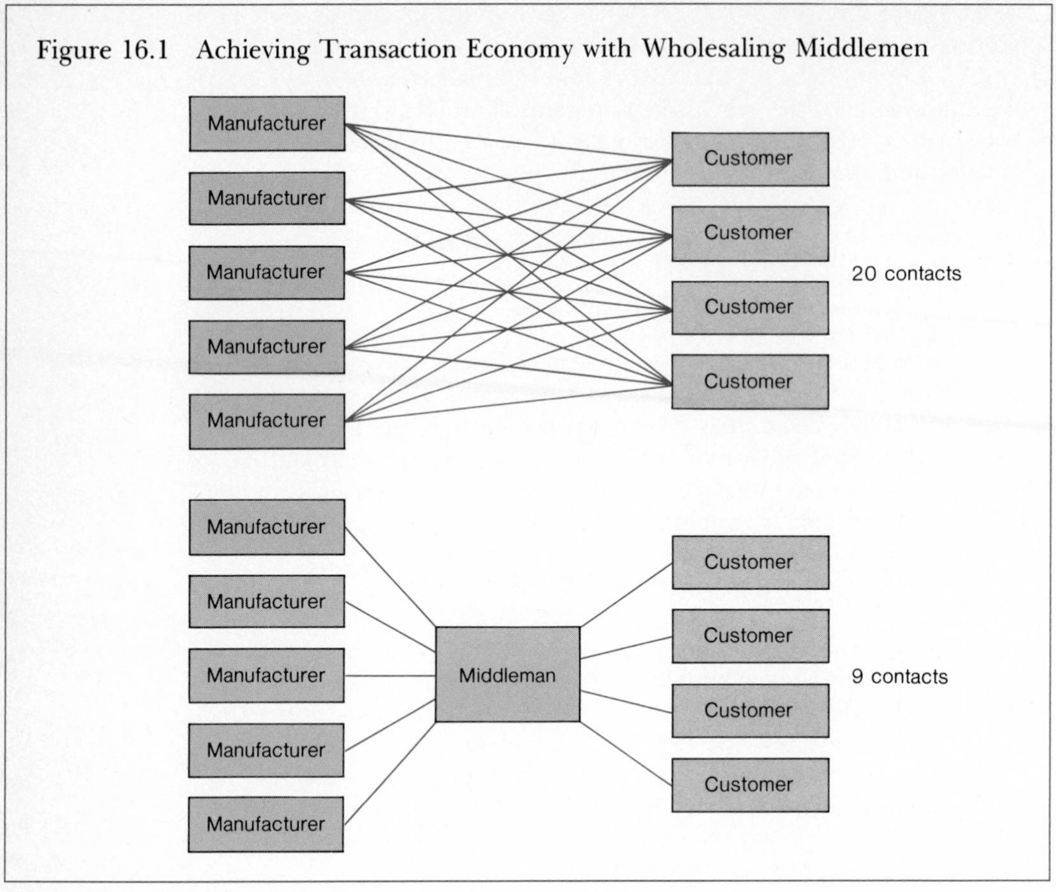

While an order from the mills may take 90 days for delivery, a service center can usually deliver locally within 24 to 48 hours. In order to attract business from key customers, such as AMF, which makes bicycles locally, Jorgensen carried inventory for them without demanding a contract. The cost and risk of maintaining the stock are assumed by the service center in order for it to provide overnight delivery service for its customers.[2]

Who Should Perform Distribution Channel Functions?

While wholesaling middlemen often perform a variety of valuable functions for their producer, retailer, and other wholesale clients, these functions could be performed by other channel members. Manufactur-

[2]Marilyn Wellemeyer, "Middlemen of Metal," *Fortune* (March 1977), pp. 163–165.

Effective Wholesaling Is Crucial to Perrier

Although Perrier's naturally carbonated mineral water has been marketed in the United States since 1903, 75 years passed before it was discovered by the American public. Prior to 1977, Perrier was distributed on a very limited basis through specialty food outlets and fine restaurants to a small number of consumers who valued either its supposed healthful properties or its snob appeal. Bruce Nevins, who headed Perrier's U.S. subsidiary, realized that drastic changes in the firm's wholesaling operations were necessary if the product was to succeed.

Nevins wanted to position Perrier as a chic alternative to cocktails and soft drinks. He noted that a number of people had switched from "browns" (bourbon and scotch) to "whites" (gin and vodka) and then to wine. According to Nevins, "The next step is away from alcohol altogether, which puts Perrier in a nice position." His challenge: to develop a distribution network that reached bars and cocktail lounges.

His second task was to tackle the enormous soft-drink market, aiming for a one percent market share. He shifted his distribution structure away from the gourmet shops and toward grocery stores.

Nevins' solution was to turn to independent wholesalers to handle distribution. Independent wholesale soft-drink bottlers were utilized to reach supermarkets and mass merchandisers such as K mart, while beer wholesalers covered liquor retailers, bars, and cocktail lounges.

All facets of the marketing mix were involved in the Perrier success. Effective promotion, retail prices in accordance with its chic appeal, and appealing packaging are important factors, but none of these was sufficient without the system of wholesale distribution designed to reach the firm's market target. The success of the Perrier marketing program is summarized in the growth of the product's sales. In 1976, prior to the implementation of the new marketing program, Perrier annual sales amounted to a mere 3.5 million bottles. Four years later, they had soared to 180 million bottles.

Source: Information from "Putting More Sparkle into Sales," *Sales & Marketing Management* (January 1979), pp. 16–17; Bob Greene, "Genius Sells Water at $2.39 a Six-Pack," *Tulsa World* (November 11, 1978); and Bernice Finkelman, "Perrier Pours into U.S. Market, Spurs Water Bottler Battle," *Marketing News* (September 7, 1979), pp. 1, 9.

ers may choose to bypass independent wholesaling middlemen by establishing networks of regional warehouses, maintaining large sales forces to provide market coverage, serving as sources of information for their retail customers, and assuming the financing function. In some instances, they may decide to push the responsibility for some of these functions through the channel on to the retailer or the ultimate purchaser. Large retailers who choose to perform their own wholesaling operations face the same choices.

A fundamental marketing principle applies to marketing channel decisions: Marketing functions must be performed by some member of the channel. They can be shifted, but they cannot be eliminated. Larger retailers who bypass the wholesaler and deal directly with the producer either assume the functions previously performed by wholesaling middlemen, or these functions will be performed by the producer. Similarly, a producer who deals directly with the ultimate consumer or with industrial buyers will assume the functions of storage, delivery, and marketing information previously performed by marketing intermediaries. Middlemen can be eliminated from the channel, but the channel functions must be performed by someone.

The potential gain for the producer or retailer is summarized in Table 16.2. The table shows the potential savings if channel members performed the wholesale functions as efficiently as the independent wholesaling middleman. Such savings, indicated in the profit as a percentage of net sales column, could be used to reduce retail prices, to increase the profits of the manufacturer or retailer, or both. However, wholesalers are specialists, and can usually perform their tasks more efficiently than others who might take over these functions.

The most revealing information in Table 16.2 is the low profit rates earned by most wholesalers. Five types of wholesalers (confectionary, dairy products, groceries, meats and meat products, and tobacco and tobacco products) earn 1.5 percent or less profit as a percentage of net sales, while the group with the highest profit as a percentage of sales (automotive parts and supplies) earned 3.7 percent.

Table 16.2 also indicates a positive relationship between annual turnover rate (as measured by total sales divided by the average inventory) and net profits as a percentage of net sales. Wholesaling middlemen, such as those in dairy and meat products, enjoyed relatively high turnover rates. These rates permitted the firms to generate sufficient financial returns with lower net profits (on a percentage of net sales basis) than many of the other intermediaries with lower turnover rates.

Types of Wholesaling Middlemen

As noted earlier, various types of wholesaling middlemen are present in different marketing channels. Some provide a wide range of services or handle a broad line of products, while others specialize in a single service, product, or industry. Figure 16.2 classifies wholesaling middlemen by two characteristics: ownership (whether the wholesaling middleman is independent, manufacturer-owned, or retailer-owned) and title flows (whether title passes from the manufacturer to the wholesaling middleman). There are, in turn, three basic types of ownership: (1) independent wholesaling middlemen, (2) manufacturer-owned sales offices and branches, (3) retailer-owned cooperatives and buying offices.

Table 16.2 Median Net Profits and Turnover Rates of Selected Wholesalers

Kind of Business	Profits as a Percentage of Net Sales[a]	Annual Turnover Rate[b]
Automotive parts and supplies	3.7%	4.7
Beer, wine, and distilled beverages	2.9	12.4
Clothing and furnishings	2.8	6.8
Confectionary	1.3	12.9
Dairy products	1.5	33.9
Drugs, proprietaries, and sundries	1.6	7.5
Electrical appliances, TV, and radio sets	2.2	5.8
Footwear	2.8	5.0
Furniture and home furnishings	2.9	6.3
Groceries, general line	1.3	12.3
Hardware	3.6	6.0
Meats and meat products	1.1	36.0
Paper and paper products	3.1	9.3
Petroleum products	2.0	27.9
Tires and tubes	2.3	5.7
Tobacco and tobacco products	0.8	15.6

[a]Return on net sales

[b]Net sales to inventory

Source: "The Ratios," *Dun's Review* (November 1981), pp. 137–149. Reprinted with special permission of *Dun's Business Month* (formerly *Dun's Review*), Copyright 1981, Dun & Bradstreet Publications Corporation.

The two types of independent wholesaling middlemen are merchant wholesalers who do take title to goods and agents and brokers who do not.[3]

Manufacturer-Owned Outlets

An increasing volume of products is being marketed directly by manufacturers through company-owned facilities for several reasons. Some products are perishable; some require complex installation or servicing; others need aggressive promotion; still others are high-unit value goods that the manufacturer can sell profitably to the ultimate purchaser. Among those who have shifted from the use of independent wholesaling middlemen to the use of company-owned channels are manufacturers of apparel, construction materials, lumber, paint, paper, and piece

[3]An interesting discussion of types of wholesaling appears in J. Howard Westing, "Wholesale Indifference," *The Courier* (Spring, 1982), pp. 3, 8.

Figure 16.2 Major Types of Wholesaling Middlemen

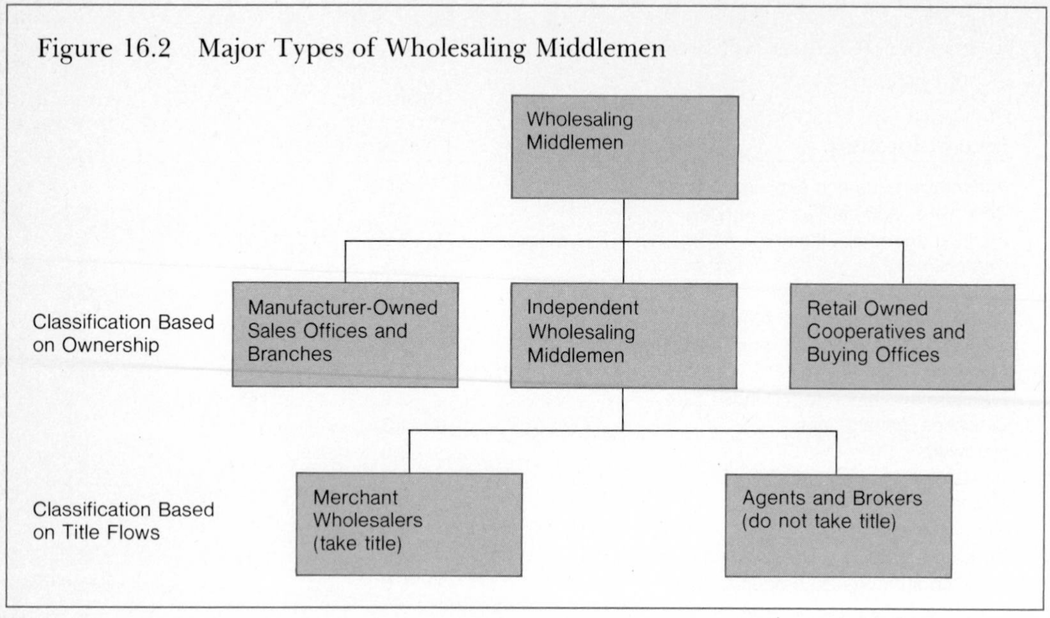

goods.[4] More than half of all industrial goods are sold directly to users by manufacturers, and slightly more than one third of all products are marketed through manufacturer-owned channels.[5]

Sales Branches and Offices The basic distinction between a company's sales branches and sales offices is that a **sales branch** carries inventory and processes orders to customers from available stock. Branches duplicate the storage function of independent wholesalers and serve as offices for sales representatives in the territory. They are prevalent in the marketing of chemicals, commercial machinery and equipment, motor vehicles, and petroleum products. Operating expenses for the 26,892 sales branches in the United States average 8.9 percent of sales. General Electric has sales branches in every major city in the United States. Its subsidiary, General Electric Supply Corporation, provides regular contacts and overnight delivery to GE retailers and industrial purchasers.

Since warehouses represent a substantial investment in real estate, small producers and even large firms developing new sales territories

[4]James R. Moore, "Wholesaling: Structural Changes and Manufacturers' Perceptions," *Foundations of Marketing Channels,* (eds.) Arch G. Woodside, J. Taylor Sims, Dale M. Lewison, and Ian F. Wilkinson (Austin, Tex.: Austin Press, 1978), pp. 118–131.

[5]Louis P. Bucklin, *Competition and Evolution in the Distributive Trades* (Englewood Cliffs, N.J.: Prentice-Hall, 1972), p. 214.

may choose to use a **public warehouse**—an independently owned storage facility. For a rental fee, producers can store their goods in any of the more than 10,000 public warehouses in the United States for shipment by the warehouses to customers in the area. Warehouse owners package goods into small quantities to fill orders and even handle billing for manufacturers. Public warehouses can also provide a financial service for manufacturers by issuing warehouse receipts for inventory. Manufacturers can use these receipts as collateral for bank loans.

A **sales office,** by contrast, does not carry stock but serves as a regional office for the firm's sales personnel. Sales offices in close proximity to the firm's customers help reduce selling costs and improve customer service. The listing of a firm in the local telephone directory often results in new sales for the local representative. Many buyers prefer to telephone the office of a supplier rather than take the time to write to distant suppliers. Since the nation's 13,629 sales offices do not perform a storage function, their operating expenses are relatively low, averaging 3.1 percent of total sales.

Other Outlets for the Manufacturer's Products. In addition to using a sales force and regionally distributed sales branches, manufacturers often market their products through trade fairs and merchandise marts. A **trade fair** (or a trade exhibition) is a periodic show where manufacturers in a particular industry display their wares for visiting retail and wholesale buyers. The New York City toy fair and the furniture show in High Point, North Carolina, are annual events for manufacturers and purchasers of toys and furniture. The cost of making face-to-face contact with a prospective customer at a trade fair is only 41 percent of the cost of a personal sales call. In addition, such exhibitions represent effective methods of generating additional sales. One study of attendees at the National Computer Conference in Anaheim, California, revealed that within the eleven months following the conference, four out of five attendees had purchased at least one product on display and the average purchase had been $254,100.[6]

A **merchandise mart** provides space for permanent exhibitions where producers rent display areas for their product offerings. The largest is the Merchandise Mart in Chicago, which is two blocks long, a block wide, and 21 floors high. Over a million items are displayed there. Retail buyers can compare the offerings of dozens of competing producers and make most purchase decisions in a single visit to a trade fair or merchandise mart.

[6]"Surveys Find Trade Shows Cost-Effective, Productive," *Marketing News* (October 3, 1980), p. 4. See also J. Steven Kelly and James M. Comer, "Trade Show Exhibiting: A Managerial Perspective," in *Evolving Marketing Thought for 1980,* (eds.) John H. Summey and Ronald D. Taylor (Southern Marketing Association, 1980), pp. 11–13.

Table 16.3 Wholesale Trade by Type of Operation

Type of Operation	Number of Establishments	Sales (in Billions)	Percentage of Total Sales
Merchant wholesalers	307,624	$ 676.1	53.7%
Manufacturers' sales branches and offices	40,521	451.9	35.9
Agents, brokers, and commission merchants	35,052	130.4	10.4
Total wholesale trade	382,837	$1,258.4	100.0%

Source: U.S. Department of Commerce, Bureau of the Census, *1977 Census of Business Wholesale Trade—Geographic Area Series 52–19* (Washington, D.C.: U.S. Government Printing Office, 1980).

Independent Wholesaling Middlemen

As Table 16.3 indicates, independent wholesaling middlemen account for 90 percent of the wholesale establishments and approximately two thirds of the wholesale sales in the United States. They can be divided into two categories—merchant wholesalers and agents and brokers.

Merchant Wholesalers The **merchant wholesaler** takes title to the goods handled. Merchant wholesalers account for slightly more than 53 percent of all sales at the wholesale level, and their sales are projected to reach the $1 trillion mark by 1985.[7] They can be further classified as full-function or limited-function wholesalers, as indicated in Figure 16.3.

Full-Function Merchant Wholesalers. A complete assortment of services for retailers and industrial purchasers is provided by full-function merchant wholesalers. These wholesalers store merchandise in convenient locations, thereby allowing their customers to make purchases on short notice and to minimize their inventory requirements. They also usually maintain sales forces to call regularly on retailers, make deliveries, and extend credit to qualified buyers. In the industrial goods market, full-function merchant wholesalers (often called industrial distributors) usually market machinery, inexpensive accessory equipment, and supplies.

Full-function merchant wholesalers prevail in industries where retailers are small and carry large numbers of relatively inexpensive items, none of which is stocked in depth. The drug, grocery, and hardware industries have traditionally been serviced by full-function merchant wholesalers.

[7]Benson Shapiro, "Improve Distribution with Your Promotional Mix," *Harvard Business Review* (March–April 1977), p. 116.

Figure 16.3 Classification of Independent Wholesaling Middlemen

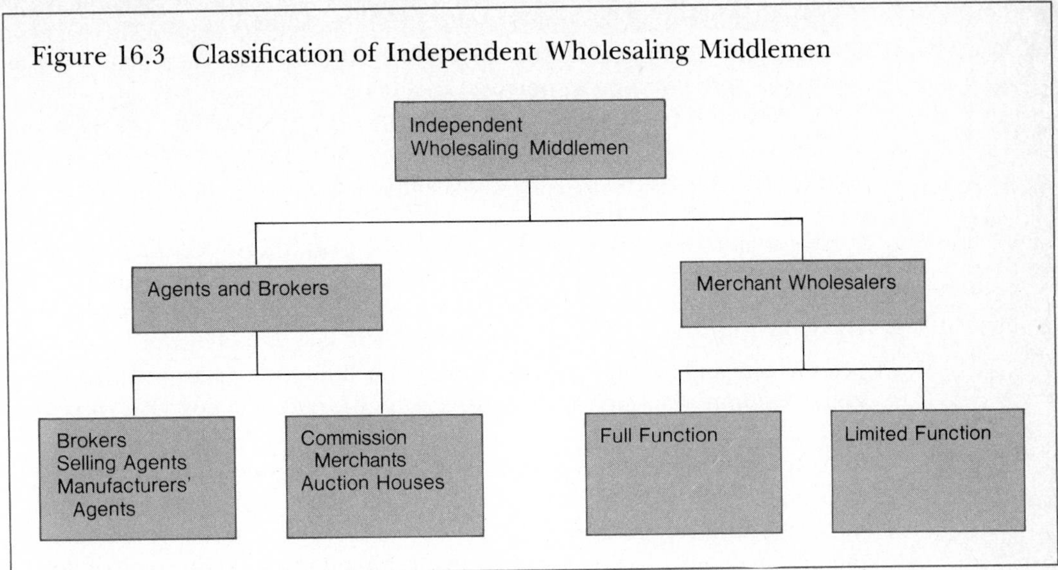

A unique type of service wholesaler emerged after World War II as grocery retailers began to stock high profit-margin nonfood items. Since store managers knew little about such products as health and beauty items, housewares, paperback books, records, and toys, the **rack jobber** provided the necessary expertise. This wholesaler supplies the racks, stocks the merchandise, prices the goods, and makes regular visits to refill the shelves. In essence, rack jobbers rent space from retailers on a commission basis. They have expanded into discount, drug, hardware, and variety stores.

Since full-function merchant wholesalers perform a large number of services, their operating expenses average nearly 13 percent, and sometimes as high as 20 percent, of sales. Attempts to reduce the costs of dealing with these wholesalers have led to the development of a number of limited-function middlemen.

Limited-Function Merchant Wholesalers. Four types of limited-function merchant wholesalers are cash-and-carry wholesalers, truck wholesalers, drop shippers, and mail-order wholesalers. The **cash-and-carry wholesaler** performs most wholesaling functions with the exception of financing and delivery. These wholesalers first appeared on the marketing scene in the grocery industry during the Depression era of the 1930s. In an attempt to reduce costs, retailers began driving to wholesalers' warehouses, paying cash for their purchases, and making their own deliveries. By eliminating the delivery and financing functions, cash-and-carry wholesalers were able to reduce their operating costs to approximately 9 percent of sales.

Although feasible for small stores, this kind of wholesaling proves to be generally unworkable for large-scale grocery stores. Chain store managers are unwilling to perform the delivery function, and cash-and-carry these days is typically one department of a regular full-service wholesaler. The cash-and-carry wholesaler has proven successful, however, in the United Kingdom, where 600 such operations produce over $1 billion a year in sales.

The **truck wholesaler,** or truck jobber, markets perishable food items such as bread, tobacco, potato chips, candy, and dairy products. Truck wholesalers make regular deliveries to retail stores and perform the sales and collection functions. They also aggressively promote their product lines. The high costs of operating delivery trucks and the low dollar volume per sale mean relatively high operating costs of 15 percent.

A **drop shipper** receives orders from customers and forwards them to producers, who ship directly to the customers. Although drop shippers take title to the goods, they never physically handle or even see them. Since they perform no storage or handling functions, their operating costs are a relatively low 4 to 5 percent of sales.

Drop shippers operate in fields where products are bulky and customers make their purchases in carload lots. Transportation and handling costs represent a substantial percentage of the total cost of such products as coal and lumber. Drop shippers do not maintain an inventory of these products, thereby eliminating the expenses of loading and unloading carload shipments. Their major service is the development of a complete assortment for customers. Since various types and grades of coal and lumber are produced by different companies, drop shippers can assemble a complete line to fill any customer's order.

The **mail-order wholesaler** is a limited-function merchant wholesaler who relies on catalogs rather than a sales force to contact retail, industrial, and institutional customers. Purchases are made by mail or telephone by relatively small customers in outlying areas. Mail-order operations are found in the hardware, cosmetics, jewelry, sporting goods, and specialty food lines, as well as in general merchandise.

Table 16.4 compares the various types of merchant wholesalers in terms of services provided. Full-function merchant wholesalers and truck wholesalers are relatively high-cost intermediaries due to the number of services they perform, while cash-and-carry wholesalers, drop shippers, and mail-order wholesalers provide fewer services and have relatively low operating costs.

Agents and Brokers A second group of independent wholesaling middlemen—**agents and brokers**—may or may not take possession of the goods, but they never take title. They normally perform fewer services than the merchant wholesalers and are typically involved in bringing together buyers and sellers. Agent wholesaling middlemen can be clas-

Table 16.4 Services Provided by Merchant Wholesalers

		Limited-Function Wholesalers			
Services	Full-Function Wholesalers	Cash-and-Carry Wholesalers	Truck Wholesalers	Drop Shippers	Mail-Order Wholesalers
Anticipates customer needs	Yes	Yes	Yes	No	Yes
Carries inventory	Yes	Yes	Yes	No	Yes
Delivers	Yes	No	Yes	No	No
Provides market information	Yes	Rarely	Yes	Yes	No
Provides credit	Yes	No	No	Yes	Sometimes
Assumes ownership risk by taking title	Yes	Yes	Yes	Yes	Yes

sified into five categories—commission merchants, auction houses, brokers, selling agents, and manufacturers' agents.

The **commission merchant,** who predominates in the marketing of agricultural products, takes possession when the producer ships goods such as grain, produce, and livestock to a central market for sale. Commission merchants act as the producer's agents and receive an agreed upon fee when the sale is made. Since customers inspect the products, and since prices fluctuate, commission merchants receive considerable latitude in making decisions. The owner of the goods may specify a minimum price, but the commission merchant will sell them on a "best price" basis. The merchant's fee is deducted from the price and remitted to the original owner.

Auction houses bring buyers and sellers together in one location and allow potential buyers to inspect the merchandise before purchasing it. Auction houses' commissions are often based on the sale price of the goods. Sotheby Parke Bernet of New York, London, and Los Angeles is a well-known auction house specializing in works of art. Other auction houses handle used cars, livestock, tobacco, fur, fruit, and other commodities.

Brokers bring buyers and sellers together. Brokers operate in industries characterized by a large number of small suppliers and purchasers—real estate, frozen foods, and used machinery, for example. They represent either the buyer or the seller in a given transaction, but not both. Brokers receive a fee from the client when the transaction is completed. Since the only service they perform is negotiating for exchange of title, their operating expense ratio can be as low as 2 percent.

Because brokers operate on a one-time basis for sellers or buyers, they cannot serve as an effective marketing channel for producers seeking regular, continuing services. A manufacturer who seeks to develop a more permanent channel utilizing agent wholesaling middlemen must evaluate the use of the selling agent or the manufacturers' agent.

Selling agents have often been referred to as independent marketing departments, since they can be responsible for the total marketing program of a firm's product line. Typically, a **selling agent** has full authority over pricing decisions and promotional outlays, and often the agent provides financial assistance for the producer. The producer can concentrate on production and rely on the expertise of the selling agent for all marketing activities. Selling agents are common in the coal, lumber, and textile industries. For small, poorly financed, production-oriented firms, they may prove the ideal distribution channel.

While producers may utilize only one selling agent, they often use a number of **manufacturers' agents**—independent salespeople who work for a number of manufacturers of related but noncompeting products and who receive commissions based on a specified percentage of sales. Although some commissions are as high as 20 percent of sales, they usually average between 6 and 7 percent. Unlike selling agents, who may be given exclusive world rights to market a manufacturer's products, manufacturers' agents operate in a specified territory.[8]

Manufacturers' agents reduce their selling costs by spreading the cost per sales call over a number of different products. An agent in the plumbing supplies industry, for example, may represent a dozen producers.

Manufacturers develop their marketing channels through the use of manufacturers' agents for several reasons. First, when they are developing new sales territories, the costs of adding salespeople to pioneer the territory may be prohibitive. Agents, who are paid on a commission basis, can perform the sales function in these territories at a much lower cost.

Second, firms with unrelated lines may need to employ more than one channel. One line of products may be marketed through the company's sales force. Another may be marketed through independent manufacturers' agents. This is particularly common where the unrelated product line is a recent addition and the firm's sales force has no experience with it.

Finally, small firms with no existing sales force may turn to manufacturers' agents in order to have access to their market. A newly organized firm producing pencil sharpeners may use office equipment and supplies agents to reach retailers and industrial purchasers.

The importance of selling agents has declined since 1940 because of manufacturers' desire to control their marketing efforts. In contrast, the volume of sales by manufacturers' agents more than doubled over

[8]For a profile of the typical manufacturers' agent, see Stanley D. Sibley and Roy K. Teas, "Agent Marketing Channel Intermediaries' Perceptions of Marketing Channel Performance," in *Proceedings of the Southern Marketing Association*, (eds.) Robert S. Franz, Robert M. Hopkins, and Al Toma (New Orleans, La.: November 1978), pp. 336–339.

Table 16.5 Services Provided by Agents and Brokers

Services	Commission Merchants	Auction Houses	Brokers	Manufacturers' Agents	Selling Agents
Anticipates customer needs	Yes	Some	Some	Yes	Yes
Carries inventory	Yes	Yes	No	No	No
Delivers	Yes	No	No	Some	No
Provides market information	Yes	Yes	Yes	Yes	Yes
Provides credit	Some	No	No	No	Some
Assumes ownership risk by taking title	No	No	No	No	No

the period of 1939 to 1977, and it now comprises 37 percent of all sales by agent wholesaling middlemen. In 1977, the nation's 20,000 agents accounted for more than $48 billion in sales. The various types of agents and brokers are compared in Table 16.5.

Retailer-Owned Facilities

Retailers have also assumed numerous wholesaling functions in an attempt to reduce costs or to provide special service. Independent retailers have occasionally banded together to form buying groups in an attempt to achieve cost savings through quantity purchases. Other groups of retailers have established retailer-owned wholesale facilities by the formation of a cooperative chain. Larger-sized chain retailers often establish centralized buying offices to negotiate large-scale purchases directly with producers for the chain members.

Costs of the Wholesaling Middlemen

Costs of the various wholesaling middlemen are calculated as a percentage of total sales. Figure 16.4 lists the costs of each major category. The primary conclusion to be drawn is that expense variations result from differences in the number of services provided by each middleman. Cost ratios are highest for merchant wholesalers and manufacturers' sales branches because both provide such services as maintenance of inventories, market coverage by a sales force, and transportation. Brokers perform only one service: bringing buyers and sellers together. As a consequence, they have the lowest expense ratios. Of course, these ratios are averages and will vary among firms within each category, depending on the actual services provided.

Figure 16.4 Operating Expenses as Percentages of Sales by Wholesaling Middlemen

Merchant Wholesalers	12.7%
Manufacturers' Sales Branches	8.9%
Manufacturers' Agents	6.6%
Commission Merchants	4.8%
Brokers	3.2%
Manufacturers' Sales Offices	3.1%
Auction Companies	3.0%

Source: U.S. Department of Commerce, Bureau of the Census, *1977 Census of Wholesale Trade*, Vol. 11, Part I, p. 8.

Independent Wholesaling Middlemen— Still an Important Marketing Institution

Many marketing observers of the 1930s felt that the end had come for the independent wholesaling middlemen as chain stores grew in importance and attempted to bypass them. Over the ten-year period from 1929 to 1939, the independent wholesalers' sales volume did indeed drop, but it has increased since then. Figure 16.5 shows how the relative shares of total wholesale trade have changed since 1929.

While the period from 1929 to the present has seen the decline in importance of agents and brokers and the increase in importance of company-owned channels, independent wholesaling middlemen are far from obsolete. In fact, they are responsible for nearly two thirds of all wholesale trade. Their continued importance is evidence of their ability to adjust to changing conditions and needs. Their market size proves their ability to continue to fill a need in many marketing channels.

Summary

Wholesalers are one of the two major institutions that make up a firm's distribution channel. They are persons or firms who sell to retailers and other wholesalers or to industrial users but who do not sell in significant amounts to ultimate consumers. The three types of wholesaling middlemen are manufacturer-owned facilities, merchant wholesalers, and

Figure 16.5 Types of Wholesale Trade Operation as a Percentage of Total Sales: 1929–1977

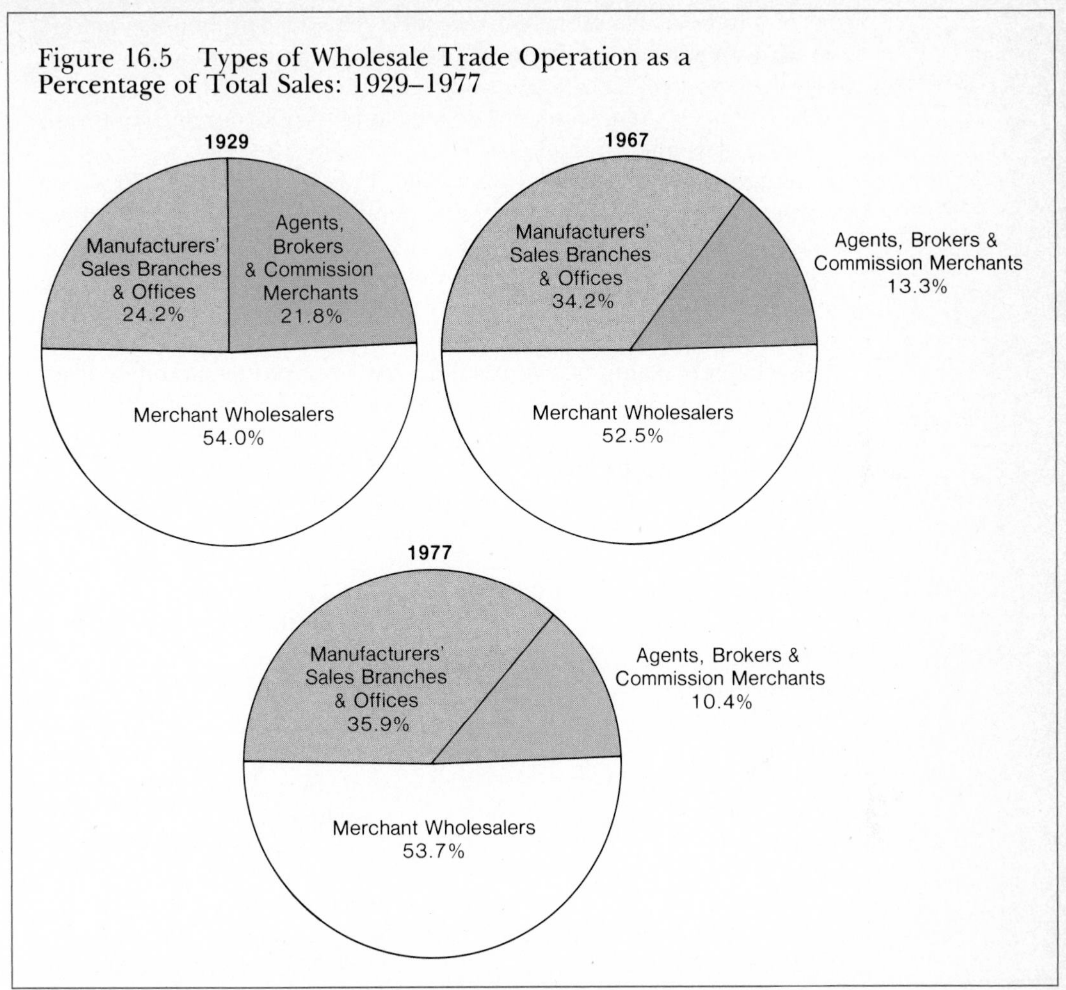

Petroleum bulk station and assembler percentages are combined with merchant wholesalers' data for 1929 and 1967 for comparison with 1977 data.

Source: 1977 data from 1977 *Census of Wholesale Trade—Geographic Area Series 52-19* (Washington, D.C.: U.S. Government Printing Office, 1980). 1929 and 1967 data from James R. Moore and Kendall A. Adams, "Functional Wholesaler Sales Trends and Analysis," in *Combined Proceedings* (Chicago, Ill.: American Marketing Association, 1976), p. 402.

agents and brokers. Merchant wholesalers take title to the goods they handle. Agents and brokers may take possession of the goods but do not take title. Merchant wholesalers include full-function wholesalers, rack jobbers, cash-and-carry wholesalers, truck wholesalers, drop shippers, and mail-order wholesalers. Commission merchants, auction houses, brokers, selling agents, and manufacturers' agents are classified as agent wholesaling middlemen because they do not take title to goods.

The operating expenses of wholesaling middlemen vary considerably depending on the services provided and the costs involved. The services include storage facilities in conveniently located warehouses, market coverage by a sales force, financing for retailers and producers, market information for retailers and producers, transportation, and, specifically for retailers, management services, retail sales training, and merchandising assistance and advice.

Although the percentage of wholesale trade by manufacturer-owned facilities has increased since 1929, independent wholesaling middlemen continue to account for 90 percent of all wholesale establishments and nearly two thirds of total wholesale trade. They accomplish this by continuing to provide desired services to manufacturers, retailers, and industrial buyers.

This chapter examined wholesaling, an important marketing institution within the distribution system. It has built on the general distribution concepts introduced in Chapter 15. The next chapter considers the other major institution in the marketing channel—retailing.

Key Terms

wholesaler
wholesaling middlemen
sales branch
public warehouse
sales office
trade fair
merchandise mart
merchant wholesaler
rack jobber
cash-and-carry wholesaler
truck wholesaler
drop shipper
mail-order wholesaler
agents
brokers
commission merchant
auction houses
selling agent
manufacturers' agent

Review Questions

1. Distinguish between a wholesaler and a retailer.
2. In what ways do wholesaling middlemen assist manufacturers? How do they assist retailers?
3. Explain how wholesaling middlemen can assist retailers in increasing their return on investment.
4. Distinguish between sales offices and sales branches. Under what conditions might each type be used?
5. What role does the public warehouse play in distribution channels?
6. Distinguish merchant wholesalers from agents and brokers.
7. Why is the operating expense ratio of the merchant wholesaler higher than that of the typical agent or broker?
8. In what ways are commission merchants and brokers different?
9. Distinguish between a manufacturers' agent and a selling agent.
10. Under what conditions would a manufacturer utilize manufacturers' agents for a distribution channel?

Discussion Questions and Exercises

1. Match each of the following industries with the most appropriate wholesaling middleman:

_____Groceries	**a.** Drop shipper
_____Potato chips	**b.** Truck wholesaler
_____Coal	**c.** Auction house
_____Grain	**d.** Manufacturers' agent
_____Antiques	**e.** Full-function merchant wholesaler
	f. Commission merchant

2. Comment on the following statements: Drop shippers are good candidates for elimination. All they do is process orders. They don't even handle the goods.
3. Prepare a brief five-page report on a wholesaler in your local area.
4. The term *broker* also appears in the real estate and securities fields. Are these brokers identical to the agent wholesaling middlemen described in this chapter?
5. Interview someone who works at a local wholesaling firm. Report to the class on this person's job within the wholesaling sector.

17

RETAILING

Chapter Objectives

1. *To relate retailing to the other variables of the marketing mix.*
2. *To outline the decision framework for retailing.*
3. *To distinguish between limited-line retailers and general merchandise retailers.*
4. *To identify and explain each of the five bases for categorizing retailers.*
5. *To identify the major types of mass merchandisers.*
6. *To explain the types of nonstore retailing.*
7. *To distingish between chain and independent retailers and to identify several industries dominated by chains.*
8. *To contrast the three types of planned shopping centers.*

It is not surprising that Revco drugstores have one of the highest profitability rates and earnings growth in the industry. The Ohio-based firm leaves little to chance when it comes to merchandising. Consider the shampoo shelf: Head & Shoulders is the nation's leading brand of shampoo, so Revco positions the standard size package of the Procter & Gamble product on the left side of the shelf. To its right, they place the Revco label, which is similar to that of the national brand. In fact, the Revco product even says, "If You Like Head & Shoulders, Try Ours." Finally, the family size package of Head & Shoulders is placed to the right of the Revco label.

Why does Revco spend so much effort lining up its shampoo? The retailer gets higher profit margins from their own private labels and larger sizes of national brands. And since most people are right handed, they are more likely to reach for one of Revco's alternatives to Head & Shoulders' standard size package.

The shampoo department is just one example of Revco thoroughness and expertise. The firm analyzes all products by inches of shelf space and develops elaborate plans for each store. Revco places the pharmacy at the front rather than the back of the store in order to reduce personnel since an additional cash register will not be needed. Similarly, Revco does not have a salesperson for cosmetics. Instead, it displays cosmetics by brand name rather than product types. Revco management concluded that most women buy cosmetics by brand name and were more likely to make additional purchases if the entire product line of a particular label was displayed together.

Revco uses what it calls "everyday discount prices" rather than weekly specials. This policy eliminates periodic pricing decisions at the store level. The company does offer a 10 percent discount for senior adults on Revco label products and prescriptions, its two highest margin items. Revco works hard to build its older clientele; it knows that seniors are three times more likely to fill prescriptions than the store's younger customers.[1] As noted earlier, Revco leaves little to chance.

The Conceptual Framework

Retailing is the third aspect of distribution to be considered here. Chapter 15 introduced basic concepts in channel strategy. Wholesaling middlemen were discussed in Chapter 16. This chapter explores retailing, which often links the consumer with the rest of the distribution channel.

Retail outlets serve as contact points between channel members and the ultimate consumer. In a very real sense, retailers are the distribution channel for most consumers, since the typical shopper has little contact with manufacturers and virtually none with wholesaling intermediaries. Retailers represent the consumer as a purchasing agent to the rest of the distribution channel. The services provided by retailers—location, store hours, quality of salespeople, store layout, selection, and the returns policy, among others—are often more important than the physical product in developing consumer images of the products and services offered. Both large and small retailers perform the major channel activities: creating time, place and possession utility.

Retailers are both customers and marketers in the channel. They market products and services to ultimate consumers, and they also are the customers of wholesalers and manufacturers. Because of this critical location in the channel, retailers often perform an important feedback

[1]Eamonn Fingleton, "Knocking Off Head & Shoulders," *Forbes* (June 7, 1982), pp. 162, 164.

role. They obtain information from customers and transmit it to manufacturers and other channel members.

Retailing may be defined as all of the activities involved in the sale of products and services to the ultimate consumer. Although the bulk of all retail sales occur in retail stores, the definition of retailing also includes several forms of nonstore retailing. Nonstore retailing involves such retail activities as telephone and mail-order sales, vending machine sales, and direct house-to-house solicitations.

The Evolution of Retailing

Early retailing can be traced to the establishment of trading posts, such as the Hudson Bay Company, and to pack peddlers who literally carried their wares to outlying settlements. The first important retail institution in the United States was the general store, a general merchandise store stocked to meet the needs of a small community or rural area. Here, customers could buy clothing, groceries, feed, seed, farm equipment, drugs, spectacles, and candy.

The basic needs that caused the general store to develop also doomed it to a limited existence. Since storekeepers attempted to satisfy the needs of customers for all types of goods, they carried a small assortment of each good. As communities grew, new stores opened, and they concentrated on specific product lines, such as drugs, dry goods, groceries, and hardware. The general stores could not compete, and their owners either converted them into more specialized, limited-line stores or closed them. Today, general stores still do exist in some rural areas. Only a few hundred stores are still operating, mostly in rural areas of the South and West.

Innovation in Retailing

Retailing operations serve as remarkable illustrations of the marketing concept in operation. The development of retail innovations can be traced to attempts to better satisfy particular consumer needs.

As consumers demanded different satisfactions from retailers, new institutions emerged to meet this demand. The supermarket appeared in the early 1930s in response to consumer desire for lower prices. Today, convenience food stores and mass merchandisers meet consumers' desires for convenience in purchasing and late-hour availability. Discount houses and catalog stores reflect consumer demand for lower prices and the willingness to give up services. Department stores meet the demands of their clientele by offering a wide variety of products and services. Vending machines, door-to-door retailing, and mail-order retailing offer the ultimate in buyer convenience. Planned shopping centers provide a balanced array of consumer goods and services and include parking facilities for their customers. The nation's two million retailing establishments are involved in developing specific marketing mixes designed to satisfy chosen market targets.[2]

Scope of the Modern Retail Market

The most recent Census of Retail Trade revealed that there were approximately 1,860,000 retail stores and about 150,000 direct-selling operations in the United States. Total retail sales amounted to $723 billion. As Figure 17.1 indicates, the Great Lakes, Mideast, and the Southeast regions account for almost 60 percent of total retail sales.

The Decision Framework for Retailing

While much of the discussion of marketing decisions so far in the text has centered upon manufacturers, the same concepts apply to retail marketers. The decision framework for retailers, like manufacturers and wholesalers, centers upon the two fundamental steps of (1) analyzing, evaluating, and ultimately selecting a *market target,* and (2) development of a *marketing mix* designed to profitably satisfy the chosen market target. The retailer must determine his or her market target. Then a product or service offering must be developed to appeal to that consumer group. Prices must be set and location and distribution decisions made. Finally, a promotional strategy has to be developed.[3]

The Market Target

Like other marketers, retailers must start by selecting the market target to which they wish to appeal. Marketing research is often used in this aspect of retail decision making. When Sears acquired Dean Witter Reynolds Inc. stockbrokerage, it was surprised when research indicated that their credit-card holders increased according to income levels. Some 76 percent of all households with a net worth of $500,000 or

[2]Gerald Albaum, Roger Best, and Del Hawkins, "Retailing Strategy for Customer Growth and New Customer Attraction," *Journal of Business Research* (March 1980), pp. 7–19; and Bert Rosenbloom, "Strategic Planning in Retailing: Prospects and Problems," *Journal of Retailing* (Spring 1980), pp. 107–120.

[3]Interesting discussions include Sak Onkvisit and John J. Shaw, "Modifying the Retail Classification System for More Timely Marketing Strategies," *Journal of the Academy of Marketing Science* (Fall 1981), pp. 436–453; and Bobby C. Vaught, L. Lyn Judd, and Jack M. Starling, "The Perceived Importance of Retailing Strategies and Their Relationships to Four Indexes of Retailing Success," in *Progress in Marketing: Theory and Practice,* (eds.) Ronald D. Taylor, John J. Bennen, and John H. Summey (Carbondale, Ill.: Southern Marketing Association, 1981), pp. 25–28.

Figure 17.1 Geographical Patterns in Retail Sales in the United States

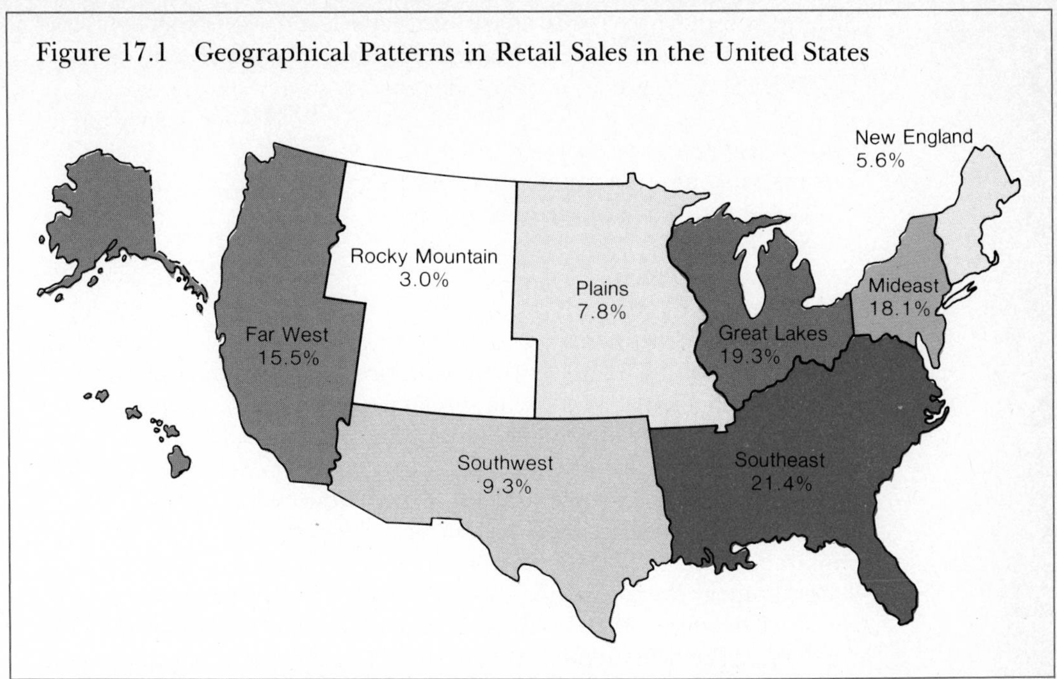

Source: Based on U.S. Department of Commerce, Bureau of the Census, *1977 Census of Retail Trade: U.S. Summary,* RC77-A 52 (Washington, D.C.: U.S. Government Printing Office, 1980).

more held a Sears credit card. Sears had always assumed its customer base had lower incomes than was actually the case.[4] This example points out the importance of marketing research in selecting a segmentation strategy.

Pittsburgh's Kaufmann's department store offers lunch-hour seminars, late hours, and career planning workshops. All of these efforts are directed at attracting working women.[5] Statistics indicate working women spend considerably more for clothing than do either men or nonworking women, so demographic segmentation helped Kaufmann's determine its prime market target.

Sometimes a retailer finds it necessary to shift its strategy. Jos. A. Banks Clothiers, Inc.—a retail outlet and mail-order firm owned by Quaker Oats—traditionally concentrated on a 45-year-old customer base. Management decided to shift its orientation to affluent 20 to 30-year-olds to take advantage of its popular new line of preppy clothing.[6]

[4]"The New Sears," *Business Week* (November 16, 1981), p. 143.

[5]Barbara Oman, "Department Stores Start Adding Seminars and Services to Attract Working Women," *The Wall Street Journal* (July 19, 1982), p. 19.

[6]"Quaker Oats Tailors for Growth," *Business Week* (July 26, 1982), p. 79.

These examples suggest that market target selection is as vital an aspect of retailers' marketing strategy as it is for any other marketer.[7]

Product/Service Strategy

Retailers must also determine their offerings with respect to:

- General product/service categories
- Specific lines
- Specific products
- Inventory depth
- Width of assortment.

The starting point is to assess their positions in the product/service matrix (shown in Figure 17.3), which relates convenience, shopping, and specialty retailers to convenience, shopping, and specialty goods. Other marketing factors can influence product and/or service offerings. For instance, the discount price policies of warehouse supermarkets forces these retailers to restrict their product offerings to 1500 to 1700 items, compared to the 15,000 found in traditional supermarkets.[8]

Montgomery Ward provides an interesting study of the evolution of a product strategy.[9] Ward's was traditionally a mass merchandiser patterned after the Sears model. When Mobil bought the retailer, management decided to move it into discounting with the Jefferson-Ward chain. Later Ward's decided to reverse that strategy.

Ward's product line is a significant aspect of their current strategy. Management has cut weak selling items from Ward's product mix wherever possible. The new Ward's products are grouped in specialty departments like a department store. Brand names like Michelin, Black & Decker, Izod, RCA, and Monroe shock absorbers have been added to boost Ward's image with customers. Product strategy will clearly play a role in the future success of Montgomery Ward.

Retail Pricing Strategy

Pricing is another critical element of the retailing mix. The essential pricing decisions concern relative price levels. Does the store want to offer higher priced merchandise like Bloomingdale's or lower priced items like Gibson's? Other pricing decisions concern markups, mark-

[7]A good discussion appears in Mary Carolyn Harrison and Alvin C. Burns, "A Case for Departmentalizing Target Market Strategy in Department Stores," in *Progress in Marketing: Theory and Practice,* (eds.) Ronald D. Taylor, John J. Bennen, and John H. Summey (Carbondale, Ill.: Southern Marketing Association, 1981), pp. 21–24.

[8]Bill Abrams, "New Worry for Manufacturers: Growth of Warehouse Outlets," *The Wall Street Journal* (May 28, 1981), p. 29.

[9]See "Ward's Latest Formula: Hybrid Discounting," *Business Week* (November 2, 1981), pp. 77, 80, 81, 83; and Steven Weiner, "Much of Old Montgomery Ward May Go as Pistner Seeks Profitability, New Image," *The Wall Street Journal* (June 15, 1981), p. 25.

downs, loss leaders, odd pricing, and promotional pricing. The retailer is the channel member with direct responsibility for the prices paid by consumers. As Chapters 13 and 14 pointed out, the prices that are set play a major role in buyer perceptions of the retail market.

Location and Distribution Decisions

Real estate professionals often point out that location may be the determining factor in the success or failure of a retail business. The location must be appropriate for the type and price of merchandise carried by the store. Stuckey's was originally set up in roadside locations to sell food and knickknacks, but the proliferation of fast-food outlets have hurt the Pet Inc. operation. Stuckey's product line may also be out of place for its location. One food franchisor critically observed, "There just isn't much of a market anymore for high quality rubber snakes."[10]

Retail Trade Area Analysis

Retail trade area analysis refers to studies that assess the relative drawing power of alternative retail locations. This task can be accomplished in a variety of ways. Shoppers might be polled as to their residence locations, driving times, frequency of shopping trips, and the like. Similarly, the credit charges of an existing store might be plotted to show the service area of an existing store.

Another technique is the law of retail gravitation, sometimes called Reilly's law after its originator, William J. Reilly.[11] The **law of retail gravitation** delineates the retail trade area of a potential site on the basis of mileage between alternative locations and relative populations. It was originally formulated in the 1920s. The formula is:

$$\text{Breaking Point in Miles from B} = \frac{\text{Miles between A and B}}{1 + \sqrt{\dfrac{\text{Population of A}}{\text{Population of B}}}}$$

Assume a retailer is considering locating a new outlet in Town A or Town B, which are located 60 miles from each other. The population of A is 80,000 and the population of B, 20,000. One of the questions that concerns the retailer is where people living in a small rural community located on the highway between the two towns 25 miles from B are likely to shop.

[10]George Salman, "IC Places Pet on a Profitable Diet," *St. Louis Business Journal* (June 6, 1982), p. 18.

[11]The following discussion of Reilly and Huff's work is adapted from Joseph Barry Mason and Morris Lehman Mayer, *Modern Retailing: Theory and Practice* (Plano, Tex.: Business Publications, Inc., 1978), pp. 486–489.

According to the law of retail gravitation, these rural shoppers would most likely shop in A even though it was 10 miles further away than B. The retail trade area of A extends 40 miles toward B, and the rural community was located only 35 miles away.

$$\text{Breaking Point in Miles from B} = \frac{60}{1 + \sqrt{\dfrac{80{,}000}{20{,}000}}} = \frac{60}{1 + \sqrt{4}} = \frac{60}{3} = 20 \text{ miles.}$$

The complete trade area for A or B could be calculated by similar calculations with other communities.

The application of this technique is limited in an area of urban sprawl, regional shopping centers, and consumers who measure distances in terms of driving time. As a result, a contemporary version of retail trade analysis has been offered by David Huff.

Huff's work is an interurban model that assesses the likelihood that a consumer will patronize a specific shopping center. The Huff model accounts for modern trends like shopping centers and the emphasis on travel time. The net result is that trading areas are expressed in terms of a series of probability contours. The probability that a consumer will patronize a specific shopping center is viewed as a function of center size, travel time, and the type of merchandise sought.[12]

Other Distribution Decisions Retailers are faced with a variety of other distribution decisions, many of which ensure that adequate quantities of stock are available when consumers want to buy. Montgomery Ward uses a 1,000-item "Never Out" program to guarantee that local stores have adequate stock and to pinpoint possible distribution channel breakdowns.[13]

Retail Image and Promotional Strategy

Retail image refers to the consumer's perception of a store and the shopping experience it provides.[14] Promotional strategy is a key element in determining the store's image with the consumer. Another im-

[12]Huff's work is described in David Huff, "A Probabilistic Analysis of Consumer Spatial Behavior," *Emerging Concepts in Marketing,* (ed.) William S. Decker (Chicago: American Marketing Association, 1972), pp. 443–461. Shopping center trade areas are also discussed in Edward Blair, "Sampling Issues in Trade Area Maps Drawn from Shopper Surveys," *Journal of Marketing* (Winter 1983), pp. 98–106.

[13]"Ward's Latest Formula: Hybrid Discounting," *Business Week* (November 2, 1981), p. 83.

[14]Retail images are discussed in a variety of articles. See, for example, Pradeep K. Korgaonbar and Kamal M. El Sheshai, "Assessing Retail Competition with Multidimensional Scaling," *Business* (April–June 1982), pp. 30–33; Jack K. Kasulis and Robert F. Lush, "Validating the Retail Store Image Concept," *Journal of the Academy of Marketing Science* (Fall 1981), pp. 419–435.

portant element is the atmosphere or amenities provided by the retailer—the so-called "atmospherics."

Consider the case of Byerly's, a Minnesota-based luxury supermarket chain that sells items as exotic as buffalo meat at $5 per pound and truffles at $45 per 7/8-ounce jar. Other luxury food retailers include Dierberg's in St. Louis, Lofino's in Dayton, Ohio, and Barlow's in Cedar Rapids, Iowa. These stores maintain their quality retail image by offering extensive services like in-store home economists and a product offering up to three times that of a conventional supermarket. Stores like Byerly's typically do little advertising but instead concentrate on their retail image.[15]

In other situations, promotional strategies can be a major determinant of retail image. Price Chopper, a discount supermarket chain in Vermont, Massachusetts, and New York, used television ads to emphasize their contributions to the community and changed the store's image.[16]

Regardless of how it is accomplished, the objective of retailer promotional strategy should be to position the consumer's perception of the store so that it is in line with other elements of the retailing mix. Retail image should also match the market target that is selected.

How Retailing Strategies Can Be Used in Categorizing Retailers

The nation's two million retailers come in a variety of forms. Since new types of retail operations continue to evolve in response to changing demands of their markets, no universal classification has been devised. The following bases can be used in categorizing them:

1. Shopping effort expended by customers
2. Services provided to customers
3. Product lines
4. Location of retail transactions
5. Form of ownership.

Any retailing operation can be classified according to each of the five bases. A 7-Eleven food store may be classified as a convenience store (category 1); self-service (category 2); relatively broad product lines (category 3); store-type retailer (category 4); and a member of a corporate chain (category 5). Figure 17.2 illustrates each basis utilized in classifying retail operations.

[15]"A New Twist: Supermarket with All the Frills," *Business Week* (August 17, 1981), p. 122.

[16]"Due to Parity of Offerings, Retail Ads Should Emphasize Employee Pride, Customer Service," *Marketing News* (October 5, 1981), pp. 5, 8.

Figure 17.2 Bases for Categorizing Retailers

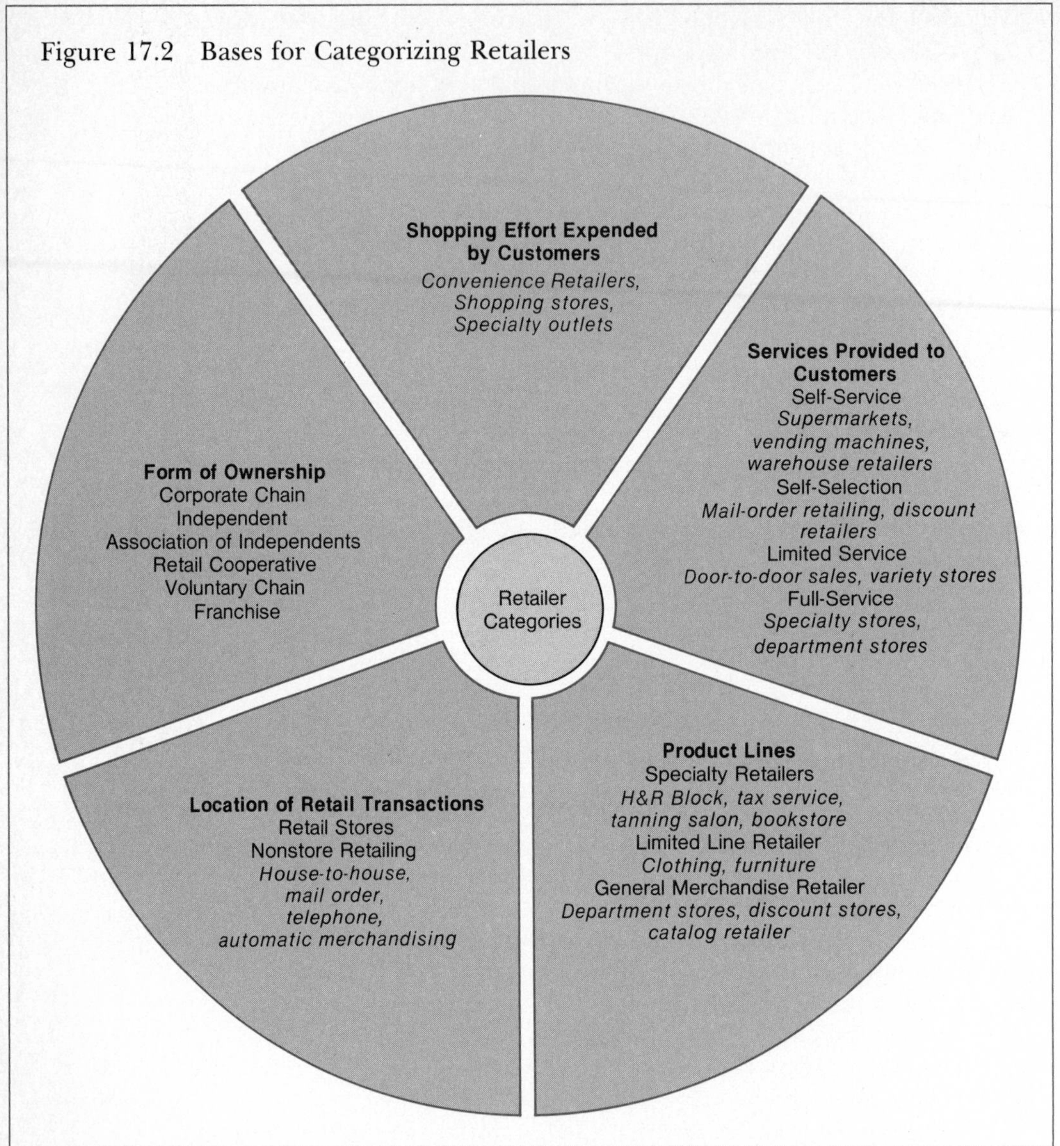

Classification by Shopping Effort

A three-way classification of consumer goods based on consumer purchase patterns in securing a particular product or service was developed earlier in the text. This system can be extended to retailers by considering the reasons consumers shop at a particular retail outlet. The result is a classification scheme in which retail outlets are categorized as convenience, shopping, or specialty.[17] This determination has a significant influence on the marketing strategies selected by a retailer. Convenience retailers focus on convenient locations, long store hours, rapid check-out service, and adequate parking facilities. Local food stores, gasoline retailers, and some barber shops may be included in this category.

Shopping stores typically include furniture stores, appliance retailers, clothing outlets, and sporting goods stores. Consumers will compare prices, assortments, and quality levels of competing outlets before making a purchase decision. Managers of shopping stores attempt to differentiate their outlets through advertising, window displays and in-store layouts, knowledgeable salespeople, and appropriate merchandise assortments.

Specialty retailers provide some combination of product lines, service, or reputation that results in consumers' willingness to expend considerable effort to shop there. Neiman-Marcus, Lord & Taylor, Tiffany & Co., and Saks Fifth Avenue have developed a sufficient degree of preference among many shoppers to be categorized as specialty retailers.

A Product/Retailer Matrix

By cross-classifying the product and retailer classifications, a matrix is created representing nine possible types of consumer purchase behavior. This matrix is shown in Figure 17.3.

Behavior patterns in each cell can be described as:

- *Convenience store—convenience good.* The consumer purchases the most readily available brand of the product at the nearest store.
- *Convenience store—shopping good.* The consumer chooses a product from among the assortment carried by the most accessible store.
- *Convenience store—specialty good.* The consumer purchases a favored brand from the nearest store carrying it.
- *Shopping store—convenience good.* The consumer is indifferent to the brand purchased; shopping is done among competing stores to secure the best services or price.
- *Shopping store—shopping good.* The consumer makes comparisons among store-controlled factors and factors associated with the product or brand.
- *Shopping store—specialty good.* The consumer purchases only a favorite brand but shops among a number of stores to obtain the best service or price.

[17]This section is adapted from Louis P. Bucklin, "Retail Strategy and the Classification of Consumer Goods," *Journal of Marketing* (January 1963), pp. 50–55, published by the American Marketing Association.

Figure 17.3 Matrix of Consumer Purchase Behavior

	Retailers		
Goods	Convenience	Shopping	Specialty
Convenience			
Shopping			
Specialty			

- *Specialty store—convenience good.* The consumer trades only at a specific store and is indifferent to the brand purchased.
- *Specialty store—shopping good.* The consumer trades only at a specific store and chooses a product from among the assortment carried by it.
- *Specialty store—specialty good.* The consumer has a strong preference for both a particular store and a specific brand.

This matrix gives a realistic picture of how people buy. The most exclusive specialty store carries handkerchiefs, and many supermarkets have gourmet food departments. The cross-classification system should help the retailer develop appropriate marketing strategies to satisfy particular market segments. The retailer who chooses either the specialty store—shopping good or specialty good cell must seek to develop an image of exclusivity and a good selection of widely accepted competing brands. The same retailer must also carry an assortment of specialty goods, such as high-fashion clothing and expensive perfumes.

Classification by Services Provided

Some retailers seek to develop a differential advantage by developing a unique combination of service offerings for the customers who comprise their market target. It is possible to distinguish various retailer types by focusing on the services they offer. Figure 17.4 indicates the spectrum of retailer services from virtually no services (self-service) to a full range of customer services (full-service retailers).

Since the self-service and self-selection retailers provide few services to their customers, retailer location and price are important factors. These retailers tend to specialize in staple convenience goods that are purchased frequently by customers and require little product service or advice from retail personnel.

Figure 17.4 Classification of Retailers on the Basis of Service Provided

	Self-Service	Self-Selection	Limited-Service	Full-Service
Characteristics	Very few services Price appeal Staple goods Convenience goods	Restricted services Price appeal Staple goods Convenience goods	Limited variety of services Less price appeal Shopping goods	Wide variety of services Fashion merchandise Specialty merchandise
Examples	Warehouse retailing Supermarkets Mail-order Automatic vending	Discount retailing Variety stores Mail-order retailing	Door-to-door Telephone sales Variety stores	Specialty stores Department stores

Source: Adapted from Larry D. Redinbaugh, *Retailing Management: A Planning Approach* (New York: McGraw-Hill, 1976), p. 12. Copyright 1976 McGraw-Hill Book Company. Used with the permission of McGraw-Hill Book Company.

The full-service retail establishments focus on fashion-oriented shopping goods and specialty items and offer a wide variety of services for their clientele. As a result, their prices tend to be higher than those of self-service retailers due to the higher operating costs associated with the services.

Classification by Product Lines

Retail strategies can also be based on the product lines that are carried. Grouping retailers by product lines produces three major categories: specialty stores, limited-line retailers, and general merchandise retailers.

Specialty Stores

A specialty store typically handles only part of a single line of products. However, this part is stocked in considerable depth for the store's customers. Specialty stores include meat markets, men's and women's shoe stores, bakeries, furriers, and millinery shops. Although some are operated by chains, most are run as independent, small-scale operations. They are perhaps the greatest stronghold of independent retailers who can develop expertise in providing a very narrow line of products for their local market.

Specialty stores should not be confused with specialty goods. Specialty stores typically carry convenience and shopping goods. The label *specialty* comes from the practice of handling a specific, narrow line of merchandise.

Limited-Line Retailers

A large assortment of one line of products or a few related lines of goods are offered in the **limited-line store.** Its development paralleled the growth of towns when the population grew sufficiently to support them. These operations include such retailers as appliance stores, furniture stores, grocery stores, hardware stores, and sporting goods stores. Examples of limited-line stores are Toys R-Us (toys); Levitz (furniture); Radio Shack and Playback (home electronics); Handy Dan and Handy Man (home repair products); Brain Factory (electronic calculators); and Lerner Shops (clothing). These retailers cater to the needs of people who want to select from a complete line in purchasing a particular product. Most retailers are in the limited-line category.

The Supermarket

A supermarket is a large-scale, departmentalized retail store offering a variety of food products, such as meats, produce, dairy products, canned goods, and frozen foods, in addition to various nonfood items. It operates on a self-service basis and emphasizes low prices and adequate parking facilities. Supermarkets offer low prices through a policy of self-service. Before the 1920s, however, food purchases were made at full-service grocery stores. Store personnel filled orders (often from customers' shopping lists), delivered goods, and often granted credit to their customers. Supermarkets exchanged these services for lower prices and quickly revolutionized food shopping in the United States and much of the world.[18]

Supermarket customers typically shop once or twice a week and make fill-in purchases between each major shopping trip. In 1982, the nearly 29,000 U.S. chain and independent supermarkets represented only 17 percent of the nation's food stores. Yet chain supermarket sales accounted for 49 percent of all food sales, and independent supermarket sales accounted for an additional 22.2 percent. The largest supermarket chains in the United States are Safeway, Kroger, Lucky Stores, American Stores, and A & P.

With profit margins averaging only about 1 percent of sales after taxes, supermarkets compete through careful planning of retail displays in order to sell a large amount of merchandise each week and thereby retain a low investment in inventory. Product location is studied carefully to expose the consumer to as much merchandise as possible (and thereby increase impluse purchases). In an attempt to fight the fast-food threat—the tendency of consumers to eat many of their meals outside the home—supermarkets have begun to feature their own del-

[18]See Thomas J. Stanley and Murphy A. Sewell, "Predicting Supermarket Trade: Implications for Marketing Management," *Journal of Retailing* (Summer 1978), pp. 13–22. See also Danny N. Bellenger, Thomas J. Stanley and John W. Allen, "Trends in Food Retailing," *Atlanta Economic Review* (May–June 1978), pp. 11–14.

icatessens. In Florida, the Publix supermarkets sell fried chicken by the bucket. Supermarkets General of New Jersey has even established cafeterias and snack shops in factories.[19]

Supermarkets carry nonfood products, such as magazines, records, small kitchen utensils, toiletries, and toys, for two reasons: consumers have displayed a willingness to buy such items in supermarkets, and supermarket managers like the profit margin on these items, which is higher than that of food products. Nonfood sales account for almost one fourth of all supermarket sales.

General Merchandise Retailers

General merchandise retailers may be distinguished from limited-line and specialty retailers by the large number of product lines they carry. The general store described earlier in this chapter is a good example of a **general merchandise retailer**—a retail establishment carrying a wide variety of product lines, all of which are stocked in some depth. Included in this category of retailers are variety stores, department stores, and such mass merchandisers as catalog retailers and discount stores.

Variety Stores Retail firms that offer an extensive range and assortment of low-priced merchandise are called variety stores. The nation's 17,000 variety stores account for only about 1 percent of all retail sales.[20] Variety stores are not as popular as they once were. Many have evolved into or been replaced by other retailing categories such as discounting.

Department Stores The **department store** is actually a series of limited-line and specialty stores under one roof. By definition, it is a large retail firm handling a variety of merchandise that includes men's and boy's wear, women's wear and accessories, household linens and dry goods, home furnishings, appliances, and furniture. It serves the consumer as a one-stop shopping center for almost all personal and household items. Department stores account for about 10 percent of all retail sales.[21]

As indicated by its name, the entire store is organized around departments for the purpose of providing service, promotion, and control. A general merchandising manager is responsible for the store's product planning. Reporting to the general manager are the department managers. These managers typically run the departments almost

[19]Christy Marshall, "Supermarkets Fight Fast-Food Challenge," *Advertising Age* (October 30, 1978), pp. 30, 34.

[20]U.S. Bureau of the Census, *Statistical Abstract of the United States: 1982–83,* 103d ed. (Washington, D.C.: U.S. Government Printing Office, 1983), p. 802.

[21]*Ibid.*

as independent businesses; they are given considerable latitude in merchandising and layout decisions. Acceptance of the retailing axiom that well-bought goods are already half-sold is indicated by the department manager's title of buyer. Buyers, particularly those in charge of high-fashion departments, spend a considerable portion of their time deciding on the inventory to be carried in their departments.

The department store has been the symbol of retailing since the construction of the nation's first department store in 1863, the A.T. Stewart store in New York City. Almost every urban area in the United States has one or more department stores associated with its downtown and major shopping areas. Macy's Herald Square store in New York City is the world's largest department store; it contains more than two million square feet of space and produces gross sales of over $360 million each year. There are about 500,000 items available in 300 selling departments.

The impact of department stores on urban life is not confined to the United States. European shoppers associate London with Harrods, Paris with Au Printemps, and Moscow with GUM. Myer is the dominant department store in both Melbourne and Sydney, Australia.

Department stores are known for offering their customers a wide variety of services, such as charge accounts, delivery, gift wrapping, and liberal return privileges. In addition, some 50 percent of their employees and 40 percent of their floor space are devoted to nonselling activities. As a result, they have relatively high operating costs, averaging from 45 to 60 percent of sales.

Department stores have faced intensified competition in the past 30 years. Their relatively high operating costs make them vulnerable to such new retailing innovations as discount stores, catalog merchandisers, and hypermarkets. In addition, department stores were usually located in downtown business districts and experienced the problems associated with limited parking, traffic congestion, and urban migration to the suburbs.

However, department stores have displayed a willingness to adapt to changing consumer desires. They have added bargain basements and expanded parking facilities in attempts to compete with discount operations and suburban retailers. They have also followed the movement of the population to the suburbs by opening major branches in outlying shopping centers.[22] They have attempted to revitalize downtown retailing in many cities by modernizing their stores, expanding store hours, attracting the tourist and convention trade, and focusing on the residents of the central cities.[23]

[22]See Eleanor G. May and Malcolm P. McNair, "Department Stores Face Stiff Challenge in the Next Decade," *Journal of Retailing* (Fall 1977), pp. 47–58.

[23]Attempts to revitalize central business districts are outlined in Louis C. Wagner, "Downtown Retailers Woo Shoppers in Effort to Reverse Sales Decline," *Marketing News* (December 25, 1981), p. 8.

Mass Merchandisers Mass merchandising has made major inroads on department stores sales during the past two decades by emphasizing lower prices for well-known brand name products, high turnover of goods, and reduced services. The **mass merchandiser** often stocks a wider line of products than department stores but usually does not offer the depth of assortment in each line. Discount houses, hypermarkets, and catalog retailers are all mass merchandisers.

Discount Houses—Limited Services and Lower Prices. The birth of the modern **discount house** came at the end of World War II, when a New York-based company called Masters discovered that a large number of customers were willing to shop at a store that charged lower than usual prices and did not offer such traditional services as credit, sales assistance by clerks, and delivery. Soon, retailers throughout the country were following the Masters formula, either changing over from their traditional operation or opening new stores dedicated to discounting. At first, discount stores sold mostly appliances, but they have spread into furniture, soft goods, drugs, and even food. Currently, more than 12 percent of all retail stores operate as discount houses.

Discount operations had existed before World War II, but the early discounters usually sold goods from manufacturers' catalogs; they kept no stock on display and often limited potential customers. The more recent discounters operate large stores, advertise heavily, emphasize low prices for well-known brands, and are open to the public. Elimination of many of the "free" services provided by traditional retailers allows these operations to keep their markup 10 to 25 percent below those of their competitors. Consumers had become accustomed to self-service by shopping at supermarkets, and they responded in great numbers to this retailing innovation. Conventional retailers such as Kresge joined the discounting practice by opening its own K mart stores. Currently, about 38 cents of every dollar spent by U.S. consumers is spent in a discount store.[24]

As discount houses move into new product areas, there has been a noticeable increase in the number of services offered. Floors in the stores are often carpeted, credit is usually available, and many discounters are even dropping discount from their name. Although they still offer fewer services than other retailers, discounters' operating costs are increasing as they begin to resemble traditional department stores.

K mart shoppers can choose from such designer labels as Calvin Klein, Sasson, Jordache, and Sergio Valente. Other brands with images of quality and style now found at the discount giant—once referred to as the "the polyester place"—include Seiko watches, Puma running shoes, Izod shirts, and Minolta and Pentax cameras.

[24]"Business Bulletin," *The Wall Street Journal* (October 26, 1978), p. 1.

The Death of Korvette's

Less than two decades ago, Korvette's was held up as the discount merchandiser that might one day rival such top retailers as Sears and J.C. Penney. In those days, Korvette's was unmatched in sales growth, suburban expansion, and its ability to pack stores with shoppers. Today, Korvette's is no longer an operating retailer. . . .

As the 1970s wore on, the public itself could get a sense of Korvette's difficulties. It eliminated once-lucrative appliance and furniture departments. It decided to deemphasize discounting and raise its markup—then reversed itself. It started an ambitious promotion—"the other Korvette's"—to stress fashion but abruptly dumped it in a cost-cutting campaign. . . .

Through the 1950s [Korvette founder Eugene Ferkauf] was one of the strongest figures in American retailing, beating the New York department stores to the suburbs with large flashy stores, underselling them on appliances and housewares and prompting price wars. . . . A Boston industry group voted him into its merchants' Hall of Fame and *Time* magazine and *Business Week* devoted cover articles to him.

But, in retrospect, critics score him for some important mistakes. He expanded too quickly, especially out of town in such cities as St. Louis, Chicago, and Detroit where locals didn't know much about Korvette's. He branched out into food (merging with Hill's Supermarkets in 1965) and into furniture (in a merger with H. Klion Inc.), both of which proved a drain that forced him to later drop them.

But his biggest failing may have been his inability to build management depth, so that he had to resort to bringing in outside top managers who produced fitful results. . . .

Wall Street analysts, who lost investment interest in Korvette's years ago, are caustic. Said one who asked not to be identified: "They started out as discounters but let their markup run up too high without giving equal value. Management slipped and image problems became serious."

In the mid-1980s, Korvette's is only a memory.

Source: Isadore Barmash, "The Last Stand and Slow Decline of E. J. Korvette," *New York Times* (October 12, 1980). © 1980 by the New York Times Company. Reprinted by permission.

Hypermarkets—Shopping Centers in a Single Store. A relatively recent retailing development has been the introduction of **hypermarkets**—giant mass merchandisers who operate on a low-price, self-service basis and carry lines of soft goods and groceries. Hypermarkets are sometimes called superstores, although this latter term has also been used to describe a variety of large retail operations.[25] The hypermarket began in

[25]Superstores are discussed in Myron Gable and Ronald D. Michman, "Superstores—Revolutionizing Distribution," *Business* (March–April 1981), pp. 14–18.

France and has since spread to Canada and the United States. Meijer's Thrifty Acres in suburban Detroit has 220,000 square feet of selling space (11 to 15 times that of the average supermarket) and more than 40 check-out counters. It sells food, hardware, soft goods, building materials, auto supplies, appliances, and prescription drugs; and it has a restaurant, a beauty salon, a barber shop, a branch bank, and a bakery. While the format might differ, more than a thousand superstores are currently in operation.

Catalog Retailers—Catalog, Showroom, and Warehouse. One of the major growth areas in retailing during the past decade has been that of catalog retailing. Catalog retailers mail catalogs to their customers and operate from a showroom displaying samples of each product handled by them. Orders are filled from a backroom warehouse. Price is an important factor for catalog store customers, and low prices are made possible by few services, storage of most of the inventory in the warehouse, reduced shoplifting losses, and the handling of products that are unlikely to become obsolete, such as luggage, small appliances, gift items, sporting equipment, toys, and jewelry. Major catalog retailers include Best Products, Service Merchandise, Giant Stores, Vornado, Zale, and Gordon Jewelry Corporation. (Mail-order catalog retailing is discussed later in the chapter.)

Classification by Location of Retail Transactions

Some retailers choose to implement their marketing strategies outside the store environment. Although the overwhelming majority of retail transactions occur in retail stores, nonstore retailing is important for many products. Nonstore retailing includes direct house-to-house sales, mail-order retailing, and automatic merchandising machines. These kinds of sales account for 2.5 percent of all retail sales.

House-to-House Retailing

One of the oldest marketing channels was built around direct contact between the seller and customer at the home of the customer—house-to-house retailing. This channel provides maximum convenience for the consumer and allows the manufacturer to control the firm's marketing channels. It is a minor part of the retailing picture, with less than 1 percent of all retail sales.[26]

[26]Leonard L. Berry, "The Time-Buying Consumer," *Journal of Retailing* (Winter 1979), pp. 58–69.

House-to-house retailing is used by a number of merchandisers, such as manufacturers of bakery products, dairy products, and newspapers. Firms emphasizing product demonstrations also tend to use this channel. Among them are companies that sell vacuum cleaners (for example, Electrolux), household items (Fuller Brush Company), encyclopedias (The World Book Encyclopedia), and insurance. Some firms, such as Stanley Home Products, Amway, and Tupperware, use a variation called party-plan selling, where a customer hosts a party to which several neighbors and friends are invited. During the party, a company representative makes a presentation of the products. The hostess receives a commission based on the amount of products sold. The five largest direct-sales retailers are Avon Products, Electrolux, Tupperware, Amway, and World Book–Childcraft International.

The house-to-house method of retailing appears to be a low-cost method of distribution. No plush retail facilities are required, no investment in inventory is necessary, and most house-to-house salespeople operate on a commission basis. However, the method actually entails very high costs. Often the distribution cost of a product marketed through retail stores is half that of the same product retailed house-to-house. High travel costs, nonproductive calls, and the limited number of contacts per day result in high operating expenses.

Mail-Order Retailing

The customers of mail-order retailing merchandisers can order merchandise by mail, by telephone, or by visiting the mail-order desk of a retail store. Goods are then shipped to the customer's home or to the local retail store. Table 17.1 identifies a number of socioeconomic, external, and competitive factors that have contributed to the growing consumer acceptance of catalog retailing.

Many department stores and specialty stores issue catalogs to seek telephone and mail-order sales and to promote in-store purchases of items featured in the catalogs. Among typical department stores, telephone and mail-generated orders account for 15 percent of total volume during the Christmas season.[27]

Mail-order selling began in 1872, when Montgomery Ward issued its first catalog to rural Midwestern families. That catalog contained only a few items, mostly clothing and farm supplies. Sears soon followed Ward's lead, and mail-order retailing became an important source of goods in isolated settlements.

In recent years mail-order sales have skyrocketed. It is estimated that 8 to 10 billion mail-order catalogs are distributed each year—300 million of which are distributed by Sears alone.[28]

[27]John A. Quelch and Hirotaka Takeuchi, "Nonstore Marketing: Fast Track or Slow?" *Harvard Business Review* (July–August 1981), p. 75.

[28]Estimated by Paul Muchnick, National Mail Order Association, 1982.

Table 17.1 Factors Contributing to the Success of Mail-Order Catalogs

Socioeconomic Factors	External Factors	Competitive Factors
More women joining the work force	Rising costs of gasoline	Inconvenient store hours
Population growing older	Availability of WATS (800) lines	Unsatisfactory service in stores
Rising discretionary income	Expanded use of credit cards	Difficulty of parking, especially near downtown stores
More single households	Low-cost data processing	"If you can't beat 'em join 'em" approach of traditional retailers
Growth of the "me generation"	Availability of mailing lists	

Source: John A. Quelch and Hirotaka Takeuchi, "Nonstore Marketing: Fast Track or Slow?" *Harvard Business Review* (July–August 1981), p. 77. Reprinted by permission of the *Harvard Business Review*.

Mail-order houses offer a wide range of products—from novelty items (Spencer Gifts) to hunting and camping equipment (L.L. Bean) to an eighteenth century Chinese screen priced at $60,000 (Horchow). Many mail-order catalog organizations also generate retail sales by having consumers buy from retail outlets of their catalog stores.

Catalog sales are extremely important to many of the nation's top retailers. Catalog sales account for about 26 percent of Montgomery Ward's business. The comparable figures at Sears and J.C. Penney are 22 percent and 13 percent, respectively.[29]

Automatic Merchandising

Automatic vending machines are a convenient way to purchase a vast array of convenience goods ranging from Pepsi-Cola to Marlboros to Michigan lottery tickets. The average American spends $1.26 a week in one or more of the approximately 6 million vending machines currently in operation. Coffee and soft-drink purchases represent about half the total dollar sales volume.[30]

Although the first vending machine dispensed holy water for a five-drachma coin in Egyptian temples around 215 B.C., the period of most rapid growth came after World War II when sophisticated new equipment was developed to keep machines working and to prevent acceptance of slugs. Products offered by automatic vending range from the mundane to the bizarre. Soft-drink machines on military bases and in college fraternity houses dispense beer rather than soda. Some bait shops sell packages of fresh worms to after-hours fishermen from coin-

[29] Suzy Hagstrom, "Consumers Turn of Page Fuels Catalog Sales Picture," *Sentinel Star* (February 23, 1982), pp. 1–E, 8–E.

[30] *The Wall Street Journal* (August 23, 1979), p. 1.

operated machines. Some flower shops have added machines to dispense corsages as last-minute gifts.

Where does the vending machine dollar go? According to the National Automatic Merchandising Association, 45.5 cents of each dollar goes for the product, 52.4 cents for operating expenses, and 2.1 cents for profit. Typically, the owner of the building receives more money from a machine for just allowing it on the premises than the owner of the machine does for installing, stocking, and servicing it.[31]

Although automatic merchandising is important in the retailing of some products, it represents less than 1 percent of all retail sales. Its future growth is limited by such factors as the cost of the machines and the necessity for regular maintenance and repair. In addition, automatically vended products are confined to convenience goods of standard sizes and weights that have a high turnover rate. Prices for many products purchased in vending machines are higher than store prices for the same products.

Classification by Form of Ownership

A final method of categorizing retailers is by ownership. The two major types are corporate chain stores and independent retailers. In addition, independent retailers may join a wholesaler-sponsored voluntary chain, band together to form a retail cooperative, or enter into a franchise arrangement through contractual agreements with a manufacturer, wholesaler, or service organization. As indicated below, each type has its own unique advantages and strategies.

Chain Stores

Chain stores are groups of retail stores that are centrally owned and managed and that handle the same lines of products. The concept of chain stores is certainly not new. The Mitsui chain operated in Japan in the 1600s.

One major advantage that chain operations have over independent retailers is economies of scale. Volume purchases through a central buying office allows such chains as Safeway, Kroger, and Lucky Stores to pay lower prices than independents. Since chains may have thousands of retail stores, they can use layout specialists, sales training, and accounting systems to increase efficiency. Advertising can also be used effectively; a single advertisement for Radio Shack in a national magazine benefits every Radio Shack store in the United States.

[31]"Vending Machine Sales Hit $13.8 Billion," *Orlando Sentinel Star* (November 29, 1981).

Table 17.2 The Ten Largest U.S. Retailers

Rank	Company	Sales in Billions	Net Income as Percentage of Sales
1	Sears (Chicago)	$27.36	2.4%
2	Safeway Stores (Oakland)	16.58	0.7
3	K mart (Troy, Mich.)	16.53	1.3
4	J.C. Penney (New York)	11.86	3.3
5	Kroger (Cincinnati)	11.37	1.1
6	F.W. Woolworth (New York)	7.22	1.1
7	Lucky Stores (Dublin, Calif.)	7.20	1.3
8	American Stores (Salt Lake City)	7.10	0.9
9	Federated Department Stores (Cincinnati)	7.07	3.7
10	Great Atlantic & Pacific Tea (Montvale, N.J.)	6.99	(loss)

Source: *Fortune,* (July 12, 1982), pp. 140–141, "The 50 largest U.S. Retailers."

About 31 percent of all retail stores are part of some chain, and their dollar volume of sales amounts to more than one third of all retail sales. Chains currently dominate four fields. They account for 92 percent of all department store sales, almost 80 percent of all variety store sales, 56 percent of all food store sales, and half of all retail shoe store sales. Table 17.2 lists the ten largest retailers in the United States.

For years, Sears has ranked as the nation's largest retailer. In fact, more than 24 million people now carry a Sears credit card. Appropriately, the firm's headquarters are located in the tallest building in the United States, the 110-story Sears Tower in Chicago.

Many of the larger chains have expanded their operations to the rest of the world. Sears has branch stores in Mexico, South America, and Spain. Safeway operates supermarkets in Australia, Germany, and the United Kingdom. J.C. Penney has retail operations in Belgium and Italy. Japanese shoppers can frequent more than 500 7-Eleven stores.[32]

Independent Retailers

Even though most retailers are small, independent operators, the larger-sized chains dominate a number of fields. The U.S. retailing structure can be characterized as having a large number of small stores, many medium-sized stores, and a small number of large stores. Even though only 7 percent of all stores have annual sales of $1 million or

[32]Tom Bayer, "7-Eleven Takes Steps to Move Beyond Image," *Advertising Age* (December 7, 1981), pp. 4, 78.

Figure 17.5 Comparison of Retail Trade by Number of Establishments and Sales Volume

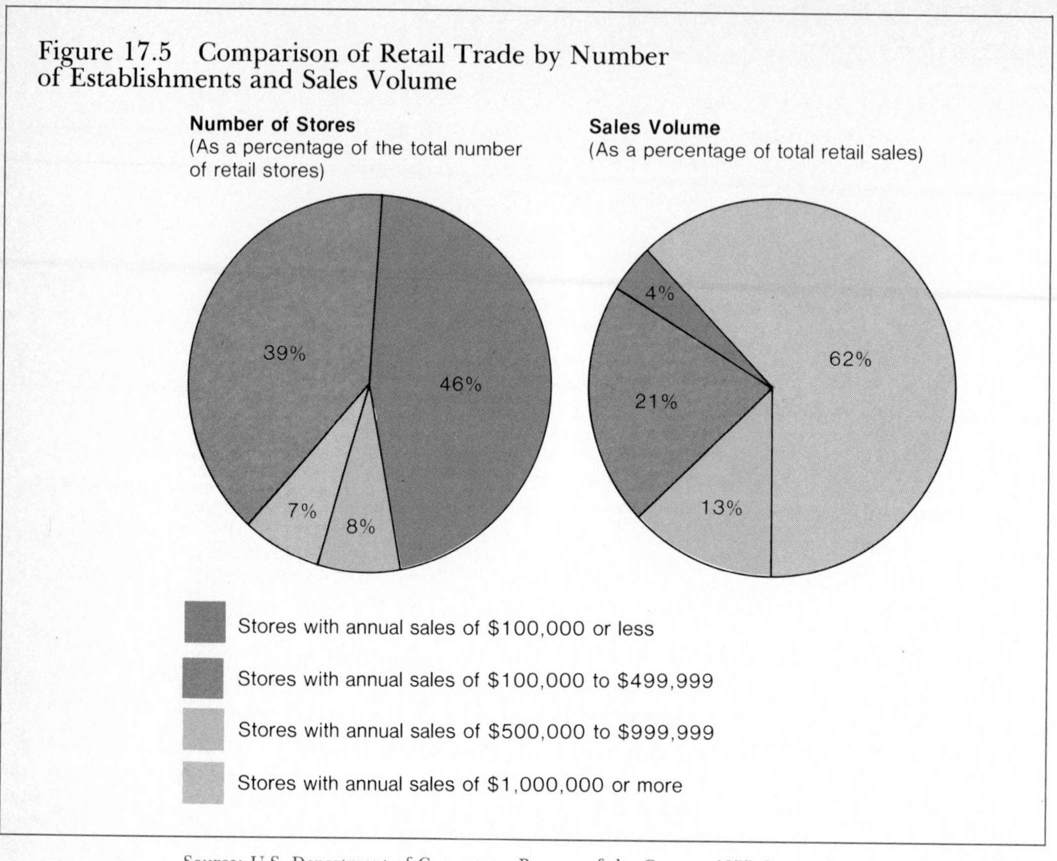

Source: U.S. Department of Commerce, Bureau of the Census, *1977 Census of Retail Trade, Establishment Size* (Washington, D.C.: U.S. Government Printing Office, 1981), pp. 1–8.

more, Figure 17.5 reveals that they account for almost two thirds of all retail sales in the United States. On the other hand, almost half of all stores in the United States have sales of less than $100,000 each year.

Independents have attempted to compete with chains in a number of ways. Some were unable to do so efficiently and went out of business. Others have joined retail cooperatives, wholesaler-sponsored voluntary chains, or franchise operations, as described in Chapter 15. Still others have remained in business by exploiting their advantages of flexibility in operation and knowledge of local market conditions. The independents continue to represent a major part of U.S. retailing.[33]

[33] "Those Mom-and-Pop Stores Are Still Going Strong," *U.S. News & World Report* (July 28, 1978), pp. 59–62; and Gerald Albaum, Roger Best and Del Hawkins, "Retailing Strategy for Customer Growth and New Customer Attraction," *Journal of Business Research* (March 1980), pp. 7–20.

Significant Developments Impacting Retailing Strategy

Two developments that have significantly altered retailing strategy in recent decades are the development of the planned shopping center and the practice of scrambled merchandising. Both have a significant impact on the retail environment in the United States.

Planned Shopping Centers

The pronounced shift of retail trade away from the traditional downtown retailing districts and toward suburban shopping centers has been building since 1950. **Planned shopping centers** are a group of retail stores planned, coordinated, and marketed as a unit to shoppers in their geographic trade area. These centers followed population shifts to the suburbs and concentrated on avoiding many of the problems associated with shopping in the downtown business district. They provide a convenient location for shoppers, as well as free parking facilities based upon the number and types of stores in the center. Shopping is facilitated by uniform hours of operation and by evening and weekend shopping hours. There are now about 23,000 shopping centers in operation.[34]

Types of Shopping Centers There are three types of planned shopping centers. The smallest and most common is the neighborhood shopping center, which is most often composed of a supermarket and a group of smaller stores, such as a drugstore, a laundry and dry cleaner, a small appliance store, and perhaps a beauty shop and barber shop. Such centers provide convenient shopping for perhaps 5,000 to 15,000 shoppers who live within a few minutes' commuting time of the center. Such centers typically contain five to fifteen stores, and the product mix is usually confined to convenience goods and some shopping goods.

Community shopping centers typically serve 20,000 to 100,000 persons in a trade area extending a few miles. These centers are likely to contain 15 to 50 retail stores, and a branch of a local department store or a large variety store is the primary tenant. In addition to the stores found in a neighborhood center, the community center is likely to have additional stores featuring shopping goods, some professional offices, and a branch of a bank or a savings and loan association.

The largest planned shopping center is the regional shopping center, a giant shopping district of at least 400,000 square feet of shopping space usually built around one or more major department stores and

[34]Lawrence Rout, "Shopping Center Glut Forces Investors to Look Elsewhere," *The Wall Street Journal* (August 12, 1981), p. 25.

as many as 200 smaller stores. In order to be successful, regional centers must be located in areas where at least 250,000 people reside within 30 minutes' driving time of the center. The regional centers provide the widest product mixes and the greatest depth of each line.

Woodfield Mall, located in Schaumburg, Illinois, is the world's largest enclosed mall. Its 230 stores occupy three stories and overlook an ice skating rink. An average of 50,000 shoppers are attracted each day, and total annual sales are estimated at $400 million. Four movie theaters, a hotel, and numerous high-rise office buildings nearby attract other residents. The mall structure and its 10,800 car parking area are situated on a site almost as large as Vatican City. Like other huge regional malls, Woodfield serves as a substitute downtown for the Illinois community.[35]

Planned shopping centers account for more than 40 percent of all retail sales in the United States. Their growth has slowed in recent years, however, as the most lucrative locations are occupied and the market for such centers appears to have been saturated in many regions. Recent trends have developed toward the building of smaller centers in smaller cities and towns.[36]

Scrambled Merchandising

A second significant development in retailing has been the steady deterioration of clear-cut delineations of retailer types. Anyone who has attempted to fill a physician's prescription recently has been exposed to the concept of **scrambled merchandising**—the retail practice of carrying dissimilar lines in an attempt to generate added sales volume. The drugstore carries not only prescription and proprietary drugs, but also garden supplies, gift items, groceries, hardware, housewares, magazines, records, and even small appliances. The modern service station is one of the biggest practitioners of scrambled merchandising. Sailboats, wood-burning stoves, and dry cleaning are now available at gas stations in Seattle. Bank card machines appear in Los Angeles service stations. Video games, snacks, and milk are often sold by these retailers. Scrambled merchandising may have come full circle at a McDonald's restaurant in Florida. It now sells gasoline.[37]

Many supermarkets fill prescriptions and stock such nonfood items as portable televisions, cameras, stereo equipment, citizen's band radios, and clothing such as jeans and T-shirts. Customers often can use bank

[35]The Woodfield Mall is described in "Shopping Centers Will Be America's Towns of Tomorrow," *Marketing News* (November 28, 1980), p. 1.

[36]An interesting discussion of conflict related to shopping centers appears in Leonard J. Konopa and Ronald L. Zallocco, "A Study of Conflict between Shopping Center Managers and Retailers within Regional Shopping Centers," *Journal of the Academy of Marketing Science* (Summer 1981), pp. 274–287.

[37]Julie Emery, "Gas Stations Offer Video Games, Groceries—and Service," *The Seattle Times* (May 2, 1982), p. A 25.

Outlet Malls–A New Type of Shopping Center

A Reading, Pennsylvania, shopping center is so popular that it draws people from a 200-mile radius. Bus tours even go to the mall. The popular attraction is none other than an outlet mall, a trend that is now sweeping the shopping center industry.

Outlet malls are shopping centers that specialize in off-price (discount) outlets for name brand merchandise. The retailers located in these malls buy overruns, seconds, and other surplus items and sell them at 20 to 60 percent discounts. All off-price retailing is a $6 billion business, and a significant amount of that is being generated in outlet malls. More than 145 of these shopping centers are in operation or being planned. Most are concentrated in the East and the South. In some cases, shopping centers with poor sales records have been successfully converted to outlet malls.

Clothing is the best selling item in outlet malls. In fact, the sales rate of off-price clothing is double that of all apparel. Other product lines that also sell well include jewelry, crystal, and linen. Even art prints are sold in such outlets. Off-price retailers have been helped recently by poor economic conditions which cause buyers to make special efforts in bargain hunting.

Outlet malls provide a welcome market for a producer with excess output, but they also create conflict in the distribution channel. Regular retailers complain that they are being undersold on name brand items. The Jack & Jill Shop in Memphis dropped the Health-Tex line of children's clothing after 23 years. The reason? Health-Tex had opened a mall outlet store and was selling the same merchandise at sizable discounts. Ship N' Shore, part of General Mills, is concerned about this conflict and decided to cut its mall outlets from 19 to 10. Despite such conflicts, outlet malls are becoming an accepted part of the retailing scene.

Source: Based on Carol Pucci, "Off-Price Retailing Booms in Bad Economic Times" *The Seattle Times* (June 8, 1982), p. D 1; and Jeffrey H. Birnbaum, "Discount Outlets Increasing in Malls, Irritating Many Full-Price Retailers," *The Wall Street Journal* (October 14, 1981), p. 31.

credit cards for payment. The best-selling product in dollar volume in drugstores is Polaroid Polacolor II film for instant movies. Other photographic materials—Kodacolor II and Polaroid SX-70 films and Sylvania flash cubes—also rank among the top ten drugstore sellers. Shoppers at Montgomery Ward's San Diego outlets can even obtain legal services.[38]

Scrambled merchandising was born out of retailers' willingness to add dissimilar merchandise lines in order to satisfy consumer demand for one-stop shopping. Consider Sears' recent purchase of Coldwell

[38]"Where Consumers Buy Legal Advice at Retail," *Business Week* (July 2, 1979), p. 44. See also Anton Rupert, "Department-Store Dentists, Lawyers Win Acceptance Despite Criticism from Peers," *The Wall Street Journal* (October 16, 1979).

Banker, a real estate firm, and Dean Witter Reynolds Inc., a stockbrokerage. Sears already has an insurance company, Allstate, operating within its stores. Scrambled merchandising complicates manufacturers' channel decisions, because attempts to maintain or increase market share will, in most instances, mean they must develop multiple channels to reach the diverse variety of retailers handling their products.

The Wheel of Retailing

Malcolm P. McNair attempted to explain the patterns of change in retailing through what has been termed the **wheel of retailing.** According to this hypothesis, new types of retailers gain a competitive foothold by offering lower prices to their customers through the reduction or elimination of services. Once they are established, however, they add more services, and their prices gradually rise. They then become vulnerable to a new low-price retailer who enters with minimum services—and the wheel turns.

Most of the major developments in retailing appear to fit the wheel pattern. Early department stores, chain stores, supermarkets, discount stores, hypermarkets, and catalog retailers all emphasized limited service and low prices. For most of these retailers, price levels gradually increased as services were added.

There have been some exceptions, however. Suburban shopping centers, convenience food stores, and vending machines were not built around low-price appeals. However, the wheel pattern has been present often enough in the past that it should serve as a general indicator of future developments in retailing.[39]

The Retail Life Cycle

Closely related to the wheel hypothesis is the concept of the retail life cycle. Just as the notion of life cycle was applied earlier to households and to products, it is also possible to apply the concept of "introduction-growth-maturity-decline" to retail institutions. Table 17.3 applies the retail life cycle concept to a number of institutions and identifies the approximate stage in the life cycle of each institution.

Retailers have demonstrated that it is possible to extend the length of their life cycles by adapting to changing environments. Such institutions as supermarkets and variety stores reached the maturity stage in

[39]For a complete discussion of the wheel-of-retailing hypothesis, see Stanley C. Hollander, "The Wheel of Retailing," *Journal of Marketing* (July 1960), pp. 37–42.

Table 17.3 Life Cycles of Selected Retail Institutions

Institutional Type	Period of Fastest Growth	Period of Inception to Maturity (Years)	Stage of Life Cycle
General store	1800–1840	100	Decline
Specialty store	1820–1940	100	Maturity
Variety store	1870–1930	50	Decline
Mail-order house	1915–1950	50	Mature
Corporate chain	1920–1930	50	Mature
Discount store	1955–1975	20	Mature
Supermarket	1935–1965	35	Mature
Shopping center	1950–1965	40	Mature
Gasoline station	1930–1950	45	Mature
Convenience store	1965–1975	20	Mature
Fast-food store	1960–1975	15	Mature
Hypermarket	1973–	—	Early growth
Warehouse retailer	1970–1980	10	Late growth
Catalog showroom	1970–1980	10	Late growth

Source: Joseph Barry Mason and Morris L. Mayer, *Modern Retailing: Theory and Practice* (Plano, Tex.: Business Publications, Inc., 1978), p. 58. © 1978 by Business Publications Inc., adapted with permission.

their life cycles several decades ago, but they have continued to function as important marketing institutions by adapting to changing consumer demands and by adjusting to meet changing competitive situations. Variety stores have countered the sales inroads of discount stores by becoming more price competitive and by providing greater depth in their product lines. Supermarkets have taken such steps as offering generic brands at lower prices, developing departments of gourmet foods to counter the competition of specialty food retailers, and adding nonfood items to meet the demand of one-stop shopping convenience.[40]

Teleshopping: The Retail Environment of the Future

Retail purchases in the future may be made at home. Sears has already converted a 236-page summer catalog to laser disc for at-home viewing.[41] Cable television provides a similar method of retailing. About 20

[40]William R. Davidson, Albert D. Bates, and Stephen J. Bass, "The Retail Life Cycle," *Harvard Business Review* (November–December 1976), pp. 89–96; and Rom J. Markin and Calvin P. Duncan, "The Transformation of Retailing Institutions: Beyond the Wheel of Retailing and Life Cycle Theories," *Journal of Macromarketing* (Spring 1981), pp. 58–68.

[41]"Sears Steps into Future with VideoDisc Mail Order Catalog," *Marketing News* (May 29, 1981), pp. 1, 3.

million households now have cable televisions, and the number is expected to grow significantly.[42] The growth of cable television will make teleshopping practical. **Teleshopping** refers to retailing done through interactive cable television. Consumers are able to buy what is displayed on their television sets.

Teleshopping is already available in some areas. Times-Mirror and Comp-U-Card have teamed up to provide "The Shopping Channel" in six metropolitan areas.[43] Warner Amex's QUBE network is another example. QUBE allows instant two-way sales communications between retailers and consumers. This cable network is currently connected to some 150,000 homes in Columbus, Cincinnati, Houston, Dallas, and Pittsburgh. When installations are completed in St. Louis, Chicago, and Milwaukee within the next three to four years, Warner Amex expects the number of subscribers to surpass the half million mark.[44]

Teleshopping obviously offers an exciting new dimension for retailing, but it is not without its drawbacks. One survey found that only 10 percent of the 2,163 respondents expressed positive attitudes about teleshopping. Reasons for the low acceptance varied, but included a desire to personally inspect the product, preference for going out to shop, and the fear of being tempted to purchase unneeded items.[45]

Teleshopping via an interactive cable system is likely to be most effective for products where sight, feel, smell, and personal service are not important in the purchase decision.[46] But as noted above, consumer resistance remains a problem. The barriers to the future development of teleshopping can be classified as consumer barriers, cable operator barriers, and cost barriers.[47]

Consumer Barriers

Teleshopping faces several consumer barriers. The *Marketing News* survey reported little interest in shopping via interactive cable television. Several other consumer-related questions have been raised:

1. Given the range of other programming, will consumers watch catalog programs?
2. How can catalog programs overcome the advantages of printed catalogs?

[42]"What TV Revolution Will Bring into Your Home," *U.S. News & World Report* (September 14, 1981), pp. 67–68.

[43]Quelch and Takeuchi, "Nonstore Marketing: Fast Track or Slow?" p. 80.

[44]This 1982 information was provided by Warner Amex.

[45]"Only 10% of Consumers Interested in Shopping at Home Via 2-Way TV," *Marketing News* (May 29, 1981), pp. 1, 3.

[46]Malcolm P. McNair and Eleanor G. May, "The Next Revolution of the Retailing Wheel," *Harvard Business Review* (September–October 1978), pp. 81–91. Another interesting article is Larry J. Rosenberg and Elizabeth C. Hirschman, "Retailing without Stores," *Harvard Business Review* (July–August 1980), pp. 103–112.

[47]The discussion that follows is adapted from Quelch and Takeuchi, "Nonstore Marketing: Fast Track or Slow?" pp. 80–83.

3. What can be done about the impersonal nature of teleshopping?
4. How can consumer perceptions of higher prices be handled?
5. Will consumers be willing to use an electronic funds transfer system?

All of the questions must be resolved if teleshopping is to be a successful retail innovation.

Cable Operator Barriers

There are about 4,500 cable stations in the United States. Few now have interactive capability and about half of the remaining ones cannot be converted. There are also two significant operator-related obstacles to the development of teleshopping. Cable operators may resist catalog programming because of their perception of consumer resistance to advertising. Cable operators have concentrated on subscription revenue rather than advertising revenues in the past. Advertising-supported cable networks like Cable News Network (CNN) and ESPN may be breaking down this barrier. The second barrier is the resistance of some public officials to cable franchise proposals that contain catalog programming. Some of these officials fear that their constituents will be influenced to buy goods on impulse and regret it later.

Cost Barriers

Teleshopping also faces significant cost barriers. The catalog marketers would have to absorb the production costs, but without the ability to divide it over many showings. These marketers would also probably be expected to pay the cable operator since the programming is essentially advertising. They could either buy air time, or give the operators a percentage of the orders received from the interactive cable setup. These costs are expected to be significant when compared to other forms of retailing.

Regardless of the barriers, teleshopping will become a regular part of the retailing environment in the next decade. In fact, the wheel of retailing seems to be rolling again.

Summary

Retailers are vital members of the distribution channel for consumer products. They play a major role in creating time, place, and possession utility. Retailers can be categorized on five bases: (1) shopping effort expended by customers; (2) services provided to customers; (3) product lines; (4) location of retail transactions; and (5) form of ownership.

Retailers must develop a marketing mix similar to other marketers. A market target must be identified, then a product/service strategy has to be developed. Retail pricing strategies start with a determination of relative price levels before proceeding to issues like markdowns, odd pricing, and promotional strategy. Location is a primary aspect of a retailer's distribution function. Retail trade area analysis can play a major role in this type of decision. Retail image refers to the consumer's perception of a store and the shopping experience it provides. Atmosphere, amenities, and promotional strategy play important roles in establishing a store's image.

Retailers, like consumer goods, may be divided into convenience, shopping, and specialty categories based upon the efforts shoppers are willing to expend in purchasing products. A second method of classification categorizes retailers on a spectrum ranging from self-service to full-service. The third method divides retailers into three categories: limited-line stores, which compete by carrying a large assortment of one or two lines of products; specialty stores, which carry a very large assortment of only part of a single line of products; and general merchandise retailers, such as department stores, variety stores, and such mass merchandisers as discount houses, hypermarkets, and catalog retailers—all handling a wide variety of products.

A fourth classification method distinguishes between retail stores and nonstore retailing. While more than 97 percent of total retail sales in the United States takes place in retail stores, such nonstore retailing as house-to-house retailing, mail-order establishments, and automatic merchandising machines are important in marketing many types of products and services.

The fifth method of classification categorizes retailers by form of ownership. The major types include corporate chain stores, independent retailers, and independents who have banded together to form retail cooperatives or to join wholesaler-sponsored voluntary chains or franchises.

Chains are groups of retail stores that are centrally owned and managed and that handle the same lines of products. Chain stores dominate retailing in four fields: department stores, variety stores, food stores, and shoe stores. They account for more than a third of all retail sales.

Retailing has been affected by the development of planned shopping centers and the practice of scrambled merchandising. Planned shopping centers are a group of retail stores planned, coordinated, and marketed as a unit to shoppers in their geographic trade area. Shopping centers can be classfied as neighborhood, community, and regional centers. Another significant development is scrambled merchandising, the practice of carrying dissimilar lines in an attempt to generate additional sales volume.

The evolution of retail institutions has generally been in accordance with the wheel of retailing, which holds that new types of retailers gain a competitive foothold by offering lower prices to their customers through the reduction or elimination of services. Once they are established, however, they add more services and their prices generally rise. Then they become vulnerable to the next low-price retailer. The evolution of retail institutions can also be explained in terms of a retail life cycle. One form of retailing that is at the introductory stage or beginning growth stage is teleshopping conducted through interactive cable television.

Chapter 17 discussed the last intermediary in the distribution channel—retailers. Earlier chapters in the discussion of the distribution channel included channel strategy and wholesaling. Attention now shifts to physical distribution in Chapter 18.

Key Terms

retailing
retail trade area analysis
law of retail gravitation
retail image
limited-line store
general merchandise retailer
department store
mass merchandiser
discount house
hypermarkets
chain stores
planned shopping centers
scrambled merchandising
wheel of retailing
teleshopping

Review Questions

1. Discuss the evolution of retailing.
2. Outline the decision framework for retailing.
3. Outline the five bases for categorizing retailers.
4. How are limited-line and specialty stores able to compete with such general merchandise retailers as department stores and discount houses?
5. Identify the major types of general merchandise retailers.
6. Give reasons for the success of discount retailing in the United States.
7. Identify and briefly explain each of the types of nonstore retailing operations.
8. Why has the practice of scrambled merchandising become so common in retailing?
9. Compare the retail life-cycle concept with the wheel of retailing hypothesis.
10. Discuss the current development and potential for teleshopping.

Discussion Questions and Exercises

1. Computers are one of the fastest growing aspects of retailing. Computer outlets include Radio Shack, Computerland, Compu Shop, Micro Age, and Computer Store. Relate this growth to the concepts discussed in Chapter 17.

2. Xerox and IBM have recently opened stores to serve small businesses and professionals like attorneys, physicians, dentists, and CPAs. How would you classify these stores?
3. Assume that a retailer was considering opening an outlet in Town A, population 144,000. The retailer wanted to know how far his trade area would extend toward Town B (population 16,000), 72 miles away. Apply the law of retail gravitation to the retailer's problem.
4. List several examples of the wheel of retailing in operation. List examples that do not conform to the wheel hypothesis. What generalizations can be drawn from this exercise?
5. What is your assessment of the future of teleshopping via interactive cable television?

18

Chapter Objectives

1. To relate physical distribution to the other variables of the marketing mix.
2. To explain the role of physical distribution in an effective marketing strategy.
3. To describe the objectives of physical distribution.
4. To discuss the problem of suboptimization in physical distribution.
5. To identify and compare the major elements or components of a physical distribution system.
6. To relate the major transportation alternatives to such factors as energy efficiency, speed, dependability, and cost.

MANAGEMENT OF PHYSICAL DISTRIBUTION

Sam Walton of Bentonville, Arkansas, knew that potential problems loomed on the horizon despite the fact that he and his family owned 16 successful Ben Franklin franchised stores. Variety stores were beginning to feel the pressure from discounters like Gibson's, which opened an outlet in nearby Fayetteville. So Walton decided to set up his own discount chain concentrating on smaller rural communities rather than the metropolitan areas favored by most discount retailers. Twenty years later, there are 500 Wal-Marts in a 13-state area. Annual sales are some $2.5 billion. Wal-Mart's net margin is 3.5 percent compared to the 2.5 percent common for discounters. Wal-Mart's 33 percent return on investment makes it one of the most profitable retailers in the country.

Physical distribution played a key role in Walton's success. Instead of building warehouses to serve existing units, Walton began with the warehouses and then located his retail outlets in clusters around them. Most Wal-Mart units are within a six-hour drive of one of the five large warehouses. The firm's 3 million square feet of warehousing allows nearly 80 percent of Wal-Mart's merchandise to pass through one of these installations.

Wal-Mart warehouses are extensively automated. Computer terminals link each store to the warehouse for faster order processing. Some 200 warehouses have a computer system tie-in with Wal-Mart to expedite shipments. Sam Walton estimates that he spends only 2 percent on shipping costs compared to 4 percent common for other discounters.

Wal-Mart's physical distribution system is not only cost effective, it is speedy. Walton's 268 trucks deliver goods to stores within 36 to 48 hours of ordering. The trucks also often pick up merchandise from vendors on the way back to the warehouse, a practice known as back-hauling. Wal-Mart's 60 percent back-hauling rate significantly cuts physical distribution costs.

Sam Walton may still drive an old Chevrolet and sometimes holds board of directors meetings in a warehouse, but his holdings in Wal-Mart are worth about $750 million. Effective physical distribution played a key role in Walton's success.[1]

The Conceptual Framework

Chapters 15 through 17 dealt with the basic concepts and marketing institutions within the channel of distribution, yet there is another side to the distribution function. An effective marketing mix also requires that products be physically moved within the channel of distribution. This chapter focuses specifically on the physical flow of goods. Improving customer service through more efficient physical distribution remains an important aspect of any organization's marketing strategy. In addition, this efficiency improvement means substantial cost savings.

Physical distribution involves a broad range of activities concerned with efficient movement of finished products from the end of the production line to the consumer. It is one of marketing's most innovative and dynamic areas. Physical distribution activities include such important decision areas as customer service, inventory control, materials handling, protective packaging, order processing, transportation, warehouse site selection, and warehousing. The term *logistics* is used interchangeably with physical distribution in this chapter.

[1]Howard Rudnitsky, "How Sam Walton Does It," *Forbes* (August 16, 1982), pp. 42–44.

Physical Distribution—A Major Cost of Marketing

Increased attention has been focused in recent years on physical distribution activities. A major reason for this attention is that these activities represent a major portion of total marketing costs. Almost half of all marketing costs result from physical distribution functions.

Management's traditional focal point for cost-cutting has been production. Historically, these attempts began with the industrial revolution of the 1700s and 1800s, where businesses emphasized efficient production, stressing their ability to decrease production costs and improve the output levels of factories and production workers. But managers have begun to recognize that production efficiency has reached a point at which it is difficult to achieve further cost savings. More and more managers are turning to physical distribution activities as a possible area for cost savings.

In a recent year, U.S. industry spent about $240 billion on transportation, more than $145 billion on warehousing, more than $95 billion for inventory carrying costs, and nearly $23 billion to administer and manage physical distribution. Physical distribution costs now account for more than 20 percent of the nation's gross national product.

Physical Distribution—A Major Determinant of the Level of Consumer Satisfaction

Another—and equally important—reason for the increased attention on physical distribution activities is the role they play in providing customer service. By storing products in convenient locations for shipment to wholesale and retail customers, firms create time utility. Place utility is created primarily by transportation. These major contributions indicate the importance of the physical distribution component of marketing.

Customer satisfaction depends heavily on reliable movement of products to ensure availability. Eastman Kodak committed a major marketing error in the late 1970s when it launched a multimillion-dollar advertising campaign for its new instant camera before adequate quantities had been delivered to retail outlets. Many would-be purchasers visited the stores and, when they discovered that the new camera was not available, bought Polaroid cameras instead.

By providing consumers with time and place utility, physical distribution contributes to implementing the marketing concept. Robert Woodruff, former president of the Coca-Cola Company, emphasized the role of physical distribution in his firm's success when he stated that his organization's policy is to "put Coke within an arm's length of desire."

The Physical Distribution System

The study of physical distribution is one of the classic examples of the systems approach to business problems. The basic notion of a system is that it is a set of interrelated parts. The word is derived from the Greek word *systema,* which refers to an organized relationship among components. The firm's components include such interrelated areas as production, finance, and marketing. Each component must function properly if the system is to be effective and if organizational objectives are to be achieved.

A **system** may be defined as an organized group of parts or components linked together according to a plan to achieve specific objectives. The physical distribution system contains the following elements:

- *Customer service:* What level of customer service should be provided?
- *Transportation:* How will the products be shipped?
- *Inventory control:* How much inventory should be maintained at each location?
- *Materials handling:* How do we develop efficient methods of handling products in the factory, warehouse, and transport terminals?
- *Order processing:* How should the orders be handled?
- *Warehousing:* Where will the products be located? How many warehouses should be utilized?

The above components are interrelated, and decisions made in one area affect the relative efficiency of other areas. Attempts to reduce transportation costs by utilizing low-cost, relatively slow water transportation may increase inventory costs, since the firm may be required to maintain larger inventory levels to compensate for longer delivery times. The physical distribution manager must balance each component so that no single aspect is stressed to the detriment of the overall functioning of the distribution system.[2]

The Problem of Suboptimization

The objective of an organization's physical distribution system is to produce a specified level of customer service while minimizing the costs involved in physically moving and storing the product from its production point to the point where it is ultimately purchased. Marketers must first agree on the necessary level of customer service, then seek to minimize the total costs of moving the product to the consumer or indus-

[2]David P. Herron, "Managing Physical Distribution for Profits," *Harvard Business Review* (May–June 1979), pp. 121–132.

trial user. All physical distribution elements must be considered as a whole rather than individually when attempting to meet customer service levels at minimum cost.

Sometimes this does not happen. **Suboptimization** is a condition in which the manager of each physical distribution function attempts to minimize costs, but, due to the impact of one physical distribution task on the others, the results are less than optimal. One writer explains suboptimization using the analogy of a football team made up of numerous talented individuals who seldom win games. Team members hold league records in a variety of skills: pass completions, average yards gained per rush, blocked kicks, and average gains on punt returns. Unfortunately, however, the overall ability of the team to accomplish the organizational goal—scoring more points than the opponents—is rarely achieved.[3]

Why does suboptimization occur frequently in physical distribution? The answer lies in the fact that each separate logistics activity is often judged by its ability to achieve certain management objectives, some of which are at cross-purposes with other objectives. Sometimes, departments in other functional areas take actions that cause the physical distribution area to operate at less than full efficiency.

Effective management of the physical distribution function requires some cost trade-offs. Some functional areas of the firm will experience cost increases while others will have cost decreases resulting in the minimization of total physical distribution costs. Of course, the reduction of any physical distribution cost assumes that the level of customer service will not be sacrificed.[4]

Customer Service Standards

Customer service standards are the quality of service that the firm's customers will receive. For example, a customer service standard for one firm might be that 60 percent of all orders will be shipped within 48 hours after they are received, 90 percent in 72 hours, and all within 96 hours. Setting the standards for customer service is an important marketing decision. Inadequate customer service may mean dissatisfied customers and the loss of future sales.

When Emery Air Freight decided to attack Federal Express's strong market position in the overnight small package delivery business, it found that its competition had high customer service standards. Federal

[3]Warren Rose, *Logistics Management* (Dubuque, Iowa: Wm. C. Brown, 1979), p. 4.

[4]James M. Daley and Zarrell V. Lambert, "Toward Assessing Trade-Offs by Shippers in Carrier Selection Decisions," *Journal of Business Logistics*, vol. 2, no. 1 (1980), pp. 35–54.

Buick Switched to Trucks

The Buick Division of General Motors provides a good illustration of cost tradeoffs in physical distribution management. Buick's assembly operation at Flint, Michigan, switched to trucks for delivery of the metal stampings it needs. The plant used to rely on rail shipments every two days. Now, the plant receives three truckloads each day. While trucking is more costly than railroads, the plant's inventory of stampings was cut from over 4,000 to 700. Apparently, GM's savings in reduced inventory carrying costs exceeded any increase in transportation costs. The automobile manufacturer's huge inventory requirement suggests that considerable cost reductions might be possible. General Motor's $9 billion inventory costs it $3 billion annually in carrying costs. At any given time, half of the corporation's inventory is in transit.

Source: John Koten, "Auto Makers Have Trouble with 'Kanban'," *The Wall Street Journal* (April 7, 1982), pp. 29, 45.

Express has on-time delivery percentages of 95 percent for its next morning shipments, and 99 percent for next afternoon deliveries. Emery responded with equally good customer service standards: 95 percent of its next morning deliveries and 98 percent of its next afternoon shipments are delivered on time.[5]

Physical distribution departments must delineate the costs involved in providing proposed standards. A conflict may arise when sales representatives make unreasonable delivery promises to their customers in order to obtain sales. In many cases, however, the need for additional inventory or the use of premium-cost transportation causes such a cost increase that the order proves unprofitable.

In an attempt to increase its share of the market, a major manufacturer of highly perishable food items set a 98 percent service level; that is, 98 percent of all orders were to be shipped the same day they were received. To meet this extremely high level of service, the firm leased warehouse space in 170 different cities and kept large stocks in each location. The large inventories, however, often mean the shipment of dated merchandise. Customers interpreted this practice as evidence of a low-quality product—or poor service.[6]

[5]Peter Nulty, "Emery Returns Federal Express's Fire," *Fortune* (May 17, 1982), pp. 120–121.

[6]Robert E. Sabath, "How Much Service Do Customers Really Want?" *Business Horizons* (April 1978), pp. 26–32. See also Arthur S. Graham, Jr., "Customer Service Measurement and Management of the 1980s," *Annual Proceedings of the National Council of Physical Distribution Management* (1980), pp. 265–275.

How American Airlines Uses Customer Service Standards

The next time you are in an American Airlines lobby, a man with a stopwatch and clipboard may well be standing around. He's there to see how long it takes you to get your ticket. The company standard says 85 percent of the passengers should not have to stand in line more than five minutes. When you land, you may find another fellow checking to see how long it takes to get the bags off the plane.

American Airlines employees are held to dozens of standards and checked constantly. Reservations phones must be answered within 20 seconds, and 85 percent of the flights must take off within five minutes of departure time and land within 15 minutes of arrival time. Cabins must have the proper supply of magazines. Performance summaries drawn up every month tell management how the airline is doing and where the problems lie. An outbreak of dirty ashtrays may be traced to a particular clean-up crew. The manager responsible for the crew will hear about it. His pay and promotion depend on meeting standards. If he fails to meet the standards for three consecutive months without extenuating circumstances, he may be looking for a job.

Constant checking has helped make American Airlines the preferred domestic line according to the latest Airline Passenger Association survey.

Source: Jeremy Main, "Toward Service Without a Snarl," *Fortune* (March 23, 1981), p. 61.

Physical Distribution System Components

The establishment of acceptable levels of customer service provides the physical distribution department with a standard which can be compared to actual operations. The physical distribution system should be designed to achieve this standard by minimizing the total costs of the following components: (1) transportation, (2) warehouses and their location, (3) inventory control, (4) order processing, and (5) materials handling.

Relative costs for each component are illustrated in Figure 18.1.

Transportation Considerations

The transportation system in the United States has historically been a regulated industry, much the same as the telephone and electric industries. Although strides toward deregulation have been made in recent years, the courts have often referred to modes of transportation as public utilities. The railroads were first regulated under the Interstate Commerce Act of 1887. This act established the Interstate Commerce Com-

Figure 18.1 Relative Costs of Physical Distribution Components

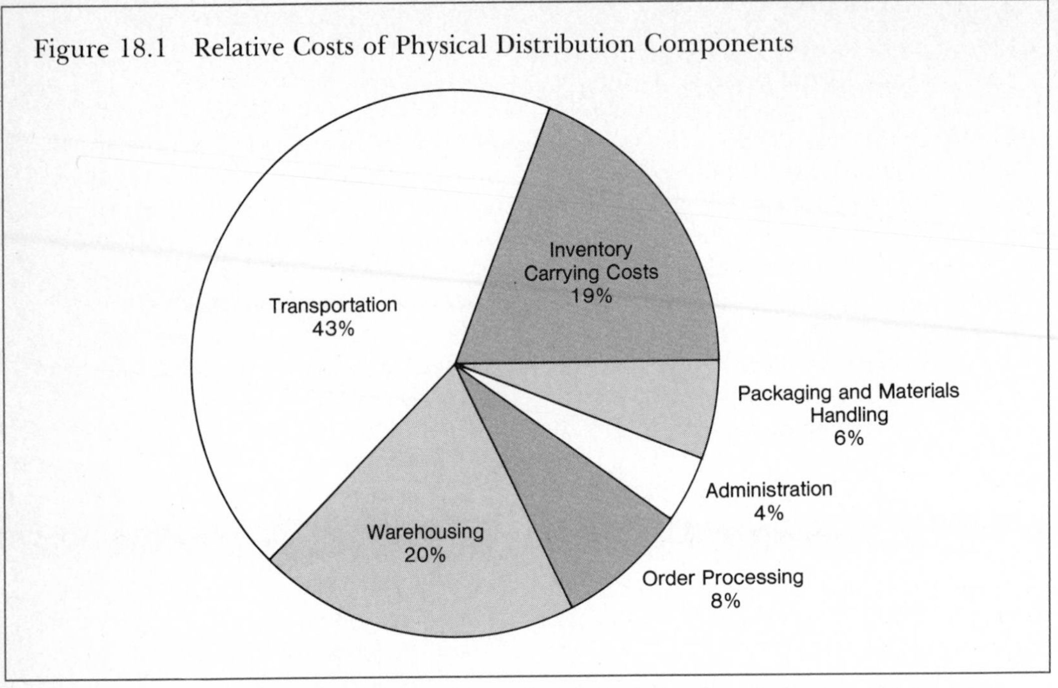

Source: Data from Herbert W. Davis, "Physical Distribution Costs: Performance in Selected Industries—1980," *Annual Proceedings of the National Council of Physical Distribution Management,* 1980, p. 35. Reprinted by permission.

mission (ICC), the first regulatory body in the United States. The ICC regulates railroads, slurry pipelines, motor carriers, and inland water carriers. The Civil Aeronautics Board regulated U.S. air carriers, and the Federal Maritime Commission regulates U.S. ocean carriers.

In general, the regulation of all the transportation modes includes a provision that the rate charged must be "just and reasonable." *Just* means that the rate must be fair to the shipper in relationship to what other shippers pay for moving similar commodities under approximately the same conditions. *Reasonable* implies that the carrier should be allowed to earn a fair return on the firm's investment. The services offered by the carriers are also regulated. Finally, the right to enter into the business of transportation historically has been restricted in most instances. Permission had to be obtained from the appropriate regulatory body before a new carrier was allowed to compete in the industry.

Rate Determination One of the most difficult problems facing the physical distribution manager who must choose a transportation service is determining the correct rate or cost of the service. The complexity results from **tariffs**—the books that are used to determine shipping charges. Tariffs take on the force and effect of statutory law when they are filed with the appropriate regulatory body. There are literally thousands of tariff books, and their number grows at a fantastic rate. One tariff expert has estimated that there are 43 trillion rates on file with the ICC and that if they were stacked one on top of another, they would be three times as tall as the World Trade Center.

There are two basic freight rates: class and commodity. The **class rate** is the standard rate that is found for every commodity moving between any two destinations. Of the two rates, the class rate is the higher. The **commodity rate** is sometimes called a special rate, since it is given by carriers to shippers as a reward for either regular use or large quantity shipments. It is used extensively by the railroads and the inland water carriers. One study showed that between 90 and 95 percent of all rail shipments were traveling under commodity rates.[7]

Deregulation in the Transportation Industry

The United States transportation industry has experienced massive federal deregulation, beginning in 1977 with the removal of regulations for cargo air carriers not engaged in passenger transportation. The following year, the Airline Deregulation Act of 1978 was passed, granting considerable freedom to the airlines in establishing fares and in choosing new routes. Passage of this act began a phase-out of the Civil Aeronautics Board that will abolish the agency in 1985.

In 1980, the Motor Carrier Act and the Staggers Rail Act significantly deregulated the trucking and railroad industries. The new laws provided transportation carriers with the ability to negotiate rates and services, eliminating much of the bureaucracy that has traditionally hampered the establishment of new and innovative rates and services. These changes are already enabling transporters to base rates on a shipper's unique needs. A large Midwest brewery, seeking to expand its Pacific Coast market, was able to negotiate a lower rate by guaranteeing a 50 percent increase in products shipped.[8]

The new transportation environment is likely to increase the importance of physical distribution managers, since their areas of responsibility are even more complex than in a highly regulated situation. It is now possible to simultaneously increase service levels and decrease transportation costs. General Foods recently negotiated a service-oriented contract with the Santa Fe Railroad in which highway trailers would be placed on railcars and transported from Houston to Chicago.

[7]Charles A. Taff, *Management of Physical Distribution and Transportation* (Homewood, Ill.: Richard D. Irwin, 1972), p. 324.

[8]"Deregulation of Railroads to Create Competitive Pricing, Better Service," *Marketing News* (May 1, 1981), p. 9.

In obtaining the contract to ship six million pounds of General Foods products each year, the railroad guaranteed the availability of sufficient truck capacity. As a bonus, it receives an additional $75 per trailer used for each month in which 90 percent of its trailers make the trip in 96 hours or less.[9]

General Electric also revised its physical distribution strategy because of deregulation. The firm wants to assign most of its shipments to two or three truckers in a particular area. The trucking companies are then expected to grant up to 29 percent price discounts because of the increased volume they will haul for GE.[10]

Classification System for Freight Carriers

Freight carriers are classified as common, contract, and private. **Common carriers,** sometimes called the backbone of the transportation industry, are for-hire carriers who serve the general public. Their rates and services are regulated, and they cannot conduct their operations without permission of the appropriate regulatory authority. Common carriers exist for all the modes of transport.

Contract carriers are for-hire transporters who do not offer their services to the general public. Instead, they contract with specific customers and operate exclusively for a particular industry (most commonly the motor freight industry). These carriers are subject to much less regulation than are common carriers.

Private carriers are not-for-hire carriers. Their operators transport products only for a particular firm and cannot solicit other transportation business. Since the transportation they provide is solely for their own use, there is no rate or service regulation.

In 1978, the ICC began to permit private carriers to also operate as common or contract carriers. Many private carriers have taken advantage of this new rule in order to operate their trucks fully loaded at all times. For instance, Nabisco Brands Inc.'s fleet of private carriers which hauls the firm's products to regional warehouses can reduce total transportation costs by transporting the products of other shippers on the return trip to the factory. Instead of returning in an empty truck, the Nabisco driver acts as a common carrier or contract carrier and receives a transport fee from the outside shipper.[11]

[9]The deregulation issue is discussed in Donald F. Wood and James C. Johnson, *Contemporary Transportation* (Tulsa, Okla.: PennWell Books, 1980), Chapter 6. See also L. L. Waters, "Deregulation —For Better or for Worse?" *Business Horizons* (January–February 1981), pp. 88–91.

[10]Michael L. King, "Transportation Official at GE Finds His Role Rises with Fuel Prices," *The Wall Street Journal* (January 31, 1981), p. 6.

[11]"Court Affirms ICC's Toto Policy, Backs Private Trucks in For-Hire Moves," *Traffic World* (July 6, 1981), pp. 129–131.

Figure 18.2 Changes in Transportation Modes as Measured by Percentage of Intercity Ton-Miles: 1940–1980

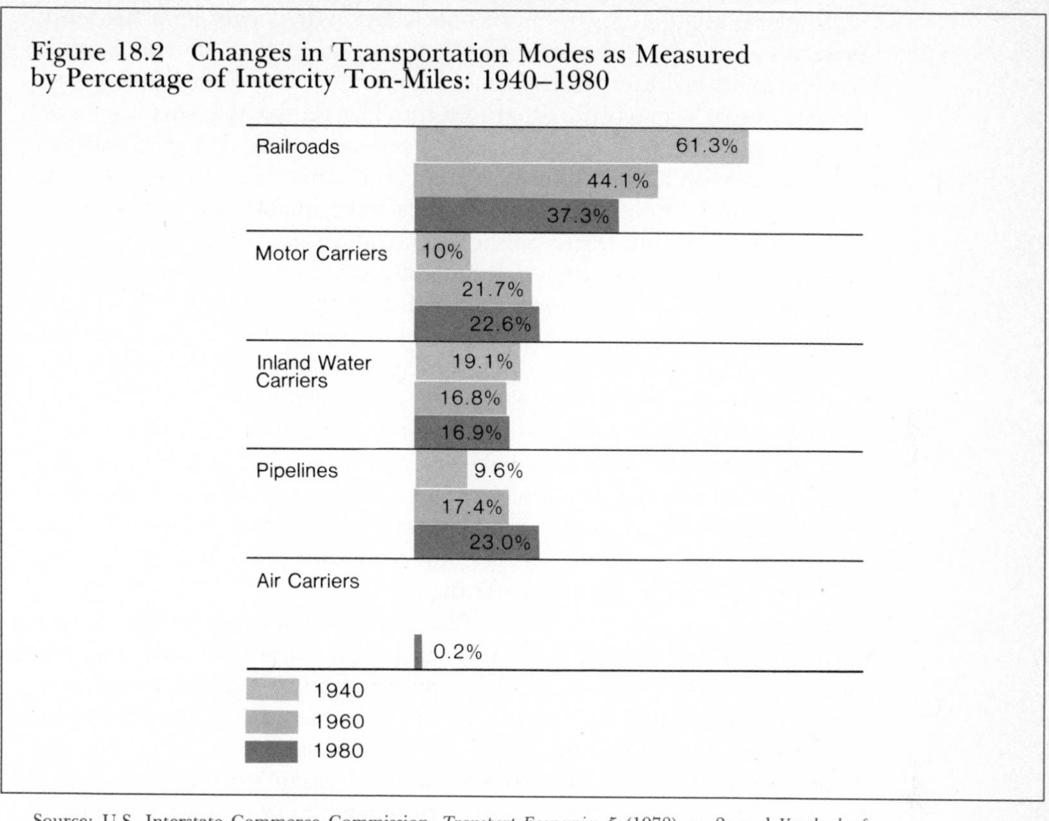

Source: U.S. Interstate Commerce Commission, *Transport Economics 5* (1978), p. 2; and *Yearbook of Railroad Facts* (Washington, D.C.: Association of American Railroads, 1981), p. 36.

Transportation Alternatives

The physical distribution manager has five major transportation alternatives: railroads, motor carriers, water carriers, pipelines, and air freight. Figure 18.2 indicates the percentage of total ton-miles shipped by each major mode. The term *ton-mile* refers to moving one ton of freight one mile. Thus a three-ton shipment moved 8 miles equals 24 ton-miles.

The water carriers' percentage has remained generally stable over the years, while railroads have experienced a significant decrease, and pipelines and motor carriers have experienced substantial increases. Air carriers are dwarfed by the other transportation alternatives, accounting for less than 1 percent of all shipments.

Railroads: The Nation's Leading Transporter The most frequently used method of transportation continues to be railroads by about a 1.5 to 1 margin over their nearest competitors. They represent the most efficient mode for the movement of bulk commodities over long distances. Recently, coal alone made up more than one fifth of the total railcar loadings in the United States. In addition, mineral products account for almost one of every two loaded railcars. The railroads have launched a drive in recent years to improve their service standards and to capture a larger percentage of manufactured and other high-value products. To accomplish their goal, the railroads have introduced a number of innovative concepts. One service innovation is run-through trains, which are scheduled to bypass completely any congested terminals. The Chicago and North Western Railroad and the Union Pacific offer a run-through train from Chicago to Los Angeles. Known as the Super Van, this train consistently covers the 2,050 miles in less than 48 hours.

Railroads are also making extensive use of unit trains to provide time and cost savings for their customers. Unit trains are used exclusively by a single customer, who pays lower rates for each shipment. The Burlington Northern Railroad operates unit coal trains for electricity utility companies in the Midwest. The railroad hauls a trainload of low-sulphur coal from Montana or Wyoming to the generating plants and then returns empty for another run.

Improved customer service is also being accomplished through an unusual method: railroad mergers. Only 42 U.S. railroad lines generate more than $50 million in annual revenues, and this number of lines is slowly shrinking due to mergers. In the past, rail shippers had to resort to interlining—using more than one rail carrier when long distances between the shipment's origin and its destination were involved. As a result, it was easy for one railroad to simply blame other connecting railroads for service problems. The increased number of rail mergers are typically "end-to-end," thereby providing shippers with single-carrier service from origin to destination.[12]

Motor Carriers: Flexible and Growing The trucking industry has shown dramatic growth over the past decades. Its prime advantage over the other modes is its relatively fast, consistent service for both large and small shipments. Trucking's service advantages also cost more. As a result, in 1980, motor carriers received approximately 16 cents per ton-mile while railroads earned 2 cents. Motor carriers concentrate on manufactured products, while railroads haul more bulk and raw material products.

Trucking's primary appeal to shippers is superior service, and the industry is working diligently to maintain this advantage. The TIME-DC trucking company is currently running schedules that just a few years ago seemed impossible. It used to require seven to ten days for a

[12]Gus Welty, "The Era of the Giants: Union Pacific, Missouri Pacific, and Western Pacific," *Railway Age* (April 27, 1981), pp. 20–26.

The Tucumcari Line

Southern Pacific had a problem. The 13,740-mile railroad line was extremely strong in California, originating as much as 50 percent of that state's rail traffic. But Southern Pacific's only route to the east was along the southern border of several western states before it could turn north to St. Louis. The more direct route—some 400 miles shorter—would have required the Southern Pacific to interline with the Union Pacific and the Rock Island lines.

Southern Pacific's solution was to purchase the Tucumcari line from Rock Island for $57 million. The company spent another $97 million upgrading the line from Tucumcari, New Mexico, to Topeka, Kansas. But a capital shortage forced Southern Pacific to abandon a similar $97 million effort to make the Kansas City to St. Louis portion of the line operable. Southern Pacific's thwarted plan suggests the extent to which firms will go to avoid interlining. The potential rewards are immense. If Southern Pacific can ever complete its California to St. Louis hookup, its estimated annual savings will be 9.8 million gallons of fuel and $33 million in expenses. The Tucumcari line could also generate $33 to $140 million in revenue for the capital-short line.

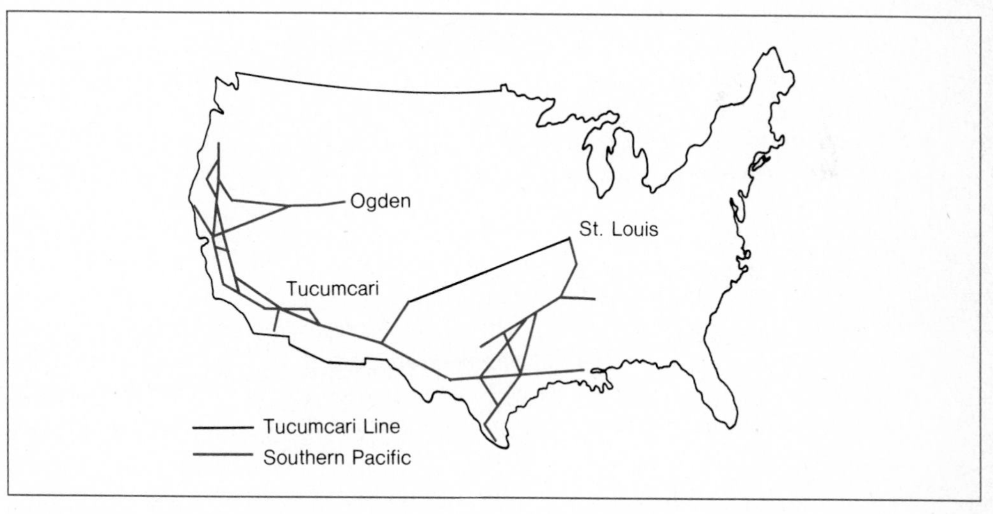

Source: James Cook, "Doomed?" *Forbes* (August 16, 1982), pp. 57–60. Original drawing by Robert Conrad.

coast-to-coast truckload shipment. TIME-DC now offers its Yellowbird Service between New York–New Jersey and Southern California in 69 hours, with delivery made the third morning after departure.

Water Carriers: Slow but Inexpensive There are basically two types of water carriers—the inland or barge lines and the ocean-going deep-water ships. Barge lines are efficient transporters of bulky, low-unit value commodities like grain, gravel, lumber, sand, and steel. A typical lower Mississippi River barge line may be more than a quarter mile long and 200 feet wide.

Ocean-going ships operate on the Great Lakes, between United States port cities, and in international commerce. Water carrier costs average 0.6 cents per ton-mile.

Pipelines: Specialized Transporters Even though the pipeline industry ranks second only to railroads in number of ton-miles transported, many people are barely aware of their existence. More than 200,000 miles of pipelines crisscross the United States. Pipelines serve as extremely efficient transporters of natural gas and oil products, as evidenced by their average revenue per ton-mile of a little less than 0.3 cents. Oil pipelines carry two types of commodities—crude (unprocessed) oil and refined products, such as gasoline and kerosene. There is also a slow but steady growth in the use of slurry pipelines. In this method of transport, a product such as coal is ground up into a powder, mixed with water, and transported in suspension through the pipeline.[13]

Although pipelines represent a low-maintenance, dependable method of transportation, they possess a number of characteristics that limit their use. Their availability in different locations is even more limited than the water carriers, and their use is restricted to a relatively small number of products that can be transported in this manner. Finally, pipelines represent a relatively slow method of transportation. Liquids travel through pipelines at an average of only three or four miles per hour.

Air Freight: Fast but Expensive The use of air carriers has been growing significantly. In 1961, U.S. airlines flew about 1 billion ton-miles. By 1980, this figure had jumped to 5 billion ton-miles. However, air freight is still a relatively insignificant percentage of the total ton-miles shipped, amounting about to one fifth of one percent.

[13]Martin T. Farris and David L. Shrock, "The Economics of Coal Slurry Pipelines: Transportation and Non-Transportation Factors," *Transportation Journal* (Fall 1978), pp. 45–57. See also James C. Johnson and Kenneth C. Schneider, "Coal Slurry Pipelines: An Economic and Political Dilemma," *ICC Practitioners' Journal* (November–December 1980), pp. 24–37.

The Nation's First Superport

Importing costly crude oil from OPEC nations has traditionally been made even more expensive due to the size of the supertankers and the inability of U.S. ports to dock them. In the past, the tankers—capable of handling 700,000-ton loads—anchored off shore and transferred their cargo to smaller vessels. The additional unloading and reloading expenses drove the high-priced crude oil even higher.

These costs were reduced in 1981 with the opening of the Louisiana Offshore Oil Port (LOOP), a $575-million installation situated 19 miles off the Louisiana Gulf Coast. LOOP, which looks like a large offshore oil drilling and pumping rig, stands on steel legs in 110 feet of water about 60 miles south of New Orleans.

Rather than pump crude oil into smaller vessels capable of navigating the Mississippi River to New Orleans, workers at the superport simply hook up hoses and pump the cargo through a 19-mile underwater pipeline. It is then fed directly into a major pipeline that crosses the nation to Chicago.

Although the facility is expensive, it reduces overall physical distribution costs. Transporters can utilize the relatively low-cost supertankers in moving the crude oil, and they avoid the added handling costs in using smaller vessels on the last few miles of the journey.

Source: The opening of the LOOP superport is described in "First Off-Shore Superport Makes Debut," *Orlando Sentinel Star* (May 8, 1981). See also "Once Again, a Plunge into Deepwater Oil Ports," *Business Week* (December 22, 1980), p. 79.

Because of air freight's relatively high cost, it is used primarily for valuable or highly perishable products. Typical shipments consist of computers, furs, fresh flowers, high-fashion clothing, live lobsters, and watches. Air carriers often offset their higher transportation costs with reduced inventory holding costs and faster customer service.

One result of airline deregulation was the simplification of regulations concerning the creation of new airline companies. In the first three years following deregulation, new air carriers such as Midway, New York Air, People Express, Muse Air, Sun Pacific, Sun Air, Pacific Express, and Air Chicago began operations. All of these carriers are primarily passenger-oriented, although some freight service is available.[14]

Table 18.1 ranks the five transport modes on several bases.

Freight Forwarders: Transportation Middlemen Freight forwarders are considered transportation middlemen because their function is to con-

[14]Peter Nulty, "Friendly Skies for Little Airlines," *Fortune* (February 9, 1981), pp. 45–53; "Upstarts in the Sky: Here Comes a New Kind of Airline," *Business Week* (June 15, 1981), pp. 78–84; and Subrata N. Chakravarty, "Power Dive," *Forbes* (June 22, 1981), pp. 64–66.

Table 18.1 The Ranking of Transportation Modes

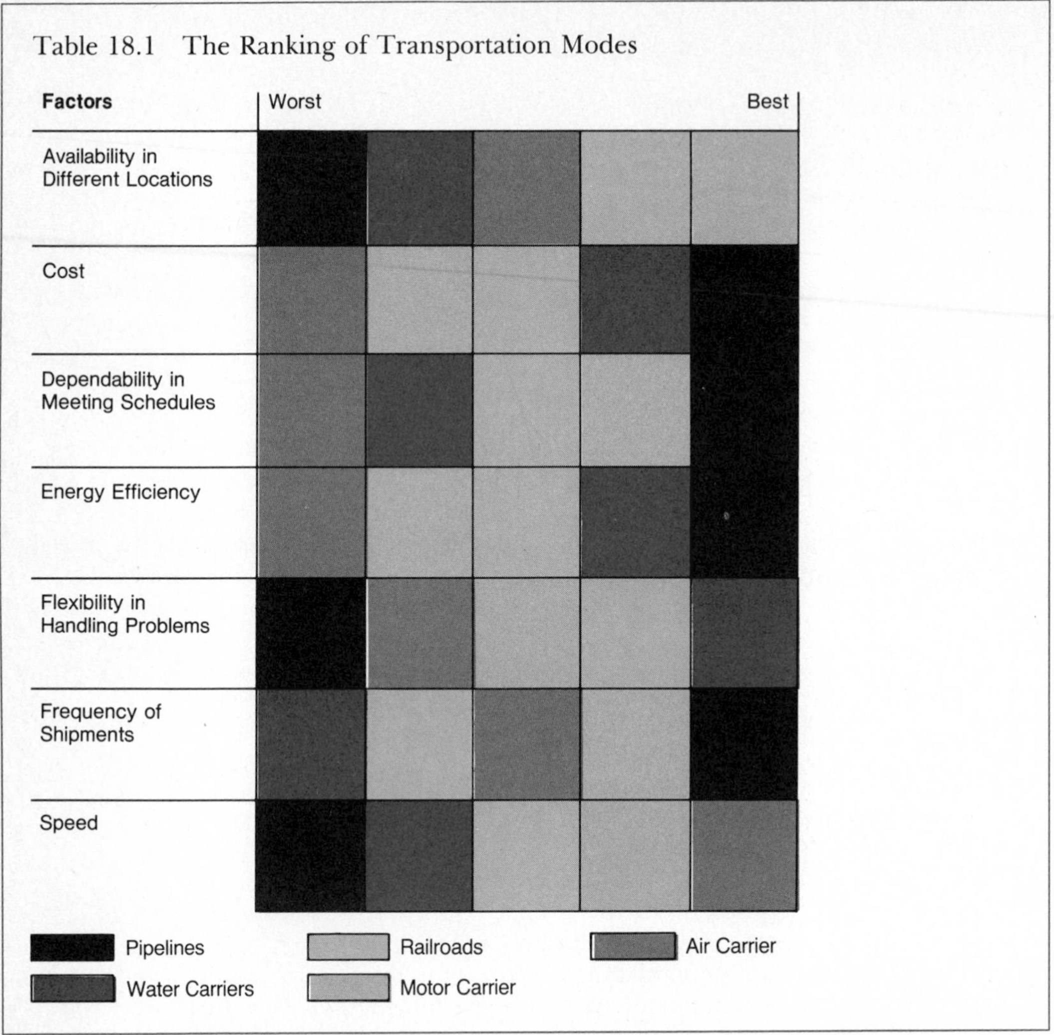

Source: The energy-efficiency rankings are reported in Eric Hirst, *Energy Intensiveness of Passenger and Freight Modes,* National Science Foundation, Oak Ridge National Laboratory, March 1972, p. 27. The other factors and rankings are based on a discussion in James L. Heskitt, Nicholas A. Glaskowsky, Jr., and Robert M. Ivie, *Business Logistics* (New York: Ronald Press, 1973), pp. 113–118. Used by permission. A similar table appears in John J. Cagle and Edward J. Bardi, *The Management of Business Logistics,* 2nd ed. (St. Paul, Minn.: West Publishing Company, 1980), p. 215.

solidate shipments in order to get lower rates for their customers. The transport rates on less-than-truckload (LTL) and less-than-carload (LCL) shipments are often twice as high on a per-unit basis as the rates on truckload (TL) and carload (CL) shipments. Freight forwarders charge less than the higher rates but more than the lower rates. They make a profit by paying the carriers the lower rates. By consolidating shipments, freight forwarders offer their customers two advantages—lower costs on small shipments and faster delivery service than the LTL and LCL shippers.

Supplemental Carriers The physical distribution manager can also utilize a number of auxiliary or supplemental carriers that specialize in transporting small shipments. These carriers include bus freight services, United Parcel Service, and the U.S. Postal Service.

Intermodal Coordination The various transport modes often combine their services to give shippers the service and cost advantages of each mode. The most widely accepted form of coordination is piggyback—railroad transportation between cities of a truck trailer carried on a rail flatcar. The motor carrier delivers and picks up the shipment.

The combination of truck and rail services generally gives shippers faster service and lower rates than either mode would individually, since each method is used where it is most efficient. Shipper acceptance of piggybacking has been tremendous. In 1955, fewer than 200,000 piggyback railcars were shipped. By 1980, more than 1.6 million cars were involved. Piggyback shipments are expected to account for 40 percent of all rail traffic by 1995. In 1981, the ICC exempted piggyback service from government regulation, a move that is expected to increase competition and improve growth prospects.[15]

Another form of intermodal coordination is birdyback. Here, motor carriers deliver and pick up the shipment, and air carriers take it over the long distance. In addition, motor carriers and water carriers have a form of intermodal coordination called fishyback.

Warehousing

Two types of warehouses exist: storage and distribution. A **storage warehouse** stores products for moderate to long periods of time in an attempt to balance supply and demand for producers and purchasers. They are used most often by firms whose products are seasonal in supply or demand.

[15]"ICC Adopts Rules Exempting Railroad Piggyback Service from Regulation," *Traffic World* (March 2, 1981), pp. 50–51.

The **distribution warehouse** assembles and redistributes products, keeping them on the move as much as possible. Many distribution warehouses or centers actually store the goods physically for less than one day.

In an attempt to reduce transportation costs, manufacturers have developed central distribution centers. A manufacturer located in Buffalo which has concentrations of customers in Charleston, South Carolina; Tampa, Florida; and Birmingham, Alabama, could send each customer a direct shipment. However, if each customer places small orders, the transportation charges for the individual shipments will be relatively high. A feasible solution is to send a large, consolidated shipment to a **break-bulk center,** a central distribution center that breaks down large shipments into several smaller ones and delivers them to individual customers in the area. For the hypothetical manager in Buffalo, the feasible break-bulk center might be located in Atlanta. Figure 18.3 illustrates the use of break-bulk centers in the United States.

Inversely, the **make-bulk center** consolidates several small shipments into one large shipment and delivers it to its destination. For example, a giant retailer like Safeway Stores may operate several satellite production facilities in a given area. Each plant can send shipments to a storage warehouse in Denver. This, however, could result in a large number of small, expensive shipments. If a make-bulk center is created in Los Angeles, as illustrated in Figure 18.3, and each supplier sends its shipments there, all deliveries bound for Denver theoretically can be consolidated into one economical shipment.

The top five distribution center cities in the United States, as measured by the total number of break-bulk distribution centers, are Chicago, Los Angeles–Long Beach, the New York City area, Dallas–Fort Worth, and Atlanta.

Automated Warehouses Warehouses lend themselves well to automation, with the computer as the heart of the operation. An outstanding example of automation at work is the Aerojet-General Industrial Systems Division warehouse in Frederick, Maryland. This huge warehouse is operated entirely by one employee who gives instructions to the facility's governing computer. The computer operates the fully automated materials handling system and generates all the necessary forms.[16]

Although automated warehouses may cost as much as $10 million, they can provide major savings to high-volume distributors such as gro-

[16]"The Ultimate in Automation," *Transportation and Distribution Management* (January 1970), p. 38. See also Kenneth B. Ackerman and Bernard J. LaLonde, "Making Warehousing More Efficient," *Harvard Business Review* (March–April 1980), pp. 94–102.

Figure 18.3 Break-Bulk and Make-Bulk Centers

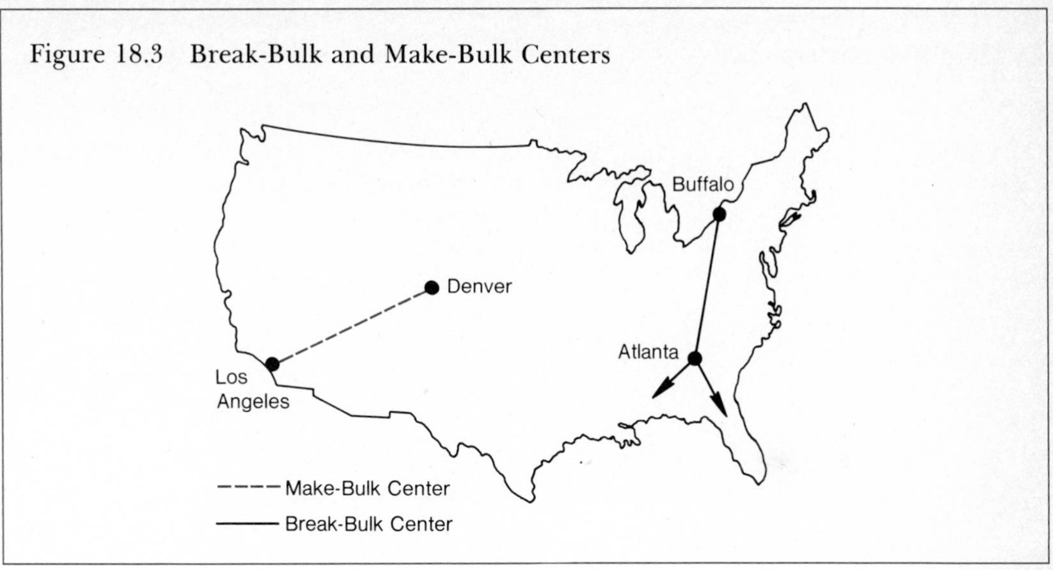

cery chains. Some current systems can select 10,000 to 300,000 cases per day of up to 3,000 different items. They can read computerized store orders, choose the correct number of cases, and move them in the desired sequence to loading docks. These warehouses reduce labor costs, worker injuries, pilferage, fires, and breakage, and they assist in inventory control.

Location Factors A major decision facing each company is the number and location of its storage facilities. The two general factors involved are warehousing and materials handling costs and delivery costs from the warehouse to the customer. The first costs are subject to economies of scale; therefore, on a per-unit basis, they decrease as volume increases. Delivery costs, on the other hand, increase as the distance from the warehouse location to the customer increases.

The two cost items are diagrammed in Figure 18.4. The asterisk in the figure marks the ideal area of coverage for each warehouse. This model helps determine the proper number of warehouses if decentralization is desired.

The specific location of the firm's warehouses presents another complicated problem. Factors that must be considered include (1) local, county, and state taxes; (2) local, county, and state laws and regulations; (3) availability of a trained labor force; (4) police and fire protection; (5) access to the various transport modes; (6) community attitude toward the proposed warehouses; and (7) the cost and availability of public utilities, such as electricity and natural gas.

Figure 18.4 Determinants of the Number of Warehouses

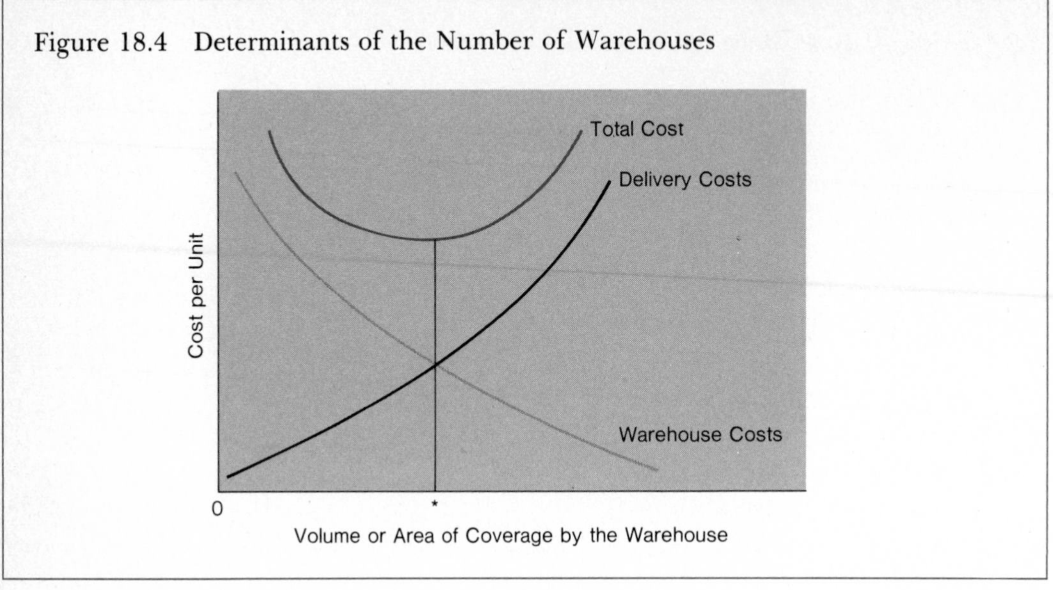

Order Processing

Like customer service standards, order processing is a logistics-type function. The physical distribution manager is concerned with order processing because it directly affects the firm's ability to meet its customer service standards. If a firm's order processing system is inefficient, the company may have to compensate by using costly premium transportation or increasing the number of field warehouses in all major markets.

Order processing typically consists of four major activities: a credit check; recording the sale, such as crediting a sales representative's commission account; making the appropriate accounting entries; and locating the item, shipping, and adjusting inventory records. An item that is not available for shipment is known as a **stock-out.** This situation requires the order-processing unit to advise the customer of the situation and the contemplated action.[17]

Inventory Control

Inventory control is a major component in the physical distribution system. Current estimates of inventory holding costs figure about 25 percent per year. This means that $1,000 of inventory held for a single

[17]Based on James C. Johnson and Donald F. Wood, *Contemporary Physical Distribution and Logistics,* 2nd ed. (Tulsa, Okla.: PennWell Books, 1982), p. 66.

Figure 18.5 The EOQ Model

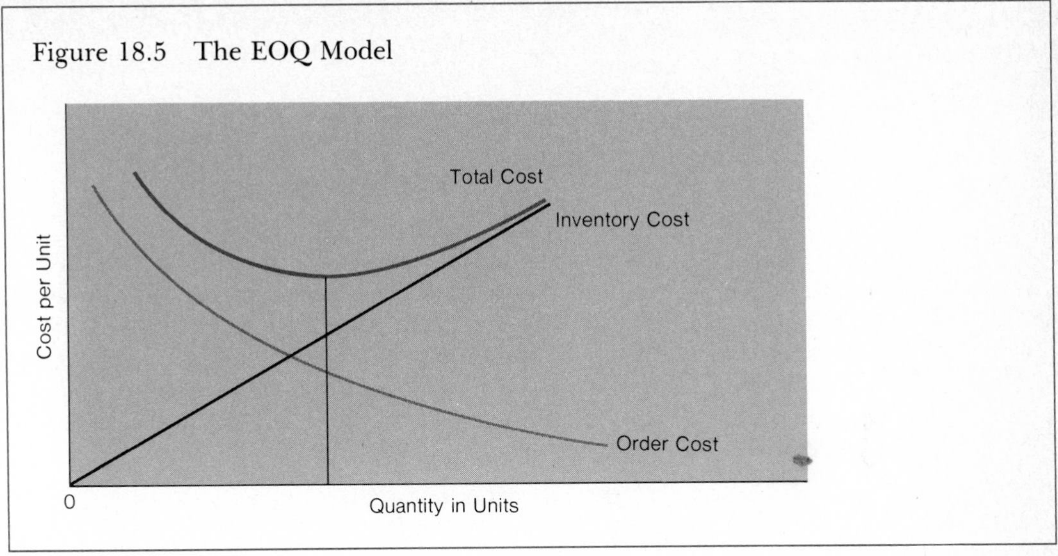

year costs the company $250. Inventory costs include such expenses as storage facilities, insurance, taxes, handling costs, opportunity costs for funds invested in inventory, and depreciation and possible obsolescence of the goods in inventory.[18]

Inventory control analysts have developed a number of techniques to help the physical distribution manager effectively control inventory. The most basic is the **EOQ (economic order quantity) model.** This technique emphasizes a cost trade-off between two fundamental costs involved with inventory: inventory holding costs that increase with the addition of more inventory and order costs that decrease as the quantity ordered increases. As Figure 18.5 indicates, these two cost items are traded off to determine the optimal order quantity of each product.

The EOQ point in Figure 18.5 is the point at which total cost is minimized. By placing an order for this amount as needed, firms can minimize their inventory costs.

The EOQ Formula

The following formula has been developed for determining the economic order quantity:

$$EOQ = \sqrt{\frac{2RS}{IC}}$$

where

[18]The impact of effective inventory control systems on company profitability is discussed in Lewis Beman, "A Big Payoff from Inventory Controls," *Fortune* (July 27, 1981), pp. 76–80.

EOQ = the economic order quantity (in units)

R = the annual rate of usage

S = the cost of placing an order

I = the annual inventory carrying cost percentage

C = the cost per unit.

In the above formula, R is an estimate based upon the demand forecast for the item. S is calculated from the firm's cost records. I is also an estimate based upon the costs of such items as depreciation, handling, insurance, interest, storage, and taxes. Since the costs of the item may vary over time, C is also likely to be an estimate. By inserting specific data into the formula, the EOQ can be determined. Consider, for example, the following data:

$$R = 5500 \text{ units}$$
$$S = \$7.50$$
$$I = 20 \text{ percent}$$
$$C = \$12.90$$

$$EOQ = \sqrt{\frac{(2)\,(5500)\,(7.50)}{(12.90)\,(.20)}}$$
$$= 178.82.$$

Although the EOQ has been calculated at approximately 178 units, other factors should be taken into account. Truckload or railroad carload shipments may consist of 200 units. In certain instances, the purchasing firm may discover that the units are shipped in special containers consisting of 175 units. In such cases, the EOQ may be adjusted to match these conditions and an order for 175 or 200 units, rather than the calculated 178 units, may be placed.

Once the EOQ has been determined, specific reorder points are determined by considering certain factors, such as the lead time required for receiving an order once it has been placed and the average daily demand. If the necessary lead time is 7 days and average daily sales consist of 5 units, orders must be placed when the available inventory reaches 35 units. Since demand may fluctuate, most organizations add a certain amount of inventory called **safety stock** to compensate for such demand fluctuations. In the above instance, a predetermined safety stock of 5 units would mean that new orders would be placed when inventory levels drop to 40 units.

Managers use the EOQ as a powerful tool in making rational decisions about inventory. The EOQ is a widely used technique as managers attempt to minimize the costs of ordering and maintaining inventory.

Materials Handling

All the activities associated in moving products within the manufacturer's plants, warehouses, and transportation company terminals are called **materials handling.** These activities must be thoroughly coordinated for both intra- and intercompany activities. The efficiency of plants and warehouses is dependent on an effective system.[19]

Two important innovations have been developed in the area of materials handling. One is known as **unitizing**—combining as many packages as possible into one load, preferably on a pallet (a platform, generally made of wood, on which products are transported). Unitizing can be accomplished by using steel bands to hold the unit in place or by shrink packaging. Shrink packages are constructed by placing a sheet of plastic over the unit and then heating it. As the plastic cools, it shrinks and holds the individual packages together securely. Unitizing is advantageous because it requires little labor per package, promotes fast movement, and minimizes damage and pilferage.

The second innovation is **containerization,** the combination of several unitized loads. It is typically a big box about eight feet wide, eight feet high, and ten, twenty, thirty, or forty feet long. Such containers allow ease of intertransport mode changes. A container of oil-rig parts, for example, can be loaded in Tulsa and trucked to Kansas City, where it can be placed on a high-speed run-through train to New York City. There, it can be placed on a ship and sent to Saudi Arabia.

Containerization also markedly reduces the time involved in loading and unloading ships. Container ships can often be unloaded in less than 24 hours—a task that otherwise can take up to two weeks. In-transit damage is also reduced, since individual packages are not handled en route to the purchaser.

International Physical Distribution

The United States has experienced rapid growth in international trade since World War II. Between 1960 and 1981, combined U.S. exports and imports grew from the equivalent of 10 percent of the nation's output to 24 percent. In 1981, the United States spent more than $273 billion on foreign imports while its exports totaled nearly $234 billion.[20] This unparalelled growth of international commerce has placed new responsibilities on physical distribution departments.

[19]For a discussion of materials handling innovations, see "Materials Handling Trends: One Expert's Viewpoint," *Traffic Management* (March 1981), pp. 36–38.

[20]"World Trade Is Pocketbook Issue for Everyone," *U.S. News and World Report* (April 26, 1982), p. 57.

A major problem facing international marketers is the flood of paperwork involved in exporting products. More than 100 different international trade documents representing more than 1,000 separate forms must be completed for each international shipment. The result is that an average export shipment requires approximately 36 employee hours for documentation and 27 employee hours for importing a shipment. Paperwork alone equals 7 percent of the total value of U.S. international trade. Many physical distribution departments are not large enough to employ international specialists, and they subcontract the work to foreign freight forwarders, wholesaling middlemen who specialize in physical distribution outside the United States.

The major impetus to exporting has been the advent of containerization and container ships. One shipping company currently has container ships that can make a round trip between New York, Bremerhaven, and Rotterdam in 14 days. Only four days are needed for crossing the Atlantic and another six for three port calls. This speed allows U.S. exporters to provide competitive delivery schedules to European markets.

Summary

Physical distribution, as a system, consists of six elements: (1) customer service, (2) transportation, (3) inventory control, (4) materials handling, (5) order processing, and (6) warehousing. These elements are interrelated and must be balanced for a smoothly functioning distribution system. The physical distribution department is one of the classic examples of the systems approach to business problems. The physical distribution system attempts to overcome the problem of suboptimization.

The goal of a physical distribution department is to produce a specified level of customer service while minimizing the costs involved in physically moving and storing the product from its production point to the point where it is ultimately purchased.

The physical distribution manager has available five transportation alternatives: railroads, motor carriers, water carriers, pipelines, and air freight. Intermodal transport systems are also available and are increasingly being used. Other elements of the physical distribution department include customer service, inventory control, materials handling, protective packaging, order processing, transportation, warehouse site selection, and warehousing. Efficient international physical distribution allows U.S. firms to compete effectively in foreign markets.

Physical distribution, by its very nature, involves keeping track of thousands of details, such as transport rates, special rate proposals, inventory locations, and customer locations. Computerization is an invaluable aid for the logistics manager.

Part Six examined the distribution element of the marketing mix, covering the topics of channel strategy, wholesaling, retailing, and physical distribution. The next section deals with the fourth aspect of marketing strategy—promotion.

Key Terms

physical distribution
system
suboptimization
customer service standards
tariffs
class rate
commodity rate
common carrier
contract carrier
private carrier
storage warehouse
distribution warehouse
break-bulk center
make-bulk center
stock-out
EOQ (economic order quantity) model
safety stock
materials handling
unitizing
containerization

Review Questions

1. Why was physical distribution one of the last areas in most companies to be carefully studied and improved?
2. Outline the basic reasons for the increased attention to physical distribution management.
3. What are the basic objectives of physical distribution?
4. What is the most effective organization for physical distribution management? Explain.
5. What factors should be considered in locating a new distribution warehouse?
6. Who should be ultimately responsible for determining the level of customer service standards? Explain.
7. Outline the basic strengths and weaknesses of each mode of transport.
8. Under what circumstances are freight forwarders used?
9. Identify the major forms of intermodal coordination and give an example of a product that is likely to use each type.
10. Determine the EOQ (economic order quantity) for the following situation:

    A firm has calculated the cost of placing orders at $4.60 per order. The annual cost of carrying the product in inventory is estimated to be 22 percent. Cost per unit estimates for the next 12 months are $8.40. Annual usage rates are estimated to be 11,500.

Discussion Questions and Exercises

1. Comment on the following statement: The popularity of physical distribution management is a fad; ten years from now it will be considered a relatively unimportant function of the firm.
2. Prepare a brief report on career opportunities in physical distribution.
3. Suggest the most appropriate method of transportation for each of the following products and defend your choices:
   a. Iron ore
   b. Dash detergent
   c. Heavy earth-moving equipment
   d. Crude oil
   e. Orchids
   f. Lumber
4. Develop an argument for the increased use of intermodal coordination. Present your argument to the marketing class.
5. Which mode of transport do you believe will experience the greatest ton-mile percentage growth during the 1980s? Why?

CASES FOR PART 6

Case 6.1
Atlas Map Company

In April of 1978, Richard J. Berlin and Roger K. Tucker, the president and vice-president of the Atlas Map Company, met at the company's headquarters in New Hampshire to review the strategy followed by their firm. Sales of the company's main product, *The Granite State Atlas,* were discouraging. Since its introduction to market in July 1977, only half of the first printing of 25,000 atlases had been sold. Several promotion campaigns failed to generate sales and the cash needed to keep the company solvent. The warehouse where the atlases were stored was sold and a new location had to be found. Several wholesalers owed the company money, but had no apparent intention of paying soon. During March 1978, the two men met several times to discuss possible solutions, but had come to no decision. This time it was clear to both men that immediate steps were necessary to assure the company's survival. Both reviewed the situation once more prior to the meeting and came prepared with several solutions, none of which had been discussed previously.

Background

The Atlas Map Company was incorporated in July 1976 to produce and market street maps of cities and towns, primarily in its home state of New Hampshire. The firm had grown from an idea of Berlin's. Richard Berlin was an insurance adjuster in the Boston area for several years prior to starting the Atlas Map Company. The adjuster's job involved traveling to clients of the company to review accidents and facilitate settlement. Berlin would generally plot on a map the locations he had to visit the next day, deriving an optimum route. Each night he spent up to half an hour planning this route. With a little experience he found he could reduce the distance traveled as well as delays caused by heavy traffic, construction, etc. Although some of his colleagues used the same method, it wasn't widespread. The chief instrument which made this possible was a book which compiled the maps and street listings of the towns in Eastern Massachusetts. It sold for $5. Berlin was able to cut hours from his workdays and still complete his assignments.

Source: This case was prepared by Professors Subhash C. Jain of the University of Connecticut and Michael V. Laric of the University of Baltimore. Reprinted by permission.

Around January 1976, Berlin was reassigned to the New Hampshire district. He found that a great deal of his time was spent finding the correct address. His attaché case bulged with individual maps, which had to be unfolded one by one in his car as he progressed from one stop to another. The maps also cost from $.75 to $1.50; the insurance company did not pay for these maps. Berlin searched for a book of maps similar to the *Boston Street Guide,* but could not find one. He believed that many salespeople, insurance agents, and adjusters, as well as other business travelers, would find such a booklet of street maps very useful.

Early in the spring of 1976, Berlin approached Roger Tucker, a high-school acquaintance, with his idea for a map book. Tucker was an engineer with connections in the printing business. The two discussed the feasibility of producing and selling an atlas with maps of New Hampshire cities and towns. Tucker was enthusiastic about the idea and stated that he could produce and publish such a product, as well as obtain financing until release of the book. The two decided that some preliminary market research should be done before committing time and resources to the project. Berlin agreed to survey several dozen salespeople, insurance people, and businesspeople to check response to the product. He was also to compile information on the maps in the present market and their characteristics. Tucker was to concurrently investigate methods of producing the maps and the optimum product with regard to layout and printing considerations. He would also produce a sample showing the basic format (no actual maps) to be used as a demonstration aid during discussions with potential sellers and buyers (retailers, potential advertisers, and potential users).

The Market

The preliminary research carried out by Berlin and Tucker revealed some information on the relevant market in New Hampshire. The only available maps of the state's cities and towns were single town maps on separate sheets, generally "fold-out" products with a street listing on the back. Most towns with large populations had maps available, but many of these were of partial areas of towns. About 90 percent of these maps were produced by two out-of-state companies: National Survey of Manchester, Connecticut, and the Charta Maps Company from Boston, Massachusetts. The remaining 10 percent were produced by various groups, such as the Lancaster Historical Society and local chambers of commerce. These maps generally had advertising messages around the margins. There were no books which compiled several towns, nor were there maps which combined several adjoining towns. The spectrum of quality and accuracy of these maps was wide, both between and within the maps produced by the two large companies. These ranged from poor to excellent. The maps of smaller towns, where there was no competition, tended to be poor. In larger cities (e.g., Manchester, Nashua, Concord) where several products were available, the quality and accuracy were much better.

The existing products were sold primarily in bookstores, drugstores, and stationery stores. The prices of the maps ranged from $.75 to $1.50. Store managers indicated they generally bought maps directly from the map companies, and only rarely through an intermediary.

Large orders were placed for proven items (i.e., those with good sales). Small quantities (15–25 copies) were purchased if the product was new and not proven. Profit margins for retailers were small (10–15 percent) even though the maps were not expensive to produce. No numbers of actual sales were available. Most of the stores surveyed reported a quick turnover and were very enthusiastic about the proposed new product. Surveyed people, who traveled about the state, were unanimously enthusiastic about the product. Each person interviewed stated he would buy the product since it would eliminate juggling several individual maps each day. Even those who traveled locally (i.e., limited to a region of the state) said they would buy the product because of the efficiency of the proposed format. A surprising number of the sample also mentioned they would probably utilize the product for nonbusiness purposes. Over one third of the sample indicated they were constantly looking for better quality maps in New Hampshire.

The survey of potential advertisers covered many types of businesses. The highest interest was indicated by realtors and bankers. They were very enthusiastic and expressed a desire to have exclusive rights to the pages containing the maps of their locales. Specifically, if a realtor bought an ad on the Nashua page, no other realtors could advertise on that page. Restaurants and motels were interested in smaller ads (less than a page), and various other individuals indicated mild interest. Several of those approached were ready to sign up for ads immediately.

A survey of alternate ways of producing and printing maps showed a wide array of alternatives. After deliberations and evaluation, Tucker chose the most cost-effective system: a two-color process. This process was both inexpensive and available at a reputable printer. The process required drawing the maps on two sheets with lines of the first color on the base and lines of the second on an overlay. Using more colors would make the matching of different colors to each other extremely difficult. The available press had a maximum size which dictated a book size no larger than 11 by 14 inches. The maps were to be hand drawn and lettered. A map of this type was as easy to read as a map produced with the expensive equipment used in cartography.

Initial Operations

After incorporation, Berlin and Tucker focused on defining their market target and course of action. They believed that business travelers were their prime target, and they required an atlas which was both very accurate and easy to use. The atlas would replace the various maps of large and small towns and cities in the user's car or attaché case. The main benefit to users would be ease of shifting from map to map without the hassle of folding and unfolding. A second benefit was that users would be able to find any street on any map without flipping back and forth from map to street listing. The atlas was to contain advertisements to cover the development and printing expenses. Profits would accrue from actual sales.

The atlas was entitled *The Granite State Atlas,* and its format was similar to the Boston atlas that Berlin and other salespeople used. Thirty towns were included, alphabetically, with the town's name in block letters on the upper right-hand corner of each map. The map was in blue with major highways and streets appearing in red. The street listings in the atlas faced each corresponding map or appeared on the succeeding page if the map covered two pages. (The Boston atlas, on the other hand, had all street listings tabulated by town on the back of the atlas.) Space was available on each page for advertisements. Advertisements were limited to one per industry per page. Realtors and bankers expressed a desire for such a limitation, and there were sufficient advertisers from different industries.

The atlas provided a major route map, a township map, and other business information. These gave the user a perspective on the location of various towns in relation to each other, as well as background information and basic statistics on the state and major towns.

The retail price for the *The Granite State Atlas* was set at $3.50. This was determined largely by profit considerations and by the cost of obtaining all the maps individually. The atlas cost *less* than a user would pay to buy all the individual maps.

Berlin and Tucker then outlined the various tasks to be accomplished and assigned responsibilities for each task. Tucker would be in charge of production, which included drawing maps, layout, integrating advertising copy, maps, street listings, and additional information. Tucker was also responsible for staffing the production portion of the business and for procurement of materials and equipment. Berlin would be responsible for sales of advertising copy and for collecting background information. He also assumed responsibility for marketing the atlas and maintaining all financial records. Both believed that businesspeople travel less in the winter and, therefore, try to make it up in the spring. They decided to plan for a March 1 release. This would provide ample time to produce the atlas, as well as allow some slack for unforeseen problems.

Tucker began experimenting with the various techniques, sizes, and papers for production. A detailed plan was devised and a part-time sales staff began approaching potential advertisers with the sample format and sales contracts which the company lawyer had drawn up.

Advertisers were enthusiastic and the space sold rapidly. The work emphasis shifted to finishing the maps and street listings in preparation for printing.

Technical problems slowed the operation somewhat. The paper selected for the overlay was found to stretch with handling, even though it was advertised as nonstretchable. This made it necessary to do special fitting of photographs before printing plates could be made. Also, the ink used on the first maps drawn was discovered to photograph unevenly. This necessitated redoing several maps with better ink. The slack time allowed in the timetable was eliminated and an extra two weeks was added to the schedule.

Berlin found that selling advertisements was much easier than collecting the actual advertising copy. Many advertisers did not send in their ads or have them ready when Berlin's staff went to pick them up. It became clear that the lack of copy would further delay publication. Berlin sent out a letter to advertisers which emphasized the new due date. This pushed the publication date to April 15. Berlin used this time to solicit ads for a special restaurant page.

During this time, the part-time sales staff committed the company to a full-color cover without consulting Tucker. This complicated production, since a full-color printing required a minimum of four base colors, and the two-color press being used was not capable of producing a full-color cover. The cover was redesigned quickly, but no press could be immediately scheduled. Publication was postponed to June 15.

Advertising for *The Granite State Atlas* appeared in various publications around the state of New Hampshire. Preliminary models of the atlas and maps always got an enthusiastic response: the atlas seemed to sell itself.

Distribution

During the delay, Berlin researched the possibility of using wholesalers to distribute the finished atlases. Berlin and Tucker were concerned about the delay in the scheduled early spring date and sought ways for quick distribution of the maps. Both believed that a great deal of time and effort could be saved by eliminating the effort required by individual sales. This, they thought, would also eliminate some cost. The sales staff was cut back during the delay because there was little to do. Using wholesalers could eliminate the need to reassemble a staff for distribution to individual outlets, and the atlas would be on the stands much sooner.

Wholesalers generally handled books and magazines of various types. The preferable kind of books, as far as the wholesaler was concerned, was the monthly publications and paperbacks. Both were inexpensive and had a stable market. The bulk of the wholesaler's effort was therefore concentrated in first pushing these two types of products. Other types of publications received less effort, and attention to any one depended on its long-term profitability. Wholesalers generally had regions of the state to themselves and did not infringe upon the territories of others. Each wholesaler had a list of such outlets as newsstands, stationery stores, and bookstores to serve. Six wholesale companies covered the entire state of New Hampshire. The operations of these wholesalers were essentially identical.

The expected gross profit from any one item was 50 percent, split between the retailers and the wholesaler. In the case of a promising new product, the wholesaler might accept a lesser profit. On items which were not periodicals, the wholesalers required exclusive selling rights within their territory to discourage competition. Most of the products were handled on half consignment; one half of the price was paid to the publisher on delivery. The remainder was due after the sale, and unsold items were returned. In practice no products were ever returned, and the wholesalers were notorious for falling behind in their payments. These two facts, however, were not known to Berlin until much later.

The Atlas Map Company decided to utilize wholesalers to get the maps to the stands quickly. A standard contract was drawn with each wholesaler in the state and with one in the greater Boston area. The atlas would be sold to the wholesalers on a half consignment basis for $2 apiece. Wholesalers received exclusive rights to distribute the book in their territories. Each wholesaler received 1,000 atlases in the first shipment. The atlases were delivered during the first part of July 1977. All payments for advertising were due with the delivery of the first set of *The Granite State Atlases* to stores. Collection of these monies covered all the short-term financing and left a small surplus for future operations. The initial payments from the wholesalers provided an additional amount of funds.

As the first printing sold, a second printing would be produced. Volumes with updated maps and new advertisements would be produced in future years.

Berlin and Tucker relaxed and waited for the sales to boom. All part-time help was laid off. Tucker began storing and organizing the original maps used in the production of the atlas. Berlin took a three-week vacation in Miami. Each enjoyed the respite after a year of hard work. The only work required in the two months which followed was preliminary gathering of information for new maps and some surveys of possible new product forms and new potential advertisers.

Initial Results

After a two-month slowdown, it became apparent to Berlin and Tucker that the anticipated sales volume had not been achieved. Not one wholesaler sent in additional money nor reordered. The two men realized that they gave up the right to distribute the maps themselves and could only push the wholesalers to get the job done. Berlin had to personally contact each wholesaler. A month of such contacts and communications with the distributors produced more promises and some token payments but no action. In October 1977, Berlin undertook the task of investigating the situation at the retail level.

The retailers were found to be enthusiastic about the atlas. The wholesalers stocked the shelves for them, and retailers had little control over what appeared on the shelf. Retailers could request that certain items be provided in greater quantity, but this was often answered by promises, not action. Specialty items got even less effort (and therefore less shelf space) than periodicals. Berlin found that many retailers had requested more of *The Granite State Atlases* but did not receive more than a few at a time. He also found that many outlets were not serviced at all by the existing wholesalers. The major wholesalers did as they pleased. Retailers approached by Berlin asked to buy atlases from the company directly. Berlin decided to market the atlases to the retailers not covered by the wholesaler. They concentrated in the larger metropolitan areas. Upon review of the wholesaler contracts with the company lawyer, they were advised that they could be in violation of the agreements and subject to legal suit if they continued direct sales to retailers. As a result of this advice, the Atlas Map Company decided on new methods of distribution. The crux of the new distribution was a line extension, which would be marketed directly.

Since most of the development costs were paid, the original maps could be used in a different format. Little work was necessary to produce smaller atlases of maps. Berlin sold several small contracts for small atlases of maps. Each had some five to seven maps, most of which were already developed. Tucker, with a reduced staff, produced the required new maps and made some minor improvements in existing ones. Berlin's new staff sold advertising for each atlas. All advertising contracts were prepaid, thus providing operating funds and some small capital for future distribution.

In February 1978, Berlin and Tucker realized that the situation with *The Granite State Atlas* affected the future of the new, smaller atlases. They received some money from the wholesalers, and several even reordered, but in spite of repeated efforts by the Atlas Map Company staff, little emphasis was placed on pushing their distribution. In addition, all the wholesalers still owed the company money. The warehouse where the remaining atlases were stored had been sold and a new location was being sought. The move would be expensive, and the company sent registered letters to all wholesalers requesting immediate payment for atlases sold or the return of those unsold. The letters were generally ignored, and little more than new promises were given by wholesalers.

During March of 1978, several alternatives were discussed and analyzed. The April meeting had to be the decisive one. Moving the atlases to a new warehouse cost Atlas Map Company some $10,000 in security deposits, transportation, packing, and storage costs. The company was on the edge of bankruptcy.

The major alternatives open to the company, according to the outline of the April meeting were as follows:

1. Sell out.
2. Take legal action against the wholesalers.
3. Continue distribution with wholesalers but distribute the smaller atlases directly to retailers.
4. Go to another state.
5. Risk litigation and sell directly to retailers.

Discussion Question

1. Propose a course of action for the Atlas Map Company.

Case 6.2 The Mass Market Paperback Book Distribution System

It is estimated that the mass market paperback book industry had annual gross sales of $425.2 million in 1974. This total amounts to over 600 million paperback books being distributed each year. To obtain this sales volume, a total of 609 million paperback books were introduced into the distribution channels. Some 230 million unsold paperback books were also removed from the retail racks and returned for full credit. Thus, at least 839 million paperbacks were handled in 1974. Returns amounted to a staggering 36 percent of gross dollar sales and 38 percent of unit volume sales. To maintain this volume, between 350–400 new paperback titles are placed in the distribution channel each month. The limited rack space available to display these books makes competition for rack space fierce. Once rack space is acquired, it is quite important that the books which occupy this space turn over many times during the year.

Source: This case was prepared by Rodger D. Collons, D.B.A., The James S. Bingay Professor of Creative Leadership, The American College, and Peter G. Betz, General Mills, Inc. Reprinted by permission.

Evolution of the System

There are four major classes of participants in the distribution of paperbacks to retailers: (1) publishers, (2) national distributors, (3) independent magazine/paperback wholesalers, and (4) jobbers. The system, as it exists today, is the product of a history of evolution beginning in 1939 when Pocket Books introduced the forerunner of today's mass-market paperback in America.

When Robert deGraff, the originator of Pocket Books, started out, his idea was to publish a relatively inexpensive (25 cents), small (pocket size) novel for a widespread readership. He solved the problem of distribution by engaging the American News Company (ANC) to distribute Pocket Books through its existing network of local newspaper and magazine wholesalers, each of which operated in exclusive geographic territories. By the late 1930s, the absolute dominance of the ANC network began to erode as various independent magazine distributors and local wholesalers began to appear, which fed tens of thousands of retail outlets with newspapers and magazines. The paperback publishers saw the opportunity for widespread distribution and convinced wholesalers to add paperbacks to their inventories. (During the 1940s and early 1950s, a publisher dealt either entirely with ANC wholesalers or entirely with independent wholesalers.) The agreement, however, called for the publisher to accept the same terms used for magazine sales: full credit for all copies returned.

By 1950, the monopolistic grip of the ANC network was broken. In its place has grown a system of national distributors and local independent magazine/paperback wholesalers (hereafter referred to as wholesalers). Although independent of the ANC organization, these wholesalers still deal in relatively exclusive geographic territories.

The jobber, the fourth class of participant, operates alongside the wholesaler, serving those retailers which the wholesaler has either failed to satisfy or decided not to serve.

The Mass-Market Paperback System Figure 1 is the model of the mass market paperback book distribution system. The solid lines in Figure 1 represent product flows. The dashed lines represent information flows confirmed in questionnaire responses. Down channel information includes promotion for new releases, offers of incentives to encourage greater efficiency and reduce returns, and suggestions for more effective merchandising techniques. Up channel information (feedback) includes sales and returns figures, initial orders for new releases, and reorders for existing titles.

The numbers to the right of the solid lines in Figure 1 are in all cases the percentage of total publisher volume flowing through the respective channel. The numbers in parentheses in each box are the discounts from cover price generally received by the respective members of the network on volume received through the respective channels. For example, note that a bookstore dealing directly with the publisher will generally receive a 40 percent discount, whereas a bookstore dealing with a wholesaler will generally receive a 30 percent discount. In the case of the national distributor, the number represents a fee based on cover price as opposed to a discount on a purchase.

Elements of the System

There are two general categories of sales by the publishers: those through a national distributor and those directly to jobbers and retailers. The national distributor is shown in Figure 1 as independent; although in the cases of five publishers, the national distributor is a wholly-owned division. There are no discernible operational differences between the two methods. One economic difference, of course, is the saving of the 8.0 percent fee for the wholly-owned distributors. In any case, each of the ten more prominent publishers deals exclusively with one national distributor for sales to wholesalers, and typically 55 percent of total sales will be through the distributor.

Direct sales to retailers and jobbers account for the other 45 percent of a publisher's business. The percentages shown in Figure 1 are derived from the survey results and will differ somewhat from company to company.

Note that nearly all of the volume handled by the national distributor is sold through independent magazine/paperback wholesalers (IDs). Survey results indicate that paperbacks represent 20–

Figure 1 Mass-Market Paperback Distribution System

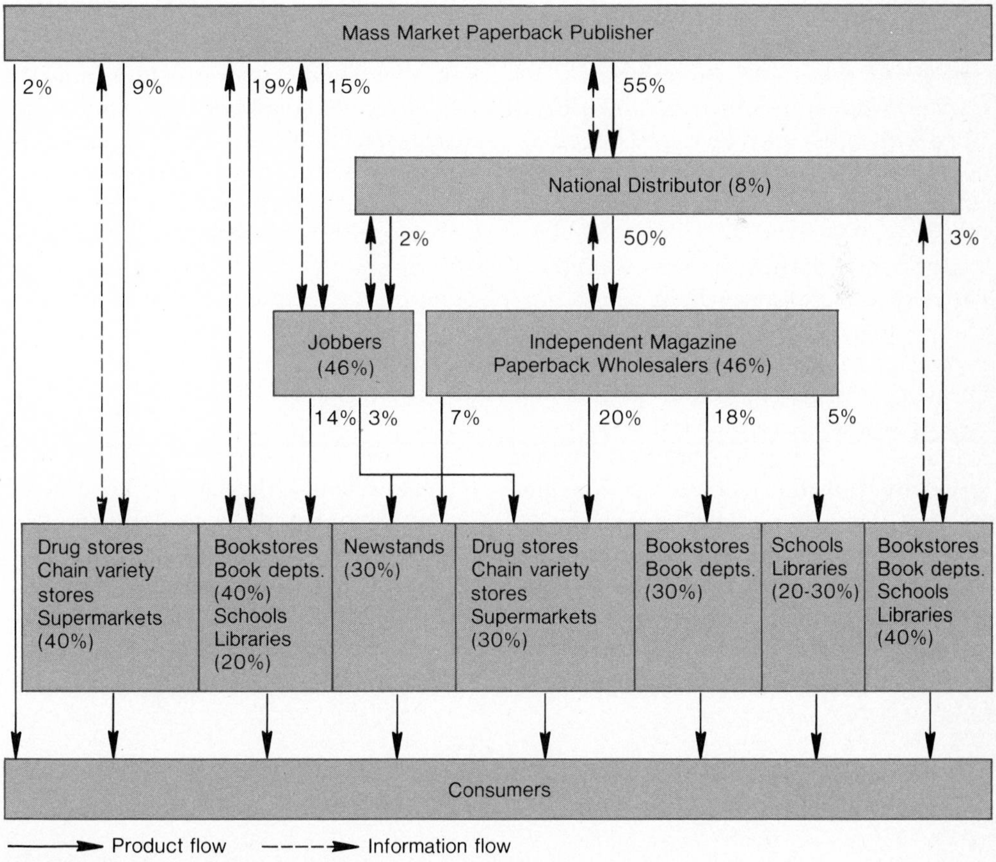

Numbers to right of product flows indicate percentage of total publisher volume.
Numbers in parenthesis indicate discounts or fees offered to a given member of the system.

35 percent of total volume for most IDs. The greatest share of their sales volume (60 percent or more) is in magazines.

Sales by the publisher to the IDs and jobbers are generally at a discount of 46 percent. Direct sales to retail accounts are at a discount of 40 percent (although 20 percent is more common for schools and libraries). Direct sales activity expanded rapidly in the late 1950s and early 1960s, a period when jobbers began to emerge and gradually increase their share of the market at the expense of the wholesalers. The wholesaler's competitive edge rests on the ability to provide a local source of supply. However, where wholesalers operated with a relatively exclusive territory, jobbers recognized no geographic boundaries. They took over accounts which became dissatisfied with wholesaler service. The jobber could provide central billing for variety store chains where the wholesaler could not.

Another major direct sales customer is the national bookstore chain which purchases directly from the publisher. The growth in chains, such as B. Dalton and Waldenbooks, has helped to increase direct sales over the years. Wholesalers responded to the erosion of their market share by providing better service, improving their merchandising techniques, and emphasizing their responsiveness as local suppliers. They are forced to offer a lower discount, however, in order to cover the additional cost of these improvements. Typically, a wholesaler offers a 30 percent discount to a given retail account as opposed to the 40 percent offered by a publisher.

Estimates for the total number of wholesalers who handle paperbacks vary from 400 to 600, for jobbers from 100 to 200, and for total mass-market paperback retailers from 60,000 to 80,000. The number of retail outlets selling paperbacks has dropped from an estimated 110,000 fifteen years ago, although the number of pockets and racks has increased.

The net result of the evolution of the various channels of distribution is that paperbacks are available to the consumer in a wide variety of retail locations. The retailer may at any one time be dealing with a wholesaler who provides immediate delivery of small paperback and magazine orders and complete rack service at a 30 percent discount, a jobber who provides the same service but only for paperbacks and with perhaps less immediate delivery at a 35 percent or 40 percent discount, and a publisher who provides no service and slow delivery at a 40 percent discount.

Discussion Questions

1. How could the channels for mass market paperback book distribution be managed to reduce the high levels of return of books?
2. What role would an improved information system play in this situation?

Daniel Starch

The comment, "I realize that fully one-half of advertising is wasted; I just don't know which half," summarizes the problem of determining the effectiveness of communications efforts. One of the pioneers in advertising effectiveness research was Daniel Starch (1884–1979).

In 1923, while teaching at the Harvard Business School, Starch published *Principles of Marketing* (Chicago: A.W. Shaw Company). In the book, Starch described a readership test. The test consisted of personal interviews with persons who had received a particular magazine. The interviewer goes through the magazine with the respondent, asking him or her to indicate advertisements that were read. On larger ads, respondents were asked whether they saw the headline, read the copy, noticed the illustration. Interviews were conducted at different locations throughout the nation, and interviewers were instructed to begin at different places in the magazine with different interviews in order to minimize any respondent fatigue factor.

Starch's technique, based on the assumption that a positive correlation exists between noting an advertisement and its effectiveness, was not widely used until pollster George Gallup reported in the late 1920s the results of a series of tests indicating its validity. Starch left the academic world during the 1930s to found Daniel Starch and Staff (now Starch INRA Hooper).

Readership tests are conducted regularly on most of the major national magazines and a number of specialized publications. Costs are reduced, since the research expenses are spread over a number of advertisers. Although the tests are occasionally criticized due to their implicit assumption that readership results in increased sales, the data provides an excellent means of comparing different advertisements.

Daniel Starch died in 1979 at the age of 95.

7

PROMOTION

Promotion is an exercise in communications. It consists of four basic elements: advertising, personal selling, sales promotion, and public relations. Each of these strategy elements is examined in the three chapters in Part Seven. Promotion's conceptual foundation in communications theory and the concept of a promotional mix are explored in Chapter 19. Chapters 20 and 21 discuss the various blends that may produce the optimal promotional mix. Chapter 20 features the nonpersonal promotional elements of advertising, sales promotion, public relations, and publicity, while Chapter 21 deals with personal selling.

19

PROMOTIONAL STRATEGY

Chapter Objectives

1. To relate the communications process to promotional strategy.
2. To explain the concept of the promotional mix and its relationship to the marketing mix.
3. To identify the primary determinants of a promotional mix.
4. To contrast the two major alternative promotional strategies.
5. To list the objectives of promotion.
6. To explain the primary methods of developing a promotional budget.
7. To defend promotion against the public criticisms that are sometimes raised.

Marketers have always been fascinated with the youth market. This group of consumers has traditionally been more receptive to new products, less likely to be brand loyal than their older consumer counterparts, and exert considerable influence in family purchase decisions. Even though the number of teenagers declined by 7 percent during the five-year period ending in 1980, their influence in household decision making greatly increased as a result of increases in the number of two-income households. More than 52 percent of mothers with children under 18 worked in 1980, compared with less than 39 percent in 1970. The percentage of teenagers involved in family food shopping grew from 49 percent in 1960 to 68 percent in 1981. And even with the 7 percent decline, teenagers spent an estimated $40 billion in 1981, over 50 percent more than in 1976. But, as *Advertising Age* points out, the most attractive part of today's youth market is undoubtedly the college segment, and it's easy to understand why:

- It is growing, currently 12 million strong and expected to increase by roughly 200,000 a year through the 1980s.
- It is affluent. The Rand Poll estimates that after college expenses are paid, the average student has roughly $2,200 a year that is almost entirely disposable income.
- It is relatively recession-proof. As one ad executive points out, "When money gets tight, parents will make every effort to keep it from affecting their kid who is away at college."

Recent surveys of the college market not only document the collegians' expected proclivity for such things as stereo equipment, electronic calculators, beer, and airline travel, but, says Mark W. Rose, vice president–marketing with CASS Student Advertising, "It has gotten to the point today that the college student is actually a mini-household . . ."

As attractive as the college market may be, efficiently delivering the marketing message to it is another matter. "College students are hard to reach because they are more active than other people," says Jeffrey Dickey, president of Alan Weston Communications, a diversified college marketing company in Los Angeles that publishes *Ampersand,* a magazine aimed at college students. "They're single, and they socialize more. They go out to parties, to concerts, to football games, to movies. They're out and around a lot, and they're not penned into situations where they can be reached by conventional media."

Several market research studies conducted in the last few years, for example, have found that college students watch about a third of the TV watching that the general population does, putting them in the lowest quartile of TV viewing audiences. . . . Given such difficulties and the growing interest of marketers in reaching the college market segment, it is not surprising that a number of efforts are under way to improve old vehicles and develop new ones that can deliver collegiate audiences.[1]

Among the more traditional vehicles are campus newspapers, direct mail, radio, direct solicitation by salespeople, in-store displays and demonstrations on campus and at nearby retail stores. Product sampling to college students has been a campus fixture for over 20 years. Gift Pax are distributed to some 3 million college students each year, while Good Stuff samples of such products as Excedrin, Pert shampoo, Listermint mouthwash, Oil of Olay, and Atra razors reach more than 1 million students on approximately 375 college campuses.

Important new means of communicating with the college market begin at registration when some 1.5 million students use University Communications' *Directory of Classes* with course listings and hundreds

[1]B. G. Yovovich, "A Game of Hide-and-Seek," *Advertising Age* (August 2, 1982), pp. M–5, M–6. Reprinted by permission of Crain Communications, Inc.

of advertisements. Both *Newsweek* and *Time* publish special college editions, offering marketers communications vehicles with less wasted advertising. When 250,000 college students arrive in Daytona Beach each spring, many of them participate in Playboy's College Expo, a week-long exposition of new and established products. At a recent College Expo, Bic Leisure Products unveiled its new sailboard, Jantzen set up a radar gun to time tennis serves, T-shirts and sun visors were given away, and Minolta gathered 2,500 students on the beach, photographed them, then mailed each participant a souvenir poster of the print.[2]

The Conceptual Framework

While the college market is more difficult to reach through traditional communications channels than many other segments, such linkages between marketer and consumer are necessary for market success. **Promotion,** the fourth variable in the marketing mix, can be defined as the function of informing, persuading, and influencing the consumer's purchase decision. Figure 19.1 depicts the relationship between the firm's promotional strategy and the other elements of the overall marketing strategy in accomplishing organizational objectives and producing utility for the consumer.

The marketing manager sets the goals and objectives of the firm's promotional strategy in accordance with overall organizational objectives and the goals of the marketing organization. Then, based on these goals, the various elements of the strategy—personal selling, advertising, sales promotion, publicity, and public relations—are formulated in a coordinated promotion plan. This becomes an integral part of the total marketing strategy for reaching selected consumer segments. Finally, the feedback mechanism, in such forms as marketing research and field reports, closes the system by identifying any deviations from the plan and by suggesting modifications for improvement.

Promotional strategy is closely related to the process of communications. A standard definition of *communications* is the transmission of a message from a sender to a receiver. **Marketing communications,** then, are those messages that deal with buyer–seller relationships. Marketing communications is a broader term than promotional strategy since it includes word-of-mouth and other forms of unsystematic communication. A planned promotional strategy, however, is certainly the most important part of marketing communications.

[2]Bob Kelly, "Students Flock to Expo," *Advertising Age* (April 26, 1982), p. 44S.

Figure 19.1 Integrating Promotion into the Total Marketing Mix

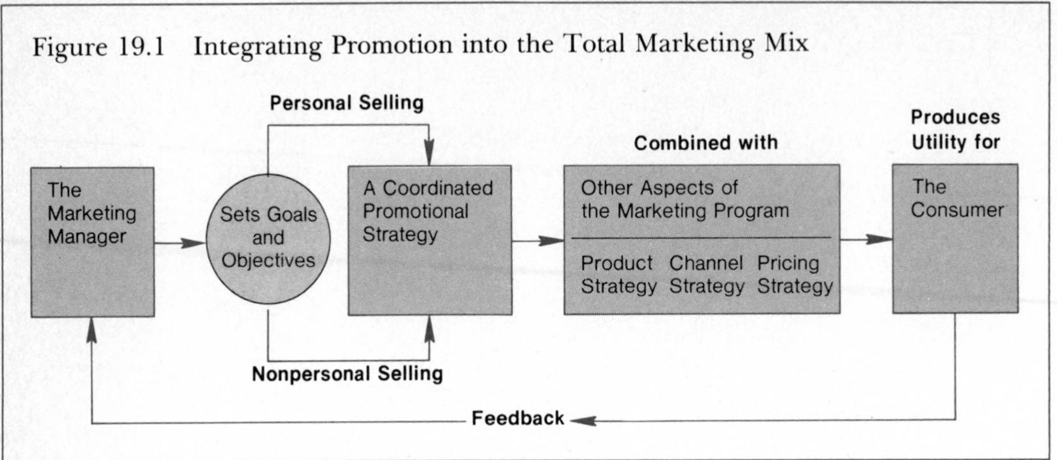

The Communications Process

Figure 19.2 shows a generalized communications process.[3] The sender is the source of the communications system since he or she seeks to convey a message (a communication of information or advice or a request) to a receiver (the recipient of the communication). The message must accomplish three tasks in order to be effective:

1. It must gain the attention of the receiver.
2. It must be understood by both the receiver and sender.
3. It must stimulate the needs of the receiver and suggest an appropriate method of satisfying these needs.[4]

The three tasks are related to the **AIDA (attention-interest-desire-action) concept** first proposed by E. K. Strong more than 50 years ago as an explanation of the steps an individual must go through prior to making a purchase decision. First, the potential consumer's attention must be gained. Once this is accomplished, the promotional message seeks to arouse interest in the product or service. If interest is aroused, the next stage is to stimulate consumer desire by convincing the would-be buyer of the product's ability to satisfy needs. Finally, the sales presentation or advertisement attempts to produce action in the form of a

[3]Similar communications processes are suggested in David K. Berlo, *The Process of Communications* (New York: Holt, Rinehart and Winston, 1960), pp. 23–38; and Thomas S. Robertson, *Innovative Behavior and Communications* (New York: Holt, Rinehart and Winston, 1971), p. 122. See also Claude Shannon and Warren Weaver, *The Mathematical Theory of Communication* (Urbana: University of Illinois Press, 1949), p. 5; and Wilbur Schramm, "The Nature of Communication Betweeen Humans," *The Process and Effects of Mass Communication*, rev. ed. (Urbana: University of Illinois Press, 1971), pp. 3–53.

[4]Wilbur Schramm, "The Nature of Communication Betweeen Humans," pp. 3–53.

Figure 19.2 A Generalized Communications Process

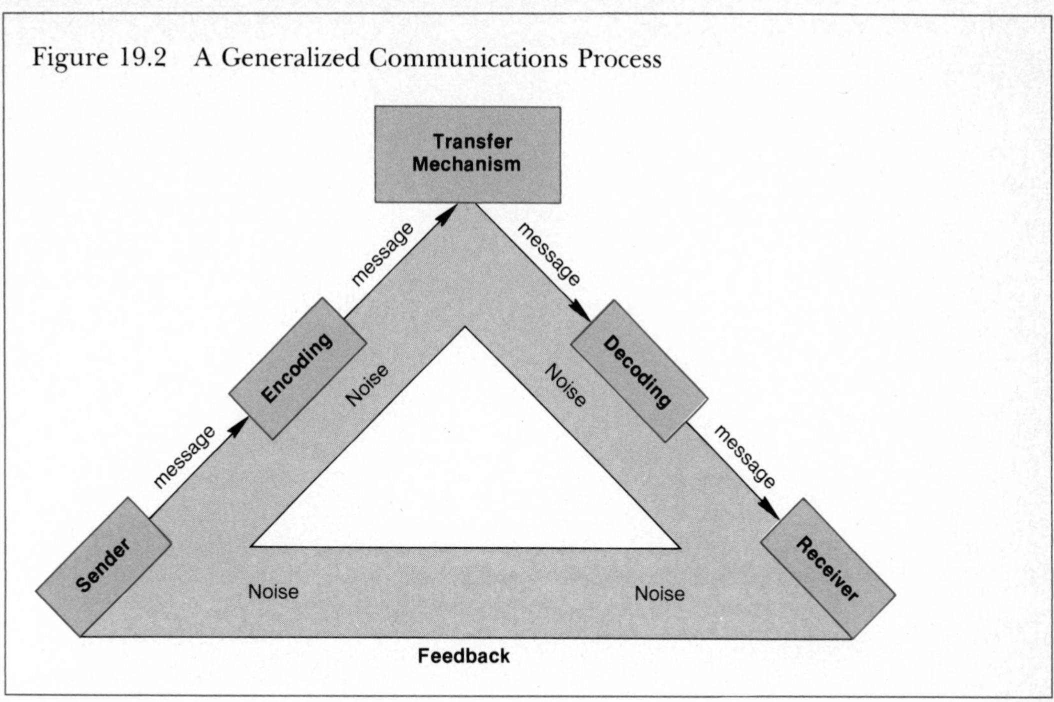

purchase or a more favorable attitude that may lead to future purchases.

The message must be *encoded,* or translated into understandable terms, and transmitted through a communications medium. *Decoding* is the receiver's interpretation of the message.[5] The receiver's response, known as *feedback,* completes the system. Throughout the process, *noise* can interfere with the transmission of the message and reduce its effectiveness.

In Figure 19.3 the marketing communications process is applied to promotional strategy. The marketing manager is the sender in the system. The message is encoded in the form of sales presentations, advertisements, displays, or publicity releases. The *transfer mechanism* for delivering the message may be a salesperson, public relations channel, or the advertising media. The decoding step involves the consumer's interpretation of the sender's message. This is often the most troublesome aspect of marketing communications since consumers do not always interpret a promotional message in the same way as its sender. Since receivers are likely to decode messages based upon their own

[5]See Patrick L. Schul and Charles W. Lamb, "Decoding Nonverbal and Vocal Communications: A Laboratory Study," *Journal of the Academy of Marketing Science* (Spring 1982), pp. 154–164.

Figure 19.3 The Process of Marketing Communications

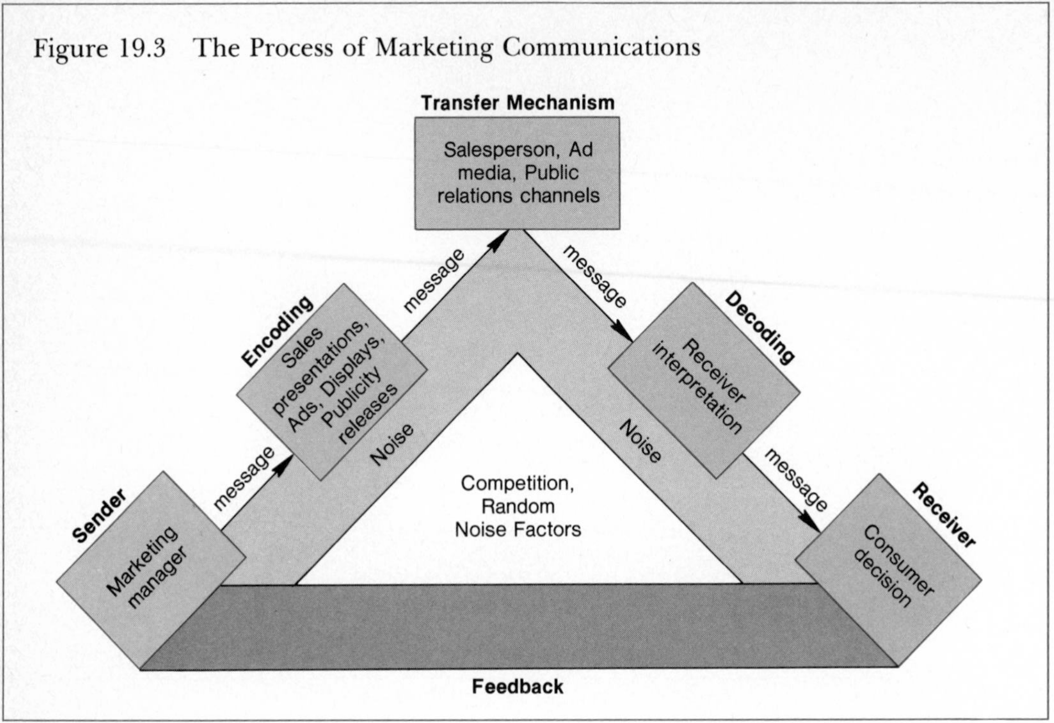

frames of reference or individual experiences, the sender must be careful to ensure that the message is encoded to match the target audience.

Feedback is the receiver's response to the message. It may take the form of attitude change, purchase, or nonpurchase. In some instances, firms may use promotion to create a favorable attitude toward its new products or services. Such attitude changes may result in future purchases. In other instances, the objective of the promotional communication is to stimulate consumer purchases. Such purchases indicate positive responses to the firm, its product/service offerings, its distribution channels, its prices, and its promotion. Even nonpurchases can serve as feedback to the sender. They may result from ineffective communication in which the message was not believed or not remembered, or the message may fail to persuade the receiver that the firm's products or services are superior to its competitors. Feedback can be obtained from such techniques as marketing research studies and field sales reports.

Noise represents interference at some stage in the communications process. It may result from such factors as competitive promotional messages being transmitted over the same communications channel, misinterpretation of a sales presentation or an advertising message, re-

Table 19.1 Examples of Marketing Communications

Type of Promotion	Sender	Encoding	Transfer Mechanism	Decoding by Receiver	Feedback
Personal selling	Sharp Business Products	Sales presentation on new model office copier	Sharp sales representative	Office manager and employees in local firm discuss Sharp sales presentation and those of competing suppliers.	Order placed for the Sharp copier
Two-for-one coupon (sales promotion)	Wendy's Hamburgers	Wendy's marketing department and advertising agency	Coupon insert to Sunday newspaper	Newspaper reader sees coupon for hamburger and saves it.	Hamburgers purchased by consumers using the coupon
Television advertising	Walt Disney Enterprises	Advertisement for a new "G"-rated animated movie is developed by Disney's advertising agency.	Network television during programs with high percentage of viewers under 12 years old	Children see ad and ask their parents to take them; parents see ad and decide to take children.	Movie ticket purchased

ceipt of the promotional message by the wrong person, or random noise factors, such as people conversing during a television commercial or leaving the room.

Table 19.1 illustrates the steps in the communications process with several examples of promotional messages. Although the types of promotion vary from a highly personalized sales presentation to such non-personal promotion as television advertising and two-for-one coupons, each form of promotion goes through each stage in the communications model.

Components of the Promotional Mix

The **promotional mix,** like the marketing mix, involves the proper blending of numerous variables in order to satisfy the needs of the firm's market target and achieve organizational objectives. While the marketing mix is comprised of product, price, promotion, and distribution elements, the promotional mix is a subset of the overall marketing mix. In the case of the promotional mix, the marketing manager is attempting to achieve the optimal blending of various promotional elements in order to accomplish promotional objectives. The components of the promotional mix are personal selling and nonpersonal selling (including advertising, sales promotion, and public relations).[6]

Personal selling and advertising are the most significant elements since they usually account for the bulk of a firm's promotional expenditures. However, all factors contribute to efficient marketing communications. A detailed discussion of each of these elements is presented in the chapters that follow. Here only a brief definition is given in order to set the framework for the discussion of promotion.

Personal Selling

Personal selling may be defined as a seller's promotional presentation conducted on a person-to-person basis with the buyer. It is a direct face-to-face form of promotion. Selling was also the original form of promotion. Today it is estimated that 6 million people in the United States are engaged in this activity.

Nonpersonal Selling

Nonpersonal selling is divided into advertising, sales promotion, and public relations. Advertising is usually regarded as the most important of these forms.

Advertising may be defined as paid, nonpersonal communication through various media by business firms, nonprofit organizations, and individuals who are in some way identified in the advertising message and who hope to inform or persuade members of a particular audience.[7] It involves the mass media, such as newspapers, television, radio, magazines, and billboards. Business has come to realize the tremendous potential of this form of promotion, and during recent decades, advertising has become increasingly important in marketing. Mass consumption makes advertising particularly appropriate for products that rely on sending the same promotional message to large audiences.

Sales promotion includes "those marketing activities other than personal selling and advertising, and publicity, that stimulate consumer purchasing and dealer effectiveness, such as displays, shows and expositions, demonstrations, and various nonrecurrent selling efforts not in the ordinary routine."[8] Sales promotion is usually practiced together

[6]See William Dommermuth, "Promoting Your Product: Managing the Mix," *Business* (July–August 1980), pp. 18–21.

[7]S. Watson Dunn and Arnold M. Barban, *Advertising: Its Role in Modern Marketing* (Hinsdale, Ill.: The Dryden Press, 1982), p. 7.

[8]Committee on Definitions, *Marketing Definitions: A Glossary of Marketing Terms* (Chicago: American Marketing Association, 1960), p. 20.

Table 19.2 Comparing Alternative Promotional Techniques

Type of Promotion	Personal or Nonpersonal	Cost	Advantages	Disadvantages
Advertising	Nonpersonal	Relatively inexpensive per contact	Appropriate in reaching mass audiences; allows expressiveness and control over message	Considerable waste; difficult to demonstrate product; difficult to close sales; difficult to measure results
Personal selling	Personal	Expensive per contact	Permits flexible presentation and gains immediate response	Costs more than all other forms per contact; difficult to attract qualified salespeople
Sales promotion	Nonpersonal	Can be costly	Gains attention and has immediate effect	Easy for others to imitate
Public relations	Nonpersonal	Relatively inexpensive; publicity is free	Has high degree of believability	Not as easily controlled as other forms

Source: Adapted from David J. Rachman and Elaine Romano, *Modern Marketing* (Hinsdale, Ill.: The Dryden Press, 1980), p. 450. Adapted by permission of the publisher.

with other forms of advertising to emphasize, assist, supplement, or otherwise support the objectives of the promotional program.

Public relations is a firm's communications and relationships with its various publics. These publics include the organization's customers, suppliers, stockholders, employees, the government, the general public, and the society in which the organization operates. Public relations programs can be either formal or informal. The critical point is that every organization, whether or not it has a formal organized program, needs to be concerned about its public relations.

Publicity concerning a company's products or affairs is an important part of an effective public relations effort. It can be defined as the nonpersonal stimulation of demand for a product, service, or organization by placing commercially significant news about it in a published medium or obtaining favorable presentation of it upon radio, television, or stage that is not paid for by an identified sponsor. In comparison to personal selling, advertising, and even sales promotion, expenditures for public relations are usually low in most firms. Since they don't pay for it, companies have less control over the publication by the press of good or bad company news. For this very reason, a consumer may find this type of news source more believable than if the news were disseminated directly by the company.

As Table 19.2 indicates, each type of promotion has both advantages and disadvantages. Even though personal selling has a relatively high cost per contact, there is less wasted effort than in such nonpersonal forms of promotion as advertising. In addition, it is often more flexible than the other forms, since the salesperson can tailor the sales message to meet the unique needs—or objections—of each potential customer.

On the other hand, advertising is an effective means of reaching mass audiences with the marketer's message. Sales promotion techniques are effective in gaining attention, and public relations efforts such as publicity frequently have a high degree of believability compared to other promotional techniques. The task confronting the marketer is to determine the appropriate blend of each of these techniques in marketing the firm's products and services.

The Promotional Mix

The blending of advertising, personal selling, sales promotion, and public relations to achieve marketing objectives is the *promotional mix.* Since quantitative measures to determine the effectiveness of each mix component in a given market segment are not available, the choice of a proper mix of promotional elements is one of the most difficult tasks facing the marketing manager. Factors affecting the promotional mix are: (1) nature of the market; (2) nature of the product; (3) stage in the product life cycle; (4) price; and (5) funds available for promotion.

Nature of the Market

The marketer's target audience has a major impact upon the type of promotion to use. In cases where there is a limited number of buyers, personal selling may prove highly effective. However, markets characterized by a large number of potential customers scattered over a large geographic area may make the cost of contact by personal salespeople prohibitive. In such instances, advertising may be extensively used. The type of customer also affects the promotional mix. A market target made up of industrial purchasers or retail and wholesale buyers is more likely to use personal selling than one consisting of ultimate consumers.

Nature of the Product

A second important factor in determining an effective promotional mix is the product itself. Highly standardized products with minimal servicing requirements are less likely to depend upon personal selling than custom products that are technically complex and require servicing. Consumer goods are more likely to rely heavily upon advertising than industrial goods. Within each product category, promotional mixes vary.

For instance, installations typically involve heavy reliance upon personal selling compared to the marketing of operating supplies. Convenience goods rely heavily upon manufacturer advertising, and personal selling plays a small role. On the other hand, personal selling is often more important in the marketing of shopping goods, and both personal selling and nonpersonal selling are important in the marketing of specialty goods. Finally, personal selling is likely to be more important in the marketing of products characterized by trade-ins.

Stage in the Product Life Cycle

The promotional mix must also be tailored to the stage in the product life cycle. In the introductory stage, heavy emphasis is placed on personal selling to inform the marketplace of the merits of the new product or service. Salespeople contact marketing intermediaries to secure interest and commitment to handle the new product. Trade shows and exhibitions are frequently used to inform and educate prospective dealers and ultimate consumers. Any advertising at this stage is largely informative, and sales promotional techniques, such as samples and cents-off coupons, are designed to influence consumer attitudes and stimulate initial purchases.

As the product or service moves into the growth and maturity stages, advertising becomes more important in attempting to persuade consumers to make purchases. Personal-selling efforts continue to be directed at middlemen in an attempt to expand distribution. As more competitors enter the marketplace, advertising stresses product differences in an attempt to persuade consumers to purchase the firm's brand. Reminder advertisements begin to appear in the maturity and early decline stages. Figure 19.4 is an example of a reminder ad used for Kool-Aid.

Price

Price of the product or service is a fourth factor in the choice of promotional mixes. Advertising is a dominant mix component for low unit value products due to the high costs per contact for personal selling. The cost of an industrial sales call, for example, is now estimated at $178. As a result, it has become unprofitable to promote lower value products and services through personal selling. Advertising, by contrast, permits a low promotional expenditure per sales unit, since it reaches mass audiences. For low value consumer products, such as chewing gum, colas, and snack foods, advertising is the only feasible means of promotion.

Figure 19.4 A Reminder Advertisement Used in the Maturity Stage of the Product Life Cycle

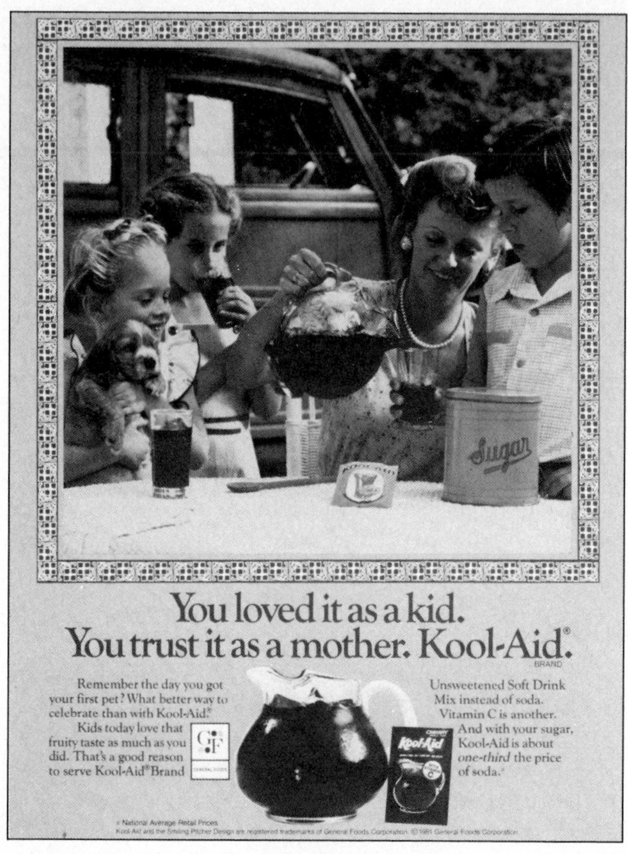

Source: Reproduced by permission of General Foods Corporation, © 1981.

Funds Available for Promotion

A very real barrier to implementing any promotional strategy is the size of the promotional budget. A 30-second television commercial on the final episode of "M*A*S*H" cost the advertiser $450,000! Even though the message was received by millions of viewers and the cost per contact was relatively low, such an expenditure would exceed the entire promotional budget of thousands of firms. For many new, smaller firms, the cost of mass advertising is prohibitive, and they are forced to seek less expensive, less efficient methods. Neighborhood retailers may not be able to advertise in metropolitan newspapers or on local radio and television stations; their limited promotional budgets may be allocated to personal selling.

Table 19.3 summarizes the factors influencing the determination of an appropriate promotional mix.

Table 19.3 Factors Influencing the Promotional Mix

Factor	Emphasis on Personal Selling	Emphasis on Advertising
Nature of the Market		
Number of Buyers	Limited number	Large number
Geographic Concentration	Concentrated	Dispersed
Type of Customer	Industrial purchaser	Ultimate consumer
Nature of the Product		
Complexity	Custom-made, complex	Standardized
Service Requirements	Considerable	Minimal
Type of Good	Industrial	Consumer
Use of Trade-ins	Trade-ins common	Trade-in uncommon
Stage in the Product Life Cycle	Introductory and early growth stages	Latter part of growth stages and maturity and early decline stages
Price	High unit value	Low unit value

Promotional Strategy—Pull or Push

Essentially, there are two promotional alternatives that may be employed: a pulling strategy and a pushing strategy. A **pulling strategy** is a promotional effort by the seller to stimulate final-user demand, which then exerts pressure on the distribution channel. In instances where marketing intermediaries stock a large number of competing products and exhibit little interest in the firm's product, a pulling strategy may be necessary to motivate them to handle the product. In such instances, personal selling by the manufacturer is largely limited to contacting intermediaries, providing requested information about the product, and taking orders. The plan is to build consumer demand for the product by means of advertising so that channel members must stock the product to meet that demand. Since most retailers want to stimulate repeat purchases by satisfied customers, the manufacturer's promotional efforts that result in shopper requests for the retailer to stock the item will usually succeed in getting that item on the retailer's shelves. Advertising and sales promotion are the most commonly used elements of promotion in a pulling strategy.

By contrast, a **pushing strategy** relies more heavily on personal selling. Here, the objective is promotion of the product to the members of the marketing channel rather than to the final user. This can be done through cooperative advertising allowances, trade discounts, personal selling efforts by the firm's sales force, and other dealer supports. Such a strategy is designed to produce marketing success for the firm's products by motivating representatives of wholesalers and/or retailers to spend a disproportionate amount of time and effort in promoting these products to customers.

While these are presented as alternative policies, it is unlikely that very many companies depend entirely upon either strategy. In most cases a mixture of the two is employed.

Timing is another factor to consider in development of a promotional strategy. Figure 19.5 shows the relative importance of advertising and selling in different periods of the purchase process. During the pretransactional period (prior to the actual sale), advertising is usually more important than personal selling. It is often argued that one of the primary advantages of a successful advertising program is that it assists the salesperson in approaching the prospect. Selling becomes more important than advertising during the transactional phase of the process. In most situations, personal selling is the actual mechanism of closing the sale. In the post-transactional stage, advertising regains primacy in the promotional effort. It affirms the customer's decision to buy a particular good or service as well as reminds the customer of the product's favorable qualities, characteristics, and performance.

Promotion Objectives

Determining the precise objectives of promotion has always been a perplexing problem for management. What specific tasks should promotion accomplish? The answer to this question seems to be as varied as the sources one consults. Generally, however, the following can be considered objectives of promotion: (1) to provide information; (2) to increase demand; (3) to differentiate the product; (4) to accentuate the value of the product; and (5) to stabilize sales.

Providing Information

The traditional function of promotion was to inform the market about the availability of a particular product. Indeed, a large part of modern promotional efforts is still directed at providing product information to potential customers. An example of this is the typical university or college extension course program advertisement appearing in the newspaper. Its content emphasizes informative features, such as the availability of different courses.

The informative function often requires repeated customer exposures. In an attempt to educate Spokane, Washington, homeowners of

Figure 19.5 Relative Importance of Advertising and Personal Selling

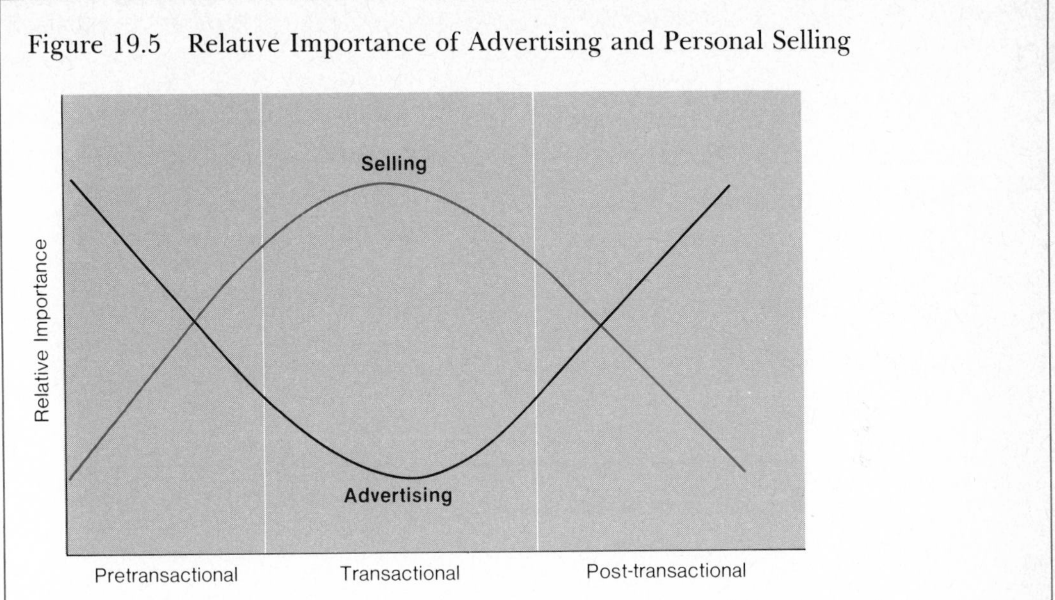

Source: Harold C. Cash and W. J. E. Crissy, "The Salesman's Role in Marketing," *The Psychology of Selling, Vol. 12* (Personnel Development Associates). Reprinted by permission.

the potential danger of termite infestation, Western Insecticide used billboards that were changed four times over a one-year period. As the photographs in Figure 19.6 indicate, each new billboard demonstrated increased termite damage until finally only the Western Insecticide's telephone number remained.

Stimulating Demand

The primary objective of most promotional efforts is to increase the demand for a specific brand of product or service. This can be shown by using the familiar demand curves of basic economics (see Figure 19.7). Successful promotion can shift demand from Schedule 1 to Schedule 2, which means greater quantities can be sold at each possible price level.

Differentiating the Product

A frequent objective of the firm's promotional effort is *product differentiation.* Homogeneous demand, represented by a horizontal line in Figure 19.8, means consumers regard the firm's output as no different from that of its competitors. In these cases, the individual firm has no control over such marketing variables as price. A differentiated demand

Figure 19.6 Using Advertising to Inform

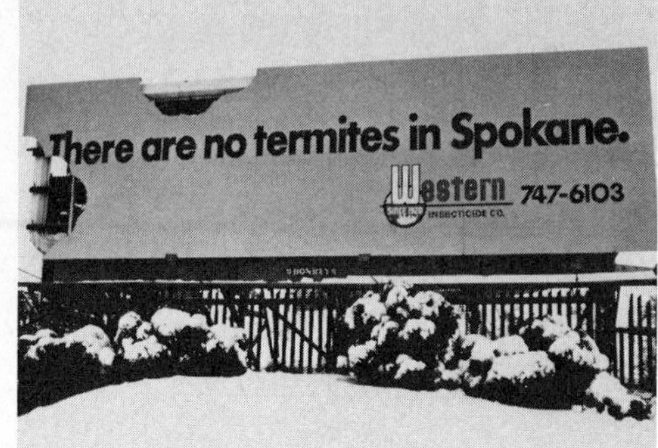

schedule, by contrast, permits more flexibility in marketing strategy, such as price changes.

For example, McCain's, a producer of high-quality frozen vegetables, advertises the dependable high quality and good taste of its products. This differentiates its products from others. Consequently, consumers who want these attributes are willing to pay a higher price for McCain's than they would for other brands. Similarly, the high quality and distinctiveness of Cross pens are advertised, resulting in Cross's ability to ask and obtain a price 100 times that of some disposable pens. With the exception of commodities, most products have some degree of differentiation, resulting in a downward-sloping demand curve. The angle of the slope varies somewhat according to the degree of product differentiation.

Accentuating the Value of the Product

Promotion can point out more ownership utility to buyers, thereby accentuating the value of a product. The good or service might then be able to command a higher price in the marketplace. For example, status-oriented advertising may allow some retail clothing stores to command higher prices than others. The demand curve facing a prestige store may be less responsive to price differences than that of a competitor without a quality reputation. The responsiveness to price differences is shown in Figure 19.9.

Stabilizing Sales

A company's sales are not uniform throughout the year. Fluctuations can be caused by cyclical, seasonal, or irregular reasons. Reducing these

Source: Reproduced by permission of Western Insecticide Company. Photographs courtesy Coons, Corker Sullivan, Agency; Dick Sperling, creator.

variations is often an objective of the firm's promotional strategy. Lee E. Preston states:

Advertising that is focused on such attitudinal goals as "brand loyalty" and such specific sales goals as "increasing repeat purchases" is essentially aimed at stabilizing demand. The prominence of such goals in the current literature

Figure 19.7 Promotion Can Help Marketers Achieve Demand Objectives

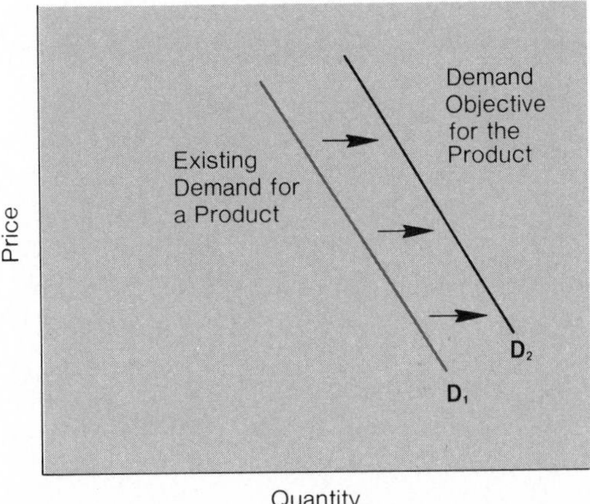

Source: *Principles of Marketing: The Management View*, 3rd ed., by Richard H. Buskirk. Copyright © 1961, 1966, 1970, by Holt, Rinehart and Winston, Inc. Adapted and reprinted by permission of Holt, Rinehart and Winston, Inc.

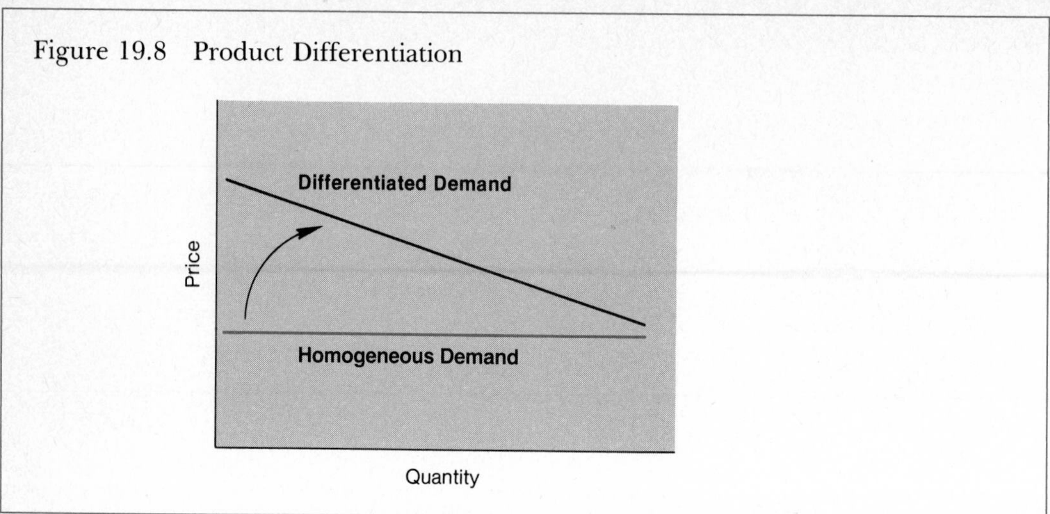

Source: *Markets and Marketing: An Orientation,* by Lee E. Preston (Glenview, Ill.: Scott, Foresman, 1970), p. 196. Copyright © 1970 by Scott, Foresman and Company. Adapted by permission.

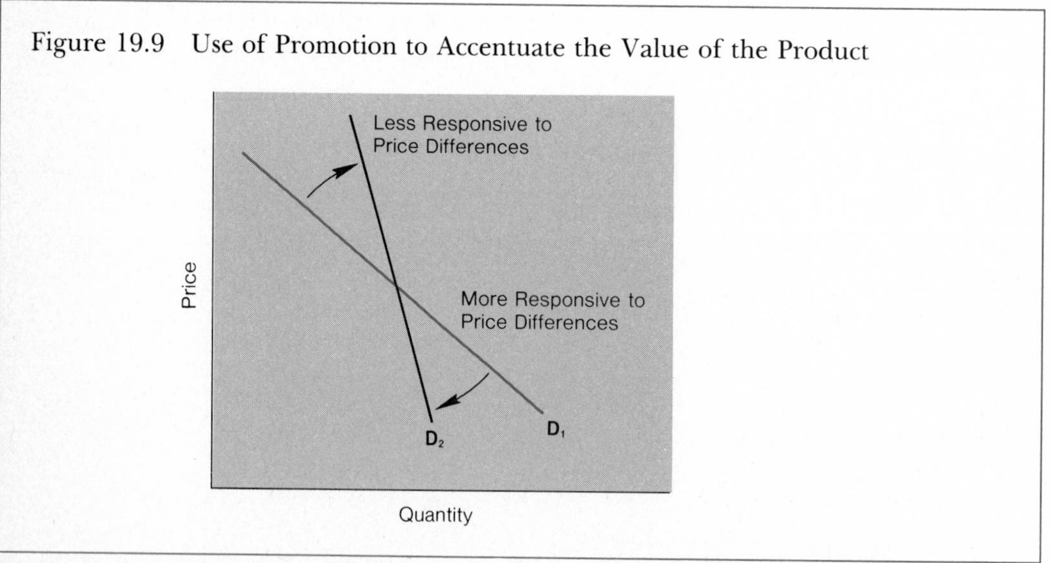

Source: *Markets and Marketing: An Orientation,* by Lee E. Preston (Glenview, Ill.: Scott, Foresman, 1970), p. 196. Copyright © 1970 by Scott, Foresman and Company. Adapted by permission.

and in advertising planning discussions suggests that stabilizing demand and insulating the market position of an individual firm and product against un-

favorable developments is, in fact, one of the most important purposes of promotional activity at the present time.[9]

Budgeting for Promotional Strategy

Promotion budgets can differ not only in amount but also in composition. Industrial firms generally invest a larger proportion of their budgets for personal selling than for advertising, while the reverse is usually true of most producers of consumer goods.

A simple model showing the productivity of promotional expenditures is shown in Figure 19.10. In terms of sales revenue, initial expenditures on promotion usually result in increasing returns. There appear to be some economies associated with larger promotional expenditures. These economies result from such factors as the cumulative effects of promotion and repeat sales.

Evidence suggests that sales initially lag behind promotion for structural reasons (filling up the retail shelves, low initial production, lack of buyer knowledge). This produces a threshold effect where there are few sales, but lots of initial investment in promotion. A second phase might produce returns (sales) proportional to a given promotion expenditure; this would be the most predictable range. Finally, the area of diminishing returns is reached when an increase in promotional expenditure does not produce a proportional increase in sales.

For example, an initial expenditure of $40,000 may result in the sale of 100,000 product units for a consumer goods manufacturer. An additional $10,000 expenditure may sell 30,000 more units, and a further $10,000 may produce the sale of 35,000 more units. The cumulative effect of the expenditures and repeat sales has resulted in increasing returns to the promotional outlays. However, as the advertising budget moves from $60,000 to $70,000, the marginal productivity of the additional expenditure may fall to 28,000 units. At some later point, the return may actually become zero or negative as competition intensifies, markets become saturated, and less effective media are employed.

To test the thesis that there is a saturation point for advertising, Anheuser-Busch once quadrupled its advertising budget in several markets. After three months, the company's distributors demanded an advertising cut. Many claimed that beer consumers came into their stores saying, "Give me anything *but* Bud."[10]

[9]From *Markets and Marketing: An Orientation* by Lee E. Preston (Glenview, Ill.: Scott, Foresman and Company, 1970), p. 198. Copyright © 1970 by Scott, Foresman and Company. Reprinted by permission of the publisher.

[10]Charles G. Burck, "While the Big Brewers Quaff, the Little Ones Thirst," *Fortune* (November 1972), p. 107.

Product Differentiation: Key to Beverage Market Success

Development of strong brand identification through a soundly conceived promotional strategy is the single greatest factor in the success of any beverage, according to Ira Herbert, executive vice-president at Coca-Cola. Herbert speaks from 30 years of experience with such products as Coke's line of soft drinks, Minute Maid orange juice and Taylor California Cellars wines.

In order to promote a brand successfully, unique product attributes must be stressed. "Whatever the characteristics, I would mold them into a distinctive image for the product that gives the consumer some definite reason to buy that particular brand," he said.

Herbert's experience with Taylor California Cellars provides a good example. In 1977, Coke entered the wine business with its acquisition of Taylor Wine Company. It was a new business for Coke, one that is capital intensive, where markets must be anticipated well in advance because grapes grow only once a year. "We had to target very specifically," he said, "concentrating on those segments with the most dynamic potential."

Coke gave special consideration to several factors. Taylor had a recognized and respected name, but it did not have an entry in the fast-growing California premium table wine market. "We decided to link Taylor—with its high-quality New York state heritage—to the two new trigger words 'California' and 'Cellars.'" The brand, which did not exist until the fall of 1978, is now the second-largest selling premium table wine in America.

Coca-Cola marketers were also successful in applying this approach to its Minute Maid frozen orange juice. The decision was made to reintroduce the essence of oils usually lost in the squeezing process, and "then we hammered home that quality message."

Source: "Brand Identity Key in Beverages: Herbert," *Advertising Age* (May 3, 1982), p. 24.

Establishing a Budget

Figure 19.10 suggests that the optimal method of allocating a promotion budget is to expand it until the cost of each additional increment equals the additional incremental revenue received. In other words, the most effective allocation procedure is to increase promotional expenditures until each dollar of promotion expense is matched by an additional dollar of profit. This procedure—called *marginal analysis*—results in the maximization of the input's productivity. The difficulty arises in identification of this optimal point, which requires a precise balancing of marginal expenses for promotion and the resulting marginal receipts.

The more traditional methods of allocating a promotional budget are by percentage of sales, fixed sum per unit, meeting the competition, and task-objective methods.

Figure 19.10 Promotion-Sales Curve

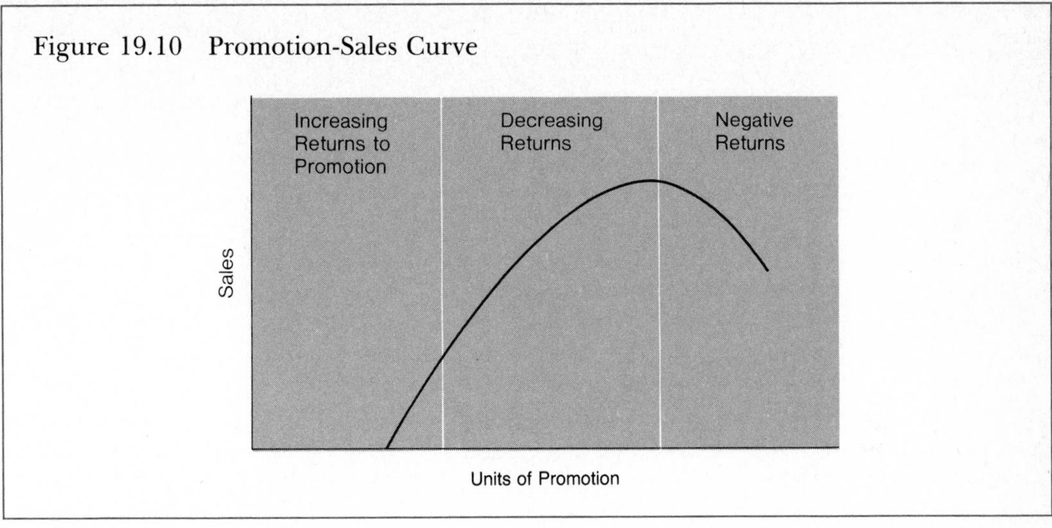

Source: *The Marketing Economy: An Analytical Approach,* by John C. Narver and Ronald Savitt, p. 294. Copyright © 1971 by Holt, Rinehart and Winston, Inc. Reprinted by permission of Holt, Rinehart and Winston, Inc.

Percentage of sales is a very common way of allocating promotion budgets. The percentage can be based on either past (such as the previous year) or forecasted (estimated current year) sales. While the simplicity of this plan is appealing, it is not an effective way of achieving the basic promotional objectives. Arbitrary percentage allocations, whether applied to historical or future sales figures, fail to allow the flexibility that is required. Furthermore, such reasoning is circular for the advertising allocation depends upon sales rather than vice versa, as it should be. Consider, for example, the implications of a decline in sales.

The *fixed sum per unit* approach differs from percentage of sales in only one respect: it applies a predetermined allocation to each sales or production unit. This can also be set on either a historical or a forecasted basis. Producers of high-value consumer durable goods, such as automobiles, often use this budgeting method.

Another traditional approach is simply to match competitors' outlays—in other words, *meet competition*—on either an absolute or a relative basis. However, this kind of approach usually leads to a status quo situation with each company retaining its percentage of total sales. Meeting the competition's budget does not necessarily relate to the objectives of promotion and, therefore, seems inappropriate for most contemporary marketing programs.

The **task-objective method** of developing a promotional budget is based upon a sound evaluation of the firm's promotional objectives, and, as a result, is better attuned to modern marketing practices. It involves two sequential steps.

Psychographic Case Study: Promoting Miller Lite

Psychographic segmentation, discussed in Chapter 4, is particularly appropriate in designing promotional messages to the firm's market target. Professors Harold Berkman and Christopher Gilson argue that one of the most popular applications of such research is in differentiating heavy users of a product category from light users and nonusers.

Take the case of beer. An early breakthrough was achieved when the Roper Research Organization discovered that 23 percent of the people who drink beer consume 80 percent of the beverage sold. The Batten, Barton, Durstine, and Osborn Advertising Agency (BBDO), impressed with this finding, began conducting group interviews with beer drinkers who downed several cans (or six-packs) a day. This "heavy" consumer became the advertising target, and BBDO's client, Schaefer Beer, adopted the positioning slogan, "The one beer to have when you're having more than one." The Schaefer campaign proved highly successful. . . .

Joseph Plummer applied AIO methodology to beer drinkers in an early study and found heavy consumers to belong to the middle class economically but to be engaged in traditional blue-collar occupations. The serious beer drinker was also revealed to be more pleasure seeking and hedonistic in his approach to life than the nonbeer drinker. He also seemed less concerned about responsibilities such as family and job and preferred physical, male-oriented activities. And he exhibited a more pronounced tendency to fantasize. Not too surprisingly, he enjoyed drinking and regarded beer as a real man's drink. . . .

When Miller Brewing Company introduced its Lite beer in the market, the promotional problem was to convince beer drinkers that the low-calorie, lighter blend fit their lifestyles just as well as the "heavy" kind. So the McCann-Erickson advertising agency decided to use ex-sports heroes as spokespeople.

As author William Flanagan noted:

1. The organization must *define the realistic communication goals* the firm wants the promotional mix to accomplish—for example, a 25 percent increase in brand awareness, or a 10 percent rise in consumers who realize that the product has certain specific differentiating features. The key is to quantitatively specify the objectives to be accomplished. They then become an integral part of the promotional plan.
2. The organization must *determine the amount (as well as type) of promotional activity required to accomplish each of the objectives* that have been set. These units combined become the firm's promotional budget.

A crucial assumption underlies the task-objective approach—that the productivity of each promotional dollar is measurable. That is why the

LITE BEER IS LIKE A QUARTERBACK.
WE CAN'T WAIT TO KNOCK ONE DOWN.
Bubba Smith and Dick Butkus.
Lite
Lite
Lite
EVERYTHING YOU ALWAYS WANTED
IN A BEER. AND LESS.
© 1982 Miller Brewing Co., Milwaukee, WI

Source: © 1982 Miller Brewing Company, Milwaukee, Wisconsin.

Everyone knows that beer and sports go together, but an obscure federal regulation prohibits using active ballplayers in beer commercials. That's why you've never seen active athletes endorse a beer. But ex-athletes proved even better. Their glories are past, frozen in time and perhaps magnified a bit—just like, well, the time you hit one over the wall, or hit the winning jump shot in the school yard. How could you find better spokesmen for a beer made for (men) who are worried about their waistlines?

Judging by the success of Miller Lite, you couldn't.

Source: Christopher Gilson and Harold W. Berkman, *Advertising* (New York: Random House, 1980), p. 115. Used by permission. Flanagan quotation from "The Charge of the Lite Brigade," *Esquire* (July 18, 1978).

objectives must be carefully chosen, quantified, and accomplished through promotional efforts. Generally, an objective like "We wish to achieve a 5 percent increase in sales" is a marketing objective, because a sale is a culmination of the effects of *all* elements of the marketing mix. Therefore, an appropriate promotional objective might be "To make 30 percent of the market target aware of the Pop Shoppe concept."

While promotional budgeting is always difficult, recent research studies and more frequent use of computer-based models make it less of a problem than it has been in the past.

Measuring the Effectiveness of Promotion

It is widely recognized that part of a firm's promotional effort is ineffective. John Wanamaker, a successful nineteenth century retailer, once observed: "I know half the money I spend on advertising is wasted; but I can never find out which half."

Measuring the effectiveness of promotional expenditures has become an extremely important research question, particularly among advertisers. Studies aimed at this measurement dilemma face several major obstacles, among them the difficulty of isolating the effect of the promotion variable.

Most marketers would prefer to use a *direct-sales results test* to measure the effectiveness of promotion. This test ascertains for each dollar of promotional outlay the corresponding increase in revenue. The primary difficulty is controlling the other variables operating in the marketplace. A $1.5 million advertising campaign may be followed by an increase in sales of $20 million. However, this increase may be due more to a sudden price hike by the leading competitor than to the advertising expenditure. Therefore, advertisers are turning to establishing and assessing achievable, measurable objectives.

With the increasing sophistication of marketing analysts, analytical techniques, and computer-based marketing information systems, historical data on promotional expenditures and their effects are being subjected to ever more scrutiny. More and more is being learned about measuring and evaluating the effects of promotional activity. While the technical literature in marketing reveals much of what is happening in this critical area, firms are reluctant to release much of this information. Not only do they wish to keep their proprietary (privately held) information about how the market works to themselves for competitive reasons, but they do not want competitors knowing the methods and decision routines used in planning promotional activity.

Other methods of assessing promotional effectiveness include sales inquiries, determination of change in attitudes toward the product, and improvement in public knowledge and awareness. One indicator of advertising effectiveness would be the elasticity or sensitivity of sales to promotion based on historical data concerning price, sales volume, and advertising expenditures.

It is difficult for the marketer to conduct research in a controlled environment as other disciplines use for research. The difficulty in isolating the effects of promotion causes many to abandon all attempts at measurement. Others, however, turn to indirect evaluation. These researchers concentrate on the factors that are quantifiable, such as recall (how much is remembered about specific products or advertisements) and readership (the size and composition of the audience). The basic problem is the difficulty in relating these variables to sales. Does extensive ad readership actually lead to increased sales? Another problem is the high cost of research in promotion. To correctly assess the effectiveness of promotional expenditures may require a significant investment.

The Value of Promotion

Promotion has often been the target of criticism. A selection of these would include the following:

- "Promotion contributes nothing to society."
- "Most advertisements and sales presentations insult my intelligence."
- "Promotion 'forces' consumers to buy products they cannot afford and do not need."
- "Advertising and selling are economic wastes."
- "Salespersons and advertisers are usually unethical."

Consumers, public officials, and marketers agree that too many of these complaints are true.[11] Some salespersons do use unethical sales tactics. Some product advertising is directed at consumer groups that can least afford to purchase the particular item. Many television commercials do contribute to the growing problem of cultural pollution.

While promotion can certainly be criticized on many counts, it is important to remember that it plays a crucial role in modern society. This point is best explained by looking at the importance of promotion on business, economic, and societal levels.

Business Importance

Promotional strategy has become increasingly important to business enterprises—both large and small. The long-term rise in outlays for promotion is well documented and certainly attests to management's faith in the ability of promotional efforts to produce additional sales. It is difficult to conceive of an enterprise that does not attempt to promote its product or service in some manner or another. Most modern institutions simply cannot survive in the long run without promotion. Business must communicate with the public.

Nonbusiness enterprises also have recognized the importance of this variable. The United States government is the twenty-sixth largest U.S. advertiser, while the Canadian government ranks as the leading advertiser in Canada, promoting many programs and concepts. Religious organizations have acknowledged the importance of promoting what they

[11]See J. Edward Russo, Barbara L. Metcalf, and Debra Stephens, "Identifying Misleading Advertising," *Journal of Consumer Research* (September 1981), pp. 119–131.

do. Even labor organizations have used promotional channels to make their viewpoints known to the public at large. The advertisement for the United Way shown in Figure 19.11 effectively points out the benefits of this organization in helping the less fortunate.

Economic Importance

Promotion has assumed a degree of economic importance, if for no other reason than the employment of thousands of people. More importantly, however, effective promotion has allowed society to derive benefits not otherwise available. For example, the criticism that promotion costs too much isolates an individual expense item and fails to consider the possible effect of promotion on other categories of expenditures.

Promotion strategies that increase the number of units sold permit economies in the production process, thereby lowering the production costs assigned to each unit of output. Lower consumer prices then allow these products to become available to more people. Similarly, researchers have found that advertising subsidizes the informational content of newspapers and the broadcast media.[12] In short, promotion pays for many of the enjoyable entertainment and educational aspects of contemporary life, as well as lowering product costs.

Social Importance

Criticisms such as "most promotional messages are tasteless" and "promotion contributes nothing to society" sometimes ignore the fact that no commonly accepted set of standards or priorities exists within our social framework. We live in a varied economy characterized by consumer segments with differing needs, wants, and aspirations. What is tasteless to one group may be quite informative to another. Promotional strategy is faced with an "averaging" problem that escapes many of its critics. The one generally accepted standard in a market society is freedom of choice for the consumer. Customer buying decisions eventually determine what is acceptable practice in the marketplace.

Promotion has become an important factor in the campaigns to achieve socially oriented objectives, such as stopping smoking, family planning, physical fitness, and the elimination of drug abuse. Promotion performs an informative and educational task that makes it extremely important in the functioning of modern society. As with everything else in life, it is how one uses promotion, not the using itself, that is critical.

[12]Francis X. Callahan, "Does Advertising Subsidize Information?" *Journal of Advertising Research* (August 1978), pp. 19–22.

Figure 19.11 Promotional Message for a Nonprofit Organization

Source: Reproduced by permission of United Way.

Summary

This chapter provided an introduction to promotion, the fourth variable in the marketing mix (product, pricing, distribution, and promotional strategies). Promotional strategy is closely related to the marketing communications system, which includes the elements of sender, message, encoding, transfer mechanism, decoding, receiver, feedback, and noise. The major components of promotional strategy are personal selling and nonpersonal selling (advertising, sales promotion, and public relations). These elements are discussed in Chapters 20 and 21.

Developing an effective promotional strategy is a complex matter. The elements of promotion are related to the type and value of the product being promoted, the nature of the market, the stage of the product life cycle, and the funds available for promotion, as well as to the timing of the promotional effort. Personal selling is used primarily for industrial goods, for higher value items, and during the transactional phase of the purchase decision process. Advertising, by contrast, is used primarily for consumer goods, for lower value items during the later stages of the product life cycle, and during the pretransactional and posttransactional phases.

A pushing strategy, which relies on personal selling, attempts to promote the product to the members of the marketing channel rather than to the final user. A pulling strategy concentrates on stimulating final user demand primarily in the mass media through advertising and sales promotion.

The five basic objectives of promotion are to (1) provide information, (2) stimulate demand, (3) differentiate the product, (4) accentuate the value of the product, and (5) stabilize sales.

Although it has become the target of much criticism, promotion plays an important role in the business, economic, and social activities of the country.

Key Terms

promotion
marketing communications
AIDA concept
(attention-interest-desire-action)
promotional mix
personal selling
advertising
sales promotion
public relations
publicity
pushing strategy
pulling strategy
task-objective method

Review Questions

1. Relate the steps in the communications process to promotional strategy.
2. Explain the concept of the promotional mix and its relationship to the marketing mix.
3. Identify the major determinants of a promotional mix and describe how they affect the selection of an appropriate blending of promotional techniques.
4. Relate the AIDA concept to the marketing communications process.
5. Explain the concept of noise and its causes.

6. Under what circumstances should a pushing strategy be used in promotion? When would a pulling strategy be effective?
7. What are the primary objectives of promotion?
8. Identify and briefly explain the alternative methods for developing a promotional budget.
9. How should a firm attempt to measure the effectiveness of its promotional efforts?
10. Identify the major public criticisms sometimes directed toward promotion. Prepare a defense for each criticism.

Discussion Questions and Exercises

1. "Perhaps the most critical promotional question facing the marketing manager concerns when to use each of the components of promotion." Comment on this statement, and relate your response to the goods classification, product value, marketing channels, price, and the timing of the promotional effort.
2. What mix of promotional variables would you use for each of the following?
   a. Champion spark plugs
   b. Weedeater lawn edgers
   c. A management consulting service
   d. Industrial drilling equipment
   e. Women's sports outfits
   f. Customized business forms
3. Develop a hypothetical promotion budget for the following firms. Ignore dollar amounts by using percentage allocations to the various promotional variables (such as 30 percent to personal selling, 60 percent to advertising, and 10 percent to public relations).
   a. National Car Rentals
   b. Holiday Inns
   c. A manufacturer of industrial chemicals
   d. Prudential Life Insurance Company
4. Many professionals, such as attorneys, physicians, and dentists, are now allowed to promote their services through media advertising. What effect is this likely to have on the practices of professionals who advertise?
5. When paperback book sales suffered a downturn, several of the major publishers adopted new promotional strategies. Fawcett Books began using 30-cents-off coupons to promote its Coventry romance series. New American Library, on the other hand, established a returns policy that rewarded dealers with high sales. The new policy also contained penalties to discourage low volume by retail book outlets. Relate these promotional strategies to the material discussed in this chapter.

20

Chapter Objectives

1. To explain the current status and historical development of advertising.
2. To identify the major types of advertising.
3. To list and discuss the various advertising media.
4. To explain how advertising effectiveness is determined.
5. To outline the organization of the advertising function.
6. To describe the process of creating an advertisement.
7. To identify the methods of sales promotion.
8. To explain the role of public relations and publicity.

ADVERTISING, SALES PROMOTION, AND PUBLIC RELATIONS

The vote by advertising professionals for the year's outstanding advertisement was not even close. And most viewers agreed: the 30-second vignette of the athlete, the little boy, and the bottle of Coke was one of the most poignant, memorable television commercials ever filmed. The athlete, recognizable to many viewers as Pittsburgh Steeler defensive lineman "Mean" Joe Greene, has removed his jersey and is painfully limping down the stadium runway to the dressing room when a small boy calls his name and offers him his bottle of Coca-Cola. Greene refuses at first, then takes it from the boy and drinks the entire contents of the bottle without stopping. The boy watches in fascination, then turns to go to his seat. Greene calls to him, says "Thanks," and tosses him his jersey.

Why was this advertisement so effective? Why was it such an effective communication when compared with the hundreds of other television ads that competed for the viewer's attention during that same day? Two marketing authorities viewed the commercial and concluded, "A child looks at 'Mean' Joe Greene drinking a Coca-Cola and subconsciously (perhaps consciously in some instances) attributes the respect and strength that the child wants in the Coke being consumed by Mr. Greene."[1] James U. McNeal, a marketing professor at Texas A&M University, discussed the ad with his marketing students and reached these conclusions:

Then I took the discussion back to the "Mean" Joe Greene ad for Coke. I asked, "What's good about it?" In concert the students said essentially that it was an unusually sensitive ad. "What's bad about it?" I next inquired. There were quiet shrugs of shoulders, and a few soft "Nothing" responses. One young woman shyly spoke up and said, "It doesn't say much about Coke, actually." I leaped at the chance. "I agree that it doesn't say much about Coke, but what does it suggest?" Among the various comments, I heard two particular ones. "It suggests that Coke really satisfies your thirst," and "It encourages sharing." I repeated those statements and then noted that the needs for thirst satisfaction and the need for social relationships were the two most common needs met by soft drinks. In essence, I explained how Coke had, in fact, communicated quite a lot, and had done so with an appealing sensitive tone. That's very good advertising, was my point. However, I made another very important point. In the case of the Coke ad, the students had judged it as good on the basis of its format and apparently not according to its message and need appeals.[2]

The Conceptual Framework

As Chapter 19 explained, promotion consists of both personal and nonpersonal elements. In this chapter the nonpersonal elements of promotion—advertising, sales promotion, and public relations—are examined. These elements play a critical role in the promotional mixes of thousands of organizations.

For most organizations, advertising represents the most important type of nonpersonal promotion. This chapter examines advertising objectives and the importance of planning for advertising. Also discussed are the different types of advertisements and media choices. Both retail advertising and manufacturer (national) advertising are discussed and the alternative methods of assessing the effectiveness of an advertisement are examined. Sales promotion and public relations—including publicity—are also discussed.

[1]James F. Engel and Roger D. Blackwell, *Consumer Behavior,* 4th ed. (Hinsdale, Ill.: The Dryden Press, 1982), p. 147.

[2]James U. McNeal, "You Can Defend Advertising—But Not Every Advertisement," *Business Horizons* (September/October 1981), p. 36. Reprinted by permission.

Advertising

If you sought to be the next member of the U.S. House of Representatives, you would need to communicate with every possible voter in your congressional district. If you had invented a new calculator and went into business to market it, your chances of success would be slim without informing and persuading students, businesspeople, and other potential customers of the usefulness of your invention. In these situations you would discover, as have countless others, the need to use advertising to communicate to buyers. In the previous chapter, **advertising** was defined as a paid, nonpersonal communication through various media by business firms, nonprofit organizations, and individuals who are in some way identified in the advertising message and who hope to inform or persuade members of a particular audience.

Today's widespread markets make advertising an important part of business. Since the end of World War II, advertising and related expenditures have risen faster than gross national product and most other economic indicators. Furthermore, about 200,000 workers are employed in advertising.

In 1981, five corporations—Procter & Gamble, Sears, General Foods, Philip Morris, and General Motors—each spent more than $400 million on advertising. Table 20.1 ranks the nation's top 20 advertisers based on spending in national media.

The total expenditure for advertising in the United States in 1981 was about $61 billion, or approximately $270 per capita was spent on advertising in a single year. Annual advertising expenditures are expected to reach $115 billion by the end of the decade. Overall, the United States accounts for about 57 percent of worldwide advertising expenditures.

Advertising expenditures vary among industries and companies. Cosmetics companies are often cited as an example of firms that spend a high percentage of their funds on advertising and promotion. Chicago management consultants Schonfeld & Associates studied over 4,000 firms and calculated their average advertising expenditures as a percentage of both sales and gross profit margin. Estimates for selected industries are given in Figure 20.1. Wide differences exist among industries, as shown in the figure. Advertising spending can range from one fifth of 1 percent in an industry like iron and steel foundries to more than 7 percent of sales in the detergent industry.

Industry in general has become somewhat advertising-oriented as other elements of promotion have grown relatively more expensive. Yet advertising's future potential remains a matter of conjecture, although it may be determined by the environmental framework within which it operates. The role of advertising in U.S. society attracts considerable public interest today.

Table 20.1 Twenty Leading National Advertisers

Rank	Company	Total Advertising Expenditures, 1981 (in Millions)
1	Procter & Gamble	$ 671.8
2	Sears, Roebuck & Co.	544.1
3	General Foods Corporation	456.8
4	Philip Morris, Inc.	433.0
5	General Motors Corporation	401.0
6	K mart Corporation	349.6
7	Nabisco Brands	341.0
8	R. J. Reynolds Industries	321.3
9	American Telephone & Telegraph Co.	297.0
10	Mobil Corporation	293.1
11	Ford Motor Co.	286.7
12	Warner-Lambert Co.	270.4
13	Colgate-Palmolive Co.	260.0
14	PepsiCo, Inc.	260.0
15	McDonald's Corporation	230.2
16	American Home Products Corporation	209.0
17	RCA Corporation	208.8
18	J.C. Penney Co.	208.6
19	General Mills Corporation	207.3
20	Bristol-Myers Co.	200.0

Source: Reprinted with permission from *Advertising Age* (September 9, 1982). Copyright 1982 by Crain Communications, Inc.

Historical Development[3]

Some form of advertising of products probably existed since the development of the exchange process. Most early advertising was vocal; criers and hawkers sold various products, made public announcements, and chanted advertising slogans like this one:

One-a-penny, two-a-penny, hot-cross buns
One-a-penny, two for tuppence, hot-cross buns.

Criers were common in colonial America. The cry of "Rags! Any rags? Any wool rags?" filled the streets of Philadelphia in the 1700s.

Signs were also used in early advertising. Most were symbolic in their identification of products or services. In Rome, a goat signified a dairy, a mule driving a mill signified a bakery, and a boy being whipped signified a school.

[3]This section follows the discussion in S. Watson Dunn and Arnold M. Barban, *Advertising: Its Role in Modern Marketing* (Hinsdale, Ill.: The Dryden Press, 1982), pp. 21–40.

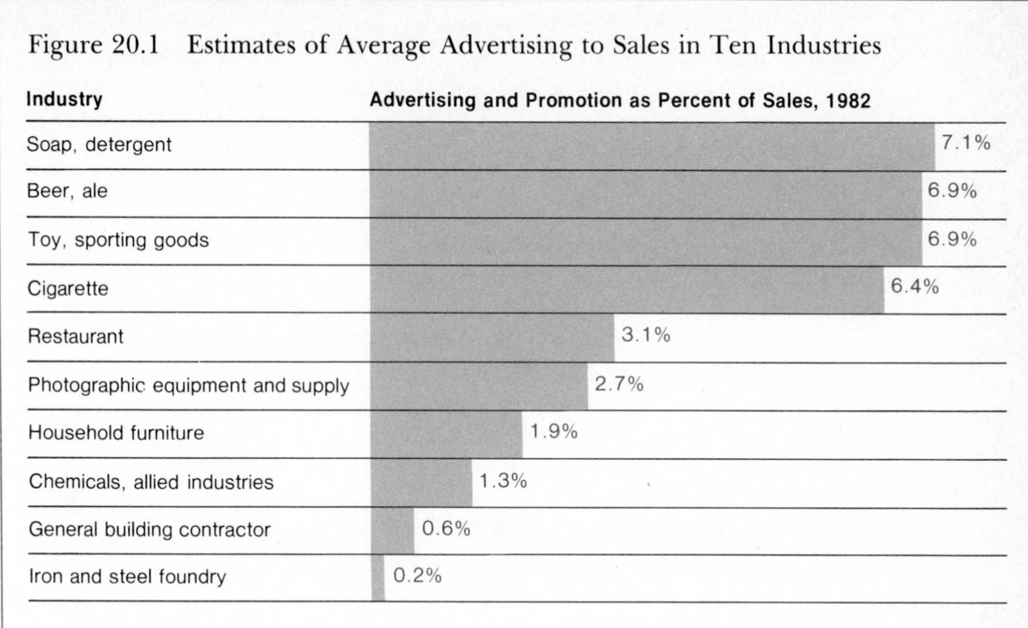

Industry
Advertising and Promotion as Percent of Sales, 1982
Soap, detergent
7.1%
Beer, ale
6.9%
Toy, sporting goods
6.9%
Cigarette
6.4%
Restaurant
3.1%
Photographic equipment and supply
2.7%
Household furniture
1.9%
Chemicals, allied industries
1.3%
General building contractor
0.6%
Iron and steel foundry
0.2%

Figure 20.1 Estimates of Average Advertising to Sales in Ten Industries

Source: Schonfeld & Associates, Inc., 120 S. La Salle St., Chicago 60603, (312) 236-5846.

Later, the development of the printing press greatly expanded advertising's capabilities. A 1710 advertisement in the *Spectator* billed one dentifrice as "the Incomparable Powder for cleaning of Teeth, which has given great satisfaction to most of the Nobility and Gentry in England." Colonial newspapers like Benjamin Franklin's *Gazette* also featured advertising. In fact, many newspapers carried it on their first page. Most of these advertisements would be called classified ads today. Some national advertisers also began to use newspaper advertising at this time. For instance, Pierre Lorillard was an early promoter of his tobacco products.

Volney Palmer organized the first advertising agency in the United States in 1841. George P. Rowell was another who pioneered in advertising. Originally, advertising agencies simply sold ad space. Services like advertising research, copywriting, and planning came later. In the early 1900s, Claude C. Hopkins used a large-scale consumer survey concerning home-baked beans before launching a campaign for Van Camp's Pork and Beans. Hopkins claimed that home-baked beans were difficult to digest and suggested that consumers try Van Camp's beans. He advocated the use of "reason-why-copy" to show why people should buy the product.

Some early advertising promoted products of questionable value, such as patent medicines. As a result, a reform movement in advertising developed during the early 1900s, and some newspapers began to screen their advertisements. Magazine publisher Cyrus Curtis began rejecting certain types of advertising, such as medical copy that claimed cures and advertisements for alcoholic beverages. In 1911, the forerunner of the American Advertising Federation drew up a code for improved advertising.

One identifying feature of advertising in the twentieth century is its concern for researching the markets that it attempts to reach. Originally, advertising research dealt primarily with media selection and the product. Then, advertisers became increasingly concerned with determining the appropriate *demographics*—such characteristics as the age, sex, and income level of potential buyers. Understanding consumer behavior has now become an important aspect of advertising strategy. Behavioral influences in purchase decisions, often called *psychographics,* can be useful in describing potential markets for advertising appeals. As described in Chapter 4, these influences include such factors as lifestyle and personal attitudes. Increased information about consumer psychographics has led to improved advertising decisions.

The emergence of the marketing concept, with its emphasis on a company-wide consumer orientation, saw advertising take on an expanded role as marketing communications assumed greater importance in business. Today, the average American is exposed to 565 advertisements daily.[4] Advertising provides an efficient, inexpensive, and fast method of reaching the much-sought-after consumer. Its extensive use currently rivals that of personal selling. Advertising has become a key ingredient in the effective implementation of the marketing concept.

Advertising Objectives

Traditionally, advertising objectives were stated in terms of direct sales goals. A more realistic approach, however, is to view advertising as having communications objectives that seek to inform, persuade, and remind potential customers of the product. Advertising seeks to condition the consumer to have a favorable viewpoint toward the promotional message. The goal is to improve the likelihood that the customer will buy a particular product. In this sense, advertising illustrates the close relationship between marketing communications and promotional strategy.

In instances where personal selling is the primary component of a firm's marketing mix, advertising may be used in a support role to assist the salespeople. Much of Avon's advertising is aimed at assisting the

[4]"The Average American," *Detroit News Magazine* (December 2, 1979), p. 13.

Figure 20.2 Use of Advertising to Assist Personal Selling

Mc Graw Hill

"I don't know who you are.
I don't know your company.
I don't know your company's product.
I don't know what your company stands for.
I don't know your company's customers.
I don't know your company's record.
I don't know your company's reputation.
Now–what was it you wanted to sell me?"

MORAL: Sales start **before** your salesman calls–with business publication advertising.

McGRAW-HILL MAGAZINES
BUSINESS • PROFESSIONAL • TECHNICAL

Source: Reprinted with permission of McGraw-Hill Publications Company.

neighborhood salesperson by strengthening the image of Avon, its products, and its salespeople. The well-known advertisement for McGraw-Hill Publications, shown in Figure 20.2, illustrates the important role advertising can play in opening doors for the sales force.

Advertising Planning

Advertising planning begins with effective research. The results of the research allow management to make strategic decisions that are translated into tactical areas, such as budgeting, copywriting, scheduling,

How Are You Going to Keep Them Down on the Farm . . . After They've Seen Alaska?

Sandwiched between the Super Bowl broadcast's beer and automobile commercials was a 30-second spot from an unusual television advertiser: Alaska. State governments normally aren't big-time media buyers, but Alaska's division of tourism decided $320,000 was a fair price to pay the Columbia Broadcasting System to put a single half-minute message into 40 million homes.

"We figured our target audience was watching the Super Bowl," says John Farnan, tourist division marketing coordinator. Who are these potential Alaska visitors? People 35 years and older with annual incomes of at least $35,000, said Farnan. "There are 21 million in the U.S. in that category who haven't been here yet," he said.

The state is spending another $1.4 million to run this spot, and a companion commercial, for five weeks in 16 major cities. "A lot of people think it's too cold here and that there's nothing to do," said Farnan, explaining why the ads, filmed in the state last September, show a handsome couple walking barefoot on a beach, flying a hot-air balloon, and dancing in a nightclub. Alaskan summers are warm, and winter temperatures often aren't as cold as in Minneapolis or Cleveland, said Farnan, and "nobody lives in igloos."

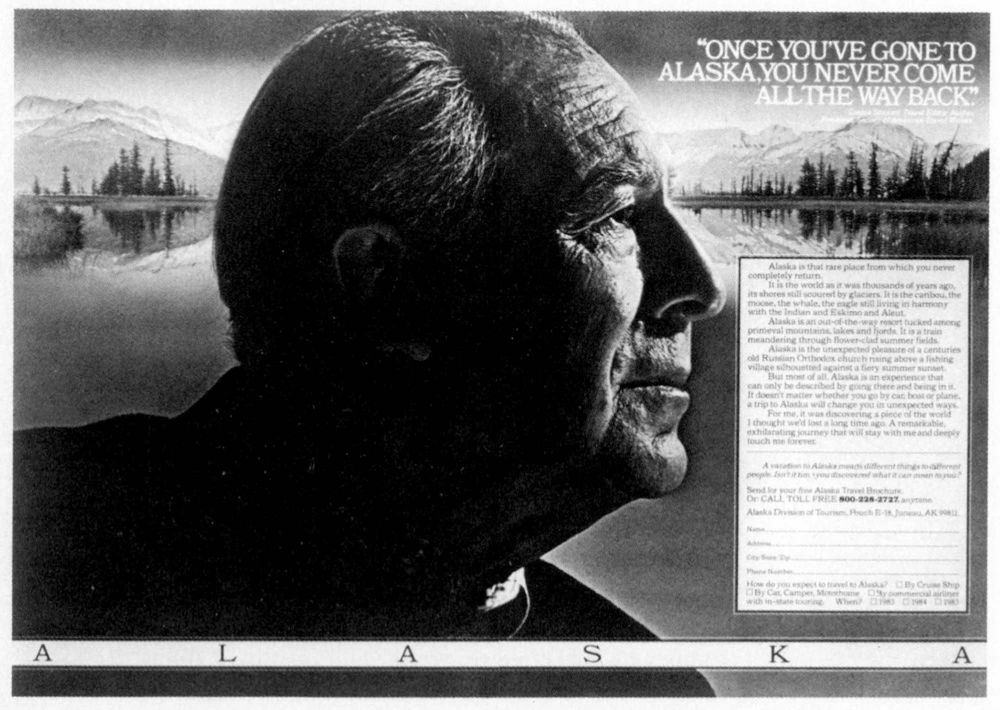

Source: "Alaska Tries Selling Itself on Television," *The Wall Street Journal* (February 2, 1982), p. 33. Reprinted by permission. Advertisement reproduced by permission of Alaska Division of Tourism.

Figure 20.3 Elements of Advertising Planning

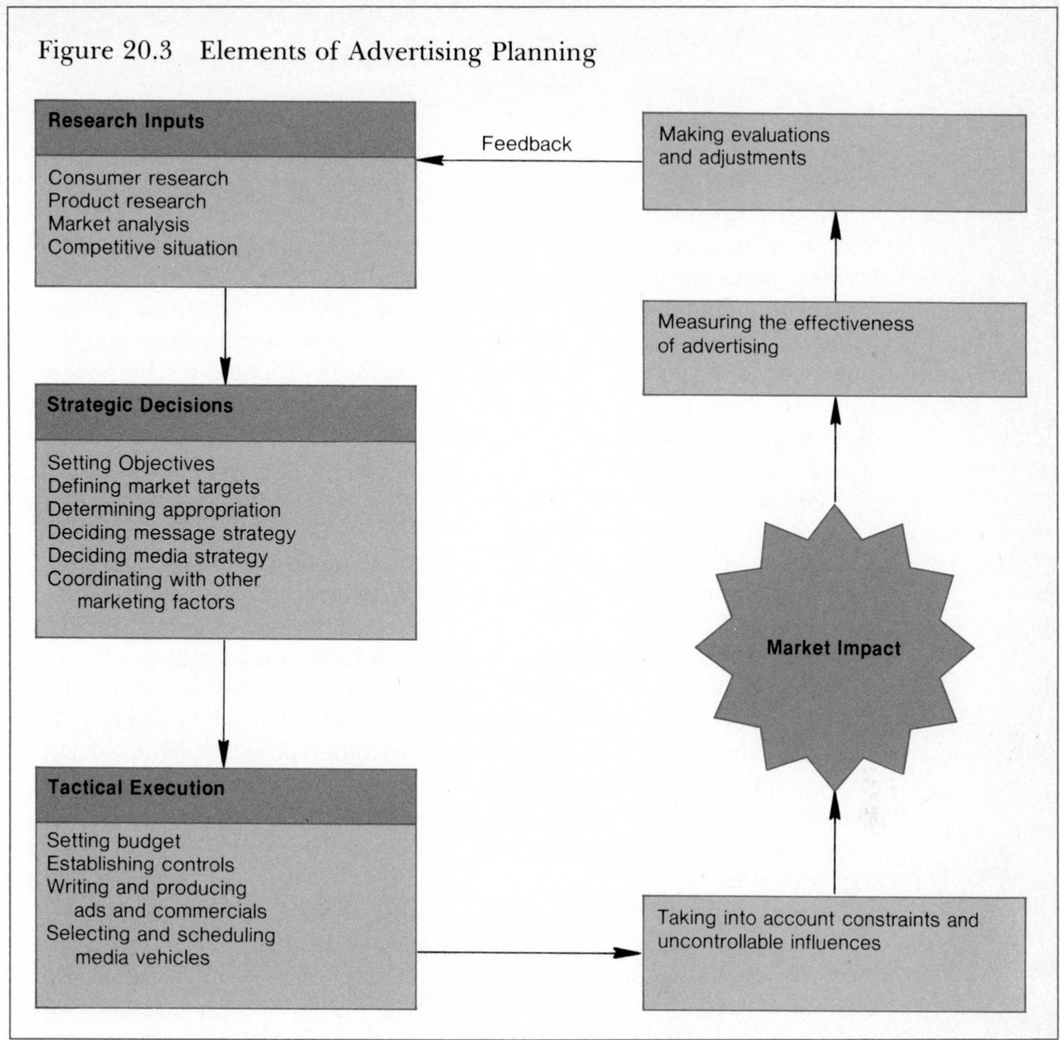

Source: *Advertising: Its Role in Modern Marketing,* p. 202, by S. Watson Dunn and Arnold M. Barban. Copyright © 1982 by CBS College Publishing. Reprinted by permission.

and the like. Finally, feedback helps to measure the effectiveness of the advertising. The elements of advertising planning are shown in Figure 20.3.

There is a real need for following a sequential process in advertising decisions. Novice advertisers are often overly concerned with the technical aspects of advertisement construction and ignore the more basic steps, such as market analysis. The type of advertisement employed in any particular situation is related in large part to the planning phase of this process.

Positioning

One of the most widely discussed strategies in advertising is the concept of **positioning,** which involves the development of a marketing strategy aimed at a particular segment of the market and designed to achieve a desired position in the mind of the prospective buyer. While advertising experts continue to debate its effectiveness and origin, positioning has been used by many firms since its inception little more than a decade ago. The strategy is applied primarily to products that are not leaders in their particular industries. These products are apparently more successful if their advertising concentrates on specific "positions" in the minds of consumers. As Professors David A. Aaker and J. Gary Shansby point out, a variety of positioning strategies is available to the advertiser. An object can be positioned:

1. By attributes. (Crest is a cavity fighter.)
2. By price/quality. (Sears is a value store.)
3. By competitor. ("Avis is only number two in rent-a-cars, so why go with us? We try harder.")
4. By application. (Gatorade is for quick, healthful energy after exercise and other forms of physical exertion.)
5. By product user. (Miller is for the blue-collar, heavy beer drinker.)
6. By product class. (Carnation Instant Breakfast is a breakfast food.)

A common positioning technique is to position some aspect of the firm's marketing mix against the leading brand. A classic example is 7-Up. With the image of being a mixer for older people's drinks, 7-Up was missing the primary market for soft drinks—children, teenagers, and young adults. So the firm developed its UnCola campaign to first identify the product as a soft drink and then to position it as an alternative to cola.

Success in positioning requires a careful, well-researched plan:

> *The selection of a positioning strategy involves identifying competitors, relevant attributes, competitor positions, and market segments. Research-based approaches can help in each of these steps by providing conceptualization even if the subjective judgments of managers are used to provide the actual input information to the position decision.*[5]

Types of Advertisements

There are essentially two types of advertisements—product and institutional. Each can be subdivided into informative, persuasive, and reminder categories.

[5]David A. Aaker and J. Gary Shansby, "Positioning Your Product," *Business Horizons* (May/June 1982), p. 62. Reprinted by permission of the publisher.

Product advertising deals with the nonpersonal selling of a particular good or service. It is the type that comes to the mind of the average person when he or she thinks about advertisements. **Institutional advertising,** by contrast, is concerned with promoting a concept, an idea, a philosophy, or the goodwill of an industry, company, or organization. It is often closely related to the public relations function of the enterprise.[6] An example of institutional advertising by The American Gas Association appears in Figure 20.4.

Informative Product Advertising Informative product advertising seeks to develop initial demand for a product. It tends to characterize the promotion of any new type of product since the objective is often simply to announce its availability. Figure 20.5 shows that informative advertising is usually used in the introductory stages of the product life cycle. In fact, it was the original approach to advertising: early shippers used to post bulletins announcing the arrival of a ship and listing the goods it carried.

Persuasive Product Advertising To develop demand for a particular product or brand is the goal of persuasive product advertising—a competitive type of promotion used in the growth period and to some extent in the maturity period of the product life cycle (see Figure 20.5). The increased competition that has characterized all marketplaces in recent years even forced a long-time hold-out, Hershey Foods Corporation, to begin to advertise.

Reminder-Oriented Product Advertising The goal of reminder-oriented product advertising is to reinforce previous promotional activity by keeping the product name in front of the public. It is used in the maturity period as well as throughout the decline phase of the product life cycle.

A good example of reminder-oriented advertising is Dewar's profiles of young, active people. Each profile gives the person's age, profession, most memorable book read, favorite quotation, and, of course, preference of Dewar's Scotch. The campaign has been running since 1969, primarily because of the extensive reader interest in the profiles that appear in mass-circulation magazines. The people are real, and their only compensation is five cases of Dewar's Scotch. By using this advertising method, Dewar's has kept its name in front of consumers and has climbed to second place in scotch sales.

[6]See Thomas F. Garbett, "When to Advertise Your Company," *Harvard Business Review* (March–April 1982), pp. 100–106.

Figure 20.4 An Example of Institutional Advertising Used by the American Gas Association

While energy costs are rising, gas still delivers America's best energy value. Because gas is America's most efficient energy system.
So when you invest in modern, high-efficiency gas appliances, America's best energy value gets even better.
Use all energy wisely. It'll save you money.
FACT:
GAS DELIVERS MORE ENERGY VALUE
Gas: The future belongs to the efficient.

Source: Copyright © 1982 by the American Gas Association. Used by permission of the American Gas Association.

Informative Institutional Advertising This type of advertising is designed to teach the message receiver about the company, organization, or agency. A few years ago, International Telephone & Telegraph Corporation (ITT) marketers began efforts to remove links among the firm's name and Watergate and the downfall of Chilean President Salvador Allende. Approximately $10 million was spent each year on informative institutional advertising. By 1982, a Roper poll of 16 large

Figure 20.5 Relationship between Advertising and the Product Life Cycle

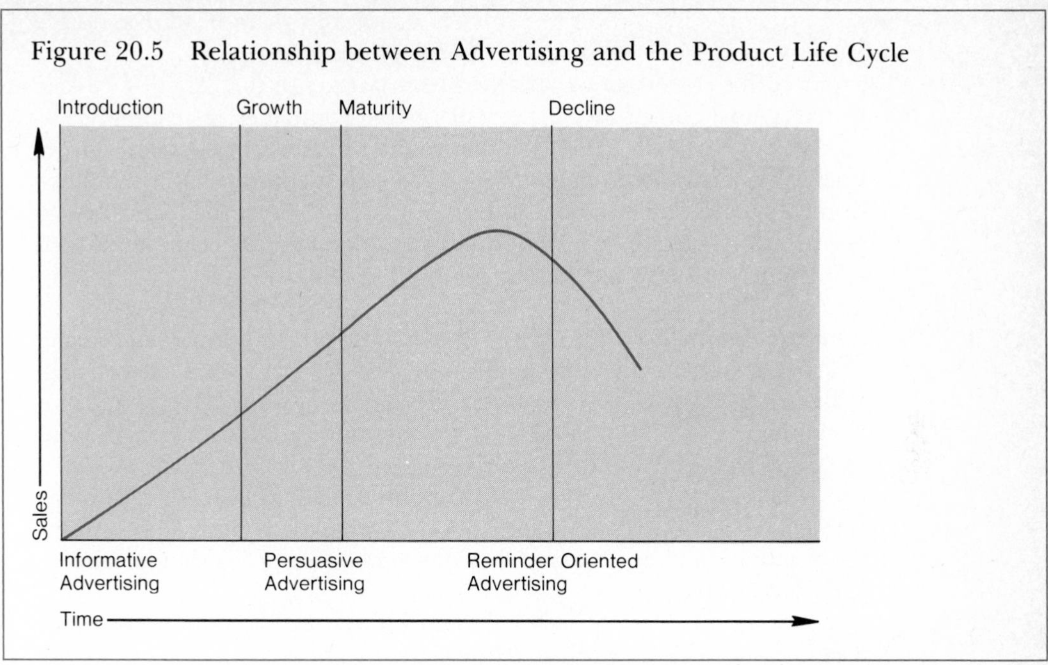

companies reported that ITT ranked eighth in the number of people who viewed it favorably. It tied with AT&T, and ranked ahead of such firms as Exxon, Chrysler, and Toyota. Today, its major institutional objectives are to reduce the general public's confusion between ITT and AT&T.[7]

Another example of this type of institutional advertising is the local United Fund's listing of all the agencies and organizations that benefit from its drive. Such advertising seeks to increase public knowledge of a concept, political viewpoint, industry, or company.

Persuasive Institutional Advertising When a firm or advertising agency wishes to advance the interests of a particular institution within a competitive environment, it often uses persuasive institutional advertising. For instance, Honda's campaign theme, "You meet the nicest people on a Honda" (1964–1967) changed people's negative stereotype of motorcyclists, thereby greatly expanding the demand for its product.

Persuasive institutional advertising may represent a significant component of the National Coffee Association's promotional efforts. The

[7]Bill Abrams, "How ITT Shells Out $10 Million or So a Year to Polish Reputation," *The Wall Street Journal* (April 2, 1982), p. 1.

task facing the industry is to reverse a major decline in per capita coffee consumption. Over a 20-year period beginning in 1962, U.S. daily per capita coffee consumption slumped from 3.12 cups to 1.92 cups. Coffee drinkers now constitute 56 percent of the population as compared to 75 percent in 1962. Young adults might constitute an enticing target for the association's attempts to increase coffee consumption since they drink less coffee than others. Industry statistics reveal that the 20 to 24 age group has a daily consumption rate of 0.86 cups as compared with a 3.21 cup consumption rate by 40 to 49 year olds.[8]

Advocacy Advertising One form of persuasive institutional advertising that has grown in use during the past decade is advocacy advertising. **Advocacy advertising,** sometimes referred to as *cause* advertising, can be defined as "any kind of paid public communication or message, from an identified source and in a conventional medium of public advertising, which presents information or a point of view bearing on a publicly recognized controversial issue."[9] Such advertising is designed to influence public opinion, to affect current and pending legislation, and to gain a following.

Advocacy advertising has long been utilized by such nonprofit organizations as Mothers Against Drunk Driving (MADD), Planned Parenthood, the National Rifle Association, and "right to life" anti-abortion groups. (Such use of advocacy advertising will be examined in Chapter 23.) In recent years, profit-seeking companies (particularly energy and resource firms) with a stake in some issue have turned to advocacy advertising. Among the firms that have used advocacy advertising in taking aggressive positions on particular issues and seeking to convince the public of their viewpoints are Mobil Oil, Bethlehem Steel, and Allied Chemical. An example of Mobil's advocacy advertisements is shown in Figure 20.6.

Reminder-Oriented Institutional Advertising Reminder-oriented institutional advertising has objectives similar to those of reminder-oriented product advertising. In most elections, for example, the nominee's early persuasive (issue directed) advertising is replaced by reminder-oriented advertising during the closing weeks of the campaign. The media abound with examples of this type of institutional advertising. The American Gas Association's message "Gas: The future belongs to the efficient" represents the industry's effort to remind the public of the importance of this vital fuel.

[8]Data supplied by the National Coffee Association of the United States.

[9]*Controversy Advertising: How Advertisers Present Points of View in Public Affairs; A Worldwide Study by the International Advertising Association* (New York: Communication Arts Books, 1977), p. 18.

Figure 20.6 Advocacy Advertisement

A 5-part series that may surprise you

Part V.
Time to cry "hard astern" on oil taxes

True or false? Oil companies are too profitable.
True or false? Oil companies don't pay enough in taxes.
In recent weeks, we've shown both statements to be false.

To sum up:

■ Oil companies earn no more than a few pennies at best on each dollar's worth of product they sell. Their return on each shareholder's dollar—a median rate of 14.3% a year since 1968—has trailed behind the median for all manufacturing—behind soap and cosmetics, newspapers, and television.

■ Tax deductions allowed other industries have been whittled away for the oils, and special taxes have been imposed, only on the oils. Percentage depletion has been virtually eliminated. Foreign tax credits have been cut, and cut again. A so-called "windfall profit" tax was slapped on in 1980. In 1982, Congress imposed an additional 5¢ tax on a gallon of gasoline, starting this month. An excise tax or an import fee on oil is being considered. And the states keep adding severance taxes, gross receipts taxes, fuel taxes, and others.

We think it's time to cry "Stop!"—in the national interest, not merely in our own. A company is simply a legal entity that invests stockholders' money in the expectation of making a profit. If that profit is constantly eroded, the business eventually fails and everybody's hurt.

In fact, it is time to cry more than "Stop." It's time for those who direct the ship of state to cry "Hard astern!" on taxes in general, and on oil taxes in particular.

The reasons are clear.

■ Oil companies pay too much in taxes now. That's basically because the politicians have stuck with the old adage "Don't tax you. Don't tax me. Tax the man behind the tree." The oil companies simply cannot go on being everybody's man behind the tree. Especially when their profits are below the average for those companies against which they have to compete for capital.

■ It especially makes no sense to heap on new taxes just as the nation is emerging from a recession. Consumers, not government, need more money in their pockets to spend and speed economic recovery. Taxes on industry are ultimately paid by the consumer. And new taxes on oil will lessen the chance of nurturing the recovery.

■ The federal government is expected to spend 25.7% of the GNP in 1983, the highest percentage since 1946. So government should be spending less, not taxing more.

■ Today's falling oil prices have been hailed as a spur to recovery, and another nail in inflation's coffin. Higher oil taxes would cut into these benefits. They would also weaken an industry which has to spend billions today to provide energy for tomorrow.

It's been said that nothing is certain except death and taxes. We would add a third certainty: unwise tax policy hastens demise, and that's as true for nations as for individual businesses or industries.

Mobil

Source: © 1983 Mobil Corporation

Media Selection

One of the most important decisions in developing an advertising strategy is media selection. A mistake at this point can cost a company literally millions of dollars in ineffective advertising. Media strategy must achieve the communication goals mentioned earlier.

Research should identify the market target to determine its size and characteristics, then match the target with the audience and the effectiveness of the available media. The objective is to achieve adequate media coverage without advertising beyond the identifiable limits of the potential market. Finally, alternative costs should be compared to determine the best possible media purchase.

There are numerous types of advertising media, and the characteristics of some of the more important ones are considered here. The advantages and disadvantages of each are shown in Table 20.2.

Newspapers Local markets continue to be dominated by newspapers with over 28 percent of total advertising revenue. Newspapers' primary advantages are flexibility (advertising can be varied from one locality to the next), community prestige (newspapers have a deep impact on the community), intensive coverage (in most places 90 percent of the homes can be reached by a single newspaper), reader control of exposure to the advertising message (unlike time media, readers can refer back to newspapers), coordination with national advertising, and merchandising services (such as promotional and research support). The disadvantages are a short life span, hasty reading (the typical reader spends only 20 to 30 minutes on the newspaper), and poor reproduction.[10]

Magazines Magazines, which are divided into such diverse categories as consumer, farm, and business publications, account for about 9 percent of national advertising, with a third of the advertising appearing in weekly magazines. The primary advantages of magazine advertising are the selectivity of market targets, quality reproduction, long life, the prestige associated with some magazines, and the extra services offered by many publications. The primary disadvantage is that magazines lack the flexibility of newspapers, radio, and television.

As Table 20.3 indicates, *Reader's Digest* is the nation's leading magazine in terms of paid subscriptions. Other leading magazines include two focusing upon the growing numbers of subscribers who are over 50, several women's magazines, one magazine targeted at young adult males, a weekly guide for television viewers, and a news magazine.

Television Television ranks first in revenue from national advertising (about 21 percent). It has an 11 percent share of local advertising revenue, making it second only to newspapers as an advertising medium. Television advertising can be divided into three categories: network, national, and local. Columbia Broadcasting System, National Broadcasting Company, and American Broadcasting Company are the three major national networks. Their programs usually account for a substan-

[10]The discussion of various advertising media is adapted from material in Dunn and Barban, *Advertising*, pp. 512–591.

Table 20.2 Advantages and Disadvantages of the Various Advertising Media

Media	Advantages	Disadvantages
Newspapers	Flexibility Community prestige Intense coverage Reader control of exposure Coordination with national advertising Merchandising service	Short life span Hasty reading Poor reproduction
Magazines	Selectivity Quality reproduction Long life Prestige associated with some magazines Extra services	Lack of flexibility
Television	Great impact Mass coverage Repetition Flexibility Prestige	Temporary nature of message High cost High mortality rate for commercials Evidence of public lack of selectivity
Radio	Immediacy Low cost Practical audience selection Mobility	Fragmentation Temporary nature of message Little research information
Outdoor Advertising	Communication of quick and simple ideas Repetition Ability to promote products available for sale nearby	Brevity of the message Public concern over esthetics
Direct Mail	Selectivity Intense coverage Speed Flexibility of format Complete information Personalization	High cost per person Dependency on quality of mailing list Consumer resistance

Source: Based on S. Watson Dunn and Arnold M. Barban, *Advertising: Its Role in Modern Marketing*, 5th ed. (Hinsdale, Ill.: The Dryden Press, 1982), pp. 513–577.

tial portion of total television advertising expenditures. A national "spot" is non-network broadcasting used by a general advertiser. Local advertising spots, used primarily by retailers, consist of locally developed and sponsored commercials. Television advertising offers the advantages of impact, mass coverage, repetition, flexibility, and prestige. Its disadvantages include relinquishing control of the promotional mes-

Table 20.3 Leading 15 Magazines in the United States[a]

Rank	Magazine	Average Paid Circulation (in Millions)
1	Reader's Digest	17.9
2	TV Guide	17.7
3	National Geographic	10.9
4	Better Homes & Gardens	8.1
5	Family Circle	7.4
6	Modern Maturity	7.3
7	American Association of Retired Persons News Bulletin	7.1
8	Woman's Day	7.0
9	McCall's	6.3
10	Ladies' Home Journal	5.5
11	Good Housekeeping	5.4
12	Playboy	5.0
13	National Enquirer	4.6
14	Redbook	4.4
15	Time	4.3

[a]Ranking based on average paid circulation

Source: List reprinted by permission from *Information Please Almanac 1983* (New York: A&W Publishers, Inc., 1983), p. 500. Data from Audit Bureau of Circulations, Publishers' Statements for six-month period ending December 31, 1981.

sage to the telecaster (who can influence its impact), high costs, high mortality rates for commercials, some public distrust, and a lack of selectivity.

Both the advantages and disadvantages of using television are illustrated by the 1982 Super Bowl telecast. CBS priced the 23 minutes of commercials at $690,000 each. While the cost was high, the broadcast reached some 110 million viewers of the game between the San Francisco 49ers and the Cincinnati Bengals. And the rates are virtually guaranteed to increase. Current estimates for advertisements during the 1985 Super Bowl are $1 million a minute.[11]

Radio Advertisers using the medium of radio can also be classified as network, national, and local. Radio accounts for about 7 percent of total advertising revenue and 5 percent of local expenditures. Its advantages are immediacy (studies show most people regard radio as the best source for up-to-date news), low cost, flexibility, practical and low-cost audience selection, and mobility. Its disadvantages include fragmenta-

[11]"Ad Folk Gasp at NFL TV Pact," *Advertising Age* (March 29, 1982), p. 92.

tion (Boise, Idaho, for example, has a population of 100,000 and 20 stations), the temporary nature of the message, and less research information than for television.

Outdoor Advertising Posters (commonly called billboards), painted bulletins or displays (such as those that appear on the walls of buildings), and electric spectaculars (large, illuminated, sometimes animated, signs and displays) make up outdoor advertising. This form of advertising has the advantages of communicating quick and simple ideas, repetition, and the ability to promote products that are available for sale nearby. Outdoor advertising is particularly effective in metropolitan and other high-traffic areas. Disadvantages of the medium are the brevity of its message and public concern over esthetics. The Highway Beautification Act of 1965, for instance, regulates outdoor advertising near interstate highways. This medium accounts for approximately 1 percent of all advertising.

Direct Mail Sales letters, postcards, leaflets, folders, broadsides (larger than folders), booklets, catalogs, and house organs (periodical publications issued by organizations) are all forms of direct mail advertising. The advantages of direct mail are selectivity, intensive coverage, speed, format flexibility, complete information, and the personalization of each mailing piece. Disadvantages of direct mail are its high cost per reader, its dependence on the quality of the mailing list, and some people's annoyance with it. This situation led the Direct Mail/Marketing Association in 1971 to establish its Mail Preference Service. This consumer service sends name-removal forms to people who do not wish to receive direct mail advertising. It also provides add-on forms for those who like to receive a lot of mail. Approximately 14 percent of total advertising is spent on direct mail.

Figure 20.7 compares the various advertising media on the basis of each medium's percentage of total advertising expenditures and shows the changes that have occurred since 1950. During the past three decades, newspapers, radio, and magazines have experienced declines in their shares of the advertising marketing, while television has grown tremendously.

Organization of the Advertising Function

Although the ultimate responsibility for advertising decision making often rests with top marketing management, the organization of the advertising function varies among companies. A producer of a technical

Figure 20.7 Percentage of Total Advertising in the Various Media: 1950–1981

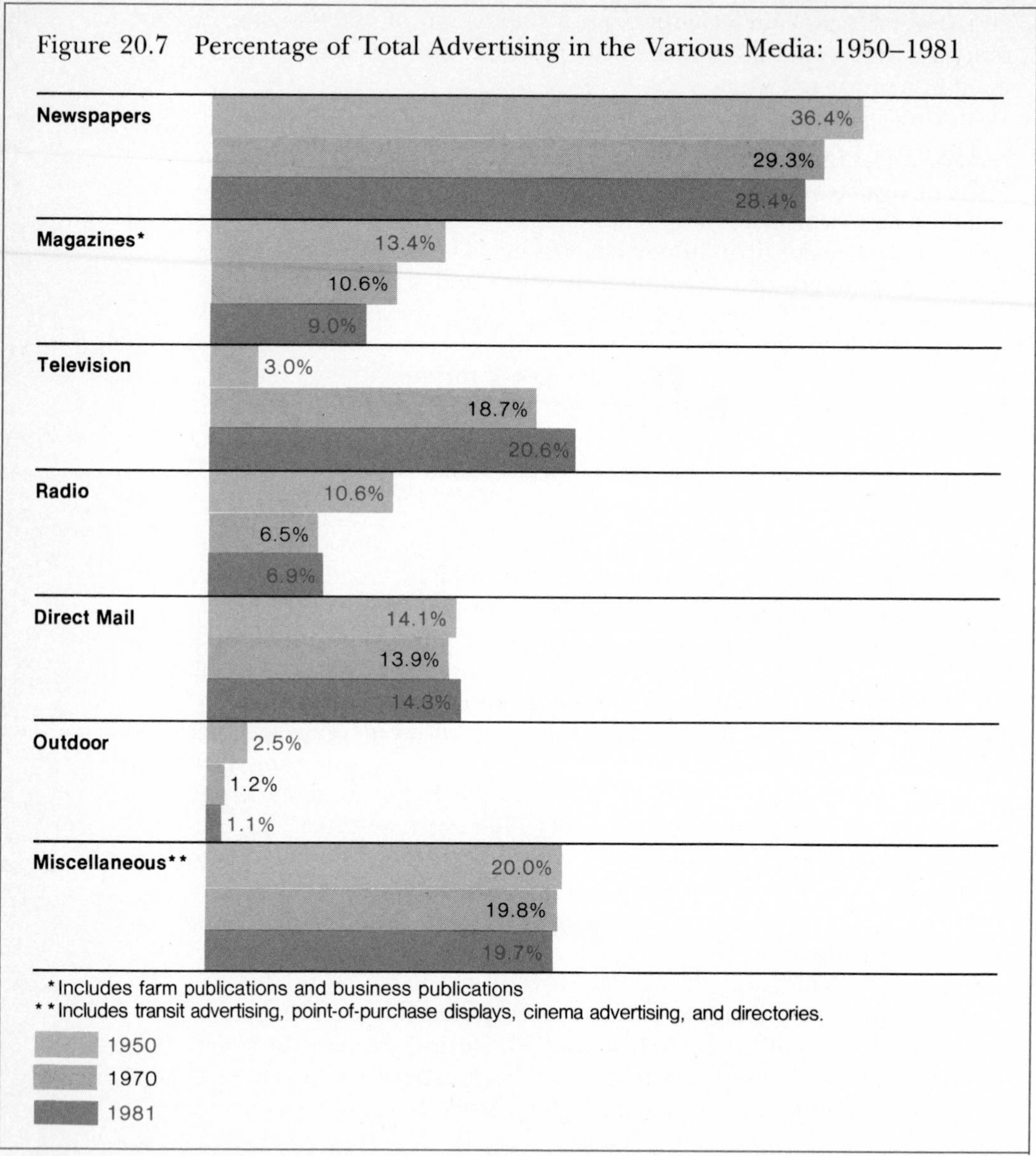

Sources: 1981 data from Robert J. Coen, "Industry Revenues Outpace GNP in '81," *Advertising Age* (March 22, 1982), p. 66. Reprinted by permission of Crain Communications, Inc. 1950 and 1970 data from *Information Please Almanac 1983* (New York: A&W Publications, Inc., 1983), p. 72.

industrial product may be served by a one-person operation primarily concerned with writing copy for trade publications. A consumer goods company, on the other hand, may have a large department staffed with advertising specialists.

The advertising function is usually organized as a staff department reporting to the vice-president (or director) of marketing. The director of advertising is an executive position heading the functional activity of advertising. The individual in this slot should be not only a skilled and experienced advertiser, but must also be able to communicate effectively within the organization. The success of a firm's promotional strategy depends upon the advertising director's willingness and ability to communicate both vertically and horizontally. The major tasks typically organized under advertising include advertising research, art, copywriting, media analysis, and, in some cases, sales promotion.

Advertising Agencies

Many major advertisers make use of one of the more than 8,000 independent advertising agencies located in the United States. The **advertising agency** is a marketing specialist firm that assists the advertiser in planning and preparing its advertisements. There are several reasons why most large advertisers use an agency for at least a portion of their advertising. Agencies are typically staffed with highly qualified specialists who provide a degree of creativity and objectivity that is difficult to sustain in a corporate advertising department. In some cases, they also reduce the cost of advertising, since they do not have many of the fixed expenses associated with maintaining an internal advertising department. Finally, since advertisers are typically compensated by the media used (typically in the form of a 15 percent discount based upon advertising expenditures), their services are available for the advertiser at little cost. However, effective use of an advertising agency requires a close relationship between advertiser and agency.

Figure 20.8 shows the organization chart for a large advertising agency. While the titles may vary from agency to agency, the major operational functions can be classified as creative services, account management, research, and promotional services. Young & Rubicam, Ted Bates Worldwide, J. Walter Thompson Company, and Ogilvy & Mather are the largest advertising agencies in the world. Each agency has worldwide billings of over $2 billion.

Since all agencies are profit-seeking, retention of existing advertisers and the addition of new clients are primary objectives. Advertising directed at these client markets represents a component of their own marketing mixes. Figure 20.9 is an advertisement by Needham, Harper & Steers which tells potential clients who their current clients are.

Figure 20.8 Organization Chart for a Large Advertising Agency

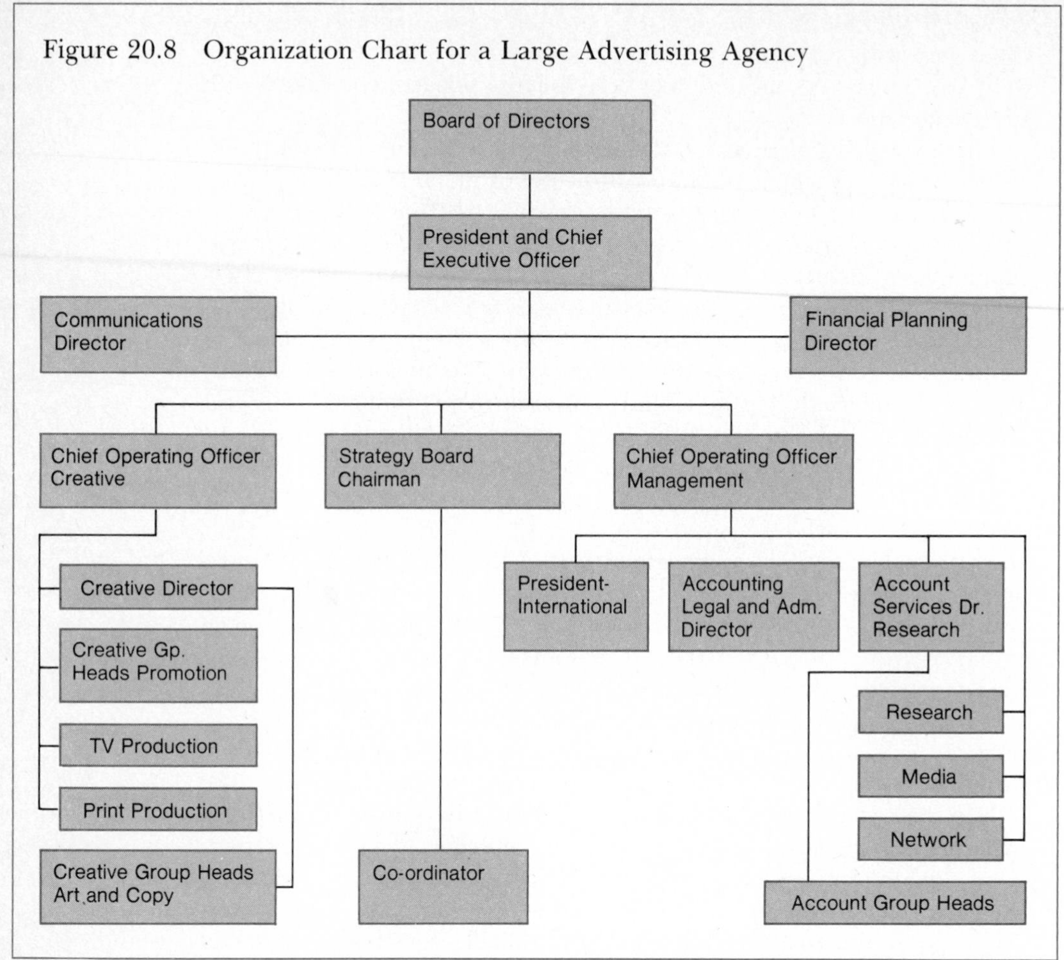

Creating an Advertisement

The final step in the advertising process is the development and preparation of an advertisement that should flow logically from the promotional theme selected. It should be a complementary part of the marketing mix with its role in total marketing strategy carefully determined. In addition, major factors to consider when preparing an advertisement are its creativity, its continuity with past advertisements, and possibly its association with other company products.

What should an advertisement accomplish? Regardless of the exact appeal that is chosen, an advertisement should (1) gain attention and

Figure 20.9 Advertising Agency Advertisement

Source: Reproduced by permission of Needham, Harper & Steers.

interest, (2) inform and/or persuade, and (3) eventually lead to buying action.

Gaining attention should be productive. That is, the reason for gaining consumers' attention should be to instill some recall of the product. Consider the case of the Gillette Company, which had a chimpanzee shave a man's face in a commercial. After tests in two cities, one Gillette spokesperson lamented, "Lots of people remembered the chimp, but hardly anyone remembered our product. There was fantastic interest in the monkey, but no payoff for Gillette."[12] The advertisement gained the audience's attention, but it failed to lead to buying action. An advertisement that fails to gain and hold the receiver's attention is ineffective.

Information and persuasion is the second factor to consider when creating an advertisement. Therefore, insurance advertisements typically specify the features of the policy and may use testimonials in attempting to persuade prospects. Stimulating buying action, however, is often difficult since an advertisement cannot actually close a sale. Nevertheless, if the first two steps are accomplished, the advertising is probably well worthwhile. Too many advertisers fail to suggest how the receiver can purchase a product if he or she so desires. This is a shortcoming that should be eliminated.

Comparative Advertising

Comparative advertising is a type of advertisement that makes direct promotional comparisons with leading competitive brands. The strategy is best employed by firms that do not lead the market. Most market leaders prefer not to acknowledge that there are competitive products. Procter & Gamble and General Foods, for instance, traditionally have devoted little of their huge promotional budgets for comparative advertising. But many firms do use it extensively. An estimated 23 percent of all radio and television commercials make comparisons to competitive products. Here are some examples:

- Scope mouthwash prevents "medicine breath," but Listerine is never mentioned.
- Minute Maid lemonade is better than the "no-lemon lemonade," a reference to General Foods' Country Time brand.
- Suave antiperspirant will keep you just as dry as Ban Ultra Dry does and for a lot less.
- Nationwide, more Coca-Cola drinkers prefer the taste of Pepsi.

Marketers who contemplate using comparative advertising in their promotional strategies should take precautions to assure that they can substantiate their claims. Comparison advertising has the potential of producing lawsuits, so practitioners must be especially careful. Advertising experts disagree about this practice's long-term effects. The conclusion is likely to be that comparative advertising is a useful strategy in a limited number of circumstances.[13]

[12]William M. Carley, "Gillette Co. Struggles as Its Rivals Slice at Fat Profit Margin," *The Wall Street Journal* (February 2, 1972), p. 1.

[13]Bill Abrams, "Comparative Ads Are Getting More Popular, Harder Hitting," *The Wall Street Journal* (March 11, 1982), p. 27. See also Linda E. Swayne and Thomas H. Stevenson, "The Nature and Frequency of Comparative Advertising in Industrial Print Media," in *A Spectrum of Contemporary Marketing Ideas,* (eds.) John H. Summey, Blaise J. Bergiel, and Carol H. Anderson (New Orleans: Southern Marketing Association, 1982), pp. 9–12.

Celebrity Testimonials: Advantages and Disadvantages

In their attempts to improve the effectiveness of their advertising, a number of marketers utilize celebrities to present their advertising messages. Well-known current examples include Sugar Ray Leonard and Magic Johnson for 7-Up, model Cheryl Tiegs for Cover Girl, James Garner and Mariette Hartley for Polaroid, former Dallas Cowboy Walt Garrison for Dodge and Skoal smokeless tobacco, and Bill Cosby for Jell-O pudding.

The primary advantage of using big-name personalities is that they may improve product recognition in a promotional environment filled with hundreds of competing 20- and 30-second commercials. (Advertisers use the term *clutter* to describe this situation.) In order for this technique to succeed, the celebrity must be a credible source of information for the item being sold. Cheryl Tiegs is an effective spokeswoman for Cover Girl, since her exuberant personality and beauty are compatible with the Cover Girl message of clean makeup aimed at young women. By contrast, sophisticated actress Ann Blyth is less effective in her advertisements for Hostess cupcakes. Celebrity advertisements are ineffective where there is no reasonable relationship between the celebrity and the advertised product or service.

Millions of Americans are currently very sports- and celebrity-oriented. Therefore, there is opportunity for firms to profitably sponsor athletes or sporting events. However, such promotion should clearly be an adjunct to existing promotional programs. There are several principles that corporate sponsors should consider before getting involved. First, they must be selective and specific. A market target should be pinpointed and a sport or celebrity carefully matched to that target and objective. Second, sports interest trends should be followed carefully. Too often firms get involved without assessing the strength of the trend. Third, they must be original and look for a special focus. Is it possible to come up with a unique concept? Fourth, firms should analyze the result in the short and long term. Sponsorship is a business decision that should pay off in profits.

Retail Advertising

Retail advertising is all advertising by stores that sell goods or services directly to the consuming public. While accounting for a sizable portion of total annual advertising expenditures, retail advertising varies widely in its effectiveness. One study showed that consumers were often suspicious of retail price advertisements. Source, message, and shopping experience seemed to affect consumer attitudes toward these advertisements.[14]

[14]Joseph N. Fry and Gordon H. McDougall, "Consumer Appraisal of Retail Price Advertisements," *Journal of Marketing* (July 1974), pp. 64–67.

The basic problem is that advertising is often treated as a secondary activity in retail stores. Advertising agencies are rarely used. Instead, store managers are usually given the responsibility of advertising as an added task to be performed along with their normal functions. The basic step in correcting this deficiency is to give one individual both the responsibility and the authority for developing an effective retail advertising program.

Cooperative Advertising **Cooperative advertising** is a sharing of advertising costs between the retailer and the manufacturer or wholesaler. For example, Ocean Pacific Sportswear may pay 50 percent of the cost of a retail store's newspaper advertisement that features their line. Cooperative advertising resulted from the media practice of offering lower rates to local advertisers than to national advertisers. Later, cooperative advertising was seen as a method of improving dealer relations. From the retailer's viewpoint, it permits a store to secure advertising that it would not otherwise have.

Assessing the Effectiveness of an Advertisement

For many firms, advertising represents a major expenditure, so it is imperative to determine whether a chosen campaign is accomplishing its promotional objectives. The determination of advertising effectiveness, however, is one of the most difficult undertakings in marketing. It consists of two primary elements—pretesting and post-testing.[15]

Pretesting

Pretesting is the assessment of an advertisement's effectiveness before it is actually used. It includes a variety of evaluative methods. To test magazine advertisements, the Batten, Barton, Durstine & Osborn ad agency cuts ads out of advance copies of magazines then "strips in" the ads it wants to test. Interviewers later check the impact of the advertisements on readers who receive free copies of the revised magazine.

Another ad agency, McCann-Erickson, uses a *sales conviction test* to evaluate magazine advertisements. Interviewers ask heavy users of a particular item to pick which of two alternative advertisements would convince them to purchase it.

Potential radio and television advertisements are often screened by consumers who sit in a studio and press two buttons—one for a positive

[15]See David Ogilvy and Joel Raphaelson, "Research on Advertising Techniques that Work—And Don't Work," *Harvard Business Review* (July–August 1982), pp. 14–15ff.

reaction to the commercial, the other for a negative one. Sometimes, proposed ad copy is printed on a postcard that also offers a free product; the number of cards returned is viewed as an indication of the copy's effectiveness. *Blind product tests* are also often used. In these tests, people are asked to select unidentified products on the basis of available advertising copy. Mechanical means of assessing how people read advertising copy are yet another method. One mechanical test uses an eye camera to photograph how people read ads: its results help determine headline placement and advertising copy length.

Post-testing

Post-testing is the assessment of advertising copy after it has been used. Pretesting is generally a more desirable testing method than post-testing because of its potential cost savings. However, post-testing can be helpful in planning future advertisements and in adjusting current advertising programs.

In one of the most popular post-tests, the *Starch Readership Report,* interviewers ask people who have read selected magazines whether they have read various ads in them. A copy of the magazine is used as an interviewing aid, and each interviewer starts at a different point in the magazine. For larger ads, respondents are also asked about specifics, such as headlines and copy. All readership, or recognition, tests assume that future sales are related to advertising readership.

Unaided recall tests are another method of post-testing advertisements. Here, respondents are not given copies of the magazine but must recall the ads from memory. Interviewers for the Gallup and Robinson market-research firms require people to prove they have read a magazine by recalling one or more of its feature articles. The people who remember particular articles are given cards with the names of products advertised in the issue. They then list the ads they remember and explain what they remember about them. Finally, the respondents are asked about their potential purchase of the product. A readership test concludes the Gallup and Robinson interview. Burke Research Corporation uses telephone interviews the day after a commercial appears on television in order to test brand recognition and the effectiveness of the advertisement.

Inquiry tests are another popular post-test. Advertisements sometimes offer a gift, generally a sample of the product, to people who respond to the advertisement. The number of inquiries relative to the cost of the advertisement is used as a measure of effectiveness. *Split runs* allow advertisers to test two or more ads at the same time. Under this method a publication's production run is split in two; half the magazines use Advertisement A, and half use Advertisement B. The relative pull of the alternatives is then determined by inquiries.

Regardless of the exact method used, marketers must realize that pretesting and post-testing are expensive, and they must, therefore, plan to use them as effectively as possible.

Sales Promotion Methods

The second type of nonpersonal selling is sales promotion. **Sales promotion** may be defined as those marketing activities, other than personal selling, advertising, and publicity, that stimulate consumer purchasing and dealer effectiveness. It includes such activities as displays, shows and exhibitions, demonstrations, and various nonrecurrent promotional efforts not in the ordinary routine.[16]

Sales promotional techniques may be used by all members of a marketing channel: manufacturers, wholesalers, and retailers. In addition, sales promotional activities are typically targeted at specific markets. For example, a manufacturer such as Texize Corporation might use trial sample mailings of a new spot remover to consumers and a sales contest for wholesalers and retailers who handle the new product. In both instances, the sales promotion techniques are designed to supplement and extend the other elements of the firm's promotional mix.

Firms that wish to use sales promotion can choose from various methods—point-of-purchase advertising, specialty advertising, trade shows, samples, coupons and premiums, contests, and trading stamps. More than one of these options may be used in a single promotional strategy, but probably no promotional strategy has ever used all of the options in a single program. While they are not mutually exclusive, promotions are generally employed on a selective basis.

Point-of-Purchase Advertising

Point-of-purchase advertising refers to displays and other promotions located near where a buying decision is actually made. The in-store promotion of consumer goods is a common example. Such advertising can be useful in supplementing a theme developed in another area of promotional strategy. A life-size display of a celebrity used in television advertising could be a very effective in-store display. Another example is the L'eggs store displays that completely altered the pantyhose industry.

[16]Committee on Definitions, *Marketing Definitions: A Glossary of Marketing Terms* (Chicago: American Marketing Association, 1960), p. 20.

Specialty Advertising

Specialty advertising is a sales promotion medium that utilizes useful articles carrying the advertiser's name, address, and advertising message to reach the target consumers. The origin of specialty advertising has been traced to the Middle Ages, when wooden pegs bearing the names of artisans "were given to prospects to be driven into their walls and to serve as a convenient place upon which to hang armor."[17]

Examples of contemporary advertising specialties carrying the firm's name include ashtrays, balloons, calendars, coffee mugs, key rings, matchbooks, pens, personalized business gifts of modest value, pocket secretaries, shopping bags, memo pads, paperweights, glasses, yardsticks, and hundreds of other items.

Advertising specialties help reinforce previous or future advertising and sales messages. An A.C. Nielsen survey found that both the general public and business were more likely to purchase from firms using specialty advertising.[18]

When Gulf Metals Industries added aluminum and copper bits to its vast selection of products, the sales department sought an effective way to bring the new products to the attention of purchasing agents in the foundry industry. The challenge was to highlight the bits, thus allowing them to stand out from the rest of the company's products—as well as those of competitors—during the introduction period. The sales department turned to specialty advertising to accomplish their mission.

Playing on the idea of "two bits," Gulf Metals embedded two clusters of the new copper and aluminum bits alongside a quarter in a clear paperweight. The highly distinctive gift-reminders were delivered either in person by salespeople or through the mail. Once in the purchasing agents' offices, these conversation piece specialities reminded the recipients again and again of the Gulf Metals sales message. An entire year's production capacity of the new metal bits was sold during the first two months of the campaign.

Trade Shows

To influence channel members and resellers in the distribution channel, it has become a common practice for sellers to participate in *trade shows.* These shows are often organized by an industry's trade association and may be part of the association's annual meeting or convention. Vendors serving the industry are invited to the show to display and demonstrate their products for the association's membership. An example is the professional meetings attended by college professors in a given discipline. Here, the major textbook publishers exhibit their of-

[17]Walter A. Gaw, *Specialty Advertising* (Chicago: Specialty Advertising Association, 1970), p. 7.
[18]*Specialty Advertising Report,* second quarter 1979, pp. 1–2.

ferings to the channel members in their marketing system. Shows are also used to reach the ultimate consumer. Home and recreation shows, for instance, allow businesses to display and demonstrate home care, recreation, and other consumer products to the entire community.[19]

Samples, Coupons, and Premiums

The distribution of samples, coupons, and premiums is probably the best-known sales promotion technique. *Sampling* is the free distribution of a product in an attempt to obtain future sales. The distribution may be done on a door-to-door basis, by mail, via demonstrations, or by inclusion in packages containing other products. Sampling is especially useful in promoting new products.

Coupons offer a discount, usually some specified price reduction, on the next purchase of a product. They are redeemable at retail outlets, which receive a handling fee from the manufacturer. Mail, magazine, newspaper, and package insertions are the standard methods of distributing coupons.[20]

Premiums are items given free with the purchase of another product. They have proved effective in motivating consumers to try new products or different brands. Premiums should have some relationship with the purchased item. For example, the service department of an auto dealership might offer its customers ice scrapers. Premiums are also used to obtain direct mail purchases. The value of premium giveaways runs into billions of dollars each year.

Contests

Firms often sponsor contests to introduce new products and services and to attract additional customers. Contests, sweepstakes, and games offer substantial prizes in the form of cash or merchandise as an inducement to potential customers. When Allied Chemical introduced a new line of Anso nylon carpeting, a $25,000 "It's on the House" sweepstakes was used. Sweepstakes participants received entry forms at department stores, furniture stores, and carpet stores and were invited to inspect the new carpet line at the same time. Figure 20.10 is one of the advertisements used in the Allied Chemical sweepstakes.

In recent years, a number of court rulings and legal restrictions have placed limitations on the use of contests. As a result, firms contemplating the use of this promotional technique should use the services of a specialist.

[19]Thomas V. Bonoma, "Get More Out of Your Trade Shows," *Harvard Business Review* (January–February 1983), pp. 75–83.

[20]See David J. Reibstein and Phyllis A. Traver, "Factors Affecting Coupon Redemption Rates," *Journal of Marketing* (Fall 1982), pp. 102–113.

Figure 20.10 Use of a Sweepstakes to Introduce a New Product

Source: Reprinted by permission of Allied Chemical.

Trading Stamps

A sales promotion technique similar to premiums is *trading stamps*. Customers receive trading stamps with their purchases in various retail establishments. The stamps can be saved and exchanged for gifts, usually in special redemption centers operated by the trading-stamp company. The degree to which the consumer benefits by trading stamps depends on the relative value of the goods offered. Trading stamps originally appeared in the 1950s, and they have been distributed by such retailers as gasoline stations, grocery retailers, mail-order houses, and savings and loan associations. The extent of their usage seems to depend on factors such as relative price levels, location of redemption centers, and legal restrictions.

Public Relations

The previous chapter defined **public relations** as the firm's communications and relationships with its various publics, including customers, employees, stockholders, suppliers, the government, and the society in which it operates. Public relations efforts date back to 1889, when George Westinghouse hired two people to publicize the advantages of alternating current, thus countering the arguments for direct-current electricity.

Public relations still remains an efficient indirect communications channel for promoting products. For instance, After Six, the tuxedo manufacturer, once rushed a pair of size 42 trousers to Buddy Hackett via a commercial airliner. Hackett's own pants had been ruined, and he had five nights remaining in a Gaithersburg, Maryland, nightclub engagement. A hurried call to After Six put a company vice-president in action, and the trousers arrived a few hours later—without a bill. Buddy Hackett has voluntarily plugged After Six ever since the firm saved his act at Gaithersburg.[21]

The public relations program has broader objectives than the other aspects of promotional strategy. It is concerned with the prestige and image of all parts of the organization. Examples of nonmarketing-oriented public relations objectives are a company's attempt to gain favorable public opinion during a long strike and an open letter to Congress published in a newspaper during congressional debate on a bill affecting a particular industry. Although in some companies the public relations department is not an arm of the marketing division, the activities of the public relations department invariably have an impact on promotional strategy.

The Growing Importance of Public Relations

Public relations is now a $2 billion industry employing 123,000 people in both the nonprofit and profit-oriented sectors. There are approximately 1,200 public relations firms in the United States ranging in size

[21]Buddy Hackett's experience is described in Urban C. Lehner, "Tuxedo Firm Thrives by Promoting Apparel that Most Men Dislike," *The Wall Street Journal* (October 14, 1975), pp. 1, 21.

from Hill & Knowlton, with over 1,000 employees, to one-person operations. Only 49 of these agencies exceed $1 million in annual revenues.

Publicity The part of public relations that is most directly related to promoting a firm's products or services is publicity. **Publicity** can be defined as the nonpersonal stimulation of demand for a product, service, or organization by placing commercially significant news about it in a published medium or obtaining favorable presentation of it upon radio, television, or stage that is not paid for by an identified sponsor.[22] Since it is designed to familiarize the general public with the characteristics, services, and advantages of a product, service, or organization, publicity is an information activity of public relations. While the costs associated with it are minimal in comparison to other forms of promotion, publicity is not entirely cost-free. Publicity-related expenses include marketing personnel assigned to creating and submitting publicity releases, printing and mailing costs, and other related expense items.

Some publicity is used to promote a company's image or viewpoint, but a significant amount provides information about products, particularly new ones. Since many consumers accept information in a news story more readily than they accept it in an advertisement, publicity releases are often sent to media editors for possible inclusion in news stories. In some cases, the information in a publicity release about a new product or service provides valuable assistance to a newspaper or magazine writer, and information of this sort eventually is published.

Public relations is now considered to be in a period of major growth as a result of increased environmental pressure for better communication between industry and the public. Many top executives are becoming involved. Lee Iacocca's efforts to publicize the justification for federal loan guarantees for Chrysler Corporation are an illustration. A survey of 185 chief executives concluded that 92 percent of them spent more time on public relations now than they did five years ago. Nearly 40 percent of the respondents reported that public relations accounted for 25 to 50 percent of their time.[23]

Publicity releases are sometimes used to fill voids in a publication, and other times are used in regular features. In either case, publicity releases serve as a valuable supplement to advertising.

Some critics have asserted that the amount of publicity a product receives is directly related to the amount of advertising revenue the firm provides the publication. This is not the case at most respected

[22]Committee on Definitions, *Marketing Definitions: A Glossary of Marketing Terms* (Chicago: American Marketing Association, 1960), p. 18.

[23]Alvin P. Sanoff, "Image Makers Worry about their Own Images," *U.S. News & World Report* (August 13, 1979), pp. 57–59.

newspapers and magazines. Some years ago, a Greyhound executive was enraged at a cartoon appearing in a Chicago newspaper that told of a character having numerous problems on a bus trip. The executive threatened to cancel future advertising in the newspaper unless the cartoon strip was stopped or changed immediately. The newspaper's curt reply was, "One more such communication from you and the alternative of withdrawing your advertising will no longer rest with Greyhound."[24]

Today, public relations has to be considered an integral part of promotional strategy even though its basic objectives extend far beyond just attempting to influence the purchase of a particular good. Public relations programs—and especially publicity—make a significant contribution to the achievement of promotional goals.

Summary

Advertising, sales promotion, public relations, and publicity—the nonpersonal selling elements of promotion—are not twentieth century phenomena. Advertising, for instance, can trace its origin to very early times. Today, these elements of promotion have gained professional status and serve as vital aspects of most organizations, both profit and nonprofit.

Advertising, a nonpersonal sales presentation usually directed to a large number of potential customers, seeks to achieve communications goals rather than direct sales objectives. It strives to inform, persuade, and remind potential consumers of the product or service being promoted.

Advertising planning starts with effective research, which permits the development of a strategy. Tactical decisions about copy and scheduling are then made. Finally, advertisements are evaluated, and appropriate feedback is provided to management. There are six basic types of advertising: (1) informative product advertising, (2) persuasive product advertising, (3) reminder-oriented product advertising, (4) informative institutional advertising, (5) persuasive institutional advertising, and (6) reminder-oriented institutional advertising. One of the most vital decisions in developing an advertising strategy is the selection of the media to be employed.

The major tasks of advertising departments are advertising research, art, copywriting, media analysis, and sales promotion. Many advertisers use independent advertising agencies to provide the creativity and ob-

[24]Gene Harlan and Alan Scott, *Contemporary Public Relations: Principles and Cases* (Englewood Cliffs, N. J.: Prentice-Hall, 1955), p. 36.

jectivity missing in their own organizations and to reduce the cost of advertising. The final step in the advertising process is developing and preparing the advertisement.

The principal methods of sales promotion are point-of-purchase advertising, specialty advertising, trade shows, samples, coupons and premiums, contests, and trading stamps. Public relations and publicity also play major roles in developing promotional strategies.

Key Terms

advertising
positioning
product advertising
institutional advertising
advocacy advertising
advertising agency
comparative advertising
retail advertising
cooperative advertising
pretesting
post-testing
sales promotion
point-of-purchase advertising
specialty advertising
public relations
publicity

Review Questions

1. Explain the wide variation in advertising expenditures as a percentage of sales in the industries shown in Figure 20.1.
2. Trace the historical development of advertising.
3. Describe the primary objectives of advertising.
4. List and discuss the six basic types of advertising. Cite an example of each type.
5. Discuss the relationship between advertising and the product life cycle.
6. What are the advantages and disadvantages associated with using each of the advertising media?
7. Discuss the organization of the advertising function. Consider all the major activities associated with advertising.
8. Under what circumstances are celebrity spokespeople in advertising likely to be effective?
9. Why is retail advertising so important today? Relate cooperative advertising to the discussion of alternative promotional strategies in Chapter 19.
10. List and discuss the principal methods of sales promotion.

Discussion Questions and Exercises

1. Develop an argument favoring the use of comparative advertising by a marketer who is currently preparing an advertising plan. Make any assumptions necessary.

2. Review the changes in the relative importance of the various advertising media between 1950 and 1981. Suggest likely explanations for the changes that have occurred during the past three decades.
3. What specialty advertising would be appropriate for the following?
   a. An independent insurance agent
   b. A retail furniture store
   c. An interior decorator
   d. A local radio station
4. Cooperative advertising results in a sharing of advertising costs between the retailer and the manufacturer or vendor. From society's viewpoint, should this kind of advertising be prohibited on the grounds that it leads to manufacturer domination of the distribution channel? Defend your answer.
5. Sweden's business practices court ordered a U.S. advertising agency and its client, a Swedish insurance company, to stop using models identified in their commercials as other people. The court ruled that this practice misled buyers. Do you agree? Why or why not?

21

PERSONAL SELLING AND SALES MANAGEMENT

Chapter Objectives

1. To explain the factors affecting the importance of personal selling in the promotional mix.
2. To identify the three basic sales tasks.
3. To list the characteristics of successful salespersons.
4. To outline the steps in the sales process.
5. To describe the major problems faced by sales managers.
6. To list the functions of sales management.

"Excuse me, would you like to buy some Girl Scout Cookies?" With those familiar words, and a sugar-sweet smile, 10-year-old Markita Andrews makes selling a piece of cake. That's all it takes to crumble such tough cookies as *Sesame Street's* Big Bird and the president of IBM and to help make Markita a super salesperson. It's also what helps keep Girl Scouts U.S.A. probably the largest selling organization in the world, with nearly 2.2 million door-to-door salespeople.

Besides her smile, Markita uses an innocent style and forthright conviction to sell cookies. Practically without knowing it, the Manhattan junior scout practices some sophisticated marketing skills. During last winter's three-week annual cookie drive, she sold 2,640 boxes, topping her previous year's 2,256 total and keeping Markita New York's number one sales scout. (She's probably number one in the country, but national statistics aren't kept.)

Markita—super salesperson

Source: *Sales & Marketing Management* (May 17, 1982), p. 39. Reprinted by permission from *Sales and Marketing Management* magazine. Copyright 1982.

What can a 10-year-old know about selling? Plenty. Here are some examples:

Experience. "I've been selling since I was six."

Market Research. "I'm selling mostly in our apartment complex [on the Upper West Side]. There are nine buildings, and they're 30 stories high, with 400 apartments in each building."

Product Research. "We sell seven different kinds of cookies, and I've tried a box of every kind."

Market Statistics and Test Marketing. "Chocolate Mints are the best selling. This year we have a new cookie, Chocolate Chunks, which were second best."

Determination. "After four years, I sold cookies to Big Bird."

Job Satisfaction and Customer Relations. "I enjoy selling because I get to meet a lot of people, and I get to see the people from last year and the year before."

Impressive Success Rate. "Only 1 out of 1,100 people said no."

Markita's inherent selling abilities have attracted a lot of media attention, as well as cookie eaters. Last year *Boardroom Reports,* a business newsletter, heard of her talents and published a list of her prescribed selling hints. The Glyn Group, a New York City corporate filmmaker, read the story, and produced an eleven-minute sales motivation film featuring Markita. *The Cookie Kid,* distributed by Walt Disney's Training and Development Division, has been shown to sales forces of more than 100 companies, including Xerox and Avon.

Markita's enthusiastic sales philosophy contains good advice for any professional. "If you don't set a goal, then you'll probably say, 'I don't want to sell that many,' " she says. "If you set a goal, then you know exactly how many you want to sell. If I know how many I have to sell, then I work harder." On that note, she reveals next year's target: 3,000 boxes.[1]

The Conceptual Framework

Although Markita Andrews has never taken a course in personal selling, the Manhattan fifth grader performs the marketing functions of informing, reminding, and persuading potential customers with enthusiasm, skill, and perseverance. These qualities are also highly valued in professional salespeople.

Personal selling was defined in Chapter 19 as a seller's promotional presentations conducted on a person-to-person basis with the buyer. It is an inherent function of any enterprise. Accounting, engineering, personnel, production, and other organizational activities are useless unless the firm's product or service match the need of a client or customer. The 6 million salespeople currently employed full-time in the United States bear witness to selling's importance in the 1980s. While advertising expenses in the average firm may represent from 1 to 3 percent of total sales, selling expenses are likely to equal 10 to 15 percent of sales. In many firms, personal selling is the single largest marketing expense.

As Chapter 19 pointed out, personal selling is likely to be the primary component of a firm's promotional mix when consumers are concentrated geographically; when orders are large; when the products or services are expensive, technically complex, and require special handling; when trade-ins are involved; when channels are short; and when the number of potential consumers is relatively small. Table 21.1 sum-

[1]"Selling Is Child's Play," *Sales & Marketing Management* (May 17, 1982), pp. 38–39. Used by permission.

Table 21.1 Factors Affecting the Importance of Personal Selling in the Promotional Mix

	Personal Selling is likely to be more important when:	*Advertising* is likely to be more important when:
consumer is:	**geographically concentrated, relatively small numbers;**	geographically dispersed, relatively large numbers;
product is:	**expensive, technically complex, custom-made, special handling required, trade-ins frequently involved;**	inexpensive, simple to understand, standardized, no special handling, no trade-ins;
price is:	**relatively high;**	relatively low;
channels are:	**relatively short.**	relatively long.

marizes the factors influencing personal selling's importance in the overall promotional mix.

Selling has been a standard part of business for thousands of years. The earliest peddlers were traders who had some type of ownership interest in the goods they sold after manufacturing or importing them. In many cases, these people viewed selling as a secondary activity.

Selling later became a separate function. The peddlers of the eighteenth century sold to the farmers and settlers of the vast North American continent. In the nineteenth century, salespeople called "drummers" sold to both consumers and marketing intermediaries. These early sellers sometimes used questionable sales practices and techniques and earned an undesirable reputation for themselves and their firms. Some of this negative stereotype remains today.[2] For the most part, though, selling is far different from what it was in the early years.

Sales Tasks

The sales job has evolved into a professional occupation. Today's salesperson is more concerned with helping customers select the correct product to meet their needs than with simply selling whatever is available. Modern professional salespeople advise and assist customers in their purchase decisions. Where repeat purchases are common, the

[2]See Alan J. Dubinsky, "Perceptions of the Sales Job: How Students Compare with Industrial Salespeople," *Journal of the Academy of Marketing Science* (Fall 1981), pp. 352–367.

salesperson must be certain that the buyer's purchases are in his or her best interest or else no future sales will be made. The interests of the seller are tied to those of the buyer.

Not all selling activities are alike. While all sales activities assist the customer in some manner, the exact tasks that are performed vary from one position to another. Three basic sales tasks can be identified as (1) order processing, (2) creative selling, and (3) missionary sales.

These tasks can form the basis for a sales classification system. It should be observed, however, that most sales personnel do not fall into any single category. Instead, we often find salespersons performing all three tasks to a certain extent. A sales engineer for a computer firm may be doing 50 percent missionary sales, 45 percent creative selling, and 5 percent order processing. In other words, most sales jobs require their incumbents to engage in a variety of sales activities. However, most selling jobs are classified on the basis of the primary selling task that is performed. We shall examine each of these selling tasks.

Order Processing

Order processing is most often typified by selling at the wholesale and retail levels. Salespeople who handle this task must do the following:

1. *Identify customer needs.* For instance, a soft-drink route salesperson determines that a store which carries a normal inventory of 40 cases has only seven cases left in stock.
2. *Point out the need* to the customer. The route salesperson informs the store manager of the inventory situation.
3. *Complete (or write up) the order.* The store manager acknowledges the situation. The driver unloads 33 cases and the manager signs the delivery slip.

Order processing is part of most selling jobs and becomes the primary task where needs can be readily identified and are acknowledged by the customer. Selling life insurance is usually not simple order processing. However, one insurance company reported that during a period of civil unrest in Belfast, Northern Ireland, one of their representatives, Danny McNaughton, sold 208 new personal accident income-protection policies in a week. McNaughton averaged one sale every 12 minutes of his working day.[3] Apparently, the need for insurance was readily recognized in Belfast.

Creative Selling

When a considerable degree of analytical decision making on the part of the consumer is involved in purchasing a product, the salesperson must skillfully solicit an order from a prospect. To do so, **creative**

[3]Reported in "Sell, Sell, Sell," *The Wall Street Journal* (September 14, 1971), p. 1.

selling techniques must be used. New products often require a high degree of creative selling. The seller must make the buyer see the worth of the item. Creative selling may be the most demanding of the three tasks.

Missionary Sales

Missionary sales are an indirect type of selling; people sell the goodwill of a firm and provide the customers with technical or operational assistance. For example, a toiletries company salesperson may call on retailers to look after special promotions and overall stock movement, although a wholesaler is used to take orders and deliver merchandise. In more recent times, technical and operational assistance, such as that provided by a systems specialist, have also become a critical part of missionary selling.

Characteristics of Successful Salespeople

The saying "Salespeople are born, not made" is untrue. Most people have some degree of sales ability. Each of us is called upon to sell others his or her ideas, philosophy, or personality at some time. However, while some individuals adapt to selling more easily than others, selling is not an easy job; it involves a great deal of practice and hard work.

Effective salespersons are self-motivated individuals who are well prepared to meet the demands of the competitive marketplace. The continuing pressure to solve buyers' problems requires that salespeople develop good work habits and exhibit considerable initiative.

Successful sales representatives are not only self-starters, they are knowledgeable businesspersons. Sales personnel are also in the peculiar position of having their knowledge tested almost continually. Sales success is often a function of how well a salesperson can handle questions. Salespeople must know their company, products, competition, customers, and themselves.

Feedback: The Responsibility of Every Salesperson

There is one function that all sales personnel perform—providing sales intelligence to the marketing organization.[4] Chapter 19 noted that field sales reports are a part of the feedback generated within the marketing system. Since the sales force is close to the market, it is often the best

[4]Joel Saegert and Robert J. Hoover, "Sales Managers and Sales Force Feedback: Information Left in the Pipeline," *Journal of the Academy of Marketing Science* (Winter/Spring 1980), pp. 33–39.

It Isn't Just Selling Anymore

The term *salesperson* all too often conjures up unpleasant visions of Arthur Miller's antihero Willy Loman in *Death of a Salesman:*

You don't understand: Willy was a salesman . . . He don't put a bolt to a nut. He don't tell you the law or give you medicine. He's a man way out there in the blue, riding on a smile and a shoeshine. And when they start not smiling back—that's an earthquake.

But the tasks of the modern salesperson are so different and so complex. Take, for example, the case of Louis J. Manara, a superb salesperson employed by American Cyanamid in New Jersey. The changes that have occurred in Manara's job over tha past decade were depicted in a recent *Fortune* article as follows:

When Manara began selling chemicals for Cyanamid in 1971, the job was relatively straightforward. As in the days of Willy Loman, the salesman was assigned a territory—Manara's was the northeastern states—and dispatched to tap every possible customer. He was told little about his division's goals, nothing about the profitability of his bag of products. His marching orders were uncomplicated: sell all you can, as fast as you can.

Back then, most industrial salespersons succeeded by nurturing close personal relationships with the customers—always a company, usually represented by a poorly paid purchasing agent who was wooed with long lunches, evening entertainment, and golf or fishing weekends. If the purchasing agent proved recalcitrant, the salesperson could try the "back door" approach of going directly to end users of the product, such as plant managers. On days when calls were finished early, the salesperson might try his luck "smokestacking,"—that is, dropping in on potential customers whose factory smokestacks were spotted while driving down the highway.

But in the past decade the salesperson's job has become vastly more complex—so much so that a number of executives believe a new job title is required. "Salesman is just too narrow a word," says one marketing manager. Gordon Sterling, Manara's division president, pinpoints the basic change. "Ten years ago, it was sales, sales, sales," he says. "Now we tell our salespeople: don't just sell—we need information. What do our customers need? What is the competition doing? What sort of financial package do we need to win the order?"

The probing for market intelligence is not the only new duty. Manara also is expected to mediate disputes between Cyanamid's credit department, newly vigilant in these times of costly money, and slow-paying customers. He has to sort out customer complaints concerning Cyanamid products. He must keep abreast of fast changes in both government regulations and world chemical markets. "Ten years ago," he sighs, "we had back-up people to handle all this. But most of them have been let go. We have to be far better informed than we were then."

Source: Hugh D. Menzies, "The New Life of a Salesman," *Fortune* (August 11, 1980), p. 173. Reprinted by permission. Quote from Arthur Miller, *Death of a Salesman* (New York: Viking, 1949).

(and most reliable) source of current marketing information upon which management decisions are based.

The marketing intelligence provided by field sales personnel is copious and varied. Sales personnel can provide timely, current assessments of competitive efforts, new product launches, customer reactions, and the like. Marketing executives should nurture and implement this valuable information source.

The Sales Process

What then are the steps involved in selling? While the terminology may vary, most authorities agree on the following sequence: (1) prospecting and qualifying, (2) approach, (3) presentation, (4) demonstration, (5) handling objections, (6) closing, and (7) follow-up.

As Figure 21.1 indicates, the steps in the personal selling process follow the attention-interest-desire-action (AIDA) concept discussed in Chapter 19. Once a sales prospect has been qualified, an attempt is made to secure his or her attention. The presentation and demonstration steps are designed to generate interest and desire. Successful handling of buyer objections should further arouse desire, and action occurs at the close of the sale.

Prospecting and Qualifying

Prospecting, the identification of potential customers, is difficult work involving many hours of diligent effort.[5] Prospects may come from many sources: previous customers, friends and neighbors, other vendors, nonsales employees in the firm, suppliers, and social and professional contacts. New sales personnel often find prospecting frustrating, since there is usually no immediate payback. But without prospecting, there are no future sales. For example, in the marketing of various types of adhesive tapes for industrial use, a representative of a tape manufacturing company, perhaps a manufacters' agent, must seek out potential users of these specialty tapes. Prospecting is a continuous process because of loss of some customers over time, as well as the emergence of new potential customers or those who have never been contacted before. Many sales management experts consider prospecting to be the very essence of the sales process.

Qualifying—determining that the prospect is really a potential customer—is another important sales task. Not all prospects are qualified

[5]For an analysis of problems involved in identifying specific decision makers in an industrial setting, see Thomas V. Bonoma, "Major Sales: Who *Really* Does the Buying?" *Harvard Business Review* (May–June 1982), pp. 111–119.

Figure 21.1 The AIDA Concept and the Steps in the Personal Selling Process

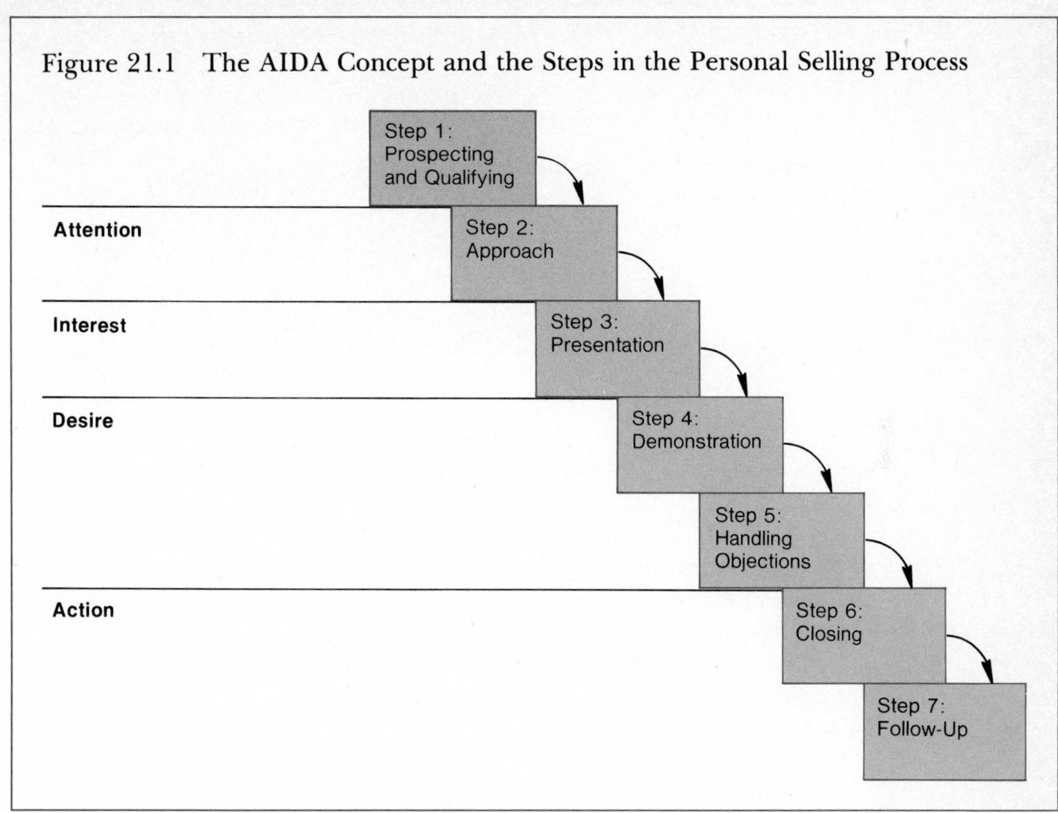

to become customers. Qualified customers are people with both money and the authority to make purchase decisions. A person with an annual income of $15,000 may wish to own a $75,000 house, but this person's ability to actually become a customer has to be questioned. Similarly, a parent with six children may strongly desire a two-seater sports car, but this would probably not be a practical purchase as the sole family vehicle.

Approach

Once the salesperson has identified a qualified prospect, he or she collects all available information relative to the potential buyer and plans an **approach**—the initial contact of the salesperson with the prospective customer. Figure 21.2 suggests that the relative aggressiveness of a sales approach usually varies inversely with the repeat-sale potential of the prospect. In other words, the lower the repeat-sale potential, the harder the approach may be and vice versa. All approaches should be based on comprehensive research. The salesperson should find out as much

Figure 21.2 The Sales Aggression Spectrum

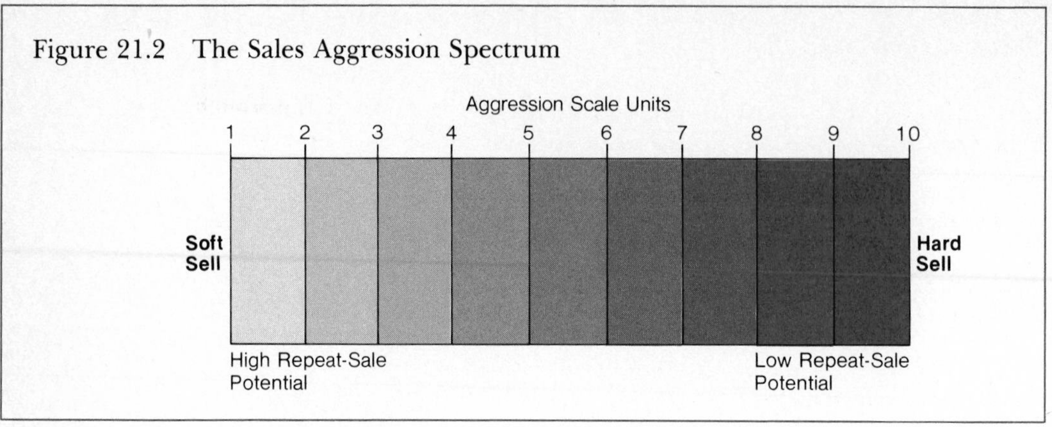

Source: Adapted from Barry J. Hersker, "The Ecology of Personal Selling," *Southern Journal of Business* (July 1970), p. 44. Reprinted by permission.

as possible about the prospect. Retail salespeople often cannot do this, but they can compensate by asking leading questions to learn more about the prospect's purchase preferences. Industrial marketers have far more data available, and they should make use of it before scheduling the first interview.

Presentation

When the salesperson gives the sales message to a prospective customer, he or she makes a **presentation.** The seller describes the product's major features, points out its strengths, and concludes by citing illustrative successes. The seller's objective is to talk about the product or service in terms meaningful to the buyer—benefits, rather than technical specifications. Thus the presentation is the stage where the salesperson relates product features to customer needs.

The presentation should be clear and concise, and it should emphasize the positive. In an attempt to increase its 18 percent share of the $1.2 billion retail market for vinyl floor covering, Mannington Mills decided to assist retail salespeople by installing an electronic salesperson who would be responsible for the initial stages of the sales presentation. The Mannington computer salesperson emits beeps to entice curious store shoppers, then asks them eight questions about their room decor, color preference, and needs. After digesting the responses, it displays style numbers of between three and ten appropriate Mannington patterns. The real-life salesperson and the customer are spared the task of searching through over 200 samples of Mannington vinyl on display. The electronic salesperson has proven satisfactory, both to Mannington marketers, who are attempting to compete with such giants as Armstrong World Industries and Congoleum, and to retail managers. By 1984, 2,000 Mannington electronic salespeople are expected to be placed in retail outlets.[6]

This approach to sales presentations is called the **canned approach,** and it was originally developed by John H. Patterson of National Cash Register Company during the late 1800s. This is a memorized sales talk used to ensure uniform coverage of the points deemed important by management. While canned presentations are still used in such areas as door-to-door *cold canvassing,* most professional sales forces have long since abandoned their use.[7] The prevailing attitude is that flexible presentations allow the salesperson to account for motivational differences among prospects. Proper planning, of course, is an important part of tailoring a presentation to each particular customer.

Demonstration

Demonstrations can play a critical role in a sales presentation. A demonstration ride in a new automobile allows the prospect to become involved in the presentation. It awakens customer interest in a manner that no amount of verbal presentation can achieve. Demonstrations supplement, support, and reinforce what the sales representative has already told the prospect. The key to a good demonstration is planning. A unique demonstration is more likely to gain a customer's attention than a typical sales presentation. A demonstration must be well planned and executed if a favorable impression is to be made. One cannot overemphasize that the salesperson should check and recheck all aspects of the demonstration prior to its delivery.

Handling Objections

A vital part of selling involves handling objections. It is reasonable to expect a customer to say, "Well, I really should check with my family," or "Perhaps I'll stop back next week," or "I like everything except the color." A good salesperson, however, should use each objection as a cue to provide additional information to the prospect. In most cases an objection, such as "I don't like the bucket seats," is really a prospect's way of asking what other choices or product features are available. A customer's question reveals an interest in the product. It gives the seller an opportunity to expand a presentation by providing additional information.

[6]Bill Abrams, "Firms Start Using Computers to Take the Place of Salesmen," *The Wall Street Journal* (July 15, 1982), p. 27.

[7]*Cold canvassing* refers to unsolicited sales calls upon a random group of people; that is, the prospecting and qualifying effort is minimal.

Closing

The moment of truth in selling is the **closing,** for this is when the salesperson asks the prospect for an order. A sales representative should not hesitate during the closing. If he or she has made an effective presentation, based on applying the product to the customer's needs, the closing should be the natural conclusion.

A surprising number of sales personnel have difficulty in actually asking for an order. To be effective they must overcome this difficulty. Methods of closing a sale include the following:

1. The *alternative-decision technique* poses choices to a prospect where either alternative is favorable to the salesperson. "Will you take this sweater or that one?"
2. The *SRO (standing room only) technique* is used when a prospect is told that a sales agreement should be concluded now, because the product may not be available later.
3. *Emotional closes* attempt to get a person to buy through appeal to such factors as fear, pride, romance, or social acceptance.
4. *Silence* can be used as a closing technique since a discontinuance of a sales presentation forces the prospect to take some type of action (either positive or negative).
5. *Extra-inducement closes* are special incentives designed to motivate a favorable buyer response. Extra inducements may include quantity discounts, special servicing arrangements, or a layaway option.[8]

Follow-up

The post-sales activities that often determine whether a person will become a repeat customer constitute the sales **follow-up.** To the maximum extent possible, representatives should contact their customers to find out if they are satisfied with their purchases. This step allows the salesperson to reinforce psychologically the person's original decision to buy. It gives the seller an opportunity, in addition to correcting any sources of discontent with the purchase, to secure important market information and to make additional sales. Automobile dealers often keep elaborate records of their previous customers so that they can promote new models to individuals who have already shown a willingness to buy from them. One successful travel agency never fails to telephone customers upon their return from a trip. Proper follow-up is a logical part of the selling sequence.

Effective follow-up also means that the salesperson should conduct a critical review of every call that is made. One should ask, "What was it

[8]These and other closing techniques are outlined in David L. Kurtz, Robert Dodge, and Jay E. Klompmaker, *Professional Selling*, 3rd ed. (Dallas, Tex.: Business Publications, 1982), pp. 221–228.

that allowed me to close that sale?" or "What caused me to lose that sale?" Such continual review results in significant sales dividends.

Retail Selling

For the most part, the public is more aware of retail selling than of any other form of personal selling. In fact, many writers have argued that a person's basic attitude toward the sales function is determined by his or her impression of retail sales personnel.

Retail selling has some distinctive features that require its consideration as a separate subject. The most significant difference between it and its counterparts is that the customer comes to the retail salesperson. This requires that retailers effectively combine selling with a good advertising and sales promotion program that draws the customer into the store. Another difference is that while store employees are sales personnel in one sense, they are also retailers in the broader dimension. Selling is not their only responsibility.

Retail sales personnel should be well versed in store policy and procedures. Credit, discounts, special sales, delivery, layaway, and return policies are examples of the type of information that the salesperson should know. One of the major complaints voiced by today's customer concerns uninformed sales personnel.

The area of retail selling exhibiting the greatest potential for improvement is the greeting. The standard "May I help you?" seems totally out of place in contemporary marketing, and yet it is interesting to observe the number of retail salespeople who still use this outdated approach. "May I help you?" invites customer rejection in the form of the standard reply, "No thanks, I'm just looking." A better method is to use a merchandise-oriented greeting such as "The fashion magazines say that this will be the most popular color this fall." The positive approach helps to orient the customer toward the merchandise or display.

Two selling techniques particularly applicable to retailing are selling up and suggestion selling. **Selling up** is the technique of convincing the customer to buy a higher-priced item than he or she originally intended. An automobile salesperson may convince a customer to buy a more expensive model than the person intended to buy. An important point is that the practice of selling up should always be used within the constraints of the customer's real needs. If the salesperson sells the customer something that he or she really does not need, the potential for repeat sales by that seller is substantially diminished.

Suggestion selling seeks to broaden the customer's original purchase with related items, special promotions, and/or holiday and seasonal merchandise. Here, too, suggestion selling should be based upon the idea of helping the customer recognize true needs rather than selling

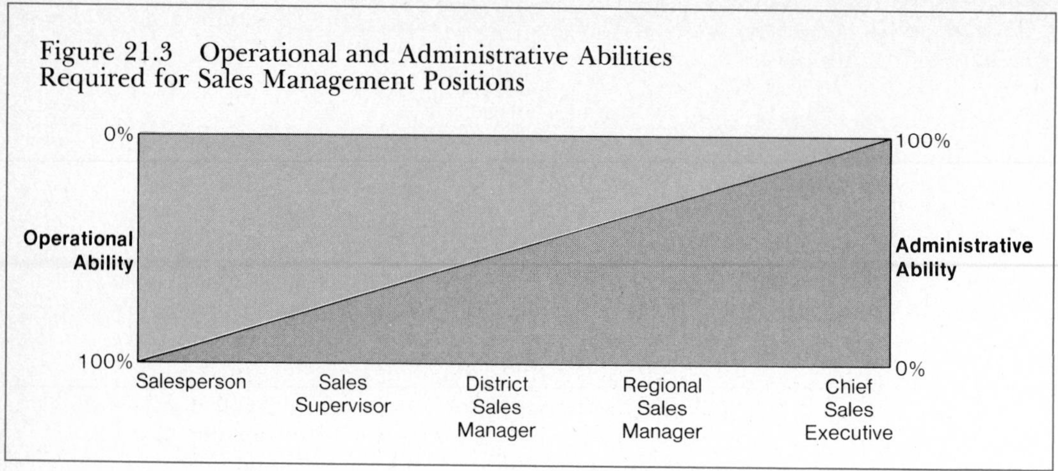

Figure 21.3 Operational and Administrative Abilities Required for Sales Management Positions

Source: Thomas R. Wotruba, *Sales Management: Planning, Accomplishment and Evaluation* (New York: Holt, Rinehart and Winston, 1971). Reprinted by permission of the author.

the person unwanted merchandise. Suggestion selling is one of the best methods of increasing retail sales and should be practiced by all sales personnel.

Managing the Sales Effort

Contemporary selling requires that **sales management** effort be exerted in the direction of securing, maintaining, motivating, supervising, evaluating, and controlling an effective field sales force. The sales manager links the salespeople, customers and prospects, and the firm's management. The sales manager has professional responsibilities in both directions. Most sales management jobs require some degree of both operational (or sales-oriented) ability and administrative (or managerial) ability. The higher one rises in the sales management hierarchy, the more administrative ability and the less operational ability is required to perform the job. Figure 21.3 diagrams this relationship.

Problems Faced by Sales Management

Sales executives face a variety of management problems. However, with few exceptions, these problems have remained largely the same over the years. Poor utilization of time and failure to plan sales effort were reported as the leading problems in both the 1959 and the 1979 surveys cited in Table 21.2. Other current major problem areas include inadequate sales training and wasted time.

Table 21.2 Major Sales Management Problems: A 20-Year Perspective

Problem Area	1979 Ranking	1959 Ranking
Poor utilization of time and failure to plan sales effort	1	1
Inadequacy in sales training	2	21
Wasted time in office by salespeople	3	6
Too few sales calls during hours	4	3
Inability to overcome objections	5	5
Indifferent follow-up	6	7
Lack of sales creativity	7	2
Meeting competitive pricing	8	15
Lack of sales drive and motivation	9	8
Recruiting and selecting personnel	10	11

Source: "Significant Trends," *Sales & Marketing Management* (October 15, 1979), p. 102. Reprinted by permission from *Sales & Marketing Management.* Copyright 1979.

Sales Management: Functions

Sales management is the administrative channel for sales personnel; it links the individual salespersons to general management. The sales manager performs seven basic managerial functions: (1) recruitment and selection, (2) training, (3) organization, (4) supervision, (5) motivation, (6) compensation, and (7) evaluation and control.

Recruitment and Selection

The initial step in building an effective sales force involves recruiting and selecting qualified personnel. Sources of new salespeople include community colleges, trade and business schools, colleges and universities, sales personnel in other firms, people currently employed in nonsales occupations, and a company's own nonsales employees.

Not all of these areas are equally productive. One of the problem areas seems to be the reluctance of high school guidance counselors to convey the advantages of a selling career to students. A successful career in sales offers satisfaction in all the five areas that a person generally looks for when deciding on a profession:

1. *Opportunity for advancement.* Studies have shown that successful sales representatives advance rapidly in most companies. Advancement can come either within the sales organization or laterally to a more responsible position in some other functional area of the firm.
2. *High earnings.* The earnings of successful salespersons compare favorably to the earnings of successful people in other professions. As Figure 21.4 indicates, the average senior salespersons now earns more than $30,000 per year.

Figure 21.4 Salespeople's Annual Compensation

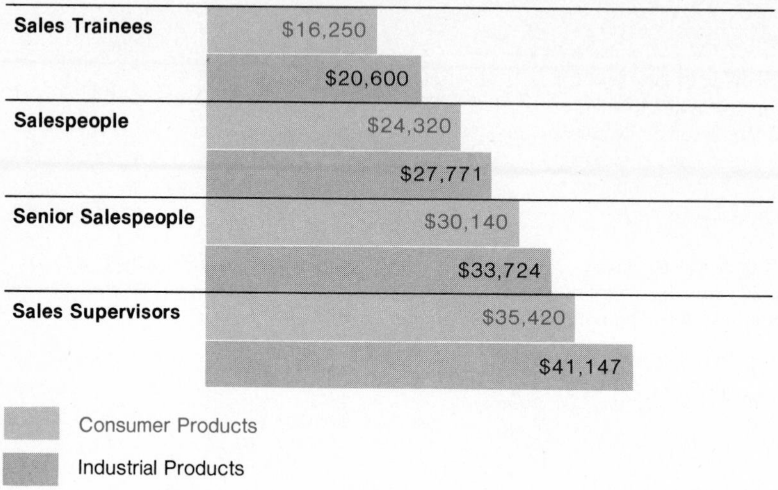

	Consumer Products	Industrial Products
Sales Trainees	$16,250	$20,600
Salespeople	$24,320	$27,771
Senior Salespeople	$30,140	$33,724
Sales Supervisors	$35,420	$41,147

Source: *Executive Compensation Service* (New York: American Management Association, 1981). Reported in *Sales & Marketing Management* (February 22, 1982), p. 70.

3. *Personal satisfaction.* One derives satisfaction in sales from achieving success in a competitive environment and from helping people satisfy their wants and needs.
4. *Security.* Contrary to what many students believe, selling provides a high degree of job security. Experience has shown that economic downturns affect personnel in sales less than those in most other employment areas. In addition, there is a continuing need for good sales personnel.
5. *Independence and variety.* Most often salespersons really operate as "independent" businesspeople or as managers of sales territories. Their work is quite varied and provides an opportunity for involvement in numerous business functions.

The careful selection of salespeople is important for two reasons. First, it involves substantial amounts of money and management time. Second, selection mistakes will be detrimental to customer relations and sales force performance, as well as costly to correct.

The selection process for sales personnel is outlined in Figure 21.5. An application screening is followed by an initial interview. If there is sufficient interest, in-depth interviewing is conducted. Next, the company may use testing in their procedure. This step could include aptitude, intelligence, interest, knowledge, or personality tests. References

Figure 21.5 Steps in the Sales Personnel Selection Process

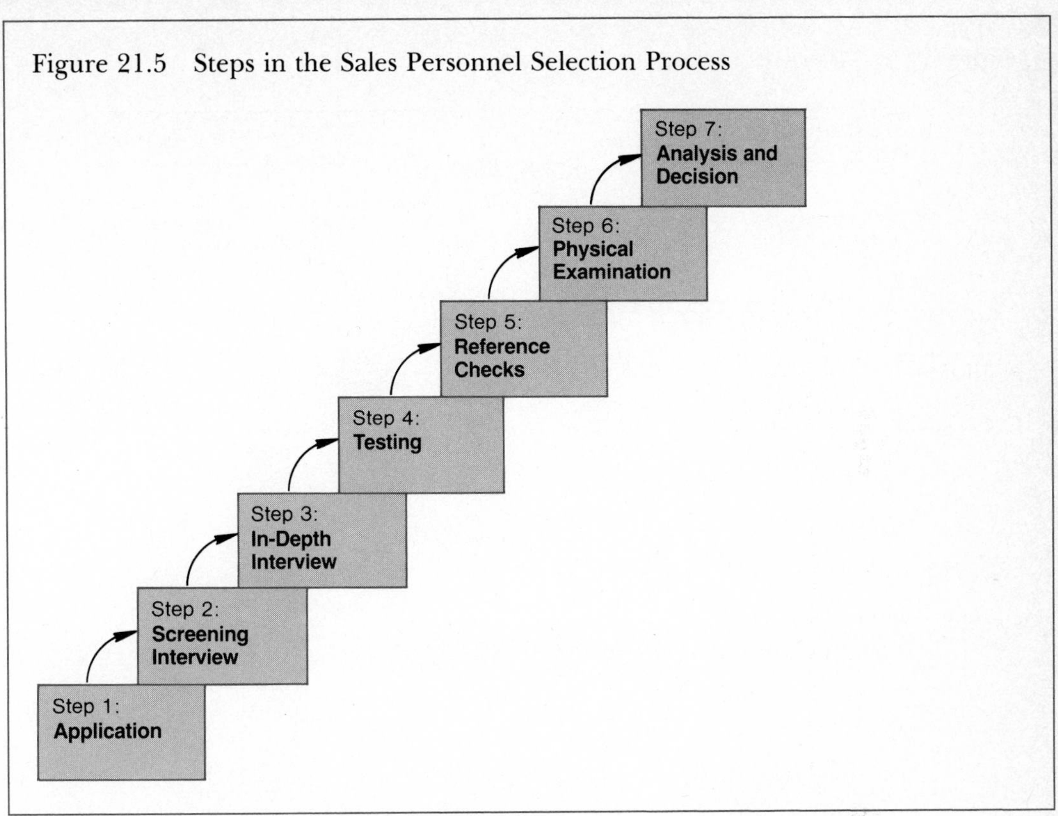

are then checked to guarantee that job candidates have represented themselves correctly. A physical examination is usually included before a final hiring decision is made.[9]

Training

To shape new sales recruits into an efficient sales organization, management must conduct an effective training program. The principal methods used in sales training are lectures, role playing, and on-the-job training.

Sales training is also important for veteran salespeople. Most of this type of training is done in an informal manner by sales managers. A standard format is for the sales manager to travel with a field sales

[9]See Wesley J. Johnston and Martha Cooper, "Industrial Sales Force Selection: Current Knowledge and Needed Research," *Journal of Personal Selling & Sales Management* (Spring/Summer 1981), pp. 49–57.

Figure 21.6 Basic Approaches to Organizing the Sales Force

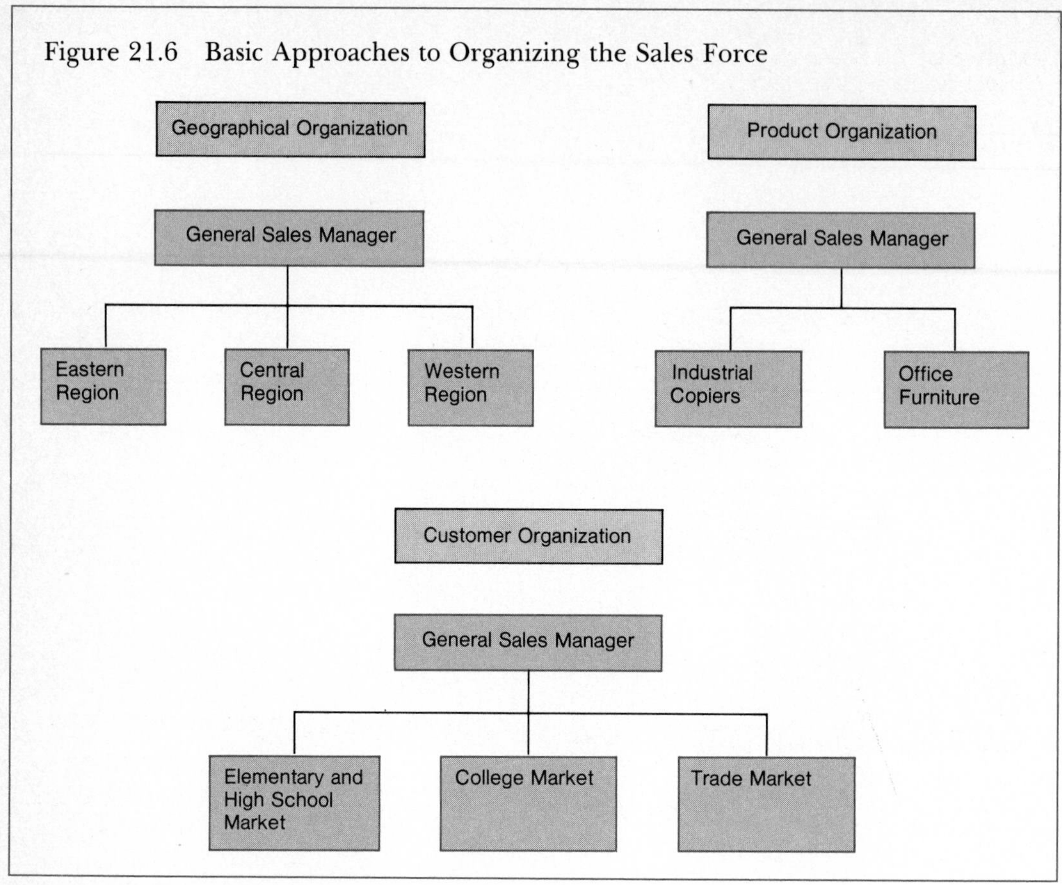

representative periodically, then compose a critique of the person's work afterward. Sales meetings are also an important part of training for experienced personnel.

Organization

Sales managers are responsible for the organization of the field sales force. General organizational alignments, which are usually made by top marketing management, can be based upon geography, products, types of customers, or some combination of these factors. Figure 21.6 presents simplified organization charts showing these alignments.

A product sales organization would have specialized sales forces for each major category of products offered by the firm. A customer organization would use different sales forces for each major type of customer served. For instance, a plastics manufacturer selling to the auto-

Figure 21.7 Relationship between Amount of Supervision and Organization Performance

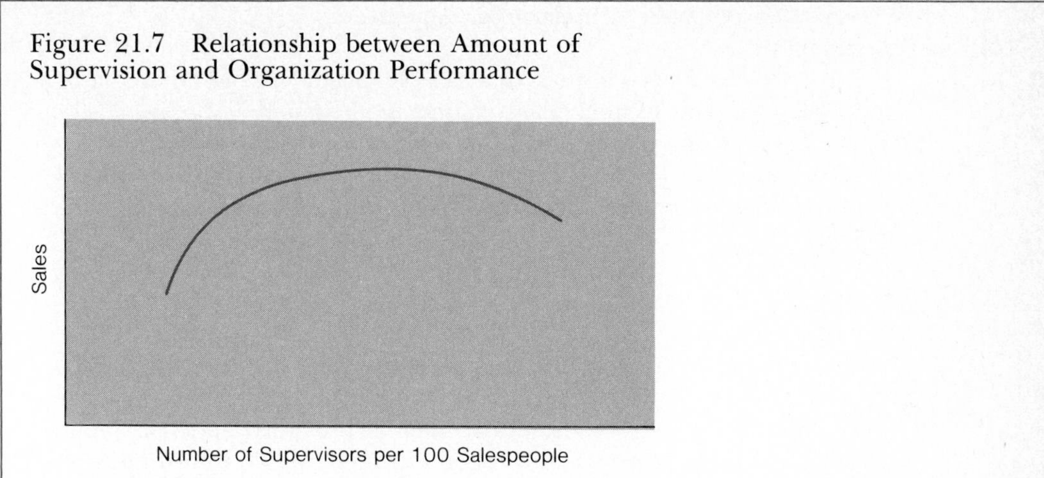

Source: *Management of the Personal Selling Function* by Charles S. Goodman. Copyright © 1971 by Holt, Rinehart and Winston, Inc. Reprinted by permission of Holt, Rinehart and Winston.

mobile, small appliance, and defense industries might decide that each type of customer requires a separate sales force.

The individual sales manager then has the task of organizing the sales territories within his or her area of responsibility. Generally, the territory allocation decision should be based upon company objectives, personnel qualifications, workload considerations, and territory potential.[10]

Supervision

A source of constant debate among sales managers is the supervision of the sales force. It is impossible to pinpoint the exact amount of supervision that is correct in each situation since this varies with the individuals involved. However, there is probably a curvilinear relationship between the amount of supervision and organizational performance (see Figure 21.7). The amount of supervision input increases sales output to some point, after which additional supervision tends to retard further sales growth.

The key to effective supervision is clear communications with the sales force. This, of course, involves effective listening on the part of the sales manager. Sales personnel who clearly understand messages from management and who have an opportunity to express their con-

[10]Territory decisions are discussed in Michael S. Hershel, "Effective Sales Territory Development," *Journal of Marketing* (April 1977), pp. 39–43.

cerns and opinions to their supervisors are usually easier to supervise and motivate.

In fact, it has been argued that sales management has entered a new era with emphasis being placed upon total human resource development. All personnel should be developed to their full abilities. One writer states, "In the long run, the total development approach may be desirable not only for humanistic reasons but also from a profit standpoint."[11]

Motivation

The sales manager's responsibility for motivating the sales force cannot be glossed over lightly.[12] Because the sales process is a problem-solving one, it often leads to considerable mental pressures and frustrations. Sales are often achieved only after repeated calls on customers and may, especially with new customers and complex technical products, occur over long periods of time. Motivation of salespeople usually takes the form of debriefing, information-sharing, and both psychological and financial encouragement. Appeal to emotional needs, such as ego needs, recognition, and peer acceptance, are examples of psychological encouragement. Monetary rewards and fringe benefits, such as club memberships and paid travel arrangements, appeal as financial incentives.

Compensation

Since monetary rewards are an important factor in motivating subordinates, compensating sales personnel is a critical matter to managers.[13] Basically, sales compensation can be determined on a straight salary plan, a commission plan, or some combination.[14]

A **commission** is a payment directly tied to the sales or profits achieved by a salesperson. For example, a salesperson might receive a 5 percent commission on all sales up to a specified quota, then 7 percent on sales beyond the quota. Commissions provide a maximum selling incentive but may cause the sales force to shortchange nonselling

[11]Leslie M. Dawson, "Toward A New Concept of Sales Management" *Journal of Marketing* (April 1970), p. 38.

[12]See Richard C. Becherer, Fred W. Morgan, and Lawrence M. Richard, "The Job Characteristics of Industrial Salespersons: Relationship to Motivation and Satisfaction," *Journal of Marketing* (Fall 1982), pp. 125–135; and Panos Apostolides, "Looking at the Age of Salespersons," *Journal of the Academy of Marketing Science* (Fall 1980), pp. 322–331.

[13]An interesting discussion appears in Gilbert A. Churchill, Jr., Neil M. Ford, and Orville C. Walker, Jr., "Personal Characteristics of Salespeople and the Attractiveness of Alternative Rewards," *Journal of Business Research* (vol. 7, 1979), pp. 25–50.

[14]Source: John P. Steinbrink, "How to Pay Your Sales Force," *Harvard Business Review* (July–August 1978), p. 113.

activities, such as completing sales reports, delivering sales promotion materials, and normal account servicing.

A **salary** is a fixed payment made on a periodic basis to employees, including some sales personnel. A firm that has decided to use salaries rather than commissions might pay a salesperson a set amount every week, for example. There are benefits of using salaries for both management and sales personnel. A straight salary plan allows management to have more control over how sales personnel allocate their efforts, but it reduces the incentive to expand sales. As a result, compensation programs combining features of both salary and commission plans have been accepted in many industries.

Evaluation and Control

Perhaps the most difficult of the tasks required of sales managers are evaluation and control. The basic problems are setting standards and finding an instrument to measure sales performance. Sales volume, profitability, and investment return are the usual means of evaluating sales effectiveness. They typically involve the use of a **sales quota**—a specified sales or profit target a salesperson is expected to achieve. A particular sales representative might be expected to sell $300,000 in Territory 414 during a given year, for example. In many cases, the quota is tied to the compensation system.

Regardless of the key elements in the program for evaluating salespeople, the sales manager needs to follow a formal system of decision rules.[15] The purpose of this system is to supply information to the sales manager for action.

What the sales manager needs to know are the answers to three general questions. First, what are the rankings of the salesperson's performance relative to the predetermined standards? In determining this ranking, full consideration should be given to the effect of uncontrollable variables on sales performance. Preferably each adjusted ranking should be stated in terms of a percentage of the standard. This simplifies evaluation and makes conversion of the various rankings into a composite index of performance easy.

Second, what are the strong points of the salesperson? One way to answer this question is to list areas of the salesperson's performance where he or she has surpassed the respective standard. Another way is to categorize a salesperson's strong points in three aspects of the work environment.

1. *Task* or the technical ability of the salesperson. This is manifested in knowledge of the product (end uses), customer, and company, as well as selling skills.

[15]This section is adapted from H. Robert Dodge, *Field Sales Management* (Dallas, Tex.: Business Publications, Inc., 1973), pp. 337–338.

Figure 21.8 Performance Evaluation Summary

Name: J. D. Jeffries
Territory: Northern Virginia
Time period covered: 1st Quarter 1984

Salesperson's Ability	
Strong points	1. Has extensive product knowledge, knows end uses. 2. Keeps up to date on company pricing policies.
Weaknesses	1. Does not have in-depth knowledge of customer requirements.
Selling Proficiency	
Strong points	1. Exceeded by 20 percent the standard for sales/call. 2. Exceeded by 12 percent the standard for sales calls/day. 3. Exceeded by 8 percent the standard for invoice lines/order.
Weaknesses	1. Overspending of expense monies (14 percent). 2. Overaggressive in selling tactics.
Sales Results	
Strong points	1. Exceeded sales quota by 3 percent. 2. Exceeded new account quota by 6 percent.
Weaknesses	1. Turnover of customers amounted to 5 percent. 2. Repeated delay in report submission.

Source: H. Robert Dodge, *Field Sales Management* (Plano, Tex.: Business Publications, Inc., 1973), pp. 337–338.

2. *Process* or the sequence of work flow. This pertains to the actual sales transaction—the salesperson's application of technical ability and interaction with customers. Personal observation is frequently used for measuring process performance. Other measures are sales calls, expenses, and invoice lines.
3. *Goal* or end results or output of sales performance. Usually this aspect of the salesperson's work environment is stated in terms of sales volume and profits.

The third and final question is, what are the weaknesses or negatives in the performance of the salesperson in question? These should be listed or categorized as much as the salesperson's strong points. An evaluation summary for a hypothetical salesperson appears in Figure 21.8.

In making the evaluation summary the sales manager should follow a set procedure.

1. Each aspect of sales performance for which there is a standard should be measured separately. This helps to avoid the halo effect, whereby the rating given on one aspect is carried over to other aspects.

2. Each salesperson should be judged on the basis of actual sales performance rather than potential ability. This emphasizes the importance of rankings in evaluation.
3. Each salesperson should be judged on the basis of sales performance for the entire period under consideration rather than particular incidents. The sales manager as the rater should avoid reliance on isolated examples of the salesperson's prowess or failure.
4. Each salesperson's evaluation should be reviewed for completeness and evidence of possible bias. Ideally this review should be made by the immediate superior of the sales manager.

While the evaluation step includes both revision and correction, the attention of the sales manager must necessarily focus on correction. This is defined as the adjustment of actual performance to predetermined standards. Corrective action with its obvious negative connotations poses a substantial challenge to the typical sales manager.

Summary

Personal selling is the seller's promotional presentation conducted on a person-to-person basis with the buyer. It is inherent in all business enterprises. The earliest sellers were known as peddlers, and some of the negative stereotyping associated with them remains today.

Three basic selling tasks exist: order processing, creative selling, and missionary selling. The successful salesperson is self-motivated and prepared to meet the demands of the competitive marketplace.

The basic steps involved in selling are: (1) prospecting and qualifying, (2) approach, (3) presentation, (4) demonstration, (5) handling of objections, (6) closing, and (7) follow-up.

Retail selling is different from other kinds of selling, primarily because the customer comes to the salesperson. Also, salespeople in stores are concerned with responsibilities other than selling. Two selling techniques particularly applicable to retailing are selling up and suggestion selling.

Sales management involves seven basic functions: (1) recruitment and selection, (2) training, (3) organization, (4) supervision, (5) motivation, (6) compensation, and (7) evaluation and control. Sales compensation can be on a straight salary plan, a commission plan, or a combination of the two. Each type of compensation has numerous advantages and disadvantages, and the most appropriate choice must be designed to meet the unique situation of each individual firm. Poor utilization of time and lack of planned sales effort rank as the leading problems faced by sales management today.

Key Terms

personal selling
order processing
creative selling
missionary sales
prospecting
qualifying
approach
presentation
canned approach
closing
follow-up
selling up
suggestion selling
sales management
commission
salary
sales quota

Review Questions

1. Identify the factors affecting the importance of personal selling in the promotional mix.
2. Identify the three basic sales tasks and give an example of each.
3. Identify the characteristics of successful salespersons.
4. What are the steps in the sales process? Relate the AIDA concept to the process.
5. Under what conditions is the canned approach to selling likely to be used? What are the major problems with this approach?
6. How is retail selling different from field selling?
7. Discuss the benefits of a sales career.
8. Describe the major problems faced by sales managers.
9. What are the primary functions of sales management?
10. Compare the alternative sales compensation plans. Point out the advantages and disadvantages of each.

Discussion Questions and Exercises

1. What sales tasks are involved in selling the following products?
   a. Lanier office equipment
   b. Support for Easter Seals to a local Rotary Club
   c. A fast-food franchise
   d. Used automobiles
   e. Cleaning compounds to be used in plant maintenance
2. How would you describe the job of each of the following salespersons?
   a. A salesperson in a retail record store
   b. Century 21 real estate sales representative
   c. A route driver for Frito-Lay (sells and delivers to local food retailers)
   d. A sales engineer for Wang Computers
3. Some critics advocate stringent regulations for telephone sales solicitations. What arguments can be made for and against such regulations?

4. Suppose that you are the local sales manager for American Bell's Yellow Pages and you employ six representatives who call upon local firms. What type of compensation system would you employ?
5. How would you evaluate the sales personnel described in Question 4?

CASES FOR PART 7

Case 7.1
Norwegian Caribbean Lines

Your agency has just been retained by Norwegian Caribbean Lines for an introductory advertising campaign for a newly acquired ship, the S.S. *Norway.*

The Company

Klosters Rederi, A/S, d.b.a. Norwegian Caribbean Lines (NCL) began sailing the Caribbean in 1966. It is one of the most innovative cruise lines in the business and is always looking for new and better ways of marketing and improving its services. It was among the first to institute a computerized reservations system like the airlines and was one of the pioneers of the nationwide fly-cruise program. The company is closely held by the Kloster family, one of Norway's most important ship-owning families.

The Service

NCL has five ships, all of which sail from Miami, Florida. The M.S. *Sunward II* offers three or four-day cruises, while the M.S. *Southward,* the M.S. *Starward* and the M.S. *Skyward* offer seven-day cruises. The fifth ship is the newly acquired S.S. *Norway* which also offers a seven-day cruise. The S.S. *Norway* is to be the focus of the ad campaign.

The S.S. *Norway* is the biggest ship in the world and previously gained public attention and traded as the S.S. *France.* The ship is 17 stories high and over 3 football fields long. Before NCL's purchase of the ship, it had been out of service since 1974. Between 1962 (when it was put to sea) and 1974, the ship (as the S.S. *France*) sailed the North Atlantic and set the world's standard for shipboard excellence. After purchasing the ship in June 1979, for $18 million, NCL gave it a $75 million refitting from bow to stern and changed it into a one-class cruise ship, doing away with much of the luxury and the crew. Knut Utstein Kloster, chairman of the company's board of directors, comments, "I'm sure you can still make money selling luxury, but I have a personal 'but' about that. As a businessman, I feel more comfortable catering to the middle class. In our world it really makes more sense."

The S.S. *Norway* sails from Miami to St. Thomas in the U.S. Virgin Islands then on to Little San Salvador (an out island in the Bahamas) before returning to Miami. The cost for one person for the seven-day cruise is an average of $900.

Source: This case was prepared by Professor Nancy Stephens of Arizona State University. Reprinted by permission.

The Market

NCL is very sophisticated in marketing research and has been able to learn a great deal about the market target. For example, they know from an awareness study that there exists some lack of consumer knowledge about the specific cruise lines and specific ships operating cruises. Based on this information, NCL feels that the introductory campaign should be fairly long (up to eight months), and should have as a goal the registration of a strong positive awareness of the S.S. *Norway* as part of the NCL fleet.

NCL's research department has also determined that only 9 to 10 percent of the adult population has even taken a cruise. They therefore feel it is important to sustain high levels of reach and frequency against target audiences.

The target, in terms of demography, is married couples earning over $25,000 a year with a college education, and 35 to 54 years of age. In terms of geography, 20 markets in the United States currently account for 60 percent of NCL's seven-day cruise business. The top five markets, in terms of past passenger production for NCL, are Los Angeles, Chicago, Miami, San Francisco, and New York.

In terms of purchase behavior, NCL has learned that the seven-day cruise is planned at least four to five months ahead of time (as opposed to three and four-day cruises, which are more of an impulse buy). It is also known that 90 percent of NCL's business is booked through travel agents.

The introduction of the S.S. *Norway* is expected to be aided by the fact that last year NCL had to turn away as many passengers as will fill the S.S. *Norway* (2,000 double occupancy). On the other hand, the new ship doesn't have the one factor that research has shown to be important for any cruise product—positive word-of-mouth advertising. A final factor is that NCL believes the decision of whether to take a cruise is affected by the economy.

The Advertising Budget

The advertising budget (exclusive of production costs) is $2,000,000 for the eight-month campaign to introduce the S.S. *Norway.*

Discussion Question

1. Recommend a media plan for Norwegian Caribbean Lines. Make any assumptions necessary.

Case 7.2
Heath Toffee Bars

The Candy Industry

Candy products are commonly grouped into five categories:

a. Bar Goods (candy bars)

b. Packaged Goods (boxed and bagged candies including assorted chocolates and miniature candy bars)

c. Specialties (examples are rolls or packets of mints and fruit drops, holiday novelties, and candy toys)

d. Bulk Goods (unpacked confections which are weighed out by the retailer for sale by the ounce)

e. Penny Goods (items, other than candy bars, intended to retail for less than five cents).

During the 1960s and early 1970s, total candy sales in the United States showed an approximately 83 percent increase—with manufacturers' shipments rising from $1.15 billion in 1959 to $2.1 billion in 1973. Per-capita consumption rose from 16.8 to 18.7 pounds per year. While all five categories showed increases, they did not share equally in the industry's gain. Percentage sales by category changed as follows:

	1959	1973
Bar Goods	34.4%	32.9%
Packaged Goods	39.2	46.7
Specialties	9.5	11.2
Bulk Goods	12.2	6.0
Penny Goods	4.7	3.1

It has been estimated that over 300 different candy bars compete for the bar goods business. Many of these are regional brands, but even among nationally distributed brands the market is divided among a large group of competitors.

Various trade publications conduct an annual survey among candy and tobacco jobbers and/or candy buyers and merchandisers for various retail outlets showing leading bars and their regional sales rankings as judged by these respondents.

The L.S. Heath Company

The L.S. Heath Company is the outgrowth of a small confectionary store in Robinson, Illinois. The store was purchased by Mr. L. S. Heath in 1918. Among the candies made and sold there was a chocolate-covered English toffee bar, and it was this product that was to transform the firm into a nationwide business.

The bar's unique flavor made it very popular locally, and customers began requesting that the store mail special orders out of town. Over a period of time, these mail order sales began to build Heath's reputation in surrounding areas.

In the early 1930s, candy brokers asked for the right to sell Heath Bars for resale in other retail outlets. A carton of 24 bars, retailing at five cents each, was set up for distribution by brokers and the product began to meet with continually

Source: This case was prepared by Professor William P. Dommermuth of Southern Illinois University at Carbondale. Reprinted by permission.

growing acceptance. As sales climbed, the Heath Company established a special plant to produce the toffee bar. By 1971, Heath's national market share in bar goods was estimated at between one and two percent, and the bars were produced in a variety of sizes and packages.

The company established an ice cream division in 1959, and a fund-raising division in 1965.

The ice cream division serves over 100 dairies, which are licensed to manufacture and sell an ice cream bar containing Heath toffee and carrying the Heath name. These dairies purchase supplies and ingredients from Heath and produce the bars according to uniform specifications.

The fund-raising division makes and sells special candies for use in fund-raising campaigns of various clubs and service organizations. Two bars are currently produced for fund-raising, a "mint melt-away" and a "coconut melt-away." The Heath Toffee Bar is not sold for this purpose.

The Heath Toffee Bar

When first introduced in the 1930s, the five-cent Heath Bar weighed one ounce compared to a more typical two or three ounces for similarly priced bars offered by competitors. Although this disparity in size met with some initial resistance by retailers, company management made an early decision to direct their major efforts toward maintaining quality rather than attempting to compete on a quantity basis. Essentially, they believed—and continue to believe—that a significant segment of the candy market shops for quality over size.

Candy prices, along with those of most products, have increased through the years. However, Heath has been able to close much of the price-quantity gap between itself and other candy bars and still maintain its original standards through technical innovation. Unlike many competitive products, the bar was originally produced almost entirely by hand labor. Breakthroughs in automation have permitted a reduction in the degree of hand labor, but the nature of the product continues to limit the degree of automation that can be used while maintaining quality.

For example, the toffee centers are still cooked in small kettles of about 25 pounds each. The technique of this cooking, along with timing and method of blending ingredients, is considered critical to producing the unique taste and texture of the bar. The skills involved make it extremely difficult for any potential competitor to satisfactorily duplicate the product.

Heath maintains rigid quality control throughout its production process as well as close checks upon both incoming materials and finished products. These checks include laboratory tests and taste tests. Since the bars require at least 48 hours of "aging" before they can be shipped, any falling outside the established standards can be recalled before shipment.

Although a number of other toffee bars have been placed on the market, none has met with anything approaching Heath's success. The largest selling similar product was estimated to have a volume less than one tenth as great.

Another toffee bar, introduced by a major food producer, was test marketed in several cities. In one test area, Tulsa-Oklahoma City, $133,000 was reportedly spent, mainly on television, radio, and newspaper advertising, over an approximate six-month period. Newspaper coupons offered one free with each bar purchased. Despite good distribution and heavy promotion in test areas, the new entry failed to achieve any significant market share.

Personal Selling and Distribution

By 1970, supermarkets, both chain and independent, accounted for roughly half of the Heath Bar's volume. Wholesale jobbers, serving mainly smaller groceries and candy stores, accounted for about another one third. Other outlets included vending machines, drugstores, and variety stores.

The company maintained no sales force of its own but sold through independent food brokers and candy brokers. These brokers received a four percent commission on their sales. Five percent is a more common commission in the candy field, but Heath was regarded as a high prestige line which raises the broker's image among his accounts. This prestige image plus the high repeat sales potential of Heath makes the product attractive from the brokers' standpoint despite the lower commission percentage.

In serving chain store accounts, some brokers employ missionary salespersons to call on individual outlets, but most have salespersons calling only on chain buying offices.

Using a 24-count pack of five-cent bars as an example, the markup pattern would run as follows:

Price to wholesaler	$ .80
Price to retailer	.87
Price to consumer	$1.20

In the above instance, the broker would receive a commission of 3.2 cents from Heath.

To assist the broker's sales force, two division persons were employed by the company. Their job was to maintain contact with brokers, insure the continued interest of brokers in Heath among the several lines they sell, and assist in solving problems in territories where sales were sagging. The division persons frequently traveled with brokers' personnel.

Distribution reached throughout the United States. Aside from U.S. military installations, there were no overseas sales. Some consideration had been given to selling in Canada, but, because of tariffs, this would require construction of manufacturing facilities in that country.

All bars were produced at one plant in Robinson, Illinois. From there they were shipped to 19 regional warehouses by leased trucks. All orders were processed through the central office in Robinson, which relayed delivery instructions to the warehouses. Invoicing and sales recording were done by computer in the central office. The minimum shipment to any account was 200 pounds.

While the company had no sales force of its own for Heath candy bars, it did employ about 35 salespersons in its fund-raising division. Each of these salespersons was assigned to a territory and represented only Heath. Fund-raising salespersons started with a salary plus expenses and moved to a straight commission basis after getting established. They contacted such organizations as the Campfire Girls, Boys Clubs, Little Leagues, and school and church clubs. The fund-raising division not only provided candy to such groups, but assisted them in developing a complete program including selling aids and public relations.

Regional and Seasonal Sales Patterns

Although sold nationally, market share positions for Heath Toffee Bars vary by region of the country. Their greatest strength tends to be in the Midwest, where the bar was first introduced. The brand also has a generally good market in California. Sales are weaker in the South, Southwest, and on the East Coast, although there are local exceptions to this pattern.

In general, the problem in weaker areas is circular in nature. Lower consumer demand leads to lower distribution coverage in retail outlets. This in turn reduces opportunities for the product to be tried and accepted by consumers. In New York City, for example, less than five percent of the available outlets carried Heath compared to almost 80 percent in the suburbs of Chicago.

The demand for immediate high turnover, considered critical by today's retailers, presents difficulties in developing weaker market areas. In the past, when retailers were less conscious of turnover and space problems, the product had time to establish itself in new markets through impulse buying and word-of-mouth advertising. Because it has no close substitutes and delivers a unique taste, the Heath Toffee Bar historically has been able to build and hold its own consumer franchise in this manner. Advertising in such consumer media as magazines, radio, and billboards has not been vital either to keeping bars in retailers' displays or to holding Heath customers. While the market might develop slowly, the product has been able to literally sell itself.

Another change that has occurred in the retailing structure finds store personnel in supermarkets, as contrasted to buying office personnel, increasingly important in securing distribution and shelf position for candy. Even though a product has been sold through chain headquarters, individual stores in the organization often choose not to stock or feature a product. This, coupled with frequent shifts in store personnel and the emphasis on quick stock turns, complicates the task of establishing a solid base for expansion in an area with low consumer demand for a given brand.

In the vending machine field, which accounts for roughly 10 percent of sales, competition for the very limited machine space is intense. A typical machine may have six or seven positions available for candy bars, with hundreds of brands vying for those positions. Given this situation, vending machine operators are highly conscious of turnover potential as well as gross margin. Bars which have demonstrated heavy demand are likely to dominate machines, although some operators, especially smaller firms, may stock lesser known brands with higher markups.

Consumer Promotion

As mentioned previously, the Heath Bar has established its market position by "selling itself." Given sufficient time in retail outlets, impulse purchases and word-of-mouth advertising have built a demand without assistance from media advertising. Amounts spent on advertising by competitors vary widely.

In the late 1950s, Heath experimented with a small amount of spot television in Terre Haute, Indiana. Results were measured on a relatively informal basis by watching sales response during the period in which the ads ran. Since this appeared to be slight, the campaign was discontinued.

In 1966, a more extensive and complex advertising test was launched. It was based on prior research conducted by the advertising agency handling the Heath account. This research indicated that the heaviest demographic purchase concentration for Heath Toffee Bars was among women in the 18 to 35-year age range. It also indicated that the product was currently getting a very small percentage of the total candy market among these women. Taken together, these findings were interpreted to suggest that the best promotional tactic would be to aim at increasing the percentage of market share among these current heavy purchasers.

The resultant campaign focused on the young homemaker and was designed to position Heath as an adult candy bar. In keeping with this aim, daytime television was selected as the most logical medium.

The plan involved scattering spot commercials among soap operas, which draw a large audience among women in the target age bracket. The copy platform stressed the high quality of the bar and treated it as a gourmet-type candy.

In conducting the advertising experiment, it was decided to measure effects of two different budget levels in areas with both high and low per-capita sales. Four test markets were selected—Grand Rapids, Michigan; Peoria, Illinois; Huntington-Charleston, West Virginia; and Oklahoma City, Oklahoma.

A payout planning approach was used for budget determination with the original payout period set at 30 months. It was found that the combination of high budget and high per-capita sales proved most effective, among the four combinations, but results in all markets were considered disappointing. Two were dropped at the end of the second year, and the other two were dropped in the third year.

Although it has not been active in consumer advertising, Heath does undertake other types of promotions to the consumer market. For example, coupons are sometimes included in bags of ten Heath bars, each coupon good for seven cents off the purchase of the next bag. Cooperative programs are offered to retailers in which they are given an allowance, based upon their purchases during a specific time period, in return for either running a special price offer on the bars and/or including it in their regular advertising. Most retailer advertising is done during holiday periods, especially Halloween.

Direct sampling to homes has also been used by Heath, mainly in territories where the company's per-capita sales are relatively low. It is believed that efforts at sampling and couponing have met with reasonably good response, although exact results are difficult to measure.

Advertising to Middlemen.

Advertisements are placed in trade journals, such as the *Candy Marketer* and *The Confectioner.* Direct-mail advertising is also used to reach approximately 9,000 corporate executives of supermarket chains, regarded as key decision makers on basic buying policies. This list is reached with five to ten mailings per year in an effort to keep the Heath name prominently before them.

Another list of about 35,000 independent retailers receives three or four mailings per year, informing them of special promotions. This effort is intended to supplement the work of local wholesalers, who are frequently too busy to fully promote all of the lines they carry.

Vending machine companies are also reached by direct mail to supplement the selling efforts of the company's broker representatives.

Discussion Questions

1. How do you account for Heath's lack of success with their test market advertising campaign?
2. What steps should the Heath management take in attempting to increase their brand's market share?

Philip Kotler

When marketing educators were polled in 1975 to determine the leading marketing educators, the person most often mentioned was Philip Kotler (1931–). Kotler, currently the Harold T. Martin Professor of Marketing at Northwestern University, is particularly qualified for such honors: he has made numerous contributions to the study of marketing and is a pioneer in the application of marketing thinking and concepts to a variety of organizations, including religious groups, hospitals, school systems, public agencies, and social cause organizations.

Kotler's thesis that marketing is a universal function of all organizations—profit and nonprofit—led to the development of the award-winning article "Broadening the Concept of Marketing." The article, coauthored with Sidney Levy, was published in the January 1969 issue of the *Journal of Marketing* and created a furor among conservatives (who thought that marketing should address itself to profit-seeking business organizations) and universalists (who believed that marketing concepts could be applied to nonprofit organizations that confront new, complex marketplace problems). His research and writing continued to focus on the methods by which the social sector could apply marketing thinking in improving their effectiveness, and he consolidated this thinking in the widely acclaimed textbook *Marketing for Nonprofit Organizations* (Prentice-Hall, 1975). Kotler's "broadening concept" attracted an increasing number of proponents during the 1970s, and many articles by scholars and practitioners probed the application of marketing thinking in nonbusiness settings. In addition, marketing courses focusing on the nonprofit sector have appeared in undergraduate and graduate business programs.

Kotler's book *Marketing Management: Analysis, Planning and Control* (Prentice-Hall, 1980) is currently in its fourth edition and continues to be a widely used marketing text in graduate business schools in the United States.

8

EMERGING DIMENSIONS IN MARKETING

The final part of *Marketing* explores important emerging dimensions in the discipline. The vital importance of the international marketplace is examined in Chapter 22. The topic of Chapter 23 is the increasingly important role of marketing in the realm of nonprofit organizations. Chapter 24 discusses the relationship of marketing and society and the final chapter focuses upon the evaluation and control of the marketing process.

22

Chapter Objectives

1. To describe the importance of international marketing.
2. To identify the international aspects of marketing strategy.
3. To describe the environment for international marketing.
4. To identify the various levels of involvement in international marketing.
5. To show how the United States is an attractive market target for foreign marketers.

INTERNATIONAL MARKETING

International marketing saved Jim Blau's company. Blau's company, Snow-Way International of Milwaukee, Wisconsin, marketed a $1,300 snowplow designed to be attached to subcompact, front-wheel-drive cars like the Volkswagen Rabbit. However, a relatively snow-free winter made Blau realize the need to broaden his customer base.

"We had to have a broader marketing base, so I took a $10,000 gamble. I flew to a trade show in Germany, taking a plow with me. I spent $2,000 for a booth. I didn't know what to expect."

He wasn't in doubt for long. Blau's patented design, which does not require remodeling of a car's front end, was an instant success. "The reception was wild," he said. "The plow was perfect for the European market, fitting in with the narrow streets. They had never seen anything like it." After he took $150,000 in orders, and even sold the plow on display, local auto dealers flocked to his hotel room. Blau, a Subaru and Volvo dealer himself, signed up eleven distributors.

Unfortunately, Blau returned to the U.S. without the vaguest idea of how to ship those orders. "I started picking brains," he said. He called friends who had export experience, the local Commerce Department office for advice and recommendations, and several freight forwarders. They all helped.

Today Blau's snowplows are sold from Australia, where they clear mudslides, to Saudi Arabia, where they are used to clear sand from driveways. Foreign sales were such a snap—"Using containers, it is as easy and inexpensive ($100) to ship a plow to Switzerland as to Portland," said Blau—that he now prefers the overseas business. About 75 percent of Snow-Way's estimated $2 million annual revenues came as a result of exports.

"It's a cleaner business. You get your money up front with the letter of credit, no worries about collections," said Blau, who spent years tinkering with other projects, including less than instant winners, such as a kit to convert motorcycles into snowmobiles, before hitting upon the successful snowplow.

He has little time to tinker these days. A recent free ad in a Commerce Department magazine produced an 8-inch stack of inquiries. Snow-Way's six employees (25 subcontractors produce parts for the plow) are hard pressed to handle the volume of incoming mail and outgoing shipments. "I'm keeping 200 to 300 people busy," said Blau, still a little awed at the profitable results of that desperation trip to Germany.[1]

The Conceptual Framework

Although international examples have been included in earlier chapter discussions of such concepts as marketing planning, segmentation, and elements of the marketing mix, most of the previous discussions have focused upon domestic marketing. Increasingly, U.S. organizations are crossing national boundaries in search of markets and profits.

Coca-Cola is one of the most readily identifiable products in the world. The Atlanta-based firm is one of the nation's most successful international marketers. Coca-Cola operates in 135 foreign countries, receiving approximately 65 percent of its sales and profits from abroad.[2]

International marketing is obviously of considerable importance to Coca-Cola and Snow-Way International. It is also important to Pfizer, Inc., since it generates over half the company's total revenues. The im-

[1]"Snowplows to Saudis," *Forbes* (April 13, 1981), p. 84. Reprinted by permission.

[2]Thomas N. Troxell, Jr., "Smiles at Coke," *Barron's* (November 5, 1979), pp. 47–48.

Table 22.1 Importance of Foreign Markets to Some U.S. Companies

Company	Percentage of 1981 Sales Abroad
Pfizer, Inc.	56.8%
Caterpillar Tractor Company	56.6
Hewlett-Packard Company	48.2
The Coca-Cola Company	45.0
Polaroid Corporation	42.4
Emhart Corporation	40.9
Minnesota Mining and Manufacturing Company	40.7
H.J. Heinz Company	39.9
General Foods Corporation	30.9
Bristol-Myers Company	29.3
AMF Incorporated	26.7
Dresser Industries, Inc.	23.0

Source: 1981 annual reports of the listed companies.

portance of international marketing for selected U.S. firms is shown in Table 22.1. Just as some firms depend on foreign sales, others depend on purchasing raw materials to use in their manufacturing operations at home. A furniture company's purchase of South American mahogany is an example.

Dominant U.S. firms are not always the most successful enterprises in foreign markets. General Motors has a 46 percent share in the United States, but only 8.5 percent worldwide. In fact, GM rates behind Toyota, Nissan, and Ford in overseas markets. The Detroit giant is currently altering its marketing strategy so as to become a more formidable competitor in foreign markets.[3]

Conversely, foreign marketers are becoming increasingly attracted to the huge U.S. market. Foreign product invasions are no longer limited to industries like automobiles, electronics, and steel. Yoshinoya & Company of Japan is opening over 200 fast-food outlets in the United States.

International trade is vital to a nation and its marketers for several reasons. It expands the market and makes production and distribution economies feasible. It can also mean more jobs at home. From 30,000 to 40,000 new jobs are supported by each billion dollars of exports.[4]

Foreign trade can be divided into **exporting**—selling goods abroad—and **importing**—buying foreign goods and raw materials. While the United States is the world's largest exporter and importer, foreign trade

[3]Bob Tamarkin, "GM Gets Ready for the World Car," *Forbes* (April 2, 1979), pp. 44–48.

[4]"Trying to Right the Balance," *Time* (October 9, 1979), p. 84.

is still less critical to it than to many other nations. In fact, U.S. exports account for a modest 7.7 percent of the nation's gross national product. The leading export for the United States is motor vehicles and parts, and the leading import is petroleum. The leading U.S. exporters in total volume are Boeing, General Motors, General Electric, Ford, and Caterpillar Tractor.[5]

Although international marketing requires implementation of marketing strategies consisting of identification of market targets, analyses of environmental influences, and development of marketing mixes, both similarities and differences between it and domestic marketing exist. This chapter examines characteristics of the international marketplace, environmental influences on marketing, and the development of an international marketing mix. It also discusses the sequential steps used by most firms in entering the international marketplace.

The International Marketplace

Many U.S. firms never venture outside their own domestic market. They feel they do not have to, because the U.S. market is huge. Even today, only about 8 percent of all domestic manufacturing firms export their products, and only 250 of these manufacturers account for 85 percent of all U.S. exports. Those that do venture abroad find the international marketplace far different from the one to which they are accustomed. Market sizes, buyer behavior, and marketing practices all vary, which means international marketers must carefully evaluate all market segments in which they expect to compete.

Market Size

In 1976, the world population passed the 4 billion mark. Only 15 years had passed since the 3 billion mark had been reached in 1961. It took 31 years to reach 3 billion from the 2 billion mark and over 300 years to reach 2 billion from the 1 billion mark. In contrast, forecasters predict the world population will reach 5 billion in 1989—just 13 years after the 4 billion mark was reached.

The United States has attained one of the highest standards of living in the history of the world, but its population size is insignificant when compared with the rest of the world. Figure 22.1 shows how the United States is dwarfed by the tremendous populations of countries such as India and China. While fully one fifth of the world's population lives in China, less than 6 percent resides in the United States.

[5]"The Fifty Leading Exporters," *Fortune* (August 24, 1981), pp. 84–85.

Figure 22.1 The World in Proportion to Population

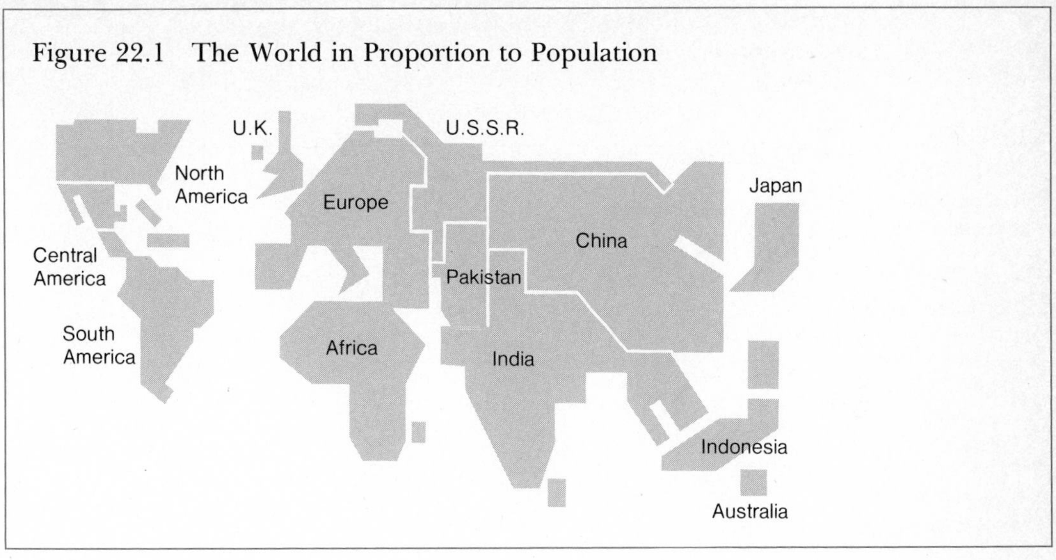

A prime ingredient of market size is population growth, and every day the world's population increases by about 200,000 people. By the year 2000, the world's population is expected to be 6.3 billion. A review of these projections produces some important contrasts. Average birthrates are dropping, but death rates are declining even faster. Population growth has fallen in industrialized nations, but it has increased in the less-developed countries. Nearly 80 percent of the population in 2000 will live in less-developed nations.

Many of the world's new inhabitants live in large cities. By the year 2000, these urban dwellers are expected to account for half the world population instead of the current 39 percent. Today, 26 cities have a population of 5 million or more. In 2000, 60 such cities will exist. Mexico City, which now ranks third in population, with nearly 9 million people, is expected to grow to 31.5 million, making it the world's largest city.

Statistical data indicates that the international marketplace will continue to grow in size and that it will become increasingly urbanized. This does not mean, however, that all foreign markets will have the same potential. Income differences, for instance, vitally affect any nation's market potential. India has a population of nearly 700 million, but its per capita income is very low. Canada, on the other hand, has only a small fraction of India's population, but its per capita income is higher than that of the United States. Table 22.2 compares population and per capita incomes for a number of the world's nations.

Table 22.2 Per Capita Income for Selected Countries and Populations

Country	Per Capita Income	Population (in Millions)
North America		
United States	$ 8,612	226.5
Canada	10,296	24.0
Mexico	1,800	71.9
Cuba	840	9.9
Dominican Republic	841	5.5
Haiti	260	5.7
South America		
Argentina	2,331	27.3
Bolivia	477	5.6
Brazil	1,523	123.0
Guyana	437	0.8
Venezuela	2,772	14.5
Europe		
Denmark	9,869	5.1
France	7,908	53.7
Italy	3,076	57.0
Portugal	2,000	9.9
Soviet Union	2,600	266.6
Sweden	9,274	8.3
Turkey	1,140	45.3
Near East		
Iran	1,986	38.0
Israel	3,332	3.8
Egypt	448	41.9
Kuwait	11,431	1.3
Saudi Arabia	11,500	9.2
Asia		
Afghanistan	168	15.8
Cambodia (Kampuchea)	90	8.8
India	162	667.3
Japan	8,460	116.7
People's Republic of China	232	1,000.0
Australia	7,720	14.6
Africa		
Angola	500	7.0
Chad	73	4.5
Liberia	453	1.8
Morocco	555	20.3
Mozambique	170	10.4

Source: *The World Almanac and Book of Facts 1982* (New York: Newspaper Enterprise Association, Inc., 1982), pp. 514–599. Reprinted by permission. Copyright 1982 NEA, Inc.

Buyer Behavior

Buyer behavior differs from one country to another. Therefore, marketers should carefully study each market before implementing a marketing strategy. Not all successful domestic marketing strategies can be exported to other parts of the world. Improved U.S.-Chinese relations will open up new markets for both nations. But the Chinese would be well advised to change some of their brand names before entering the American market: for example, "White Elephant" batteries and "Maxi-puke" playing cards.[6]

Marketers must also be careful that their marketing strategies comply with local customs, tastes, and buying practices. In some cases, even the product itelf has to be modified. General Foods, for instance, offers different blends of coffee for each of its overseas markets. One variety goes to British consumers, who prefer considerable quantities of milk in their coffee; another goes to the French, who usually drink coffee black; still another mix goes to Latin Americans, who prefer a chicory taste.[7]

Different buying patterns mean that marketing executives should do considerable research before entering a foreign market. Sometimes, the research can be done by the marketer's own organization or a U.S.-based research firm. In other cases, a foreign-based marketing research organization should be used. The advertisement shown in Figure 22.2 is an example of a marketing research firm which specializes in Arab countries.

Foreign research firms are often innovative. For example, Audits, Ltd., of Great Britain, pioneered in the field of home audits of package goods. The British firm provided its respondents with a special trash container rather than relying on a diary of purchases. Discarded packages were then studied to determine consumer buying patterns.[8]

The Environment for International Marketing

Various environmental factors can influence international marketing strategy. Marketers should be as aware of these influences as they are of those in domestic markets.

Cultural, Economic, and Societal Factors

International marketing is often influenced by cultural, economic, and societal factors. The economic status of some countries makes them less or more likely candidates for international business expansion. Nations

[6]"Teaching Management to Marxists," *Fortune* (March 23, 1981), p. 103.

[7]David A. Ricks, Marilyn Y. C. Fu, and Jeffrey S. Arpan, *International Business Blunders* (Columbus, Ohio: Grid, 1974), pp. 17–18.

[8]Ralph Z. Sorenson, II, "U.S. Marketers Can Learn from European Innovators," *Harvard Business Review* (September–October 1972), p. 97.

Figure 22.2 Independent Marketing Research Firm Specializing in Research in Arab Countries

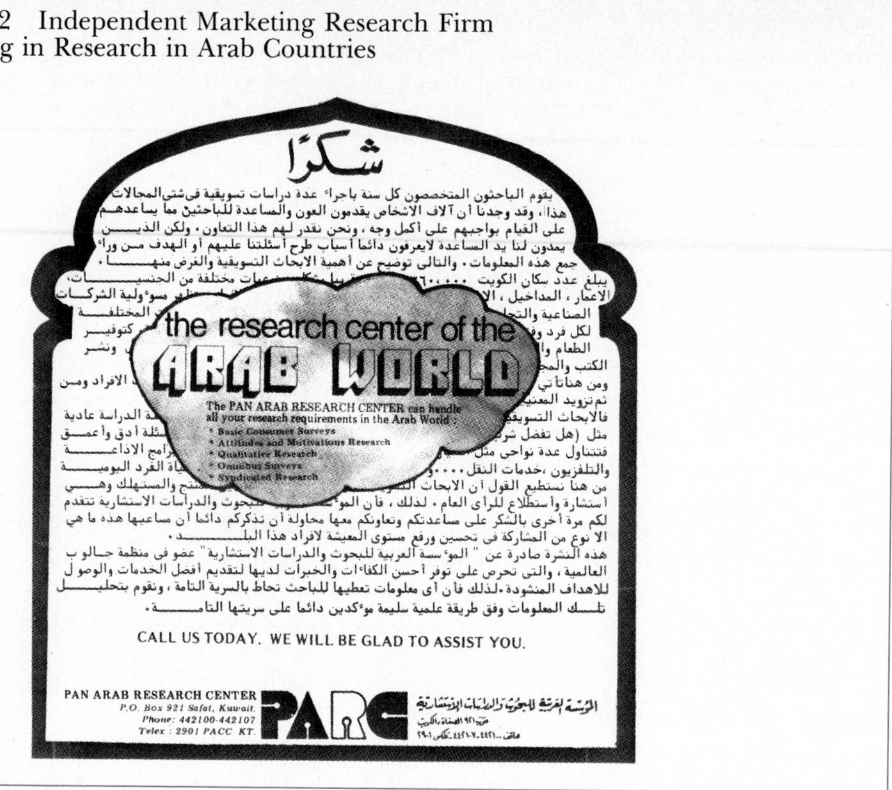

Source: Reprinted by permission of Pan Arab Research Center.

with low per capita income may be poor markets for expensive industrial machinery but good markets for agricultural hand tools. These nations cannot afford the technical equipment necessary in an industralized society. Wealthier countries can prove to be prime markets for the products of many U.S. industries, particularly those involved with consumer goods and advanced industrial products.

Many products have failed abroad simply because the producing firm tried to use the same marketing strategy that was successful in the United States. Consider, for example, an advertising strategy based primarily on the use of print media and featuring testimonials. Such a campaign would offer dim prospects in a less-developed nation with a high degree of illiteracy.

U.S. products sometimes face consumer resistance abroad. American automobiles, for example, have traditionally been rejected by European drivers, who complain of poor styling, low gasoline mileage, and poor handling. But the new, smaller cars from Detroit are making moderate inroads into European markets. This reversal suggests that it is not always possible to determine the precise impact of cultural, economic, or societal factors prior to entering a foreign market. Japanese tea drinkers for centuries have preferred natural tea, but Boston Tea Company's blended, spiced, and herbed tea is now selling well in Japan.

Trade Restrictions

Assorted trade restrictions also affect world trade. These restrictions are most commonly expressed through **tariffs**—taxes levied against imported products. Some tariffs are based on a set tax per pound, gallon, or unit; others are figured on the value of the imported product. They can be classified as either revenue or protective tariffs. *Revenue tariffs* are designed to raise funds for the government. Most of the revenue of the early U.S. government came from this source. *Protective tariffs* are designed to raise the retail price of an imported product to match or exceed a similar domestic product. Protective tariffs are usually higher than revenue tariffs. In the past, it was believed that a country should protect its infant industries by using tariffs to keep out foreign-made products. Some foreign goods entered, but the addition of a high tariff payment made domestic products competitive in price. Recently, it has been argued that tariffs should be raised to protect employment and profits in domestic U.S. industry.

The **General Agreement on Tariffs and Trade (GATT),** an international trade accord, has sponsored several tariff negotiations that have reduced the overall level of tariffs throughout the world. The latest series, the so-called *Tokyo Round,* began in 1974 and concluded in 1979. The Tokyo Round reduced tariffs by about 33 percent over an eight-year period. The agreement also lessened nontariff barriers, such as government procurement regulations, that discriminated against foreign marketers.

There are also other forms of trade restriction. An **import quota** sets limits on the amount of products in certain categories that can be imported. Import quotas seek to protect local industry and employment and to preserve foreign exchange. The ultimate quota is the **embargo,** the complete ban on the import of certain products. In the past, the United States has prohibited the import of products from some Communist countries. The United States has also used export quotas. In 1982, for example, President Reagan enforced trade sanctions against Argentina for its actions against Great Britain in the Falkland Islands dispute.

Foreign trade can also be regulated by exchange control through a central bank or government agency. **Exchange control** means that firms gaining foreign exchange by exporting must sell this exchange to the central bank, or other agency, and importers must buy foreign exchange from the same organization. The exchange control authority can then allocate, expand, or restrict foreign exchange according to existing national policy.

Dumping: A Contemporary Marketing Problem

Dumping is the practice of selling a product at a lower price in a foreign market than it sells for in the producer's domestic market. In the late 1970s, Bethlehem Steel ran advertisements to protest what it viewed as dumping in the steel industry. It is often argued that foreign governments give substantial export support to their own companies. Such support may permit these firms to extend their export markets by offering lower prices abroad.

Products that have been dumped on U.S. markets can be subject to additional import tariffs to bring their prices in line with domestically produced products. For instance, a 32 percent dumping duty was assessed against five Japanese steel sellers. However, businesses often complain that charges of alleged dumping must go through a lengthy investigative and bureaucratic procedure before duties are assessed. In an attempt to speed up the process in the steel industry, a *trigger pricing system,* which established a set of minimum steel prices, has been used. Japanese production costs, the world's lowest, were used in these calculations. Any imported steel selling at less than these rates triggers an immediate Treasury Department investigation. If dumping is substantial, additional duties are imposed.

Steel is not the only product to involve allegations of dumping. Similar allegations have been leveled against foreign makers of products as diverse as hockey sticks, cement, and motorcycles.

Demands for protection against foreign imports are common in all countries, particularly during periods of economic uncertainty. Firms ask for protection against sales losses, and unions seek to preserve their members' jobs. Overall, however, the long-term trend is in the direction of free trade among nations.

Political and Legal Factors

Political factors greatly influence international marketing. The election of Socialist Francois Mitterand as president of France initially caused furor among international marketers. Earlier political turmoil in South Korea, Nicaragua, El Salvador, and Iran also suggests how volatile this environmental factor can be in international markets. In fact, many U.S. firms have set up internal political risk assessment (PRA) units or turned to outside consulting services to evaluate the political risks of the marketplace in which they operate. Sometimes marketing strategies have to be adjusted to reflect the new situation. For example, when Colgate-Palmolive introduced Irish Spring in England, it marketed the soap as Nordic Spring.[9]

[9]"Off the Record," *Detroit News* (February 28, 1975), p. 1.

Setting Quotas for Japanese Cars

Imported cars nearly brought the U.S. domestic auto industry to its knees at the beginning of the decade. Imports, particularly Japanese models, accounted for 29 percent of the U.S. automobile market. About 240,000 U.S. auto workers—nearly 20 percent of the United Auto Workers membership—were laid off. The U.S. companies and the union called for help from Washington.

The flood of imported Japanese cars set off one of the biggest public debates over international trade ever. Both the Carter and Reagan administrations considered the issue. Proponents of government assistance argued that it would reduce the severe unemployment in the industry and in states like Michigan; it would provide domestic manufacturers the necessary money and time to make the industry competitive; and failure to act would retard the nation's economic recovery. Opponents argued that federal intervention would be only a short-term fix, and limiting Japanese models would be inflationary. Federal assistance was also counter to the free-market philosophy of the Reagan administration, which made the final decision.

The debate was resolved in 1981 when the Japanese, under the threat of mandatory U.S. import limits, agreed to hold their exports to 1.68 million in the next year and to tie second- and third-year exports to the growth of U.S. sales. However, Japanese exporters substantially increased their U.S. inventories prior to the agreement so some of the reduction would be inventory cuts and not imports. Whether the U.S. manufacturers will ever recover their market dominance is an unresolved marketing question of the 1980s.

Source: Steve Posner, "In Japanese Plants, the Workers Help Manage," *Seattle Business Journal* (March 9, 1981), p. 20; Herbert Zeltner, "Sounding Board Surveys Impact of the Imports on U.S. Marketing," *Advertising Age* (December 8, 1980), p. 55; Jerry Flint, "Less than Meets the Eye," *Forbes* (May 25, 1981), p. 38; and John F. Stacks, "The Administration's Split on Auto Imports," *Fortune* (May 4, 1981), pp. 156–158, 162, 166.

Many nations try to achieve political objectives through international business activities. Japan, for instance, has openly encouraged its firms' involvement in international marketing, because much of the nation's economy is dependent on overseas sales.

Legal requirements complicate world marketing. Indonesia has banned commercial advertisements from the nation's only television channel. It was feared that the advertisements would cause the 80 percent of the population living in rural areas to envy those who resided in cities. All commercials in the United Kingdom and Australia must be cleared in advance. In the Netherlands, ads for candy must also show a toothbrush. Some nations have *local content laws* that specify the portion of a product that must come from domestic sources. These examples suggest that managers involved in international marketing must be well versed in legislation affecting their specific industry.

The legal environment for U.S. firms operating abroad can be divided into three dimensions: (1) U.S. law, (2) international law, and (3) legal requirements of host nations. International law can be found in the treaties, conventions, and agreements that exist among nations. The United States has many **friendship, commerce, and navigation (FCN) treaties,** agreements that deal with many aspects of commercial relations with other countries, such as the right to conduct business in the treaty partner's domestic market.

Other international business agreements concern international standards for various products, patents, trademarks, reciprocal tax treaties, export control, international air travel, and international communication. The International Monetary Fund has been set up to lend foreign exchange to nations that require it to conduct international trade. These agreements facilitate the whole process of world marketing.

The legal requirements of host nations affect foreign marketers. For example, some nations limit foreign ownership in their business sectors. International marketers in general recognize the importance of obeying the laws and regulations of the countries within which they operate. Even the slightest violations of these legal requirements are setbacks for the future of international trade.

International marketing is subject to various trade regulations, tax laws, and import/export requirements. One of the best-known U.S. laws is the Webb-Pomerene Export Trade Act (1918), which exempted various combinations of U.S. firms acting together to develop foreign markets from antitrust laws. The intent was to give U.S. industry economic power equal to that possessed by *cartels,* the monopolistic organizations of foreign firms. Companies operating under the Webb-Pomerene Act cannot reduce competition within the United States and cannot use "unfair methods of competition." Generally, Webb-Pomerene associations have not been significant in the growth of U.S. trade.[10]

The Foreign Corrupt Practices Act

The most important new legislation is the *Foreign Corrupt Practices Act,* which makes it illegal to bribe a foreign official in an attempt to solicit new or repeat sales abroad. The act also specifies that adequate accounting controls be installed to monitor internal compliance. Violations can result in a $1 million fine for the firm and a $10,000 fine and

[10]See Igal Ayal, "Industry Export Performance: Assessment and Prediction," *Journal of Marketing* (Summer 1982), pp. 54–61.

five years' imprisonment for individuals involved.[11] This law has been quite controversial since several companies have reported that the paperwork involved has caused them to lose overseas sales.

Designing Marketing Mixes for International Markets

Marketing practices vary throughout the world. These practices must be taken into consideration when an "outside" firm decides to launch a marketing campaign. A high illiteracy rate, for example, may substantially limit the types of advertising campaigns employed. Aggressive sales efforts may be regarded negatively in some foreign cultures. Business customs and traditions may restrict a firm's distribution strategy to certain marketing channels. A brief consideration of each marketing strategy component will illustrate the differences that exist in marketing practices overseas.

Product Strategy

Although baseball may be known as an American pastime, Mizuno Corporation of Osaka, Japan, has developed an innovative product strategy for the U.S. market. About 400 professional baseball players in the United States now use custom-fitted Mizuno baseball gloves. Mizuno imports leather from the United States, then tans, cures, and shapes it into a baseball glove that does not need to be broken in. Mizuno has spent $3 million on research and development of an entire line of baseball equipment. The line includes plexiglass catcher's masks, an electronic umpire-to-scoreboard relay system, strike zone sensors, and electronic foul lines.[12]

Mizuno has chosen to offer an innovative product mix to the marketplace, but sometimes existing products can be modified to meet consumer needs. Successful adaptation can significantly extend the market for a product. Sometimes, the product itself has to be modified; in other cases, it is the packaging; in still others, it is the product's identi-

[11] "The Antibribery Bill Backfires," *Business Week* (April 17, 1978), p. 143. Also see Frederick L. Neumann, "Corporate Audit Committees and the Foreign Corrupt Practices Act," *Business Horizons* (June 1980), pp. 62–71; Jack G. Kaikati and Wayne A. Label, "American Bribery Legislation: An Obstacle to International Marketing," *Journal of Marketing* (Fall 1980), pp. 38–43; David N. Ricchiute, "Illegal Payments, Deception of Auditors, and Reports on Internal Control," *MSU Business Topics* (Spring 1980), pp. 57–62; and Mark Pastin and Michael Hooker, "Ethics and the Foreign Corrupt Practices Act," *Business Horizons* (December 1980), pp. 43–48.

[12] "Japanese Company Invades U.S. Sporting Goods Market with Futuristic Baseball Gear," *Marketing News* (March 20, 1981), p. 18.

fication. Consider the many products that use the word *mist* as part of their name. But imagine the difficulty of marketing such a product in Germany, where *mist* means "manure."[13]

Promotional Strategy

While effective personal selling continues to be vital in foreign markets, advertising has gained in importance. The wider availability of media such as radio and television has enhanced advertising's contribution to the overall promotional effort. However, many U.S. advertising approaches are not really adaptable overseas. Promotional strategies tend to be strictly regulated in many foreign marketplaces.

Distribution Strategy

Distribution is a vital aspect of overseas marketing. Proper channels must be set up and extensive physical distribution problems handled. Transportation systems and warehousing facilities may be unavailable or of poor quality. International marketers must adapt speedily and efficiently to these situations if they are to profit from overseas sales.

Sears, one of the most effective retailers in the United States, met its match in Seibu, a large Japanese retailer with 600 outlets. So Sears turned to Seibu to sell its catalog merchandise in Japan. The venture was so successful that Allstate Insurance, a Sears subsidiary, began marketing its life insurance policies through Seibu's retail locations.[14]

Nissan automobiles are the leading seller in oil-rich Saudi Arabia (where gasoline sells for 23 to 25 cents per gallon). Its large market share is credited to the excellent organization of local distributors, who were recruited in the early 1960s. The Japanese firm sought out Saudi entrepreneurs who had sufficient investment capital and who were skilled managers and marketers.[15] The strategy was obviously effective.

Pricing Strategy

Pricing in foreign markets can be a critical ingredient in overall marketing strategy. Pricing practices in overseas markets are subject to considerable competitive, economic, political, and legal constraints. International marketing managers must clearly understand these requirements if they are to succeed.

The most significant development in pricing strategy for international marketing has been the emergence of commodity marketing or-

[13]William Mathewson, "Trademarks Are a Global Business These Days, but Finding Registerable Ones Is a Big Problem," *The Wall Street Journal* (September 4, 1975), p. 26.

[14]"Sears Adds Insurance to Its Line of Exports," *Business Week* (August 4, 1975), p. 39.

[15]"Nissan Competes with the Camel," *Business Week* (May 26, 1975), p. 44.

Advertising in the Soviet Union

Who ever would have thought that more than 100 advertising agencies would be plying their trade today in the Soviet Union? Certainly not Marx! According to traditional Marxist-Leninist doctrine, advertising is a tool of capitalistic exploitation. It siphons off the surplus value belonging to underpaid workers and puts it in the hands of overpaid white-collar workers who are nonproductively employed writing jingles.

Yet there has been an impressive growth of advertising agencies in the Soviet Union. The initial argument was that these agencies exist to develop advertising to support Soviet goods in export markets where it is necessary to compete against Western and other nations. But many advertisements also appear in print and broadcast media reaching Russian consumers. Another rationale was established at the 1957 Prague Conference of Advertising Workers of Socialist Countries, which made three points as to how advertising was to be used: (1) to educate people's tastes, develop their requirements, and thus actively form demand; (2) to help the consumer by providing information about the most rational means of consumption; and (3) to help to raise the culture of trade. Furthermore, Soviet advertising is to be ideological, truthful, concrete, and functional. The Soviets claim that their advertising does not indulge in devices used in the West. Their ads will not use celebrities—only experts will be used to promote a product. They will not use mood advertising. They will not create brand differentiation when none exists.

Experts think that the main use of Soviet advertising is to help industry move products that come into excess supply where the Soviets do not want to do the logical thing, cut prices.

Source: Courtland L. Bovee and William F. Arens, *Contemporary Advertising* (Homewood, Ill.: Richard D. Irwin, 1982), p. 119. Reprinted by permission. Photograph courtesy of Pepsico.

ganizations that seek to control prices through collective action. OPEC (the Organization of Petroleum Exporting Countries) is the best example of these collective export organizations, but a variety of others exist.

Levels of Involvement in International Marketing

Several levels of involvement in international marketing can be identified: casual or accidental exporting, active exporting, foreign licensing, overseas marketing, and foreign production and marketing.[16]

Casual or accidental exporting is a passive level of involvement in international marketing. A U.S. company may export goods without even knowing it if its goods are bought by resident buyers for foreign companies. In other cases, a firm may export only occasionally when surplus or obsolete inventory is available.

When a firm actually makes a commitment to seek export business, it engages in *active exporting*. While the exact extent of the commitment may vary, the term implies that the firm is making a continuing effort to sell its merchandise abroad.[17]

Foreign licensing occurs when a firm permits a foreign company to produce and distribute its merchandise under a formal agreement. Licensing has several advantages over exporting, among them the availability of local marketing information and distribution channels and protection from various legal barriers. Sometimes it is the best way to get into a particular market. For instance, Hughes Tool Company of Houston has negotiated a licensing agreement that will provide drill bits to the People's Republic of China.[18]

A firm that maintains a separate marketing or selling operation in a foreign country is involved in *overseas marketing*. Examples are foreign sales offices and overseas marketing subsidiaries. The product may be produced by domestic factories, foreign licensees, or contract manufacturers, but the company always directly controls foreign sales.

Foreign production and foreign marketing, the ultimate degree of company involvement in the international market arena, can be accomplished in the following ways:

1. The firm can set up its own production and marketing operation in the foreign country.

[16]These levels are suggested in Vern Terpstra, *International Marketing*, 3d ed. (Hinsdale, Ill.: The Dryden Press, 1983).

[17]Small-scale exporting is discussed in Ralph A. Rieth, Jr., and Edward T. Ryan, Jr., "A Study of the Perceptions of Selected Small Massachusetts Manufacturers toward Exporting," in *Developments in Marketing Science*, (ed.) Venkatakrishna V. Bellur; (co-editors) Thomas R. Baird, Paul T. Hertz, Roger L. Jenkins, Jay D. Lindquist, and Stephen W. Miller, vol. VI (Marquette, Mich.: Academy of Marketing Science, 1981), pp. 97–100.

[18]"No Great Leap Forward for U.S. Exports," *Business Week* (May 26, 1980), p. 67.

2. It can acquire an existing firm in the country in which it will do business.
3. It can form a **joint venture,** in which the risks, costs, and management of the foreign operation are shared with a partner who is usually a national of the host country.

Multinational Marketing

Switzerland's Nestlé now operates in 65 national markets with 146,000 employees and 300 plants. Sales total approximately $14 billion. Nestlé gets 41 percent of its revenue from Europe, 24 percent from Third World nations, and the remainder primarily from the United States and Japan.[19]

Multinational corporations are firms with significant operations and marketing activities outside their home country. Examples of multinationals include General Electric, Siemens, and Mitsubishi in the heavy electrical equipment industry; Caterpillar and Komatsu in large construction equipment; and Timex, Seiko, and Citizen in watches. As these examples reveal, not all multinationals are U.S. firms. In fact, according to the Conference Board, the United States has continued to decline as the home for such worldwide corporations. Now only 47 percent of the world's largest corporations are based in the United States, down from 58 percent in 1971 and 67 percent in 1963. Germany ranked second with 13 multinationals in the most recent listing.[20]

Hewlett-Packard provides an illustration of how a multinational firm can operate effectively. The California-based electronics company sells nearly as much abroad as it does in the United States. How does Hewlett-Packard do it? The company encourages its European subsidiaries to run autonomously with European management. Subsidiaries are told to use local technical talent to produce export products. Hewlett-Packard's German subsidiary has been particularly successful, deriving more than half of its revenues from non-German markets. Some German executives now manage Hewlett-Packard operations in California.[21]

Multinationals have been the subject of considerable public scrutiny both in the United States and abroad. Some U.S. multinationals have been criticized for their involvement in South Africa. These firms typically respond that they are contributing to social and economic progress in all the nations in which they operate. Some nations—Australia and Canada, for example—have occasionally expressed concern about the multinationals' domination of some domestic markets. Similar complaints have been expressed in the United States about the inroads

[19]Robert Ball, "Nestle Revs Up Its U.S. Campaign," *Fortune* (February 13, 1978), pp. 80–83.

[20]"U.S. Industrial Lead Wanes as Foreign Multinationals Gain," *Marketing News* (May 29, 1981), p. 1.

[21]"Hewlett-Packard's Buffer against Recession," *Business Week* (July 7, 1980), p. 32.

made by Japanese automobile firms. While criticism of multinational practices is likely to continue, it is obvious that multinational corporations have become fixtures in the international marketplace.

Multinational Economic Integration and World Marketing

A noticeable trend toward multinational economic integration has developed since the close of World War II. The Common Market, or European Economic Community (EEC), is the best known of these multinational economic communities.

Multinational economic integration can be set up in several ways. The simplest approach is a *free trade area,* where participating nations agree to free trade of goods among themselves. All tariffs and trade restrictions are abolished between the nations involved. A *customs union* establishes a free trade area, plus a uniform tariff for trade with nonmember nations. The EEC is the best example of a customs union. A true *common market* or *economic union* involves a customs union and also seeks to bring all government regulations affecting trade into agreement. The EEC has been moving in the direction of an economic union.

Multinational economic communities have played a significant part in international business. United States firms invested heavily in Western Europe in the 1960s basically because of the attraction of larger markets offered by the EEC. Multinational economic integration is forcing management to adapt its operations abroad, and it is likely that the pace will accelerate.

The United States as a Market for International Marketers

The United States has become an increasingly inviting target for foreign marketers. It has a large population, high levels of discretionary income, political stability, an attitude generally favorable to foreign investment, and economic ills that are relatively controlled in comparison to those in many other countries. Figure 22.3 shows U.S. goods and services produced by foreign-owned companies.

A number of foreign-owned competitors have found the United States an attractive market. Retailing has been a recent target of foreign companies. All of the following U.S. retailers are owned in full or in part by an overseas firm: A&P (Germany), Grand Union (France), Gimbel Brothers (United Kingdom), Fed Mart (Germany), Bi-Lo (Nether-

Figure 22.3 U.S. Goods and Services Produced by Foreign-Owned Companies

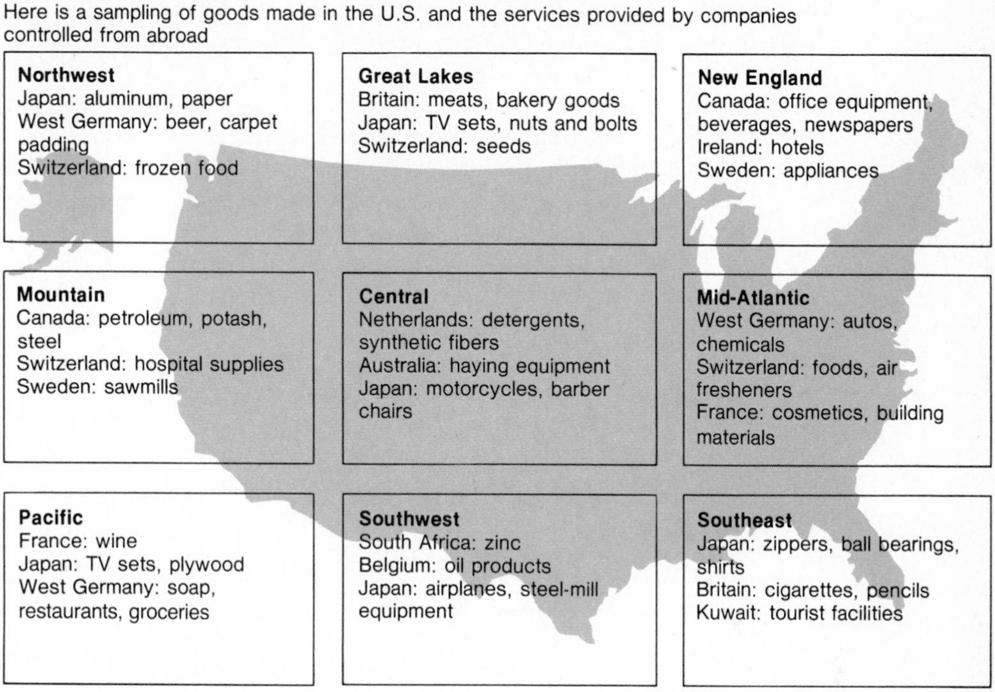

Here is a sampling of goods made in the U.S. and the services provided by companies controlled from abroad

Northwest
Japan: aluminum, paper
West Germany: beer, carpet padding
Switzerland: frozen food

Great Lakes
Britain: meats, bakery goods
Japan: TV sets, nuts and bolts
Switzerland: seeds

New England
Canada: office equipment, beverages, newspapers
Ireland: hotels
Sweden: appliances

Mountain
Canada: petroleum, potash, steel
Switzerland: hospital supplies
Sweden: sawmills

Central
Netherlands: detergents, synthetic fibers
Australia: haying equipment
Japan: motorcycles, barber chairs

Mid-Atlantic
West Germany: autos, chemicals
Switzerland: foods, air fresheners
France: cosmetics, building materials

Pacific
France: wine
Japan: TV sets, plywood
West Germany: soap, restaurants, groceries

Southwest
South Africa: zinc
Belgium: oil products
Japan: airplanes, steel-mill equipment

Southeast
Japan: zippers, ball bearings, shirts
Britain: cigarettes, pencils
Kuwait: tourist facilities

Source: "Foreign Firms: Covering the U.S.," reprinted from *U.S. News & World Report* (July 24, 1978), p. 54. Copyright 1978 U.S. News & World Report, Inc.

lands), Kohl (United Kingdom), Fuir's (Germany), Dillard Department Stores (Netherlands), Red Food Stores (France), F.A.O. Schwartz (Switzerland), Maurices (Netherlands), and Winn's Stores (Germany).

Some buyers have shown a preference for foreign products over domestic competitors. Foreign sports cars, English china, and French wine all hold sizable shares of the U.S. market. Some foreign products, such as Porsche sports cars, are sold in the United States because of the quality image. Others sell on the basis of a price advantage over domestic competition.

U.S. marketers must expect to face substantial foreign competition in the years ahead. The United States' high level of buying power is sure to continue its considerable appeal abroad, and the reduction of trade barriers and expanded international marketing appear to be long-run trends. U.S. marketers no longer face the choice of whether to compete with foreign firms; their continued long-term success depends to a great extent on their ability to compete.

Summary

International marketing has become increasingly important to the United States. Many U.S. firms depend on their ability to market their goods abroad, while others depend on buying raw materials from other countries.

Competing in overseas markets is often considerably different from competing in domestic markets. Market size, buying behavior, and marketing practices may all differ. International marketers must make significant adaptations in their product, distribution, promotional, and pricing strategies to fit different markets abroad.

Several levels of involvement in international marketing can be identified: casual or accidental exporting, active exporting, foreign licensing, overseas marketing, and foreign production and foreign marketing. The world's largest firms are usually multinational in their orientation. Such companies operate in several countries and view the world as their market.

Various environmental factors can influence international marketing strategy. Cultural, economic, and societal factors can hinder international marketing. So can assorted trade restrictions and political and legal factors.

Since the end of World War II, there has been a noticeable trend toward multinational economic integration. Three basic formats for integration are free trade areas, customs unions, and common markets.

The United States is now viewed as an attractive market for marketers from abroad. U.S. firms can expect to face growing foreign competition in the domestic market.

Key Terms

exporting
importing
tariff
General Agreement on Tariffs and Trade (GATT)
import quota
embargo
exchange control
dumping
friendship, commerce, and navigation (FCN) treaties
foreign licensing
joint venture
multinational corporation

Review Questions

1. Why is international marketing important to U.S. firms? To the U.S. economy?
2. What type of products are most often marketed abroad by U.S. firms?
3. In what ways is the international marketing mix likely to be different from a marketing mix used in the domestic country?

4. Describe the environment for international marketing.
5. Identify the various levels of involvement in international marketing.
6. Explain how trade restrictions may be employed to restrict or to stimulate international marketing activities.
7. Distinguish between import quotas and embargoes.
8. Explain the international marketing practice of dumping? Why does dumping sometimes occur?
9. Identify and briefly explain the three basic formats for economic integration.
10. Why is the United States such an attractive market target for foreign marketers? What does this mean for U.S. firms?

Discussion Questions and Exercises

1. Comment on the following statement: It is sometimes dangerous for a firm to attempt to export its marketing strategy.
2. Outline the basic premises behind the operation of a multinational corporation. Why do you think the term has a negative connotation?
3. Some people argue that foreign investment in the United States should be limited. Would you agree with a plan that would limit such investment in a particular firm to some specified amount? Explain.
4. Give an example—hypothetical or actual—of a firm operating at each level of international marketing:
   a. Casual or accidental exporting
   b. Active exporting
   c. Foreign licensing
   d. Overseas marketing
   e. Foreign production and foreign marketing
5. Relate specific international environmental considerations to each of the following aspects of a firm's marketing mix:
   a. Brands and warranties
   b. Advertising
   c. Distribution channels
   d. Discounts to middlemen
   e. Use of comparative advertising

23

Chapter Objectives

1. To identify the primary characteristics of nonprofit organizations that distinguish them from profit-seeking organizations.
2. To describe the evolution of the broadening concept.
3. To explain the types of nonprofit organizations.
4. To explain how a marketing mix might be developed in a nonprofit setting.
5. To identify the variables used in evaluation and control of a nonprofit marketing program.

MARKETING IN NONPROFIT SETTINGS

To survive in these financially perilous times, David Gockley, the director of the Houston Grand Opera, has put as much emphasis on earnings, product development, and marketing as on arias, librettos, and falsettos. The company must perform well on the stage and on the balance sheet, Gockley said. Unlike the heads of many opera companies that have retrenched in recent years to make ends meet, Gockley believes growth and diversification are the keys to his company's long-term survival.

"Companies that stay small and specialized are going to have far greater difficulty surviving in the years ahead," Gockley said, unaesthetically. "With increasing competition, ever-escalating production costs, and reduced government subsidies, the future of an organization like ours will depend on our ability to aggressively market a broad range of products to more and more people."

Toward that end, Gockley is trying to ease opera's highbrow image and pitch the marketing of it to a mass audience. He has advertised the

Houston Grand Opera on T-shirts and television commercials, taken it on the road to such unlikely places as Eagle Pass, Texas, and Broadway, and presented it in forms ranging from traditional European classics to contemporary rock musicals. "They're the P. T. Barnum of opera," said Scott Heumann, a correspondent for *Opera News,* a trade publication. "They'll beat drums, do somersaults, or whatever else it takes to bring people into the theater."

Purists sniff at Gockley's unorthodox methods but not at the results. At a time when many U.S. opera companies are struggling financially and a few recently have shut down—such as Artists Internationale in Providence, Rhode Island, and Opera St. Paul in St. Paul, Minnesota—the Houston Grand Opera is flourishing. Over the past decade, season subscriptions have risen to 13,500 from 4,113; the total number of performances has increased to more than 400 from 27; and the annual budget has ballooned to $7 million from $420,000.

Besides explosive growth, another trademark of the Houston Grand Opera has been its aggressive diversification. Since becoming director ten years ago, Gockley has brought back neglected works and commissioned new ones. He has produced a new series of operettas, or light operas, which are sung in English, and a few highly controversial stagings of operas featuring nudity on stage. He has established the country's only free, full-staged outdoor opera, a junior touring company (sort of a "farm team" for young singers), and, to train fledgling artists, the Houston Opera Studio at the University of Houston. "There aren't many companies that offer the diversity of programs they do," said Maria Rich, executive director of Central Opera Service, an information trade group. "And all of (the programs) are run on a fiscally responsible basis."

Indeed, the Houston Grand Opera considers the term *fiscal responsibility* a company matter and has it emblazoned on the company's brochures, programs, and fact sheets. That's because Gockley, a former opera singer and a graduate of the Columbia University Graduate School of Business, is convinced the greatest challenge of any arts organization today is to produce "shows of artistic excellence while still managing to live within its means."[1]

The Conceptual Framework

In Chapter 1, marketing was defined as the development and efficient distribution of goods, services, ideas, issues, and concepts for chosen consumer segments. Although much of the text concentrated on orga-

[1]George Getschow, "Houston's 'P. T. Barnum of Opera' Thrives by Emphasizing Marketing, Bottom Line," *The Wall Street Journal* (March 9, 1982), p. 25. Reprinted by permission.

nizations that operate for profit, the activities of the Houston Grand Opera are as representative of modern marketing activities as the marketing programs of Burger King, Wendy's, and McDonald's. Our definition of marketing is sufficiently comprehensive to encompass nonprofit as well as profit-seeking organizations.

A substantial portion of the U.S. economy is composed of **nonprofit organizations**—those whose primary objective is something other than returning a profit to its owners. An estimated one of every ten service workers and one of six professionals in the U.S. is employed in the nonprofit sector. The nonprofit sector includes 350,000 religious organizations, 37,000 human service organizations, 6,000 museums, 5,800 private libraries, 4,600 secondary schools, 3,500 hospitals, 1,500 colleges and universities, 1,100 symphony orchestras, and thousands of other organizations, such as government agencies, political parties, and labor unions.[2] Figure 23.1 illustrates a portion of the marketing efforts of two of these organizations—the National Rifle Association and the Friends of Animals.

Nonprofit organizations can be found in both public and private sectors of society. Federal, state, and local governmental units and agencies whose revenues are derived from tax collection have service objectives not keyed to profitability targets. The Department of Defense provides protection. A state's department of natural resources regulates conservation and environmental programs. The local animal control officer enforces ordinances that protect both persons and animals. Some public-sector agencies may be given revenue or behavior goals. A bridge or turnpike might be expected to pay maintenance costs and retire its bonds out of tolls, for example. Yet society does not expect these units to routinely produce a surplus that is returned to the taxpayers.

The private sector offers an even more diverse array of nonprofit settings. Art institutes, Notre Dame's football team, labor unions, hospitals, private schools, the United Fund, the Lion's Club, and the local country club all serve as examples of private-sector, nonprofit organizations. Some, like Notre Dame's football team, may return a surplus to the university that can be used to cover other activities, but the organization's primary goal is to win football games. The diversity of these settings suggests how pervasive organizational objectives—other than profitability—really are in a modern economy.

The market offering of the nonprofit organization is frequently more nebulous than the tangible goods or service provisions of profit-seeking firms. Table 23.1 lists social issues and ideas ranging from gay rights to the use of motorcycle helmets that represent the offerings made by some nonprofits to their publics.

[2]Don Bates, "Special Demand on Nonprofit PR," *Public Relations Journal* (August 1976), p. 24.

Figure 23.1 Examples of Advertising by Nonprofit Organizations

The diversity of these issues suggests the size of the nonprofit sector and the marketing activities involved in accomplishing their objectives. What makes them different from their profit-seeking counterparts?

Characteristics of Nonprofit Organizations

Nonprofit organizations have a special set of characteristics that impact the marketing activities of these entities. Like the profit-oriented service offerings discussed in Chapter 12, the product offered by a nonprofit organization is often intangible. A hospital's diagnostic services exhibit

Source: NRA advertisement courtesy of National Rifle Association of America. "Six-Pack Strangler" advertisement courtesy of Friends of Animals, Inc.

marketing problems similar to those inherent in marketing a life insurance policy.

A second feature of nonprofit organizations involves multiple publics. As Professor Philip Kotler points out:

Nonprofit organizations normally have at least two major publics to work with from a marketing point of view: their clients and their funders. The former pose the problem of resource allocation *and the latter, the problem of* resource attraction. *Besides these two publics, many other publics surround the nonprofit organization and call for marketing programs. Thus a college can direct marketing programs toward prospective students, current students,*

Table 23.1 Social Issues Marketed by Nonprofits

Abortion rights	Family planning	Nudism
Affirmative action	Fire prevention	Peace Corps
Alcoholism control	Fluoridation	Physical fitness
Birth defects	Forest fire prevention	Police, support of
Blood	Foster parenthood	Pollution control
Blue laws	Fraternal organizations	Population control
Buy American goods	Free enterprise	Prayer in schools
Cancer research	Freedom of the press	Prison reform
Capital punishment	Fundraising	Religion
CARE packages	Gay rights	Save the whales
Carpooling	Gun control	Seat belt use
Child abuse	Legalized gambling	Solar energy
Child adoption	Literacy	Space program
Consumer cooperatives	Littering prevention	Suicide hot line
Crime prevention	Mass transportation	Tax reform
Draft registration	Mental health	UNICEF
Drunk driving	Metric system	United Way
Energy conservation	Military recruiting	VD hotline
Equal Rights Amendment	Motorcycle helmets	55-mph speed limit
Euthanasia	Museums	911-emergency number
	Nuclear energy	

Source: These issues are listed in Seymour H. Fine, *The Marketing of Ideas and Social Issues* (New York: Praeger, 1981), pp. 13–14.

parents of students, alumni, faculty, staff, local business firms, and local government agencies. It turns out that business organizations also deal with a multitude of publics but their tendency is to think about marketing only in connection with one of these publics, namely their customers.[3]

A customer or service user may wield less control over the destiny of a nonprofit organization. A government employee may be far more concerned with the opinion of a member of the legislature's appropriations committee than of a service user. Furthermore, nonprofit organizations often possess some degree of monopoly power in a given geographical area. An individual might object to the United Fund's inclusion of a crisis center among its beneficiary agencies. But a contributor who accepts the merits of the United Fund appeal recognizes that a portion of total contributions will go to the agency in question.

Another problem involves the resource contributor, such as a legislator or a financial backer, who interferes with the marketing program. It is easy to imagine a political candidate harassed by financial support-

[3]Philip Kotler, *Marketing for Nonprofit Organizations* (Englewood Cliffs, N.J.: Prentice-Hall, 1982), p. 9.

ers who want to replace an unpopular campaign manager (the primary marketing position in a political campaign).

Perhaps the most commonly noted feature of the nonprofit organization is its lack of a *bottom line* (business jargon referring to the overall profitability measure of performance). While nonprofit organizations may attempt to maximize their return from a specific service, less exact goals such as service level standards are the usual substitute for an overall evaluation. The net result is that it is often difficult to set marketing objectives that are alligned specifically with overall organizational goals.

A final characteristic is the lack of a clear organization structure. Nonprofit organizations often refer to constituencies that they serve, but these are often considerably less exact than, for example, the stockholders of a profit-oriented corporation. Nonprofit organizations often have multiple organizational structures. A hospital might have an administrative structure, the professional organization consisting of medical personnel, and a volunteer organization that dominates the board of trustees. These people may sometimes work at cross-purposes and not be totally in line with the marketing strategy that has been devised.

While the above factors may also characterize some profit-oriented organizations, they are certainly prevalent in nonprofit settings. These characteristics impact the implementation of marketing efforts in such organizations and must be considered in the development of an overall strategy.

The Broadening Concept

The current status of nonprofit marketing is largely the result of an evolutionary process that began in the early 1960s, when several writers suggested that marketing should be concerned with issues beyond the traditional profit-oriented domain. Marketing was beginning to be seen as having wider application than was normally the case.

A major breakthrough came in 1969 with the publication of Kotler and Levy's classic article that argued that the marketing concept should be broadened to include the nonprofit sector of society.[4] The theoretical justification for this view was that marketing was a generic activity for all organizations.[5] In other words, marketing was a function to be performed by any type of organization. Thus, the **broadening concept**

[4]Philip Kotler and Sidney J. Levy, "Broadening the Concept of Marketing," *Journal of Marketing* (January 1969), pp. 10–15. For a description of this evolution, see Philip D. Cooper and William J. Kehoe, "Marketing's Status, Dimensions, and Directions," *Business* (July–August 1979), pp. 14–15.

[5]Philip Kotler, "A Generic Concept of Marketing," *Journal of Marketing* (April 1979), pp. 46–54.

was an extension of the marketing concept to nontraditional exchange processes.

The broadening concept was not unanimously accepted by marketers. Luck argued that it was an unwarranted extension of the marketing concept.[6] More recently, Laczniak and Michie argued that a broadened marketing concept could be responsible for undesirable social changes and disorder.[7] Despite some dissent, the broadening concept is enjoying wide acceptance among nonprofit organizations and various students of marketing.

Types of Nonprofit Organizations

Although nonprofit organizations are at least as varied as profit-seeking organizations, it is possible to categorize them based upon the type of offerings they provide. The three major types of marketing among nonprofits are person marketing, idea marketing, and organization marketing.

Person Marketing

Person marketing refers to efforts designed to cultivate the attention, interest, and preference of a market target toward a person.[8] This type of marketing is typically employed by political candidates and celebrities.

The 1980 presidential campaign between Ronald Reagan and Jimmy Carter is a good example of person marketing.[9] Republican candidate Reagan chose a former marketing researcher, Richard B. Wirthlin, as his marketing manager. Wirthlin, whose business clients include Sears, Standard Oil of Ohio, Coors, G.D. Searle, and Armour-Dial, based his marketing recommendations upon the findings of $1.3 million spent on voter research. These findings, contained in a 176-page "Black Book," dealt with voter segments and strategies to reach them. In order to expand the Reagan base of voter support, Wirthlin identified four market targets on which the campaign should concentrate: southern

[6]David J. Luck, "Broadening the Concept of Marketing—Too Far," *Journal of Marketing* (July 1969), pp. 53–55.

[7]This interesting series of exchanges appears in the *Journal of Academy of Marketing Science* (Summer 1979). See Gene R. Laczniak and Donald A. Michie, "The Social Disorder of the Broadened Concept of Marketing," pp. 214–232; Sidney J. Levy and Philip Kotler, "Toward a Broader Concept of Marketing's Role in Social Order," pp. 232–238; and Laczniak and Michie, "Broadened Marketing and Social Order; A Reply," pp. 239–242.

[8]Philip Kotler, *Marketing for Nonprofit Organizations* (Englewood Cliffs, N.J.: Prentice-Hall, 1982), p. 482.

[9]Jack Honomichl, "The Marketing of a Candidate," *Advertising Age* (December 15, 1980).

white Protestants; blue-collar workers in industrial states; urban ethnics; and rural voters in upstate New York, Ohio, and Pennsylvania. He also identified the key states that could decide the election. The campaign was then based upon this information.

Idea Marketing

The second type of nonprofit marketing deals with causes and social issues rather than an individual. **Idea marketing** refers to the identification and marketing of a cause to chosen consumer segments.[10] A highly visual marketing mix element frequently associated with idea marketing is the use of *advocacy advertising,* discussed earlier in Chapter 20. The importance of wearing seat belts is currently being marketed by the American Insurance Association. The National Organization for the Repeal of Marijuana Laws (NORML) is attempting to affect voter and legislative attitudes in order to legalize marijuana.

As Figure 23.2 indicates, different organizations may use advocacy advertising in marketing different viewpoints for the same social issue. When the Maryland affiliate of Planned Parenthood ran the advertisement on the right (developed by Planned Parenthood of New York City) in several Maryland newspapers and in a regional edition of *Newsweek,* the Catholic archdiocese of Baltimore responded with the advertisement on the left. The parody advocating the opposite point of view was part of the Catholic archdiocese's campaign to increase support for anti-abortion legislation.

Organization Marketing

The third type of nonprofit marketing, **organization marketing,** attempts to influence others to accept the goals of, receive the services of, or contribute in some way to an organization. Included in this category are *mutual benefit* organizations, such as churches, labor unions, and political parties; *service* organizations, such as colleges and universities, hospitals, and museums; and *government* organizations such as military services, police and fire departments, and the post office. Figure 23.3 illustrates the efforts of the U.S. Postal Service to serve some of its collector clients through a broadened product and service mix. Other recent innovations include self-service stamp vending machines in shopping centers and office buildings, Express Mail for overnight delivery, and promotional efforts designed to encourage ZIP code usage.[11]

[10]An excellent discussion of idea marketing appears in Jagdish N. Sheth and Gary L. Frazier, "A Model of Strategy Mix Choice for Planned Social Change," *Journal of Marketing* (Winter 1982), pp. 15–26.

[11]David J. Rachman and Elaine Romano, *Modern Marketing* (Hinsdale, Ill.: The Dryden Press, 1980), p. 576. The delineation of person, idea, and organization marketing are proposed by Professors Rachman and Romano.

Figure 23.2 Idea Marketing: The Case For—and Against—Abortion

THE DECISION TO HAVE A BABY IS NOT MADE IN THE SENATE, BUT IN THE HOUSE.
YOUR HOUSE.

THE ARCHDIOCESE OF BALTIMORE

HAVING A BABY IS SOMETHING PERSONAL. PROTECT A PERSON'S RIGHT TO LIFE.

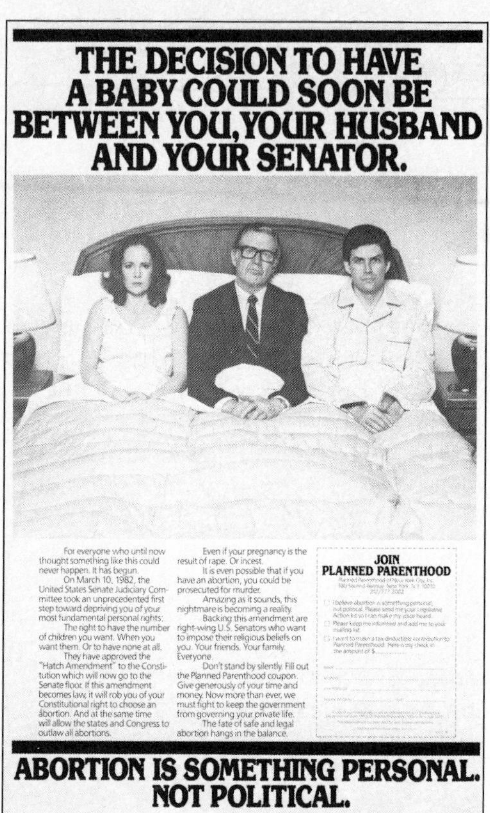

Source: Reprinted by permission of the Archdiocese of Baltimore and Planned Parenthood of New York City.

Defining Marketing in Nonprofit Settings

One of the most pervasive problems in nonprofit marketing is the way in which marketing is defined. In many cases, marketing is taken to mean simply promotion. Other components of the marketing mix—product development, distribution, and pricing strategies—are largely ignored. Marketing, defined as aggressive promotion, is seen as a short-lived, surface-level solution for a variety of organizational problems and objectives.

Professor Seymour H. Fine recently conducted a survey of nonprofit organizations to assess the degree of marketing sophistication present. His findings, illustrated in Table 23.2, revealed that many respondents were unaware of, or at least reluctant to admit, the presence of marketing efforts in their organizations.

Figure 23.3 Advertisement for Commemorative Stamp

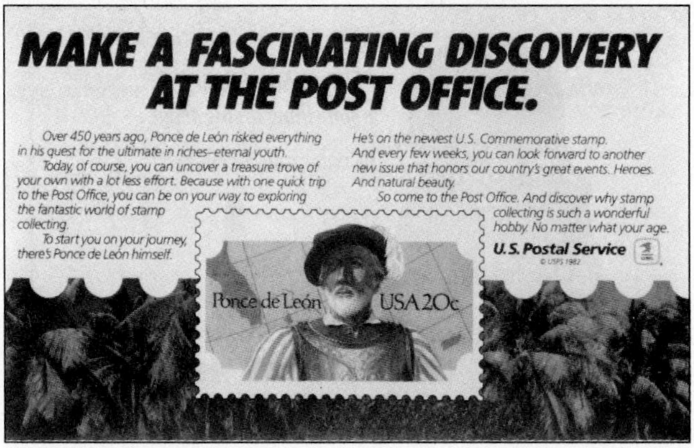

Source: Courtesy of U.S. Postal Service.

Few nonprofit organizations take the time to develop a comprehensive marketing approach that includes an analysis of its market, resources, and mission. Strategies should be devised only after these basic parameters have been identified and studied. Of course, there are exceptions. The University of Houston, for example, conducted a comprehensive marketing audit that designated strong and weak areas in its product mix (program offerings).

The Importance of Marketing to Nonprofit Organizations

Marketing is a late arrival to the management of nonprofit organizations. The practices of improved accounting, financial control, personnel selection, and strategic planning all were implemented before marketing.[12] Nevertheless, nonprofit organizations have accepted it enthusiastically. Dozens of articles and speeches attest to marketing's popularity. Some colleges and universities now offer courses in nonprofit marketing. Meanwhile, university administrators attend seminars and conferences to learn how to better market their own institutions.

[12]This section is based on and used with permission from Philip Kotler, "Strategies for Introducing Marketing into Nonprofit Organizations," *Journal of Marketing* (January 1979), pp. 37–44, published by the American Marketing Association.

Table 23.2 Responses of Selected Nonprofit Organization Representatives

Nonprofit Organization	Response to the Question: "Do you have a marketing department or equivalent?"
Public health service official	"Marketing fluoridation is not a function of government—promotion and public awareness is."
Administrator of regional League of Women Voters	"We have never thought of ourselves as marketing a product. We have people who are assigned ERA as their 'item.' "
Group crusading for the rights of the left-handed	"Don't understand the term (marketing); we do lobbying, letter writing to appropriate government and commercial concerns."
A national center for the prevention of child abuse	"We disseminate information without the marketing connotation. Besides, demand is too great to justify marketing."
National Guard recruiting officer	"Not applicable."

Source: Adapted from Seymour H. Fine, *The Marketing of Ideas and Social Issues* (New York: Praeger, 1981), p. 53.

Philip Kotler, one of the persons most responsible for this new direction, has published a textbook in this area.[13]

Marketing's rise in the nonprofit sector could not be continued without a successful track record. While it is often more difficult to measure results in nonprofit settings, marketing can already point to examples of success. The Presbyterian-affiliated Church of the Covenant in Cleveland credits a 10 percent increase in average attendance to a series of radio commercials.[14] And a Midwestern hospital's marketing analysis allowed it to reposition itself as a provider of tertiary care services rather than as a community hospital. Marketing is now an accepted part of the operational environment of most successful nonprofit organizations. Figure 23.4 is a hypothetical job description for a marketing director at a college or university.

Developing a Marketing Strategy

The need for a comprehensive marketing strategy rather than merely increasing promotion expenditures was noted earlier. Substantial op-

[13]Philip Kotler, *Marketing for Nonprofit Organizations* (Englewood Cliffs, N.J.: Prentice-Hall, 1982).

[14]Margaret Yao, "Big Pitch for God: More Churches Try Advertising in Media," *The Wall Street Journal* (December 31, 1979), pp. 1, 7. See also Fred L. Miller and Phillip B. Niffenegger, "Television Evangelists: Fast Food Marketing Strategies in the Religion Industry," in *A Spectrum of Contemporary Marketing Ideas,* (eds.) John H. Summey, Blaise J. Bergiel, and Carol H. Anderson (New Orleans: Southern Marketing Association, 1982), pp. 253–256.

Figure 23.4 Job Description: Director of Marketing for a University

Position Title: Director of Marketing

Reports to: A vice president designated by the president

Scope: University-wide

Position Concept: The director of marketing is responsible for providing marketing guidance and services to university officers, school deans, department chairmen, and other agents of the university.

Functions: The director of marketing will:

1. Contribute a marketing perspective to the deliberations of the top administration in their planning of the university's future.
2. Prepare data that might be needed by any officer of the university on a particular market's size, segments, trends, and behavioral dynamics.
3. Conduct studies of the needs, perceptions, preferences, and satisfactions of particular markets.
4. Assist in the planning, promotion, and launching of new programs.
5. Assist in the development of communication and promotion campaigns and materials.
6. Analyze and advise on pricing questions.
7. Appraise the workability of new academic proposals from a marketing point of view.
8. Advise on new student recruitment.
9. Advise on current student satisfaction.
10. Advise on university fundraising.

Responsibilities: The director of marketing will:

1. Contact individual officers and small groups at the university to explain services and to solicit problems.
2. Prioritize the various requests for services according to their long-run impact, cost saving potential, time requirements, ease of accomplishment, cost, and urgency.
3. Select projects of high priority and set accomplishment goals for the year.
4. Prepare a budget request to support the anticipated work.
5. Prepare an annual report on the main accomplishments of the office.

Major Liaisons: The director of marketing will:

1. Relate most closely with the president's office, admissions office, development office, planning office, and public relations department.
2. Relate secondarily with the deans of various schools and chairmen of various departments.

Source: Reprinted with permission from Philip Kotler, "Strategies for Introducing Marketing into Nonprofit Organizations," *Journal of Marketing* (January 1979), p. 42, published by the American Marketing Association.

portunities exist for effective, innovative strategies since there has been little previous marketing effort in most nonprofit settings.

Marketing Research

Many decisions in nonprofit settings are based on little if any research. An Illinois hospital opened an adult day-care center for elderly people requiring ongoing attention and personnel services, based solely as a result of the observation that many seniors lived within a three-mile radius. Only two patients were admitted at the daily fee set by hospital administrators.[15]

Adequate marketing research can be extremely important in a variety of nonprofit settings. Resident opinion surveys in many cities have proven valuable to public officials. Consumer surveys currently play an important role in product liability lawsuits. The analysis of projected population trends has led to tentative decisions to close obstetric units at some hospitals.

Product Strategy

Nonprofit organizations face the same product decisions as profit-seeking firms. They must choose a product, service, person, idea, or social issue to be offered to their market target. They must decide whether to offer a single product or a mix of related products. They must make product identification decisions. The United Way symbol and the Red Cross trademarks illustrate the similarity in the use of product identification methods.

A common failure among nonprofit organizations is the assumption that heavy promotional efforts can overcome a poor product strategy or marketing mix. Consider the number of liberal arts colleges that tried to use promotion to overcome their product mix deficiencies when students became increasingly career-oriented. Successful institutions adjust their product offerings to reflect customer demand.

Antal Dorati, of the Detroit Symphony Orchestra, recognizes the importance of product strategy in a nonprofit setting. The orchestra's ticket sales and donations were on the decline when Dorati took over as conductor. While the maestro is known as an aggressive promoter, he also is a very adept product manager. Dorati expanded the orchestra's season to include a festival highlighting a specific period or composer. He coordinated festival concerts with lectures delivered by guest musicians, critics, and the like. Dorati has taken the Detroit Symphony Orchestra on a European tour. Domestic tours, including a New York appearance, are planned. The conductor also secured a recording contract for the orchestra, and its first album became a best seller. Dorati understands the importance of developing an appropriate product mix.[16]

[15]Kotler, "Strategies for Introducing Marketing into Nonprofit Organizations," p. 40. See also Richard Homans and Franklin S. Houston, "Marketing Research for Public Health: A Demonstration of Different Responses to Advertising," *Journal of the Academy of Marketing Science* (Fall 1981), pp. 380–398.

[16]Leonard M. Apcar, "Detroit's Antal Dorati, Master Merchandiser, Thrives on Promoting," *The Wall Street Journal* (January 22, 1980), pp. 1, 17. See also Julian W. Vincze, "A Model of the Marketing Management Process for the Performing Arts," and John E. Robbins and Stephanie S. Robbins, "Marketing the New Orleans Symphony to Blacks: A Strategic Analysis," in *A Spectrum of Contemporary Marketing Ideas,* (eds.) John H. Summey, Blaise J. Bergiel, and Carol H. Anderson (New Orleans: Southern Marketing Association, 1982), pp. 229–237.

Pricing Strategy

Pricing is typically a very important element of the marketing mix for nonprofit organizations. Pricing strategy can be used to accomplish a variety of organizational goals in nonprofit settings. These include:

1. *Profit maximization.* While nonprofit organizations by definition do not cite profitability as a primary goal, there are numerous instances in which they do try to maximize their return on a single event or a series of events. The $1,000-a-plate political fund raiser is a classic example.
2. *Cost recovery.* Some nonprofit organizations attempt only to recover the actual cost of operating the unit. Mass transit, publicly supported colleges, and bridges are common examples. The amount of recovered costs is often dictated by tradition, competition, and/or public opinion.
3. *Providing market incentives.* Other nonprofit settings follow a penetration pricing policy or offer a free service to encourage increased usage of the product or service. Seattle's bus system charges no fare in the downtown area to reduce traffic congestion, encourage retail sales, and minimize the effort required to use downtown public services.
4. *Market suppression.* Price is sometimes used to discourage consumption. In other words, high prices are used to accomplish societal objectives and are not directly related to the costs of providing the product or service. Illustrations include tobacco and alcohol taxes, parking fines, tolls, and gasoline excise taxes.[17]

Distribution Strategy

Distribution channels for nonprofit organizations tend to be short, simple, and direct. If middlemen are present in the channel, they are usually agents such as an independent ticket agency or a specialist in fund raising. A major distribution decision involves the specific location of the nonprofit organization.

Nonprofit organizations often fail to exercise caution in the planning and execution of the distribution strategy. Organizers of recycling centers sometimes complain about lack of public interest, when their real problem is an inconvenient location or lack of adequate drop-off points. Urban hospitals located in declining areas sometimes find it difficult to attract suburban patients.[18] By contrast, some public agencies like health and social welfare departments have set up branches in neigh-

[17]This section is based on Philip Kotler, *Marketing for Nonprofit Organizations*, 1982, pp. 306–309. Adapted by permission of Prentice-Hall, Inc., Englewood Cliffs, New Jersey. See also Chris T. Allen, "Self-Perception Based Strategies for Stimulating Energy Conservation," *Journal of Consumer Research* (March 1982), pp. 381–390.

[18]Daniel J. Fink, "Marketing the Hospital," *MBA* (December 1978/January 1979), p. 50.

borhood shopping centers to be more accessible to their clientele. Nonprofit marketers must carefully evaluate the available distribution options if they are to be successful in delivering their product or in serving their intended consumer.

Promotional Strategy

It is common to see or hear advertisements from nonprofit organizations such as educational institutions, churches, and public service organizations. A striking example of nonprofit advertising is Figure 23.5, a magazine advertisement for the United Negro College Fund.

The effectiveness of marketing communications and promotional strategy is impacted by a variety of factors including relative involvement in the nonprofit setting, pricing, and perceived benefits.[19] But overall, promotion is seen by many nonprofit managers as the primary solution to their marketing problems. As noted earlier, this view is often naive, but it does not diminish the importance of promotion in a nonprofit setting.

All types of promotional strategy components have been utilized. The U.S. armed services have used television advertising to attract enlistments. University development officers rely on personal selling to build endowments. Fund-raising drives often rely on publicity and public relations efforts like TV talk shows to promote their product, but charitable groups have used badges, paper flowers, and other specialty advertising items to identify donors or contributions and to promote their particular cause. Promotion is likely to remain the key ingredient of most marketing strategies devised within nonprofit settings.

Evaluation and Control of Nonprofit Marketing

A comprehensive discussion of the evaluation and control of marketing activities is presented in Chapter 25. However, there are several variables that can be used to measure the effectiveness of nonprofit marketing efforts. Some of these include total market response, market share, cost per dollar of market response, efficiency measures, and market attitudes.[20]

Total market response is a measurement of numbers; examples of this measurement could be enrollment applications at a university or season ticket sales to the ballet. The actual market response can then be com-

[19]Michael L. Rothschild, "Marketing Communications in Nonbusiness Situations or Why It's So Hard to Sell Brotherhood Like Soap," *Journal of Marketing* (Spring 1979), pp. 11–20.

[20]These variables are outlined in Philip Kotler, *Marketing for Nonprofit Organizations,* 1975, pp. 250–251. Adapted by permission of Prentice-Hall, Inc., Englewood Cliffs, New Jersey.

Figure 23.5 A Promotional Strategy for the United Negro College Fund

Source: Reprinted by permission of the United Negro College Fund.

pared to forecasted response. The data can also be broken down into categories, like first-year, transfer, and first-time season ticket purchasers.

Market share is a comparative measure that allows a nonprofit agency to assess its performance against the competition. Symphony, ballet, and theater season ticket sales could be measured on a market-share basis.

Cost per dollar of market response is an evaluation measure often used in charitable fund raising. Solicitation costs are cited as a percentage of each dollar collected in such efforts.

Efficiency measures are also common in the evaluation and control of nonprofit marketing activities. Number of donor contacts per day, percentage of lost contributions, acceptance rates, and other measures are common in nonprofit settings.

Market attitudes can be evaluated by conducting consumer surveys among those whom the agency serves. A hospital, for example, might attempt to assess patients' attitudes toward its services, food, and personnel by sending them a questionnaire after their release. Colleges and universities often gauge student attitudes toward services like the dining halls, health center, intramural facilities, parking, and placement office.

Regardless of how the evaluation is stated and conducted, it is essential that nonprofit agencies be subject to a degree of control similar to that found in profit-oriented institutions. An evaluation and control system forms an integral part of an effective marketing program.

The Future of Nonprofit Marketing

While marketing has gained increasing acceptance in the nonprofit sector of society, it is still viewed with suspicion by many of the people involved. The heavy emphasis on promotion is one reason. But in a broader sense, marketing efforts in nonprofit organizations often lack the sophistication and integration found in the marketing of profit-oriented industries. Marketing is too often seen as the quick-fix solution to a more basic problem. To combat this, marketers must market their discipline in a realistic and socially responsible manner. The client must be made to understand the opportunities, benefits, behavior modifications, and commitment involved in the adoption of the marketing concept in a nonprofit setting.

Summary

Nonprofit organizations are those enterprises whose primary objective is something other than returning a profit to the owners. Nonprofit organizations are often characterized by the intangible nature of many of their services; multiple publics; minimal control by customers; professional rather than organizational orientation of their employees; involvement of resource contributors; lack of an overall bottom line; and the lack of a clear organizational structure. Person, idea, and organization marketing are the three types of nonprofit marketing.

The introduction of marketing into nonprofit settings has been associated with the broadening concept, which extends the marketing concept to nontraditional exchange processes. The broadening concept was introduced by Philip Kotler and Sidney J. Levy in 1969.

Marketing is now viewed as integral to many nonprofit settings, although it is too often defined largely in terms of promotional strategy.

Nonprofit agencies require a comprehensive marketing mix based upon accurate marketing research. An effective evaluation and control system must be set up to monitor the marketing strategy. This system might be based on one or more of the following variables: total market response, market share, cost per dollar of market response, efficiency measures, and market attitudes.

Key Terms

nonprofit organization
broadening concept
person marketing
idea marketing
organization marketing

Review Questions

1. What are the primary characteristics of nonprofit organizations that distinguish them from profit-seeking organizations?
2. Describe the evolution of the broadening concept.
3. What is person marketing? Contrast it with marketing of a consumer good such as magazines.
4. Why is idea marketing more difficult than organization marketing?
5. Identify the types of organization marketing and give examples of each.
6. Why is marketing sometimes defined inaccurately in a nonprofit organization?
7. Contrast the product strategy of nonprofit marketing with that of marketing for profit.
8. Identify the pricing goals that are commonly found in nonprofit enterprises.
9. Compare distribution and promotional strategies of nonprofit organizations with profit-seeking enterprises.
10. Explain the variables used in evaluating and controlling a nonprofit marketing program.

Discussion Questions and Exercises

1. What type of nonprofit organization does each of the following represent:
   a. United Auto Workers
   b. Glenn for President committee
   c. New York Public Library
   d. San Diego Zoo
   e. Save the Whales Foundation
   f. U.S. Girl Scouts
   g. Easter Seals
2. Table 23.2 reveals that many nonprofit organization executives have negative attitudes toward marketing. What must be done to change this?

3. Cite several examples of circumstances when penetration pricing might be practiced by public utilities.
4. How would you assess the marketing performance of the following:
   - **a.** Your university
   - **b.** March of Dimes
   - **c.** United Mine Workers
   - **d.** Planned Parenthood
   - **e.** Re-election committee of a U.S. senator
5. Outline the marketing program of your college or university. Make any reasonable assumptions necessary. Where are the major strengths and weaknesses of the current program? What recommendations would you make for improving it?

24

Chapter Objectives

1. To describe marketing's contemporary environment.
2. To outline the need for measuring social performance.
3. To identify the three major current issues in marketing.
4. To explain how the contemporary issues in marketing might be resolved.

MARKETING AND SOCIETY

Marketers at Boots Pharmaceuticals, Inc., achieved considerable success in attempting to employ a *pulling* promotional strategy in an industry where a *pushing* strategy is expected. But in implementing their innovative strategy, they stirred controversy among physicians who prescribe the products to their patients. It all started when Boots marketers decided to enter the $700 million U.S. market for prescription anti-arthritic drugs with a $1.50 rebate to consumers on bottles of Rufen—their brand of the generic drug ibuprofen. The furor caused by this traditional marketing technique was described by a *Business Week* reporter as follows:

Boots' marketing tactic has been described reluctantly by U.S. competitors as "clever" and "unique," but also has been criticized as unethical. The traditional way to introduce a new drug to the market is through a sales force, known in the ethical, or prescription, drug industry as a "detail" force, which markets the drug directly to physicians and pharmacists. Many pharmaceutical companies give physicians generous samples of the drug to pass along to patients. Advertising is done through professional journals. It is an expensive but time-honored way to introduce a new product.

Instead, Boots opted to spend the money normally allocated to marketing on lowering the cost of the medicine, says John D. Bryer, president. . . . To reach physicians, Boots sent product information to 46,000 physicians and 26,000 pharmacists, explaining that Rufen is the chemical equivalent of Motrin (Upjohn Company's brand whose annual sales exceed $200 million). Given Upjohn's extensive sales of Motrin, Boots did not feel the need to offer samples and has done little advertising. Says Bryer: "We figured we could take the money away from Madison Avenue and give it to the consumer."

Moreover, it appears to be working. Bryer says that in four months Rufen has captured about a six percent share of all new prescriptions for ibuprofen and that almost 19,000 rebate coupons have been returned to the company. A spokeswoman for Gray Drug Fair, a 365-unit subsidiary of Cleveland-based Sherwin Williams Co., said sales of Rufen "have gradually increased" since the promotion began. "For those who have to take it on a regular basis, the lower price will be a very big factor," she added. Consumer interest is sure to heighten as Bryer completes a promotional tour that includes television and radio talk shows.

But by marketing directly to the consumer, say some critics, Boots is interfering with the physician-patient relationship. In a letter published in the New England Journal of Medicine, *Dr. William M. O'Brien asserts: "If patients taking Motrin for arthritis know that other patients are getting rebates for using a less-expensive brand of ibuprofen, they may pressure their physicians to change their prescription to Rufen. A consumer-initiated switch from one brand of ibuprofen to another may involve nothing but costs; but imagine the physician's dilemma if they should get the same sort of request from patients currently taking another ("rebateless") nonsteroidal drug. In such a situation, a switch, however appealing to the patient, might simply be medically unwise."*[1]

The Conceptual Framework

It should be clear by now that the marketing decision maker develops a marketing mix based on an analysis of the target *and* the environmental factors that affect the consumer and the marketing mix. Chapter 2 outlined the key environmental considerations from that perspective.

There is a further environmental dimension that goes beyond the previous considerations. This is the role that marketing plays in society itself and the consequent effects and responsibilities of marketing activities. Since marketing is such a visible force in society, the issue is im-

[1] "Tumult Over a Drug Rebate," *Business Week* (February 1, 1982), p. 55. Reprinted by permission.

portant to all. General Motors, Pillsbury, J.C. Penney, and General Electric have all set up committees from their boards of directors to decide in which social programs the companies should engage.[2] W. Michael Blumenthal, former chairman and president of Bendix Corporation, and others have advocated a code of professional ethics for business executives.

What do these firms and executives have in common? All are attempting to act responsibly in regard to contemporary business and societal issues. And marketing has a key role to play in the resolution of these matters. The text has consistently stressed that marketing is a most dynamic business activity. Marketing's relationship to society in general and to various public issues is subject to constant scrutiny by the public. It may, in fact, be reasonably argued that marketing typically mirrors changes in the entire business environment. Since marketing is the final interface between the business enterprise and the society in which it operates, it is understandable that marketers often carry much of the responsibility for dealing with various social issues affecting their firms.

This chapter provides a framework within which you can constructively evaluate the marketing system. As you will see, the question "does the marketing system serve consumers well?" cannot easily be answered. You will, however, be helped to evaluate the marketing system for yourself.

The Contemporary Environment of Marketing

Marketing operates in an environment external to the firm. It reacts to its environment and is, in turn, acted upon by it. These environmental relationships include relationships with customers, employees, the government, vendors, and society as a whole. While they are often a product of the exchange process, these relationships are coincidental to the primary sales and distribution functions of marketing.

External relationships form the basis of the societal issues confronting contemporary marketing. Marketing's relationship to its external environment has a significant effect on the relative degree of success achieved by the firm. Marketing must continually find new ways to deal with the social issues facing our competitive system.

Historically, marketing has neglected some environmental relationships. Various regulations and license requirements have been enacted to limit door-to-door selling, which had become excessive in some areas.

[2]Michael L. Lovdol, Raymond A. Bauer, and Nancy H. Treverton, "Public Responsibility Committees on the Board," *Harvard Business Review* (May–June 1977), p. 40. See also Kenneth E. Goodpaster and John B. Matthews, Jr., "Can a Corporation Have a Conscience?" *Harvard Business Review* (January–February 1982), pp. 132–141.

The government has banned some children's toys because they were unsafe.

The Federal Trade Commission has accused numerous firms of using misleading advertising and, as discussed in Chapter 2, has occasionally required them to use corrective advertising to inform consumers of the misrepresentation. For 50 years, Warner-Lambert promoted Listerine mouthwash as a cold and sore-throat remedy. During the 1970s, the FTC ruled that the product would not relieve sore throats or colds and required the firm to spend more than $10 million in advertising making the statement, "Listerine will not help prevent colds or lessen their severity."

The competitive marketing system is a product of our drive for materialism, but it is important to note that materialism developed from society itself. Most U.S. culture, with its acceptance of the work ethic, has viewed the acquisition of wealth favorably. The motto of this philosophy seems to be "More equals better." A better life has been defined in terms of more physical possessions, although that may be changing.

Evaluating the Quality of Life

One theme runs through the arguments of marketing's critics: materialism (as exemplified by the competitive marketing system) is concerned only with the quantities of life and ignores the quality aspect. Traditionally, a firm was considered socially responsible in the community if it provided employment to its residents, thereby contributing to its economic base. Employment, wages, bank deposits, and profits, the traditional measures of societal contribution, are quantity indicators. But what of air, water, and cultural pollution? The boredom and isolation of mass assembly lines? The depletion of natural resources? The charges of neglect in these areas go largely unanswered simply because we have not developed reliable indices by which to measure a firm's contribution to the quality of life.

An Indictment of the Competitive Marketing System

An indictment of the competitive marketing system would contain at least the following:

1. Marketing costs are too high.[3]
2. The marketing system is inefficient.

[3]This issue has been debated in such works as Paul M. Mazur, "Does Distribution Cost Enough?" *Fortune* (November 1947), pp. 138–139, 192, 194, 197–198, 200; R. S. Vaile, E. T. Grether, and Reavis Cox, *Marketing in the American Economy* (New York: Ronald Press Company, 1952); Stanley C. Hollander, "Measuring the Cost and Value of Marketing," *MSU Business Topics* (Summer 1961), pp. 17–27; and Reavis Cox, *Distribution in a High-Level Economy* (Englewood Cliffs, N.J.: Prentice-Hall, 1965). One widely cited study of marketing costs concluded that high distribution costs should be blamed on consumers as well as marketers. See Paul W. Steward and J. Frederick Dewhurst with Louise Field, *Does Distribution Cost Too Much?* (New York: The Twentieth Century Fund, 1939), p. 348.

3. Marketers (the business system) are guilty of collusion and price fixing.
4. Product quality and service are poor.
5. Consumers receive incomplete and/or false and misleading information.
6. The marketing system has produced health and safety hazards.
7. Unwanted and unnecessary products are promoted to those who least need them.

Almost anyone could site specific examples where these charges have been proven. But each of us has a somewhat different set of values, so it should be recognized that we all evaluate the performance of the marketing system we experience within our own frames of reference.

Bearing this in mind, and taking the system as a whole, we can evaluate the success or failure of the competitive marketing system in serving the needs of consumers. Most of us will likely arrive at the uncomfortable and not terribly satisfying conclusion that the system usually works quite adequately, although there are some aspects of it that we would like to see changed.

How can we change and regulate the system so that it is more in line with what we want for our society? What is the consumer interest? How much change do we really want?

Current Issues in Marketing

Marketing faces many diverse social issues. The current issues in marketing can be divided into three major subjects: consumerism, marketing ethics, and social responsibility. While the overlap and classification problems are obvious, the framework provides a foundation for systematically studying the issues.

Consumerism

Despite factors that tend to inhibit development of strong consumer groups, business practices and changing societal values have led to the consumerism movement. Today everyone—marketers, industry, government, the public—is acutely aware of the impact of consumerism on the nation's economy and general well-being. **Consumerism** has been defined as a social force within the environment designed to aid and protect the consumer by exerting legal, moral, and economic pressure on business.[4] Professors George Day and David Aaker argue that con-

[4]David W. Cravens and Gerald G. Hills, "Consumerism: A Perspective for Business," *Business Horizons* (August 1970), p. 21.

sumerism includes "the widening range of activities of government, business, and independent organizations that are designed to protect individuals from practices that infringe upon their rights as consumers."[5] It is a societal demand that organizations apply the marketing concept.

The Consumer Interest

The consumer interest lies in the development of a system that represents the interests of individuals in their roles as consumers as well as in their roles as suppliers of labor and owners of capital.[6] Groups such as the Consumer Federation of America, Common Cause, Action for Children's Television, and Ralph Nader's Public Citizen emerged out of consumers' frustrations that business and other interest groups were not serving their interests as well as they might.

Businesses do not overtly try to displease consumers. In fact, since most business activities take place in the relatively free market system, firms that do not satisfy consumers often go out of business eventually or are less profitable than they could be. Yet the many regulatory laws that have been introduced indicate that there are areas where consumers believed that the system needed improvement. Consumer groups have succeeded in strengthening consumer rights.[7]

The Consumer's Rights

Not all consumer demands are met. A competitive marketing system is based upon the individualistic behavior of competing firms. Our economic system requires that reasonable profit objectives be achieved. Business cannot meet all consumer demands if it is to generate the profits necessary to remain viable. This selection process is one of the most difficult questions facing society today. Given these constraints, what should the consumer have the right to expect from the competitive marketing system?

The most frequently quoted statement of **consumer rights** was made by President John F. Kennedy in 1962. While it was not a definitive statement, it is a good rule of thumb to explain basic consumer rights:

1. The right to choose freely
2. The right to be informed

[5]George S. Day and David A. Aaker, "A Guide to Consumerism," *Journal of Marketing* (July 1970), p. 12.

[6]J. D. Forbes and S. M. Oberg, "The Consumer Interest," (Faculty of Commerce and Business Administration, University of British Columbia, mimeo, 1981).

[7]Paul N. Bloom and Stephen A. Greyser, "The Maturing of Consumerism," *Harvard Business Review* (November–December 1981), pp. 130–139.

3. The right to be heard
4. The right to be safe.

These rights have formed the conceptual framework of much of the consumer legislation passed since then. However, the question of how best to guarantee these rights remains unanswered.

The Right to Choose Freely The first consumer right is the right to free choice in the marketplace and to a range of products and services that best suit the individual consumer. To exercise this right as a responsible consumer, everyone should be able to evaluate products rationally and choose the product that will give them the most satisfaction. Consumer policies should provide education and information to enable individuals to be responsible consumers, as well as to maintain markets that allow an adequate range of goods and services. In those cases where freedom of choice is restricted, for example, where monopolies are given to privately or publicly owned utilities, governments should establish regulatory bodies to ensure these monopolies do not misuse their power. There is much criticism of such controls and of their major impact on consumers.

The Right to Be Informed The second consumer right is to be provided with adequate product/service information to be able to make an informed choice. Controversy often surrounds government imposition of rules specifying information that sellers must provide to consumers.

Some consumer advocates work on the principle that more information is better; others are skeptical of this point of view. While more may be better, consumers have difficulty processing masses of information unless they understand the relationships between the various product/service attributes and are able to analyze information rationally.

There is much we do not know about how to assist consumers in exercising their right to be informed. Marketers are conducting a great deal of research about information, its form, the importance of format, and its availability during the buying process. Packaging and labeling regulations and "false and misleading advertising" provisions of federal, state, and local laws have contributed to increased information and decreased deception in recent years. With the research in progress, more effective information for consumers can be provided.

The Right to Be Heard The third consumer right is being able to express legitimate displeasure over the inability to obtain goods and services or the terms of trade under which they are purchased. While the marketplace *may* produce the quality of product in the place and at the time desired by the consumer, there is no guarantee. In addition, products may not perform as the consumer wanted or the manufacturer intended. In the vast majority of cases, the dissatisfied consumer need only discuss the matter with the provider of the goods or service to obtain satisfaction. It is those infrequent, but often important, situations where an effective system for redress is unavailable even though the consumer's complaint is valid that cause frustration.

While it is the consumer's responsibility to do what is possible on an individual level to sound off and exercise his or her rights, the system for redress may be unavailable or available only at a cost out of proportion to the damage involved; for instance, a faulty cabinet on a television set may involve only $100 damage, but to collect that amount from the manufacturer may cost $300 in legal fees and personal time. A few firms have produced faulty products knowing that consumers do not believe it worthwhile to complain.

Another potent consumer weapon is the **class action suit,** which allows private citizens to join together and sue individuals and firms on behalf of any group of consumers for damages resulting from unfair business practices. Litigation, however, is not always the solution to society's problems. The recent medical malpractice crisis illustrates some unpleasant side effects of corrective actions based largely on litigations. Many physicians, for example, dropped malpractice insurance altogether because of major premium increases. Others raised their fees substantially to offset the increases.

Large consumer products organizations, departments of consumer and corporate affairs at federal, state, and municipal levels of government, and several consumer assistance groups have set up systems of handling consumer complaints to assist and expand the consumer's right to be heard. Even so, the systems do not work as well as many consumers desire.

The Right to Be Safe The fourth basic consumer right is a high degree of assurance that a product will neither be injurious to health nor present undue risks of injury through normal use. Products for general consumption should be designed so the average consumer can use them safely.

Enlightened design by manufacturers, coupled with safety and health regulations and government inspections, has made consumers in the 1980s significantly better protected than they were even 15 or 20 years ago. However, some people believe there are so many regulations that costs to minimize the risks to health and safety significantly exceed any consumer benefits provided. This point is understandably a contentious issue, and it is difficult to prove either side of the argument.

A further specification of the four consumer rights has been made by Professor Hans Thorelli (Figure 24.1). Thorelli suggests that com-

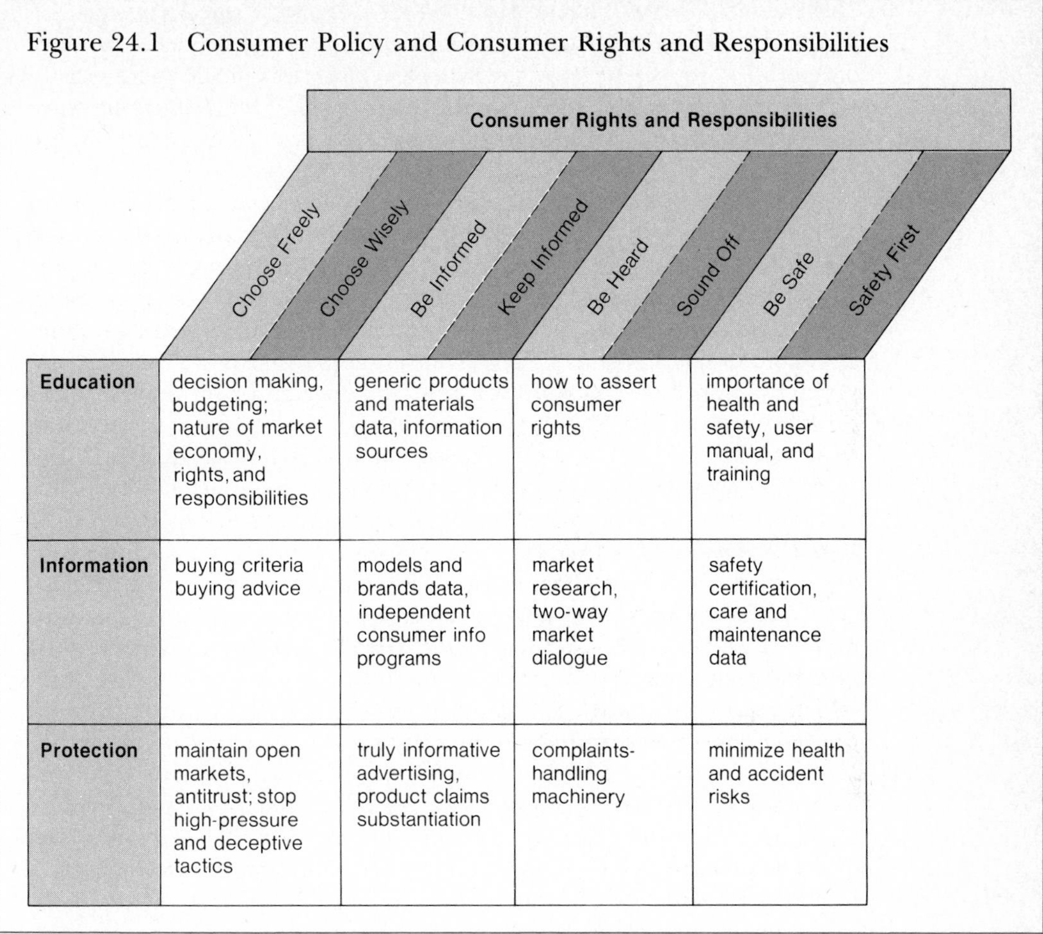

Figure 24.1 Consumer Policy and Consumer Rights and Responsibilities

Consumer Rights and Responsibilities	Choose Freely / Choose Wisely	Be Informed / Keep Informed	Be Heard / Sound Off	Be Safe / Safety First
Education	decision making, budgeting; nature of market economy, rights, and responsibilities	generic products and materials data, information sources	how to assert consumer rights	importance of health and safety, user manual, and training
Information	buying criteria buying advice	models and brands data, independent consumer info programs	market research, two-way market dialogue	safety certification, care and maintenance data
Protection	maintain open markets, antitrust; stop high-pressure and deceptive tactics	truly informative advertising, product claims substantiation	complaints-handling machinery	minimize health and accident risks

Source: Hans B. Thorelli, "Improving Policies Affecting Marketers, Consumer Groups, Universities and Governments," in Mel S. Moyer, *Marketers and Their Publics: A Dialogue* (Toronto: Faculty of Administrative Studies, York University, 1978), p. 22.

panies, consumer groups, and governments can develop useful consumer policies of education, information, and protection related to each consumer right. Such a scheme may focus the efforts of those concerned. Finally, there is a role for consumers.

Consumers also have some responsibility to provide feedback to companies, government, and others to encourage useful change. Consumer apathy does little to improve the system. A third dimension of the matrix would show the makers of consumer policy, including consumer organizations, other citizen groups, business, government, educational institutions, and the mass media.

Consumer Characteristics and Interest Representation[8]

There are characteristics of consumers and consumer groups that make it difficult to represent their broadly based interests in the political process. It is easier to look after the narrower special interests (of business and professional groups, for example).

Consumer Role Secondary An individual's role as a consumer is almost always secondary to that same individual's role as a producer. It is in the individual's interest to devote more time to furthering the producer role than the consuming role. Labor union members devote much more time and receive much more immediate returns from activities affecting them as workers than from attempts to have producers improve food product labels. In the role of a lawyer, a consumer receives greater personal benefits from participating in the local law society than from participating in a study to determine the quality of fabrics and apparel construction.

Diffuse Nature of Consumerism The consumer purchases a wide range of products, few of which constitute a large proportion of the total budget. Goods and services are purchased from firms and individuals who have much greater product knowledge than the consumer. This usually puts the consumer at a disadvantage. The automobile salesperson who sells several cars a week is obviously more expert than the individual who purchases a car once every five years.

Expertise and Information Costs The relative benefits to an individual consumer of becoming expert on all he or she consumes are low, given the diffuse nature of the consumer interest. Just as our lawyer finds it relatively unproductive to become expert in fabrics and apparel construction, so each of us can ill afford the time required to become expert in all fields. Individually, we have neither the resources nor the time to investigate all products.[9]

These three consumer characteristics—the consumer role being secondary, diffusion resulting from buying many products, and problems of expertise and information costs—have led to demands for more effective consumer representation in public policy making to improve the consumer's position in relation to producers.

Consumers periodically believe that their interests and rights are under attack and are being eroded in the political process by special interest groups. Governments sometimes are less than vigorous in further-

[8]The extensive contribution of Professor J. D. Forbes to the balance of the chapter is gratefully acknowledged.

[9]Anthony Downs, *An Economic Theory of Democracy* (New York: Harper and Row, 1957).

ing the consumer interest. Sometimes there is no effective consumer interest advocate to counteract the lobbying activities of special interest groups, and public policy can insidiously and incrementally drift toward the more organized, effective lobbying group. This is not a nefarious plot but results from characteristics of the groups being represented in the political process.[10]

Special Interests Special interest groups, such as industry trade associations, unions, and professional associations, compete with general interests, such as those of consumers. Governments are organized along special interest lines: the Commerce, Transportation, and Agriculture Departments are concerned with specific issues and usually represent the interests of specific segments of the population. Special interest groups have fewer, more specific goals and generally can obtain resources more easily than consumer groups.[11]

Public Goods and Consumer Interest There is little personal incentive for individuals to join ad hoc consumer groups since any gains by those groups are distributed to all consumers rather than just to members of the particular consumer group. This characteristic is not unique to consumer groups but illustrates the public goods nature of large, mass-oriented, latent interest groups including groups such as women, the poor, the elderly, and the young, to name some of the more prominent ones.

Contrast the consumer group to clothing manufacturers, for example, who benefit directly from import restrictions that protect them from foreign competition. They receive direct benefits from contributing and participating in industry associations which represent their interests to government.

Marketing Ethics

Environmental considerations have led to increased attention to the subject of marketing ethics. **Marketing ethics** are the marketer's standards of conduct and moral values. They are concerned with matters of right and wrong: the decision of the individual and the firm to do what is morally right. A discussion of marketing ethics highlights the

[10]See Downs, *An Economic Theory of Democracy;* and Mancur Olson, *The Logic of Collective Action* (Cambridge, Mass.: Harvard University Press, 1971).

[11]Olson, *The Logic of Collective Action,* 1971.

types of problems faced by individuals in their role as marketers.[12] Such problems must be considered before we suggest possible improvements in the marketing system.

People develop standards of ethical behavior based upon their own systems of values. Their individual ethics help them deal with the various ethical questions in their personal lives. However, when they are put into a work situation, a serious conflict may materialize. Individual ethics may differ from the organizational ethic of the employer. An individual may believe that industry participation in developing a recycling program for industrial waste is highly desirable, but the person's firm takes the position that such a venture would be unprofitable. Similar conflicts are not difficult to imagine.

How can these conflicts be resolved? The development of and adherence to a professional ethic may provide a third basis of authority. This ethic should be based on a concept of professionalism that transcends both organizational and individual ethics. It depends on the existence of a professional peer association that can exercise collective sanctions over a marketer's professional behavior. The American Marketing Association (the major international association of marketers), for example, has developed a code of ethics that includes a provision to expel members who violate its tenets. The code is shown in Figure 24.2.

A variety of ethical problems faces the marketer every day. While promotional matters have received the greatest attention recently, ethical questions concerning the research function, product management, channel strategy, and pricing also arise.

Ethical Problems in Marketing Research

Marketing research has been castigated because of its alleged invasion of personal privacy. Citizens of today's urban, mechanized society seek individual identity to a greater degree. Personal privacy is important to most consumers and has therefore become a public issue.

Ethical Problems in Product Management

A few years ago, Chevrolet engines were installed in 128,000 new Oldsmobiles, Buicks, and Pontiacs as a result of unexpected demand for the medium-priced models. General Motors reasoned that the Chevrolet engines were the same size and horsepower and that a switch of this

[12]Excellent discussions of ethics appear in Douglas J. Lincoln, Milton M. Pressley, and Taylor Little, "Ethical Beliefs and Personal Values of Top Level Executives," *Journal of Business Research* (December 1982), pp. 475–487; Gene R. Laczniak, Robert F. Busch, and William A. Strang, "Ethical Marketing: Perception of Economic Goods and Social Problems," *Journal of Macromarketing* (Spring 1981), pp. 49–57; and James Weber, "Institutionalizing Ethics into the Corporation," *MSU Business Topics* (Spring 1981), pp. 47–52.

Figure 24.2 A Marketing Code of Ethics

Our Code of Ethics

As a member of the American Marketing Association, I recognize the significance of my professional conduct and my responsibilities to society and to the other members of my profession:

1. By acknowledging my accountability to society as a whole as well as to the organization for which I work.
2. By pledging my efforts to assure that all presentations of goods, services, and concepts be made honestly and clearly.
3. By striving to improve marketing knowledge and practice in order to better serve society.
4. By supporting free consumer choice in circumstances that are legal and are consistent with generally accepted community standards.
5. By pledging to use the highest professional standards in my work and in competitive activity.
6. By acknowledging the right of the American Marketing Association, through established procedure, to withdraw my membership if I am found to be in violation of ethical standards of professional conduct.

Source: American Marketing Association, *Constitution and Bylaws*, rev. ed. (Chicago: American Marketing Association, 1977), p. 20. Reprinted by permission.

nature was an acceptable marketing practice. But buyers were not informed of the switch, and consumer complaints and legal cases resulted. General Motors was ordered by the court to make restitution in what the media labeled the "Chevymobile" case.[13] This incident suggests the changing nature and growing importance of ethical decisions in product management. Accepted marketing practice in this case was no longer acceptable to consumers.

Product quality, planned obsolescence, brand similarity, and packaging questions are significant concerns of consumers, management, and governments. Competitive pressures have forced marketers into packaging practices that may be considered misleading, deceptive, and/or unethical in some quarters. Larger than necessary packages are used to gain shelf space and customer exposure in the supermarket. Odd-size packages make price comparisons difficult. Bottles with concave bottoms give the impression that they contain more liquid than is actually the case. The real question seems to be whether these practices can be justified in the name of competition. Growing regulatory mandates appear to be narrowing the range of discretion in this area.

Ethical Problems in Pricing

Pricing is probably the most regulated aspect of a firm's marketing strategy. As a result, most unethical price behavior is also illegal. When asked to identify unethical practices they wanted eliminated, fewer ex-

[13]Terry P. Brown, "GM, State Aides Due to Disclose Accord for $200 Rebates in 'Chevymobile' Case," *The Wall Street Journal* (December 19, 1977), p. 16.

ecutives specified issues such as price collusion, price discrimination, and unfair pricing in a 1976 survey than a similar group had in a 1961 study. This suggests that tighter government regulations exist in these areas now than in the past.[14]

There are, however, some gray areas in the matter of pricing ethics. For example, should some customers pay more for merchandise if distribution costs are higher in their areas? Do marketers have an obligation to warn customers of impending price, discount, or returns policy changes? All these questions must be dealt with in developing a professional ethic for marketing.

Ethical Problems in Distribution Strategy

A firm's channel strategy is required to deal with two kinds of ethical questions:

1. What is the appropriate degree of control over the channel?
2. Should a company distribute its products in marginally profitable outlets that have no alternative source of supply?

The question of control typically arises in the relationship between a manufacturer and franchised dealers. Should an automobile dealership, a gas station, or a fast-food outlet be required to purchase parts, materials, and supplementary services from the parent organization? What is the proper degree of control in the channel of distribution?

Furthermore, should marketers serve unsatisfied market segments even if the profit potential is slight? What is marketing's ethical responsibility to serve retail stores in low-income areas, users of limited amounts of the firm's product, or the declining rural market?

These problems are difficult to resolve because they often involve individuals rather than broad segments of the general public. An important first step would be to assure that channel policies are enforced on a consistent basis.

Ethical distribution practices usually return a dividend, but often the returns are not readily measurable and are seen only in the long run.

Ethical Problems in Promotional Strategy

Promotion is the component of the marketing mix where the majority of ethical questions arise. Personal selling has always been the target of ethically based criticisms. Early traders, pack peddlers, greeters, drummers, and the twentieth century used-car salesperson, for example, have all been accused of marketing malpractice ranging from exagger-

[14]See Steven N. Brenner and Earl A. Mollander, "Is the Ethics of Business Changing?" *Harvard Business Review* (January–February 1977), pp. 61–62; and Jeffrey Sonnenfeld and Paul R. Lawrence, "Why Do Companies Succumb to Price Fixing?" *Harvard Business Review* (July–August 1978), pp. 145–157.

ating product merits to outright deceit. Gifts, bribes, and the like were identified as the primary ethical abuses in studies done in 1961 and 1976.[15]

Advertising, however, is even more maligned than the salesperson. It is impersonal and hence easier to criticize. In fact, a study by the American Association of Advertising Agencies showed that it ranked second (along with clothing and fashion) in a list of "things in life that we enjoy complaining about but we may not really be serious about our complaints."[16]

While these studies may suggest that much of the criticism of advertising is overstated, there is ample evidence and legitimate concern regarding advertising. Charges of overselling, uses of fear-based advertising messages (of social rejection, of growing old), sexism, and the like are common.

The portrayal of women in advertising has been of particular concern to marketers. Too often, it is argued, women have been portrayed as frivolous individuals or assigned stereotyped housewife roles in radio and television commercials and other media. Advertisers are making a concerted effort to show women in varied situations, especially in nontraditional work roles, such as bus drivers, bank officers, and heavy-equipment handlers. Figure 24.3 is a good example of avoiding stereotypical portrayals of women in advertising.

Another ethical concern surrounds advertising to children. Some critics fear that television advertising exerts an undue influence on children.[17] They believe children are easily influenced by toy, cereal, and snack food commercials. Correspondingly, there is the assumpion that children then exert substantial pressure on their parents to acquire these items. In recognition of this concern, the Canadian Association of Broadcasters has formulated a comprehensive broadcast code for advertising to children. No similar code exists in the United States. The Canadian code, which applies to advertising directed at children age 12 or under states:

The purpose of the Code is to serve as a guide to advertisers and agencies in preparing messages which adequately recognize the special characteristics of the children's audience. Children, especially the very young, live in a world

[15]Steven N. Brenner and Earl A. Mollander, "Is the Ethics of Business Changing?" *Harvard Business Review* (January–February 1977), p. 62. See also Alan J. Dubinsky, Eric N. Berkowitz, and William Rudelius, "Ethical Problems of Field Sales Personnel," *MSU Business Topics* (Summer 1980), pp. 11–16.

[16]*Rebuttal to Some Unfounded Assertions about Advertising* (New York: American Advertising Foundation, 1967), p. 13.

[17]Children's advertising is discussed in Jay D. Lindquist, "Measuring Children's Attitudes toward TV Commercials: An Instrument Reliability Test," *Journal of the Academy of Marketing Science* (Fall 1981), pp. 409–418; Glen Riecken and A. Coskun Samli, "Measuring Children's Attitudes toward Television Commercials: Extension and Replication," *Journal of Consumer Research* (June 1981), pp. 57–61; and Seymour Banks, "Children's Television Viewing Behavior," *Journal of Marketing* (Spring 1980), pp. 48–55.

Figure 24.3 Advertisement with Woman in Nonstereotyped Role

She earns $46,000.
He makes $33,000.
Who in this family should have the most life insurance?
In many of today's families, both the husband and wife are income producers. And, because they have adjusted their lives around two incomes, the loss of either can present major difficulties.
Does this describe your family situation? Well, New York Life insurance can't replace you or your spouse. But a well-designed program could certainly help your family carry on.
Who, then, should have the most life insurance...the husband?...the wife?...the one with the higher income? It depends on your family's particular circumstances. But, the person who can help you answer the question precisely is your New York Life Agent. A good person to know in your community.
New York Life. For all of your life.
NEW YORK LIFE
NEW YORK LIFE

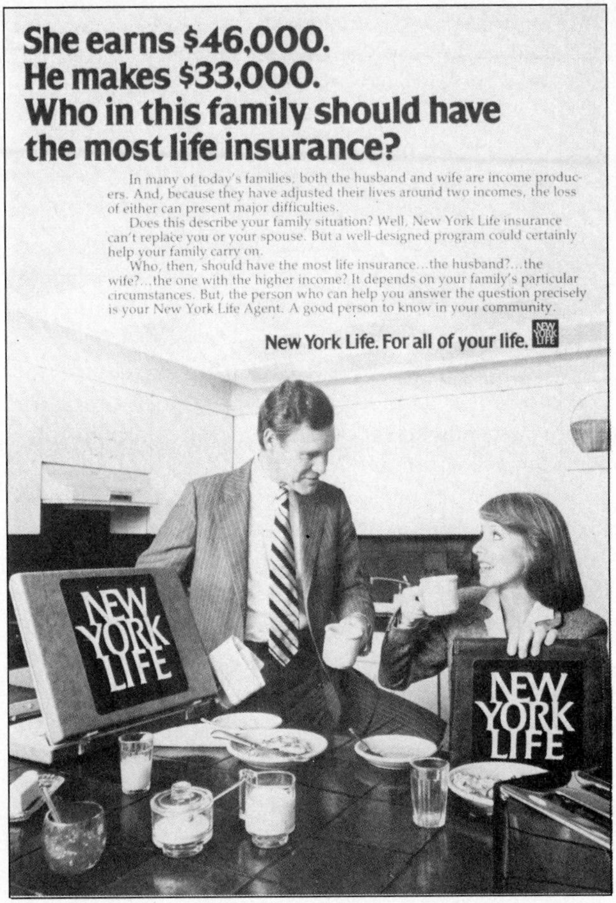

Source: Reproduced by permission of New York Life Insurance Company.

that is part imaginary, part real, and sometimes do not distinguish clearly between the two. Advertisements should respect and not abuse the power of the child's imagination.[18]

Some specific clauses of the Code are:

1. No commercial may employ any device or technique that attempts to transmit messages below the threshold of normal awareness.
2. To clearly establish relative size, something from the child's actual

[18] *Broadcast Code for Advertising to Children* (Ottawa: The Canadian Association of Broadcasters, 1982), pp. 1–5.

Some Hypothetical Situations Involving Ethical Questions

A study conducted by the Bureau of Business Research at the University of Michigan posed a series of action situations to a sample of 401 marketing research directors and chief marketing executives. The respondents were told that the marketing research director of a company had taken some particular action. The participants were then asked, "Do you approve or disapprove of the action taken?" A sample of these situations and the resulting responses are shown. How would you have replied?

One-Way Mirrors

One product of the X Company is brassieres, and the firm has recently been having difficulty making some decisions on a new line. Information was critically needed concerning how women put on brassieres. So the marketing research director designed a study in which two local stores cooperated in putting one-way mirrors in their foundations dressing rooms. Observers behind the mirrors successfully gathered the necessary information.

	Approve	Disapprove
Research directors	20%	78%
Line marketers	18	82

Advertising and Product Misuse

Some recent research showed that many customers of X Company are misusing Product B. There's no danger; they are simply wasting their money by using too much of it at a time. But yesterday, the marketing research director saw proofs on Product B's new ad campaign, and the ads not only ignored the problem of misuse but actually seemed to encourage it. The director quietly referred the advertising manager to the research results, well known to all involved with B's advertising, and let it go at that.

	Approve	Disapprove
Research directors	41%	58%
Line marketers	33	66

General Trade Data to Citizens' Group

The marketing research department of X Company frequently makes extensive studies of its retail customers. A citizens' group working to get a shopping center in their low-income area wanted to know if they could have access to this trade information. But since the firm had always refused to share this information with trade organizations, the marketing research director declined the request.

	Approve	Disapprove
Research directors	64%	34%
Line marketers	74	25

Source: Based on and quotes with permission from C. Merle Crawford, "Attitudes of Marketing Executives toward Ethics in Marketing Research," *Journal of Marketing* (April 1970), pp. 46–52, published by the American Marketing Association. Reprinted from the *Journal of Marketing*, published by the American Marketing Association. Another excellent discussion of marketing research ethics is found in Robert Bezilla, Joel B. Haynes, and Clifford Elliot, "Ethics in Marketing Research," *Business Horizons* (April 1976), pp. 83–86.

world, e.g., a child, coins, marbles—must appear with the product itself.

3. Drugs, proprietary medicines, and vitamins . . . must not be advertised to children.
4. Commercials must not directly urge children to purchase, or urge them to ask their parents to make inquiries or purchases.
5. Any single product, premium or service must not be promoted more than once during any half-hour period, except in the event of full program sponsorship.
6. Puppets, persons, and characters (including cartoon characters) well-known to children or featured on children's programs must not be used to endorse or personally promote products, premiums, or services. This promotion does not apply to characters created by an advertiser for promotional purposes, to professional actors or announcers who are not featured on children's programs, or to factual statements about nutritional or educational benefits.
7. Price and purchase terms, when used, must be clear and complete. When parts or accessories, that a child might reasonably suppose to be part of the normal purchase, are available only at extra cost, this must be made clear, both orally and visually. The cost must not be minimized as by the use of "only," "just," "bargain price," etc.
8. Toy advertisements shall not make direct comparisons with the previous year's model, or with competitive makes even when the statements or claims are valid—because such references may undermine the child's enjoyment of present possessions or those that may be received as gifts.
9. Advertising must not imply that possession or use of a product makes the owner superior, or that without it the child will be open to ridicule or contempt.

Social Responsibility

Another major issue affecting marketing is the question of social responsibility.[19] In a general sense, **social responsibility** is the marketer's acceptance of the obligation to consider profit, consumer satisfaction, and societal well-being of equal value in evaluating the performance of the firm. It is the recognition that marketers must be concerned with the

[19]Social responsibility issues are examined in Ed Timmerman, "The Concept of Marketing's Corporate Social Responsibility," in *1981 Southwestern Marketing Proceedings,* (eds.) Robert H. Ross, Frederic B. Kraft, and Charles H. Davis (Wichita, Kan.: The Southwestern Marketing Association), pp. 188–191.

more qualitative dimensions of consumer and societal benefits as well as the quantitative measures of sales, revenue, and profits by which marketing performance is traditionally measured.

As Professors Engel and Blackwell point out, social responsibility is a more easily measured concept than marketing ethics:

Actions alone determine social responsibility, and a firm can be socially responsible even when doing so under coercion. For example, the government may enact rules that force *firms to be socially responsible in matters of the environment, deception, and so forth. Also, consumers, through their power to repeat or withhold purchasing, may* force *marketers to provide honest and relevant information, fair prices, and so forth. To be ethically responsible, on the other hand, it is not sufficient to act correctly; ethical intent is also necessary.*[20]

The locus for socially responsible decisions in organizations has always been an important question. Who should be specifically accountable for the social considerations involved in marketing decisions? The district sales manager? The marketing vice-president? The firm's president? The board of directors? Probably the most valid assessment is to say that *all marketers,* regardless of their stations in the organization, are accountable for the societal aspects of their decisions.

A related aspect of this question is how should socially responsible decisions be made? Figure 24.4 presents a decision making flow chart that illustrates the types and levels of social responsibility decision making. It also provides a framework for dealing with these critical issues.

Marketing's Responsibilities

The concept of business responsibility has traditionally concerned the relationships between the manager and customers, employees, and stockholders. Management had the responsibility of providing customers with a quality product at a reasonable price, the responsibility of providing adequate wages and a decent working environment for employees, and the responsibility for providing an acceptable profit level for stockholders. Only on occasion did the concept involve relations with the government and rarely with the general public.

Today, the responsibility concept has been extended to the entire societal framework. A decision to continue operation of a profitable but air-polluting plant may be responsible in the traditional sense. Customers receive an uninterrupted supply of the plant's products, employees do not face layoffs, and stockholders receive a reasonable return on their investment in the plant. But from the standpoint of contemporary business ethics, this is not a socially responsible decision.

[20]James F. Engel and Roger D. Blackwell, *Consumer Behavior,* 4th ed. (Hinsdale, Ill.: The Dryden Press, 1982), p. 668.

Figure 24.4 Flow Chart for Socially Responsible Decisions

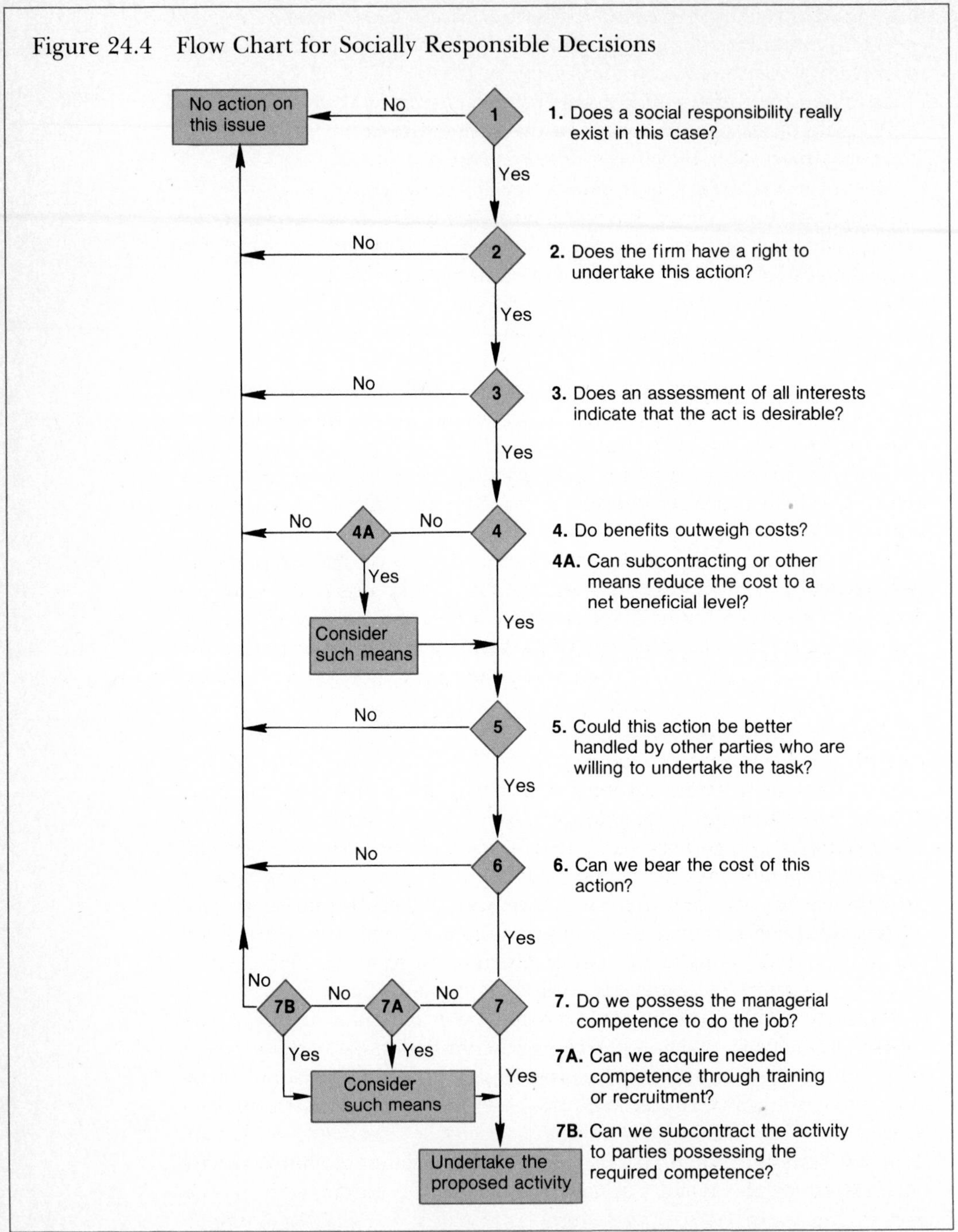

Source: Ramon J. Aldag and Donald W. Jackson, Jr., "A Managerial Framework for Social Decision-Making," *MSU Business Topics* (Spring 1975), p. 34. Reprinted by permission of the publisher, Division of Research, Graduate School of Business Administration, Michigan State University.

Similarly, a firm that markets foods with low nutritional value may satisfy the traditional concept of responsibility, but such behavior is questionable in the contemporary perspective. This is not to say that firms should distribute only foods of high nutritional value; it means only that the previous framework for evaluation is no longer considered comprehensive in terms of either scope or time.

Contemporary marketing decisions must now regularly involve consideration of the external societal environment. Decisions must also account for eventual, long-run effects. Socially responsible decisions must consider future generations as well as existing society.

Marketing and Ecology

Ecology is an important aspect of marketing. The concept of **ecology**—the relationship between humanity and the environment—appears to be in a constant state of evolution.

There are several aspects of ecology that marketers must deal with: planned obsolescence, pollution, recycling waste materials, and preservation of resources.

The original ecological problem facing marketing was **planned obsolescence**—a situation where the manufacturer produced items with limited durability. Planned obsolescence has always represented a significant ethical question for the marketer. On one side is the need for maintaining sales and employment; on the other is the need for providing better quality and durability.

A practical question is whether the consumer really wants or can afford increased durability. Many consumers prefer to change styles often and accept less durable items. Increased durability has an implicit cost. It may mean fewer people can afford the product.

Pollution is a broad term that can be applied to a number of circumstances. It usually means making unclean. Pollution of such natural resources as the water and the air is of critical proportions in some areas.

Recycling—the reprocessing of used materials for reuse—is another important aspect of ecology. The marketing system annually generates billions of tons of packaging materials, such as glass, metal, paper, and plastics, that add to the nation's growing piles of trash and waste. The theory behind recycling is that if these materials can be processed so as to be reusable, they can benefit society by saving natural resources and energy as well as by alleviating a major factor in environmental pollution.

Tire manufacturers have built artificial fish reefs out of used tires. Minnesota Mining and Manufacturing Company has printed outlines for splints on the corrugated shipping cartons destined for hospitals. The cartons are then used by emergency and rescue teams for temporary splints. The beverage industry is using more aluminum cans because of the relative ease of recycling aluminum.

Recovery rates for reusable materials vary by industry. For instance, the rate for copper is 50 percent, for iron and steel 30 percent, for paper and paper products 20 percent, and for glass only 4 percent. In many instances, the recovery rates are now less than they were in the mid-1950s. Yet it is estimated that extensive recycling could produce 40 percent of the materials needed by manufacturers.[21]

The biggest problem in recycling is getting the used materials from the consumer back to the manufacturer who will handle the technological aspects of recovery. These "backward" channels are limited, and those that do exist are primitive and lack adequate financial incentives.[22] Marketing can play an important role by designing appropriate channel structures.

Another ecological problem concerns the preservation of natural resources. The natural gas and fuel oil shortages during the 1970s illustrate the urgent need for effective policies for both conserving and finding new sources of these resources.

Some critics claim that business spends more money publicizing its ecological expenditures than it does meeting specific ecological problems. In many cases, the criticism is valid, but experience has shown that consumers are also at fault in that they sometimes fail to support ecology-inspired products.

Controlling the Marketing System

When the marketing-economic system does not perform as well as we would like, we attempt to change it. We hope to make it serve us better by producing and distributing goods and services in a fairer way. Most people believe that the system is working sufficiently well to require no major changes and relatively minor adjustments can achieve a fair distribution.

Four ways in which we control or influence the direction of the marketing system and try to rid it of imperfections are: (1) assisting the competitive market system to operate in a self-correcting manner, as Adam Smith suggested; (2) consumer education; (3) regulation; and (4) political action.

[21]Liz Roman Gallese, "Art of Turning Waste into Useful Fuel Gains in Popularity Rapidly," *The Wall Street Journal* (August 4, 1977), pp. 1, 20.

[22]William G. Zikmund and William J. Stanton, "Recycling Solid Wastes: A Channels-of-Distribution Problem," *Journal of Marketing* (July 1971), pp. 34–39. Also see Donald A. Fuller, "Recycling Consumer Solid Waste: A Commentary on Selected Channel Alternatives," *Journal of Business Research* (January 1978), pp. 17–31; and Peter M. Ginter and Jack M. Starling, "Reverse Distribution Channels: Concept and Structure," in *Proceedings of the Southern Marketing Association,* (eds.) Robert S. Franz, Robert M. Hopkins, and Al Toma (New Orleans, La., 1978), pp. 206–208.

The competitive market system operates to allocate resources and provide for our needs most of the products we purchase. While we may hear many complaints against the system, most of the goods and services we purchase or use flow through the system with little difficulty. Competition works if the conditions of many buyers and sellers and other technical requirements of the free market economic model allow it. We have attempted, sometimes with limited success, to restore competition in instances where monopolies have reduced it.

Combined with the free market system, consumer education can lead to wise choices. As products become more complex, diverse, and plentiful, the consumer's ability to make wise decisions must also expand. Educational programs and efforts by parents, schools, business, government, and consumer organizations all contribute to a better system.

Political Action

One function of government is satisfaction of the desires of society. Therefore, all regulation is the consequence of political action. The effectiveness of business lobbies in directing the economic system is often noted in daily life, but the political activities of groups representing consumer interests are becoming increasingly visible and effective, too. These groups are attempting to make the system more responsive to consumers. Since marketers are the interface between business and consumers, a knowledge of consumer groups and their views on consumer interests and rights can be quite helpful in avoiding confrontation. As citizens we should understand interest group participation in the political process, and how large, broadly based interest groups, such as consumers, differ from smaller, narrowly based special interest groups in having their points of view adequately represented in the political process.

Ethics and Values—The Enemy Is Us

In previous chapters on consumer behavior and marketing segmentation, you became aware of the wide range of individual attitudes and desires to be satisfied by our marketing system. Walk through apparel shops in any large metropolitan area and you can see the wide diversity of products that are offered to satisfy individual needs. The ethics and values that we hold as a society also have a wide range of diversity. Why else would we elect members of the Democratic, Republican, or other political parties if we did not have a wide range of values that we want to be represented within our system of government?

Some values, such as the sanctity of human life and the rule of law, are common to all of us. At the other end of the scale are areas where we disagree, such as what is normal product promotion and what is false and misleading advertising. For example, is saying that your product is the best in the world a statement that has to be supported by a researched fact? Or can you reasonably expect consumers to take such a statement with a grain of salt?

In the very broadest sense, the function of a government is to express the collective values of the citizenry through laws. Marketing is only one of a number of systems that reflect society's desires. If marketing as a system is to be indicted, then we must all be defendants, since we find it impossible to differentiate among ourselves as members of society, as consumers, and as elements in the business system that serves us.

Adam Smith, the champion of capitalism, argued that people's desire to serve their own best interests would act as an "invisible hand" in guiding the economy. The resulting maximization of output would improve life and society by improving the standard of living. Smith saw competition as the watchdog that kept the economy on the correct course. He also observed that any time two or more businesspeople got together there was a tendency to cooperate to use the system to their advantage. For this reason, competition was necessary so that no individual or group could misuse the system.

Adam Smith could not foresee our present day economic systems with large international businesses, large governments, and large labor unions, all of which have the potential to abuse the system for their own advantage. As society has become more complex, we have tried to develop control mechanisms so that the interests of society members are well reflected in the way it operates.

Consumerism, the Individual, and the Marketer

In our daily lives we are mainly consumers. Only when participating directly in the role of producers of goods and services do we switch into a situation of possible conflict. Because of the wide range and diversity of values, some of us may not fully subscribe to some particular stand of broadly based interest groups like consumer groups. However, it is not surprising that most people agree with such activities.

As marketers, we should view the reactions of consumers and various consumer groups as a reflection of how well our views and actions match expectations in the marketplace. Businesses that could not or would not change some of their actions have been the root cause of legislation and regulation to change that behavior. Conflicts between individual, organizational, and industry values and ethics will continue, as they have throughout history. The individual will still be required to resolve these conflicts within his or her value system. It is small consolation that we are not alone in the difficult choices each of us must face. It is for just these reasons that we may disagree in answer to the question: does marketing serve our nation well?

Resolving Contemporary Issues in Marketing

The resolution of the contemporary issues of consumerism, social responsibility, and marketing ethics is one of the most crucial tasks facing marketing in the years ahead. Three courses of action are available: increased regulation, better public information, and a more responsible marketing philosophy. Progress in these areas is essential if the competitive marketing system is to survive at all.

Few marketers doubt that increased regulation will become a reality in the marketplace unless reforms are instituted. History has shown that government, in response to consumer pressures, has always moved to fill voids created by business apathy and neglect. Improved self-regulation by marketers is needed if stricter governmental controls are to be avoided.

Better public information is a solution that applies to many contemporary issues. In many cases, issues arise simply because the public was not informed or was informed incorrectly. Package labeling is a good example of where improved public information has taken place. Unit pricing, explained in Chapter 14, was widely debated as a method of providing better information before it was adopted by major food chains. **Open dating,** which sets the last date a perishable or semiperishable food can be sold, involves similar discussion.[23] To what type of information should consumers be entitled? Is better public information worth the cost? How can marketers improve the information consumers receive? Many of these questions will have to be answered in the decades ahead.

A more responsible marketing philosophy is also needed in contemporary society. Incidents like the following one reflect badly on marketers and their firms:

One unhappy patron who discovered bedbugs in his hotel bed and complained bitterly in writing to the company received a mollifying reply to which had been attached, accidentally, a scribbled note from some executive to his secretary that said: "Alice, send this guy the bedbug letter."[24]

A responsible marketing philosophy should encourage consumers to voice their opinions. These comments can result in significant improvements in the products and services offered by the seller. One company with a responsible attitude toward consumer complaints featured its critics in television advertisements. The critics and the company spokesperson discussed the various issues surrounding the company and its service area. Surveys showed that the public adopted a more favorable attitude toward the company's position of these matters after seeing the advertisements.

[23]Open dating is examined in Prabhaker Nayak and Larry J. Rosenberg, "Does Open Dating of Food Products Benefit the Consumer?" *Journal of Retailing* (Summer 1975), pp. 10–20.

[24]A. T. Baker, "Louder!—The Need to Complain More," *Time* (July 3, 1972), p. 33.

The marketing concept must include social responsibility as a primary function of the marketing organization. Social and profit goals are compatible, but they require the aggressive implementation of an expanded marketing concept. Explicit criteria for responsible decision making must be adapted in all companies. This is truly marketing's greatest challenge.

Summary

At the interface between business and society, the marketer often takes the brunt of criticisms of the operation of the market system. There are many important issues in contemporary marketing's societal environment. Marketing's environmental relationships have expanded in scope and importance. The current issues in marketing can be categorized as consumerism, marketing ethics, and social responsibility.

Criticisms of the marketing system are often justified and result from a broad range of ideas about what is and what is not ethical business activity. It is much too easy to point the finger at marketers or at business as the perpetrators of the evils of the system rather than recognizing that the system is *us*. The system is what its members want it to be, and when the system does not respond as we would like it to, the result is government-instituted regulations and controls to correct the situation.

Attempts to make the system more responsive to the desires of society have resulted in increased regulation and the emergence of groups representing consumer interests. Basic consumer rights to choice, to information, to be heard, and to safety and health, and consumers' interests in maintaining these rights are most commonly ensured by competition in the marketplace. When the marketplace has inadequately ensured the consumer rights and interests, government has responded to public pressure and intervened to improve the situation. Consumer groups have developed to spur business and government in this action and to counteract the natural advantage that special interest groups have in representing their interests in the political process at the expense of more broadly based consumer interests.

Increased regulation, better public information, and a more responsible marketing philosophy are possible avenues for resolving these issues. All are expected to play a greater role in the years ahead.

The marketer must recognize that increasingly his or her decisions are made within a highly interactive system. Contemporary marketing decisions must regularly involve consideration of the external societal environment. However, it is difficult to foresee less regulation of the marketplace, and the marketer will face constraints that aim to make the system more responsive to society's needs.

Key Terms

consumerism
consumer rights
class action suit
marketing ethics
social responsibility
ecology
planned obsolescence
pollution
recycling
open dating

Review Questions

1. Examine Adam Smith's thoughts on competition. How have these views affected the marketing system?
2. Explain the causes of the consumerism movement. Does the rise of consumerism suggest that the marketing concept has failed?
3. Evaluate consumerism's indictment of the competitive marketing system.
4. Discuss the problems involved in setting up "backward" channels of distribution for recycling used packages.
5. Distinguish among individual, organizational, and professional ethics.
6. Describe the ethical problem related to:
   a. Marketing research
   b. Product management
   c. Distribution strategy
   d. Pricing
   e. Promotional strategy
7. Describe the main avenues open for the resolution of contemporary issues facing the marketing system.
8. How would you have responded to each of the situations described in the section on ethical problems in marketing research? Explain.
9. Describe the conflict that exists between the consumer's desire for product durability and the ecology movement.
10. The marketing concept marked the advent of the age of consumerism. Do you agree with this statement? Why or why not?

Discussion Questions and Exercises

1. Should the United States ban advertising aimed at children?
2. Some have suggested that the majority of U.S. consumers are consumer illiterates. How would you suggest alleviating this problem?
3. Henry Ford II has argued that in a competitive market system, a firm cannot afford to meet the expense of environmental improvements unless competitors are also legally required to follow the same standards. Discuss.
4. Unit pricing and open dating increase distribution costs and thus prices. Therefore, these policies are undesirable from a consumer's viewpoint. Comment on these statements.
5. Some have suggested a deposit for all beverage containers be made a national law in an attempt to reduce roadside litter. Do you agree? Why or why not?

25

Chapter Objectives

1. To explain the steps in the marketing evaluation and control process.
2. To describe the use of sales analysis and marketing cost analysis.
3. To identify the strengths and limitations of return on investment as an evaluative technique.
4. To describe the major ratios used in evaluating marketing performance.
5. To explain the concept of the market audit and the major steps involved.

EVALUATION AND CONTROL

The marketing plan at Best Foods called for personal contact by its 400 sales representatives on the 32,000 individual retail stores, retail chain headquarters, and wholesale accounts. Those 32,000 grocery accounts (out of a total of more than 180,000 in the United States) generate 75 percent of total grocery sales in the United States. Marketing managers at Best Foods, whose products range from Skippy peanut butter to Hellmann's mayonnaise, expect each sales representative to make an average of 6.5 daily calls on his or her 100 accounts and to visit each store every seven to thirty days, depending on the store's sales volume. The sales representative is responsible for maintaining good relationships with store personnel, in-store product displays and other promotional activities, and feedback to area managers about changes in the marketplace that might require adjustments in Best Foods' sales-call frequencies. Each sales call costs an average of $25.

How could Best Foods sales managers establish a system of evaluating and controlling the activities of its sales force? The starting point was the establishment of quantifiable standards for account coverage, case sales, number of calls on promising new accounts, and promotional activities, such as building in-store displays. Since the sales force works in two-month promotion periods, meetings among the district manager, area managers, and sales representatives result in the establishment of priorities for each representative prior to each period. Area managers are intimately involved with the goal-setting process for each of their representatives, and they continue to meet informally with each salesperson on a biweekly basis throughout the period.

In order to minimize paperwork, Best Foods managers developed a computerized call reporting system called SCORE (Sales Call Objective Report and Evaluation). After each sales call, the salesperson completes a brief report of sales and promotional activities on a machine-readable form. These are mailed to company headquarters in Englewood Cliffs, New Jersey, two times a week, where they are read by optical scanners and processed by computer. Within five to seven working days after receiving them, headquarters supplies the sales managers and individual salespersons with a weekly productivity report. These reports are combined into a bimonthly call summary at the end of each promotion period. The summary makes such comparisons as scheduled versus actual calls, average number of presentations and success rates, and accounts where no sales have been made during the past four months. Such accounts are candidates for careful study and possible deletion from the customer list. Best Foods sales vice-president Cliff Jennewein is enthusiastic about SCORE as a tool in evaluation and control: "SCORE helps us determine just what (the salesperson) is achieving . . . giving sales reps and managers quantifiable standards of performance and results."[1]

The Conceptual Framework

The desire of Best Foods marketers to obtain feedback of actual performance and compare it with expected results is one shared by marketing managers in every organization. Evaluation and control are essential components in the firm's marketing strategy. They determine whether marketing plans are being implemented and whether organizational objectives are being achieved. They are a part of a sequential process that begins with the original analysis of a marketing opportu-

[1]Sally Scanlon, "Best Foods Knows the Score," *Sales and Marketing Management Sales and Marketing Plans* (New York: Bill Brothers, 1978), p. 30.

nity. While marketing planning, first discussed in Chapter 3, refers to the establishment of objectives and the development of strategies, **evaluation and control** refer to the establishment of standards of performance and the comparison of actual results with planned results to determine whether actual performance matches marketing plans. This chapter examines a number of techniques by which marketing performance may be measured and compared with expectations. Such methods as sales analysis, marketing cost analysis, return on investment, ratio analysis, and marketing audits are important tools in evaluation and control.

The Need for Evaluation and Control

The evaluation and control phase provides a feedback mechanism that keeps marketing planning and implementation of plans on track. The control sequence allows marketers to assess whether corrective actions are needed. In some cases, uncontrollable variables such as technological breakthroughs by a competitor, a recession, a major factory closing, or the development of a lower priced substitute for the firm's product may adversely affect sales and profits. In such instances, volume or profitability targets will have to be reevaluated, and new, more realistic goals set. In other situations, the firm's plans may be judged as accurate, but the marketing program may require adjustments. A third possible outcome is that both plans and their implementation may require adjustments. Finally, in instances where the original marketing opportunity analysis was faulty, the option may be to abandon the project entirely. Regardless of the final result, the most important contribution of evaluation and control is that it allows the marketer to keep his or her marketing planning on target.

The Evaluation and Control Process

Figure 25.1 is a model of the evaluation and control process. Since marketing planning and control are closely related components of an effective marketing program, the figure shows how evaluation and control guide performance to conform to the plan.

A number of elements must be present for evaluation and control to be effective. First, as Figure 25.1 indicates, organizational goals must result in the establishment of standards of performance. Such standards become reference points against which actual performance can be compared. They may take such forms as expected number of sales calls per

Figure 25.1 Steps in the Process of Evaluation and Control

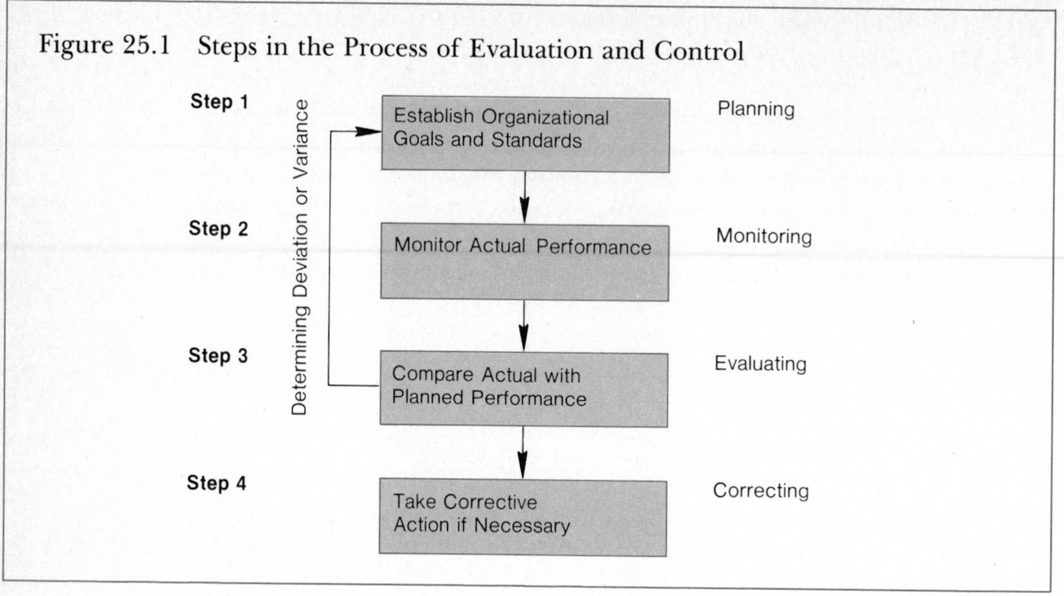

month, sales, profit, or market share expectations, or even consumer awareness rankings.

The second step of evaluation and control is monitoring actual performance. Decisions must be made concerning what activities and/or individuals are to be measured and how to measure them. The third step is comparison of actual and planned performance. At this point, decisions must be made about the degree of permissible deviations from standards.

Taking corrective action if significant deviations exist between planned and actual performance is the final step. It consists of two elements: identifying the cause of the deviation and implementing the corrective action.

Methods of Evaluation and Control

A multitude of evaluative methods exist for measuring and controlling marketing performance. Some are based on the use of financial ratios such as return on investment. These calculations are outlined in later sections of this chapter. Other evaluations employ extensive field tests. McDonald's, for example, tested one new sandwich, the McFeast, for two years.[2] Another evaluative favorite is simply hard questioning

[2]Paul Ingrassia, "McDonald's Fast Track Drops Quinlan into the Hot Seat as Competition Sizzles," *The Wall Street Journal* (February 21, 1980), p. 14.

Putting Greyhound Back on Schedule

The gasoline shortages of the mid-1970s and the accompanying price increases should have been good news for Greyhound, the nation's leading bus transportation company. Greyhound's capacity measure is passenger miles, a rate determined by multiplying passenger loads by the number of bus miles driven. In 1974, the measure stood at 9.2 billion passenger miles. Four years later, the number had declined to 7.5 billion passenger miles.

Other feedback also indicated problems. An analysis of letters from customers and employees revealed a growing number of complaints about poor security at stations, dirty buses, many buses with defective air conditioners, and problems with reservations.

Greyhound's top executives decided that something had to be done. A task force of 15 company representatives began a thorough investigation using a checklist to rate such activities as condition of bus stations and buses, driver courtesy, baggage handling, and reservation systems. A number of changes resulted from their findings. Off-duty policemen were hired to improve security at many terminals. A new computer telephone reservation system was installed. The size of the Greyhound repair departments was increased. Local managers were given more authority to handle rider complaints. Within a year of these actions, Greyhound passenger miles increased to 8.2 billion.

Source: The Greyhound changes are described in John Quirt, "How Greyhound Made a U-Turn," *Fortune* (March 24, 1980), pp. 139–140.

about organizational achievements. August Busch III, chairman of the board at Anheuser Busch, likes to hold 7 a.m. meetings in the dining room of his St. Louis brewery, where he questions executives about company operations.[3] The critical factor is not how it is done, but the fact that the organization does have some procedure for evaluating its marketing plans and programs.

Using Control Charts

Marketing evaluation and control involves making a comparison of actual performance against some standard or target that has been set. Most organizations set upper and lower control limits on the evaluative standards they employ. Marketers expect some random fluctuations in actual performance; the key to effective control is keeping these variations within the control limits.

[3]Thomas O'Hanlon, "August Busch Brews Up a New Spirit in St. Louis," *Fortune* (January 15, 1979), p. 92.

Figure 25.2 The Standard Control Chart Model

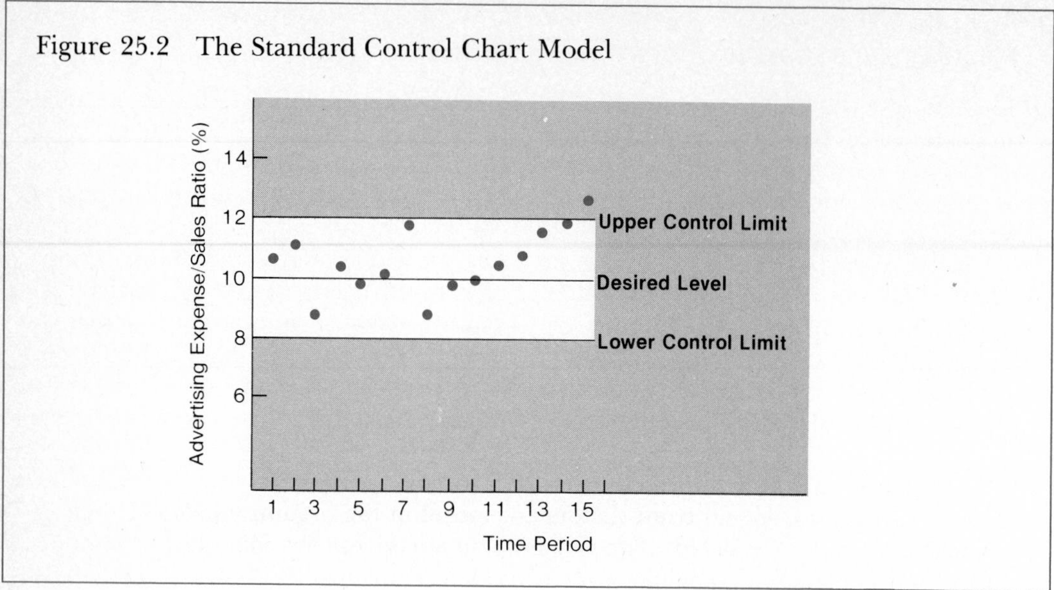

Source: Reprinted from Philip Kotler, *Marketing Decision Making: A Model Building Approach* (New York: Holt, Rinehart and Winston, 1971), p. 635. Reprinted by permission of the author.

Marketers have adapted techniques long used in quality control efforts. **Control charts**—diagrams that plot actual performance against established control limits—are especially useful in marketing evaluation and control.

Figure 25.2 shows a control chart used to monitor the advertising expense/sales ratio. This control chart has specified that advertising expenditures should constitute 10 percent of sales, but that normal variation can range between 8 and 12 percent. Figure 25.2 indicates that only in time period 15 did the ratio go beyond the acceptable range.

Control charts can be very useful tools in marketing evaluation and control. They provide an excellent graphic display of actual against planned performance and also highlight the need for corrective action.

Assessing Marketing Performance

Standards for marketing performance vary widely. When Coca-Cola entered the wine market with its acquisition of the Taylor label, it set a ten-year sales volume target of $1 billion.[4] Miller Brewing marketers

[4]"Coca-Cola: A Spurt into Wine that Is Altering the Industry," *Business Week* (October 15, 1979), pp. 126, 131.

have turned their attention to profits rather than simply growth. As one Miller executive expressed it, "We are in the beer business for profit, not primarily for volume."[5] Most marketing objectives and performance standards can be categorized as either volume-oriented or profitability-oriented.

Which type of standard is correct? How should organizations evaluate marketing performance? Most evaluation and control processes involve one or more of the following methods of assessing marketing performance: sales analysis, marketing cost analysis, return on investment, ratio analysis, and marketing audits. Typically, most organizations use a combination of evaluative methods to assess marketing performance.

Sales Analysis

Important evaluation and control facts are found in the organization's sales records. Analysis of this data can provide a basis for obtaining an overall view of marketing effectiveness.

Basic financial statements are often too broad to be very useful in marketing evaluation and control. Where nondetailed accounts are used, their main contribution is that they assist the marketer in raising more specific questions. The income statements in Table 25.1 show that the company earned a profit for the period being considered, and that selling expenses represent approximately 13 percent of sales.

$$\text{Cost/sales ratio} = \frac{\$753{,}000}{\$5{,}783{,}000} = 13 \text{ percent.}$$

Comparison of the 13 percent selling expense/sales ratio with previous years may hint at possible problems, but it will not specifically reveal the cause of the variation. To discover the cause, a more detailed breakdown is necessary.

Table 25.2 shows a typical breakdown of sales by territories. This kind of classification forms part of an overall sales analysis. The purpose of the **sales analysis**—the in-depth evaluation of a firm's sales—is to obtain meaningful information from existing data.[6]

Easily prepared from company invoices stored on computer tapes, the sales analysis can be quite revealing for the marketing executive. As Table 25.2 shows, the sales force in District 4 has a much higher cost/sales ratio than the sales force in other districts.

[5] Allan F. Hussey, "Philip Morris Calling," *Barron's* (December 10, 1979), p. 52.

[6] See J. Irwin Peters and Robert O'Keefe, "Marketing and Customer Analysis for Sales Management," *The Journal of Personal Selling & Sales Management* (Spring/Summer 1981), pp. 44–48. For an application of sales analysis in a retail setting see Ed Weymes, "A Different Approach to Retail Sales Analysis," *Business Horizons* (March–April 1982), pp. 66–74.

Table 25.1 Income Statement for Horizon Manufacturing Company

Horizon Manufacturing Company
Income Statement
for the Year Ended December 31, 1984

Sales		$5,783,000
Cost of goods sold		3,291,000
Gross margin		2,492,000
Expenses:		
Selling expenses	$753,000	
Other expenses	301,000	1,054,000
Profit before taxes		1,438,000
Income taxes		719,000
Profit after taxes		$ 719,000

Table 25.2 Sales and Expense Analysis by Territory

District	Average Compensation	Average Expenses	Total Sales Costs	Total Sales	Cost/ Sales Ratio
1	$23,600	$10,400	$34,000	$654,000	5.2%
2	21,900	12,800	34,700	534,000	6.5
3	27,200	13,100	40,300	790,000	5.1
4	25,700	12,300	38,000	180,000	21.1
5	24,200	11,700	35,900	580,000	6.2

In order to evaluate the performance of the salespeople in the five districts, the marketing executive must have a standard of comparison. District 4, for example, may be a large area but with relatively few industrial centers. Consequently, the costs involved in obtaining sales will be higher than for other districts.

The standard by which actual and expected sales are compared typically results from a detailed sales forecast by territories, products, customers, and salespersons. Once the **sales quota**—the level of expected sales by which actual results are compared—has been established, it is a simple process to compare the actual results with the expected performance. Table 25.3 compares actual sales with the quota established for each person in District 4.

Even though Kahn had the smallest amount of sales for the period, her performance was better than expected. However, the district sales manager should investigate Collins' performance since it resulted in the district's failure to meet its quota for the period.

Table 25.3 Sales Breakdown by Sales Representatives in District 4

Salesperson	Quota	Actual	Performance to Quota
O'Brien	$136,000	$128,000	94%
Fitzgerald	228,000	253,000	111
Kahn	118,000	125,000	106
Collins	246,000	160,000	65
Total	$728,000	$666,000	91%

The Iceberg Principle The performance of the salespersons in District 4 provides a good illustration of the **iceberg principle,** which suggests that important evaluative information is often hidden by aggregate data. The tip of the iceberg represents only one tenth of its total size. The remaining nine tenths lies hidden beneath the surface of the water. Summaries of data are useful, but the marketer must ensure that summaries do not actually conceal more than they reveal. If the sales breakdown by salesperson for the district had not been available, Collins' poor performance would have concealed the unexpectedly high sales performances by Fitzgerald and Kahn.

Other Classifications. Other possible breakdowns for sales analysis include customer type, product, method of sale (mail, telephone, or personal contact), type of order (cash or credit), and size of order. Sales analysis is one of the least expensive and most important sources of marketing information, and any firm with data-processing facilities should include a sales analysis as part of its evaluation and control system.

Marketing Cost Analysis

Marketing cost analysis is the evaluation of such items as selling costs, billing, warehousing, advertising, and delivery expenses in order to determine the profitability of particular customers, territories, or product lines.

Marketing cost analysis requires a new way of classifying accounting data. **Functional accounts** (representing the purpose for which an expenditure is made) replace the traditional **natural accounts** used in financial statements. These natural accounts—such as salary—must be reallocated to the pertinent functional accounts. A portion of the original salary account, for example, will be allocated to selling, inventory control, storage, billing, advertising, and other marketing costs. In the

Table 25.4 Allocation of Marketing Costs

	By Customer		By District		
Marketing Costs	Large	Small	A	B	C
Advertising	$14,000	$30,000	$20,000	$10,000	$14,000
Selling	52,000	62,000	38,000	38,000	38,000
Physical distribution	33,000	26,000	28,000	14,000	17,000
Credit	400	2,600	1,600	600	800
Total	$99,400	$120,600	$87,600	$62,600	$69,800

same manner, an account such as supply expenses will be allocated to the functions that utilize supplies.

The costs allocated to the functional accounts will equal those in the natural accounts. But instead of showing only total profitability, they can show the profitability of, say, particular districts, products, customers, salespersons, and order sizes. The most common reallocations are to products, customers, and territories or districts. Table 25.4 shows how allocations can be made.

The marketing decision maker can then evaluate the profitability of particular customers and districts on the basis of the sales produced and the costs incurred in producing them.

Table 25.5 indicates that District B is the most profitable and District A is unprofitable. Attention can now be given to plans for increasing sales or reducing expenses in this problem district to make market coverage of the area a profitable undertaking. Marketing cost analysis is similar to sales analysis in that both provide warning signals of deviations from plans and allow the marketing executive the opportunity to explain and possibly correct the deviations.[7]

Return on Investment: A Commonly Used Evaluative Technique

Evaluation is one of the most challenging tasks facing the marketing manager. The basic problem is to find an instrument capable of measuring marketing performance—actual and planned. Historically, sales volume was first used in this capacity; later, profitability became the accepted yardstick. More recently, **return on investment (ROI)** has gained popularity as an effective evaluative device. It is particularly useful in evaluating proposals for alternative courses of action.

[7]An excellent discussion of marketing cost analysis is presented in Patrick M. Dunne and Harry I. Wolk, "Marketing Cost Analysis: A Modularized Contribution Approach," *Journal of Marketing* (July 1977), pp. 83–94.

Table 25.5 Income Statement for Districts A, B, and C

	District			
	A	B	C	Total
Sales	$260,000	$200,000	$191,000	$651,000
Cost of sales	175,000	135,000	120,000	430,000
Gross margin	85,000	65,000	71,000	221,000
Marketing expenses	87,600	62,600	69,800	220,000
Contribution of each territory	($ 2,600)	$ 2,400	$ 1,200	$ 1,000

ROI is a quantitative tool that seeks to relate the activity or project's profitability to its investment. It is equal to the rate of profit multiplied by the turnover rate. ROI can be calculated as follows:

$$\text{ROI} = \frac{\text{Net Profit}}{\text{Sales}} \times \frac{\text{Sales}}{\text{Investment}}$$

In other words:

$$\text{ROI} = \text{Rate of Profit} \times \text{Turnover.}$$

A brief example shows how ROI might be used as an evaluative device. Consider a new product idea for which the firm estimates that a $200,000 investment will be required. The company expects to reach $500,000 in sales, with a net profit of $40,000. The proposed project's ROI is calculated in the following manner:

$$\text{ROI} = \frac{\$40,000}{\$500,000} \times \frac{\$500,000}{\$200,000}$$
$$= 0.08 \times 2.5 = 20 \text{ percent.}$$

Whether or not this expected performance is acceptable depends on the ROI of alternative uses of corporate funds. It would not be viewed favorably at Gould, Inc., for instance. This major industrial goods manufacturer wants all new products to generate a return on investment of 40 percent before taxes.

ROI is often used in conjunction with other evaluative tools. For example, Gould also specifies that its new products should generate profits of 30 percent before taxes and 15 percent annual sales and profit growth. It also insists on a $20 million sales potential within five years following introduction and a total market potential of about $50 million.[8]

[8]The Gould example is reported in "Industrial Newsletter," *Sales & Marketing Management* (April 3, 1978), p. 32.

The Limitations of ROI ROI should be used with caution and in conjunction with other evaluative tools in assessing marketing performance. A variety of factors can affect ROI calculations: book value of assets, depreciation, industry conditions, time periods, and transfer pricing. Consider how these factors could impact an attempt to judge the overall effectiveness of different divisions within a large corporation.

Book Value of Assets. If an older division is using assets that have been largely written off, both its current depreciation charges and its investment base will be low. This will make its ROI high in relation to newer divisions.

Depreciation. ROI is very sensitive to depreciation policy. If one division is writing off assets at a relatively rapid rate, its annual profits and, hence, its ROI will be reduced.

Industry Conditions. If one division is operating in an industry where conditions are favorable and rates of return are high, whereas another is in an industry suffering from excessive competition, such environmental differences may cause the favored division to look good and the unfavored division to look bad, quite apart from any differences in their respective managers. External conditions must be taken into account when appraising ROI performance.

Time Periods. Many projects have long gestation periods—expenditures must be made for research and development, plant construction, market development, and the like; such expenditures will add to the investment base without a commensurate increase in profits for several years. During this period, a division's ROI could be seriously reduced; without proper constraints, its division manager could be improperly penalized.

Transfer Pricing. In most corporations some divisions sell to other divisions. At General Motors, for example, the Fisher Body Division sells to the Chevrolet Division; in such cases, the price at which goods are transferred between divisions has a fundamental effect on divisional profits. If the transfer price of auto bodies is set relatively high, then Fisher Body will have a relatively high ROI and Chevrolet a relatively low ROI.

Tying ROI to Profit Centers Dresser Industries, a diversified $5 billion manufacturer, illustrates how return on investment can be used to evaluate a marketing program. Dresser has a profitability goal of increasing earnings by an average of 10 to 15 percent annually. To stay on target, Dresser has set up 500 separate profit centers worldwide. A **profit cen-**

ter is any administrative unit whose contribution to corporate earnings can be measured. The company's objective is to make the smallest possible operational unit responsible for its own performance. Dresser requires that each profit center report operating results to its Dallas headquarters by the fourth day of business each month. Any profit center reporting an ROI of less than 25 percent is immediately studied, and corrective action is taken if necessary.[9] ROI is a major evaluative tool at Dresser Industries.

Ratio Analysis

In addition to the market share and ROI calculations outlined earlier in this chapter, there are a variety of ratios useful in the evaluation and control process. These ratios are especially helpful in the analysis of specific aspects of marketing performance. The starting place for such analysis is with the firm's *income statement.* This financial statement (sometimes referred to as the operating statement or the profit and loss statement) presents a summary portrait of the firm's revenues and expenses over a period of time. The time period may be a month, quarter, year, or any period selected by the firm's management. The second primary type of financial statement, the *balance sheet,* shows the financial condition of the firm at one period by examining its assets, liabilities, and net worth. While the balance sheet provides a snapshot view of the organization at one point in time, the income statement is similar to a motion picture, focusing on activities—income and expenditures—over a time period.

The income statement is particularly useful for marketing decision makers in focusing on overall sales and the costs incurred in generating these sales. Moreover, it indicates both whether a profit or loss was incurred and the amount of this loss or profit. For nonprofit organizations, the income statement provides specific indications of the ability of the organization's revenues and contributions to cover the cost involved in its operation. Finally, the income statement provides the basic data required to calculate numerous ratios used by the marketing decision maker.

Table 25.6 shows the operating statement for Ski Colorado, a relatively small Denver retailer marketing ski equipment, ski clothing, group ski tours, and ski instructions. Since the firm is a retailer, the operating statement contains a net purchases subsection under the cost of goods sold section. The operating statement for a manufacturer would include a section labeled *cost of goods manufactured* in addition to purchases of raw materials and component parts. Otherwise, the in-

[9] Grover Herman, "Jack James Directs Dresser's Destiny, Texas-Style," *Nation's Business* (November 1979), pp. 68–72, 75–76.

come statements for manufacturers and marketing intermediaries (retailers and wholesalers) are similar.

Table 25.6 may be divided into the following major sections:

Net sales	$110,000
Minus: Cost of goods sold	−54,200
Equals: Gross margin	55,800
Minus: Expenses	−43,300
Equals: Net income before taxes	12,500
Minus: Taxes	−4,000
Equals: Net income	$ 8,500

Net sales was calculated by subtracting merchandise returned by customers from total sales revenue. In some cases, overall sales are reduced when the retailer refunds a portion of the sales price (a sales allowance) on an item that is damaged or partially defective. In other instances, returned merchandise must be subtracted from the total sales figure to accurately reflect net sales.

Cost of goods sold by Ski Colorado is somewhat more complicated. At the beginning of the operating period, total inventory of $26,000 was on hand. In addition, Ski Colorado managers purchased $52,000 in inventory during 1984 to add to the beginning inventory, but received a purchase discount of $1,000 from one firm for quantity purchases. Delivery charges of $1,200 for the new purchases resulted in total net delivered purchases of $52,200. When this was added to the cost of beginning inventory, the total cost of products available for sale amounted to $78,200.

At the end of the operating period, some $24,000 was still on hand, indicating that the cost of goods sold during 1984 was $54,200 ($78,200 minus $24,000). Total *gross margin* ($110,000 net sales less $54,200 cost of goods sold) amounted to $55,800.

In order to determine net income for 1984, Ski Colorado managers must deduct the various selling and general expenses incurred from the $55,800 gross margin total. *Selling expenses* include salaries and commissions paid to store personnel, advertising, sales supplies, delivery expenses, and such miscellaneous selling expenses as telephone charges, depreciation, insurance, and utilities allocated to sales. *General expenses* include salaries of office personnel; supplies; special services such as consultants, accounting services, or legal fees; insurance; postage; and depreciation. Total expenses for Ski Colorado in 1984 were $43,300.

Net income before taxes amounted to $12,500 ($55,800 gross margin less $43,300 total expense). After subtracting $4,000 for taxes, Ski Colorado earned a total *net income* of $8,500 for 1984.

Analytical Ratios By analyzing the operating statement shown in Table 25.6, Ski Colorado managers can use a number of ratios in critically evaluating their performance and comparing it with the performance

Table 25.6 Ski Colorado Income Statement for Year Ending December 31, 1984

Revenues			
Gross sales		$112,000	
Less: Sales returns and allowances	$ 2,000		
Net sales			$110,000
Cost of Goods Sold			
Beginning inventory, January 1 (at cost)		26,000	
Gross purchases during year	52,000		
Less: Purchase discounts	1,000		
Net purchases	51,000		
Plus: Freight in	1,200		
Net purchases (total delivered cost)		52,200	
Cost of goods available for sale		78,200	
Less: Ending inventory, December 31 (at cost)		24,000	
Cost of goods sold			54,200
Gross Margin			55,800
Expenses			
Selling expenses			
Sales salaries and commissions	17,000		
Advertising	4,500		
Sales supplies	2,000		
Delivery expenses	1,000		
Miscellaneous selling expenses	3,500		
Total selling expenses		28,000	
General expenses			
Office salaries	12,000		
Office supplies	1,000		
Miscellaneous general expenses	2,300		
Total general expenses		15,300	
Total expenses			43,300
Net Income before Taxes			12,500
Taxes			4,000
Net Income			$ 8,500

of previous periods and with that of similar firms in the industry. Four important analytical ratios are the gross margin percentage, the net profit percentage, the selling expense ratio, and the operating expense ratio.

Gross margin percentage. The **gross margin percentage** is the ratio of gross margin to net sales. It indicates the percentage of revenues available for covering expenses and earning a profit after the payment of the cost of products sold during the period. The gross margin percentage for Ski Colorado is calculated as follows:

$$\text{Gross Margin Percentage} = \frac{\text{Gross Margin}}{\text{Net Sales}}$$

$$= \frac{\$\ 55{,}800}{\$110{,}000} = 50.7 \text{ percent.}$$

Net Profit Percentage. As its name indicates, the **net profit percentage** reflects the ratio of net profit to net sales. It is calculated as follows:

$$\text{Net Profit Percentage} = \frac{\text{Net Income}}{\text{Net Sales}}$$

$$= \frac{\$\ \ 8{,}500}{\$110{,}000} = 7.7 \text{ percent.}$$

In comparing the 7.7 percent net profit percentage with those of previous periods and of other firms, it is important to note that taxes have been deducted from the net income figure. In some instances, other firms may use net income before taxes in their calculation. Valid comparisons can be made only if the ratios use the same formula.

Selling Expense Ratio. The **selling expense ratio** reveals the relationship between major sales expenses and total net sales. It is calculated by dividing total selling expenses by net sales.

$$\text{Selling Expense Ratio} = \frac{\text{Total Selling Expenses}}{\text{Net Sales}}$$

$$= \frac{\$\ 28{,}000}{\$110{,}000} = 25.5 \text{ percent.}$$

Operating Expense Ratio. The **operating expense ratio** combines both selling and general expenses and compares them with overall net sales. The operating expense ratio for Ski Colorado is calculated as follows:

$$\text{Operating Expense Ratio} = \frac{\text{Total Expenses}}{\text{Net Sales}}$$

$$= \frac{\$\ 43{,}300}{\$110{,}000} = 39.4 \text{ percent.}$$

Whether or not these ratios are considered acceptable depends primarily upon industry averages, the firm's past performances, and the alternatives available to the company. In any case, sales analysis, cost analysis, return on investment, and ratio analysis can be enlightening to marketing management in providing concrete, quantifiable comparisons with actual and expected performances.

The Marketing Audit

A comprehensive marketing audit can provide a valuable—and sometimes disquieting—perspective on a firm's marketing performance. Consider the pharmaceutical firm that was delighted with an 83 percent awareness rating for an advertising campaign, but shocked upon learning that this amounted to only a 28 percent intent-to-buy figure.[10]

All marketing organizations need to evaluate their operations and performance periodically. Such a review is invaluable not only in identifying the tasks that the organization does well, but also in highlighting its failures. Periodic review, criticism, and self-analysis are crucial to the vitality of any organization. They are particularly critical to a function that is as diverse and dynamic as marketing.

Marketing audits are especially valuable in pointing out areas in which managerial perceptions differ sharply from the reality. Table 25.7 reports some of the things that were learned in marketing audits at various pharmaceutical enterprises.

The Marketing Audit: A Definition William S. Woodside, the president of American Can Company, has been quoted as saying: "The roughest thing to get rid of is the Persian Messenger Syndrome, where the bearer of bad tidings is beheaded by the king. You should lean over backward to reward the guy who is first with the bad news. Most companies have all kinds of abilities to handle problems, if they only learn about them soon enough."[11]

If the marketing organization is to avoid the Persian Messenger Syndrome, as Woodside calls it, it must not only institute periodic program reviews, but must also be willing to accept the objective results of such evaluations. For most organizations, this means the use of a **marketing audit**—a thorough, objective evaluation of an organization's marketing philosophy, goals, policies, tactics, practices, and results.[12]

The marketing audit goes beyond the normal control system. The control process for marketing essentially asks: are we doing things right? The marketing audit extends this question to: are we also doing the right thing?[13]

Marketing audits are applicable to all organizations—large or small, profitable or profitless, and nonprofit or profit-oriented. Audits are particularly valuable when they are performed for the first time or when they are conducted after a long absence from the managerial process. Not all organizations have implemented marketing audits, but the number of firms using them is expected to grow. One study found that 28 percent of the firms surveyed had used a marketing audit. Table 25.8 reflects the use of audits in different industries.

[10]Ed Roseman, "An Audit Can Make the 'Accurate' Difference," *Product Marketing* (August 1979), pp. 24–25.

[11]Quoted in Arthur R. Roolman, "Why Corporations Hate the Future," *MBA* (November 1975), p. 37.

[12]The basis of this section and the next was taken from an excellent discussion of marketing audits appearing in David T. Kollat, Roger D. Blackwell, and James F. Robeson, *Strategic Marketing* (New York: Holt, Rinehart and Winston, 1972), pp. 498–500.

[13]Kollat, Blackwell, and Robeson, *Strategic Marketing*, p. 500.

Table 25.7 Staff Assumptions about Marketing Variables as Compared with Audit Findings

Focus	Marketing Staff Assumptions	Audit Findings
Personal Selling		
Scale of efforts	6.5 calls daily	4.0 calls daily
Quality of effort	Full presentation, 100 percent of calls	Full presentation, 70 percent of calls
Message integrity	100 percent accuracy	65 percent accuracy
Communication with sales force	100 percent readership	82 percent readership; 81 percent accuracy; 2.7 retail calls daily
Advertising		
Ad agency interface	Harmonious	Disharmonious
Message integrity	100 percent accuracy	62 percent accuracy
Message impact		83 percent awareness; 28 percent acceptance
Product		
Manufacturing cost	No change	11 percent increase
Market growth	7 percent growth	2 percent growth
Penetration	45 percent accepting; 25 percent neutral; 10 percent rejecting	28 percent accepting; 57 percent neutral; 15 percent rejecting
Intra-company		
Interface processing	No problems	Communication and cooperation problems
Marketing intelligence system	Satisfactory	Unsatisfactory
Approval processing	1 working day	3–14 working days; average, 9 working days

Source: Ed Roseman, "An Audit Can Make the 'Accurate' Difference," *Product Marketing/Cosmetic & Fragrance Retailing* (August 1979), p. 24. Reprinted by permission.

Selecting the Marketing Auditors Selection of the auditors is a critical aspect of conducting a marketing audit. Three potential sources of auditors are regular corporate executives, special marketing audit staffs, and outside marketing consultants.

Some firms prefer to assign selected executives to perform marketing audits on a periodic basis. The difficulties in such an arrangement include the time pressure of the executives' regular duties and the problem of maintaining impartiality. Other organizations set up a separate marketing staff if their size permits such a structure. This arrangement can provide an excellent balance between impartiality and extensive inhouse knowledge. Marketing consultants are often recommended for marketing audits because they enter the evaluation with an independent viewpoint that is valuable. Consultants also may be able to offer the most up-to-date evaluation methodology.

Table 25.8 Marketing Audit Usage by Industry

Type of Company	Percentage Conducting Marketing Audits
Industrial goods manufacturers	36%
Consumer goods manufacturers	19
Manufacturers of consumer and industrial goods	22
Service related firms	28
Total of all firms	28

Source: Adapted from Louis M. Capella and William S. Sekely, "The Marketing Audit: Usage and Applications," in *Proceedings of the Southern Marketing Association,* (eds.) Robert S. Franz, Robert M. Hopkins, and Alfred G. Toma (New Orleans, La.: Southern Marketing Association, November 1978), p. 412. Used by permission of the Southern Marketing Association. All rights reserved.

Conducting a Marketing Audit Marketing audits are probably as diverse as the people who conduct them. Some auditors follow only informal procedures. Others have formulated elaborate checklists, questionnaires, profiles, tests, and related research instruments. Regardless of the tools employed, all marketing audits follow four major steps.

1. Securing agreement between the auditor and the organization on the audit's objectives and scope.
2. Developing a framework for the audit.
   - **a.** Studying the company's external environment.
   - **b.** Profiling the major elements of the marketing system.
   - **c.** Examining the key marketing activities.
3. Preparing an audit report with findings and recommendations.
4. Presenting the report in a manner that will lead to action.[14]

These steps can be implemented in a variety of ways. Certainly, some basic questions can be raised under each topic, and they must be answered if a proper audit is to be made. For instance, during the initial stage, the auditor and the organization should agree on the goals to be achieved by the audit, the audit's coverage and depth, and the provision of data sources for the audit. Similar vital questions can be raised during each of the other stages of the marketing audit.

The real value of a marketing audit may not emerge until considerably after the final report has been prepared and presented. As one author has pointed out:

The marketing audit can function as a catalyst to start management discussion as to where the company should be going. The final actions taken may

[14]This section is adapted from an address by Philip Kotler to the Chicago chapter of the American Marketing Association. Reported in "Kotler Presents Ways, Hows of Marketing Audits for Firms, Nonprofit Organizations," *Marketing News* (March 26, 1976), p. 21.

vary from those recommended, but the audit has served its purpose in starting the needed dialogue about the company's marketing strategy.[15]

Such an audit can make a significant contribution to improved marketing productivity in virtually all organizations. The starting point, as noted earlier, is to stop beheading the Persian Messenger.

Summary

The control process is an important part of marketing. *Evaluation and control* refers to all the various assessments that marketers employ to determine if the marketing opportunity analysis, the objectives and the standards set during the marketing planning phase, and/or the implementation of the marketing program itself have been effective. Evaluation and control permits marketers to determine whether corrective actions are needed. Control charts are sometimes used to set both upper and lower control limits for such assessments.

Chapter 25 examined the question of how marketing performance should be measured. Several techniques or procedures are useful in marketing evaluation and control. Sales analysis is an in-depth evaluation of a firm's sales designed to obtain meaningful information from existing data. Marketing cost analysis is the evaluation of such items as selling costs, billing, warehousing, advertising, and delivery expenses in order to determine the profitability of particular customers, territories, or product lines. ROI is a quantitative tool that seeks to relate the activity or project's profitability to its required investment. Also, the calculation of various ratios helps in analyzing specific aspects of marketing performance. The marketing audit, which entails a thorough study of a firm's marketing program, is extremely useful in improving overall effectiveness.

Key Terms

evaluation and control
control charts
sales analysis
sales quota
iceberg principle
marketing cost analysis
functional accounts
natural accounts
return on investment (ROI)
profit center
gross margin percentage
net profit percentage
selling expense ratio
operating expense ratio
marketing audit

[15] *Marketing News* (March 26, 1976), p. 21.

Review Questions

1. Explain the steps in the marketing evaluation and control process.
2. Explain the role of sales quotas in sales analysis.
3. Compare sales analysis and marketing cost analysis.
4. Distinguish between functional accounts and natural accounts.
5. Identify the primary benefits of return on investment (ROI) in evaluation and control. What are the major limitations?
6. Identify and briefly explain the major ratios used in marketing evaluation and control.
7. How would a marketer decide whether the ratios for his or her firm are satisfactory?
8. Compare the marketing audit with the typical control system in an organization.
9. Who should conduct the marketing audit?
10. Identify the major steps in a marketing audit.

Discussion Questions and Exercises

1. If Great Lakes Enterprises had a gross margin of $4 million on net sales of $9 million, what is its gross margin percentage?
2. What is the net profit percentage for a store with a net income of $72,000 on net sales of $900,000?
3. El Paso Industries had total selling expenses of $85,000. The firm's net sales were $440,000. What was the selling expense ratio for El Paso Industries?
4. Bridgeport Standard ($4 million in net sales) had total expenses of $1.6 million. What was the firm's operating expense ratio?
5. A marketing vice-president is considering a new product idea. The firm estimates that a $600,000 investment will be required. The company expects to achieve sales of $3 million with a net profit of $300,000. What is the proposed project's ROI?

CASES FOR PART 8

Case 8.1
The Central Department Store

The Central Department Store is the largest retail organization in Thailand and Southeast Asia. In recent years management has become increasingly aware of several legal and ethical issues involving the purchase of merchandise from local dealers and manufacturers and has sought out ways to reorganize and control such purchasing.

Problems with Repeat Buying of Merchandise

During 1978, the merchandising vice-president of the Central Department Store (CDS) had been confronted by the increasing corruption among the merchandise buyers of his company. As the profitability and the overall success of the CDS have to a large extent depended upon the efficiency and honesty of these buyers, the merchandising vp was alarmed and ready to explore new methods to control the buying operations. He believed that the company's carefully planned, integrated marketing efforts would be hampered by the gradual accumulation of overpriced and/or uncompetitive merchandise obtained by corrupt or inefficient buyers. He therefore wanted to halt the threatening decline of confidence in the ability of the company to control its merchandise buying system.

It has for a long time been acknowledged that the buyers have the most crucial positions in the retail business. In order to attain the twin company objectives of profitability and consumer satisfaction, buyers had to obtain merchandise of acceptable quality at competitively low prices. The prevailing problem of corruption among them has seriously threatened the CDS's long-term marketing and merchandising strategy. Two recent events have focused the executives' attention on this issue.

The head of the luggage department in one of the company's stores had to be fired because it was discovered that he was taking bribes from suppliers. Although the merchandising vp had been responsible for all initial negotiations determining the prices, terms, and conditions of delivery from new suppliers, heads of departments routinely placed repeat orders whenever consumer demand necessitated the replenishing of

Source: This case was prepared by Dr. Thomas J. Seres, Associate Professor at the University of Southern California. Reprinted by permission.

stocks. The heads of these departments have therefore also acted as buyers for repeat orders.

During the mid-1970s, the CDS obtained the major part of its traveling bags and luggage items from six local manufacturers. Competition among these suppliers had been fierce, and business ethics had been based on the realities of the prevailing atmosphere in the country. Eventually, one of the suppliers approached the head of the luggage department with gifts to persuade him to increase the volume of repeat purchases from a favored manufacturer. When this actually happened, repeat orders from the other manufacturers had to be curtailed since the aggregate consumer demand had not increased sufficiently. The other manufacturers refused to accept the relative loss in their market share and made similar offers to the corrupt buyer. One supplier offered him a monthly "buying-bonus" of 800 baht (about $40 U.S. currency), while another one wanted to pay him 5 percent commission on all future repeat orders from his company. When it became impossible to satisfy all suppliers at the same time, the dissatisfied manufacturers leaked the word to CDS executives that the buyer was corrupt. An investigation followed, and the evidence led to the immediate dismissal of this buyer.

Another suspected case of corruption was highlighted by the puzzling behavior of one of the other buyers. This employee was assigned to a new task in another CDS outlet, representing promotion to a higher position with increased basic salary but no buying duties. Instead of the satisfaction and gratitude that the company expected, the buyer resigned. Management considered this resignation as astonishing evidence of a corrupt buying system that obviously provided unscrupulous buyers with more money than the salaries of some of their superiors.

On the basis of these two unrelated incidents, the merchandising vp was forced to conclude that corruption and inefficiency among the buyers were more serious and widespread than previously believed. The question was to find adroit ways and means to stop this deplorable practice that had started to assert noticeably negative influences on the company's marketing programs.

The Management Structure and Operations of the Central Department Store

The Central Department Store Company, Ltd. was the largest retail organization in Southeast Asia with 18 wholly owned subsidiaries, total assets of about $30 million (U.S. currency), and annual reventues of between $45–$50 million during the mid- and late 1970s. Tiang Chirathivat started a one-room retail shop in Bangkok in the days following World War II, and his family successfully continued to expand the retail operations until in 1977, the consolidated sales of the CDS companies placed the group among the top 25 industrial and commercial firms in Thailand. The group operated marketing and manufacturing subsidiaries as well as a complex of four department stores in Bangkok. The largest and the newest of these stores was located at Chitlom with total floor space of 18,000 square meters; two others were in the Wang Burapha section in Chinatown; and one was on Silom Road in the center of Bangkok. Total floor space in the four stores amounted to 26,200 square meters. This family-controlled group operated on the basis of the high volume–low profit margins marketing philosophy. Many items sold in these stores were manufactured by the wholly owned subsidiaries, which helped maintain profitability while at the same time allowing the CDS to sell at competitively low prices.

Buying from these subsidiaries of course presented no problem with corruption, since neither directly imported merchandise from various countries. The core of this problem was the existing system of repeat buying from local suppliers in Thailand. The main strength of CDS's management structure was the efficient, hard working, and impeccably honest group of family members who occupied the top executive positions in the company.

According to this management structure, the problem of dishonest buyers should have been handled by the merchandising vp, but he needed the help of his executive colleagues as well. According to some observers, most stores in Thailand were experiencing the same difficulties with their buyers. Among the most important attributes good buyers were required to have were intelligence, experience, and integrity. However, the realities of modern city life, the exigency of maintaining an acceptable standard of living under inflationary conditions, the decline of traditional moral values in a fast-changing society, and the constant temptation to obtain strongly advertised, comfort-providing but costly gadgets created an atmosphere where it was extremely difficult to find buyers who were both scrupulously honest and intelligent.

On one hand, buyers had to be intelligent, alert to changes in fashion and in other consumer preferences, experienced in dealing with a variety of skillful suppliers, as well as knowledgeable about prices and qualities. All these characteristics required a relatively sophisticated employee with considerable foresight about market trends, so that the store would not be burdened with a great deal of unsold stock at the end of each season. Management fully realized that no amount of adroit personal selling, heavy advertising, or other marketing methods would be able to sell the type of dead merchandise for which consumer demand was sluggish from the beginning, or was unfashionable, overpriced, or otherwise uncompetitive.

On the other hand, the buyers' honesty, loyalty, and integrity were just as vital. The unhappy example of the head of the luggage department indicated the type of difficulties that could result from a dishonest handling of the buyers' duties and responsibilities. The merchandising vp therefore decided to investigate the whole system of buying in general and the position of the buyers at the CDS in particular. He first interviewed a trusted employee who had been with the company for a long time and who seemed to quietly and informally observe the method of buying and buyers' behavior at CDS. The man reported as follows:

When a new buyer is appointed, he will work hard and will usually be honest to begin with. After a while, however, one or two suppliers will approach him with gifts to persuade him to order larger quantities or to provide more prominent shelf space and display for the merchandise in question.

If the buyer becomes approachable, the suppliers try to further enlist his services with a variety of "kickbacks." They might offer him a certain commission on the extra quantity ordered or even pay him a fixed salary on the condition that he continue to order large quantities and provide bigger and better display space.

As the tempting conditions further corrupt the buyer, he will no longer order from suppliers who fail to pay him bribe money, and he will find new and ingenious ways to extract larger amounts from the competing suppliers. He might, for instance, issue private lottery tickets to sell his car or camera or any of his secondhand belongings. These lottery tickets would be offered to the suppliers and would normally provide the enterprising buyers with money far in excess of the value of the article. Suppose he has a used car that would fetch $300 (U.S. currency) under normal market conditions. The buyer would then persuade his eager suppliers to pay $20 for each lottery ticket. If he manages to sell, say, 50 tickets, he will receive $1000 for his car.

Other buyers will organize a birthday party for one of their many close relatives and invite the suppliers to attend. Apart from birthdays, there are many other occasions for these parties, such as housewarmings, weddings of relatives, and other family events. Nearly always, the invited suppliers do not have any ideas about the personal requirements of these unknown family members, so they give cash gifts instead that would invariably end up as an indirect "kickback" for the corrupt buyer.

More audacious buyers simplify the bribery transaction and borrow money directly from the suppliers. As these salesmen dare not jeopardize their supply position with the buyer, they conveniently forget about the loan and consider it as a necessary expenditure to ensure continuity of the orders from CDS.

The merchandising vp was horrified to discover the extent and scope of the various bribery methods pervading among the buyers and proceeded with his investigation by reviewing the whole system of buying and repeat buying at CDS.

The Existing System of Obtaining Supplies

The CDS had basically three different methods of obtaining supplies of merchandise for its stores:

1. CDS's own sources from manufacturing operations controlled by its own subsidiaries. The company operated four factories at Wang Burapha, Silom, Chitlom, and at Klong Tan, manufacturing such items as dresses, blouses, skirts, sportswear, and underwear. Some of the world-famous merchandise, such as Manhattan shirts, Wrangler jeans, and Jockey underwear were also produced locally under license agreements by these CDS subsidiaries. Naturally, obtaining supplies from these wholly owned subsidiaries was the simplest form of merchandising.
2. Direct importing from abroad. CDS's foreign suppliers were located mainly in Hong Kong, Taiwan, U.S.A., Japan, Italy, Germany, England, France, and China. There were three methods of dealing with these foreign suppliers:
   a. CDS buyers, who traveled abroad visiting the factories and headquarters of the manufacturers, attending fashion shows in Paris, London, or Dusseldorf to obtain better insight into new fashion trends as well as to examine new merchandise offerings from manufacturers. Since import regulations by the Thai government changed from time

to time, these buyers had to be fully aware of the various restrictive measures, taxes, and duty charges for the products they considered buying for CDS.

b. CDS foreign representatives, who operated and were located permanently in cities such as London, New York, Hong Kong, or Toyko. These representatives bought merchandise in these places on behalf of the CDS within the limitations of their contracts with the company.

c. Representatives and salesmen of foreign producers who traveled to Bangkok to show samples and catalogs to CDS executives. This method of buying presented certain advantages for the company compared with importing via CDS's own traveling buyers. Firstly, it reduced overhead costs related to the direct buying of imported merchandise, as the CDS buyers' traveling expenditure was eliminated, particularly if it could be assumed that the prices obtained by either type of foreign ordering remained the same. Secondly, it placed the responsibility of negotiating terms and conditions with foreign suppliers into the hands of the merchandising vice-president or some of his trusted assistants.

3. Local suppliers, who could be either manufacturers or wholesalers of locally produced goods or local agents and importers of foreign merchandise. CDS used two methods to obtain products from these local suppliers: either buying on consignment or buying as a definite purchase.

a. Consignment buying was naturally less risky for CDS because the merchandise that remained unsold would eventually be returned to the suppliers. In such an arrangement CDS paid only for the goods already sold at the end of each month. There were two systems of selling goods on consignment in the CDS:

i. When the suppliers organized their own sales operations with their own sales force at their own counters located in CDS outlets. This system was used primarily by cosmetics suppliers such as Max Factor, Coty, or Kanebo, who were responsible for their own stocks, shortages, pilferage, and damages and paid a 25 percent fee on their sales to CDS for the location facilities.

ii. When consignment goods were sold by the CDS sales force and the unsold merchandise was returned to the suppliers. In this case, CDS's share of profit was greater than in the first type, since by using its own sales force CDS assumed full responsibility — and therefore greater risk — for shortages and damages.

b. The greatest risk for CDS and the greatest opportunity for dishonest buyers were, however, definite purchases of merchandise from manufacturers, when CDS fully committed itself to total payment for the entire order regardless of the sales progress in the stores. In order to reduce such risk, CDS bought only the most popular and fast-selling consumer goods, such as detergents, canned foods, toothpaste, or shampoo, under these arrangements. CDS obtained favorable terms and discounts from these suppliers mostly on the basis of the company's oligopolistic position in the Bangkok marketplace. Only two truly large department stores competed for shares in the retail business during the 1970s: CDS and Dai Maru. As CDS aggregate sales were large, the company was able to obtain special prices from local suppliers. Although the terms of sales varied a great deal, most suppliers provided one-month credit for definite purchases, one percent or two percent special discount on large quantity orders, and a further two percent discount for cash payment. In addition to this, CDS charged a fee for display space whenever the local manufacturers wanted to promote their merchandise (particularly new or improved versions of products) in the company's stores.

All these discounts and business favors between the manufacturers and the retail distributors have given the dishonest buyers frequent opportunities to exploit their position for personal gain. Although orders for new products remained the responsibility of the merchandising vice-president or his chief buyers, they could not personally deal with the large number of repeat buying orders, which were carried out by various department heads who also acted as buyers. As the two recent examples of corruption indicated, the problem of honesty, mostly among the heads of departments, caused serious headaches for the merchandising vice-president, who was ultimately responsible for control of the whole system of buying.

The basic salaries paid by CDS to these buyers and chief buyers were considered fair during the period under review; they received approximately \$100–\$150 and \$200–\$250 (U.S. currency) respectively. These monthly salaries represented after-tax incomes and compared with approximately \$600–\$800 (U.S. currency) for the executives of the company. It was estimated that during 1978 a household of four people would have probably needed \$100–\$150 (U.S. currency) per month to cover basic living expenditures in the lower income groups and perhaps \$200–\$300 (U.S. currency) per month in the middle-income strata.

In addition to these take-home salaries, CDS had generously provided fringe benefits for its employees. Depending on the number of service years, bonuses of up to six-months salary per year were given, although one-month per year bonuses had probably been more common. Over 2,000 employees were entitled to free medical services and mothers received one month's full salary after each child delivered. CDS offered free tuition for many of the employees' children and provided rent-free dormitory facilities for some of the single employees. When a lifetime of service came to an end, some retired key employees were rewarded with a house. All these extra advantages were offered by CDS in a country where social security gains and fringe benefits were far less frequently provided than in Western Europe or North America.

The merchandising vice-president had therefore concluded that the main motivation behind the corruption among the buyers was more likely greed than desperation. Although the basic salaries of these employees appeared to be low compared with compensations received for similar work in more developed countries, many people doing more dangerous, difficult, or higher qualified work received even less in Thailand. It seemed to the merchandising vp that simply increasing the basic salaries of the buyers could not eliminate the deeply rooted corruption. He was, therefore, searching for more ingenious and original solutions that would take into account the peculiar socioeconomic and ethical circumstances prevailing in Thailand during the late 1970s. He believed that forces beyond the control of his company might have orchestrated the overall mood that tempted the buyers working for retail outlets in his country.

The question was to recommend the most practical steps to the board of directors that could conceivably reduce the extent of corruption among these employees and to raise the level of efficiency in the buying operations to that of the selling and marketing.

Discussion Questions

1. What practical measures would you recommend for the CDS to deal with the existing corruption among its buyers?
2. If corruption and bribery could not be completely eliminated from the system, what marketing steps would you suggest that could minimize the effect of inefficient and uncompetitive buying?
3. If you were one of the competing manufacturers (domestic or foreign) trying to sell to the CDS under the prevailing conditions, how would you organize the marketing of your merchandise without paying bribery to corrupt buyers?

Case 8.2
Sunrise Hospital

Present

David R. Brandsness, a young dynamic administrator at Sunrise Hospital, turned in his swivel chair and stared out over the hospital parking lot and pondered some thoughts. He had just looked at figures that indicated that the hospital was underutilized on the weekends. The figures, in part, revealed that the 486 beds at Sunrise had only 60 per-

Source: This case was prepared by Professors Henry A. Sciullo, Eddie H. Goodin, and Philip E. Taylor. Dr. Sciullo (now deceased) was a member of the faculty at the University of Nevada, Las Vegas, where Dr. Goodin and Dr. Taylor are currently faculty members. Reprinted by permission.

cent occupancy on weekends, compared with turnaway business on weekdays. This was a recurrent problem. David Brandsness muttered in frustration, "Our weekend census is below 300 and I know that by Tuesday night we will be turning patients away." Brandsness wondered aloud, "How can we have increased utilization of our outstanding equipment and skilled personnel on weekends which will eventually result in a reduction of patient costs and allow us to offer health services at the lowest rates of any private acute care hospital in Las Vegas?"

Background

Sunrise Hospital is a fully accredited private acute care hospital with a licensed capacity of 486 beds. Since it opened in 1958, it has shown a consistent growth in both capacity and census.

These expansions have been accompanied by the development of an extensive range of ancillary services designed to meet both inpatient and outpatient demands. As a result of these programs, the hospital's share of the Las Vegas market had grown to approximately 46 percent of the total patient days recorded.

Market Demographics

Over the past 15 years, the population of Clark County (Las Vegas), Sunrise Hospital's primary service area, has grown 162 percent for a compound annual growth rate of 7.12 percent. It is the largest and fastest growing county in the state of Nevada, and projections indicate it will continue to grow at a 5 percent rate through 1985, adding approximately 188,000 residents in that ten-year span.

Market Share

Perhaps the most important measure of Sunrise Hospital's success is that its average daily census has increased at an 8 percent compound average rate (263 average daily census to 363 average daily census), while total patient days recorded for all Las Vegas hospitals has grown at a compound rate of 4.74 percent. Sunrise Hospital has grown to dominate the Las Vegas market.

Sunrise has achieved the present market position by aggressively marketing its services to the medical and general community. Recent innovations, such as a satellite outpatient testing center, 24-hour pharmacy, and a laboratory pickup and delivery service for physicians' offices, are indicative of some of the marketing efforts.

As Sunrise Hospital's market share approaches the 50 percent level, it gives a significant degree of stability to the operations. The broad base of support required to sustain this dominance indicates that Sunrise is not overly dependent on any single group of physicians and can continue to exercise leadership in providing medical services over a broad range of specialties.

Sunrise Hospital has always been a financially stable operation. Some factors which have contributed to this success are:

1. The maintenance of a prestigious position as "the hospital" in Las Vegas.
2. The relatively low (35 percent) number of governmental reimbursement-type patients.

Medical Staff

The history of the Sunrise Hospital medical staff can be classified into three phases. At its inception, the primary support of Sunrise Hospital came from general practitioners, a limited number of internists, and fewer than six general surgeons. During the 1960s, a concentrated effort was made to attract specialists. This effort was primarily directed, in the initial stages, toward internists and subsequently moved on to other areas, including the subsurgical specialties.

The medical staff consists of 403 members. Of this total, over 50 percent are located within a one-mile radius of Sunrise Hospital. Another major concentration of physicians is located between Sunrise Hospital and Southern Nevada Memorial Hospital, or a distance of less than four miles. These physicians, like most physicians in Las Vegas, have multiple hospital staff memberships. Approximately 70 physicians limit their practice to Sunrise exclusively.

Present

David Brandsness took his eyes off the parking lot and got up from his chair and declared, "Why didn't I think of this before?" He thought to himself: "Other industries such as hotels and airlines offer special rates during certain times of the week to achieve overall efficiency, so why shouldn't an investor-owned hospital do the same?"

After a careful economic analysis by his staff, David Brandsness announced a revolutionary new health care policy: cash rebates for patients admitted on Fridays and Saturdays. The program would guarantee a 5.25 percent cash rebate on the total hospital bill of every patient admitted to Sunrise Hospital on Fridays and Saturdays.

Brandsness stressed that the rebate program "will be paid directly to the patient by Sunrise Hospital and will have no effect on insurance claims." If a patient is admitted on a Friday or Saturday and is confined for one week, a month, or longer, the patient will receive a cash rebate covering the entire length of stay. Brandsness further stressed that the rebates "will amount, in all cases, to 5.25 percent of the entire hospital bill—not just for Fridays and Saturdays."

Within eight months the program had boosted weekend occupancy by between 15 and 30 percent, and more than 2,200 patients had received $190,000 in rebates, for an average of more than $85 per patient. One of the largest amounts paid to a patient under the program was a juvenile involved in an auto accident whose bill totaled more than $22,000. The insurance company provided 100 percent coverage, thus paying the entire bill, and Sunrise Hospital rebated $1,164 to the patient.

Almost everyone was most happy with the plan. Doctors, who in the past were only "on call" on the weekends, now found themselves on the job. Doctors and nurses knew from the start that they would have to work a seven-day week. The biggest critic of the program, however, had been the insurance industry, distressed that rebates go to patients instead of insurers. Other hospitals in the area seemed skeptical of the whole idea.

The rebate program was abruptly stopped by Sunrise Hospital after eleven months of operation. Brandsness stated that the "revolutionary" cash rebate plan was suspended because large insurance companies were keeping the 5.25 percent intended rebate for themselves. However, the hospital is pursuing legal action and intends to reinstate the program when possible, he pointed out.

"The rebate worked far better than we expected," he said, adding that Sunrise made no price increases in the eleven months since the program began. "I don't know of another hospital in the western United States that can say that." The rebates amounted to $350,000 for patients coming in on Friday and Saturday, according to Brandsness.

He said the insurance companies believed that since they were insuring the patients, they should be the beneficiaries of the rebate. But Brandsness said that wasn't true because it was hospital profits that were to be redistributed to the patients and not insurance money. What eventually killed the program, he said, was the insurance companies deducting the rebate themselves before they paid expenses to the hospital. Some companies, he charged, even conspired to get patients to boycott the hospital.

It was Brandsness' belief that hospitals must be allowed to initiate any cost-cutting innovations they can and not be hampered by outmoded concepts in hospital administration. "The health industry just tends to move at a slower rate . . . other companies have offered rebates and felt no repercussions," he said.

David Brandsness now had to face the same problem over again, i.e., how to get potential patients to check in on Friday or Saturday. He approached this by announcing that a drawing would be offered to those patients who check in on Friday or Saturday. The winner of the drawing, to be held on Monday, would win an all-expense-paid vacation for two, worth $4,000, to the vacation spot selected. There would be a drawing every Monday—52 weeks a year—for those patients who checked in the previous Friday or Saturday. Brandsness hoped this new idea would be as successful as the cash rebate but without the repercussions from the insurance companies.

Discussion Questions

1. Make recommendations to Brandsness designed to increase weekend hospital utilization.
2. Evaluate the use of drawings for vacations as a promotional device.

APPENDIX
Careers in Marketing[1]

Seventeen-year-old Nicholas Di Bari had to make a decision. The Boston Red Sox had offered the young pitcher a minor league contract. But Di Bari picked a second option. He became a marketing major at the University of Dayton. As it turned out, he clearly made the right decision.

Twenty years later, Nicholas Di Bari was the senior vice president of marketing for Comdisco, a major computer leasing company. His total annual earnings exceed $1.2 million—more than Reggie Jackson receives. Di Bari's net worth is about $5 million.[2] While not every marketing student can achieve Di Bari's level of success, his example illustrates how far one can reach in this most vital of all business disciplines.

This appendix focuses on careers in marketing. A variety of aspects are considered. They include the following:

1. The kinds of positions available, offering brief descriptions of the responsibilities attached to each.
2. The academic training and other preparation needed for marketing employment.
3. Marketing employment trends and opportunities.
4. Marketing employment for women and minorities.

Positions in Marketing

The text has examined the great extent and diversity of the components of the marketing function. The types of marketing occupations required to fulfill these tasks are just as numerous and diverse. Indeed,

[1]This appendix was prepared with the assistance of Dinoo T. Vanier of San Diego State University.
[2]"Macro Marketer," *Money* (November 1982), pp. 36, 40.

with the growth of industrial society, marketing occupations have become more complex and specialized. Students intending to pursue a marketing career may be bewildered at the range of employment opportunities in marketing. How can they find their way through the maze of marketing occupations and concentrate on the ones that best match their interests and talents? A convenient starting point is an understanding of the different positions and the duties required of each.

Marketing personnel are classified as either sales force personnel or marketing staff personnel. They are employed in such service and staff functions as advertising, product planning, marketing research, purchasing, and public relations. The precise nature of their responsibilities and duties varies among organizations and industries. Marketing tasks may be undertaken in-house by company marketing personnel or subcontracted to outside sources. Indeed, a large number of organizations are available to support in-house marketing efforts. Among them are advertising agencies, public relations firms, and marketing research agencies. Marketing employment can be found in a variety of organizations—manufacturing firms, distributive enterprises such as retailers and wholesalers, service suppliers, and research agencies.

All of these organizations have managerial positions. The specific duties of the positions vary with the size of the organization, the nature of its business, and the extent to which marketing operations are departmentalized or centralized. Marketing management jobs generally require the individual to formulate and assist in the formulation of the organization's marketing policies and to plan, organize, coordinate, and control marketing operations and resources. Some of the typical marketing management positions (the particular titles of which may differ) and descriptions of their responsibilities follows.

The Chief Marketing Executive The person who oversees all the marketing activities and is ultimately responsible for the success of the marketing function is the chief marketing executive. All other marketing executives report through channels to this person.

The Product Manager The person in charge of marketing operations for a particular type of product—such as clothing, building materials, or appliances—is the product manager. This person also assumes responsibility for some or all of the functions of the marketing executive, but only as they pertain to particular products.

The Brand Manager The brand manager performs functions similar to those of the product manager, but only with regard to a specific brand.

The Marketing Research Director The marketing research director determines the marketing research needs of the organization and plans and directs various stages of the marketing research process. These stages include formulation of the problem, research design, data collection, analysis, and interpretation of results. On the basis of marketing research, the director also helps formulate marketing policy and strategies pertinent to any of the marketing variables.

The Sales Manager The person responsible for managing the sales force is the sales manager. Some of the manager's specific duties are establishing sales territories; deploying the sales force; recruiting, hiring, and training salespeople; and setting sales quotas.

The Advertising Manager The person who plans and arranges for the promotion of the company's products or services is the advertising manager. Among that person's duties are formulating advertising policy, selecting advertising agencies, evaluating creative promotional ideas, and setting the advertising budget.

The Public Relations Officer The public relations officer directs all the activities that project and maintain a favorable image for the organization. This person arranges press conferences, exhibitions, news releases, and the like.

Purchasing or Procurement Manager The purchasing manager controls all purchasing and procurement activities involved in acquiring merchandise, equipment, and materials for the organization.

The Retail Buyer The retail buyer is responsible for the purchase of merchandise from various sources—manufacturers, wholesalers, and importers, among others—for resale through retail outlets.

The Wholesale Buyer The person who buys products from manufacturers, importers, and others for resale through wholesale outlets is the wholesale buyer. This buyer's duties are similar to those for the retail buyer but within the specific context of wholesale distribution.

Physical Distribution Manager The trend for firms to consolidate physical distribution activities under a single managerial hierarchy has resulted in a significant increase in the importance of the physical distribution manager. This person is involved with such activities as transportation, warehousing, inventory control, order processing, and materials handling.[3]

The discussion so far has spotlighted the top management level of each type of work. Depending on company size, however, there may be

[3]An interesting discussion appears in Bernard J. LaLonde and Jerome J. Cronin, "Distribution Career Patterns," *Distribution Worldwide* (March 1979), pp. 67–72.

several other levels within each of the categories described. For every management position, there are several other marketing occupations that involve the "doing" of specific tasks that are supervised and controlled by the managers; their exact number varies considerably from organization to organization. In the area of marketing research, for instance, employees engage in field work, information collection, editing, coding, tabulation, and other statistical analyses of data.

In advertising, the copywriter gathers information on the products and customers or likely customers and then writes copy—creating headlines, slogans, and text for the advertisements. The media planner is often a time and space buyer who specializes in determining which advertising media will be most effective. The advertising layout person decides the exact layout of illustrations and copy that make up the finished advertisement.

The majority of people in marketing are in the area of sales. Sales representatives sell at the manufacturing, wholesale, or retail level. Their job descriptions vary somewhat with the types of products and customers. Sales positions are a common entry point for people desiring promotion to other marketing positions.

Career Preparation

What are the requirements for obtaining a marketing job? What are the typical positions at which marketing careers begin? What are the usual patterns of progression to the top spots in marketing management?

The starting point should be a sound education. Certainly, collegiate coursework does not guarantee entrance into any career field. During a recent ten-year period, one out of four college graduates accepted employment in a position previously staffed by someone with less education.[4] This bleak employment picture suggests the importance of effective career planning. The more one knows about business, careers, employment trends, and the like, the better prepared he or she is when entering the labor force. In fact, according to one study, business administration leads other disciplines as an undergraduate major cited by first-year college students, being selected by 24 percent of the respondents. The humanities, education, and natural sciences tie in a distant second place, each being named by 8 percent.[5]

Completion of a basic marketing course is a good step toward preparing for the job marketplace. Employers tend to seek those persons

[4]U.S. Department of Labor, Bureau of Labor Statistics, *Occupational Outlook Handbook, 1982–1983 Edition* (Washington, D.C.: U.S. Government Printing Office, Bulletin 2200, 1982), p. 14.

[5]"The Golden Passport," *Newsweek* (May 14, 1979), p. 110.

with knowledge applicable to the real world. But marketing education is not enough. George Rosenbaum, executive vice-president of Chicago-based Leo J. Shapiro & Associates, has observed: "A marketing graduate must not only learn business skills, but also must know what English, history, and political science majors know. This will enable them to compete with these same people in terms of communication skills, creative energy, and ability once they are in an actual business setting."[6]

Employment Projection to 1990

Table A.1 reports the Bureau of Labor Statistics employment projections to 1990. Market research analysts, securities sales workers, real estate agents and brokers, and automobile sales workers are all expected to experience above average employment opportunities.

Marketing Compensation

Table A.2 shows the median salaries of various marketing positions based on a survey of 528 firms. This research indicated that marketing compensation is based on such factors as the extent of responsibility, location, customer type, experience, education, and the supervisory responsibility level.[7]

Marketing Employment Opportunities for Women and Minorities

In recent years, strong nondiscriminatory legislation and supportive social commitment have protected the employment rights of women and minorities.[8] The Supreme Court of the United States, for example, has held that the consequences of an employer's action—not the intent—determine whether discrimination has occurred.[9] As a result, companies have been actively attempting to fill positions with qualified women and minorities. These efforts have produced marked increases in the employment options available to women and minorities.

Advertising, marketing research, and retailing are marketing occupations in which women have traditionally held jobs. Women often en-

[6]Rosenbaum is quoted in "Execs Tell Educators: We Want Grads Who Love Business," *Marketing News* (August 22, 1980), p. 10.

[7]*Summary of Survey of Income in Sales/Marketing Management* (Abbott, Langer & Associates).

[8]Excellent discussion appers in Ann Foote Cahn, ed., *Women in the U.S. Labor Force* (New York: Praeger Publishers, 1979).

[9]Griggs *v.* Duke Power Company, 401 U.S. 424 (1971).

Table A.1 Marketing Employment Projection to 1990

Marketing Occupation	Recent Employment	
Advertising workers	100,000	15-27%
Automobile sales workers	157,000	28-49%
Buyers	150,000	15-27%
Insurance agents and brokers	325,000	15-27%
Manufacturers' sales workers	440,000	15-27%
Market research analysts	29,000	28-49%
Public relations workers	87,000	15-27%
Purchasing agents	172,000	15-27%
Real estate agents and brokers	580,000	28-49%
Retail trade sales workers	3,300,000	15-27%
Securities sales workers	63,000	28-49%
Wholesale trade sales workers	1,100,000	15-27%

Source: U.S. Department of Labor, Bureau of Labor Statistics, *Occupational Outlook Handbook, 1982–1983 Edition* (Washington, D.C.: U.S. Government Printing Office, Bulletin 2200, 1982), pp. 27–28, 46–47, 109–110, 194–195, 236, 239–240, 242, 244, 248–251, 254.

Table A.2 Median Annual Compensation for Various Marketing Positions

Marketing Position	Median Annual Compensation
Vice-president sales/marketing	$50,000
General sales manager	43,800
Regional sales manager	40,805
District sales manager	33,420
Product manager	37,000
Top marketing research manager	36,300
Top sales promotion manager	34,200
Top advertising manager	32,552

ter these fields by way of retail sales, where they outnumber men by a ratio of nearly three to one (as shown in Table A.3). Women also account for a high percentage of the total employees in real estate sales, service and construction sales, and buyers in the wholesale and retail trade.

Table A.3 Distribution of Marketing Employment by Sex and Race

Occupation	Percent Male	Percent Female	Percent White	Percent Nonwhite
Sales workers	54.7%	45.3%	94.9%	5.1%
Insurance agents, brokers, and underwriters	74.8	25.2	93.8	6.2
Real estate agents and brokers	49.3	50.7	97.9	2.1
Sales representatives, manufacturing industries	81.1	18.9	97.0	3.0
Sales representatives, wholesale trade	89.4	10.6	97.0	3.0
Sales clerks, retail trade	28.9	71.1	92.8	7.2
Sales workers (except clerks), retail trade	80.5	19.5	96.3	3.7
Salespersons, service and construction	58.1	41.9	92.8	7.2
Stock and bond sales agents	83.6	16.4	97.8	2.2
Sales managers	74.3	25.7	95.5	4.5
Buyers, wholesale and retail trade	57.4	42.6	95.3	4.7
Purchasing agents and buyers	71.7	28.3	94.3	5.7

Source: U.S. Bureau of the Census, *Statistical Abstract of the United States: 1981*, 102nd ed. (Washington, D.C., 1981), p. 402.

Although there have been gains in women's employment, an earnings gap between men and women employees still exists. The average pay for a woman is still lower than that for a man in most fields.

A similar situation confronts minorities. Nonwhite employment in marketing is often less then five percent of any particular marketing job category, as illustrated by Table A.3. Similar to the female marketing employment situation, a higher proportion of nonwhites are employed as retail sales clerks (7.2 percent) or as salespersons in service and construction (7.2 percent) than in any other category of sales workers; but 4.5 percent of sales managers are nonwhites. Few nonwhites hold other marketing managerial positions, but, as is the case with women, nonwhite participation in marketing employment is expected to grow.

GLOSSARY

Accelerator Principle (9) The disproportionate impact that changes in consumer demand has upon industrial market demand.

Accessory Equipment (10) In the industrial market, capital assets that are less expensive and shorter-lived than installations. Examples include office machinery and hand tools. *See also* Installations.

Active Exporting (22) In international marketing, the activities of a firm that has made a commitment to seek export business.

Adoption Process (10) A series of stages in a consumer's relationship with a new product, beginning with awareness of the product to the ultimate decision to purchase the product regularly or to reject it.

Advertising (19, 20) A paid, nonpersonal communication through various media by business firms, nonprofit organizations, and individuals who are in some way identified in the advertising message and who hope to inform or persuade members of a particular audience.

Advertising Agency (20) Independent businesses used to assist advertisers in planning and implementing advertising programs.

Advocacy Advertising (20) A paid public communication or message that presents information or a point of view bearing on a publicly recognized controversial issue.

Agent (16) A middleman who performs wholesaling functions but does not take title to the goods handled.

AIDA Concept (19) Acronym for attention-interest-desire-action; traditional explanation of the steps an individual must go through prior to making a purchase decision.

AIO Statements (4) A collection of statements contained in a psychographic study to reflect activities, interests, and opinions of the respondents.

Approach (21) The initial contact of a salesperson with a prospective customer.

Asch Phenomenon (7) An occurrence first documented by the psychologist S. E. Asch, which illustrates the effect of the reference group on individual decision making.

Aspirational Group (7) A sub-category of a reference group where the member desires to associate with a group.

Attitude (8) One's enduring favorable or unfavorable evaluations, emotional feelings, or pro or con action tendencies.

Auction House (16) An establishment that brings buyers and sellers together in one location for the purpose of permitting buyers to examine merchandise before purchasing it.

Bartering (22) The exchange of one product for another instead of for money.

Basing Point System (14) An obsolete pricing system under which the buyer's costs included the factory price plus freight charges from a basing point nearest the buyer.

BCG Matrix (3) A matrix developed by the Boston Consulting Group that enables a firm to classify its products in terms of the industry growth rate and their market share relative to competitive products. The matrix is comprised of four segments: *cash cows* (high market share, low market growth brands); *stars* (high market share, high market growth brands); *dogs*, (low market share, low market growth brands); and *question marks* (low market share, high market growth brands).

Benefit Segmentation (4) Dividing a population into homogeneous groups based on the benefits the consumer expects to derive from the product.

Bid (9) In the industrial market, a written sales proposal from a vendor to a firm that wants to purchase a good or service.

Bottom Line (23) Business jargon referring to the overall profitability measure of performance.

Brand (11) A name, term, sign, symbol, design, or some combination used to identify the products of one firm and to differentiate them from competitive offerings.

Brand Insistence (11) A consumer's preference for a specific brand to the point where the consumer will accept no alternatives and will search extensively for the product.

Brand Name (11) That part of the brand consisting of words or letters that comprise a name used to identify and distinguish the firm's offerings from those of competitors.

Brand Preference (11) A consumer's choice of one product over the competing brands, based on previous experience with the product.

Brand Recognition (11) A consumer's awareness and familiarity with a specific brand.

Break-bulk Center (18) A facility at which large shipments are divided into many smaller ones and delivered to individual customers in the area, in the interest of reducing transportation expenses.

Breakeven Analysis (13) In pricing strategy, a method for comparing the profit potential of various prices.

Broadening Concept (23) An idea introduced by Philip Kotler and Sidney J. Levy, suggesting that marketing is a generic function to be performed by all organizations.

Broker (16) An independent wholesaling middleman who does not take title or possession to goods, and whose primary function is bringing buyers and sellers together.

Buyer's Market (1) A market with an abundance of goods and/or services.

Buying Center (9) Refers to everyone who participates—in some fashion—in an industrial buying action.

Canned Approach (21) A memorized sales talk used to ensure uniform coverage of the points management deems important.

Cannibalizing (11) A product that takes sales from another offering in a product line. Marketing research should take steps to see that cannibalizing is minimized or at least anticipated.

Capital Items (9) Long-lived business assets that must be depreciated over time.

Cartels (22) The monopolistic organizations of some foreign firms.

Cash-and-carry Wholesaler (16) One who performs most wholesaling functions except financing and delivery.

Cash Discount (14) A price reduction made for prompt payment of a bill.

Casual Exporting (22) The activities of a firm that takes a passive level of involvement in international marketing.

Catalog Retailer (17) A merchant who operates from a showroom displaying samples of the product line. Customers order from the store's catalog and orders are filled from a warehouse, usually on the premises.

Celler-Kefauver Antimerger Act (1950) (2) Federal legislation amending the Clayton Act to include restrictions on the purchase of assets, where such purchase would decrease competition. Previously, only "acquiring the stock" of another firm was prohibited, if it lessened competition. *See also* Clayton Act.

Census (6) The collection of data from all possible sources in a population or universe.

Chain Store (17) A group of retail stores that are centrally owned and managed and that handle essentially the same product lines.

Channel Captain (15) The dominant and controlling member of a marketing channel.

Charter (10) A document drawn up by a manufacturing firm specifically defining the functions, operating procedures, and other guidelines for a venture team. Also known as a *venture team charter.*

Class Action Suit (24) A legal case brought by private citizens on behalf of any group of consumers for damages caused by unfair business practices.

Class Rate (18) The standard rate that is found for every commodity moving between any two destinations.

Clayton Act (1914) (2) A federal statute that strengthened antitrust legislation by restricting such practices as price discrimination, exclusive dealing, tying contracts, and interlocking boards of directors.

Closed Sales Territories (15) Restricted geographic selling regions ordered by a manufacturer for its distributors.

Closing (21) The point in personal selling at which a salesperson asks a customer to make a purchase decision.

Cluster Sample (6) A sampling technique where areas or clusters are selected, then all or a sample within them become respondents.

Cognitions (8) An individual's knowledge, beliefs, and attitudes about certain events.

Cognitive Dissonance (8) The postpurchase anxiety that results when an imbalance exists among an individual's cognitions (knowledge, beliefs, and attitudes).

Combination Plan (21) A method of compensating sales personnel by using a base salary along with a commission incentive.

Commission Merchant (16) One who takes possession of goods when they are shipped to a central market for sale, acts as the producer's agent, and collects an agreed-upon fee at the time of sale.

Commodity Rate (18) Sometimes called a special rate, since it is given by carriers to shippers as a reward for either regular use or large quantity shipments.

Common Carriers (18) Freight transporters that offer shipping service to the public at large.

Common Market (22) In international marketing, a format for multinational economic integration involving a customs union and continuing efforts to standardize trade regulations of all governments. *See also* Customs Union.

Community Shopping Center (17) A group of 15 to 50 retail stores, often including a branch of a department store as the primary tenant. This type of center typically serves 20,000 to 100,000 persons within a radius of a few miles.

Comparative Advertising (20) Nonpersonal selling efforts that make direct promotional comparisons with leading competitive brands.

Competitive Bidding (14) A process in which potential suppliers submit price quotations to a buyer for a proposed purchase or contract.

Competitive Environment (2) The interactive process that occurs in the marketplace.

Component Parts and Materials (10) In the industrial market, the finished industrial goods that actually become part of the final product.

Concentrated Marketing (5) The directing of all of a firm's marketing resources into a small segment of the total market.

Concept Testing (11) In new-product development, the consideration of a product idea prior to its actual development.

Consolidated Metropolitan Statistical Area (CMSA) (4) Major population concentrations; includes the 25 or so urban giants like New York, Chicago, and Los Angeles.

Consumer Behavior (7, 8) The acts of an individual in obtaining and using goods or services, including the decision processes that precede and determine these acts.

Consumer Goods (4, 9) Products purchased by the ultimate consumer for personal use.

Consumer Goods Pricing Act (1975) (2) Federal legislation that halted all interstate usage of resale price maintenance agreements.

Consumer Innovator (10) In new-product development, those individuals who purchase a new product almost as soon as it is placed on the market.

Consumerism (24) A social force within the environment designed to aid and protect the consumer by exerting legal, moral, and economic pressure on business.

Consumer Market (9) Individuals who purchase goods and services for personal use.

Consumer Product Safety Act (1970) (2) A federal statute that set up the Consumer Product Safety Commission, authorizing it to specify safety standards for most consumer products.

Consumer Rights (24) As stated by President John F. Kennedy in 1962, the consumer should have the following rights: to choose freely, to be informed, to be heard, and to be safe.

Containerization (18) One of two important innovations developed in the area of materials handling. It involves the combination of several unitized loads into a container.

Contract Carriers (18) Freight transporters who are contracted to certain firms and operate exclusively for a particular industry.

Control Charts (25) Diagrams that plot a firm's actual performance against established limits.

Convenience Goods (10) Products that the consumer wants to purchase frequently, immediately, and with a minimum of effort.

Convenience Retailer (17) One who sells to the ultimate consumer and focuses chiefly on a central location, long store hours, rapid checkout, and adequate parking facilities.

Convenience Sample (6) A nonprobability sample based on the selection of readily available respondents.

Cooperative Advertising (20) A sharing of advertising costs between a retailer and the manufacturer of a good or its vendor.

Corrective Advertising (2) A policy of the Federal Trade Commission, under which companies found to have used deceptive promotional messages are required to correct their earlier claims with new messages.

Cost-plus Pricing (13) In pricing strategy, the practice of marking up a base cost figure (per unit) to cover unassigned costs and to provide a profit. *See also* Markup.

Cost Trade-offs (18) A concept in physical distribution whereby some functional areas of the firm will experience cost increases while others will have cost reductions, but the result will be that total physical distribution costs will be minimized.

Coupons (20) A sales promotion method in which a specially marked slip of paper entitles the bearer to a discount on the purchase of a particular product.

Cues (8) Any objects existing in the environment that determine the nature of the response to a drive.

Culture (7) A complex of values, ideas, attitudes, and other meaningful symbols created by people to shape human behavior and the artifacts of that behavior as they are transmitted from one generation to the next.

Customary Prices (13) In pricing strategy, the traditional costs of products.

Customer Service Standards (18) The quality of service that a firm intends to offer its customers.

Customs Union (22) In international marketing, a format for multinational economic integration that sets up a free trade area for member nations and a uniform tariff for nonmember nations.

Data (6) Refers to statistics, opinions, facts, or predictions categorized on some basis for storage and retrieval.

Decoding (19) In marketing communications, the receiver's interpretation of a message.

Demand Variability (11) In the industrial market, the impact of derived demand on the demand for interrelated products used in producing consumer goods.

Demarketing (2) The process of cutting consumer demand for a product to a level that can be supplied by the firm.

Demographics (20) Characteristics, such as age, sex, and income level, of potential buyers.

Demographic Segmentation (7) Dividing a population into homogeneous groups based on characteristics such as age, sex, and income level.

Department Store 17) A large retail firm handling a variety of merchandise, including clothing, household goods, appliances, and furniture.

Depreciation (9) The accounting concept of charging a portion of a capital item as a deduction against the company's annual revenue for purposes of determining its net income.

Derived Demand (9) In the industrial market, the demand for an industrial product that is linked to demand for a consumer good.

Detailers (21) Special representatives of firms in the health-care industry, who familiarize physicians and hospitals with the firms' products.

Differentiated Marketing (5) A practice employed by a firm that produces numerous products with different marketing mixes designed to satisfy numerous market segments.

Diffusion Process (10) The acceptance of new products and services by the members of a community or a social system.

Direct-sales Results Test (19) A tool for measuring the effectiveness of promotional expenditures, by ascertaining the increase in revenue per dollar spent.

Disassociative Group (7) A sub-category of a reference group, one in which an individual does not want to be identified with by others.

Discount House (17) A store that charges lower-than-normal prices but may not offer many typical retail services, such as credit, sales assistance by clerks, and home delivery.

Distribution Channel (15) Refers to the various marketing institutions and their interrelationships responsible for the physical and title flow of goods and services from producer to consumer or industrial user.

Distribution Strategy (1) An element of marketing decision making dealing with the physical handling of goods and the selection of marketing channels.

Distribution Warehouse (18) A facility for assembling and redistributing products.

Drive (8) Any strong stimulus that impels action.

Drop Shipper (16) One who receives orders from customers and forwards them to producers who ship directly to the customers.

Dumping (22) The controversial practice of selling a product in a foreign market at a lower price than it would receive in the producer's domestic market.

Ecology (24) The relationship between humanity and the environment.

Economic Environment (2) A setting of complex and dynamic business fluctuations that historically tended to follow a four-stage pattern: 1) recession, 2) depression, 3) recovery, and 4) prosperity.

Elasticity (13) A measure of responsiveness of purchasers and suppliers to a change in price.

Embargo (22) A complete ban on the importing of a specific product.

Encoding (19) In marketing communications, the translation of a message into understandable terms and its transmittal through a communication medium.

Engel's Laws (4) Statements on spending behavior, comprised of three generalizations: as family income increases, 1) a smaller percentage of income goes for food; 2) the percentage spent on household operations, housing, and clothing remains constant; and 3) the percentage spent on other items increases.

Environmental Protection Act (1970) (2) Federal legislation establishing the Environmental Protection Agency and giving it the power to deal with pollution issues.

EOQ (Economic Order Quantity) Model (18) A tool that helps control inventory by attempting to equalize or balance two costs associated with inventory—inventory holding costs and order costs.

Equal Credit Opportunity Act (1975–77) (2) Federal legislation banning discrimination in lending practices based on sex, marital status, race, national origin, religion, age, or receipt of payments from a public-assistance program.

Escalator Clause (14) In pricing, part of many bids allowing the seller to adjust the final price, based upon changes in the costs of the product's ingredients, between the placement of the order and the completion of construction or delivery of the product.

Ethics (24) *See* Marketing Ethics.

Evaluation and Control (25) The various assessments that marketers employ to determine if all phases of a marketing program have been effective.

Evaluative Criteria (8) In consumer decision making, the features considered in a consumer's choice of alternatives.

Evoked Set (8) In consumer decision making, the number of brands that a consumer actually considers before making a purchase decision.

Exchange Control (22) In international marketing, a method used to regulate the privilege of international trade among importing organizations.

Exchange Process (1) The process by which two or more parties give something of value to one another to satisfy felt needs.

Exclusive Dealing Agreement (15) An understanding between a manufacturer and a middleman that prohibits the middleman from handling the product lines of the manufacturer's competitors.

Exclusive Distribution (15) A policy under which a firm grants exclusive rights to a wholesaler or retailer to sell in a particular geographic area.

Expected Net Profit (14) A formula used in competitive bidding to determine which bid shows the greatest chance of generating the most revenue.

Expense Item (9) Industrial products and services that are used within a short period of time.

Experience Curve (25) The idea that higher market shares reduce costs because of factors like learning advantages, increased specialization, higher investment, and economies of scale.

Experiment (6) A scientific investigation in which a researcher controls or manipulates a test group or groups and compares the results with that of a control group that did not receive the controls or manipulations.

Exploratory Research (6) Discussing a marketing problem with informed sources within a firm and with wholesalers, retailers, customers, and others outside the firm and examining secondary sources of information.

External Data (8) In marketing research, the type of secondary data that comes from sources outside a firm.

Facilitating Agencies (15) Institutions, such as insurance companies, banks, and transportation companies, which provide specialized assistance to channel members in moving the product from producer to consumer.

Fads (10) Fashions with abbreviated life cycles. Examples include disco, punk, and new wave.

Fair Credit Reporting Act (1970) (2) Federal legislation providing for individuals' access to credit reports about them and the opportunity to change information that is incorrect.

Fair Debt Collection Practices Act (1978) (2) Federal legislation outlawing harassing, deceptive, or unfair collection practices by debt-collecting agencies.

Fair Packaging and Labeling Act (1967) (11) A federal statute requiring the disclosure of product identity, the name and address of the manufacturer or distributor, and information concerning the quality of the contents.

Fair Trade Laws (2) Statutes permitting manufacturers to stipulate a minimum retail price for a product.

Family Brand (11) A name used for several related products. An example is the Johnson & Johnson line of baby products.

Family Life Cycle (4) The process of family formation and dissolution. The cycle includes many subcategories and five major stages: 1) young single people, 2) young married people without children, 3) other young people, 4) middle-aged people, and 5) older people.

Fashions (10) Currently popular products that tend to follow recurring life cycles.

Federal Trade Commission Act (1914) (2) Federal legislation that prohibited "unfair methods of competition" and established the Federal Trade Commission to oversee the various laws dealing with business.

Feedback (19) In marketing communications, the receiver's response to a message.

Fixed Sum Per Unit (19) A budget allocation method under which a predetermined promotional amount is allocated, either on a historical or forecasted basis.

Flammable Fabrics Act (1953) (2) Federal legislation prohibiting the interstate sale of flammable fabrics.

Flanker Brands (11) The introduction of new products into the market in which the company has established positions in an attempt to increase overall market share. For example, Butcher's Blend Dry Dog Food is Ralston Purina's flanker to their Dog Chow line.

FOB Plant (14) "Free on board," a price quotation that does not include shipping charges. The buyer is responsible for paying them.

Focus Group Interview (6) A marketing research information-gathering procedure that typically brings eight to twelve individuals together in one location to discuss a given subject.

Follow-up (21) The post-sales activities that often determine whether an individual will become a repeat customer.

Food, Drug, and Cosmetic Act (1938) (2) Federal legislation strengthening the Pure Food and Drug Act, to prohibit the adulteration and misbranding of food, drugs, and cosmetics.

Foreign Corrupt Practices Act (22) Federal legislation that prohibits bribing an official in attempting to solicit new or repeat sales in a foreign nation.

Foreign Freight Forwarders (18) Transportation middlemen who specialize in physical distribution outside the United States.

Foreign Licensing (22) In international marketing, an agreement between a firm and a foreign company, whereby the foreign company produces and distributes the firm's goods in the foreign country.

Form Utility (1) The want-satisfying power created by the conversion of raw materials into finished products.

Franchise (15) A contractual arrangement in which a dealer agrees to meet the operating requirements of a manufacturer.

Free Trade Area (22) In international marketing, economic integration between participating nations, without any tariff or trade restrictions.

Freight Absorption (14) A pricing system under which the buyer of goods may deduct shipping expenses from the cost of the goods.

Freight Forwarders (18) Transportation middlemen who consolidate shipments in order to reduce shipping costs for their customers.

Friendship, Commerce, and Navigation (FCN) Treaties (22) In international marketing, agreements that deal with many aspects of commercial relations with other countries.

Full Cost Pricing (13) A pricing procedure in which all costs are considered in setting a price, allowing the firm to recover all of its costs and realize a profit.

Full Service Research Supplier (6) An independent marketing research firm that contracts with a client to conduct the complete marketing research project. They define the problem or conceptual stage; work through the research, design, data collection, and analysis stages; and prepare the final report to management.

Functional Accounts (25) Income statement expense categories representing the purpose for which an expenditure is made.

Fur Product Labeling Act (1951) (2) Federal statute requiring that the name of the animal from which a fur garment was derived be identified.

General Agreement on Tariffs and Trade (GATT) (22) An international trade agreement that has helped to reduce world tariffs.

General Merchandise Retailer (17) An establishment carrying a wide variety of product lines, all of which are stocked in some depth.

Generic Name (11) A brand name that has become a generally descriptive term for a product (for example, nylon, zipper, and aspirin). When this happens, the original owner may lose exclusive claim to the name.

Generic Product (11) A food or household item characterized by plain labels, little or no advertising, and no brand name.

Geographic Segmentation (4) Dividing a population into homogeneous groups on the basis of location.

Goods-Services Continuum (12) An imaginary line or spectrum, along which products are arranged in a sequence from tangible (good) to intangible (service).

Green River Ordinances (24) Local statutes enacted in some communities to limit door-to-door selling.

Gross Margin Percentage (25) An evaluative technique indicating the percentage of revenues available for covering expenses and earning a profit after the payment of the production costs of products sold during a certain time period.

House-to-house Retailing (17) A distribution strategy under which the transaction occurs between the seller and the consumer in the consumer's home.

Hypermarket (17) A giant mass merchandiser who operates on a low-price, self-service basis and carries lines of soft goods and groceries.

Hypothesis (6) A tentative explanation about some specific event. A hypothesis is a statement about the relationship between variables and carries clear implications for testing this relationship.

Iceberg Principle (25) A theory that suggests that important evaluative information is often hidden by collected data when it exists in a summary format.

Idea Marketing (23) The identification and marketing of a cause to chosen consumer segments.

Import Quota (22) A trade restriction that limits the amount of certain products that can enter a country for selling purposes.

Impulse Goods (10) Products purchased by a consumer after little or no conscious deliberation. These items are often located near the cashier in a store, to induce spur-of-the-moment purchases.

Incremental Cost Pricing (13) A pricing procedure in which only the costs directly attributable to a specific output are considered in setting a price.

Individual Brand (11) The strategy of giving each item in a product line its own brand name, rather than identifying it by a single name used for all products in the line. An example would be the many detergents marketed by Procter & Gamble—Tide, Cheer, Oxydol, among others. *See also* Family brand.

Individual Offerings (11) One of the primary components of a product mix, it consists of single products.

Industrial Distributors (10) In the industrial market, wholesalers who represent a manufacturer of accessory equipment in the sale and distribution of the manufacturer's product.

Industrial Goods (4, 9) Products purchased for use either directly or indirectly in the production of other goods for resale.

Industrial Goods Market (9) A marketplace made up of customers who purchase goods and services for use in producing other products for resale. Examples include manufacturers, utilities, government agencies, retailers, wholesalers, contractors, mining firms, insurance and real estate firms, and institutions, such as schools and hospitals.

Inflation (2) A rising price level that results in reduced purchasing power for the consumer.

Information (6) Data which is relevant to the marketing manager in making decisions.

Input-Output Models (3) Quantitative forecasting techniques first developed by Wassily Leontif which show the impact on supplier industries of production changes in a given industry and which can be utilized in measuring the impact of changing demand in any industry throughout an economy.

Installations (10) In the industrial market, such specialty goods as factories, heavy machinery, or other major capital assets.

Institutional Advertising (20) Promoting a concept, an idea, a philosophy, or the goodwill of an industry, company, or organization.

Intensive Distribution (15) A policy under which a manufacturer of a convenience good attempts to saturate the market with the product.

Internal Secondary Data (6) In marketing research, the type of information that is found in records of sales, product performances, sales force activities, and marketing costs.

Inventory Adjustments (11) Changes in the amounts of raw materials or goods in process a manufacturer keeps on hand.

Inventory Turnover (25) An evaluative figure showing how many times the average value of a firm's stock of merchandise is sold in a year.

Job-order Production (15) A production system in which products are manufactured to fill customer orders.

Joint Demand (9) In the industrial market, the demand for an industrial good as related to the demand for another industrial good that is necessary for the use of the first item.

Joint Venture (22) In international marketing, a firm that establishes a foreign operation, sharing risks, costs, and management responsibilities with a partner who is usually a citizen of the host nation.

Judgment Sample (6) A nonprobability sample of people with a specific attribute.

Jury of Executive Opinion (3) A qualitative sales forecasting method which combines and averages the outlook of top executives from such functional areas as finance, production, marketing, and purchasing.

Kefauver-Harris Drug Amendments (1962) (2) Amendments to the Pure Food and Drug Act, requiring generic labeling of drugs and a summary of adverse side effects.

Label (11) The descriptive part of a product's package, listing such items as the brand name, or symbol, the name and address of the manufacturer or distributor, the ingredients, the size or quantity of the product, and/or recommended uses, directions, or serving suggestions for the product.

Lanham Act (1946) (10) A federal statute requiring that registered trademarks not contain words in general use: such *generic words* are descriptive of a particular type of product—such as "automobile" or "suntan lotion"—and thus cannot be given trademark protection.

Law of Retail Gravitation (17) Sets the retail trade area of a potential site on the basis of mileage between alternative locations and relative populations.

Learning (8) Any changes in behavior, immediate or expected, that occur because of experience.

Life-cycle Costing (9) In the industrial market, the cost of using a product over its lifetime.

Life-style (4) The mode of living of consumers.

Limited-line Store (17) An establishment that offers a large assortment of one-product lines, or a few related product lines.

Limited Service Research Supplier (6) Organization that specializes in a limited number of marketing research activities.

Line Extension (11) A new product that is closely related to existing product lines.

List Price (14) A rate normally quoted to potential buyers.

Local Content Laws (22) In international marketing, legislation requiring that a certain portion of a product come from domestic sources.

Loss Leader (14) A retail good priced at less than cost in an attempt to attract customers who will then buy other merchandise at regular prices.

Magnuson-Moss Warranty Act (1975) (9) A federal statute authorizing the Federal Trade Commission to develop regulations on warranty practices.

Mail Order Wholesaler (16) Limited-function merchant wholesalers who utilize catalogs instead of a sales force to contact their customers in an attempt to reduce operating expense.

Make-bulk Center (18) A facility at which several small shipments are consolidated into a large shipment and delivered to a central destination, in an attempt to reduce transportation costs.

Manufacturers' Agent (16) An independent salesperson who works for a number of manufacturers of related but noncompeting products; the salesperson receives a commission based on a specified percentage of sales.

Marginal Analysis (13, 19) A budgeting procedure, the objective of which is to allocate the same amount for an expenditure (such as promotion) that the expenditure will generate profits.

Markdown (13) A reduction in the price of an item.

Market (4) A group of people who possess purchasing power and the authority and willingness to purchase.

Marketing (1) The development and efficient distribution of goods, services, ideas, issues, and concepts for chosen consumer segments.

Marketing Audit (25) A thorough, objective evaluation of an organization's marketing philosophy, goals, policies, tactics, practices, and results.

Marketing Channels (1, 15) The steps a good or service follows from producer to final consumer.

Marketing Communications (19) The messages that deal with buyer-seller relationships.

Marketing Concept (1) A company-wide consumer orientation with the objective of achieving long-run success.

Marketing Cost Analysis (25) The evaluation of such items as selling costs, billing, and advertising, to determine the profitability of particular customers, territories, or product lines.

Marketing Ethics (24) The marketer's standards of conduct and moral values.

Marketing Information System (MIS) (6) A set of procedures and methods designed to generate an orderly flow of pertinent information for use in making decisions, providing management with the current and future states of the market, and indicating market responses to company and competitor actions.

Marketing Mix (1) Blending the four strategy elements of marketing decision making—product, pricing, distribution, and promotion—to satisfy chosen consumer segments.

Marketing Myopia (1, 12) A term coined by Theodore Levitt in his argument that executives in many industries fail to recognize the broad scope of their business. According to Levitt, future growth is endangered because these executives lack a marketing orientation.

Marketing Planning (3) The implementation of planning activity as it relates to the achievement of marketing objectives.

Marketing Research (6) The systematic gathering, recording, and analysis of data about problems relating to the marketing of goods and services.

Marketing Strategy (3) The overall company program for selecting a particular market segment and then satisfying consumers in that segment through the elements of the marketing mix.

Market Price (14) The amount a consumer or middleman pays for a product.

Market Segmentation (4, 7) The process of dividing the total market into several relatively homogeneous groups with similar product interests, based on any number of characteristics.

Market Share (25) The percentage of a market controlled by a firm or its product.

Market Share Objective (13) Pricing objectives linked to achieving and maintaining a stated percentage of the market for a firm's product or service.

Markup (13) In pricing strategy, the amount added to the cost of an item to determine its selling price.

Mass Merchandiser (17) A merchant who stocks a wider line of goods than that offered by a department store, but usually does not offer the same depth of assortment.

Materials Handling (18) All the activities associated with the moving of products within the manufacturer's plants, warehouses, and transportation company terminals.

Megalopolis (4) An extensive contiguous strip of urban-suburban population.

Membership Groups (7) A sub-category for a reference group, where the members of the reference group belong to, say, a country club.

Merchandise Mart (16) A facility in which manufacturers rent space for relatively permanent exhibits of their product offerings.

Merchant Wholesaler (16) An independent wholesaling middleman who takes title to the goods handled.

Metropolitan Statistical Area (4) Large free-standing urban areas like Sheboygan, Wisconsin, and Syracuse, New York.

Middleman (15) A business firm, either wholesale or retail, that operates between the producer of goods and the consumer or industrial user.

Miller-Tydings Resale Price Maintenance Act (1937) (2) Federal antitrust legislation that exempted interstate fair trade contracts from compliance with antitrust requirements.

Missionary Sales (21) An indirect type of selling; people promote the goodwill of the firm, often by providing the customer with assistance on product use.

Missionary Salesperson (15) An individual who aids wholesalers and retailers by providing information about a firm's products, and generally acts as a management consultant for members of the channel.

Modified Breakeven Analysis (13) A pricing technique that combines the traditional breakeven analysis model with an evaluation of consumer demand.

Modified Rebuy (9) A situation where industrial purchasers are willing to reevaluate their available options in a repurchase of the same product or service. Lower prices, faster delivery, or higher quality may be buyer desires in this type of purchase situation.

Monopolistic Competition (13) A market structure involving a heterogeneous product and product differentiation, allowing the marketer some degree of control over prices.

Monopoly (13) A market structure involving only one seller of a product for which no close substitutes exist.

Motive (8) An inner state that directs people toward the goal of satisfying a felt need.

MRO Items (10) Supplies for an industrial firm, so called because they can be categorized as maintenance items, repair items, or operating supplies.

Multinational Corporation (22) In international marketing, a company that operates in several nations and literally views the world as its market.

National Brands (11) Products offered by a manufacturer. Also known as *manufacturers' brands.*

Natural Accounts (25) Expense categories traditionally listed on an organization's income statement. An example is salary expenses.

Need (8) The lack of something useful; a discrepancy between a desired state and the actual state.

Neighborhood Shopping Center (17) A geographical cluster of stores, usually consisting of a supermarket and about 5 to 15 smaller stores. The center provides convenient shopping for 5,000 to 15,000 shoppers in its vicinity.

Net Profit Percentage (25) An evaluative technique reflecting the ratio of net profits to net sales for an organization.

New Product Task Force (11) An interdisciplinary group on temporary assignment that works through functional departments. Its basic task is to coordinate and integrate the work of these functional departments on some specific project.

New Task Buying (9) Refers to first time or unique industrial purchase situations that require considerable effort on the part of the decision makers.

Noise (19) In marketing communications, interference in a transmitted message.

Nonprobability Sample (6) Sample chosen in an arbitrary fashion in which each member of the population does not have a representative chance of being selected.

Nonprofit Organization (23) A firm whose primary objective is something other than the return of a profit to its owners.

Odd Pricing (14) A pricing policy based on the theory that a price with an uncommon last digit is more appealing than a round figure. An example would be a price of $9.99 (rather than $10.00).

Oligopoly (13) A market structure involving relatively few sellers and, because of high start-up costs, significant entry barriers to new competitors.

Open Dating (24) The system of marking a perishable or semiperishable food item with the last date it can be sold.

Operating Expense Ratio (25) An evaluative technique that combines both selling and general expenses and compares them with overall net sales.

Opinion Leader (7) An individual in a group who serves as an information source for other group members.

Order Processing (21) Selling at the wholesale and retail levels; specifically, identifying customer needs, pointing out the need to the customer, and completing the order.

Organization Marketing (23) Marketing by *mutual benefit organizations* (churches, labor unions, and political parties), *ser-*

vice organizations (colleges, universities, hospitals, museums), and *government organizations* (military services, police and fire departments, post office) that seeks to influence others to accept the goals of, receive the services of, or contribute in some way to that organization.

Overseas Marketing (22) In international marketing, a firm's maintaining of a separate selling operation in a foreign country.

Ownership Utility (1, 15) A want-satisfying power created by marketers when title to a product is transferred to the customer at the time of purchase.

Party-plan Selling (17) A distribution strategy under which a company's representative makes a presentation of the product(s) in a party setting. Orders are taken and the host or hostess receives a commission or gift based on the amount of sales.

Penetration Pricing (14) A pricing policy under which a manufacturer sets an entry price much lower than the intended long-term price, on the theory that this initial low price will help secure market acceptance.

Percentage of Sales (19) A budget allocation method under which a fixed percentage of funds, based on past or forecasted sales volumes, is allocated for promotion.

Perception (8) The manner in which an individual interprets a stimulus; the often highly subjective meaning that one attributes to an incoming stimulus or message.

Perceptual Screen (8) The perceptual filter through which messages must pass.

Personal Selling (19, 21) A seller's promotional presentation conducted on a person-to-person basis with the buyer.

Person Marketing (23) Marketing efforts designed to cultivate the attention, interest, and preference of a market target toward a person. Person marketing is typically employed by political candidates and celebrities.

Physical Distribution (18) The activities associated with the efficient movement of finished products from the end of the production line to the ultimate consumer. Also known as *logistics*.

PIMS Study (13) Acronym for Profit Impact of Market Strategies, a research project that discovered that market share and return-on-investment figures are closely linked.

Place Utility (1, 15) A want-satisfying power created by marketers who have products available where consumers want to buy them.

Planned Obsolescence (24) The deliberate production of an item with limited durability.

Planned Shopping Center (17) A group of retail stores planned, coordinated, and marketed as a unit to shoppers in a geographic trade area.

Planning (3) The process of anticipating the future and determining the courses of action to achieve company objectives.

Point-of-Purchase Advertising (20) Displays and other promotions located near where a buying decision is actually made.

Political and Legal Environment (2) Component of the marketing environment consisting of laws and interpretation of laws that require firms to operate under competitive conditions and to protect consumer rights.

Pollution (24) Commonly, the spoiling or making unclean of natural resources.

Population (6) The total group that the researcher wants to study. For a political campaign, the population would be eligible voters.

Positioning (20) Developing a marketing strategy aimed at a particular market segment and designed to achieve a desired position in the mind of the prospective buyer.

Possession Utility (1, 15) *See* Ownership Utility.

Post-testing (20) The assessment of an advertisement after it has been used.

Premiums (20) Items given free with the purchase of a specified good or service.

Presentation (21) A description of a product's major features and the relating of them to a customer's problems or needs.

Prestige Goals (13) A pricing objective based on setting relatively high prices so as to maintain an image of quality.

Pretesting (20) The assessment of an advertisement before it is actually used.

Price (13) The exchange value of a good or service.

Price Elasticity of Demand (13) A measure of responsiveness of purchasers to changes in price; calculated as the percentage change in the quantity of a product or service demanded divided by the percentage change in its price.

Price Elasticity of Supply (14) A measure of responsiveness of suppliers to changes in price; calculated as the percentage change in the quantity of a product or service supplied divided by the percentage change in price.

Price Flexibility (14) The policy of maintaining a variable price for a product in the market.

Price Lining (14) The practice of marketing merchandise at a limited number of price ranges.

Pricing Policy (14) A general guideline based upon pricing objectives and intended for use in specific pricing decisions.

Pricing Strategy (1) An element of marketing decision making that deals with the methods of setting profitable and justified exchange values on goods or services.

Primary Data (6) Information or statistics being collected for the first time during a marketing research study.

Primary Metropolitan Statistical Area (PMSA) (4) Major urban areas within a CMSA. Long Island's Nassau and Suffolk counties would be examples.

Private Brand (11) A product that carries the name of the retailer offering it; a brand promoted by a retailer as its own. An example is the Kenmore line of appliances sold by Sears.

Private Carriers (18) Freight transporters who operate only for a particular firm and cannot solicit business from others.

Probability Sample (6) A sample in which every member of the population has an equal chance of being selected.

Producers (9) Industrial customers who purchase goods and services for the production of other goods and services.

Product (10) A bundle of physical, service, and symbolic attributes designed to produce consumer want satisfaction.

Product Advertising (20) The nonpersonal selling of a good or service.

Productivity (12) The output of a worker or a machine.

Product Liability (11) Refers to the concept that manufacturers and marketers are responsible for injuries and damages caused by their products.

Product Liability Risk Reduction Act (1981) (11) It authorizes producers to set up their own insurance firms to protect them from product liability complaints.

Product Life Cycle (10) The stages in the life of a product—introduction, growth, maturity, and decline.

Product Line (11) The various related goods offered by a firm.

Product Manager (11) An individual in a manufacturing firm who is assigned a product or a product line, and is given complete responsibility for determining objectives and establishing marketing strategies.

Product Mix (5, 11) The assortment of product lines and individual offerings available from a marketer.

Product Positioning (11) Refers to the consumer's perception of a product's attributes, use, quality, and advantages and disadvantages.

Product Strategy (1) An element of marketing decision making comprising package design, branding, trademarks, warranties, guarantees, product life-cycles, and new-product development.

Profit Center (14, 25) Any part of an organization to which revenue and controllable costs can be assigned.

Profit Impact of Market Strategies (13) *See* PIMS Study.

Profit Maximization (13) In pricing strategy, the point at which the additional revenue gained by increasing the price of a product equals the increase in total cost.

Promotion (19) The function of informing, persuading, and influencing the consumer's purchase decision.

Promotional Allowance (14) An advertising or sales promotion grant by a manufacturer to other channel members in an attempt to integrate promotional strategy in the channel.

Promotional Mix (19) The blending of personal selling and nonpersonal selling (including advertising, sales promotion, and public relations) by marketers in an attempt to accomplish promotional objectives.

Promotional Price (14) A lower-than-normal price used as an ingredient of a firm's selling strategy.

Promotional Strategy (1) An element of marketing decision making that involves appropriate blending of personal selling, advertising, and sales promotion.

Prospecting (21) The function of identifying potential customers.

Psychographics (4) Behavioral profiles developed from analyses of activities, opinions, interests, and life-styles that may be used to segment consumer markets.

Psychological Pricing (14) A pricing policy based on the belief that certain prices or price ranges are more appealing than others to buyers.

Psychophysics (8) The relationship between the actual physical stimulus and the corresponding sensation produced in the individual.

Public Health Cigarette Smoking Act (1971) (2) Federal legislation restricting tobacco advertising on radio and television.

Publicity (19, 20) Stimulation of demand by placing commercially significant news or obtaining favorable presentation not paid for by an identified sponsor.

Public Relations (19, 20) A firm's communications and relationships with its various publics.

Public Responsibility Committee (24) A permanent group within the board of directors of a firm that considers matters of corporate social responsibility.

Public Warehouse (16) An independently owned storage facility.

Pulling Strategy (19) A promotional effort by the seller to stimulate final user demand, exerting pressure on the distribution channel.

Pure Competition (13) A market structure characterized by homogeneous products, in which there are so many buyers and sellers that none has a significant influence on price.

Pure Food and Drug Act (1906) (2) Federal legislation that prohibits the adulteration and misbranding of foods and drugs in interstate commerce.

Pushing Strategy (19) A promotional effort by the seller of a product to members of the marketing channel to stimulate personal selling of a product.

Qualifying (21) The act of determining that a prospect is actually a potential customer.

Quantity Discount (14) A price reduction granted for large volume purchases.

Quota (21) A specified sales or profit target that a salesperson is expected to achieve.

Quota Sample (6) A nonprobability sample that is divided so that different segments or groups are represented in the total sample.

Rack Jobber (16) A service wholesaler whose services to retailers include supplying a display case, pricing the merchandise, stocking the case, and returning regularly to replenish the case.

Raw Materials (10) In the industrial market, farm products and natural resources used in producing the final manufactured goods.

Rebate (14) A refund for a portion of the purchase price, usually granted by the manufacturer of a product.

Reciprocity (9) In the industrial market, the highly controversial practice of extending purchasing preference to suppliers who are also customers.

Recycling (24) The reprocessing of used materials for their reuse.

Reference Group (7) A group with which an individual identifies, to the point where the group dictates a standard of behavior for the individual.

Referral Sample (6) Referred to as the Snowball Sample. It is a sample which is done in waves as more respondents with the requisite characteristics are identified.

Regional Shopping Center (17) The largest type of planned cluster of retail stores, usually involving one or more major department stores and as many as 200 other stores. A center of this size typically is located in an area with at least 250,000 people within 30 minutes driving time of the center.

Reinforcement (8) The reduction in drive that results from an appropriate response.

Research Design (6) A series of advanced decisions that, when taken together, comprise a master plan or a model for conducting marketing research.

Response (8) An individual's reaction to cues and drive.

Retail Advertising (20) All nonpersonal selling by stores that offer goods or services directly to the consuming public.

Retailer (15) One who sells products or services to the ultimate consumer and not for resale.

Retail Image (17) Refers to the consumer's perception of a store and the shopping experience it provides.

Retailing (17) All of the activities involved in the sale of products and services to the ultimate consumer.

Retail Life Cycle (17) The concept that retail institutions pass through a series of stages in their existence—introduction, growth, maturity, and decline.

Retail Trade Area Analysis (17) Refers to studies that assess the relative drawing power of alternative retail locations.

Return on Investment (ROI) (14, 16, 25) A measure of profitability equal to the rate of profit multiplied by the organization's or department's inventory turnover.

Reverse Channel (15) The path goods follow from consumer to manufacturer, in an effort to recycle used products or by-products. *See also* Recycling.

Reverse Reciprocity (9) The practice of extending supply privileges to firms that provide needed supplies.

Robinson-Patman Act (1936) (2) Federal legislation prohibiting price discrimination that is not based on a cost differential. The act also prohibits selling at an unreasonably low price in order to eliminate competition.

Roles (7) Behavior that members of a group expect of individuals in a particular position within the group.

Safety Stock (18) In inventory control, a certain quantity of merchandise kept on hand to protect a firm from fluctuations in demand and to prevent depletion of inventory.

Salary (21) A fixed payment made on a periodic basis to an employee, including some sales employees.

Sales Analysis (25) The in-depth evaluation of a firm's sales.

Sales Branch (16) An installation of a firm that carries inventory and processes customer orders from available stock.

Sales Force Composite (3) A qualitative sales forecasting method in which sales estimates are based upon the combined estimates of the firm's sales force.

Sales Forecasting (3) An estimate of company sales for a specified future period.

Sales Management (21) The activities of securing, maintaining, motivating, supervising, evaluating, and controlling an effective sales force.

Sales Maximization (13) The practice of setting as a minimum the lowest acceptable profit level, and then seeking to enlarge sales within this framework. Under this policy, marketers believe that increased sales are more important than immediate high profits in the long run.

Sales Office 16) A regional installation for a firm's sales personnel.

Sales Promotion (19, 21) All marketing activities (other than personal selling, advertising, and publicity) that stimulate consumer purchasing and dealer effectiveness. Examples are displays, shows and expositions, demonstrations, and various nonrecurrent selling efforts.

Sales Quota (25) The level of expected sales against which actual results are compared.

Sampling (20) The free distribution of a product to consumers in an attempt to obtain future sales.

Scrambled Merchandising (17) The practice of carrying dissimilar product lines in an attempt to generate added sales volume.

Secondary Data (6) Previously published data.

Selective Distribution (15) A policy under which a firm chooses only a limited number of retailers to handle the product line.

Selective Perception (8) The idea that consumers are consciously aware of only those incoming stimuli they wish to perceive.

Self-Concept (8) A mental conception of oneself, comprised of four components: real self, self-image, looking-glass self, and ideal self.

Seller's Market (1) A market with a shortage of goods and/or services.

Selling Agent (16) Agent middleman responsible for the total marketing program of a firm's product line.

Selling Expense Ratio (25) An evaluative technique revealing the relationship between selling expenses and total net sales.

Selling Up (21) The sales technique of convincing a customer to buy a higher-priced item than he or she originally intended to buy.

Semantic Differential (8) A measurement tool using bipolar adjectives—like *hot* and *cold*—to gauge consumer attitudes.

Services (12) Intangible tasks that satisfy consumer and industrial user needs when efficiently developed and distributed to chosen market segments.

Shaping (8) The process of applying a series of rewards and reinforcement so that more complex behavior can evolve over time.

Sherman Antitrust Act (1890) (2) Federal antitrust legislation that prohibits restraint of trade and monopolization, and subjects violators to civil suits as well as to criminal prosecution.

Shopping Goods (10) Products purchased only after the consumer has made considerable comparisons between items on such bases as price, quality, style, and color.

Shopping Store (17) An establishment at which customers typically compare prices, assortments, and quality levels with those of competing outlets before making a purchase decision.

Simple Random Sample (6) The basic type of probability sample where every item in the relevant universe has an equal opportunity of being selected.

Skimming Pricing (14) A pricing policy based on the theory that setting an initially high entry price will permit the manufacturer to recover its new-product costs quickly, before competition eventually drives the price down.

Social and Ethical Considerations (13) A pricing objective based on certain societal and ethical factors such as ability to pay.

Social Class (7) The relatively permanent divisions of a society into which individuals or families are categorized on the basis of prestige and community status.

Social Responsibility (24) Those marketing philosophies, policies, procedures, and actions that have the advancement of society's welfare as one of their primary objectives.

Societal/Cultural Environment (2) Component of the marketing environment consisting of the relationship between the marketer and society and its culture.

Sorting (15) The contribution of distribution channels in securing a balanced stock of goods available to match the needs of customers. It consists of accumulating, allocating, assorting, and sorting out goods.

Specialty Advertising (20) A sales promotion medium that involves the use of articles—such as key rings, calendars, and ball-point pens—bearing the advertiser's name, address, and advertising message.

Specialty Goods (10) Products purchased for their unique characteristics as they are perceived by the consumer. Such items are typically branded and high-priced.

Specialty Retailer (17) One who provides a combination of product lines, service, and/or reputation in an attempt to attract customer preference.

Specialty Store (17) An establishment that typically handles only part of a single line of products.

Specifications (9) In the industrial market, a written description of a product or a service needed by a firm. Prospective bidders use this description initially to determine whether they can manufacture the product or deliver the service, and subsequently to prepare a bid.

Speculative Production (15) Production based on the firm's estimate of the demand for its product.

SSWD (4) Acronym for single, separated, widowed, divorced; a term applied to single-person households, an emerging market segment.

Stagflation (2) A situation in which an economy has both high unemployment and a rising price level.

Standard Industrial Classification (SIC) (9) A classification system developed by the U.S. government for use in collecting detailed information about the various industries comprising the industrial market.

Status (7) The relative position of any individual member in a group.

Status-quo Objectives (13) In pricing strategy, goals based on the maintenance of stable prices.

Stock Out (18) An item that is not available for shipment.

Stock Turnover (13) The number of times the average inventory is sold annually.

Storage Warehouse (18) A facility for holding goods for moderate to long periods of time in an attempt to balance supply and demand for producers and purchasers.

Straight Rebuy (9) A recurring industrial purchase decision where an item that has performed satisfactorily is purchased again by a customer.

Strategic Business Units (SBU) (3) Related product groupings or classifications within a multi-product firm, so structured for optimal planning purposes.

Strategic Planning (3) The process of determining an organization's primary objectives, and allocating funds and proceeding on a course of action to achieve those objectives.

Strategic Window (3) The limited periods during which the "fit" between the key requirements of a market and the particular competencies of a firm is at an optimum.

Stratified Sample (6) A probability sample that is constructed so that randomly selected sub-samples of different groups are represented in the total sample.

Subculture (7) A subgroup of a culture with its own distinguishing mode of behavior.

Subliminal Perception (8) A subconscious level of awareness.

Suboptimization (18) A physical distribution concept describing a condition in which each manager attempts to minimize costs, but due to the interrelatedness of the various physical distribution tasks, the results fall short of the desired goal.

Suggestion Selling (21) A form of selling that attempts to broaden the customer's original purchase with related items, special promotions, and holiday or seasonal merchandise.

Supermarket (17) A large-scale departmentalized retail store offering a variety of food products and various nonfood items. It typically operates on a self-service basis and emphasizes low prices and adequate parking facilities.

Supplies (11) In the industrial market, regular expense items necessary for a firm's daily operations, but not part of the final product. An example would be office stationery.

Survey of Buyer Intentions (3) A qualitative sales forecasting method in which sample groups of present and potential consumers are surveyed concerning their purchase intentions.

Syndicated Service (6) An organization that offers to provide a standardized set of data on a regular basis to all who wish to buy it.

System (18) An organized group of parts or components linked together according to a plan to achieve specific objectives.

Systematic Sample (6) A probability sample that takes every Nth item on a list.

Tactical Planning (3) The implementation of activities necessary in the achievement of a firm's objectives.

Target Return Objective (13) A short-run or long-run pricing goal, usually stated as a percentage of sales or investment.

Tariffs (18, 22) In international marketing, a tax levied against imported products; also, an official publication used in determining shipping charges.

Task Objective Method (19) A promotional budget allocation method, under which a firm defines its goals and then determines the amount needed to accomplish them.

Technological Environment (2) The applications of knowledge based upon discoveries in science, inventions, and innovations to marketing.

Teleshopping (17) An innovative method of shopping by which consumers order merchandise that is displayed on their television sets.

Tertiary Industries (12) The businesses that specialize in the production of services.

Test Marketing (6, 11) The process of selecting a specific city or television-coverage area considered reasonably typical of the total market and introducing the product with a total marketing campaign in this area.

Time Utility (1, 15) A want-satisfying power created by marketers having products available when consumers want to buy them.

Tokyo Round (22) A series of international trade negotiations intended to reduce the amount of tariffs throughout the world.

Total Cost Approach (18) The idea that all factors of physical distribution should be considered as a whole and not individually.

Trade Discount (14) A payment to a channel member or buyer for performing some marketing function normally required of the manufacturer. Also known as a *functional discount.*

Trade Fair (16) A show, at which manufacturers of a particular industry display their wares for visiting wholesale and retail buyers. Also known as a *trade show.*

Trade-in (14) A credit allowance given for an old item when a customer is purchasing a new item. An example is a used car that a customer "sells" to a car dealer in partial payment for a new car.

Trade Industries (9) Organizations such as retailers and wholesalers who purchase for resale to others.

Trademark (11) A brand that has been given legally protected status. The protection is granted solely to the brand's owner.

Trading Stamps (20) A sales promotion technique involving redeemable stamps. The stamps are given as a purchase premium in some retail establishments. They may be collected and redeemed for cash or gifts at special redemption centers operated by the trading stamp company.

Transfer Mechanism (19) In marketing communications, the means of delivering a message.

Transfer Price (14) The cost of sending goods from one company profit center to another.

Trend Analysis (3) A quantitative sales forecasting method in which estimates of future sales are determined through statistical analyses of historical sales patterns.

Trigger Pricing System (22) In international marketing, a protective measure taken by a country to combat the practice of dumping. When a price level for a commodity dips below a preordained figure, it sets off an immediate investigation by a government agency. *See also* Dumping.

Truck Wholesaler (16) One who markets perishable food items. Also known as a *truck jobber.*

Truth-In-Lending Act (1968) (2) Federal legislation requiring disclosure of the annual interest rates on loans and credit purchases.

Turnover (13) The number of times the average inventory is sold annually. The turnover rate is often frequently used as a sales efficiency measure.

Tying Agreement (15) An understanding between a dealer and a manufacturer that requires the dealer to carry the manufacturer's full product line in exchange for an exclusive dealership

Undifferentiated Marketing (5) A practice employed by a firm that produces only one product and markets it to all customers using a single marketing mix.

Unfair Trade Laws (2) State laws requiring sellers to maintain minimum prices for comparable merchandise.

Uniform Delivered Price (14) A pricing system under which all buyers are quoted the same price (including transportation expenses).

Unitizing (18) The practice of combining as many packages as possible into one load, preferably on a platform.

Unit Pricing (14) A pricing policy under which prices are stated in terms of a recognizable unit of measurement or a standard numerical count.

Unit Trains (18) A time and money-saving service provided by railroads to large-volume customers, in which a train is loaded with the shipments of only one company and transports solely for that customer.

Universal Product Code (11) Special codes on packages that can be read by optical scanners. The scanner can print the item and its price on a sales receipt and simultaneously maintain a sales and inventory record for the retailer or shipper.

Utility (1) The want-satisfying power of a product or service.

Value Added by Manufacturing (11) The difference between the price charged for a manufactured good and the cost of the raw materials and other inputs.

Venture Team (11) An organizational strategy for developing new product areas by combining the management resources of technological innovation, capital, management, and marketing expertise.

Vertical Marketing System (VMS) (15) A professionally managed and centrally programmed marketing channel network structured to achieve operating economy and maximum impact.

Want Satisfaction (9) A state of mind achieved when a consumer's needs have been met as the result of a purchase.

Warranty (10) A guarantee to the buyer of a product that the manufacturer will replace the product or refund the purchase price if the product proves defective during a specified time period.

Webb-Pomerene Export Trade Act (1918) (2, 22) Federal legislation that excludes voluntary export trade associations from restrictions of the Sherman Act, but only in their foreign dealings.

Weber's Law (8) The proposition that the higher the initial intensity of a stimulus, the greater the amount of the change in intensity that is needed for a difference to be perceived.

Wheeler-Lea Act (1938) (2) A federal statute amending the FTC Act so as to ban deceptive or unfair business practices per se.

Wheel of Retailing (17) A hypothesis by M. P. McNair stating that new types of retailers gain a competitive foothold by offering lower prices through reduction or elimination of services. Once they are established, however, they add more services and their prices gradually rise. They then are vulnerable to the emergence of a new low-price retailer with minimum services.

Wholesaler (16) A middleman who takes title to the goods he or she handles.

Wholesaling (15) The activities of those who sell to retailers, other wholesalers, and industrial users, but not in significant amounts to ultimate consumers.

Wholesaling Middleman (16) Channel members who take title to the goods they handle; also, agents and brokers who perform important wholesaling activities without taking title to the goods.

Wool Product Labeling Act (1939) (2) Federal legislation requiring that the kind and percentage of each type of wool in a product be identified.

Zone Pricing (14) A pricing system under which the market is divided into various regions and a different price is set in each region.

ZPG (4) Acronym for zero population growth, the point at which the number of live births in a year equals that year's death rate.

NAME INDEX

SUBJECT INDEX